SLUMMING

 HISTORICAL STUDIES OF URBAN AMERICA

Edited by Timothy J. Gilfoyle, James R. Grossman, and Becky M. Nicolaides

ALSO IN THE SERIES:

Parish Boundaries: The Catholic Encounter with Race in the Twentieth-Century Urban North
by John T. McGreevy

Modern Housing for America: Policy Struggles in the New Deal Era
by Gail Radford

Smoldering City: Chicagoans and the Great Fire, 1871–1874
by Karen Sawislak

Making the Second Ghetto: Race and Housing in Chicago, 1940–1960
by Arnold R. Hirsch

Faces along the Bar: Lore and Order in the Workingman's Saloon, 1870–1920
by Madelon Powers

Streets, Railroads, and the Great Strike of 1877
by David O. Stowell

The Creative Destruction of Manhattan, 1900–1940
by Max Page

Brownsville, Brooklyn: Blacks, Jews, and the Changing Face of the Ghetto
by Wendell Pritchett

My Blue Heaven: Life and Politics in the Working-Class Suburbs of Los Angeles, 1920–1965
by Becky M. Nicolaides

In the Shadow of Slavery: African Americans in New York City, 1626–1863
by Leslie M. Harris

Building the South Side: Urban Space and Civic Culture in Chicago, 1890–1919
by Robin F. Bachin

Places of Their Own: African American Suburbanization in the Twentieth Century
by Andrew Wiese

Downtown America: A History of the Place and the People Who Made It
by Alison Isenberg

Block by Block: Neighborhoods and Public Policy on Chicago's West Side
by Amanda I. Seligman

The Elusive Ideal: Equal Educational Opportunity and the Federal Role in Boston's Public Schools, 1950–1985
by Adam R. Nelson

Chicagoland: City and Suburbs in the Railroad Age
by Ann Durkin Keating

City of American Dreams: A History of Home Ownership and Housing Reform in Chicago, 1871–1919
by Margaret Garb

Millennium Park: Creating a Chicago Landmark
by Timothy J. Gilfoyle

The New Suburban History
edited by Kevin M. Kruse and Thomas J. Sugrue

Selling the Race: Culture, Community, and Black Chicago, 1940–1955
by Adam Green

Colored Property: State Policy and White Racial Politics in Suburban America
by David M. P. Freund

The Flash Press: Sporting Male Weeklies in 1840s New York
by Patricia Cline Cohen, Timothy J. Gilfoyle, and Helen Lefkowitz Horowitz in association with the American Antiquarian Society

Chicago Made: Factory Networks in the Industrial Metropolis
by Robert Lewis

The Problem of Jobs: Liberalism, Race, and Deindustrialization in Philadelphia
by Guian McKee

SLUMMING

*Sexual and Racial Encounters
in American Nightlife, 1885–1940*

CHAD HEAP

The University of Chicago Press   Chicago and London

CHAD HEAP is associate professor of American studies at The
George Washington University. He is a contributor to *The Encyclopedia
of Chicago* and curator and catalog author of the Regenstein Library
exhibition Homosexuality in the City: A Century of Research at the
University of Chicago (2000).

The University of Chicago Press, Chicago 60637
The University of Chicago Press, Ltd., London
© 2009 by Chad Heap
All rights reserved. Published 2009
Printed in the United States of America
16 15 14 13 12 11 10 09   1 2 3 4 5

ISBN-13: 978-0-226-32243-8 (cloth)
ISBN-10: 0-226-32243-2 (cloth)

Library of Congress Cataloging-in-Publication Data
Heap, Chad C., 1967–
     Slumming : sexual and racial encounters in American nightlife,
  1885–1940 / Chad Heap.
       p. cm.
     Includes bibliographical references and index.
     ISBN-13: 978-0-226-32243-8 (cloth : alk. paper)
     ISBN-10: 0-226-32243-2 (cloth : alk. paper) 1. New York (N.Y.)—
  Social life and customs. 2. Chicago (Ill.)—Social life and customs.
  3. Slums—Social aspects—New York (State)—New York—
  History. 4. Slums—Social aspects—Illinois—Chicago—History.
  5. City and town life—New York (State)—New York—History.
  6. City and town life—Illinois—Chicago—History. 7. New
  York (N.Y.)—Race relations. 8. Chicago (Ill.)—Race relations.
  9. Sex customs—New York (State)—New York—History.
  10. Sex customs—Illinois—Chicago—History. I. Title.
F128.5.H43 2009
305.8009773'11—dc22   2007010881

♾ The paper used in this publication meets the minimum requirements
of the American National Standard for Information Sciences—
Permanence of Paper for Printed Library Materials, ANSI Z39.48-1992.

Contents

Illustrations

Acknowledgments

Because this book has been more than a decade in the making and its completion has sometimes seemed in doubt, I have not only accumulated a long list of debts which must be acknowledged here but have also exasperated more than a few individuals whom I must thank for their indulgence and patience. Let me begin by expressing my gratitude to those who were there at the project's conception. As the chair of my dissertation committee, George Chauncey proved an invaluable advisor and friend throughout graduate school and beyond. From the insider information he shared about particular archives and sources to the time he invested in commenting on drafts and helping to secure funding for my research, his support has been unwavering, and his creative and scrupulous scholarship has provided a model and foundation for my own. I am also indebted to Leora Auslander for our long conversations about the theoretical dimensions of sexuality and gender, to Tom Holt for his insights into the "marking" of race, and to Kathleen Conzen for her advice on the little urban history research project that grew up to be a book. In addition, I am grateful to my University of Chicago compatriots, Gabi Arredondo, Matti Bunzl, Elisa Camiscioli, David Churchill, the late Charles Clifton, Eduardo Contreras, Laurie Green, Dawne Moon, Greta Rensenbrink, Michael Schreffler, Dana Seitler, Nayan Shah, and Red Tremmel, for sharing their ideas about history, identity, and sexuality, and for providing an occasional—and necessary—escape from the academic world of Hyde Park.

Over the years, my work on this project has been supported financially by a number of sources, including the Mellon Postdoctoral Research Fellowship at the Newberry Library, the James C. Hormel Dissertation Fellowship in Lesbian and Gay Studies from the Lesbian and Gay Studies Project of the Center for Gender Studies at the University of Chicago, the Sexuality Research Fellowship from the Social Science Research Council with funds provided by the Ford Foundation, and the Freehling Research and Summer Mellon Research grants from the Department of History at the University of Chicago. I am beholden to each of these generous benefactors, as well as to Nina and Tim Zagat, who provided extended part-time employment at Zagat Survey whenever I needed to supplement my graduate-student research budget in New York. For granting me academic leave, financial support, and extended time to complete this book, I must also thank Donald Lehman, Executive Vice President for Academic Affairs at The George Washington University, as well as the following deans and interim dean of GWU's Columbian College of Arts and Sciences: Lester Lefton, William Frawley, Peg Barratt, and Diana Lipscomb.

Because any historical work is only as good as the sources upon which it is based, I am indebted to the many archivists and librarians who have facilitated my research over the years. The late Archie Motley of the Chicago Historical Society (now the Chicago History Museum) deserves special mention both for his encyclopedic knowledge of Chicago history and archives and for his unwavering encouragement of hundreds of young researchers, myself included. I am also particularly grateful to Archie's colleague, Linda Evans, to Melanie Yolles of the Manuscripts and Archives Division of the New York Public Library, to Dan Meyer and Alice Schreyer of the Special Collections Research Center at the University of Chicago, to Gonzalo Gomez in the Gelman Library interlibrary loan office at The George Washington University, and to scores of others who have pointed me toward countless resources and photocopied reams of documents for further consultation. For tracking down missing citations and illustrations and assisting with miscellaneous research tasks in Chicago, New York, and Washington, I thank P. J. Brownlee, Leslie De-Grande, Wynn Hansen, Sandra Heard, Maureen Kentoff, Mike Phillips, Kyle Riismandel, Jason Steinhauer, Tim Stewart-Winter, and especially Jeremy Hill. In addition, I would like to express my gratitude to the many scholars I have met in archives, at conferences, and online, who have generously shared relevant materials from their own research, including Andrew Diamond, J. D. Doyle, Scott Elliott, Mara Keire, William Straw, Sharon Wood, and particularly Beth Clement, with whom I enjoyed a long-running exchange of photocopies, notes, and ideas as we completed our dissertations and revised them for publication.

The feedback I received when presenting portions of my ongoing research at conferences and seminars over the past several years proved invaluable in refining the arguments presented here. Although space does not permit a full accounting of all the venues and their participants, I would like to single out Cynthia Blair, Mona Domosh, Leslie Fishbein, Ramón Gutiérrez, Philip Brian Harper, Marya McQuirter, Darryl Moore, Siobhan Somerville, Susan Strasser, Michael Trask, and Hal Wolman. I am also grateful to Sara Austin, Eduardo de Jesús Douglas, Jim Grossman, Toby Higbie, Richard John, Dale Kramer, Bethel Saler, Susan Sleeper-Smith, Helen Thompson, and Lisa Voigt for the collegiality, intellectual stimulation, and pertinent insights they provided during my year at the Newberry Library. Over the past eight years, this project has also been generously supported by my students at The George Washington University, as well as by my colleagues in the American Studies Department, including Libby Anker, Jim Horton, Melinda Knight, Kip Kosek, Richard Longstreth, Melani McAlister, Barney Mergen, Jim Miller, Elaine Peña, Suleiman Osman, and John Vlach. Their unremitting encouragement and the department's genial atmosphere continues to make teaching and research a distinct pleasure.

A host of friends and colleagues in Chicago, New York, Washington, and elsewhere has also been integral to the completion of this book, often simply by providing an encouraging word or a much-needed diversion from the seemingly all-consuming tasks of research, writing, and revision. Thanks to Paul Baum, Wallace Best, Caroline Corbin, Magda Hernandez, Richard Isbrucker, Sue Legro, Sean McGinn, Richard McKewen, Larry Pick, James Polchin, Jenny Schuessler, Brooke Shipley, Michael Thaddeus, and Michael Waugh for weathering far too many years when I was focused on little more than slumming; I promise to have something new to talk about when next we meet. Thanks also to Hannah Joyner for convincing me that I was cut out to be a historian in the first place, and to David Johnson, Theresa Mah, and Rebecca Zorach for the years of unshakable support, keen intellectual insights, and pleasurable diversions they have so willingly provided.

In the final stages of revision, this book was strengthened immeasurably by friends and colleagues who took time out of their schedules to provide detailed comments on large sections of the work. I am indebted to Tom Guglielmo and John Sweet for their close readings of several chapters, to Tim Gilfoyle and John Howard for their comprehensive and discerning reader's reports on the whole manuscript, and to Lois Leveen for her shrewd, judicious, and often droll assistance with copy-editing the entire book. My editors at the University of Chicago Press—Doug Mitchell and Tim McGovern—not only helped me produce the best book possible but also displayed extraordinary patience with my seemingly unending, and ultimately futile, quest to get it all right. More than to anyone else, however, I am beholden to my friends (and former department chairs) Terry Murphy and Phyllis Palmer, who stepped in when the completion of this book seemed increasingly unlikely to provide a valuable mix of admonition, encouragement, and practical suggestions for organization and revision. While I take full responsibility for any remaining errors in the text, I know that the book is better—indeed, that it exists at all—because of their timely and compassionate intervention.

Finally, I am grateful to my family—especially my mother, Clydia Heap; my father, the late Jerry Heap; and my grandparents, Fern Cottrell, Ralph Heap, and the late Edna Heap—for their long-standing support and indulgence as I followed an academic life that was unfamiliar to all of them and often seemed insufficiently remunerative to several. Although they have not all lived to see the book they heard about for years, I know they would be proud that it is finally in print.

This book is dedicated to my partner, Jérôme Bernard, who came into my life during dark hours when I was nearly ready to cast this work aside and became the loving and inordinately supportive bulwark I needed to see the project through. I look forward to many post-*Slumming* years with you.

Introduction

For most Americans, the notion of "slumming" conjures up images of well-to-do whites' late-night excursions to the cabarets of Prohibition-era Harlem. Like the African American chanteuse Bricktop, they likely recall a time when "Harlem was the 'in' place to go for music and booze," and "every night the limousines pulled up to the corner," disgorging celebrities and hundreds of other "rich whites . . . all dolled up in their furs and jewels." The more socially and politically attuned might recollect scenes of interracial camaraderie, in which white jazz musicians and aficionados eagerly interacted with beloved black performers and patrons at Small's Paradise or budding civil rights activists attended fundraisers for the National Association for the Advancement of Colored People (NAACP) at the popular Lenox Club. Yet when Americans think about slumming, in all likelihood they imagine scenes that emphasize the more pejorative aspects of this once-popular cultural practice. Recalling Jim Crow establishments such as the Cotton Club and Connie's Inn, they probably envision segregated crowds of inebriated, well-to-do "Nordics" being entertained by a host of scantily clad, light-skinned chorus girls and darker-skinned musicians. Or perhaps they imagine even more bawdy scenes, in which otherwise "respectable" white women and men ventured into Harlem's lower-scale dives in search of supposedly more authentic black entertainment, cross-racial sexual encounters, and the anonymity necessary to allow themselves to indulge in the "primitive" behaviors and desires they associated with blacks.[1]

From the best intentioned to the most horrifyingly exploitative, each of these scenarios depicts some aspect of what slumming has come to represent in U.S. cultural memory. But the tendency to remember this complex practice as a Prohibition-era, New York–centered encounter between whites and blacks hardly does justice to the crucial role slumming played in shaping the popular conceptualization of race, sexuality, and urban space in the United States over the course of the late nineteenth and early twentieth centuries. The practice of slumming began some three decades before Prohibition became effective nationwide in 1920, and it persisted well beyond the repeal of the Eighteenth Amendment in 1933. Moreover, while the U.S. version of slumming probably started in Manhattan and certainly reached its apogee in that city, in one form or another this cultural phenomenon materialized in every major U.S. urban center and many smaller ones, and its effects on the ways that Americans thought about urban life and the different types of people who resided in U.S. cities resonated even in the most sparsely populated areas of this sprawling nation.

The social dynamics of this voyeuristic, oft-demeaning but always revealing practice also extended well beyond the parameters of any preconceived notion of crossing a presumed white/black racial divide. From the mid-1880s until the outbreak of the Second World War, an overlapping progression of slumming vogues encouraged affluent white Americans to investigate a variety of socially marginalized urban neighborhoods and the diverse populations that inhabited them. In its earliest formulation, slumming prompted thousands of well-to-do whites to explore spaces associated with working-class southern and eastern European immigrants, Chinese immigrants, and blacks. But successive generations of such pleasure seekers set their sights instead on the tearooms of "free-loving" bohemian artists and radicals, the jazz cabarets of urban blacks, and the speakeasies and nightclubs associated with lesbians and gay men. As they did so, slummers gave lie to the commonly held notion that U.S. cities of the late nineteenth and early twentieth centuries were little more than urban congeries of highly segregated racial and sexual communities. Moreover, they spurred the development of an array of new commercialized leisure spaces that simultaneously promoted social mixing and recast the sexual and racial landscape of American urban culture and space.[2]

By focusing on the nightlife of New York and Chicago, this book delineates the crucial historical moment when slumming captured the popular imagination—and the pocketbooks—of well-to-do white Americans, demonstrating how this distinctive cultural practice transformed racial and sexual ideologies in the United States. As a heterosocial phenomenon through which substantial numbers of white middle-class women first joined their male counterparts to partake of urban leisure and public space, slumming provided a relatively comfortable means of negotiating the shifting contours of public gender relations and the spatial and demographic changes that restructured most U.S. cities during the late nineteenth and early twentieth centuries. Yet slumming accomplished more than simply creating places where affluent whites were encouraged to cross preconceived racial and sexual boundaries. By opening spaces where people could explore their sexual fantasies outside the social constraints of their own neighborhoods and where those who engaged in same-sex and cross-racial relationships could publicly express their desires, this popular phenomenon played an extensive role in the proliferation of new sexual and racial identities. In charting the full range of such complex cultural dynamics over a period of more than five decades, this book argues that slumming contributed significantly to the emergence and codification of a new twentieth-century hegemonic social order—one that was structured primarily around an increasingly polarized white/black racial axis and a hetero/homo sexual binary that were defined in reciprocal relationship to one another.[3]

When well-to-do whites went slumming in turn-of-the-century U.S. cities, crossing the neighborhood boundaries that separated their daily lives from the urban poor, they built on a long tradition of similar excursions. Since at least the mid-1830s, New York's wealthier residents and occasional sightseers regularly visited impoverished urban areas, such as the lower Manhattan neighborhood known as Five Points. Like later-nineteenth-century slumming parties, these early visitors walked the streets and examined the hovels and low-down dives of immigrant and working-class New York. But in several important respects, their explorations of urban poverty and immorality differed from the slumming excursions that became so popular in New York and Chicago over the course of the late nineteenth and early twentieth centuries.[4] First, in the mixed landscape of the mid-nineteenth-century walking city, where the homes of affluent and poor were jumbled together in close proximity not only with each other but also with a variety of commercial enterprises, these early ramblings usually covered no more than a few blocks. As such, they were more investigations of pockets of degradation and illicit activities in affluent whites' own neighborhoods than ventures into separate urban districts. Only after the mid-1850s, but especially during the Gilded Age building boom that followed the Civil War, did this relatively integrated urban environment give way to the increasingly hierarchical arrangement of urban culture and space, which provided the basis for affluent whites to imagine their journeys into immigrant and working-class New York neighborhoods as slumming excursions into wholly distinct—even foreign—urban districts. In the younger city of Chicago, this requisite reorganization of urban space occurred even slightly later, during the massive reconstruction efforts undertaken following the famous 1871 conflagration.[5]

The cultural context of mid-nineteenth-century journeys into the immigrant and working-class sections of New York and Chicago also set them apart from later slumming excursions. Although some mid-nineteenth-century New Yorkers and Chicagoans clearly ventured into these areas simply to satisfy their curiosity about local social and moral conditions, the vast majority of the women and men who toured Five Points and similar districts in Chicago did so in conjunction with two well-defined urban institutions: the evangelical Protestant moral reform movement and the more boisterous, class-integrated sporting culture of urban men.

At a time when a new white middle-class ideology of separate spheres required women to structure their lives around hearth and home, fundamentally ceding the public realm of the city to men, the moral reform work carried out by evangelical Protestants provided mid-nineteenth-century women with their only respectable entrée into urban working-class life. To preserve their good reputations, under nearly all circumstances "respectable" women steered clear of poverty-stricken urban neighborhoods, rarely venturing into public at all without a male escort, in order to distance themselves from any association with "public women," or prostitutes. But because the Protestant reform movement drew upon women's domestic expertise, it provided an opportunity for religious-minded women to carve out a public role for themselves, undertaking a series of "home visits" to local tenements to teach immigrant and workingwomen the "proper" methods of housekeeping and child rearing. Other female reformers called upon their reputations for religious piety to address the moral conditions of the cities' tenement districts. Descending upon local brothels in the company of like-minded men, they launched a program of "active visiting," endeavoring to convert local prostitutes to their particular brand of Christianity and providing refuge in newly founded missions and safe houses to those women whom they were able to coax away from the demimonde. Yet even though this work encouraged white middle-class women to interact with the urban underworld, its religious impetus and accomplishments clearly set such cross-class encounters apart from those that would come to characterize slumming at the century's end.[6]

The sporting culture of mid-nineteenth-century New York and Chicago shared even more in common with slumming, but it, too, differed in significant ways. Organized around access to liquor, gambling, pugilism, and cockfighting, sporting-male culture provided a means for white middle- and upper-class men to join their working-class brethren in the rough-and-tumble environs of the Bowery and comparable working-class districts in Chicago. Yet even as such interactions promoted a sense of fraternity and mutual respect among a wide range of urban men, the possibilities that the sporting life presented for crossing the social and cultural boundaries of the city remained restricted almost entirely to the male domain. Grounded in an atmosphere of rowdy male homosociality, sporting-male culture usually permitted the entry of women only if they were sexually available and never if they insisted upon maintaining a sense of decorum and respectability. In fact, as important as drinking and gambling were to the establishment of a sense of cross-class camaraderie, that camaraderie's very existence was maintained in large part by men's shared access to the sexual favors and paid services of working-class women.[7] Such interactions persisted, of course, with the advent of slumming in the mid-1880s. But because this latter practice was part and parcel of the increasing heterosocialization of urban leisure, in which the public dance hall and other "cheap amusements" supplanted the all-male environs of the saloon, it afforded respectable women of all classes with a range of new opportunities for crossing the social and cultural boundaries of the city.[8] Participating in New York's nascent bohemian subculture of writers, actors, and artists, a handful of actresses and society matrons got a jumpstart on this trend during the 1870s, visiting Chinatown opium dens and popular Bowery and Tenderloin concert halls. But for most affluent white women in Chicago and New York, the chance to partake of such pleasure-oriented excursions into the cities' immigrant and working-class districts became available only at the end of the nineteenth century.[9]

To a significant degree, then, the practice of slumming emerged from the consolidation of these two earlier traditions of cross-cultural encounter, combining the reform movement's engagement of respectable white middle-class women with the sporting-male culture's unabashed pursuit of pleasure. Indeed, in its earliest formulations, the very notion of

1   According to the original caption this engraving shows two well-to-do white women and
     their male escort "doing the slums" of the Five Points district of New York under police su-
     pervision. Before such respectable white women began to venture into the city's immigrant
     and working-class resorts in the late nineteenth century, they often toured the streets of
     local slums to observe the impoverished conditions of New York's poorest residents.
     (Reprinted from *Frank Leslie's Illustrated Newspaper*, December 5, 1885. Collection of the
     Prints and Photographs Division, Library of Congress.)

slumming often retained some sense of the benevolent work undertaken
by nineteenth-century female reformers.[10] Such was certainly the case
when an 1888 tract on female and child labor reported that "Mrs. Dr.
Clinton Locke . . . has, perhaps, done more real charity for the Chicago
poor" by going " 'slumming' . . . into the holes and hovels . . . where she
personally taught ignorant Irish, Polish, Swedish, German, and Italian
mothers how to make broth from scraps, gruels from chaff, and tempting cookies from cheap flours."[11] But as an increasing number of well-to-
do whites set out to "do the slums" of New York and Chicago (figure 1),
the popular definition and practice of slumming shifted more definitively toward the pursuit of amusement. In an emerging heterosocial
permutation of the earlier sporting-male culture, slumming actively encouraged middle- and upper-class white women to join their husbands,
boyfriends, and brothers as active participants in the rambunctious environs of the cities' immigrant and working-class resorts.

Yet this new cultural practice accomplished more than simply open-ing a previously all-male realm of cross-cultural camaraderie to so-called respectable white women. It also served as a mechanism through which affluent whites could negotiate the changing demographic character-istics and spatial organization of modern U.S. cities. Encompassing an even broader cultural terrain than its predecessors, slumming became central to the emergence of the commercialized leisure industry, prompt-ing the creation of a variety of new public amusements that promoted the crossing of racial and sexual boundaries. This development in turn fueled the advent of more intense urban reform campaigns that were de-signed to police the cross-cultural and sexual interactions that took place in these spaces and to reinforce traditional nineteenth-century notions of social and sexual propriety and respectability. But as reformers fought an uphill—and ultimately unwinnable—battle, white middle- and upper-class New Yorkers and Chicagoans began to embrace slumming even more heartily—not only as a means to ground the changing popular con-ceptualization of race and sexuality in particular urban spaces but also as an opportunity to shore up their own superior standing in the shifting racial and sexual hierarchies by juxtaposing themselves with the women and men they encountered on their slumming excursions.

The late nineteenth and early twentieth centuries were a highly con-tentious period in U.S. history. The rapid urbanization of an increas-ingly varied and expanding population—exemplified by the massive immigration of southern and eastern Europeans and the unprecedented migration of Southern blacks and single women and men to Ameri-can cities—created a sense of tremendous flux. Indeed, the very basis of American nationality was openly and vociferously debated. Histori-ans have described the antagonistic efforts undertaken by so-called old-stock Americans—those of northwestern European descent—to solidify the boundaries that separated them from the supposed danger posed by these new urban populations. An ever-expanding array of public and private reform organizations battled to control the moral construction of the urban landscape, stigmatizing and criminalizing the social and sexual behavior of immigrants, blacks, and single women and men, while attempting to Americanize them through the imposition of the standards of middle-class respectability.[12]

U.S. cities were also marred by the rebirth of particularly virulent strains of nativism and racism. The Red Scare that followed the First World War painted Italian and Russian—especially Jewish—immigrants as po-tent, socialistic threats to the Anglo-American way of life. Native-born whites led a campaign for legislative quotas, slowing eastern and southern European immigration to a trickle and completely excluding the entry of Asian immigrants into the United States.[13] During this same period, the Ku Klux Klan experienced dramatic growth, especially in Northern U.S. cities, where the animosity of its estimated four to five million members was directed primarily against adherents to the "alien" religions of Catholicism and Judaism. The Klan's historical reign of violence against African Americans also continued; lynchings occurred with frightening frequency well into the 1930s, enforcing racial, class, and gendered hierarchies of power through sheer force of terror. When Southern blacks migrated to northern cities in search of better economic and social conditions, they were greeted with still more violence—at the workplace, in the streets, and in an extraordinary wave of urban riots during the late 1910s and early 1920s.[14]

The hostility of old-stock Americans was also directed at the single women and men who flooded U.S. cities during the late nineteenth and early twentieth centuries. Although the women's suffrage movement overcame strong opposition to achieve passage of the Nineteenth Amendment in 1920, its supporters were increasingly lesbian-baited because of their expressed opposition to women's traditional roles. Other "New Women," single men, and urban bohemians were castigated for their supposed sexual immorality and promiscuity. Their support for birth control measures, engagement in sexual relations for pleasure, and other transgressions against reproductive sexuality rendered them social outcasts on par with prostitutes and so-called sexual inverts.[15]

Such developments marked the extremes in the struggle to maintain or reorganize the structure of power in early-twentieth-century U.S. cities, but similar battles occurred on a daily basis in the more mundane reaches of urban life—on neighborhood streets, for example, and in local workplaces, housing, and public amusements. During the late nineteenth and early twentieth centuries, the slumming venues of New York and Chicago furnished a unique space for such everyday struggles by encouraging middle- and upper-class whites to *choose* to interact with the women and men who lived in the cities' socially marginalized districts. In the absence of any fixed biological or cultural notions of race and sexuality, this decision to go slumming provided a powerful means to naturalize changing notions of racial and sexual difference by "marking" them into the material culture and physical spaces of U.S. cities. That is, as well-to-do whites interacted with the inhabitants of increasingly racialized and sexualized urban neighborhoods, slumming made the abstractions of race and sexuality seem more stable and "real."[16]

This book's first two chapters trace the spatial dimensions of this phenomenon, documenting both the shifting cultural geography of slumming and the range of regulatory mechanisms that white middle-class
reformers and municipal officials devised to police the social and sexual
interactions that took place in these spaces. Concocted as a way for well-
to-do whites to observe and sometimes interact with the most "foreign"
residents of late-nineteenth-century New York and Chicago, slumming
began as a place-based activity focused on the so-called slums and red-
light districts inhabited by recent southern and eastern European immigrants, blacks, and Chinese. Yet even as this unique cultural practice
prompted affluent whites to participate in the bustling public culture of
these districts, it also reified the notion of the slum as a container for the
degradation and immorality commonly associated with such racialized
populations. However, when reformers successfully effected the closure
of the cities' red-light districts in the early- to mid-1910s, slumming became detached from the specific urban locale of the slum and assumed
the status of an activity in and of itself. Rather than describing affluent
white pleasure seekers' participation in the dance halls and saloons of the
cities' immigrant and working-class districts, slumming became a type
of amusement that they used to negotiate subsequent demographic and
spatial changes in the city. As sizable new populations of "free-loving"
bohemian artists and radicals, blacks, and lesbians and gay men appeared
in New York and Chicago, they each became the subjects of successive
new slumming vogues. These vogues in turn helped to associate each of
the new populations with particular urban spaces, simultaneously establishing them in the public's mind as exotic others—as the residents of
the immigrant and working-class districts before them had been—while
downgrading the urban spaces with which they were associated by casting them in terms of the slum.

Building on this cultural geography, the final four chapters of this
book critically examine the everyday racial and sexual negotiations that
took place among the participants during each of four successive slumming vogues. Beginning with affluent whites' turn-of-the-century excursions into the slums and red-light districts of Chicago and New York, the
chapters focus sequentially on slummers' search for "bohemian *thrillage*,"
their increasing fascination with the "Negro vogue," and the emergence
of the "pansy and lesbian craze." From the mid-1880s until the outbreak
of the Second World War, these vogues prompted the development of a
range of public amusements where the ongoing transformation of racial
and sexual ideologies in the United States could be intimately experienced and where participants were encouraged to use their slumming

excursions to mark emerging conceptions of race and sexuality in the popular culture and space of U.S. cities.

As recent historical studies by Mathew Frye Jacobson, Robert Orsi, David R. Roediger, and others have demonstrated, the residents of late-nineteenth-century U.S. cities had a very different perception of "race" and racial difference from that which would become hegemonic by the middle of the twentieth century. Rather than viewing all individuals as either white or black, they operated within a racial framework that cast recent immigrants from southern and eastern Europe—especially Italians and Jews—as a sort of nonwhite "in-between" group of peoples, situated above blacks in the racial hierarchy of the United States but beneath old-stock whites.[17] They likewise possessed a different understanding of sexual normalcy and difference than that defined by the hetero/homo sexual dyad that also consolidated its cultural hegemony in the mid-twentieth century. As scholars such as George Chauncey, Lisa Duggan, and Jonathan Ned Katz have shown, in the late nineteenth century—and among many immigrant and working-class communities well into the first decades of the twentieth century—sexual abnormality was defined not by the expression of one's sexual desire for a person of the same sex but by one's adoption of the mannerisms, public comportment, and even sexual roles commonly associated with members of the so-called opposite sex. That is, "mannish women" and feminine male "fairies" were considered to be sexually abnormal, but their more normatively gendered sexual partners were not. Feminine women and masculine men who abided by the sexual and other cultural roles conventionally ascribed to their sex could engage in same-sex sexual encounters without risking stigmatization or the loss of their status as purportedly normal women and men.[18]

Mapping the complex relationship between racial formation and sexual classification in the United States over the course of the late nineteenth and early twentieth centuries, this book details the crucial role that slumming played both in making visible and in facilitating the transition from one racial and sexual regime to the next. In addition, it demonstrates that the transformation from a gendered sexual regime to the now-hegemonic hetero/homo sexual binary was inextricably linked to the emergence of an increasingly polarized white/black racial axis—and vice versa. As successive slumming vogues encouraged affluent white women and men to position themselves in relation to a shifting series of racial and sexual "others," slumming provided a mechanism through which its participants could use both race and sexual encounters to mediate their transition from one system of sexual classification to another. Moreover, by creating spaces where Jewish and Italian immigrants could begin to consolidate their claim to whiteness by simultaneously emulating and differentiating themselves from the sexual permissiveness and "primitivism" they had come to associate with black urban culture, slumming also ensured that shifting notions of sexual propriety and respectability became integral to the definition of race. That is, despite its occasional egalitarian impulses, slumming proved to be largely complicit both in the efforts of previously nonwhite or "in-between" racial groups to secure whiteness at the expense of black subjugation and in the refashioning of sexual normalcy and difference from a gendered system of marginalized fairies and mannish women to a cultural dyad that privileged heterosexual object choice.[19]

A few words are in order about the book's terminology and its title. Although slumming clearly had derogatory connotations in the United States during the late nineteenth and early twentieth centuries, many of which persist today, I have chosen to retain—and even emphasize—this term for several important reasons. Foremost among these is the prevalence with which turn-of-the-century Americans relied upon the notion of slumming to describe their participation in activities that encouraged them to venture into the city's more socially marginalized neighborhoods. In its most demeaning formulation, some affluent white pleasure seekers no doubt used the term consciously to reinforce their sense of social and moral superiority over the residents of the districts that they visited. But following the precedent of its British origins, *slumming* also lent itself to more well-meaning uses, whether describing the benevolent work that charitable organizations undertook in impoverished urban neighborhoods or the practice of living among the residents of the slum in settlement houses or religious missions.[20] More often, however, Americans simply employed the term mindlessly, embracing it as casually as they did each of the popular slumming crazes while paying little or no attention to how their language—or even the practice of slumming itself—was received by the women and men who became the objects of such cultural fascination.

In an effort to avoid such thoughtless usage of the term, this book critically examines both the rhetoric and the practice of slumming, giving as much attention to the way that socially marginalized groups resisted slummers' incursions into their neighborhoods as to the actions and ideas of the slummers themselves. But at the same time, it embraces the term's flexibility and its historical application to a wide array of activities, finding in the notion of slumming a useful shorthand (especially in the absence of any more applicable term) to encapsulate the full range of cross-racial and sexual encounters that took place in New York and Chicago over the course of the late nineteenth and early twentieth centuries. This is not to say that all the activities encompassed in this study constituted a form of slumming in any classical, voyeuristic sense. Most settlement house workers and moral reformers, for example, were motivated to visit the cities' immigrant and working-class neighborhoods less to indulge in sexual or racialized thrills than to participate in well-meaning projects of social uplift. Yet by linking such sincere cross-cultural encounters with their more voyeuristic cousins, the rubric of slumming plays an important analytical role—that of reminding readers that no matter how different an individual's motivations for visiting socially marginalized urban districts might initially seem, they often prove more similar upon closer examination.[21] For instance, although white jazz musicians ventured to Harlem and Bronzeville more out of a sincere appreciation of black rhythms and performance techniques than from any fascination with the alleged primitivism of black urban life, their interactions with black entertainers could be every bit as exploitative as the actions of more typical slummers. Indeed, many black jazz performers accused their white compatriots of stealing and capitalizing upon their musical innovations.

Throughout the book, readers will also encounter a number of derogatory terms that white Americans used to denote racial and sexual others during the late nineteenth and early twentieth centuries. As with the rhetoric of slumming, I have used such terms advisedly both to give a feeling of the historical era under consideration and to provide critical insight into the racial and sexual dynamics of turn-of-the-century American culture. Following well-established traditions in the history of U.S. sexuality, for instance, I have employed historically accurate terms such as *fairy*, *pansy*, *bulldagger*, and *queer* in order to call attention to the differences between our present-day understanding of sexual identities and practices and those that were commonplace a century ago. (To avoid the repetitive use of the rather clinical-sounding *homosexuals* and *homosexuality*, however, I have sometimes resorted to the somewhat anachronistic use of *gay men and lesbians* and have occasionally employed the adjective *queer*, as used by present-day queer theorists to encompass an even broader range of nonnormative or *anti*normative sexual identities and practices.) Although also endeavoring to document a racial landscape significantly different from that of the present day, for the most part I have avoided the use (except in direct quotations) of historically accurate terms such as *Hebrews*, *Chinamen*, *Negroes*, and even more derogatory racial references. Hewing to the traditions and conventions of historical studies of race and ethnicity, I have opted instead for the present-day parlance of *Jewish, Chinese, black,* and *African American*—although the last is used only when it can be applied with certainty, since a significant number of urban blacks in early-twentieth-century New York and Chicago were West Indian immigrants.

Two additional parameters of the study also require some explanation: the book's geographic focus and the scope and limitations of the primary sources upon which its arguments are based. While slumming played a significant role in the nightlife of many (if not all) U.S. cities, this study focuses on the sexual and racial encounters that took shape in the public amusements of Chicago and New York. It does so primarily to take advantage of both the extensive documentation and the complex social dynamics of these urban centers. As the two largest cities in the country during the late nineteenth and early twentieth centuries, New York and Chicago were the subjects of extensive studies by urban sociologists and private anti-vice organizations.[22] Indeed, the voluminous unpublished field reports of these organizations comprise a significant portion of the evidence that appears in this book. But more importantly, the diverse populations of these two cities provide an opportunity to explore the widest variety of slumming's permutations—from affluent whites' excursions into the dives frequented by southern and eastern European immigrants, Chinese immigrants, and blacks to their subsequent explorations of bohemian tearooms and masquerades, black-and-tan cabarets, and the nightclubs and drag balls frequented by lesbians and gay men.

In assessing the relative significance of the phenomenon of slumming in both New York and Chicago, the unpublished correspondence, memoirs, and reminiscences of prominent writers, musicians, and socialites have proved invaluable. Yet in an attempt to document the interactions that took place among ordinary women and men in the cities' more marginal nightspots, this book employs a much wider variety of sources, including local government records, sociological studies, novels, newspapers, and trade magazines. Perhaps the most important—and certainly the most plentiful—evidence, however, comes from the field reports of undercover investigators employed by private anti-vice organizations such as the Committee of Fourteen in New York and the Juvenile Protective Association in Chicago. These documents provide particularly valuable descriptions of urban slumming venues and the activities that occurred within them. Read at face value, they offer some sense of the white middle-class objections to slumming, but they also yield important insights when read against the grain. Mindful of their prejudices and moral assumptions, I have attempted to do just that, compensating for the relative paucity of first-person responses to slumming by teasing out the reactions of immigrants, blacks, bohemians, and homosexuals as recorded, either directly or indirectly, in such investigative reports. I have also used these reports on occasion to document the actions and beliefs of the slummers themselves, having found that the distinction between thrill seeking and investigative expeditions was often a narrow one indeed.

Finally, given the subject of this study, it seems imperative to say a few words about the book's relation to the phenomenon under examination. Drawing on often-explicit primary source material in order to provide a glimpse into the intimate history of cross-racial and sexual encounters in the nightlife of late-nineteenth- and early-twentieth-century New York and Chicago, this book clearly runs the risk of promoting some version of "armchair slumming" among its readers. No doubt some will find parts of this book titillating and sensationalistic. But in critically analyzing and historically contextualizing even the most salacious accounts of past social and sexual interactions, this book seeks to make productive use of the voyeuristic aspects of such research in order to reveal the complex, sometimes exploitative and often erotic processes through which racial and sexual ideologies were constructed more than a century ago and through which they continue to find their power today. If the result of this enterprise is as pleasurable and stimulating as it is informative, so much the better.

PART ONE

The Spatial Dynamics of Slumming and the Emergence of Commercial Leisure

ONE

Into the Slums: The Spatial Organization, Cultural Geography, and Regulation of a New Urban Pastime

In the mid-1880s, affluent white New Yorkers embraced a new form of urban amusement, forming "slumming parties," as they called them, to explore the immigrant and working-class districts of the city's Lower East Side. Copying the latest London trend, they would gather a small group of male and female friends, hire a police escort and, according to one newspaper account of these early excursions, set out to "see for themselves how the poorer classes live." These late-night sojourns guided well-to-do whites into the crowded tenements of the "Italian and Hungarian colonies on the east side," through the Jewish immigrant commercial and residential districts located along Baxter and Hester streets, "and thence on a regular tour of the dives," including the Bowery's bustling concert halls and the nearby "Celestial eating houses" and "opium joints" of Chinatown.[1]

Heralding the advent of this new urban phenomenon, the *New York Times* predicted in the autumn of 1884 that "the latest fashionable idiosyncrasy in London—i.e., the visiting of the slums of the great city by parties of ladies and gentlemen for sightseeing—" was certain to "become a fashionable dissipation . . . among our belles." Although warning about the possible dangers associated with such excursions, the *Times* quickly embraced the trend and suggested a number of other urban districts that might provide some degree of amusement for the intrepid slummer. In addition to the crowded tenements of the Lower East Side, the *Times* recommended "the west side, south of Cortlandt-street and west of Broadway, . . . a populous neighborhood, offering many attractions to the sight-seeking slummer, as also the line and neighborhood of the elevated railroad in South Fifth-avenue." To this already substantial list, the newspaper added the west-side Tenderloin, New York's preeminent red-light district, including "the 'colored' colony between Twentieth and Thirtieth streets" that nestled into its midst. "A few minutes' walk" in this region, the *Times* noted, "will take the 'slummer' from the Oriental splendor of the Hoffman House," a hotel located at Broadway and Twenty-fifth Street, "to some of the lowest beer saloons in the city, dingy and dirty, frequented by the vilest characters of both sexes."[2]

Successive slumming parties soon discarded the police escort, but other elements of these early expeditions quickly became standard—not only in New York, but also in Chicago and other major U.S. cities. Nearly all early slumming excursions included both women and men, reflecting the growing trend toward the heterosocialization of public leisure.[3] These expeditions likewise maintained the early focus on the cities' Jewish and Italian tenement districts, Chinatowns, and the black communities that overlapped the cities' principal red-light districts. During the late nineteenth century, middle- and upper-class whites sometimes intruded into the very living quarters of the urban poor. By the turn of the century, however, such unwelcome incursions were usually omitted from the typical slumming itinerary. Instead, slummers rambled through neighborhood streets, visited immigrant restaurants and shops, and heartily indulged in the liquor and easy social and sexual interactions available in the districts' colorful dance halls and saloons.

A popular new cultural amusement, slumming made manifest the profound physical and demographic transformations that reshaped U.S. cities during the late nineteenth and early twentieth centuries. While encouraging well-to-do white pleasure seekers to venture beyond the protective confines of their own neighborhoods, the practice reinforced the public perception of the American city as a segregated place. As the term suggests, slumming was centered on the "slum," designating both a physical urban space and a white middle-class idea about that space and the people who inhabited it. The emergence of slumming thus revealed more about the women and men who participated in this activity than about the inhabitants of the urban geographies they visited. Ultimately, the pastime demonstrated the extent to which prosperous New Yorkers and Chicagoans bought into the misguided notion that the slum and the red-light district were spaces where degradation and immorality could be safely cordoned off from their own families and homes.

While reform-minded middle- and upper-class whites eventually forced the closure of the red-light districts and slum resorts that attracted affluent thrill seekers in turn-of-the-century New York and Chicago, attempts to police these areas and to regulate the behavior of their inhabitants often served to reinforce their appeal. The presence of reformers—especially female reformers—on the streets and in the tenements and dives of these districts paradoxically suggested that such spaces were safe for popular congregation, and reformers' activities in the cities' slums and red-light districts were often remarkably similar to those of their pleasure-seeking compatriots. Whether they took the form of benevolent uplift, sociological investigation, or the mere pursuit of pleasure, intrusions into the slums were first and foremost the product of a particular bourgeois conception of the spatial dynamics and organization of U.S. cities during the late nineteenth and early twentieth centuries.

The Slum, the Red-Light District, and the Spatial Origins of Slumming

Slumming was an activity that emerged from the dramatic social and spatial reconfiguration of U.S. cities during the latter decades of the nineteenth century. Given its connotations of venturing beneath one's own social standing and beyond the parameters of one's local neighborhood, the practice marked both the cultural ascendancy of a vibrant and sizable urban middle class and the increasing geographic segregation of U.S. cities along class lines. In short, slumming was a practice that required the advent of the slum—as an identifiable urban space and as an ideological concept that carefully separated the lives and homes of well-to-do white women and men from the deprivation and degradation associated with urban poverty.[4]

The idea of the slum as a vast, identifiable, even menacing, district of urban poverty was a direct outgrowth of the economic transformations and technological innovations of Gilded Age urban America. In New York and Chicago, for instance, an unprecedented building boom gave rise to hundreds of new commercial structures, including massive urban department stores and high-rise office buildings, that initially benefited the cities' elite and burgeoning middle classes. But as these expanding commercial districts encroached upon neighboring dwellings, most of the white middle- and upper-class residents of New York and Chicago departed the central cities. Taking advantage of the introduction of new modes of mass transit that made commuting downtown to work more affordable, they relocated to exclusive new suburban communities or to the elaborate apartment buildings that were being constructed in uptown Manhattan and along the lakefront on Chicago's North Side.[5]

Although this movement of affluent whites to class-segregated residential enclaves created an unprecedented geographic divide between the urban poor and the elite, working-class migration also contributed to the emergence of the slum. When the development of large-scale manufacturing led to the creation of industrial suburbs on the outskirts of New York and Chicago, thousands of workingmen and women—especially those of native birth or of German or Irish parentage—chose to leave the cities' centers in pursuit of increased economic opportunities, all but abandoning the dwellings of the central city to the most dissolute and impoverished of urban residents, as well as to those unskilled laborers who comprised the bulk of the cities' most recent arrivals.[6]

Inhabited primarily by this motley crew of urban "failures" and newcomers unfamiliar with the ways of the city, the slum became associated in the minds of most Americans with extreme poverty and abjection. Yet the area's degenerating reputation was not simply a product of its changing residential composition; it was a direct outgrowth of the slum's unique physical environs. Although the emerging new central business districts of New York and Chicago had swallowed up substantial portions of their urban cores, the uneven commercial development of these districts had subjected other sections of the cities' centers to dereliction and neglect. Holding out for the higher profits associated with the area's wholesale transformation, real estate owners were often reluctant to make even the most minor repairs to decaying buildings in the central city. Instead, they encouraged the subdivision of these dwellings into lodging houses and tenements, seeking short-term gains by packing increasing numbers of residents into the homes that had been abandoned by the cities' more prosperous residents.[7]

As these dilapidated neighborhoods lay fallow for extended periods of time, property owners sought to wrench even more revenue from them by building additional structures in vacant lots and in the rear yards of existing tenements, intensifying the congestion and urban blight that so alarmed reformers. In New York, this process produced an increasingly high-rise, brick-clad district of twenty-five-foot-wide "dumb-bell" tenements that, according to the New York State Tenement House Commission of 1900, routinely squeezed "as many as 100 to 150 persons in one building, extending up six or seven stories into the air." In Chicago, however, the physical landscape of the slum was somewhat different. Although New York–style tenement buildings began to appear in the slums of the Windy City at the turn of the century, most of Chicago's tenement districts were characterized by ramshackle two- and three-story wooden houses that had been subdivided to accommodate multiple families. Despite these differences, reformers generally agreed that the tenements of both cities shared several distinctive qualities, including "lack of light and ventilation, insufficient protection against fire, [and] surroundings so unclean and uncomfortable as to make home life almost impossible." Yet even as the physical crowding of bodies and structures made the cities' slums seem more noxious and uninviting, it produced a sense of containment that served both to convince affluent white New Yorkers and Chicagoans that their daily lives were safely isolated from these districts and to provoke their curiosity and concern about the goings-on in such spaces.[8]

From the mid-1880s through the early 1910s, this concomitant curiosity and concern about the social and moral conditions of the slum motivated thousands of well-to-do white women and men to participate in a range of cross-class interactions, each of which operated under the general rubric of "slumming." As the *Chicago Tribune* noted in a 1907 editorial, urban Americans considered the activities of "members of religious organizations like the Salvation Army," who visited the "slum districts" of the city "with the hope of finding people who have been reported to them as lost to home and friends," to be a form of slumming. But they also employed the term to describe the endeavors of "sociological workers" who labored to understand the social and physical conditions of poverty, "in order that intelligent action may be taken in the direction of remedy or restraint." Thus, slumming encompassed both the fact-gathering expeditions of the nation's earliest urban sociologists and the home visits and educational campaigns that women reformers established in tenement districts. Even the muckraking journalism of Jacob A. Riis, George Kibbe Turner, and others was perceived as a type of slumming—albeit one that prompted readers to partake of a little "armchair slumming" of their own as they followed such authors on their sensationalistic forays into the cities' immigrant and working-class neighborhoods.[9]

At the turn of the last century, however, the term was far more commonly used to describe those excursions into the cities' slums for which the *Chicago Tribune* could find "no excuse." Composed of "well dressed and apparently respectable" white women and men, who appeared to be motivated by little more than "vulgar curiosity" and "a morbid desire to find out how the underworld lives," these slumming parties left the newspaper's editors both irritated and perplexed. Other types of slumming might be justified by the participants' desires to improve—or at least to document—the social and moral ills that Americans came to associate with the slum. But the *Tribune* found absolutely no benefit in the exploits of affluent whites who ventured "from one resort to another intent upon seeing the sights," when "there are enough people who must be brought into contact with the evil of the world without needlessly increasing the number." Yet even as the newspaper's editors lobbied for the "slumming party as an amusement . . . [to] be frowned down," their rhetoric made explicit the basic premise that united all turn-of-the-century slumming excursions: namely, that the slum constituted an identifiable and uniform region of urban poverty, congestion, and decay that was segregated, both geographically and morally, from the residential districts inhabited by middle- and upper-class whites.[10]

This image of the slum was, of course, at odds with that held by many of the immigrant and working-class women and men who called these districts home. Although some slum dwellers, such as the rural Italian immigrant Leonard Covello, bemoaned the fact that "the endless monotonous rows of tenement buildings . . . shut out the sky" in New York, replacing "sunlight and fresh air" with "four walls and people over and under and on all sides of us," many others viewed these districts as vibrant, bustling communities that afforded immigrants and black migrants from the rural South with a unique opportunity to establish a toehold in the urban world. From a white middle-class perspective, the living conditions that residents encountered in the tenement districts of both New York and Chicago were far from acceptable, but for the immigrant or working-class migrant who had only recently arrived in the city, they provided cheap, reliable accommodation in a central location. The slums of New York and Chicago afforded easy access to the employment opportunities available in the cities' new central business districts, including unskilled work in warehouses and transportation terminals, and the neighborhoods' lower rents enabled residents to save up funds either to finance their own eventual return home or to subsidize the subsequent migration of family and friends. The slums were made more appealing, too, by the opportunities they provided new residents to live in close proximity to others who spoke the same native language, practiced the same religion and customs, and ate the same foods. Doubtless each of these benefits was undercut by the more commonly recognized disadvantages of the neighborhoods' crowded and dilapidated quarters. Yet "in spite of all the difficulties that are thrown in their way by economic struggle and municipal neglect," more than one reformer noted that "in a large majority of cases" the immigrant and working-class residents of such districts lived "a clean and decent life."[11]

Slummers, of course, lacked such a nuanced understanding of the tenement districts. Whether intended primarily for the sake of amusement or freighted with more lofty social goals, the success of slumming depended upon the existence of relatively stable districts of the presumed urban squalor and immorality that piqued the curiosity and concern of the cities' more prosperous residents. Yet just as the white middle-class notion of the "slum"—in cultural historian Alan Mayne's formulation—routinely "obscured and distorted the varied spatial forms and social conditions to which it was applied," the practice of slumming, firmly embedded in bourgeois ideology, actively created the very balance of pleasure and danger that, in alternate guises of benevolent reform and amusement seeking, it both pretended to rectify and exploited. Indeed, the practice of slumming was responsible not only for helping to naturalize the middle-class conception of the slum that permeated the popular imagination of turn-of-the-century America but, to a significant extent, for its very creation.[12]

Whether reform oriented or amusement driven, however, slumming excursions into the tenement districts of New York and Chicago were less a product of class difference than an outgrowth of the shifting racial landscape of urban America.[13] In New York and Chicago, this transformation could be attributed, in part, to the steady growth of the cities' black populations. In the thirty-year period from 1880 to 1910, according to the U.S. Census Bureau, the "Negro population" of Chicago grew nearly sevenfold, from 6,480 to 44,103, while in Manhattan it more than tripled, from 19,663 to 60,534. The emergence of a small but clearly identifiable Chinese urban community during these same years also contributed to the changing racial landscape of New York and Chicago. The Chinese population of Manhattan swelled from 731 in 1880 to 3,476 in 1910, and the rate of increase was even more dramatic in Chicago, from 171 to 1,778.[14]

The most significant factor in these cities' racial transformations, however, was the influx of Italians, Jews, and other immigrants who began arriving from southern and eastern Europe during the last two decades of the nineteenth century. As late as the mid-1880s, these "new" immigrants constituted less than a quarter of the people entering the United States each year, but by 1896 and for more than two decades thereafter, these groups comprised the vast majority of new arrivals. A substantial proportion of these new immigrants took up residence in New York and Chicago, radically transforming the demographic profiles of these two cities. In 1890, only 39,951 Italians lived in Manhattan. By 1910, the number had grown to 199,757, not counting their American-born children. Although more difficult to measure, the Jewish population also rose considerably during this period. U.S. census figures documenting the growth of Manhattan's Russian-born population, the vast majority of which was Jewish, provide a rough estimation of this expansion—from 48,790 residents in 1890 to 285,198 in 1910. While smaller in absolute numbers, the growing concentration of Italian and Jewish immigrants in Chicago was equally remarkable: the Italian-born population grew nearly eightfold, from a meager 5,685 residents in 1890 to 45,169 in 1910, while the city's Jewish population (as estimated through census figures for Russian-born immigrants) experienced an even more dramatic expansion, from 7,683 residents in 1890 to 121,786 in 1910. Because these figures do not include American-born offspring of these groups, they necessarily underestimate both the size of new immigrant communities in New York and Chicago and their impact on the racial dynamics of the two cities.[15]

The extraordinary degree of fascination with which slummers approached the tenement districts inhabited by these sizable new racialized urban populations was prominently exhibited in the popular press of the day. Whether in magazine articles or in book-length exposés, reformers and muckraking journalists alike provided vivid glimpses into the elaborate and seemingly distinct social worlds that blacks, Chinese, Jewish, and Italian immigrants constructed in the dilapidated slums of New York and Chicago. Foremost among these accounts was Jacob A. Riis's *How the Other Half Lives* (1890), which introduced readers to the variety of new immigrant and working-class groups that had begun to settle on the Lower East Side of New York. But Riis's book was only one of an astonishing array of publications that offered armchair slummers an intimate tour of the lively street life and ramshackle dives of the black districts popularly known as "Niggertowns" or "Little Africas"; the joss houses, chop sueys, and opium dens of local "Chinatowns"; the Yiddish theaters, secondhand shops, and dance halls of the Jewish "Ghettoes"; and the Italian groceries and beer saloons of the cities' "Little Italies." These were accompanied by urban guidebooks, such as Louis Schick's *Chicago and Its Environs: A Handbook for the Traveler* (1891), which recommended touring through the South Clark Street slum district inhabited by "Italians, Greeks, Chinamen, Negroes, Hebrews, with an occasional German store keeper" on Sunday afternoons, when "almost all the inhabitants are to be seen out of doors and the variety of costumes and the diversity and brilliancy of color fully make the scene worth witnessing." Still other publications, including Rand, McNally & Company's travel guides to New York and Chicago, provided detailed instructions for undertaking "A Nocturnal Ramble" through the cities' tenement districts.[16]

Nevertheless, the mere presence of new immigrants and blacks in the cities' tenement districts did not always elicit attention from local slummers. Neither the southern Italian tenements of New York's East Harlem nor the slum district on Chicago's Near North Side, where a considerable population of southern Italian immigrants lived in close proximity to a small but identifiable black community, became significant slumming destinations. Both areas lacked the reputation for illicit sex that attracted pleasure seekers and reformers alike.[17]

In New York and Chicago, slumming was relegated to those immigrant and working-class neighborhoods that were coincident with the cities' red-light districts. These areas earned their colorful designation in the late nineteenth century when local brothels began to advertise to passersby by illuminating their doorways in shades of red, by covering their hall lamps with ruby-colored glass globes or hanging red curtains over the transom so that the light filtering onto the street took on a rosy hue. In due course, the term "red-light district" became shorthand for any relatively segregated urban neighborhood where prostitution flourished openly in brothels and on the streets or where illicit sexual encounters could be arranged in local saloons or dance halls.[18]

Unlike New Orleans, where the 1897 Story Ordinances established legally sanctioned sex districts, Chicago and New York never passed legislation codifying the locations of their red-light districts, nor did they manage to contain prostitution and other illicit sexual activities to particular neighborhoods. Yet in the minds of local residents and authorities, the red-light districts were clearly identifiable urban spaces. In New York, these districts were often little more than hyped-up entertainment locales where elaborate systems of graft prompted police officers to turn a blind eye to the presence of prostitution and other illicit activities. But in Chicago, municipal officials actively encouraged the extralegal persistence of the city's red-light districts, adopting an unofficial policy of segregation that sought to isolate prostitution from the city's commercial center and affluent white residential neighborhoods. So intent were they on this policy that, until the early 1910s, Chicago's elected officials and businessmen often publicly debated exactly where the geographic boundaries of the restricted districts should be drawn. Despite these different approaches, in both New York and Chicago the result was much the same: by the late nineteenth century, the cities' red-light districts usually overlapped that handful of neighborhoods where immigrants and blacks were able to locate housing and work—a development that surely heightened the districts' appeal to urban thrill seekers while it intensified the sense of danger and the threat of immorality that others associated with these neighborhoods.[19]

This conflation of the slum and the red-light district—both in the physical layout of the city and in the minds of well-to-do whites—was hardly accidental. It was the product of a complex interplay of several important social and cultural factors. These included the organization of urban space and public amusements that blacks and Chinese and southern and eastern European immigrants encountered upon their arrival in New York and Chicago, the patterns of these groups' migrations to U.S. cities, and the sexual cultures that they brought with them. But the spatial consolidation of the slum and the red-light district also reflected white urban residents' preconceived notions about the cities' most recent arrivals. Having already decided that prostitution and sexual indiscretion were an inevitable part of city life that could best be controlled through spatial confinement to select neighborhoods, many native-born whites easily assumed that these same neighborhoods should become home to those groups whom they believed were "naturally" inclined to such illicit activities.[20]

This assumption was particularly pronounced with respect to blacks. The 1911 report of the municipally funded Chicago Vice Commission asserted, "The history of the social evil in Chicago is intimately connected with the colored population. Invariably the larger vice districts have been created within or near the settlements of colored people." In New York, blacks often found themselves pushed into neighborhoods already associated with prostitution and other illicit activities. As the burgeoning population of Italian immigrants displaced blacks from the small community that they had established near the intersection of Thompson and Third streets on the Lower East Side, one of the few districts in which they were able to secure alternative accommodations was New York's most notorious red-light district. Remarking on this development in 1898, the Reverend P. Butler Tompkins of St. James Presbyterian Church noted that "the district known as the 'Tenderloin District,' . . . might now be called 'Little Africa,' [given] the change in the character of the residents" in the region that "extends west of Sixth Avenue and between Twenty-sixth and Fifty-second Streets."[21]

The segregation of the cities' latest arrivals to its tolerated red-light districts, however, was hardly limited to blacks. Much to the displeasure of the more "respectable" immigrants who had recently settled in New York and Chicago, by the turn of the century, the cities' Jewish "Ghettoes," "Little Italies," and "Chinatowns" were all widely associated with illicit sexual activity. In the preface to *The Spirit of the Ghetto*, Hutchins Hapgood's 1902 collection of sketches documenting the more positive and dynamic aspects of "Yiddish New York," the author acknowledged the growing perception among white New Yorkers that the city's "Jewish quarter" was a central locus of "immorality," "where 'red-lights' sparkle at night, [and] where the people are queer and repulsive." Others asserted that the presence of prostitution and other illicit activities among the cities' latest immigrants was a result of preexisting conditions in the districts where they settled. "The new immigrant," federal investigator Kate Holladay Claghorn remarked, whether "an unsophisticated Italian peasant or a poor Hebrew of quiet family life and moral traditions," had often been forced to settle in districts where "vice has been developed through years of a sifting process which has taken elsewhere the successful of the former generation of immigrants and left the failures." Such was the case, in Claghorn's estimation, on New York's Lower East Side, where Italian and Jewish immigrants had been "thrown in with the corrupt remnants of Irish immigration which now make up the beggars, the drunkards, the thugs, and thieves of those quarters." According to this scenario, it was little wonder that "lately . . . the Jews and Italians [were becoming] street-walkers and rowdies," since "everything [was] arranged to favor their becoming so."[22]

The practice of prostitution in immigrant communities did not reflect any inherent moral shortcomings so much as it evidenced how circumstances shaped the needs, desires, and demographics of the cities' new immigrant populations. With the exception of Bohemians, Moravians, and "Hebrews" (as U.S. officials began in 1899 to describe Jews, regardless of their national origin), the immigrants who arrived in the United States during the late nineteenth and early twentieth centuries were disproportionately male in composition. Whether single male laborers or married men who had, at least temporarily, left their wives behind, these men comprised a relatively transient population who, for the most part, were situated at the sexual prime of life. This pattern was especially pronounced among the cities' Italian and Chinese immigrants. Between 1880 and 1910, roughly 80 percent of the Italians who arrived in the United States each year were men, the vast majority of whom were between the ages of 14 and 44. Among Chinese immigrants, the sex ratio was even more sharply skewed. Because the Page Law of 1875, designed ostensibly to prohibit the importation of Chinese women into the United States for the purpose of prostitution, had in practice been used to prevent nearly all female Chinese immigrants from entering the country, Chinese men constituted as much as 96 percent of the total Chinese immigrant population in the United States between 1880 and 1910. Like the Italians, these men were almost uniformly of marriageable age; indeed, many of them were already married. Yet married or not, because many Chinese and Italian men intended to be in the United States for only a short period of time before returning to their home countries, they were often loathe to establish long-term romantic relationships in their American communities. For these men, the more casual sexual and romantic encounters that were fostered by the brothels, dance halls, and resorts of the cities' red-light districts provided an important and viable alternative for securing companionship or sexual release.[23]

Following the nineteenth-century model of male homosocial public leisure, industrious immigrant and working-class entrepreneurs opened saloons and gambling halls that catered to the districts' disproportionately male population and established brothels that specialized in providing women to service their own immigrant and racial communities. Amid the "bachelor society" of this predominantly male world, enterprising individuals even founded a number of "fairy" resorts, where female impersonators and other feminine men provided musical entertainment and sexual favors for an appreciative and lucrative male audience. Yet they also established a variety of public amusements that allowed immigrant and working-class women to socialize with local men as they searched for companionship amid the anonymity of the city. By the turn of the century, the resulting dance halls, nickelodeons, and other sexually integrated amusements had come to rival and, on occasion, even remake the predominantly male atmosphere of the traditional nineteenth-century concert hall and saloon. Documenting some of the more tangible effects of this trend toward the heterosocialization of urban leisure, a correspondent for the *National Police Gazette* reported in 1899 that "the concert hall of the Bowery to-day is not what it was years ago." Rather, he insisted, it had become "less pretentious, and has gotten to be simply a resort for people of both sexes—a sort of meeting place, as it were," a standard component in the commercialized leisure industry that grew in prominence in early-twentieth-century U.S. cities.[24]

This new emphasis on heterosocial commercial amusements fueled the influx of slummers into the immigrant and working-class districts of New York and Chicago. As public dance halls replaced private formal balls, and nickelodeons and amusement parks provided new alternatives to the opera and legitimate stage, the commercial resorts of the cities' new "bright-light districts" introduced well-to-do white pleasure seekers to a wide range of immigrant and working-class cultural productions—including ragtime, "tough dancing," vaudeville, and burlesque—that soon became mainstays in the popular culture of the United States. No doubt a persistent double standard inhibited the full participation of many affluent white women in these pleasurable diversions, especially if they were unescorted. But from the mid-1880s through the early 1910s, the increasing presence of respectable white women in the districts' more popular resorts clearly signaled an ongoing shift in the gendered dynamics of access to urban public spaces. As slumming helped to normalize this development by furnishing middle- and upper-class whites with a means to justify their participation in the new world of commercial amusements, it simultaneously catapulted the activity to the forefront of American culture. Whether living in the country's bigger cities or in its smaller rural communities, by the turn of the century, most adult Americans were familiar with not only the general practice of slumming but also the particular sections of New York and Chicago that had come to be so closely identified with it.

The Amusements of Slumming: Turn-of-the-Century Excursions through New York's Bowery and Tenderloin, Chicago's Levee Districts, and the Chinatowns of Both Cities

From the mid-1880s through the early 1910s, when affluent white Americans set out to go slumming, there was no more popular destination than the Bowery. Running roughly parallel to Broadway on the east side of lower Manhattan (figure 2), the street was New York's most vital working-class thoroughfare. By day, it bustled with immigrants and "floaters" shuffling in and out of its lodging houses, cheap restaurants, and secondhand shops, and at night, beneath the glare of brash electric signage, the street continued to writhe with activity. Boisterous crowds of working-class women and men covered its length, spilling in and out of the many immigrant theaters and concert saloons that rendered this mile-long stretch of pavement an exemplar of urban commercial leisure. Making their way

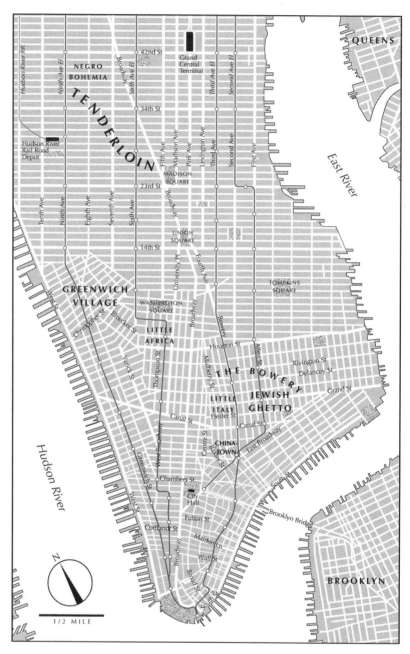

QUEENS

Hudson River RR

NEGRO
BOHEMIA

TENDERLOIN

Hudson River
Rail Road
Depot

42nd St

Ninth Ave El

Sixth Ave El

Broadway

Broadway

34th St

Grand
Central
Terminal

Third Ave El

Second Ave El

East River

Fifth Ave

Madison Ave

Park Ave

Lexington Ave

Third Ave

Second Ave

First Ave

MADISON
SQUARE

23rd St

Tenth Ave

Ninth Ave

Eighth Ave

Seventh Ave

Sixth Ave

Broadway

UNION
SQUARE

14th St

University Pl

Fourth Ave

TOMPKINS
SQUARE

GREENWICH
VILLAGE

WASHINGTON
SQUARE

Broadway

Bowery

Christopher St

Bleecker St

LITTLE
AFRICA

Varick St

Thompson St

Mulberry St

Houston St

Allen St

Rivington St

Delancey St

THE BOWERY

Grand St

LITTLE
ITALY

JEWISH
GHETTO

Hester St

Canal St

Centre St

Canal St

West Broadway

Greenwich St

CHINA-
TOWN

Baxter St

East Broadway

West St

Chambers St

City
Hall

South St

Fulton St

Brooklyn Bridge

Cortlandt St

Broadway

Maiden Ln

Wall St

Hudson River

N

Broad St

South St

BROOKLYN

1/2 MILE

2   This map of lower Manhattan illustrates the close proximity of the slums and red-light
    districts that fascinated turn-of-the-century slummers—principal among them, the Bowery,
    the Tenderloin, and Chinatown.

from the Bowery's southern terminus at Chatham Square to its northern-most point at Cooper Union, visitors to the district might encounter more different urban types than in any other part of the city. From respectable young clerks, "factory girls," and immigrant families to roughhousing sailors, hooligans, and streetwalkers, the habitués of the Bowery gave the district a unique, worldly feel, easily justifying its reputation among plea-sure seekers as what the poet and editor of *Puck* magazine Henry Cuyler Bunner described in 1894 as "the alivest mile on the face of the earth."[25]

Yet as Bunner noted, "properly speaking," the Bowery was more "a place . . . than a street or avenue," and slummers were initially drawn to the district not only by the dance halls and saloons that lined its raucous path but also by the immigrant restaurants, shops, and crowded tenements that occupied the surrounding blocks of New York's Lower East Side. Arriving by hansom cab, private brougham, or even by the Third Avenue elevated train, which connected the Bowery to the Upper East Side in 1893, uptown New Yorkers and tourists alike routinely ex-plored the neighborhoods situated on both sides of the busy thorough-fare. West of the Bowery, they pushed their way through the congested Italian quarter of Mulberry Bend, where, by day, noisy street vendors hawked bread, fruit, crockery, and clothing to industrious Neapolitan women, and by night, "half-dressed men and women" were said to come "staggering through the open doorways bearing pails of stale beer." One block further west, slummers often found themselves dodging the "pullers-in" at the "quaint and busy shops" where eastern European Jews had "enter[ed] into the old-clothes traffic," seeking instead to ex-plore the crowded Jewish Ghetto east of the Bowery. In the shabby tene-ments and busy cafés of Chrystie, Forsyth, and Orchard streets, among others, visitors were certain to encounter a remarkable array of Jewish men and women: Hungarian, Bohemian, and Portuguese Jews; "Polish Jews with their back-yards full of chickens"; and those to whom Bunner referred somewhat derisively as "Anarchist Russians."[26]

During their explorations of the residential sections of the district, some of the Bowery's earliest slummers apparently took the dictum to see how the other half lived quite literally. Like the novelist Wil-liam Dean Howells and his companion, who visited New York's "He-brew quarter" in the mid-1890s, these slummers deliberately chose to mimic the behavior of local reformers, whose "at home" visits to the tenements were intended to improve the residents' general living condi-tions. Arriving unannounced, these curiosity seekers randomly knocked on doors or simply pushed their way into the residents' living quar-ters. Yet as they nosed around even the shabbiest of the overburdened tenements, the interlopers were often pleasantly surprised to find that they were "not as dirty as one would think." Their curiosity satisfied, such visitors usually departed with little more than a casual thought about remedies for the impoverished circumstances in which so many recent immigrants found themselves. On occasion, one of the slummers might hand out "some small silver" as recompense for the inconvenience they had caused. But more often than not, they departed with nary a word, perhaps justifying their lack of compensation as Howells did, by finding "an unseemliness in it, as if it were an indignity added to the hardship of their lot . . . unless I gave all my worldly wealth to them."[27]

Not all visitors to the Bowery thought it unseemly to contribute to the local economy. Rather than barging into the homes of local residents, these slummers visited the area's restaurants and shops, sampling the food, clothing, and imported wares favored by the district's latest residents. A tiny cellar café located near the corner of Second Avenue and East Houston Street, for instance, became especially popular with well-dressed "clubmen" and other "inhabitants of the upper West Side" who sought to satisfy what one New York newspaper labeled their "Hungarian habit." Drawn by the sweet wines, "guylash" and the "wild, weird melodies" performed by the café's colorful "gypsy players," these well-heeled interlopers began arriving in such extraordinary numbers that, during the spring of 1899, the café's owners expanded their forty-seat establishment to accommodate as many as two hundred at a time.[28]

Other visitors to the area focused their culinary and shopping tours on the Italian district in Mulberry Bend. There, as one observer noted, they found "trays and bins . . . containing dozens and dozens of things that you would never guess were meant to eat if you didn't happen to see a ham or a string of sausages . . . among them," as well as "every article of apparel, external or private and personal, that [a woman] ever heard of, and some that she never heard of," available for purchase in almost "any shade or hue." Nevertheless, the majority of women who went slumming sought more than properly gendered activities, such as shopping. Like their male counterparts, these women slummers longed for a glimpse of the more ribald dimensions of immigrant and working-class life.[29]

On the Bowery, where Irish, Italian, and Jewish proprietors ran the vast majority of resorts, the attraction remained much the same from the 1890s though the early 1910s. At concert saloons, such as The Manhattan, located at 104 Bowery, male and female patrons were treated to an evening of unvarnished variety entertainment. Presented on a simple platform in the back room of the resort, The Manhattan's shows usually featured a series of suggestive comedy skits performed by waiters doubling as actors. But their main attractions were the popular, high-kicking, song-and-dance routines performed by women "dressed in short skirts and very low-necked waists and bare arms." In between performances, slummers were free to drink and carouse to their hearts' content. For some, this time was spent in further observation, ogling the dive's immigrant and working-class patrons as they engaged in conversation or "spieling," a popular dance style in which, according to one observer, couples held each other close, chins on shoulders, to "pivot or spin, around and around with the smallest circle that can be drawn around them." For others, however, it was a time for participation. More than a few of the well-to-do white women and men who visited such establishments chose to take a spin on the dance floor themselves. Still others pursued a course that hewed much more closely to the district's original red-light charms. "Invited by the waiter to go up in the boxes and sit with the ladies" who had just left the stage, The Manhattan's more prosperous male clientele were able to purchase female companionship at a price equal to the cost of the cigarettes and champagne the women consumed, while negotiating additional fees for any further favors they desired. [30]

For the particularly adventuresome male amusement seeker, the Bowery offered a number of even more bawdy attractions. On Bayard Street, for instance, in a relatively nondescript "three-story brick house, with green blinds," one habitué of the district recalled that slummers could "danc[e] with a bevy of girls" who appeared nearly nude in the ground-floor parlor. Known as a "tight house" because of "the fleshings all its inmates must wear," such resorts proved especially popular with those young men who preferred a bit of carousing with friends before heading upstairs for more intimate encounters. But for those less desirous of such niceties, the Jewish immigrant–run brothels of the Lower East Side provided more businesslike transactions, efficiently pairing up the thrill-seeking men who wandered through the Ghetto with the women who solicited on the district's streets and from the doorways and second-floor windows of neighborhood buildings. On Allen and Rivington streets, in particular, this practice became so prevalent—and so tolerated by local authorities—that the captain of the surrounding police precinct casually acknowledged that "men that are looking for that sort of thing"—whether local residents or curious slummers—"can find plenty of it" on the city's Lower East Side.[31]

Even more sensational entertainment could be found by those amusement seekers who chose to venture west of the Bowery, where the northward expansion of Little Italy into the black working-class settlement situated along Sullivan, Thompson, and Macdougal streets gave rise to a number of "black and tans," or, racially integrated resorts. As historian Elizabeth Clement has noted, these neighborhood dance halls and saloons were intended primarily as spaces of "interracial sociability" rather than "interracial spectacle"—that is, as places where local residents of all colors could interact with each other more as neighbors than as voyeurs seeking sensationalized entertainment. Yet as early as the mid-1880s, at least some well-to-do whites had already begun to patronize such dives, hoping to catch a glimpse of—or maybe even participate in—the couplings of "Negro men and white girls and white men and negro wenches" that were said to characterize these resorts. No doubt the double standard of the day discouraged most "respectable" white women from joining the slumming trade that patronized these early black and tans, but throughout the 1890s, such dives proved increasingly popular with the affluent white men who set out to see the city's sights.[32]

Enterprising slummers could locate still more opportunities for cross-racial encounters in "the Chinese colony in Mott, Pell, and Doyers Streets," situated just west of the southernmost blocks of the Bowery. At their most extreme, these interactions included visits to Chinatown brothels, where a handful of Chinese women and significantly more white female prostitutes serviced a mixed clientele of local Chinese men, immigrant and white male laborers, and occasional thrill-seeking male slummers. But during the late 1880s and early 1890s, most of the district's cross-racial encounters occurred in its infamous basement opium dens, where affluent white women and men alike smoked themselves into stupors alongside local Chinese addicts. By the mid-1890s, however, when Chinatown began to attract thousands of well-to-do whites with its promise of an exotic Oriental city-within-the-city, even these impulsive interactions became extremely rare. Rather than partaking of the brothel or the pipe, slummers found themselves instead ushered into fake opium joints where a handful of Chinese men and white women—the latter often legal wives of the former—staged "scenes of all sorts of iniquity" for the benefit of paying spectators.[33]

Although slummers might also visit the Chinese theater, the local joss house, and a smattering of neighborhood shops that marketed medicinal herbs and colorful silks, by the late 1890s, Chinatown's principal attractions were its restaurants and Bowery-style resorts. In 1898, one popular guide to the district noted that no tour of Chinatown was ever really considered complete until slummers had not only "drop[ped] in" on a local eatery "to see the natives eating their food with their chop sticks [*sic*]" but also visited one of the region's more notorious dives, such as the Chatham Club on Doyers Street or the Pelham Café at 12 Pell Street. Ironically, as the former served to reinforce Chinatown's particular appeal to slummers, the latter subtly undermined it. Because nearly all local resorts that permitted routine entry to non-Chinese patrons were operated by Irish, Jewish, and Italian proprietors, the general atmosphere that they promoted differed little from that available on the neighboring Bowery. Combined with the districts' close geographic proximity, this similarity in their appeal virtually ensured that both Chinatown and the Bowery became staples on nearly every New York slumming excursion.[34]

In fact, at the turn of the century, the only other section of New York that appealed to slummers to any considerable degree was the notorious Tenderloin. Concentrated between Fifth and Eighth avenues across a swath of converted brownstones that stretched from Twenty-third Street as far north as Fifty-seventh, the Tenderloin was New York's preeminent red-light district from the 1870s through the early 1910s. Its faro tables and roulette wheels offered the city's "young men, clerks, students, bookkeepers, and tradesmen" an upscale alternative to the more rough-and-tumble dives of the Bowery and Chinatown, and its concert halls and brothels promised access to more beautiful and refined women. Because the Tenderloin was located in close proximity to the Metropolitan Opera House and several other prominent theatrical establishments, the district's wine joints and dance halls also attracted a substantial number of affluent white *female* patrons, whose search for after-theater desserts or other diversions provided the impetus for numerous slumming excursions. Escorted by their male companions or husbands to resorts such as the Tenderloin's infamous Haymarket (figure 3), these women might opt to waltz the night away to the tune of the resort's small band. Or they could take a seat at one of the resort's many intimate tables to sip "claret lemonade" or even harder spirits while getting better acquainted with their escorts.[35]

For unaccompanied men, the Haymarket offered still more possibilities. According to one observer, "women walked about the place soliciting the different men, not interfered with in any way by anybody in charge of the place." No doubt prostitutes and other sexually available working-class women accounted for the vast majority of the Tenderloin's female patrons, but as the proprietor of a neighboring resort noted in 1898, "There is [also] a great many nice people go into all these places." Indeed, the *New York Times* reported that the Haymarket was so popular

3   The Haymarket, located in an old playhouse at the corner of Sixth Avenue and Thirtieth
     Street, was one of the Tenderloin's most notorious resorts. With some minor interruptions,
     this popular dance hall operated from 1878 to 1913, reaching the height of its popular-
     ity with slummers under the management of Edward Corey from the late 1890s until the
     resort's final closure. (Reprinted with permission from the Collection of The New-York
     Historical Society, negative 78887d.)

that during the calendar year of 1903, "its paid admissions" reputedly
"aggregated 1,900,000 . . . at a quarter apiece and 35 cents on Saturday
night."[36]

This is not to say that the Tenderloin lacked more risqué attractions
for adventuresome slummers. By the 1890s, observers noted that a section of West Thirty-ninth Street was "known all over the country" by

the sobriquet "Soubrette Row," because its bordellos were owned and operated by French immigrants who had a reputation for engaging in "unnatural practices." The Tenderloin's black resorts likewise attracted curious white interlopers in search of ragtime music and cross-racial sex. In the 1890s, most of these nightspots were situated in a relatively segregated portion of the Tenderloin, located along West Twenty-fifth and Twenty-seventh streets between Sixth and Seventh avenues. But by the 1910s, the "black Tenderloin" or "Negro Bohemia," as the section was popularly known, had relocated to Twenty-eighth and Thirtieth streets between Seventh and Eighth avenues and also encompassed large portions of the area bounded by West Thirty-fifth and Forty-first streets between Seventh and Ninth avenues. Although most of the resorts in this section were patronized exclusively by black residents and tourists, a few of the district's black-operated clubs, including Baron Wilkins's Café, Diggs' Place, William Banks's Keystone Café, and Edmund's Theatrical (or Douglas) Club, were "very popular," according to one observer, "and attract many young people—white and colored—who are induced to go there for past time [sic]."[37]

In Chicago, a similar combination of sexual and racialized attractions fueled the slumming expeditions of the late nineteenth and early twentieth centuries. As in New York, two of the earliest slumming destinations were the bustling Jewish Ghetto and Little Italy that emerged on Chicago's Near West Side (figure 4). A guide distributed by the Chicago Association of Commerce suggested that "the average visitor looking for the unusual" would enjoy the "Ghetto Market" on Jefferson Street between Twelfth and Fourteenth streets, "though it is squalid and dirty to a degree." Local slummers were also attracted to the pawnshops, open-air markets, restaurants, and Yiddish and Italian theaters situated on the city's West Side. Yet despite their inclusion in an 1889 *Sporting Club House Directory* and their apparent popularity with at least some male slummers, the brothels and saloons of the neighboring West Side Levee—as the restricted sex district bounded by West Lake, Monroe, Sangamon, and Halsted streets was commonly known—remained the nearly exclusive province of recent Jewish and Italian immigrants and the down-and-out hobos who gathered nightly along the "main stem" of West Madison.[38]

When it came to nighttime adventures in Chicago, affluent white residents and tourists turned their attention instead to the city's South Side Levee, the bustling red-light district located just south of the Loop, the city's central business district. Although it was one of three levee districts in Chicago at the turn or the century, the area was so popular

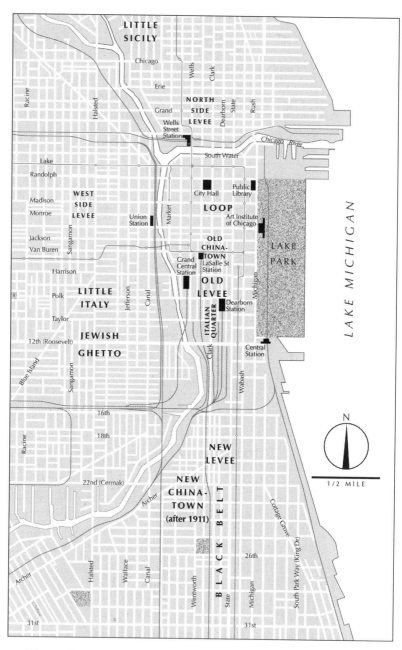

LITTLE SICILY

Chicago

Erie

NORTH SIDE LEVEE

Grand

Wells Street Station

Wells

Clark

Dearborn

State

Rush

Chicago River

South Water

Lake

Randolph

WEST SIDE LEVEE

Madison

Monroe

Jackson

Van Buren

Harrison

Polk

Taylor

12th (Roosevelt)

LITTLE ITALY

JEWISH GHETTO

Racine

Halsted

Sangamon

Union Station

Market

Jefferson

Canal

City Hall

Public Library

LOOP

Art Institute of Chicago

OLD CHINA-TOWN

Grand Central Station

LaSalle St Station

OLD LEVEE

ITALIAN QUARTER

Dearborn Station

Michigan

LAKE PARK

Central Station

Blue Island

Sangamon

Clark

Wabash

16th

18th

NEW LEVEE

Racine

22nd (Cermak)

NEW CHINA-TOWN (after 1911)

Archer

BLACK BELT

Cottage Grove

26th

Archer

Halsted

Wallace

Canal

Wentworth

State

Michigan

South Park Way (King Dr)

31st

31st

LAKE MICHIGAN

N

1/2 MILE

4   This map of central Chicago depicts the shifting geography of turn-of-the-century slum-ming destinations—from the old Levee district, Chinatown, and Italian quarter that drew white thrill seekers to the area just south of the Loop as early as the mid-1880s, to the new Levee district and Chinatown that took shape near the city's Black Belt in the early twen-tieth century and the expanding immigrant districts of Little Italy and the Jewish Ghetto located on the city's Near West Side.

that it was often referred to simply as "the Levee." Named after the disorderly levee districts of American river towns, this designation had originally been reserved for a particularly rough section of South State Street between Harrison and Taylor streets, but by the 1890s, it was used to denote an area of "about a half mile square," situated along the eastern bank of the Chicago River and bound by State Street on the east and Van Buren and Twelfth (now Roosevelt) streets on the north and south, respectively. Located within walking distance of the major department stores and corporate offices of the Loop, the Levee was much more easily accessible to Chicago residents and visitors than any of New York's red-light districts were to that city's white middle- and upper-class inhabitants. In fact, many visitors to the Windy City unknowingly found themselves in the midst of the Levee immediately upon their arrival in Chicago. As one local newspaper noted in 1891, "two of the finest railroad stations in the country, the Wisconsin Central and Northern Pacific, and Polk Street Depot" were located well inside the parameters of this notorious district.[39]

The Levee's extraordinary popularity and international reputation dated from the 1893 World's Columbian Exposition, when its location between the fair and the prominent hotels of the Loop left it uniquely situated for tourists' late-night ramblings. Sporting guides of the day advised their male readers that ribald entertainment and female companionship could be easily procured in most of the district's brothels, concert halls, and saloons. These ranged from the rough-and-tumble environs of the Park Theatre on South State Street and Vina Fields's house of black prostitution on Custom House Place (now Federal Street) to the opulent, gilded mansions of Carrie Watson on South Clark Street and Lizzie Allen on South Dearborn Street. Allen's brothel was said to have been so elaborate that it attracted not only the usual "visitors to 'joy houses' " but also occasional male and female slummers who hoped simply to gain a glimpse of the brothel's elaborate interior decoration and "rare treasures of art." Despite such ostensibly proper justifications for venturing into the Levee, however, throughout the 1890s muckraking exposés continued to advise respectable white women to steer well clear of the district's rowdy nightlife. Yet as in the Tenderloin and Bowery districts of New York, heterosocial slumming parties became increasingly common in Chicago's most prominent red-light district as the decade wore on.[40]

The participation of female slummers further increased during the first years of the twentieth century, as real estate interests and moral reformers forced the relocation of the Levee nearly one mile south. After

5   This drawing by H.G. Maratta titled *Chicago's "Levee District" at Night* shows the bustling
and well-illuminated street life of the district. Wending their way between popular dance
halls and saloons, hundreds of women and men nightly traversed South Clark Street in
search of pleasure of various kinds. Many of them doubtless took advantage of the "clean
rooms" advertised on the upper floors of several local resorts. (Reprinted from *Harper's
Weekly*, February 12, 1898. Collection of the author.)

the opening of the South Clark Street trolley in late 1895, a series of
complaints about the flagrant displays of prostitution along a route
that "citizens . . . were compelled to use . . . as transportation to and
from business" prompted municipal authorities to clean up the original
South Side Levee. The result: the district's brothels and resorts decamped
to the half square mile bounded by Clark Street, Wabash Avenue, and
Eighteenth and Twenty-second streets. This new Levee actually proved
even more popular with slummers, encompassing, as it did, a cluster of
well-known working-class dance halls and saloons, such as The Owl,
The Erin, and other resorts depicted in an 1898 illustration for *Harper's
Weekly* (figure 5). Without a doubt, male slummers continued to make
solo calls at the district's high-class brothels—the famed Everleigh Club,
located at 2131–33 South Dearborn Street, foremost among them. But
more and more often, they invited female companions—even their
wives—to join them as they sampled the liquor, ragtime, and "tough
dancing" that were so plentiful in the Levee. In fact, aside from the
Everleigh sisters' establishment, no Levee enterprise garnered more
public renown than Freiberg's Dance Hall and Theatre, at 180–82 East

Twenty-second Street. During the first decade and a half of the century, thousands of slummers visited this nightspot where, according to one local official, the "couples seemed to compete with each other in trying to undertake suggestive steps."[41]

While the casual intimacy of the Levee's dance halls and the district's reputation for flagrant prostitution made the area a "must-see" for many slummers, the Levee's association with immigrants and blacks also contributed to its popularity. Most contemporary observers thought of the Levee as a "segregated vice district," but the area was much more than that. Just as the Bowery's brightly lit amusements were accompanied by side-street tenements abounding with varied ethnic and racial groups, Chicago's Levee served simultaneously as red-light district and as residential neighborhood to a host of recent arrivals to the city. One Baptist missionary, who claimed to have documented more than four hundred saloons and five hundred houses of prostitution in the district during the early 1890s, noted "a mixed multitude who lived here: Americans, Africans, Italians, Spanish, French, Germans, Swedes, Jews, Arabians, and Syrians." Like New York's Tenderloin, the Levee was especially associated with its French inhabitants and their "cunning, brazen, Parisian licentiousness." But, of the many new residents who found their way to the Levee, none were more closely identified with the area than the Chinese and blacks, two groups that were largely segregated to the same district that the city had already set aside for prostitution and other illicit activities.[42]

At the turn of the century, Chicago's principal Chinese settlement was encompassed by the Levee. Located along a one-block segment of South Clark Street between Van Buren and Harrison streets, this early Chinatown was distinguished primarily by its grocers, gambling halls, and crowded "bachelor" quarters, so called because of the virtual absence of Chinese women in Chicago. But even this one block was not exclusively Chinese. As late as 1907, the Hip Sing Tong, one of the city's two principal Chinese mutual aid associations, was still headquartered above an Italian grocery and next door to a German restaurant. Nevertheless, Orientalist fantasies shaped the visits of most whites who arrived in the district hoping to gain entrée to the elusive opium dens that were said to populate the street's basements. One exposé noted that it was a "fad 'to hit the pipe just once' by some adventure seeking people in other walks of life." But the vast majority of slummers stopped far short of this, settling instead for a visit to a local chop suey restaurant before returning home with the general impression that Chinatown was, as one visitor recalled, "the most respectable, or rather the least disreputable, part of the Levee."[43]

The creation of a new Chinatown at the intersection of Archer Avenue and Twenty-second Street after 1912 reinforced the connection between the city's Chinese residents and its South Side red-light district. Pushed southward by many of the same economic and moral forces that had reconfigured the Levee, Chinese immigrants began settling along Archer Avenue west of State Street in the early 1900s. But in 1912, breaking away from rival Hip Sing, the On Leong Tong engineered the mass relocation of many of Chinatown's restaurants, stores, and flats to Twenty-second Street, where the tong had secured ten-year leases on more than forty local buildings. Set apart from the surrounding neighborhood by railroad lines and vacant lots, this new Chinatown acquired a much more discrete identity—one that was reinforced by the construction of a new temple and the addition of ornamental balconies to many existing buildings. But the district remained close enough to the Levee to allow slummers to visit both on the same night.[44]

Avid pleasure seekers could also explore both the city's premier red-light district and the people and establishments of its emerging "Black Belt" in a single evening. Stretching southward from the Loop in a narrow band "wedged between the railroad yards and industrial plants just west of Wentworth Avenue and the fashionable homes east of Wabash Avenue," the Black Belt was largely coincident with, though not fully contained within, both the old and new Levee districts. But the overlapping geography of these districts meant that many of the area's black leisure establishments, including Pony Moore's Turf Exchange on Twenty-first Street and John V. "Mushmouth" Johnson's resort on South State Street, became part of the spectacle that drew slummers to the Levee. While many of these resorts catered chiefly to local black residents, the more financially successful among them welcomed growing numbers of white patrons, collaborating in the spectacularization of blackness that added to the Levee's appeal. For the most part, this collaboration consisted primarily of allowing white slummers to sample the ragtime music and dance steps performed by black entertainers in the back rooms of local saloons. But in a few instances, black entrepreneurs also chose to cater to their white customers' more carnal desires. According to one observer, Vina Fields kept between thirty and forty women "all colored, but all for white men," at her resort on Custom House Place, while another noted that Black May's, located on Armour Avenue between Cullerton and Twenty-first streets, not only "provided light-skinned Negro girls for white men" but also staged "the most bestial circuses," or, live sexual performances, "ever seen in the United States."[45]

While not nearly as common as these areas' other sights, by the early 1890s, the "circus" was an integral part of the spectacle that attracted well-to-do whites to the red-light districts of Chicago and New York. In both the Levee and the Tenderloin, its existence was widely celebrated. Indeed, according to one account, several resorts even "made it a specialty, advertising it as one of their regular nightly attractions." But unlike most of the districts' attractions, which were easily accessible to the public, circuses were intended for a more restricted audience. Staged in local brothels and parlor houses, at costs ranging from $15 to $75, these performances were not only outside the social boundaries of what was permissible for slumming women, but they were also priced well beyond the budgets of most local men. They were designed, instead, to appeal to the affluent white businessman or the visiting tourist out to see the sights.[46]

More accessible to the average slummer were the "dens of the sexual pervert of the male sex," as one disgusted Chicagoan called them. "Found in the basements of buildings in the most crowded, but least respectable parts of certain streets, with immoral theaters, cheap museums, opium joints, and vile concert saloons surrounding them," these Levee resorts were characterized by some spectators as "the blackest holes of iniquity that ever existed in any country since the dawn of history." Others who visited the district, however, took a more benign view, considering such amusements simply a part of the general mix of ribald entertainments that were constantly on display in the Levee. Just as the female entertainers in local concert saloons offered a glimpse of leg, décolletage or even more, so the "fairy" entertainers of the district exhibited their own special talents. In a typical "State street resort, across from the old and unsavory Park Theatre," one observer noted, "the stage is given to performances of 'female impersonators,' who pose in all the lewd and disgusting attitudes, as exhibitors of Oriental phenomena." Yet no matter how off-color such performances might have seemed, within the context of the district's sex circuses or the nude after-hours dances staged by chorus girls at the Park Theatre, they were hardly shocking.[47]

In New York, similar dives became an illustrious staple of the city's red-light districts during the 1890s. "On the Bowery alone," an officer of the Reverend Charles Parkhurst's City Vigilance League reported in 1899, "there is to my knowledge certainly six [such] places." Primary among these was Columbia Hall (also called "Paresis Hall"), located at 392 Bowery near Fifth Street, but the resorts also included the Palm Club on Chrystie Street, Manilla Hall, the Black Rabbit at 183 Bleecker Street, a Delancey Street dive, and "a place called 'Little Buck's,' at the Bowery . . . diagonally opposite from Paresis Hall." At the last of these, an investigator reported, "they used to give what they called 'the circus,'" but by 1899, they were more likely to feature three or four "male degenerates" who sang and "danced the rag time" before an enthusiastic audience of men and women. The ever-popular Paresis Hall, however, provided an even more elaborate spectacle for curiosity seekers visiting the Bowery. With "degenerate men [or 'fairies'] there in large number, . . . from twenty-five to fifty," and "a woman . . . they call a hermaphrodite," the resort's patrons furnished as much or more amusement for adventuresome slumming parties as any organized entertainment ever could have. Describing the antics that went on in the joint, in the presence of no less than "some congressman or assemblyman," local reformers expressed their disdain for the "men that conduct themselves there." "They act effeminately," one of the reformers noted, "most of them are painted and powdered; they are called Princess this and Lady So and So and the Dutchess [sic] of Marlboro, and get up and sing as women, and dance; ape the female character; call each other sisters and take people out for immoral purposes."[48]

Even as such exposés prompted occasional crackdowns on the social and sexual interactions documented by Parkhurst's investigators, the fairy resort and its patrons remained an integral part of the slumming craze that prompted affluent whites to visit the immigrant and working-class districts of turn-of-the-century U.S. cities. While the Bowery's establishments were by far the most visible of such joints in New York, several Tenderloin resorts and at least one Chinatown dive also earned reputations as popular hangouts for both "the Nancys and fairies" and the slummers who came to gawk at or have sex with them. In Chicago, the presence of similar resorts became so pronounced by 1910 that the city's municipal Vice Commission launched a sweeping investigation of the "definite cult" of feminine men and female impersonators who were said to frequent the Levee's popular concert halls and saloons.[49]

Such regularized amusements were not the only means by which slummers encountered the "male degenerates" of New York and Chicago, however. By the early 1890s, affluent white curiosity seekers had also begun to pursue such encounters by crowding into the galleries of the annual masquerades that were held in the cities' principal red-light districts. A young medical student from North Carolina by the name of Charles Nesbitt was introduced to the renowned balls held at New York's Walhalla Hall after striking up a conversation with "Princess Toto," the "social queen of this group" of "male perverts" whom he met in a Bowery resort. But such personal introductions to these events were hardly necessary. In Chicago, one observer noted, "a series of annual balls held by the 'fruits' and the 'cabmen' [were] advertised by placards extensively all over the city."[50]

Whether in the Levee or on New York's Lower East Side, the attractions at these masquerades were much the same. "At these disreputable gatherings," Chicagoan L. O. Curon reported in an 1899 reform-oriented exposé, "the pervert of the male persuasion displays his habits by aping everything feminine. In speech, walk, dress, and adornment they are to all appearances women." In fact, Curon found the men's feminine presentation so indistinguishable from that of the female denizens of the Levee, who were also in attendance at the ball, that he insisted that "the uniformed observer" might have no idea "what a seething mass of human corruption he is witnessing." At New York's Walhalla Hall, Charles Nesbitt labored under no such illusions while watching nearly five hundred same-sex couples, including a good many women accompanied by "masculine looking women in male evening dress," as they took to the dance floor. Unlike Curon, who found the very existence of these masquerades profoundly unsettling, Nesbitt's account of the happenings at the Walhalla affair suggested that the balls' popularity with local slumming parties stemmed from their inversion of a familiar and highly regarded upper-class leisure pursuit. If one overlooked the masquerades' transgressive cross-dressing, Nesbitt claimed, "one could quite easily imagine oneself in a formal evening ball room among respectable people."[51]

Urban Reform and the Regulation of Slumming

As the commercialized leisure industry began to remake both the slum and the red-light district in ways that made them increasingly palatable to middle- and upper-class whites, it set in motion a showdown between members of the middle and upper class who would seek to embrace the districts' cheap amusements and those who would seek to control or police them. At issue was the future not only of the restricted and tolerated sex districts of Chicago and New York but also the very existence of hundreds—if not thousands—of popular neighborhood resorts in the Bowery and Tenderloin of New York, the Levee district of Chicago, and the Chinatowns of both cities. Although the last decades of the nineteenth century saw occasional crackdowns on the cities' red-light districts, for the most part, local authorities turned a blind eye to the districts' pleasurable pursuits. Abiding by the common belief that prostitution and the resorts that sheltered it were necessary evils in modern urban life, such resorts often tolerated these establishments, provided, that is, they remained confined to designated sections of the city. Some reformers even suggested that the persistence of sex districts served to safeguard the public. The secretary of New York's Committee of Fourteen, for example, undercut his organization's expressed desire to suppress such spaces by insisting that prostitution could never be fully eliminated without instigating "a terrible increase in the crimes of rape and seduction and abortions and illegitimate births."[52]

Whether or not this was actually the case, the continued toleration of discrete red-light districts in New York and Chicago probably had more to do with financial incentives than moral imperatives. Bowery "places paid for and enjoyed ample police protection," one frequent visitor to the district's dives later recalled. Only those dives that failed to pay up "were sure to be subjected to a spectacular police raid in the sacred name of civic virtue."[53] The underground economy of bribes and protection money proved so lucrative that it purportedly provided the basis for the Tenderloin's famous moniker. "I've been having chuck steak ever since I've been on the force," police captain Alexander S. Williams was said to have remarked upon his transfer to New York's Twenty-ninth Precinct in 1876, "and now I'm going to have a bit of tenderloin." The allusion seemed so apt to New Yorkers familiar with the inner workings of the city's commercialized sex industry that the name stuck.[54]

As more white middle-class women and men undertook slumming expeditions into the red-light districts of New York and Chicago, community leaders began to reevaluate their uneasy acceptance of these immigrant and working-class amusements. Although the regulatory campaigns of urban reformers rarely targeted the practice of slumming directly, for many, the increasing prevalence of this pastime at the turn of the century served as both sign and symbol of at least three broader challenges to the cities' social and moral order. First, because slumming prompted thousands of well-to-do whites to venture into red-light districts, it became inevitably entangled with reformers' renewed attempts to address the burgeoning "social evil" of female prostitution. This proved especially true by the middle of the twentieth century's first decade, when such reform efforts ballooned into an international crusade against "white slavery." Based on the belief that immigrant and working-class men were using urban saloons and dance halls as a forum through which to ensnare white native-born women in lives of involuntary sexual servitude, this white slavery panic dovetailed all too neatly with the growing popularity of slumming. Not only did the latter provide evidence of the increasing likelihood that white middle-class women would find themselves in close contact with unfamiliar immigrant and working-class men, but the synergy of the two also seemed to confirm reformers' fears that slumming would ultimately undermine middle-class morality by encouraging otherwise respectable women to engage in a range of disreputable activities.[55]

Second, by promoting affluent whites' participation in working-class amusements, slumming played into social reformers' more general objections to the emergence of commercialized leisure. In Chicago, for example, reformer Jane Addams expressed considerable dismay that "the old dances on the village green in which all of the older people of the village participated" were being replaced by dance halls, "gin-palaces," and other resorts that "confus[ed] joy with lust, and gaiety with debauchery." In Addams's view, such amusements simultaneously permitted urban youth to skirt the restraints of community supervision in a "feverish search for pleasure" and also exploited young women and men for financial gain, having been designed expressly "to empty pockets" for the consumption of liquor and musical entertainment.[56]

Finally, slumming also appeared to place a substantial number of middle- and upper-class whites at loggerheads with reformers' efforts to combat the immigrant political machine and the resulting corruption of municipal government. Because the most popular resorts were either owned by or paid tribute to Democratic city councilmen or other local party officials, slumming provided an economic wellspring for the urban machine at the very moment that middle-class progressives were organizing politically to take back their cities.[57]

To address this interlocking inventory of urban issues, concerned activists adopted a variety of reform tactics, each of which affected the continuing practice and prevalence of slumming at the turn of the century. Among the earliest and most visible of the reform campaigns were those led by evangelical Protestant reformers, including the Reverend Charles Parkhurst and the British editor and publisher William T. Stead. As minister of the Madison Square Presbyterian Church, Parkhurst instigated perhaps the most publicized anti-vice crusade in American history during the spring of 1892, and Stead, the son of a Congregationalist parson, published a scathing review of social and labor conditions at the close of Chicago's 1893 World's Columbian Exposition. To gather evidence for their respective projects, both men adopted the guise of the stereotypical male slummer, gaining entrée to some of the cities' most notorious dives, details of which they later reported in courtroom testimony, speeches, sermons, and books. Yet even as their investigations spurred a fervent revival of urban reform, which prompted the advent of anti-vice organizations such as Parkhurst's City Vigilance League and Chicago's Civic Federation, they also fueled the furor for urban slumming. The newspaper coverage of Parkhurst's courtroom testimony and the cottage industry of publications that emanated from his slumming expeditions around New York provided readers with a virtual map of illicit resorts to visit. The same was true of Stead's 1894 publication, *If Christ Came to Chicago!*, which included a map of the numerous brothels and saloons that occupied one two-block stretch of the South Side Levee.[58]

A similar combination of revelry and reform also characterized a number of state-financed investigations of urban immorality and corruption in Chicago and New York. Realizing the futility of appealing to Tammany Hall's immigrant-dominated Democratic political machine to improve the social and moral conditions of New York, on no fewer than two occasions during the 1890s, Manhattan reformers convinced members of the state legislature to launch an investigation of the systems of municipal graft and sexual exploitation sanctioned by the city's police. The first of these, known as the Lexow Committee after its chair, New York state senator Clarence Lexow, constituted a state-sponsored attempt to verify Parkhurst's initial findings. Established in 1894 and funded by a grant from the Chamber of Commerce (after the governor vetoed the committee's intended state financing), Lexow's hearings generated substantial publicity, as well as five volumes of testimony that included such graphic details of police collusion in the city's underworld that Tammany lost control of the mayoralty later that same year. Yet by 1899, with Tammany back in control, state Republican Party leader Thomas Platt felt compelled to order a second investigation, this time headed by assemblyman Robert Mazet. Like the Lexow Committee before it, the Mazet Committee produced another five hefty volumes of testimony that, in sections, read more like a rambling guide to the city's red-light districts than an instrument of earnest reform. In reality, it was likely both, since the daily press printed much of the testimony heard by these two committees, including the names and addresses of popular resorts.[59]

In Chicago, at least initially, similar investigations produced more prudent results. Following the success of New York's Lexow Committee, the Republican-controlled Illinois Senate authorized two separate investigations of police corruption and sexual exploitation under Chicago's

Democratic administration. The first committee, chaired by Illinois state senator Orville F. Berry and authorized during a special session of the Illinois Legislature in 1897, issued its final report in February 1898, finding "that crime was protected and lewdness tolerated" by the Chicago police force. According to one summary of the Berry Committee's findings, the force proved not only to be "a powerful ally of the criminal classes" but also "practically made an unofficial livelihood off unfortunate women of the town, thieves and their fences, gambling resorts and their keepers, and the patrons and keepers of the all night saloons." A second Illinois Senate investigation, known as the Baxter Committee, after its chair, Illinois state senator Delos W. Baxter, uncovered similar conditions through hearings that began in May 1899. But neither of these two committees issued substantive reports that provided addresses or descriptions of the goings-on in local resorts that could be exploited by would-be thrill seekers. Rather, it was left to the municipally funded Chicago Vice Commission, formed more than a decade later under pressure from local reformers by the Republican mayor, Fred A. Busse, to detail the social and sexual environs of the city's brothels, dance halls, and saloons. But even the commission's scandalous 1911 report, *The Social Evil in Chicago*, proved somewhat of a disappointment to readers with ulterior motives, since the commission had replaced the names and street addresses of local resorts with codes, perhaps anticipating the report's possible secondary uses.[60]

Although municipally funded, the Chicago Vice Commission displayed a level of tact in reporting on its investigation of urban moral conditions that was more often associated with the numerous privately financed civic organizations that came to dominate urban reform after the turn of the century. Exemplars of the Progressive Era, these private anti-vice societies adopted a businesslike approach that mirrored the professional practices both of the academics and social workers who sat on their boards and of the business tycoons who provided much of their funding. Confronting the system of extortion that allowed red-light districts to thrive under the protection of political machines, they established alternative frameworks of surveillance and regulation, endeavoring to improve urban conditions while imposing their own conception of morality and social order on the people and institutions that fell under their widening influence. Turn-of-the-century Chicago and New York were homes to a wide array of such organizations, whose deliberate focus on achieving significant social change meant that their activities and publications yielded few particulars about the cities' notorious resorts that could be easily co-opted by curiosity seekers. While none of these organizations was established specifically to police the social and sexual encounters associated with slumming, the activities of each contributed to the regulation of the physical places and general atmosphere that made this popular pastime possible.[61]

In New York, the two principal private anti-vice organizations that shaped the terrain of urban slumming were the Committee of Fifteen and its successor, the Committee of Fourteen. Organized in 1900 by the Chamber of Commerce, New York's Committee of Fifteen was charged with investigating "the present alarming increase of gambling and the Social Evil," as well as its political and financial beneficiaries. Of particular concern to the committee was the proliferation of prostitution in the resorts and saloons of the city's immigrant and working-class districts, including the Bowery, Chinatown, and the Tenderloin. Ironically, the committee's investigations were focused, in large part, on a condition precipitated by earlier reform efforts. When the New York State Assembly passed the Raines Law in 1896, restricting Sunday sales of liquor to hotels with ten or more beds, it had intended to curtail liquor consumption and prostitution by forcing the Sunday closure of every saloon in New York. But, as interpreted by saloonkeepers and Tammany politicians, the law had the opposite effect; saloons simply subdivided their backrooms or upper floors into "hotel rooms" that became ideal places of assignation and tempting diversions for affluent white male pleasure seekers. For more than a year, the committee employed a corps of undercover investigators to gather evidence against such resorts, hoping to pressure local authorities to shut them down. But with the defeat of Tammany in 1901 (the Committee of Fifteen's true objective), the group resolved to disband, presuming that the city's new reform-minded mayor, Seth Low, would see that such resorts were adequately policed.[62]

The new mayor's term proved short, however, and the continued proliferation of so-called Raines Law hotels under the return of Tammany prompted the organization of the Committee of Fourteen in 1905. Funded by wealthy industrialists, including Andrew Carnegie and John D. Rockefeller Jr., this group of prominent male and female reformers resumed the fight against prostitution in the city's saloons. Assembling a team of undercover investigators, ranging from well-heeled medical students to more humble immigrant men and women, the Committee of Fourteen amassed an astonishing volume of evidence that documented the prevalence of prostitution and other casual sexual encounters in New York's immigrant and working-class hotels, saloons, and other popular places of amusement. In doing so, of course, it also chronicled the expanding participation of middle- and upper-class whites in many of these activities, heightening concern among the city's reformers about the perils of slumming. Although the committee's secretary, Frederick H. Whitin, generally accepted the idea that prostitution could never be fully eliminated without instigating "a terrible increase in the crimes of rape and seduction and abortions and illegitimate births," he advocated the suppression of its most visible and public forms with the hope of insulating the city's middle-class residents as much as possible from the moral contamination threatened by such displays. In the eyes of the committee's investigators, this goal was made even more imperative by the increasing frequency with which the practice of slumming exposed respectable, well-to-do white women to the city's flagrant underworld.[63]

In Chicago, two similar organizations, the Committee of Fifteen and the Juvenile Protective Association, spearheaded a privately financed drive to eliminate the system of police extortion that encouraged the proliferation of prostitution and other unsavory activities in the city's Levee districts. Begun informally in 1907 but not incorporated until May 1911, about a month after the publication of the Chicago Vice Commission's influential report, the Committee of Fifteen was charged specifically with "aid[ing] the public authorities in the enforcement of all laws against pandering and to take measures calculated to suppress the 'white slave' traffic." By the summer of 1912, however, it had become a staunch leader of a widespread civic campaign to liquidate the Levee, wholeheartedly embracing the commission's findings that the "segregation of commercialized vice was a failure, . . . and ultimate suppression the only possible remedy." To accomplish this objective, one of the organization's founding members recalled, the Committee of Fifteen launched a direct assault on "the keepers of houses in the segregated district." The immediate result was the closure not only of five "open houses of prostitution" but also of the pejoratively nicknamed "Dago" Frank Lewis and Harry Cusick's popular Imperial Café on Armour Avenue—a development that highlighted the organization's decision to focus its resources against the very resorts that attracted slummers to the Levee. By early 1914, after adopting the unorthodox tactic of publishing the "names of the owners of real estate" in which "immoral resorts" were conducted, the committee's superintendent boasted that the group had shamed property-holders into evicting hundreds of unsavory tenants, resulting in the closure or dramatic reform of no fewer than seventy-three "disorderly saloons," many of which had earlier stood at the center of the Levee slumming craze.[64]

Chicago's other major private anti-vice organization, the Juvenile Protective Association (JPA), had a somewhat different mission and, as a result, a different impact on the terrain of slumming in the Windy City. The only major anti-vice organization in either Chicago or New York to be managed by a woman and to include more than a token number of female reformers on its governing board, the JPA was incorporated in June 1909 as a direct outgrowth of the community reform work that had culminated in the establishment of the country's first juvenile court in 1899. Formed, as its name suggests, to protect Chicago's youth and "to remove as far as possible the temptations and dangers, which carelessness and greed place about too many children," the JPA operated both as a social casework agency, directly assisting endangered and incorrigible youths, and as an investigatory organization. It was in this latter capacity that the group most directly affected the contours of slumming. After undertaking extensive campaigns to document the immoral conditions of the dance halls, cabarets, and soda parlors frequented by the young women and men of Chicago, the JPA invoked a mantle of maternalism to pressure local authorities to crack down on these popular Levee resorts.[65]

Ironically, reformers' attempts to curtail the practice of slumming and shutter the resorts associated with it often promoted the very social and sexual interactions that they sought to prevent. In the autumn of 1909, for instance, when evangelist Rodney "Gipsy" Smith, an Englishman of Romany descent, mobilized "an army of 10,000 Christian workers" to rally support for the permanent closure of the Levee by parading through the district with a brass band, as many as 100,000 spectators flocked to the South Side to watch the proceedings. Doubtless many of those who visited the Levee that night had long been familiar with its dance halls and saloons, but the *Chicago Record-Herald* reported that the crowd also included scores of "school children, girls not out of their teens and youths who never before had witnessed the sights of Chicago's underworld." The parade, likewise, attracted hundreds of curious "'slumming parties,' in which," the newspaper noted, "the young women fell in behind their escorts and elbowed their way up and down the streets," taking in every available sight, including popular Levee resorts such as Buxbaum's, Freiberg's, Gaffney's and Fred Train's, each of which claimed to be "doing a 'business' such as . . . they have not had in years."[66]

Even when reformers managed to convince local authorities to crack down on the goings-on in popular slumming destinations, they were often less than successful in curbing the appeal that such places held for urban tourists. By the turn of the century, in fact, police raids had simply become part of the spectacle that slummers identified with red-light districts. When uniformed officers arrested more than three hundred individuals in the spring of 1905 during one of the biggest raids ever to hit Chinatown, the *New York Times* reported that "thousands of persons" witnessed the event, including dozens of women and men dressed "in their Easter finery" on "several of the big 'Seeing Chinatown by Night' automobiles." According to the *Times*, "The women at first feared that they were going to be arrested, but when assured that there was no danger settled back and watched the police work. They got a bargain counter quantity of excitement for their fare," the newspaper later remarked, seemingly endorsing affluent Americans' pursuit of such thrills.[67]

In the early 1910s, however, whatever tacit acceptance slumming expeditions to the immigrant and working-class districts of New York and Chicago might have enjoyed was effectively terminated. Exploiting a rising tide of anti-immigrant hysteria in the first decade of the twentieth century, social reformers launched an unprecedented campaign against urban political machines, attacking not only the immigrant influence in municipal politics but also the saloons and dance halls that provided their political and economic base. In short order, this effort expanded to include a nationwide cleanup of urban red-light districts, fueled by the increasingly inflammatory rhetoric of white slavery that blamed immigrants from southern and eastern Europe for both the proliferation of commercialized sex and the supposed corruption of white American womanhood. By the mid-1910s, this so-called Progressive crusade had virtually eradicated open prostitution in New York, Chicago, and other cities, bringing an end to the vibrant nightlife that attracted slummers to red-light districts in the first place. Although a handful of the districts' more popular resorts managed to survive the persistent crackdowns, the threat of raids and the anti-immigrant sentiment that instigated them made the practice of slumming seem less pleasurable, if not downright dangerous, for well-to-do whites, precipitating a decline in their ventures to these districts.[68]

The termination of slumming excursions to the immigrant and working-class resorts of New York and Chicago did not, however, bring an end to affluent whites' participation in the emerging commercialized leisure industry of the two cities. Instead, thrill seekers set out for the more sophisticated cabarets that had recently opened in the bright-light districts of midtown Manhattan and Chicago's Loop. In these more respectable middle-class amusements, well-to-do whites could finally dance and socialize publicly without having to venture into working-class neighborhoods or exposing themselves to the purported threats of violence and white slavery associated with such spaces. As the next chapter shows, however, the impulses that led to the original slumming craze recurred in slightly modified form throughout the early decades of the twentieth century, resulting in three subsequent waves of thrill-seeking forays into racialized and sexualized urban spaces. Even as well-to-do whites left off visiting the slums that gave the pastime its name, their new pursuits—of "bohemian *thrillage*" in the 1910s and 1920s, the "Negro vogue" in the 1920s and 1930s, and the "pansy and lesbian craze" of the late 1920s through the early 1940s—reciprocally responded to and shaped demographic and geographic transformations of urban space.[69]

TWO

Beyond the Slums: Commercial Leisure and the Reorganization and Policing of Urban Space

With the relatively definitive closure of the red-light districts of Chicago and New York, affluent white pleasure seekers increasingly repaired in the early 1910s to the more respectable environs of the cabaret. Heralded by the *Chicago Tribune* as "a further refinement in civilization," this popular new institution combined upscale public dining with commercial leisure opportunities previously available only in the cities' immigrant and working-class dance halls. The cabaret further enhanced its reputation among well-to-do white consumers by resituating late-night public amusements in the safer and more refined locales of midtown Manhattan and Chicago's Loop—two districts with which most cabaret goers were already well accustomed through their employment in nearby office buildings or shopping excursions to local department stores. In such familiar locations, the *Tribune* noted approvingly, the cabaret practically "brings your amusement to you."[1]

To insure its continued success and perceived respectability among middle- and upper-class whites, the cabaret also facilitated the "refinement" and modification of popular dance steps. Most famously, at Louis Martin's New York café and, later, in their own Castles in the Air, the husband-and-wife team Irene and Vernon Castle developed and demonstrated less sensual versions of the "tough dancing" that had attracted many slummers to the cities' red-light resorts. Transforming the bunny hug, the turkey trot, and the grizzly bear of the Levee and the Tenderloin into the less animalistic and more graceful one-step waltz, long Boston, and eponymous Castle glide, this popular duo provided a primer for refined participation in urban nightlife—both through their cabaret exhibitions and with the publication of their 1914 manual entitled *Modern Dancing*. On the heels of the Castles' success, a host of ambitious cabaret impresarios in both Chicago and New York soon followed suit, employing their own exhibition dancers to provide instruction to patrons who wished to master the latest in respectable amusement.[2]

Not all New Yorkers and Chicagoans welcomed these developments. Well into the second decade of the twentieth century, private anti-vice organizations and reform-minded politicians in both cities continued to monitor cabarets. They passed legislation to regulate perceived excesses and prompted raids on establishments that refused to conform to reformers' only slightly revamped notions of nineteenth-century propriety and respectability. In Chicago, for instance, during the summer of 1913 when Rector's cabaret presented female performers attired in flesh-colored tights, Mayor Carter G. Harrison Jr. grew so incensed that he pushed legislation through the city council prohibiting such performances and forbidding the patrons of restaurants and cafés to dance on the premises. In 1913 and again in 1914, New York mayors William Jay Gaynor and John Purroy Mitchel attempted to address similar concerns by imposing curfew laws that set clear limits on the extent to which middle- and upper-class whites could participate in the nightlife of the city. For the most part, however, such regulations proved ineffective, unenforceable, and ultimately unnecessary—not only because many of the well-heeled constituents of these mayors patently ignored them, but also because the reemergence of slumming soon made the cabaret seem decidedly tame.[3]

Responding to continued shifts in urban demographics and spatial organization during the mid-1910s, affluent whites began to venture once again into areas associated with significant new urban populations. In a series of three slumming vogues that ran, successively, from the mid-1910s into the early 1940s, parties visited first the bohemian tearooms of New York and Chicago, then the black-and-tan cabarets of the cities' rapidly expanding black communities, and finally the speakeasies and nightclubs frequented by the cities' increasingly visible homosexual populations. Simultaneously legitimizing the attendance of well-to-do white pleasure seekers at the more respectable cabarets of New York and

Chicago, while allowing slummers to indulge their enduring appetite for the latest in urban thrills, these new excursions echoed the original craze for the cities' red-light districts and slum resorts. But unlike the cities' first slumming vogue, these later crazes were not focused on the geographic space of the slum itself. Rather, they were centered on the *amusement* of slumming. This activity continued to suggest a sense of social and physical boundary crossing in urban America, but instead of the place defining the activity, with each successive vogue the practice of slumming came more and more to define the urban districts upon which it converged.

The Bohemian *Thrillage* of Greenwich Village and Towertown

As the outbreak of the First World War slowed the influx of new immigrants and inflamed already simmering nativist tensions, those in search of exotic diversions began to look beyond the slums of New York and Chicago. In the bohemian tearooms and cabarets of New York's Greenwich Village and Chicago's Towertown, they soon discovered a suitable alternative. Characterized by radical politics and artistic and sexual experimentation, these districts offered a spectacle at once strange enough to excite slummers and sufficiently familiar to seem harmless. By early 1917, one Manhattan high-society journal announced that it was now "considered monstrously amusing to dine 'down town' and then 'do' the rounds" in Washington Square. Within a few years, Chicago guidebooks followed suit, informing locals and tourists alike that "a district containing numerous restaurants of Bohemian character, each with its own 'atmosphere' and special features" was available for exploration on the city's Near North Side.[4]

Greenwich Village earned its reputation for bohemian radicalism and sexual nonconformity during the first decades of the twentieth century. In the late nineteenth century, after the city's northward expansion fully encompassed this formerly rural district, the area had been all but abandoned to the city's working class. A few clusters of elite whites remained in the area, but most repaired to the outlying suburbs or to the luxury apartment buildings that had recently been constructed along the perimeter of Central Park. Thousands of Italian immigrants soon replaced the departing whites, joining a number of longer-term black and Irish residents and making their homes in the district's newly constructed tenements and subdivided brownstones. By 1900, the neighborhood's transformation was so complete that locals referred to it, like many other immigrant districts, simply by its political designation: the

Ninth Ward. Only after substantial numbers of white middle-class artists and radicals began moving into the area in the following years did the district's original name reemerge, giving rise to "the Village" of popular mythology (figure 6).[5]

Rejecting the comfort and respectability of white middle-class life, thousands of young bohemian women and men took up residence in Greenwich Village during the first quarter of the twentieth century. In its narrow, winding streets and hidden mews, they found a promis-

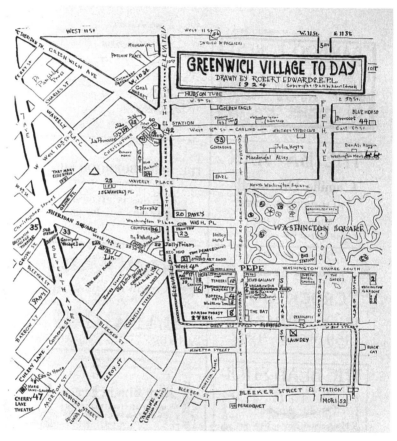

6   This 1924 map, titled "Greenwich Village To Day" and drawn by Robert "Bobby" Edwards, was intended to provide slummers and other readers of the bohemian magazine *The Quill* with a modest overview of the district. Although the map's key no longer exists, it is still possible to make out the location of colorful Village nightspots, such as the Wind Blew Inn (#5), the Mad Hatter (#19), the Pirate's Den (#41), and the Brevoort Hotel and the Blue Horse (both near #44). (Reprinted with permission from the Theater Collection of the Museum of the City of New York.)

ing retreat from the insistent demands of an increasingly capitalistic and mechanized world. The district's European flavor and inexpensive housing only added to its charm, encouraging many young writers and painters to cultivate a romanticized life of poverty. Tucked away in their studios and garrets, they dabbled at prose, oils, and clay before smoking and drinking their way into the wee hours of yet another morning. But not all aspects of bohemian life were reducible to such exaggerated theatrics. Like similar bohemian districts across the country, the Village made possible an entirely new way of life. Its cheap flats and colorful tearooms and shops provided enterprising young women and men with a rare opportunity to fashion lives outside the constraints of both traditional family networks and the industrial economy. Whether eschewing salary for creativity or exchanging the benefits of spousal relations for individual freedom, the district's artists, anarchists, and intellectuals carved out a unique place for themselves in the social landscape of New York, and at times even managed to build alliances with their working-class neighbors by interacting with each other in local restaurants and saloons.

A nearly identical process was underway in a similar neighborhood on the Near North Side of Chicago. During the first decades of the twentieth century, writers, actors, artists, and radicals began to pour into the furnished-room district that had only recently begun to take shape among the abandoned mansions and stables of the city's elite. After the Great Fire of 1871, many of Chicago's earliest settlers and society scions had rebuilt their spacious homes along Ohio, Erie, Rush, and Cass (now Wabash) streets, but by the late 1880s, they had decided to move further north. Distancing themselves both from the expanding immigrant workforce of Irish, Germans, Swedes, and southern Italians that lived and toiled in the industrial area along the north bank of the Chicago River and from the incursion of commerce along North State and Dearborn streets, the well-to-do constructed new homes on the outskirts of Chicago or took up residence in the exclusive lakefront hotels and private residences of the city's new "Gold Coast." In the wake of their departure, the district's once-resplendent housing was subdivided by local entrepreneurs, and the neighborhood—an area bounded roughly by Division Street and Grand Avenue to the north and south and Michigan Avenue and Clark Street to the east and west—soon became Chicago's busiest lodging house district. By the early twentieth century, the Near North Side had been colonized by thousands of single working women and men who had only recently arrived from rural America and more than twenty foreign lands in search of their fortune. It was in this already unconventional atmosphere of cheap rents and working-class

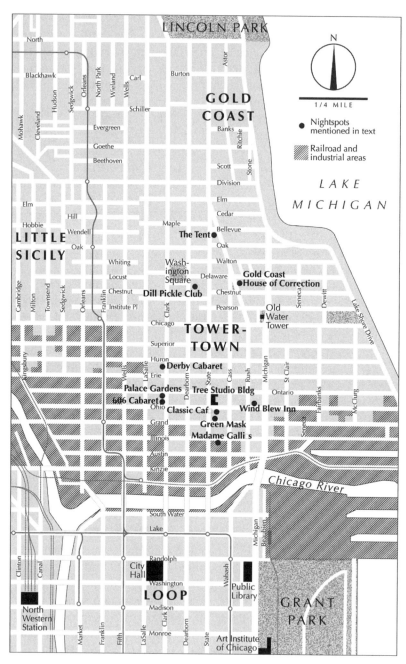

North

LINCOLN PARK

N

Blackhawk

Orleans

Hudson
Sedgwick

North Park
Wieland
Wells

Carl

Burton

Astor

GOLD
COAST

Schiller

1/4 MILE

Mohawk
Cleveland

Evergreen

Goethe

Beethoven

Banks

Ritchie

Scott

Stone

● Nightspots
   mentioned in text

▨ Railroad and
   industrial areas

Elm

Hill

Hobbie

Wendell

LITTLE
SICILY

Oak

Division

Elm

Cedar

Maple

Bellevue

The Tent ●

Oak

LAKE
MICHIGAN

Whiting

Locust

Cambridge
Milton
Townsend
Sedgwick
Orleans
Franklin

Chestnut

Institute Pl

Chicago

Wash-
ington
Square

Delaware

Chestnut

Clark

Pearson

Walton

Gold Coast
● House of Correction

Old
Water
Tower

Seneca

Dewitt

Lake Shore Drive

Dill Pickle Club ●

Superior

TOWER-
TOWN

Kingsbury

Huron ● Derby Cabaret

Erie

Wells

LaSalle

Palace Gardens Tree Studio Bldg

Dearborn

State

Cass

Rush

Michigan

St Clair

606 Cabaret ●

Ohio

Classic Caf ●

Grand

Illinois

Austin

Kinzie

Classic Caf ●   ● Wind Blew Inn

● Green Mask

Madame Galli s ●

Ontario

Fairbanks

Seneca

St Clair

McClurg

Chicago River

South Water

Lake

Michigan

Beaubien

Clinton
Canal

Randolph

City
Hall

Washington

LOOP

Madison

North
Western
Station

Market
Franklin
Fifth

Monroe

LaSalle
Clark
Dearborn

State

Wabash

Public
Library

Art Institute
of Chicago

GRANT
PARK

7   This map situates Towertown's most popular tearooms and cabarets in relation to the sur-
     rounding districts.

restaurants and saloons that bohemian artists and radicals began to explore their creative energies, leftist leanings, and yearnings for free love.
Renaming the district "Towertown" (figure 7) in honor of the city's old
water tower, located at Michigan and Chicago avenues, they created a
lively new world—a world in which the convergence of working-class
spaces and intellectual interests in art, literature, and politics became
less the exception and more the rule.[6]

No doubt the amalgamation of cultures and social types in Towertown and Greenwich Village accounted for much of their appeal to
nonconformist bohemian youth, but it also contributed significantly to
affluent whites' increasing fascination with these same neighborhoods
during the mid-1910s and 1920s. For slummers, the appearance of substantial numbers of white middle-class artists and radicals in these districts previously dominated by immigrants and workers rendered them
safer for popular consumption while still perpetuating the sense of mystery and difference that had attracted an earlier generation of pleasure
seekers to similar working-class resorts in the Bowery, the Tenderloin,
and the Levee.[7] Whether at the Village's Golden Swan Saloon, located at
Sixth Avenue and Fourth Street, or at Madame Galli's Italian restaurant,
at 18 East Illinois Street in Towertown, bohemians' interactions with
local residents helped smooth the rougher working-class edges of long-
standing neighborhood amusements, making them immediately more
palatable for the curious elite. But slumming expeditions to the Village
and Towertown were by no means focused simply on such integrated
environments. They also embraced the strange spectacles of art, politics,
and sexual titillation created by the bohemians themselves. In the dank,
unfinished basements of New York's Greenwich Village and the shabby
wooden cottages and alleyway stables of Chicago's Near North Side, slummers sampled a colorful new world of bohemian tearooms and cafés, the
brightly painted walls of which were often reflected in their names. The
Green Mask, the Blue Fish, and the Red Lantern of Towertown and the
Village's Purple Pup, Yellow Fish, Black Cat, and Blue Horse were but a
few of the popular nightspots that attracted visitors to these districts.[8]

While a number of enterprising local entrepreneurs actively stimulated the public's budding obsession with bohemian *thrillage,* the arrival
of astonishing numbers of affluent white pleasure seekers in these once-
ramshackle districts was also a product of larger political and commercial
forces. In New York, for instance, the 1917 extension of Seventh Avenue
across the Village from Eleventh Street to Houston and the related construction of an Interborough Rapid Transit (IRT) subway station in Sher-
idan Square transformed the once-secluded Village into one of the most

central and easily accessible neighborhoods in the city. In 1920, the completion of the Michigan Avenue Bridge similarly altered the public perception of Chicago's Near North Side by prompting the development of a new, magnificent, mile-long strip of retail shops and businesses immediately adjacent to the city's bohemian district. Suddenly, the Village and Towertown were not only more accessible and inviting to white middle- and upper-class pleasure seekers in search of an evening's entertainment, but also provided more convenient residences for women and men working in New York's downtown financial district or in one of the many new office buildings being constructed north of the Chicago River. "Scores of old, disreputable houses [on Chicago's Near North Side] were made over into studios," Alfreda Gordon recalled, "but not for artists. They were fitted with French windows, over-ornamented fireplaces, ceiling beams and various 'quaint' and 'artistic' gew-gaws—and rented to businessmen and assorted dalliers who adored north light sentiment." During this same period in the Village, editor Sam Putnam recalled, "commercial tearooms and similar enterprises were flourishing, rents were mounting, and the bond salesman and the advertising man were moving in."[9]

Thus, the changing physical infrastructure of the cities and the fashionableness of these districts generated by their role as popular slumming destinations combined to strip Towertown and the Village of whatever vestiges of the immigrant and working-class slum they might otherwise have maintained. Far from reinforcing the districts' association with poverty, degradation, or illicit sex, the slumming vogue for bohemian *thrillage* actually led to what might be considered one of the earliest examples of urban gentrification. Yet the importance of these developments in promoting the bohemian nightlife of New York and Chicago paled in comparison to the inadvertent enticements generated by another contemporaneous development: the ratification of the Eighteenth Amendment in 1919 and its implementation under the Volstead Act at the stroke of midnight on January 16, 1920.

With the passage of Prohibition, middle-class progressives intended to enhance their ability to police public social interactions and reform municipal government by closing the immigrant and working-class saloons that provided the foundation of urban machine politics. (This is why the amendment outlawed the *sale* of liquor rather than its consumption; those with access to private stashes and private property on which to consume it, such as the Yale Club of New York, which had reportedly laid in a fourteen-year supply of liquor, could continue to drink with impunity.[10]) But in practice, Prohibition not only failed to limit immigrants' political influence but it also diminished the power of local

police and anti-vice organizations to regulate public sociability, especially across class and racial lines. Because the criminalization of liquor
effectively rendered all urban nightlife illegal, the distinction that many
middle-class whites had earlier drawn between attending high-class cabarets and undertaking slumming expeditions to less reputable establishments became increasingly irrelevant. In both New York and Chicago,
the loss of legitimate liquor revenues drove most of the respectable, upscale nightspots out of business, leaving middle-class pleasure seekers
with little alternative but to turn to the speakeasies operated or controlled by Irish, Italian, and Jewish "gangsters." Chief among these, during the earliest years of Prohibition, were the bohemian tearooms and
cabarets of Greenwich Village and Towertown, which were uniquely positioned to capitalize on the changing dynamics of urban nightlife. They
were situated in close proximity to the Italian restaurants, groceries, and
drugstores that became the cities' primary purveyors of homemade red
wine during Prohibition, and their minimal decoration, low capital in-
vestment, and location in dark alleyways and basements provided strategic advantages that were later adopted by speakeasy owners in other
districts in an effort to avoid local and federal regulation and to trim
their losses in the event that failed to do so.[11]

The readily available bootleg liquor undoubtedly enhanced many
slumming excursions to the Village and Towertown by lowering inhibitions and lubricating social interactions, but it was hardly the neighborhoods' primary attraction. Intrepid drinkers could easily lay their hands
on bathtub gin or moonshine at any one of hundreds of speakeasies
(and more than a few local juice joints, candy shops, and drugstores),
but only the cities' bohemian districts promised a glimpse into the everyday lives of starving artists and radical politicos. When they visited
Chicago's Dill Pickle Club, located in Tooker Alley, or Polly's Restaurant
on Washington Square in the Village, middle- and upper-class whites
got an eyeful of bohemia's "long-haired men and short-haired women,"
their colorful clothing, and provocative, avant-garde art. In one bohemian tearoom they might listen intently to recitations of modern verse
or ukulele tunes, while in others their ears could ring with heated debates over anarchism, socialism, or reproductive freedom.

The association of bohemia with radical politics was so widely held that
during and immediately after the First World War, federal officials carefully investigated the potentially dangerous influence that such nightspots might have on the women and men who visited them. Chicago's
Dill Pickle Club came under particular scrutiny both because of its supposed association with "Bolsheviki, Anarchists and like radicals" and

because its owner, Jack Jones, was the former husband of Industrial Workers of the World (IWW) organizer Elizabeth Gurley Flynn. Attending a masquerade ball sponsored by the club in April 1919, an investigator from the Military Intelligence Division of the War Department displayed the government's almost-ridiculous fears of political subversion, noting not only that masks "were necessary in order to gain admittance," but that "red carnations were worn by all attendants, as it was explained by members that red is the color of the club." A later report from informants associated with the Patriotic American League, however, apparently dispelled the War Department's concerns by suggesting that young women and men visited the Dill Pickle Club more for sexual than political thrills. "They were there for anything that came off," the informants reported. "Girls were observed smoking cigarettes, one sat on a mans [sic] lap and there was much freedom" of the "free-love" sort.[12]

To most of the pleasure seekers who patronized bohemian tearooms and cabarets, this sense of sexual freedom constituted the very essence of Towertown and Greenwich Village. Interpreting free love more as casual promiscuity than as the idealized and sexually equitable relationships that most bohemians intended, slummers expected to stumble upon sexual discussions and carefree social interactions on their expeditions to these districts. Usually they were not disappointed. "On galactic Summer nights" during the late 1910s, one bohemian regular recalled, visitors to the Dill Pickle Club were likely to encounter "pale girls with daring bobbed heads . . . and tortoise-shelled glasses discuss[ing] Nietzsche and Prudhomme [sic] and Havelock Ellis with boys whose eyes dreamed and visioned." Such intellectual conversations about sex and philosophy thrilled those who came looking for subtle expressions of forbidden desire, but slummers were even more fascinated by the apparent nonchalance with which bohemians publicly discussed their sexual relationships. At the Black Parrot in Greenwich Village, one observer noted the ease with which a woman named Bessie confessed her earlier sexual involvement with one of the tearoom's male patrons while talking to his new flame: "Oh, we are old friends," she told the woman in a tone loud enough to be heard across the small tearoom. "I lived with John once. Didn't I?"[13]

But the sexual spectacle that most intrigued visitors to Towertown and the Village extended well beyond words. Although only a handful would ever lay eyes on the nude models that they imagined to be regular fixtures in every bohemian studio, more than a few eventually caught a glimpse of human flesh during their slumming adventures. Attendance at one of the districts' elaborate masquerade balls offered one of the surest opportunities to see skin. In Chicago, the Dill Pickle Club's annual St. Patrick's Day and Halloween dances often featured women and men in scanty attire, enthusiastically competing to win the prize for the "best Adam and Eve Costume." Similarly risqué attire was often on display at the Village masquerades held regularly at Webster Hall. At the Liberal Club Ball in February 1917, for instance, a young medical student reported that several of the balls' female participants cavorted in "filmy transparent things through which one could see easily" or in one-piece men's bathing suits "with one breast exposed." But women did not provide the only eye candy at Webster Hall: "Egyptian costumes are very popular" among the men, one participant remarked, "with just the diaper effect and the rest of the body painted."[14] Even in the bohemian tearooms of Chicago and New York, tourists were sometimes treated to the "rather suggestive" dances and informal actions of their fellow patrons and entertainers. On one occasion, slummers watched attentively as a male patron at the Greenwich Village Hearth "spre[a]d his legs out and asked [a nearby woman] to fan him between his legs" to cool him off. "All enjoyed while she was doing that," an observer recalled.[15]

Bohemia's exhibition of free love extended to displays of same-sex desire and affection, providing yet another attraction for curious interlopers. As historian George Chauncey has noted, in the late 1910s droves of fairies regularly flocked to the masquerades at Webster Hall, donning evening gowns, make-up, and wigs to call attention to their femininity and court more masculine companions. They could "be seen practising their little peculiar tricks with men," a guest at one ball confirmed, "going through their antics which at once mark them for what they are," and even "hugging and kissing each other." In fact, their attendance became so integral to the spectacle associated with such balls that a man attending the Greenwich Village Carnival in the spring of 1917 commented on the presence not only of "the usual crowd of Homosexuals . . . decoratively attired" but also of "the usual crowd who go expecting to find this type there." By the early 1920s, slummers' expectations could also be met by the entertainers featured in a number of bohemian tearooms. Celebrating the Fourth of July in 1922, for instance, the Village nightspot known as The Jungle (located at 11 Cornelia Street) presented "a jazz band and two male performers Rosebud and Countess," whose campy antics drew the hearty applause of a mixed crowd of slummers, male "degenerates" and "lady lovers [lesbians] of the Greenwich Village type." Later that same year, Towertown tourists visiting the Derby Cabaret at 680 North Clark Street were treated to a similar, "amateur" performance of "a man, garbed as a woman and singing in a high soprano voice."[16]

While the mere existence of such spectacles unsettled many urban reformers, local authorities were generally prepared to ignore the eccentricities of bohemian artists and radicals as long as their challenges to social and sexual norms were confined strictly to the bounds of their own communities. But as bohemian balls and tearooms grew in popularity among middle- and upper-class whites, reformers' hackles rose sharply. "As long as the attendance at the balls was confined to the residents of the Village, we did not feel that much harm was done," the general secretary of New York's Committee of Fourteen told an associate in late 1917, "but they are becoming more and more commercialized." Still, reformers' concerns about the alleged dangers that bohemian unconventionality posed to slummers differed markedly from those that had fueled their earlier efforts to regulate slumming in the cities' red-light districts and immigrant neighborhoods. Chicago's Committee of Fifteen remained sufficiently concerned about "the immoral cabaret" to lobby successfully for the passage of a 1917 "law regarding indecent shows and entertainments," but for the most part, urban reformers no longer opposed the mere existence of public amusements or believed that they were especially incompatible with middle-class respectability. Some, like Greenwich House founder Mary Simkhovitch, found even the bohemian nightspots of the Village to be relatively inoffensive. "A great many of the restaurants and so forth in the neighborhood are very nice, harmless, jolly, innocent places," she informed New York's mayor John F. Hylan after a group of "old-fashioned, conservative, respectable neighbors" urged him to crack down on the district's amusements. "Tastes of the two groups are very different and they do not understand each other," she continued. "But as a matter of fact, there are several good people among the restaurateurs and artists who have come into the neighborhood and there are also some pretty bad customers to be found among the old neighbors."[17]

The involvement of significant numbers of middle-class whites—although, admittedly, rebellious ones—in the creation and maintenance of the spectacle presented in bohemian establishments also appears to have tempered reformers' attempts to regulate slumming in Towertown and the Village. The rhetoric of white slavery that anti-vice societies had used so effectively both to warn female slummers away from and to rally public sentiment against the immigrant and working-class resorts of the cities' red-light districts held little weight in bohemian tearooms that were often run by native-born white women and frequented by middle-class writers, painters, and radicals. Even reformers' continuing and concerted crusade against female prostitution became more complicated in bohemia. Recognizing that the closure of the wide-open sex districts of New York and Chicago during the mid-1910s had pushed many prostitutes into the more covert environs of the call house and the cabaret, investigators for the Committee of Fourteen and the JPA, among other organizations, diligently attempted to document the role of bohemian nightspots in facilitating commercialized sex. On occasion, undercover men reported that, "after spending some time in her company" or buying a drink or two, one of the female patrons or entertainers in an establishment such as the 606 Cabaret on North Clark Street in Chicago would directly solicit them, quoting a price for her services and "a room up the street." More often, however, the scenario was more opaque, and the solicitations more closely resembled "charity" (providing sexual favors in return for being treated to drinks, entertainment, or material goods) than prostitution. After a Miss Delys smiled at him from across the room at the Greenwich Village Hearth on Macdougal Street, Harry Kahan, an investigator for the Committee of Fourteen, "called her over to sit down at my table." Expecting a solicitation, Kahan reported instead, "She told me, that she was a dancer and instructs strictly private either in her apartment on West 48th Street or down here, price $2.50 per hour or lesson." Judging from the fact that Miss Delys had to put Kahan off until the next day, because "she had to meet a man tonight with whom she made previous arrangment [sic]," it seems likely that she meant to offer more than a fox trot for her fee. But it is equally clear that her offer did not meet the standard required either to charge her with prostitution or to close the tearoom for "violating decency laws."[18]

Acknowledging the difficulties that these legal distinctions posed in gathering evidence for police raids and closures of bohemian tearooms and cabarets, anti-vice organizations adopted more creative strategies for regulating the social interactions in these spaces. In New York, the Committee of Fourteen proposed changes in the municipal licensing of public amusements to decrease the number of resorts while increasing the frequency with which they were subject to official review. As early as 1918, the committee's general secretary advocated the introduction of cabaret licenses (which were not required until 1926) to provide leverage against tearooms and other establishments that featured live entertainment but were not technically subject to dance hall regulations, and later proposed that "the best way to handle the Village problem . . . is with temporary licenses" rather than the standard two-year, bonded licenses granted to most dance halls. In Chicago, when the Committee of Fifteen found the local police and courts hesitant or unwilling to prosecute disorderly cabarets, it strategically exploited the Federal Injunction

Law to move such cases into federal court. "Wherever vice was found to be extant with liquor," the committee's superintendent reported, "our investigators secured the necessary evidence for the issuance of temporary injunctions." Yet the increasing difficulty that many investigators reported in singling out prostitutes from "charity girls" and free lovers made the regulation of bohemian tearooms and cabarets a relatively unproductive venture for private anti-vice societies that sought to have the biggest impact on commercialized sex that their limited budgets would allow. Throughout the 1920s, New York's Committee of Fourteen maintained sporadic oversight of Village cabarets. But in Chicago similar investigations became less of a priority; after 1924, the Committee of Fifteen focused its energies exclusively on houses of prostitution, while the JPA undertook only one concerted investigation of local cabarets during the Century of Progress World's Fair in 1933–34.[19]

For the most part, when local authorities chose to crack down on slummers' searches for bohemian *thrillage*, they did so for one of two reasons: either to protect the morals of minors, especially young women below the age of 18, or to placate residents who had become annoyed with the nightly invasion of their neighborhoods. The former provided justification for the New York Police Department's spectacular, headline-grabbing, January 1923 raid on Robert Cushman's restaurant and dance hall at 160 West Fourth Street. After observing a large number of apparently underage women and men in the resort, detectives ordered the bust, arresting twenty patrons including "eleven girls between the ages of 16 and 18," two "Princeton boys" and a young girl of 15 whose presence resulted in the conviction of the establishment's proprietor for "impairing the morals of a girl under 16 years."[20] "The complaint against some of these newer Village cafés," the *New York Times* later reported:

is that they rob the cradle. They advertise the lure of Bohemia in school and college papers; and it has an awful pull for collegians and schoolboys, and youths in their teens who would like to be mistaken for collegians and schoolboys, and girls in their teens who think it would be merry sport to tell mother that they're going to the movie around the corner, and then beat it down to West Fourth Street to meet college youths in a romantic and Bohemian way.[21]

In Chicago, the JPA expressed similar concerns. At a time when the Dill Pickle Club and several other Towertown resorts regularly advertised in student publications at the University of Chicago, Northwestern University, and the School of the Art Institute, the organization's leadership thought it prudent to take preemptive action against such nightspots' potential corruption of the city's youth. In the spring of 1922, they actively lobbied local authorities to close the popular Wind Blew Inn at 116 East Ohio Street, not because they had observed any "disorderly" actions on its premises but because its "very bad" atmosphere regularly drew a crowd of wide-eyed youths. Several raids soon followed, but the tearoom continued to operate until it caught fire in late April.[22]

Aside from occasional federal crackdowns on illegal liquor sales in the Village and Towertown and an unprecedented, two-year series of raids and closures of popular slumming destinations initiated by Chicago's newly elected, reform-minded mayor, William E. Dever, in 1923, the only other significant crackdowns on bohemian slumming occurred at the behest of disgruntled neighbors.[23] On several occasions in the early 1920s, after conservative, long-time residents and business owners complained that Village nightspots were "disturb[ing] the slumbers of the peaceful," New York's Mayor Hylan launched a series of crackdowns on the "early hour revelries" of bohemian nightspots. The subjects of these raids were not the artists and radicals who called the district home but rather the "boys and girls from other sections" of the city who, according to the executive secretary of the Washington Square Neighborhood Association, came "to revel in the artificial bohemian atmosphere they themselves created."[24] Mayor Dever charted a similar course in the Windy City. Responding to a petition signed by thirty-eight Near North Side residents in late April 1925, he ordered the padlocking of Vincenc Noga's Gold Coast House of Corrections, apparently hoping to encourage the cabaret's patrons—whom the local police captain described as "not of the rowdy or tough class" but "what might be termed, 'Slummers' or those who seek the odd and unusual"—to refrain from attending such places.[25]

When they survived judicial review, padlocks provided local authorities with an effective way to close a particular nightspot or two that neighbors or reformers found especially offensive, but their effect on the more general atmosphere of bohemian nightlife was relatively minimal. When one cabaret closed, another sprang up in its place, often operating in the same location under different owners or at a new address under the shuttered cabaret's proprietor. Because padlock cases were notoriously difficult to prosecute and often involved months of legal maneuverings, authorities hoping to rein in entire entertainment districts usually resorted to simpler tactics, including the stepped-up enforcement of city-mandated closing hours: 1:00 a.m. in Chicago and an hour later in New York. Such actions not only appeased neighbors who complained about noise and unruliness well beyond official closing hours but also proved unusually effective in briefly curtailing the very practice of slumming, which usually took place well after local theaters and more mainstream cabarets had closed. During the spring of 1923, a waiter at Towertown's Palace Gardens confirmed the effectiveness of this technique when asked why the cabaret "has been poorly patronized of late." "Oh! I don't know," he told an undercover investigator from the JPA. "Now that they are trying to close us up at one o'clock, I suppose the people don't want to come around because they think it isn't worth while." Yet a crackdown on slumming in one neighborhood often had the unintended effect of promoting the activity in another. In the midst of Towertown's increased regulation, the waiter pointed out that "they get the big crowds over at the black and tan joints on the south side," indicating both the unevenness of urban policing and white revelers' renewed fascination with black culture.[26]

The "Negro Vogue": Harlem and Bronzeville

The 1920s marked the high point of white slummers' preoccupation with the black neighborhoods and nightlife of Chicago and New York. On Chicago's South Side, popular cabarets, such as the Plantation and Sunset cafés, drew record crowds of "sophisticated high school youngsters, cynical office clerks, and effusive representatives of produce houses, who," *Variety* observed, "seem to relish the carefree atmosphere" and the "loud, wailing and pulsating" music that they found in these clubs. The crowds were even larger in New York, where Harlem "acquired a worldwide reputation" for "being exotic, colorful, and sensuous; a place of laughing, singing, and dancing; a place where life wakes up at night." African American writer and activist James Weldon Johnson noted that "New Yorkers and people visiting New York from the world over go to the night-clubs of Harlem and dance to such jazz music as can be heard nowhere else; and they get an exhilaration impossible to duplicate." During Prohibition, this sense of jazz-induced exhilaration became the chief pursuit of many pleasure-seeking whites. According to African American poet Langston Hughes, this was the era "when the Negro was in vogue" with urban whites who could not get enough of black nightlife, music, and dance.[27]

The popular fascination with black-and-tan resorts that played a role in slummers' earlier ventures to the Tenderloin and the Levee provided a precedent for the Negro vogue. But unlike the multifaceted focus of the earlier craze, this new vogue was centered exclusively on black nightlife and on the sizable new black neighborhoods that began to take shape in Harlem and on Chicago's South Side during the mid-1910s. These new communities were a direct result of the outbreak of the First World War. As hostilities brought southern and eastern European immigration to a virtual standstill, northern industrialists turned to the rural South and the Caribbean in an effort to offset the growing shortage of unskilled labor in cities like Chicago and New York. Responding to these entreaties, tens of thousands of Southern blacks and a significant number of West Indian immigrants soon packed their bags and headed north. For rural Southern migrants, the North signified a "land of hope," an opportunity not only to secure better-paying industrial or service-oriented jobs but also to escape the prejudice, discrimination, and threat of violence that marked their daily lives in the Jim Crow South. The reality of urban life often proved much more complex than they had ever imagined, but the unprecedented Great Migration of Southern blacks and influx of West Indians soon transformed the racial environments of New York and Chicago. Quickly overflowing the traditional bounds of the black sections of the Tenderloin and the Levee, these new residents fueled the rapid development of bustling black communities in Harlem and on Chicago's South Side, making black nightlife and culture more visible than ever before in the urban North and attracting a whole new generation of curious white slummers.[28]

Harlem had been home to a small number of black New Yorkers since at least the 1830s, when it was little more than an isolated, rural town located well outside the boundaries of New York City. As middle- and upper-class whites transformed Harlem into an affluent suburb of brownstones and exclusive apartment buildings during the last decades of the nineteenth century, still more blacks moved into the area, seeking work as domestic servants. But the emergence of Harlem as the nation's premier black community did not begin in earnest until the first decade of the twentieth century, when speculative construction reached astonishing proportions in that neighborhood, far outpacing the market for new housing. For black New Yorkers, this overabundance of vacant buildings provided a unique opportunity to improve their living conditions and eventually establish the largest black community in early-twentieth-century America.[29]

Around 1904, the Afro-American Realty Company, founded by black real estate agent Philip A. Payton Jr., began to acquire five-year leases on white-owned property in Harlem. Renting these apartments to blacks who sought to escape the dilapidated housing of the Tenderloin, Payton's company sparked the establishment of a vibrant new black community

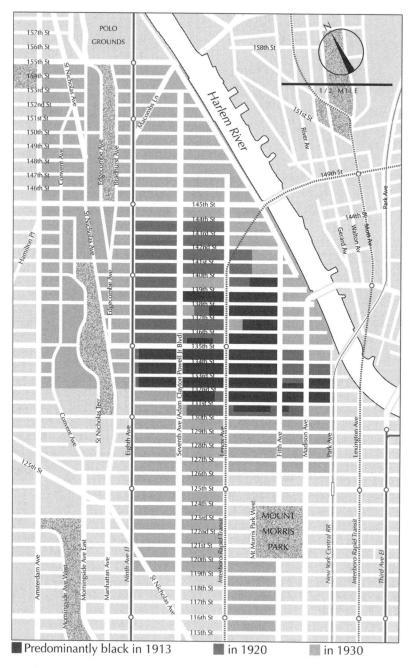

POLO
GROUNDS

MOUNT
MORRIS
PARK

Harlem River

■ Predominantly black in 1913   ■ in 1920   ■ in 1930

8   This map illustrates the dramatic expansion of Harlem's black population from the early
1910s to 1930.

centered along 135th Street between Lenox and Seventh avenues (figure 8). By 1914, nearly 50,000 blacks had settled in the neighborhood, and tens of thousands more followed in their wake, most of them newly arrived from the rural South and the West Indies during and immediately after the First World War. By 1920, Harlem was not only New York's principal black residential and commercial district but also the largest urban concentration of blacks anywhere in the country. Extending from 144th Street to 128th and occupying most of the area between Fifth and Eighth avenues, black Harlem became a city unto itself during the mid-1920s and fostered a thriving literary and artistic movement now commonly referred to as the Harlem Renaissance. While the books, paintings, and journals produced by Harlem's artists attracted significant attention to the district, in the eyes of most urban whites, the city's vibrant new black community was soon equated with all-night cabarets and the syncopated beat of jazz.[30]

The Great Migration hastened a similar transformation of the black community of Chicago (figure 9). In 1910, the South Side neighborhood known by whites as the "Black Belt" was little more than a narrow strip running along State Street from the Loop for about thirty blocks south. Only a few blocks wide, except at its northern end, the district housed some 34,335 black residents—about 78 percent of the city's total black population. By 1920, however, as Southern migrants began to pour into the area, the black community pushed significantly further south, and Thirty-first Street, a commercial strip where several popular cabarets were located, effectively became its northern border. Nicknamed "Bronzeville" by local residents, the community came to occupy all the space between the city's lakefront and the railroad located west of State Street, stretching as far south as Fortieth Street, in addition to two further parcels that branched down from that core: the first ran along the original narrow State Street strip to near Fifty-seventh Street, and the second formed a slightly broader wedge between Cottage Grove Avenue and South Parkway (now Martin Luther King Drive), extending as far as Forty-ninth Street. As the district's population continued to swell throughout the 1920s, reaching a total of more than 200,000 by the end of the decade, Bronzeville swallowed up still more of the surrounding territory and soon gained a reputation as one of the country's most vibrant black communities, as well as one of its premier jazz destinations. Along "The Stroll" on South State Street, the cabarets were so thick that one white musician claimed that "around midnight you could hold an instrument in the middle of the street and the air would play it."[31]

9　This map displays the demographic transformation on Chicago's South Side associated with an unprecedented influx of black migrants who transformed the city's early-twentieth-century "Black Belt" into a vibrant neighborhood known as Bronzeville in the 1920s and 1930s.

Although it is tempting now to imagine these districts as the slums they became in later years, at the height of the Negro vogue, Harlem and Bronzeville were hardly dilapidated centers of poverty or immorality. Rather, they were bustling black commercial and residential hubs, filled with a wide array of black- and white-owned restaurants, shops, and cabarets, as well as an extraordinarily diverse black population. Whether professional or blue collar, homeowner or renter, nearly all black New Yorkers and Chicagoans lived in the same general geographic vicinity during the 1920s—a predictable outcome given the Jim Crow real estate practices of the era. True, there were pockets of Harlem and Bronzeville that resembled turn-of-the-century slums, where once-magnificent houses and apartment buildings were subdivided into rooming houses and small "kitchenettes" for which tenants paid significantly higher rents than the open market would have permitted for similarly decaying properties in other neighborhoods. But there were also elegant residences and well-maintained apartment buildings that provided shelter to black professionals, business leaders, and commercially successful artists and musicians. In Harlem, one particularly posh block of brownstones on 138th and 139th streets earned the nickname of "Strivers' Row" among locals, and similar residences could also be found in Bronzeville.

The urban black community that attracted slummers, then, was by no means a slum; rather, it was a destination for the consumption of commercialized leisure. In fact, most of the affluent whites who visited Harlem and Bronzeville did so only late at night, when the popular black-and-tan cabarets and basement speakeasies were alive and pulsating with jazz. Yet it was this type of slumming excursion that came to define the black communities of New York and Chicago in the minds of most white Americans and other visitors to these districts. While the harshness of daylight revealed the stark inequalities that continued to separate most black and white residents in northern U.S. cities, the cover of darkness promoted a romanticized sense of toleration, equality, and fraternization among the various types who reveled in the black and tans of Bronzeville and Harlem. British stage actress Gracie Fields confirmed this contrast between Harlem by day and by night, telling an American newspaper that "she had not had many thrilling experiences as yet" but was planning a late-night visit to Harlem. "I drove around that section of your city the first day I arrived," she reported, but "found it singularly drab and unexciting. I'm sure it must look more romantic at night."[32]

Whatever romanticism white slummers found in Harlem and Bronzeville could be directly attributed to the boom in black nightlife precipitated by the Great Migration. Disproportionately youthful in composition, Southern migrants arrived in New York and Chicago at the very moment that dance halls and cabarets were reaching the height of their popularity among working- and middle-class youth. In short order, this influx of young people overwhelmed the existing public amusements in both cities, prompting the establishment of a barrage of new saloons, cabarets, and dance halls designed to cater to the black residents of Harlem and Bronzeville. When the granting of entertainment licenses failed to keep pace with the growing demand of blacks for leisure space, the districts' officially licensed amusements were augmented by hundreds of impromptu "buffet flats" that operated above storefronts and in private apartment buildings in surrounding neighborhoods. In the late nineteenth century, these informal establishments had served primarily as black alternatives to discriminatory white-owned hotels, but during the Great Migration they increasingly assumed the role of neighborhood centers of drinking, gambling, and prostitution. In due course, the buffet flats of Harlem and Bronzeville also began to attract the attention of curious whites, who found in these more clandestine environs an even greater degree of cross-racial interaction than that which so unsettled white urban reformers in the districts' more prominent black-and-tan cabarets.[33]

Ironically, as reformers struggled to police this white escape from sexual and racial convention, it was one of their most resounding achievements—namely, the passage of national Prohibition—that actually fostered the development and expansion of the Negro vogue. Much as it had expedited the earlier search for bohemian *thrillage*, the criminalization of liquor sales encouraged gin-deprived white urban residents and tourists to flock to black neighborhood establishments in an effort to quench their thirst. In comparison with the speakeasies of Greenwich Village and Towertown, however, those located in Harlem and Bronzeville often proved to be even more reliable providers of bootleg liquor, since local authorities were usually content to allow such illicit activities to flourish in black neighborhoods. Except for periodic crackdowns, which often coincided with municipal elections, slummers in Bronzeville and Harlem drank to their hearts' content, protected by the largely Jewish- and Italian-dominated underground economy that operated unhindered in these neighborhoods.[34]

The underground economies of Harlem and Bronzeville also provided white pleasure seekers with easy access to illegal drugs. Upon the closure of the Levee, Chicago's thriving black market for drugs relocated to nearby Bronzeville, and by the early 1920s was securely ensconced within the black nightlife district located between Thirty-first and Thirty-fifth streets. This same period witnessed similar transformations in New York, prompting one entertainment weekly to report that a stretch of Harlem's Fifth Avenue, between 132nd and 138th streets, had become so drug-infused by the late 1920s that it had garnered the nickname "Coke village." While these developments were part and parcel of local authorities' attempts to contain all manner of illicit behavior within the confines of the cities' black neighborhoods, they also provided white slummers with yet another social lubricant to lower their inhibitions as they crossed over the infamous color line. The prospect of such recreational participation in Harlem's drug culture was suggested by *Variety*'s announcement that "many of the be-ermined and high-hat white gentry entering the area are on the bay for 'hop,'" or, opium. Others insisted that visitors to Harlem and Bronzeville preferred "tea" or "reefer," as marijuana was known in the parlance of the day, to enhance their sense of escape into the revelry of local black and tans. Yet whatever the drug of choice, by the late 1920s, white thrill seekers increasingly associated their participation in black nightlife with an indulgence in illegal substances. In the words of black journalist Edgar M. Grey, they "sought the great fire-eating gift of black folk to the American scene: Sex served scientifically with Jazz, and washed down by poisonous liquors and more poisonous drugs."[35]

As the closure of the cities' segregated red-light districts pushed prostitution under cover in call houses and cabarets, there was no denying that it, too, became disproportionately concentrated in the cities' black neighborhoods. Upon arrival in New York and Chicago, southern black migrants found themselves face to face with hundreds of prostitutes, both black and white, recently displaced from the Tenderloin and the Levee. Although local authorities increased their surveillance of Harlem and Bronzeville, spurring periodic crackdowns on the prostitution that flourished in these districts, for the most part, they turned a blind eye to these neighborhoods. In part, this was the result of a shortage of black anti-vice investigators and police officers who could more easily gather evidence in the cities' black neighborhoods without raising suspicions. But it was also the product of the containment strategies promulgated by the cities' white-run police departments and private anti-vice organizations. As with the segregated red-light districts of old, officials in New York and Chicago essentially resolved to tolerate the persistence of prostitution in the cities' black residential districts in order to minimize its presence in affluent white neighborhoods.

What little policing of black-and-tan cabarets local authorities did undertake was prompted primarily by the inability of white urban reformers to conceptualize cross-racial interactions outside a sexualized framework. Assuming that no respectable white woman could possibly desire to participate in cross-racial dancing or socializing, they routinely equated the mere presence of white women in the cities' black and tans with prostitution. In a report to Chicago's JPA, one investigator made this equation particularly clear. "White fellows . . . dance with negro prostitutes," he wrote of the interactions he observed at one Bronzeville cabaret, "and white girls, *or rather prostitutes*," he corrected himself, "dance with colored men." Indeed, the linkage between prostitution and racial mixing was so complete in the minds of authorities that, as New York's Committee of Fourteen reported, two young white women were arrested on Broadway in early 1922 merely for entering a cab with a male acquaintance bound for "135th Street and Seventh Avenue, the vicinity of the colored resorts." Although a judge later dismissed this case for lack of any evidence that the women had actually exchanged sex for money, he praised the New York policeman who made the arrests for intervening in a situation that "had given every appearance of evil."[36]

Throughout the early 1920s, municipal authorities routinely invoked such appeals to protect the sanctity of white womanhood in an effort to discourage the growing white middle-class fascination with black urban culture which they believed threatened to disrupt the cities' fragile racial order. In December 1922, for instance, New York officials proudly proclaimed that they had heeded "numerous complaints from parents that their daughters were visiting [black and tans]" by raiding Harlem's Shuffle Inn and arresting eighty-three of its youthful white patrons. Yet in rescuing young white women from the supposed dangers of cross-racial sexuality, authorities further demonstrated their resolve to reinforce the spatial segregation of the city. Although the "usual custom in such cases [was] to discharge the prisoners with a reprimand," according to the black-owned *Chicago Whip*, the judge overseeing this case held each of the youths on $500 bail and "injected the race question into a moral question" by informing them that "there were sufficient white cabarets for white folk to visit without going to places maintained by Negroes."[37]

Local officials in New York and Chicago also advocated the regulation or prohibition of cross-racial interaction as a means of preventing racial unrest. The segregation of public amusements along a black/white axis was considered so integral to the maintenance of public order that, as late as the autumn of 1927, New York's Committee of Fourteen continued to insist that the racial integration of Harlem's cabarets not only created a "moral hazard to young people of both races," but also "may ultimately, if not checked, lead to the probability of serious race riots."[38] In Chicago, where "the intimate association of Negroes and whites in the cabarets of the South Side" had been cited as a contributing factor in the city's August 1919 race riot, such rhetoric held even greater sway. Despite protestations from local black newspapers that "persons who dance together are not so likely to fight as persons who stand at a distance and call each other bad names," the white press maintained that Bronzeville's black and tans posed a significant threat not only to the purity of white womanhood but also to the surety of continued white political dominance.[39] Describing local black and tans as "a potent breeder of race hatred, which may explode into a race riot at any moment," white reporters attempted to rally voters against the city's black-supported Republican party during the mayoral campaign of 1923. Calling attention to Mayor "Big Bill" Thompson's alleged protection of Bronzeville's underground trade in sex, liquor, and gambling, they threw their political might behind the reform-minded Democratic challenger, Judge William E. Dever, who had publicly pledged to curtail such activities while subtly conveying his intentions to strengthen white control over the city's government. Less than two months after taking office, the victorious Dever followed through on his pledge, ordering the closure of no fewer than ten prominent Bronzeville black and tans.[40]

Lest voters should suspect that these closures constituted payback to the black supporters of Dever's Republican rival, the city's white newspapers and government officials reignited public concerns about the threat that such cabarets posed to white social and sexual respectability. William Randolph Hearst's *Chicago American* reported that "improper dancing between black and white patrons and habitués" was regularly observed in each of the padlocked cabarets, while the *Chicago Tribune* upped the ante by relating the "soul kisses between colored men and white women" that supposedly characterized the goings-on in these spaces. Chicago's assistant corporation counsel Leonard J. Grossman further insisted that the city was forced to eliminate these "haven[s] for wily sensualists and debauchees," because they attracted and furthermore produced "mongrel hybrid nondescripts."[41] In an attempt to not only counteract such threats of miscegenation but also secure the right to reopen their cabaret, the Jewish owners of the Entertainers' Café offered to "whitewash" their Bronzeville establishment, "prohibit[ing] all colored persons from entering the cafe." Ultimately, however, such Jim Crow strategies proved unnecessary. Although a few Bronzeville resorts managed to safeguard their continued operation by limiting or banning black patrons in the months following Dever's raids, in some cases, even gaining a seal of approval from reform organizations such as the JPA, most of the raided black and tans simply resumed their previous operations after obtaining legal injunctions against the city. In the case of at least two prominent Bronzeville cabarets, however, even these tactics fell short of their mark.[42]

Shortly before Dever's 1927 rematch against Thompson, Chicago police arrested both the black proprietor of the Dreamland Café, Virgil Williams, and the Jewish owner of the Sunset and Plantation cafés, Joe Glaser, on charges of contributing to the delinquency of white teenage girls. Throughout the campaign, Dever used these two examples to remind white voters of his willingness to crack down on the illicit activities which Thompson had allowed to fester in Bronzeville, as well as to suggest that a return to Thompson's mayoral rule would imperil the sanctity and purity of white womanhood as never before. "Only a few days ago one, Glaser, who runs the Sunset Cabaret was arrested for contributing to the delinquency of a fourteen year old school child," Dever exhorted white supporters in an overtly racist stump speech that conflated the alleged danger that Jewish men like Glaser posed to white females with the supposedly inherent sexual menace of black men. "The army of nigger vagrants that haunt every street and every doorway [of the Black Belt]," Dever insisted in his very next statement, "is eternally on the outlook for white girls."[43]

Although such tactics failed to secure Dever's victory in the March election, his rhetoric of a sexualized racial threat probably helped cement Sunset Café proprietor Joe Glaser's conviction and "sentence to the penitentiary for the rape of a child," a development which the JPA proudly announced in its annual report for 1927. Moreover, when coupled with federal Prohibition agents' expanded policing of Chicago's illicit nightlife, it made black-and-tan slumming an increasingly less desirable indulgence, even under the relatively permissive reign of the recently reempowered Thompson administration. In the year following the election, federal authorities repeatedly closed the Plantation Club and several other popular black and tans, eventually placing the Plantation under permanent federal padlock in February 1928 and prompting the Harlem-bound departure of many of the district's most prominent black jazz musicians. In the aftermath of these developments, *The Light and "Heebie Jeebies,"* a black Chicago weekly, noted that only "one honest-to-goodness so-called 'black and tan' cabaret" still operated in the district. Indeed, those slummers who braved the closures and rhetorical threats by continuing to undertake slumming excursions to Bronzeville increasingly found themselves shuttled into mere "holes in the wall," which *The Light*'s anonymous rambling columnist reported "ha[d] come out like stars in the evening" since the reelection of Mayor Thompson.[44]

In New York, former Bronzeville musicians like Joe "King" Oliver encountered a more lively black-and-tan scene in 1927 and 1928. Yet Harlem's cabarets also faced diminishing white attendance, because federal authorities brought the new enforcement techniques they were perfecting in Chicago to New York, and local officials were becoming increasingly alarmed by the growing white presence in the city's bustling black entertainment district. In early 1927, New York's Committee of Fourteen announced that the "morbid curiosity" of white New Yorkers was "being capitalized by exploiters of both races" in Harlem at an unprecedented pace. Securing funding from the Rockefeller-supported Bureau of Social Hygiene to document its suspicions, the committee hired its first full-time black investigator, Raymond A. Claymes, to gather evidence in Harlem cabarets and buffet flats where the committee's white investigators either were already well known or easily aroused suspicions. From mid-March to the end of July 1928, Claymes visited eighty-five mainly white-owned and operated black-and-tan speakeasies, in addition to fifty buffet flats "operated mostly by negro men or negro women with negro and white 'girls' for negro and white patronage." During the course of these investigations, the committee claimed that Claymes uncovered rates of prostitution that were "four or five times as prevalent as in other sections of the city," sparking outrage among both white and black reformers.[45]

These findings also prompted substantial changes in the regulation of slumming venues during New York's Negro vogue. While not more than six Harlem nightspots had been raided, according to Claymes, during his four-and-a-half-month investigation, immediately after the public release of the committee's resulting 1928 annual report, the police secured warrants against "thirty-five [Harlem] places in one batch." In addition, following the example and recommendation of the committee, New York police commissioner Grover A. Whalen agreed to establish a "carefully selected and intelligent squad of plain clothes colored policemen" to expedite the gathering of evidence in black establishments. The immediate result of these actions was that Harlem's buffet flats and black and tans became subject to more frequent raids by local authorities, and New York slummers began to experience the growing discomfort and unpredictability that had characterized Chicago's black-and-tan nightlife for nearly two years. At the same time, the apparently increased willingness of federal and local authorities to go after syndicate-connected Harlem nightspots further destabilized New York's Negro vogue. In early 1929, slummers discovered that such traditionally protected nightspots as the white-owned Swanee Club, where the former "Floradora Girl" Evelyn Nesbit served as hostess, were increasingly prone to police harassment.[46]

Even in the face of such increased policing, the vogue for New York's black-and-tan nightlife maintained most of its spark until the Depression set in more fully in the early 1930s. *Variety* reported in mid-October 1929 that Harlem had "never . . . been more popular," boasting "11 class white trade night clubs," over five hundred "colored cabarets, of lower ranks," and two buffet flats "for every apartment building in the black belt." But by late 1930, no more than four of these major night clubs were still operating, and the few slummers who continued to head uptown were increasingly ushered into the district's smaller speakeasies and secluded, black-owned buffet flats. In its usual year-end summary of the nightlife of 1930, *Variety* proclaimed in typical slang-filled prose that "Harlem with its numerous hot spots no longer offers much in the way of opposish [opposition] to the Broadway joints." This was an observation confirmed not only by entertainment reporters but also by members of the white bohemian crowd who had made Harlem a favored slumming destination in earlier years. In a letter to his parents in 1931, the writer and former Harlem regular Max Ewing remarked, "Harlem is a dead city and I never go there any more. The depression has put an end to nearly everything."[47]

The Pansy and Lesbian Craze: Greenwich Village, Times Square, Towertown, and the Black and Tans of Harlem and Bronzeville

Despite the economic constraints of the Depression, by the early 1930s, the last of the great slumming vogues was in full flower. Known as the "pansy and lesbian craze," this vogue created a spectacle of homosexuality and was fueled by the public's growing curiosity about the many lesbians and gay men who began settling in residential enclaves in New York and Chicago during the previous decade.[48] Part of a broader cultural trend in which homosexual characters and topics became surprisingly common in popular fiction, theatrical productions, film, and tabloid newspapers, the pansy and lesbian craze provided slummers with an occasion to visit some of the nightspots identified with this sizable new urban population. From the late 1920s through much of the following decade, the cities' pansy and lesbian cabarets—with their colorful entertainment and plentiful sexual opportunities—became favored destinations for thrill-seeking middle- and upper-class whites. Many urbanites saw such excursions as little more than a logical extension of their growing familiarity with mass-media representations of homosexuality. In Chicago, for instance, one young woman told a local retailer that she and a female friend "decided to go on a sluming [sic] party to one of the places" after they "had read of homosexual life in books," including Radclyffe Hall's *The Well of Loneliness* (1928). Their decision to visit the Ballyhoo Café, a Near North Side speakeasy popular with both lesbians and gay men, mirrored the actions of thousands of their contemporaries whose insatiable appetite for novelty provided a ready audience for this dazzling but short-lived vogue.[49]

Because there was no sure and easy way for the average slummer to identify residential concentrations of homosexual women and men in the neighborhoods of New York and Chicago, this final interwar craze carried to its furthest extreme the general progression of slumming from a place-oriented activity to an amusement that determined the character of the spaces upon which it converged. True, even the most casual observer could recognize the presence of extremely feminine men and masculine women on neighborhood streets and in other public urban spaces. But as the gendered framework of sexuality gave way to the now-dominant binary of heterosexuality and homosexuality, many affluent white pleasure seekers understood that the highly gendered pansies and lesbians they encountered in New York and Chicago were but a portion of the cities' homosexual population. With no reliably visible markers to help identify the more normatively gendered segments of the cities' burgeoning homosexual communities, slummers turned instead to the nightclubs and speakeasies that featured discernibly queer entertainers as a way of investigating and incorporating this new urban population into their cosmopolitan conception of the city.

Slummers' participation in the pansy and lesbian craze took them over much of the same terrain covered by earlier slumming vogues. Their journey led them to queer reincarnations of the ramshackle tearooms and speakeasies that had attracted a previous generation to the bohemian *thrillage* of Greenwich Village and Towertown. It also carried them into the remnants of the old Tenderloin—a segment of which had been rechristened as Times Square and had become a center of mainstream commercial amusements in the early 1910s with the emergence of the cabaret—as the economic crunch of the early 1930s encouraged local impresarios to embrace the pansy and lesbian trend in an effort to boost short-term revenues. (To a similar but lesser extent, the same conditions applied to the mainstream cabarets of Chicago's Loop and its popular Rush Street entertainment district, the latter of which, as bohemia's eastern boundary, was always little more than a spruced-up extension of Towertown.) Finally, the quest for spectacles of homosexuality took well-to-do whites back to the black-and-tan cabarets of Harlem and Bronzeville. Like the mainstream, all-white venues of Times Square and the Loop, many of these cabarets employed female impersonators and mannish "bulldaggers" (as lesbians were known in the black argot of the day) in an effort to supplement the spectacles of blackness and cross-racial sexuality that had long been presented to slummers.

As it turns out, the nightlife venues that slummers frequented during this popular slumming craze were for the most part situated in the very neighborhoods that lesbians and gay men favored as residential centers. In the Village, Towertown, and Times Square, this was the result of the districts' long-standing reputations for sexual unconventionality, as well as the presence of numerous neighborhood lodging houses and studio apartments, which made it possible for single men and women to live apart from their families or in same-sex rooming situations that aroused relatively little suspicion among neighbors. As early as the late 1910s, in the midst of the vogue for bohemian *thrillage*, the Village had already acquired a reputation for welcoming, or at least tolerating, women and men who sought out sexual and romantic relations with members of the same sex. When local artists and radicals began to flee the growing commercialization of the neighborhood, white lesbians and gay men seized upon the opportunity to take their place. By the mid-1920s, the district's queer reputation was firmly cemented, and a popular ditty heard in local tearooms boldly proclaimed, "Fairyland's not far from Washington Square."[50]

In Chicago, white lesbians and gay men exploited similar commercial and demographic transformations in bohemian Towertown and the surrounding Near North Side rooming-house district. Moving into the alleyway studios and "vermilion kitchenette apartment[s]" abandoned by local artists, they began to establish a queer residential enclave that became visible to outsiders primarily through the local speakeasies that sought to capitalize on their presence. During the 1930s, in an unprecedented effort to document Towertown's increasing association with homosexual residents, University of Chicago sociologists and their students visited local cabarets to gather the life histories of the lesbians and gay men whom they encountered there. In the most comprehensive of these investigations, including interviews with more than fifty-three gay men, graduate student Earle W. Bruce discovered that more than two-thirds (thirty-four men) rented rooms or apartments in this section of the city, and nearly all the others spent the majority of their leisure hours in the public nightspots and private parties that defined the "Near North Side homosexual world."[51]

Meanwhile, in New York, where the homosexual population was, perhaps, larger than in any other U.S. city during this period, middle-class gay men began to move into the once-fashionable bachelor apartments and subdivided row houses of the West Forties and Fifties, to the north and east of Times Square. The district's cheap lodging houses, transient hotels, and "theatrical boarding houses" also provided housing for many working-class homosexual men whose employment in the scores of hotels, restaurants, and theaters around the square encouraged them to settle nearby. While the Village remained the address of choice for most New York lesbians during this period, it is likely that they also settled near the Square—especially those who worked beside their male counterparts in the neighborhood's public amusements. By 1930, the district had acquired enough of a reputation as a public rendezvous for "lady lovers" to prompt one theatrical weekly to warn that "seductions of this type on Broadway are one of its most serious problems."[52]

In Harlem and Bronzeville, the development of a homosexual enclave was less a matter of choice than of necessity. Like their heterosexual counterparts, black lesbians and gay men were almost always denied entrée into lodging houses and apartments in predominantly white residential districts. As a result, they carved out a place for themselves within the segregated black worlds of New York and Chicago. Because they shared a history of racial discrimination and residential segregation with their heterosexual neighbors, black lesbians and gay men often experienced a greater level of acceptance, or at least toleration, in their broader community than white homosexuals did. But in the complex, class-integrated black worlds of Harlem and Bronzeville, where prominent business leaders and professionals were forced to live in close proximity to the most recent migrants from the rural South, the level of acceptance shown to lesbians and gay men was often class-inflected. As evidenced particularly in the gossip columns of local black newspapers, the districts' more prosperous and better-educated residents often expressed disdain for the unabashed visibility of black working-class homosexuals in the public venues and residential quarters of Harlem and Bronzeville.[53]

Though there is a lack of comprehensive data documenting black homosexuals' residential patterns, the columns' snide remarks provide unique insights into the process by which lesbians and gay men staked out a place for themselves amid the limited housing options of the city's principal black enclaves. For instance, the surprise that the *Chicago Whip*'s "Nosey" columnist expressed upon discovering a man attired in a woman's dressing gown during a visit to a Bronzeville lodging house demonstrates that, as early as 1921, pansies were living quite openly in black working-class environments. A catty columnist for New York's *Inter-State Tattler* suggested that a seemingly more prosperous black male couple had been forced to *"secretly* leas[e] an apartment in 141st Street" together. Yet even amid Harlem's more affluent and reserved residents, it seems likely that these men also experienced some degree of toleration, provided they kept their sex lives relatively private, in accordance with middle-class notions of proper decorum.[54] Although the black press seldom commented on the living arrangements of lesbians, the sociological fieldwork conducted by E. Franklin Frazier during the early 1930s suggests that they, too, were a visible—though possibly less tolerated—part of the Bronzeville community. One of Frazier's young female informants pointed out the presence of such women in a nearby apartment house, noting that her sister had told her to steer clear of the building because it "ain't nothin' but for . . . (female homosexuals)."[55]

The pansy and lesbian craze, however, was premised not on visiting the urban districts inhabited by significant numbers of homosexuals but on patronizing those nightspots that specialized in presenting queer entertainment for curious onlookers or fellow homosexuals. As early as 1925, *Variety* reported that at least twenty Village tearooms were converted to "'temperamental' resorts," both to capitalize on the recent influx of white lesbians and gay men into the district and to showcase the unique spectacle that they provided, in an effort to woo back a substantial slumming trade from Harlem. For most bohemian entrepreneurs and habitués, sociologist Caroline Ware argued in her landmark study of the neighborhood, this "passing on from free love to homosexuality" constituted merely the latest in a series of "obvious manifestations which were successively adopted to mark the outposts of revolt." In Chicago, this transition was made no more evident, perhaps, than by the evolving list of entertainments presented at the long-running Dill Pickle Club. For years the popular tearoom had hosted lectures and debates on such explicitly sexual topics as "Buzzing a Broad in Bohemia" and "Capturing a Millionaire by One who lost one." But from the mid-1920s on, these events became increasingly queer, featuring a "guy called Theda Bara talking about his life as a homosexual," Elizabeth Davis "read[ing] her paper from Lesbos 'Will Amazonic Women Usurp Man's Sphere?'" and an appearance by attorney William H. Seed and Towertown cabaret owner Jack Ryan in a debate entitled, "Shall Society accept Intermediates?"[56]

By the spring of 1930, as the Depression began to exact its toll on commercial leisure, the pansy and lesbian craze moved into the more

mainstream nightspots of New York's Times Square. Acting on the recommendation of newspaper columnist Mark Hellinger, cabaret proprietors Louis and Arkie Schwartz hired one of the Village's most popular
female impersonators, Imogene Wilson (who had adopted the name of
one of the most popular Ziegfeld Follies showgirls), to headline their
Club Abbey, a popular West 54th Street speakeasy with connections to
gangster Owney Madden. But when the newly employed entertainer arrived at the Abbey sans drag and calling himself Jean Malin (an Americanization and feminization of his given name, Victor Eugene James
Malinovsky), this sharp-witted pansy performer quickly set the trend
for Broadway entertainment.[57] By the end of the year, no fewer than
six Times Square nightspots cashed in on the queer cachet that Malin
lent to the district. At the Club Abbey, Malin was joined first by Village
drag entertainer Francis Dunn, who appeared as Helen Morgan Jr., and
then by Lestra LaMonte, a female impersonator whose claim to fame
was his extensive wardrobe of papier-mâché costumes. Owners of the
nearby Club Calais copied the Abbey's success, inviting Village personalities Jackie Maye and Arthur "Rose" Budd to transport their carefully
honed female impersonation acts from the cellar dives of the downtown
district to the opening of this new Broadway nightspot. Similarly, at the
Coffee Cliff and the Club D'Orsay management hustled to put together
a passel of relatively unknown drag entertainers, eventually installing
Chicago radio personality and male impersonator Edna "Eddye" Adams
as the headline act at the latter cabaret.[58]

Perhaps the most stunning development occurred when two grand
dames of female impersonation stepped out of the dimming lights of
vaudeville to assume their rightful place among the pansy personalities of Times Square's latest nightlife craze. For a brief period during
the winter of 1930–31, vaudeville legend Francis Renault brought his
elaborate gowns and dead-on impersonations to the popular Everglades,
while the renowned "Creole Fashion Plate," Karyl Norman, recreated
his near-perfect illusions of current-day flappers at his newly opened
Pansy Club at 48th and Broadway. Unlike Renault, who maintained a
traditional theatrical approach to female impersonation, Norman embraced the trend of the times. He named his club so that it clearly signaled the latest slumming craze and surrounded himself with a group of
"Pansies on Parade."[59]

The early 1930s were witness to a similar blossoming of the pansy
and lesbian craze in Chicago. During this period, "tea shops and bootleg
joints . . . cater[ing] to lesbians" dotted the Near North Side, drawing
curious middle-class slummers to, among other places, the Roselle Inn

on North Clark Street and the Twelve-Thirty Club on North Clybourn. But clubs oriented toward a gay male clientele or featuring flamboyant pansy entertainers and female impersonators were far more abundant and popular. In December 1930, *Variety* noted the appearance of "some 35" Near North Side "pansy parlors" in the space of only six months. These "dim lit tea rooms, operated by boys who won't throw open the doors until at least two hours have been spent adjusting the drapes just so" featured "waitresses who are lads in gal's clothing." Although they attracted a reliable patronage from Towertown's growing homosexual population, *Variety* was far more impressed by the appeal that these speakeasies seemed to hold for local slummers. Even a number of Chicago's notorious "gun toting lads," *Variety* reported, "are supporting them nobly for the laughs."[60]

By the end of 1931, the Near North Side was so closely identified with the vogue for such entertainments that one New York tabloid warned promoters of the city's upcoming 1933 World's Fair that they might want to think twice before shining "their publicity spotlight on . . . [the city's] bohemian section," as the "real truth about the near north side" might be something that "Chicagoans would [not] like revealed." Despite such warnings, local officials apparently resolved that Chicago's pansy and lesbian nightspots provided a profitable and worthy diversion for the hordes of expected tourists. In anticipation of the fair, enterprising businessmen opened a smattering of even more upscale cabarets to showcase this latest slumming craze. The arrival of Karyl Norman and his protégé Leon LaVerde from New York in February 1932 heralded this sea change in Chicago nightlife. "Female impersonations in night life here have been confined mostly to the smaller spots on the near North Side," one reviewer noted as Norman staked his claim to a popular Loop cabaret located at Clark and Lake streets, "but Norman's engagement at the Kentucky Club is probably a forerunner of this form of entertainment on a large scale." Indeed, during the run-up to the opening of the Century of Progress World's Fair in 1933, a number of Near North Side pansy and lesbian cabarets rose in prominence with the slumming crowds, the K-9 Club at 105 East Walton Place foremost among them. "During the World's Fair—1933–34 editions," the nightlife critic for Hearst's *Chicago American* recalled, "the K-9 never had a night without a capacity crowd, and most evenings, the spot did a sell-out volume from opening time until the boys and girls of the show were dismissed for the night—'long about 5 a.m."[61]

In the face of such extraordinary popularity, and despite strong moral reservations about the spectacle on display in such spaces, until the mid-1930s, local authorities permitted the pansy and lesbian resorts of Greenwich Village, Times Square, and Towertown to operate relatively unimpeded. Their decision to do so was shaped by two principal factors: first, the absence of a sufficient force of federal agents to take over the enforcement of Prohibition regulations that the urban political machines of New York and Chicago largely ignored, and second, the lack of funds to subsidize any sustained regulatory campaigns by the cities' private anti-vice organizations. When a concerned New Yorker lodged a complaint in 1931 about the growing presence of homosexuals in local nightclubs, including the employment of "so-called 'Pansies' as masters of ceremonies," the Committee of Fourteen regretfully responded that "there seemed to be nothing to do about it." The police usually would not intervene in such operations, the organization's secretary reported, because the clubs "kept just within the law." Ultimately, however, it was the economic crisis of the Depression that spelled the end for the city's once illustrious Committee of Fourteen. Acknowledging its growing inability to raise funds or control the city's increasingly sexualized public amusements and popular culture, the committee closed its doors for good in 1932 (although not before mounting a last-ditch fundraising effort that highlighted the supposed dangers associated with the city's lesbian and pansy cabarets).[62]

Yet as historian George Chauncey shows, by the mid-1930s, the loss of the committee's leadership in the policing of urban nightlife and morality was more than offset by the repeal of Prohibition. Almost counterintuitively, Repeal ushered in an era of increased surveillance and control, reinvigorating the state's power to police urban sexuality through the passage of new liquor regulations that effectively outlawed the presence of homosexuals, prostitutes, gamblers, and other "undesirables" in the taverns of New York. Under the enforcement of the State Liquor Authority (SLA), these regulations sounded an ultimate death knell for the pansy and lesbian revues that once dominated Times Square. In July 1936, the last remaining survivor—the Club Richman, featuring Jack Mason's female impersonator revue—was unceremoniously shuttered. Announcing the closure of the cabaret, SLA Chairman Henry E. Bruckman cited "an investigation by State inspectors and the police [which] disclosed criminals congregating on the premises, the sale of liquor during prohibited hours and other violations." In due course, these "criminals" were revealed to be the club's drag entertainers and homosexual patrons, an allegation which the club's owner Morris Eisbrouch challenged unsuccessfully in court by insisting that "the police had no right to stop men from dressing as women and that if the police charges against the nitery were at all true they should have caused arrests when they investigated the club last October."[63]

In Chicago, where city and state officials fought over which governmental body should regulate liquor sales and where anti-vice organizations still held considerable sway, the Towertown version of the pansy and lesbian craze met its ultimate demise in a manner more closely resembling the end of previous slumming vogues. Throughout the Century of Progress World's Fair in 1933–34, social reformers vigorously protested what they perceived to be the exposition's corrupting influence on local nightlife and, by association, on the morals of Chicago's youth. "During the months of a Century of Progress," the JPA indignantly reported at the fair's conclusion, "several saloon-taverns 'amused' their patrons with spectacles of perversion . . . includ[ing] not only 'impersonators' in the floor shows, but also 'male hostesses' employed to sit and drink with patrons." While municipal officials chose to ignore these lapses in morality and decorum during the fair's two-year run, allowing the city's Depression-era economy to benefit from the increased revenues that such sexualized entertainment generated, they took an increasingly less obliging stance toward these amusements upon the closure of the exposition in the fall of 1934.[64]

As the tourist trade dried up, Mayor Edward J. Kelly gave in to reformers' demands to clean up Chicago's nightlife.[65] In December 1934, in a move that coincided with his decision to run for election to the seat he had assumed after Mayor Anton J. Cermak's 1933 assassination, Kelly launched an aggressive campaign to rid the city's cabarets and theaters of both striptease acts and male and female impersonators. Several burlesque theaters and Near North Side nightclubs quickly fell victim to his purge of fan dancers, but Chicago's queer nightlife took the hardest hit. By early 1935, pansy and lesbian entertainment was virtually eradicated from the city's Near North Side. Both the K-9 Club, "known throughout the midwest for its femme impersonators," and the Ballyhoo Café, which featured campier female and male impersonation, were padlocked by police "on charges of bawdiness," shutting slummers and queer patrons alike out of the city's two most popular pansy venues. Lesbian nightlife also suffered a major setback when two nightspots popular with both mannish women and heterosexuals—the Twelve-Thirty Club and the Roselle Inn—were shut down as part of the mayor's attack on "night clubs catering to women who prefer men's attire." Calling these cabarets "a disgrace to any city," Mayor Kelly vowed to purge Chicago of "every joint of such character" and announced that he would insist that the city council pass "an ordinance forbidding the impersonation of one sex by the opposite sex on any stage or place of amusement in the city of Chicago."[66]

Despite the virtual eradication of pansy and lesbian venues that such crackdowns brought to Towertown, Times Square, and the Village, the pansy and lesbian craze of Chicago and New York managed to survive this stepped-up policing, at least temporarily, by relocating to the black entertainment districts of Bronzeville and Harlem. In some instances, this relocation was literal, as white lesbian and pansy entertainers and entrepreneurs set up shop in the cities' black neighborhoods, performing in racially mixed cabaret revues and organizing drag balls in the districts' more permissive dance halls. But as increasing numbers of affluent white slummers began to make their way to Harlem and Bronzeville to partake of such amusements, the pansy and lesbian craze took on a distinctively brown hue. Simultaneously revitalizing the "Negro vogue" and capitalizing on slummers' ongoing fascination with queer amusements, black lesbian performers and female impersonators—including Gladys Bentley, the Sepia Gloria Swanson, and the Sepia Mae West—became the headline attractions in a renewed rage for things homosexual.

This "darkening" of the pansy and lesbian craze built on nearly a decade of similar entertainments in Harlem and Bronzeville that catered more to a local audience than to the handful of adventurous white slummers they attracted. Central among these were the districts' popular masquerades. By the late 1920s and well into the 1930s, Harlem's renowned annual Hamilton Lodge Ball and the interracial drags held at Chicago's Coliseum Annex drew even more white participants and observers than blacks. But during the early- to mid-1920s, they were largely community affairs.[67] The same held true for the small local speakeasies that introduced pansy and lesbian acts to Bronzeville and Harlem. When the Sepia Gloria Swanson (née Walter Winston), a prize winner at several Chicago drag balls, became a "permanent fixture" in his "net and sequin evening gowns" at the Book Store in 1928, nary a white slummer could be found. Only after he transferred his act to the nearby Pleasure Inn the following spring, making James H. Pleasure's cabaret "one of the town's chief spots of interest for those who don't care what," did he begin to entice a smattering of adventurous white thrill seekers.[68] Likewise, the earliest Harlem ventures of the "huge, voluptuous, chocolate colored" Gladys Bentley, who began performing in a tuxedo and top hat at Hansberry's Clam House in 1929, attracted only the most daring and

10   While this humorous 1932 map of Harlem nightclubs, drawn by African American illustra-
      tor E. Simms Campbell, included a number of uptown staples, such as the Cotton Club,
      Connie's Inn and Small's Paradise, it also highlighted the district's embrace of the pansy
      and lesbian craze during the early 1930s. Tuxedoed Gladys Bentley, the headliner at The
      Clam House, is featured prominently, as are a number of other Harlem speakeasies that
      attracted a queer clientele or provided queer entertainment for slumming audiences—
      including Dickie Wells's Theatrical Grill, where the Sepia Gloria Swanson held court; the Log
      Cabin, which was popular with Harlem's pansy and lesbian crowd; and the Club Hot-Cha,
      which gained a reputation, according to one Broadway tabloid, for being "ultra-lavender."

jaded white slummers (figure 10). When she moved to the eponymous
Gladys' Exclusive Club in 1931, Bentley's white following expanded
significantly, but it was still meager compared to the crowds she would
draw later in the decade.[69]

   Only after the repeal of Prohibition did the pansy and lesbian craze
definitively relocate to Harlem and Bronzeville, bringing with it the
throngs of affluent slummers who still could not get enough of the homosexual spectacle, and prompting local entrepreneurs to open a series
of upscale black and tans designed specifically to showcase queer black
entertainment. Moving from Bronzeville to Harlem in the summer of
1933, the Sepia Gloria Swanson was soon ensconced as the headliner
at one of these new cabarets (the black-owned Theatrical Grill on West
134th Street), where he dazzled appreciative audiences with a host of
ribald ditties, including his roof-raising rendition of "I'm a Big Fat Mama
With the Meat Shaking on My Bones."[70] The following spring, he was
joined by Gladys Bentley, as she returned from a short downtown engagement to recapture the Harlem spotlight at the opening of the lav-

ish Ubangi Club. Here, according to one fan, "Gladys toned her songs down somewhat" so that they were simply "risqué," but accompanied by a chorus line of "six gentlemen with a dash of lavender," her act was more unquestionably queer than ever.[71] Yet Swanson and Bentley were only the two most prominent among scores of black queer acts that captivated Harlem residents and slummers during the mid-1930s.

In 1934 alone, entertainers ranging from Swanson and Bentley to the lesbian comedian Jackie (later "Moms") Mabley, the male impersonator Lillian Brown, and the Sepia Clara Bow and his Fairyland Revue made almost monthly appearances on the stages of Harlem's vaudeville theaters. Such theatrical spectacles paled, however, in comparison to the number of similar acts, including the female impersonators Clarenz (née Clarence Henderson), "Daisy Navarro," and the Sepia Mae West (née Dick Barrow), who joined these entertainers to perform in local cabarets, such as the 101 Ranch, the Rosebud, and Small's Paradise.[72] In the spring of 1935, the violence of Harlem's race riot cast a decided chill over the district's nightlife, but not even this could deter the most dedicated slummers from making the trip uptown.[73] Throughout 1936, that bastion of metropolitan taste known as *The New Yorker* listed the Ubangi Club starring Gladys Bentley as a favored after-theater hot spot in its "Goings On About Town" column (a designation that had previously been afforded to only two other Harlem cabarets, the Cotton Club and Connie's Inn). Even as late as 1937, Harlem's queer entertainment was prominent and profitable enough for a study of the local business economy to remark that "The men who look and act like women have about reached a state of respectability, *for commercial purposes, at any rate*. They are featured entertainers in many of the night clubs and are clamored for on the programs of societies. People come from hundreds of miles for the annual 'pansie' [*sic*] or 'fairy' ball."[74]

Yet by the spring of 1937, Harlem's pansy and lesbian craze had largely run its course. In sporadic raids over a period of nearly three years, local authorities picked off the district's popular queer nightspots one by one, citing them for violations of the state's new liquor code or for permitting cross-dressed entertainment, despite municipal authorities' ban on the same. Not even the famed Ubangi Club was immune to this increased regulation. Although maintaining the tuxedoed Gladys Bentley as their headline act, in February 1935 management bowed to police demands that they replace the club's popular pansy chorus line with a bevy of beautiful chorines. "At last it's happened!" *New York Age* entertainment columnist Lou Layne exclaimed upon hearing the news. "This week the Ubangi goes normal." However, the final death knell for Harlem's pansy and lesbian craze did not sound for at least two more years, when the Ubangi Club's liquor and entertainment licenses were revoked in April 1937—not because of the cabaret's association with homosexual patrons and entertainers, but for the much more easily proved violation of selling liquor during prohibited hours early one Sunday morning.[75] Coupled with the personal calamities of two of Harlem's most popular female impersonators—the March 1936 suicide of the twenty-six-year-old Clarenz and the repeated hospitalization of the Sepia Gloria Swanson from late 1936 until his death in 1940 at age thirty-three—the Ubangi Club's closure signaled the end of an era.[76] As late as December 1938, a handful of "'high-voiced' entertainers" continued to perform at the Brittwood, but by the following spring even the annual Hamilton Lodge Ball met its ultimate demise, unable to secure the necessary permits from the municipal government despite months of planning.[77]

In Bronzeville, however, the craze persisted. From its quiet beginnings in late 1933, when the Sepia Mae West and the Sepia Peggy Hopkins Joyce (née Sam Fouchee) began performing at the 7–11 Club on the corner of 31st Street and Indiana Avenue, the district's reputation for pansy and lesbian entertainment only intensified over the course of the following decade. During the summer of 1934, enterprising local businessmen opened a number of new black and tans designed specifically to take advantage both of the city's newfound fascination with homosexuality and of Bronzeville's unbeatable location at the southern perimeter of the Century of Progress fairgrounds. At the newly established Annex Buffet, the Sepia Mae West soon lived up to his chosen persona, "Doin' 'Em Wrong in Her Own Musical Revue, 'The Gay Nineties.'" Similar female impersonation acts drew still more slummers to "Big" Nat Ivy's nearby Cozy Cabin Club, where the floorshow featured the blues stylings of Luzetta Hall, the soubrette act of "Joan Crawford" (née George Manus), and "Gilda Gray's" rousing impersonation of the fan dance made famous by Sally Rand at the nearby world's fair. Incorporating gay argot in his local newspaper advertisements, Ivy even suggested that a visit to this popular black and tan was an essential part of Chicago's nightlife experience. "When you have seen our Floor Show and 'camped' in the Cozy Cabin Club," the ads told potential patrons, "you have seen Chicago at its Best."[78]

When Mayor Kelly clamped down on the pansy and lesbian craze on Chicago's Near North Side in late 1934 and early 1935, Bronzeville's version of this popular slumming vogue continued to thrive. After producing the Annex Café's elaborate spring "Easter Parade," the Sepia Mae West crossed over to the local competition, joining Nat Ivy at his renewed Cabin Inn (now minus the "Cozy") when it relocated to a more esteemed State Street address. Even the prominent Club DeLisa got in on the act that summer, featuring the drag stylings of Valda Gray, as did the newly opened DeLuxe Café, located just a few short blocks up the State Street Stroll. Responding, perhaps, to the flurry of white slummers who headed south to partake of such amusements (especially after their eviction from Towertown), in late October 1935 local authorities launched a campaign to clean up the city's popular black and tans. According to a story released by the Associated Negro Press, when police raided the DeLuxe Café and the Cabin Inn, they "ordered the impersonators to 'either put on pants or go to jail with the management.'" At the Cabin Inn, the entertainers apparently followed orders, and those patrons who had not been scared off by the raid "were treated to the unusual sight of impersonators wearing genuine male dress." Within a week, both resorts resumed normal operations, allegedly bribing their way out of their legal difficulties, but only the Cabin Inn remounted its queer-oriented floor-show. Yet in early December, the police descended on Bronzeville once again, ordering the popular Club DeLisa to terminate Sam Fouchee's performance as Peggy Hopkins Joyce and citing the Cabin Inn for staging a floorshow that violated its entertainment license.[79]

While this crackdown effectively drove both the Club DeLisa and the Deluxe Café out of the queer entertainment business—and encouraged the Sepia Mae West to accept a yearlong series of engagements in Los Angeles—it by no means spelled the end of the pansy and lesbian craze in Bronzeville. By the autumn of 1936, the Cabin Inn resumed its position as the city's premier slumming destination, this time with Valda Gray at the helm of its elaborate productions.[80] When University of Chicago graduate student Conrad Bentzen visited the popular black and tan in March 1938, he reported, "Every night we find the place crowded with both races, the black and the white, [and] both types of lovers, the homo and the hetro [sic]." Indeed, the Cabin Inn and its performers became such a visible and accepted part of Bronzeville nightlife that even the rather conservative *Chicago Defender* asked them to perform at its annual Christmas benefit shows throughout the late 1930s. Chicago health officials likewise acknowledged their presence and importance in the Bronzeville entertainment and sex economy, targeting the Cabin Inn's "painted boys" along with the female prostitutes working out of other local cabarets, to receive questionnaires, free blood tests, and treatment as part of the city's intensive campaign against syphilis during the late 1930s.[81] In early 1938, no fewer than four additional Bronzeville cabarets got in on the popular pansy and lesbian craze, including the popular Swingland Café, where the "curvy male impersonator" Gladys Bentley played a short engagement on her way to the West Coast.[82]

Yet by decade's end, this last slumming vogue had largely run its course. The Cabin Inn closed its doors in early 1940, and Dickie "Mae West" Barrow began to play it as straight as it was possible for him to do as the emcee of variety performances in local cabarets. During the war, Valda Gray's elaborate drag productions would reemerge a bit further south in Bronzeville at Joe's DeLuxe Café (6323 South Parkway), but this time when the "girls" got together, they were performing primarily for a local audience. The slumming trade had largely disappeared.[83]

The advent of new liquor licensing following the repeal of Prohibition combined with the outbreak of the Second World War to achieve what evangelical Protestant reformers, private anti-vice organizations, mayors, and municipal police departments had been unable to accomplish for the previous half century: the virtual elimination of the popular amusement known to Americans by the rather peculiar appellation of *slumming*. Notwithstanding this rather definitive development, the regulation of the social, sexual, and urban transformations associated with each of the four successive slumming vogues had, to a significant extent, already been enacted by the slummers themselves. Rather than simply running amok in the cities' red-light resorts or bohemian tearooms, in their colorful black and tans or fanciful queer cabarets, white pleasure seekers usually shouldered the responsibility of policing the reconfiguration of social and sexual boundaries. Whether emulating the risqué behaviors they associated with the women and men they encountered in slumming venues or naturalizing their own changing conceptions of sexual and racial norms in relation to the sexual "perversions" and racialized "defects" they attributed to the objects of their observation, slummers seemed focused only on pursuing immediate pleasures and satisfying personal curiosities. Yet taken collectively, their actions helped shape American ideas about race and sexuality in the late nineteenth and early twentieth centuries.

At a crucial historical moment when previously gendered notions of sexual normativity were slowly giving way to the now-dominant hetero/homo sexual binary and when the Great Migration of Southern blacks shifted the earlier racialized landscape of immigrant-filled northern U.S. cities along an increasingly black/white axis, slumming provided a means to translate these transformations into mass cultural forms, grounding them in specific urban spaces and behaviors. It is to this everyday process of racial and sexual negotiation that I now turn, closely examining the shifting popular conceptualizations of race and sexuality that took shape within the context of an emerging commercialized leisure industry and the popularization of four distinct slumming vogues in the cities of Chicago and New York in a period ranging from the mid-1880s until the outbreak of the Second World War.

PART TWO

The Changing Conceptualization of Sexuality and Race in the Slumming Vogues of Chicago and New York

THREE

Adventures in the Slums and Red-Light Districts

As the first chapter demonstrated, the earliest wave of slum-ming expeditions in Chicago and New York focused prima-rily on their immigrant and working-class neighborhoods—especially those that were coincident with the cities' more renowned red-light districts and inhabited by their least as-similated populations. The so-called new immigrants from southern and eastern Europe, who were arriving in unprec-edented numbers at the turn of the century, proved a particu-lar source of fascination for affluent white thrill seekers, as did the smaller but substantial populations of blacks and Chinese immigrants who resided in many of the same neighborhoods. Slummers were also captivated by the districts' dance halls, opium dens, and black-and-tan resorts—both because of their unabashed association with illicit sex and because of the en-trée such spaces provided to the new realm of commercialized public leisure. These competing but often complementary attractions not only prompted well-to-do whites to think of their excursions into Chicago's Levee district and the Bowery and Tenderloin of New York in increasingly racialized and sexualized terms, but also created popular venues where the formation of modern racial and sexual hierarchies could be concurrently visualized and intimately experienced.

Because the neighborhoods that slummers visited were commonly associated with prostitution, casual sex, and sex-ual spectacle, they provided affluent whites with an opportu-nity to explore new social and sexual terrain. The more adven-turous among these urban thrill seekers actively participated in the sexual culture of the districts' immigrant and working-class resorts. But many others simply observed the antics that took place in these spaces or exploited the anonymity they provided to become more publicly intimate with middle-class dates. Whatever the case, slummers' excursions into the cities' red-light districts challenged Victorian notions of social and sexual reserve by broadening the categories of leisure and sexual behavior considered acceptable for elite whites and simultaneously blurring the boundary that ordinarily separated white middle-class respectability from the so-called moral improprieties of the working class.

Even as the sexual mechanics of slumming threatened to undermine the social and moral standing of well-to-do whites, however, the racial dynamics of this popular pastime usually served to reestablish their rank and respectability. Whether inhabited by Chinese immigrants and blacks (whose "racial difference" was usually apparent to even the most casual observer) or by southern and eastern European immigrants (whose popular racialization was a complicated matter that went well beyond the mere color of skin), the neighborhoods that slummers visited were those that were most clearly marked as nonwhite. As such, these spaces provided white pleasure seekers with an opportunity to shore up their position atop the American racial hierarchy by contrasting any perceived improprieties in their social and sexual activities with the less "civilized" behaviors of the racialized objects of their amusement. That is, slumming excursions refashioned popular conceptions of race and sexuality in a reciprocal manner that reinforced white middle-class sexual propriety and social respectability by casting racialized immigrant and working-class groups as "primitive," highly sexed populations.

The women and men who found themselves on the receiving end of this practice did not always take kindly to the primitivism that slumming reified. Nor were they generally pleased by the seemingly constant traffic of outsiders that surged through neighborhood streets and into local restaurants, dance halls, and shops. In the Bowery, the Tenderloin, Chinatown, and the Levee, residents regularly resisted slummers' incursions, forbidding them entrance to the districts' tenements and resorts and simply taunting them on the streets. Yet because there was significant money to be made from affluent white pleasure seekers, many immigrant and working-class saloonkeepers and restaurateurs chose to overlook the more derogatory aspects of slumming, focusing instead on its potentially positive economic effects. Even some of those residents who did not profit directly from the slumming trade also found reasons to tolerate its existence. For whether slummers set out to participate in the rough-and-tumble environs of working-class amusements or to refine them, to investigate social conditions or to regulate them, the insatiable drive of these well-to-do white pleasure seekers to cross the neighborhood boundaries that separated their daily lives from the urban poor clearly seemed preferable to the rising nativist tide that was beginning to wash over turn-of-the-century U.S. cities.

From Benevolence to Amusement: The Making of "Slummers"

Since its initial coinage in the mid-1880s, the word *slumming* has always implied some sense of venturing not only beneath one's own social standing but also beyond the parameters of one's local neighborhood. Well-to-do white women and men were said to "go slumming" whenever they left behind the safety of their own relatively segregated residential districts to journey into the older, more dilapidated working-class sections of Chicago and New York. But the appeal of slumming was never simply a matter of crossing the social and geographic boundaries that separated "respectable" white urbanites from their new immigrant and working-class neighbors; it was also a matter of balancing pleasure and danger.

For nearly thirty years, this balance was secured in large part by the wide array of social and cultural activities—ranging from benevolence and social reform to sociological inquiry and, increasingly, the mere pursuit of amusement—that operated under the general rubric of slumming. As the participants in these various activities jostled each other to observe how the other half lived and played in the cities' slums and red-light districts, they revealed much about the changing conception of white middle-class social and sexual propriety and respectability. But they also contributed to the emerging practice of using such interactions, simultaneously, as cover for social and sexual experimentation and as the foil against which particular notions of sexual respectability could be naturalized vis-à-vis the perceived improprieties of slum dwellers. The red-light excursions of these competing constituencies—whether ministers and members of evangelical Protestant organizations, urban reformers and sociologists, or still more casual and trendy thrill seekers—reinforced the overarching process of emulation and differentiation that characterized turn-of-the-century slumming, yet they also necessarily undermined it. Although each of the different groups of slummers generated its own unique set of social and sexual comparisons, taken together, they inevitably revealed the absence of any clear notion of white middle-class social and sexual norms.

The white evangelical Protestants who journeyed into the slums and red-light districts of late-nineteenth-century Chicago and New York constituted, perhaps, the most visible and self-assured slummers of their day. Dressed in dour clothes of black or gray, with religious tracts and Bibles in hand, they approached their slumming expeditions with a sense of rectitude so intense that it prompted them to evangelize even as they established themselves as moral arbiters of everyday urban life. The more stalwart of these self-appointed judges routinely castigated the cities' middle- and upper-class whites for partaking of the extravagances and immoral dalliances associated with midnight pleasure trips to the slums. But for the most part, this group of exceedingly pious white women and men directed its zealotry toward saving the souls of the urban poor. Whether converting the "heathen" Chinese, Jewish, or Catholic immigrants who had taken up residence in the cities' slums or "rescuing" the "fallen women" who plied their trade in the brothels and streets, by the early 1890s, according to one New York observer, these "little bands of missionaries . . . of whom the majority are nearly always women" were fast becoming "familiar sights to the police and night loungers of the Chinese district and elsewhere in the slums." In Chicago's Levee, evangelists from the local Midnight Mission further increased their visibility by delivering late-night sermons and distributing religious tracts on the doorsteps of the district's more infamous resorts (figure 11). Even attendees at national conventions of the Women's Christian Temperance Union and other religiously oriented reform organizations regularly joined the cause, arranging their own excursions through the Levee. When participants at the annual meeting of the National Purity Federation held "an impromptu revival service on the floor of Freiberg's notorious dance hall" in the fall of 1906, the *Chicago Tribune* proclaimed it "the most picturesque 'slumming tour' denizens of the levee have ever witnessed."[1]

Sociology and divinity students from Yale, Columbia, the University of Chicago, and other institutions of higher learning also made regular tours of the slums and red-light districts of New York and Chicago. Taught to avoid taking any moral stance on the goings-on that they observed on these excursions, students were encouraged instead to "enlarg[e] their sociological knowledge by examining various institutions" that catered to the cities' immigrant and working classes. Under the guidance of esteemed members of Yale's sociology faculty, beginning in the late 1890s, groups of twenty to seventy undergraduates undertook annual spring visits to New York's Bowery for such educational purposes. After lodging overnight at the Mills Hotel for transient men on Bleecker Street, the students toured local settlement houses, the city prisons, and the

11   The Reverend Ernest A. Bell led a series of evangelical Protestant prayer services outside
     popular Levee resorts during the early 1900s. Along with fellow missionaries from the
     Midnight Mission, located at 2136 Armour Avenue, Bell sought to provide Christian
     charity and spiritual guidance to the district's prostitutes and immigrant residents. Public
     rallies such as these eventually became part of the spectacle that slummers expected to
     encounter. (Reprinted from Clifford G. Roe, *The Great War on White Slavery; or Fighting
     for the Protection of Our Girls* [Clifford G. Roe & B.S. Steadwell, 1911]. Collection of the
     author.)

state asylum on Ward's Island. During the May 1906 excursion, the *New
York Times* reported, Professor William B. Bailey's class also "passed a
few hours studying the noodle industry in Stanton Street, the effects of
tenement life upon the Italian temperament, and the naturally demoral-
izing influence of [the] saloon environment in the Bowery." Inevitably,
the annual tours of these academic slummers culminated in a visit to the
chop suey restaurants, opium joints, and lowdown resorts of Chinatown,
where they were said to witness "'rag-time' ball[s]" and "the horrors of
underground China." But Professor Bailey instructed his charges that "it
is with no morbid curiosity that you must look at these things, but rather
with the feeling, though it may be one of aversion, that here we uplift
the mirror of distorted nature and read the truth."[2]
    As the amusement of slumming became more and more popular with
affluent white New Yorkers and Chicagoans, the activities of religious,
sociological, and reform organizations became increasingly indistinguishable from those of thrill seekers visiting these same neighborhoods.
College students' sociological expeditions, in particular, elicited skepticism and occasional mockery for being little more than pleasure trips

masquerading under the thinnest of academic veneers. The *New York Times* lampooned one Yale student's "expressed . . . desire to study the effect of diluted liquor at a certain place, that he might make an exhaustive report on the same" to his professor. Theatrical critic Alexander Woolcott likewise recalled with wry humor the prevalence with which "Nigger Mike's" Chinatown resort appeared "in the hidden notebooks of those Columbia students where it was prominently mentioned as an excellent laboratory for those extra-curriculum studies in sociology not required by [university president] Nicholas Murray Butler." But youthful undergraduates were by no means the only subjects of such indictments. Critics also accused the clergy and professional social workers of crossing the boundaries of respectability on occasion by descending to the level of casual thrill seekers as they investigated urban red-light districts and slums.[3]

Newspapermen began to question and ridicule the motives and tactics of evangelical reformers as early as 1892, when the Reverend Charles H. Parkhurst undertook his infamous undercover investigation of the illicit activities that Tammany Hall allowed to flourish in late-nineteenth-century New York. After witnessing a "French Circus" on West Fourth Street and visiting the Golden Rule Pleasure Club on West Third, where male visitors were solicited by a "youth, whose face was painted, eye-brows blackened, and whose airs were those of a young girl," Parkhurst indignantly railed against municipal corruption. But his later admission that he had "sip[ped] at a glass of beer" in Hattie Adams's Tenderloin resort while watching his hired male guide engage in a "celebrated 'leap-frog' episode" with naked women quickly elicited accusations of having stooped to the level of an inordinately notorious sinner in a misguided effort to conquer the very same sin. "The fact that any sum of money was offered and paid to bring about such an immoral and disgusting performance is not to the credit of the over-zealous friends of morality," the *Washington Post* editorialized in April 1892, "and it will not be at all strange if it is discovered that the doctor has seriously injured the cause he is seeking to serve." The author of a fictionalized guide to the resorts of Chicago's Levee district, *Side Lights on Darkest Chicago* (1899), similarly argued that such tactics were both morally questionable and usually counterproductive. "Your professional preacher slummer does nothing to relieve the misfortune" of the residents of the red-light district, P. J. Duff insisted. "Rather, the spasmodic raids of a leap frog Parkhurst into the scarlet houses of the *demi-monde* tends to excite the passions of the morbid."[4]

By the early twentieth century, such public questioning of the efficacy of slumming for achieving moral uplift or social reform became even more pronounced as a steadily expanding number of self-proclaimed reformers appeared to further blur the boundary that supposedly separated benevolence from amusement. In one particularly notorious incident, the curate of St. Matthew's Episcopal Church in New York was arrested in March 1907 by two undercover police detectives who had watched him, dressed in ordinary civilian clothes, "accompany a mulatto girl whom he met in Seventh Avenue . . . to a house near by." Convinced that the curate's visit was prompted by the same desires that led most men to participate in such interactions, especially after overhearing his protests that the young woman was trying to rob him, the detectives were adamant that the minister was nothing more than a common john. But when he appeared before a local magistrate and in the presence of his loyal wife, the clergyman successfully defended himself by insisting that he had been drawn to the Tenderloin only by "a desire to study sociology." Similar claims met with even more incredulity in Chicago. When several prominent associates of Jane Addams's Hull House were arrested in a raid on a Levee resort in 1912, their plea that they were merely "investigating vice conditions" initially held little sway with local coppers. "That's what they all say," the arresting detective replied. "Hand that 'con' to the sergeant. You'll have to wait for the wagon."[5]

While the profusion of "reformers" investigating the conditions of the cities' slums and red-light districts provided ready cover for any thrill seeker who chose to invoke them, affluent white men went slumming on a variety of pretexts. Muckraking journalists and novelists, including Stephen Crane, Theodore Dreiser, Hutchins Hapgood, George Ade, and Josiah Flynt, sometimes justified their trips through the tenements, streets, and dance halls of the Bowery, the Tenderloin, and the Levee by claiming that their excursions were motivated by nothing more than the desire to gather material for well-meaning newspaper articles or artistically crafted novels exposing the detriments of urban poverty and immorality. Actors and writers similarly defended their decisions to partake of an occasional toke from the pipe during visits to Chinatown opium dens by insisting, as New Yorker James L. Ford did, that such indulgences provided for them opportunities to master the slang of the "bunco-steerers, gamblers, prostitutes, 'con' men and thieves" for use in later stage performances and publications.[6]

From the early 1890s through the mid-1910s, however, the patronage of well-heeled white men in the red-light resorts of Chicago and New York was so widespread that they rarely bothered to offer any excuse for their presence in the districts. Religious enthusiasts and sociologists alike lamented the presence of "young men . . . from banks, offices, stores, factories, schools and colleges, . . . many of them to our positive knowledge from rich and honored homes on the boulevards and in the suburbs," in the notorious resorts of Chicago's Levee. Nor were urban and suburban residents the only men to partake of such revelry. In his 1894 exposé of moral conditions in Chicago, William T. Stead noted that the city's largest wholesale houses routinely employed guides to escort their "country customers" around "the sights of the town" when they came to make their purchases. Conventioneers were also "irresistibly drawn, if only by curiosity" to the red-light districts of New York and Chicago. "When the Shriners . . . held a convention here," Chicago reformer Ernest A. Bell remarked, "their red fezzes and Arabian symbols were seen by the hundred in the 'levee' towards midnight."[7]

Acknowledging the nearly universal embrace of slumming by well-to-do white men in both New York and Chicago, evangelical ministers and urban reformers adopted a range of scare tactics designed to discourage male pleasure seekers from visiting the cities' red-light districts and slums. First, they appealed to the men's sense of physical safety and financial security, emphasizing the dangers that were said to lurk in the regions' dark alleyways—from the female prostitutes whose seductive powers often served as a ruse for lifting watches and wallets to the urban ruffians who were believed to relish violence as much as burglary. But when guidebooks to both cities refuted such scenarios by suggesting that, as long as a man left his "silk hat, diamond studs and kid gloves" at home, he could travel almost anywhere he chose "without worrying himself a particle as to his safety," reformers changed tactics. They focused instead on the dangers that men's visits to the dives and dance halls of the cities' red-light districts posed to morality and health by bringing men "into contact with vile, depraved characters" who might infect them with venereal diseases that would "curse innocent wives and unborn babies." Nevertheless, their appeals generally fell on deaf ears, and slummers continued to participate, with little or no reservation, in the urban revelry available in New York's Bowery and Tenderloin, Chicago's Levee, and the Chinatowns of both cities.[8]

Men's relatively unfettered participation in the earliest slumming craze, however, was premised in large part on the persistence of a double standard. While well-to-do white men could venture into the cities' slums and red-light districts with impunity, any woman who attempted to do the same was considered to be disreputable or immoral. Slumming thus reinforced the distinction between the pleasurable pursuits that men of social standing could undertake with "respectable" women of their own class and those that they might undertake on their own or in the company of male friends. In a memoir of his experiences in Chicago in the 1890s, author Theodore Dreiser demonstrated how this custom played out in practical terms. While on sojourn in the Windy City, one of Dreiser's friends spent his days playing the gentleman, "visiting certain friends . . . and calling on certain girls who could be taken with only the most serious and conservative formality." But when darkness fell, Dreiser recalled, the same friend "explained his deepest desire was to reconnoiter the great red light district," where he might exchange the formality and propriety of courting for more casual social and sexual interactions. The double standard thus preserved the reputations of respectable young women while granting supposedly reputable young men freer access to such spaces, since none of their wifely prospects were likely ever to observe their red-light antics.[9]

Despite—or, perhaps, because of—this persistent double standard, by the early 1890s an increasing number of middle- and upper-class white women began to express their desire to undertake nighttime excursions into the slums and red-light districts of New York and Chicago. In fact, respectable white women's interest in slumming became so pervasive that a reader of *The Ladies' Home Journal* wrote in to the magazine's "What You Want to Know" column in December 1891 asking the editors to clarify exactly what the practice entailed. "Slumming usually means the going through the parts of a large city where the wretched, sinful and the destitute live," columnist Ruth Ashmore replied on the magazine's behalf. "Sometimes it is done with the intention of helping them; sometimes, under the care of the police, it is simply a visit of curiosity." In either case, Ashmore assured her readers, such undertakings were "certainly not to be commended." Commendable or not, women began to seek such "visits of curiosity" with increasing frequency. Whether to satisfy their desires to learn more about the districts' "wretched" and "destitute" immigrant and working-class residents or simply to partake of the "sinful" pleasures that some came to associate with the districts' commercial leisure, affluent white women set out to identify a number of safe, reliable ways that they could partake of this new urban pastime.[10]

Because the double standard still threatened to label as disreputable any woman who dared to venture into the slums and red-light districts on her own, women generally sought to undertake such journeys only in the company of men of upstanding character. For some, this entailed hiring a local policeman or private detective to escort a small group of friends or social acquaintances through the tenements and low dives of the Bowery or the Levee. But for many others, it meant engaging one of the commercial tour companies that arose to satisfy what one New York newspaper called "the silly affectations of society people toward an interest in their lowly neighbors." As early as 1891, a group of enterprising New Yorkers had established a corporation designed to capitalize on the growing belief that "slumming is the most absorbing of diversions," by guaranteeing "full protection" to any woman or man who cared to procure their services for a tour through "the slums and poorer quarters of New York." The company not only provided sightseers with a souvenir map of the city "on which the slums are indicated by dark shading," but also promised them safe nighttime glimpses of "the poor man in his home, the laborer in his hovel, the opium joint, fan tan games and Italian dens where at times thirty people live together in a room twenty feet square." In both New York and Chicago, an array of similar organizations soon followed suit, popularizing a range of walking tours and horse-drawn excursions through the cities' working-class districts. These were followed in turn, during the first decade of the twentieth century, by a range of touring cars that harnessed the increasing automation of mass transportation to carry still larger groups of sightseers through the same regions. Even as such organized tours continue to grow in popularity with out-of-town visitors well into the twentieth century, local women and men sought out ever more intimate ways to experience the pleasures and dangers of the cities' slums.[11]

By the turn of the century, as slumming excursions became an acceptable part of the social lives of affluent white women and men, most New Yorkers and Chicagoans discarded the guided slumming tour in favor of more independent adventures. For some, these individually organized excursions continued to be primarily group affairs, in which a number of women and men set off together to explore unfamiliar urban quarters. Such was the case when H. S. Pingree Jr., the son of Michigan's governor, and a number of his Yale classmates accompanied a group of fifteen visiting nurses from Pingree's home state on a "jolly spree" through New York's Lower East Side. "Down through Pell, Doyers, Mott, and Mulberry streets," the *Chicago Tribune* reported in 1898, "the fifteen gaily danced, astonishing the natives and causing the policemen to gape." For white "Bohemian folk bent on an evening of enjoyment and song," not even the more refined black-and-tan resorts of New York's black Tenderloin were considered off-limits. By 1908, advertising executive George B. Van Cleve freely remarked that he took his wife and "a number of very prominent men and their wives" to the Marshall Hotel at 127 West 53rd Street both "to listen to the colored singers and banjo players" and to partake of a bit of intimacy and raucousness unavailable within the context of more traditional high-society functions.[12]

For others, slumming became a more intimate pastime. During the first decade of the twentieth century, as well-to-do white women and men looked for unchaperoned public spaces where they could begin to "date"—a term that was only beginning to come into wide usage—outside the prying and protective eyes of parents and neighbors, slumming excursions seemed to provide an ideal prospect. A 1905 guide to New York's edgier amusements suggested that "a party of four is about right" for visiting Chinatown, because such a group "can get lost in a crowd without attracting the attention which follows the usual sightseer." In Chicago's Levee district (figure 12), slummers embraced the same impulse to disappear amid the bustling crowd in more intimate pairings. Every Saturday night, observers noted, "well dressed and apparently respectable" white couples ventured "from one resort to another intent upon seeing the sights."[13]

Recognizing the growing tendency of white middle- and upper-class women to accompany their boyfriends, husbands, and brothers into the red-light districts and slums of New York and Chicago, reformers expressed their objections with extraordinary vehemence. As early as 1891, the authors of *Chicago's Dark Places*, an exposé underwritten by the Women's Christian Temperance Union, decried the existence of concert halls that attracted both women and men with their seemingly innocent music and entertainment. "Before long," the report ominously asserted, "the vile influences that dwell in such holes take hold upon [the resorts' patrons] and drag them into the fearful vortex of dissipation and sensuality. The music is the bait which allures the victim to drink and lustful pleasures." An array of anti-vice authorities expressed similar concerns, citing the unsavory mix of music, dance, and liquor consumption in the public resorts of the Levee and the Tenderloin as particular threats to the purity and sanctity of white middle-class womanhood. In the public dance halls of Chicago, some insisted, "many young girls go whirling down the road to ruin in twostep time," finding themselves in a place "where drink and degeneracy are inseparable evils" or where otherwise respectable young women were unwittingly "lured to prostitute life."[14]

Acknowledging the relative ineffectiveness of such scare tactics, a number of social critics began to adopt more subtle strategies to dissuade white women from participating in pleasure-oriented slumming excursions. "It is hard to understand how any pure minded man would take a pure minded woman into places of disreputable character," the

12   Originally used as an illustration in former Chicago police detective Clifton R. Wooldridge's
      1901 exposé of the city's preeminent red-light district, this drawing by W. Layman titled
      Night Scenes on the Levee depicted the full range of illicit activities slummers might
      encounter: gambling, dime hotel rooms, prostitutes, all-night saloons, and public smoking
      and drinking, especially by women. (Reprinted from Clifton R. Wooldridge, *Hands Up! In
      the World of Crime* [Chicago: Police Publishing Company, 1901]. Collection of the author.)

editors of the *Chicago Tribune* opined in the spring of 1907. To do so not only called into question the respectability of white middle-class womanhood but also contributed to the blurring of the spatial boundaries that ordinarily separated the city's illicit immigrant and working-class spaces from its more affluent white residential districts. Sounding a nativist tone, the *Tribune* further suggested that by encouraging interactions between "old-stock" white Americans and the unassimilated masses of immigrants who inhabited these districts, such slumming excursions threatened to undermine American democracy. "The sharper the distinction between the home and the 'red light district,'" the newspaper's editors insisted, "the better for the interests of good citizenship."[15]

Ironically, reformers' concerted efforts to protect respectable white women from the perceived dangers of the slum and the red-light district became a circular and somewhat self-defeating enterprise. During the earliest years of the twentieth century, as affluent white women grew ever more determined to explore the most notorious resorts of New York and Chicago, their increasing presence in these spaces spurred a particularly zealous campaign to eradicate the cities' sex districts. But even as reformers labored to eliminate the threat that they believed such districts posed to unsuspecting women slummers, the growing presence of male and female reformers and police officers patrolling these spaces fostered a sense of safety for visitors. Knowing that the public dance halls and saloons of Chicago's Levee and New York's Bowery and Tenderloin were under such protective supervision likely emboldened affluent white pleasure seekers, especially women, to explore the very resorts that reformers found so objectionable.

Slumming expeditions provided respectable white women and men with their first taste of urban nightlife while simultaneously allowing these curious thrill seekers to contrast themselves with the depravity and dilapidation that they associated with immigrant and working-class neighborhoods. By 1909, the author of a guidebook to "the new New York" remarked that the Bowery was the place where slummers went "to laugh at the absurd and the queer, or to get sociological statistics in exaggerated form" before returning "back to [their] up-town home[s] better satisfied, perhaps, with [their] own quarters." But slumming comprised more than the mere opportunity for native-born middle- and upper-class whites to reconfirm their sense of social superiority. The pastime also encouraged slummers to emulate the sense of social and sexual freedom they attributed to the districts' immigrant and working-class inhabitants by publicly romancing, dancing, and drinking with each other, even as they shored up their position at the head of the cities' racial, sexual, and class hierarchies. This seemingly contradictory process reflected a limited but definite movement away from nineteenth-century Anglo-American ideals of social and sexual restraint toward a more modern and relaxed conception of social interaction, public intimacy, and rugged masculinity. But the new positioning of the white urban middle class was not merely a result of its seeming embrace of the sexual and gender norms of the immigrant and working classes. It was also the product of the formation and maintenance of a complex racial ideology that naturalized the cultural fiction of whiteness by defining and redefining its contours in relation to the shifting range of nonwhite residents and newcomers who lived in turn-of-the-century U.S. cities.[16]

Marking and Understanding Race in Working-Class New York and Chicago

To present-day Americans, the definition of "whiteness" as a racial category may seem obvious—even if they have come to think of race as a social construction rather than a biological fact. But at the turn of the century, the formulation of whiteness—especially the sort of unequivocal whiteness claimed by so-called old-stock Americans—was a matter of some contention. Never simply a matter of skin color or of the legal rights that came with being designated "white" by judges or immigration officials, for most turn-of-the-century urban Americans, whiteness was a complex cultural construction developed in relation to the wide range of peoples who inhabited U.S. cities. Rather than merely reflecting phenotype and physical appearance, whiteness represented an amalgamation of an individual's relative social status, class standing, national origin, citizenship, and length of residence in the United States.

By these criteria, although many of the more affluent white women and men who went slumming were undeniably and unmistakably white, many of those who accompanied or followed them were not. This was true especially of pleasure seekers who had only recently risen into the middle class from more humble immigrant or working-class beginnings. But it also pertained to some of the prosperous nouveau riche whose presence in the United States was, in whole or part, a byproduct of the massive waves of Irish and German immigration that began in the mid-nineteenth century. Only decades before, for example, the Irish were viewed as racialized others who occupied a position in the American racial hierarchy somewhere between whiteness and blackness. The popular press depicted them with simian features and routinely referred to the "dirty Irish" who lived in squalor and close proximity to blacks and whose Catholicism purportedly posed a dangerous threat to American democracy. Germans, too, were often distinguished from old-stock whites, despite their shared Protestantism and tendency to "become good and industrious citizens." As late as 1883, New York residents commented on the "'east side' look" of Germans and German Americans, "both in garb and features," and described their fondness for beer in almost genetic terms. "The lager . . . flow[s] from inexhaustible founts into the insatiable and indefinitely expansible interiors of Teuton and Hibernian," one visitor to the Bowery remarked, invoking a language of race that linked the Germans and Irish while simultaneously setting them apart from Anglo-Americans.[17]

As Irish and German Americans ventured into the slums of turn-of-the-century New York and Chicago alongside undeniably white old-stock Americans, the irony of the situation was not lost on the most trenchant observers of the period. They suggested that the participation of such women and men in the popular new practice of slumming had the potential to unveil the latter's more base social origins, thus revealing the ultimate instability of the middle-class whiteness into which so many native-born Americans of Irish and German ancestry had only recently been assimilated. "Slumming bids fair to become popular," the *Brooklyn Daily Eagle* noted in 1884, "but it is open to more or less danger in New York. So many of our high class society people lived in the slums a few years ago, that awkward recognitions might occur." An 1891 description of a slumming tour through Mulberry, Hester, and Delancey streets adopted a similar tone, perhaps betraying the resentments of newspapermen whose economic standing had been eclipsed by these relative newcomers. Mocking the "tremendous ado about the novelty" of venturing through the tenements of the Lower East Side, the newspaper insisted that many of the young slummers could have asked their parents instead to give them "points about the life of the people from personal experience."[18]

The danger of exposure no doubt lessened over time, as the nouveau riche became less "new" and the descendants of mid-nineteenth-century German and Irish immigrants were more fully assimilated into the native-born white middle class. But as late as 1915, travelogues still called attention to the recent vintage of some slummers' claims on Americanness, whiteness, and economic privilege. In his "intimate" guide to New York, James Huneker even suggested that slumming was a particular preoccupation of those women and men whose families had only recently risen above their immigrant or working-class roots. Hoping to distinguish themselves from these forebears, Huneker observed, "fashionable slummers whose fathers wore leathern aprons and drank their beer from tin pails" comprised a substantial proportion of those who visited the "gaudy" resorts of the Lower East Side to "sip champagne."[19]

Although champagne sipping did not exactly conform to white middle-class Protestant standards of restraint and respectability, it did allow upwardly mobile thrill seekers to establish a sense of sophistication that set them apart from the racialized residents of the slums and red-light districts. Many of these young slummers had separated themselves geographically from the cities' tenement districts when either they or their parents took advantage of Gilded Age economic prosperity to work their way out of the slums and into the newly constructed white middle-class neighborhoods of the cities' professional and managerial classes. But slumming provided them with yet another means of solidifying their fragile hold on whiteness and "civilization" by positioning them in stark contrast to the "primitive" blacks and Chinese and southern and eastern European immigrants who constituted the bulk of the residents inhabiting popular slumming destinations.[20]

As noted in the first chapter, one key element in this process of racial differentiation and stabilization was the designation of slumming destinations in terms of their foreign or racialized character. Popular guidebooks of the era, such as Ernest Ingersoll's *A Week in New York* (1891), suggested that slummers might undertake "A Nocturnal Ramble" that included Baxter Street's Jewish commercial district, Mulberry Bend's "Little Italy," "Chinatown," the Bowery, the "Russian Quarter," and the city's bustling and crowded "Judea," where he estimated that "nine tenths are Germans or Germanized Jews and Bohemians." *Rand, McNally & Co.'s Handy Guide to Chicago and the World's Columbian Exposition* (1893), produced by Ingersoll's publisher, laid out an equally colorful tour that suggested that the city's South Side Levee was divided into distinct racialized segments. If slummers walked south from the Loop along Clark Street, the guidebook promised, they would glimpse, in fairly quick succession, "the haunt of color and habitat of Chinamen," "gin-mills" catering to "huge 'buck niggers'" and the "ebony Venus," various other "disreputable" Levee resorts, and an Italian settlement nestled along the Twelfth Street viaduct. A separate excursion to Chicago's West Side was required if visitors hoped to see the city's Polish and Hungarian neighborhoods, its "Judea," or the local beer halls that were said to be frequented by "long-haired" socialists and anarchists "of alien birth."[21]

Including "Little Africa" among the "foreign colonies" that tourists should plan to visit, other guides to New York and Chicago were even clearer about the extent to which they considered these districts to be racially coded sections of the city. The 1898 guidebook prepared by New York's Siegel-Cooper department store, ostensibly for local residents as well as tourists, encouraged visitors "to see the curious sections of the city almost exclusively peopled with those of alien birth or tongue." The store's list of "foreign colonies" included "Little Germany," "Little Italy," "China," "Judea," and "Africa," the last of which, it noted, was located at "Thompson st. north of Canal st. . . . where the colored brother shines in full glory." Such equations of blackness with foreignness and of immigrant status with racial difference recurred among travel writers and reformers alike, as they made frequent references that linked the entire immigrant regions of Chicago and New York to Africa. Acknowledging the extraordinary diversity of immigrant and working-class residents in New York's Bowery district, for instance, journalist Allan Forman insisted that "the lower east side of the city is as much of a *terra incognita* to the banker or merchant as the interior of Africa." Reform-minded authors in Chicago echoed this sentiment, one of them comparing his investigations of the city's diversely populated Levee district with the enterprise undertaken by Henry Stanley when he "visited the heart of the Dark Continent and wrote 'In Darkest Africa.'"[22]

The naming of these districts, however, was not simply a reflection of their designation as the residence of already racialized inhabitants. Rather, their creation as identifiable places associated with particular racial groups was part of the process of racialization. While slummers and reformers spoke of visiting Chinatown, Little Africa, the Jewish Ghetto, and Little Italy, the inhabitants of these sections of New York and Chicago experienced no such cohesive, racially organized communities. In reality, the immigrant and working-class groups living in the vicinity of New York's Bowery and Chicago's South and West Side Levee districts spilled into and over each other. Sometimes members of one group occupied a building on a block or street otherwise dominated by another group. Sometimes multiple groups lived in close proximity, creating a virtual Tower of Babel within a particular tenement. When Jane Addams and her associates at Chicago's Hull House set out in 1895 to map the "nationalities" of their thirty-five block West Side neighborhood, they failed to locate even one cohesive block in the district, much less an exclusive "colony" of immigrants from a single country. Yet they, like their less reform-minded contemporaries, continued to refer to distinct Jewish and Italian districts when describing their findings.[23]

In the face of such incredible diversity, the insistence on referring to various sections of the city as specifically and solely Jewish, Italian, Chinese, or African reflected a desire to contain these racialized groups and their "alien" ways to particular geographic locations—both on the physical map of the city and, more importantly, in the imaginations of urban residents and visitors. When sightseers chose to visit these districts, they became complicit in this process of racialization and containment. Slumming in the Ghetto, Little Italy, Chinatown, or Little Africa reified the racial differences that were commonly associated with the districts' residents and reinforced the notion that racialized others could be safely cordoned off in discrete urban spaces where they could be visited—or avoided—at will. Moreover, it allowed well-to-do whites to ground their understanding of racial ideologies and stereotypes in the concrete examples of apparent "racial types" that they encountered in these districts.[24]

Although turn-of-the-century slummers believed that race could be readily identified by sight—principally by reference to skin color, but also as demarcated by particular facial features or other bodily characteristics—they also relied upon other stereotypes that cast blacks and Chinese, Jewish, and Italian immigrants as racial inferiors. As cultural historian Gail Bederman and others have noted, at the turn of the last century, this othering process centered primarily around the establishment of old-stock Americans and northwestern Europeans—especially the English but also increasingly the Germans and Irish—as a "civilized" race rightfully located at the top of a hierarchy peopled by more and more "primitive" races, ranging from southern and eastern Europeans to Asians and finally to Africans and African Americans.[25]

To white elites, including new members of the middle class, being civilized required a sense of maturity, cultural sophistication, and social and sexual restraint. Because each of these qualities was relative, however, they could assume definite shape and acquire clear meaning only by being defined against the presumed primitivism of racialized populations—a primitivism that slummers and other affluent whites usually perceived in terms of childishness (represented by what "civilized" observers identified as an almost natural state of happiness and apparent satisfaction with impoverished conditions), sensuality (expressed through supposed bawdiness as well as fecundity), and a closer relation to nature (indicated by so-called animalistic behavior and other bestial qualities). Because slumming placed the "civilized" and the "primitive" in direct contact with each other and allowed the former to observe how and where the latter lived and played, it provided affluent white Americans with a unique opportunity to instantiate this racial ideology, giving it a seemingly flesh-and-blood reality as well as a specific place in the urban landscape. This process was never clearer than when slummers visited the black districts, or Little Africas, of Chicago's Levee or New York's Tenderloin and Lower East Side.[26]

Setting out in the late summer of 1886 "to 'do' the negro quarter" located "in the classic shades of [New York's] Thompson street, and extending round about into Bleecker, Mercer, South Fifth avenue and Greene," journalist Allan Forman called attention to the ongoing process of racialization in American cities by explicitly contrasting the black district located near South Fifth Avenue with "its more northerly and fashionable namesake." "One is respectable and dull," Forman wrote of the uptown bastion of white wealth and respectability, while "the other is always unique and sometimes amusing." Part of the amusement that Forman and other slummers located in the black districts of New York and Chicago arose simply from the presumed differences associated with the skin color and physical characteristics of a people only a few short decades removed from slavery. While insisting, on occasion, that the "Northern negro . . . [was] distinct from the Southern" and deserved to be treated differently, many northern white urbanites continued to refer to their darker neighbors by derogatory terms, such as "darkey" or "dusky," that referenced their skin tones or called attention to their "kinky" hair, broad noses, or full lips in ways that reinforced nineteenth-century "scientific" notions of an Ethiopian race set apart from and beneath that of Caucasians. In a slightly more innocuous form, such physical distinctions were also referenced by the lyrics to a popular 1890s "coon song" that at least one slummer overheard while visiting one of the white-owned resorts of Chicago's Levee. "God made the black man, / He made him at night," the song insisted. "He made him in a hurry, / And He did'nt [sic] make him right."[27]

But as slummers explored both the recesses and commercial centers of black life in New York and Chicago, they increasingly recognized that skin color and physical characteristics were not sufficient markers of racial difference and inferiority. Journalist Allan Forman reported that color gradations among New York's black population were so pronounced that they generated a "strong caste feeling" within the black community. Reversing traditional accounts of lighter-skinned blacks' supposed disdain for darker members of their group, Forman reported that "the genuine full-blooded negro looks with scorn upon his lighter brother. 'Saddle-colored smoke,' 'salmon-colored nigger,' 'bleeched [*sic*] darkey' are some of the epithets I have heard applied to the lighter-colored denizens of Little Africa by this coal-black aristocracy." In the face of such unreliable markers of racial difference, slumming promised to produce a more cohesive conception of blackness grounded in a physical urban space. Thus, Forman suggested that despite their differences, blacks were all the same, "liv[ing] like animals rather than as human beings . . . in the tall tenements squalid, unventilated and breeding disease."[28]

Relying on presumed notions of primitive black sexuality, bawdiness, and obscenity, slummers also grounded their conception of blackness in the performances that they observed in the resorts of New York's Tenderloin and Chicago's Levee. White undercover investigators for private anti-vice organizations routinely commented on the apparently carefree interactions that took place in local black resorts, as well as on their supposed sexual content, whether expressed directly by raised skirts and exposed body parts or indirectly through suggestive ragtime lyrics. After visiting the black Tenderloin resort known as Bernie's Place, located on the northeast corner of 47th Street and Seventh Avenue, one white investigator for New York's Committee of Fourteen reported that "a nigger wench was dancing & singing Oh my lemmon, my little lemmon I will squeeze you &c."—lyrics that the investigator identified as so sexual and so unsettling to his notions of propriety that he "did not feel strong enough to go in" but instead "stood at the basement door" to watch and document the proceedings. Other white observers suggested that the sensuality of blacks was so primal and uncontained that "little or no home life" could be found in the black districts of New York and Chicago, where, as Allan Forman put it, "The family relation is but lightly held, and marriage is the exception rather than the rule."[29]

Even when urban blacks did comport themselves in ways that middle- and upper-class whites might have recognized as properly restrained and respectable—as Forman acknowledged many of them did, although "the outsider does not see them" because "they stay at home with their families"—the racial ideology of black inferiority and primitivism was so pronounced among white Americans that it rendered such displays of comportment and "civilization" as mere performances or flawed imitations of whiteness. A fictionalized guidebook titled *The Real New York* (1904) suggested as much when it mocked the city's wealthiest blacks by referring to the section of the Tenderloin where they lived as the "Darkey Fifth Avenue" and pointed out that "the dances given by the colored aristocrats," like the more rowdy black resorts of the neighboring district, "often attract white audiences, who find great amusement in the profound dignity of the couples" whom they believed were literally "aping" white convention.[30]

In a similar fashion, slumming excursions to the Chinatowns of New York and Chicago provided affluent whites with a way to root their conception of the "Chinese race" in a particular urban place. In contrast to the hypersexualized stereotype of blacks, the Chinese were perceived as secretive, inscrutable, and potentially dangerous. Visitors to these districts repeatedly referenced the facial characteristics of the "almond-eyed people" or "slant-eyed yellow men" who stared at them as they made their way past the colorfully decorated buildings, draped in paper lanterns and "effigies of all manner of repulsive beasts and reptiles."[31] One French visitor to New York's Chinatown carried his description of the "racial characteristics" of the "yellow men" to almost ridiculous extremes, describing them as a beautiful but potentially menacing threat to American cities:

Short and fragile, with smooth faces under their round hats, with black braids of hair rolled up underneath in an oily chignon, they come and go silently. . . . This sort of delicate-featured dwarfs, with their loop-shaped eyes, so black in their cooper-colored skin, their high cheek-bones, the triangular framework of their faces, and their flat noses, gives the impression of an invasion of beasts that would spread over all the city, gain and gain and destroy everything.[32]

A host of other observers commented on their silent movement, "cat-like tread," and "secretiveness," suggesting that the Chinese residents of New York and Chicago were simply biding their time in darkened basements and tenements before pouncing on their unsuspecting prey. "You happen upon them in dark hallways," one slummer recalled without bothering to excuse his uninvited entrance into their domestic spaces, "or find them looking at you from strange crannies of ramshackle structures like night-blooming felines."[33]

In contrast to the ease with which white slummers defined the racial differences of blacks and Chinese immigrants, the racial status of the vast numbers of southern and eastern European immigrants that they encountered in the cities' slums and red-light districts proved more challenging to define. Italians and eastern European Jews were considered white by state and federal government agencies. Miscegenation laws did not forbid their intermarriage to native-born whites, and immigration authorities classified them as white and therefore eligible for naturalization. Nevertheless, many native-born whites insisted on the racial difference of these immigrant groups. Indeed, although late-nineteenth-century racial ideologies centered less on *color* than on biological notions of *race* linked to particular national or regional groups, slummers who visited the Jewish Ghetto and Little Italy often perceived both color and culture as markers of racial difference.[34]

Writing about his slumming tour of Chicago's South Side Levee in the winter of 1892, the Reverend Dr. Frank M. Bristol reported entering a dark cellar where he discovered "seven to ten black, grinning, unkempt, head-scratching, jabbering Italians huddled about a little, broken, smoking stove, or squatted on the floor, eating their nasty food out of their nasty hands." When he ventured farther into the Italian Quarter to a tenement housing at least three hundred recent immigrants, he further racialized the district's residents by comparing them to vermin, "apparently little higher in their tastes and ambitions than so many fleas, or cockroaches, or rats." The dilapidated conditions of the Italian tenements on New York's Mulberry Bend led observers to similar conclusions, describing the "six storied 'dumb bells,'" as being "alive with vermin, both human and insect," while allusions to the primitive sexuality of "black eyed, buxom, full breasted women, who sit on doorsteps and curbstones unconcernedly nursing their babes," seemed to further the association of Italians with African Americans who were often characterized in similar ways.[35]

Others in New York and Chicago positioned Italians somewhere between blacks and whites in the urban racial hierarchy. References to "swarthy, low browed Italians" in many popular periodicals attempted to ground the supposed racial characteristics of these immigrants in somatic differences. Focusing on the black hair and olive skin common to many southern Italians, such allusions to their "swarthiness" were intended to cast them, at the very least, as "off-white," although some commentators went even further to insinuate that the darker skin and hair of Sicilians, especially, could be traced to African ancestry. Still others called attention to the in-between racial status of Italians in more subtle ways. For instance, when an investigator from New York's Committee of Fourteen visited Goldberg's saloon at 13 Bayard Street on the Lower East Side, he reported finding "a double back room, both parts of which was occupied by a number of whites, Italians and negros [sic] among whom were several women." Whether referring to color gradations or to more complex cultural and linguistic differences, this investigator clearly excluded Italians from his conception of both "whites" and "Negroes."[36]

The eastern European Jews whom slummers encountered in the Ghettoes of Chicago and New York occupied a similarly complex racial position. Like the cities' Italian residents, Jewish slum-dwellers and storekeepers were often described as being "swarthy." Outside a secondhand shop on New York's Baxter Street, for instance, one passerby reported being accosted by a particularly persistent "puller-in," a "Jewish woman, swarthy, strong, and eager," while another male visitor to the Ghetto noted the presence of more sexually enticing "bright-eyed and red-lipped Jewish maidens," under the watchful protection of "their swarthy, stalwart brothers and fathers." Indeed, male slummers' accounts of their journeys through the Lower East Side often took on an Orientalist dimension suggestive of the presumed sexual availability—or at least the fecundity—of the district's women. "These are mostly Germans and Poles," French author Paul Bourget noted of the Jews that he encountered on his ramble through the Bowery's environs in the mid-1890s, but they were "just like . . . what I have seen in the lanes of Tangier and Beyrout and Damascus . . . . There are swarms of children, attesting that fruitfulness which the Book promised 'as the sand of the seashore.'" He later added, "Many of these little ones have eyes of magnetic Oriental brilliancy, and we see it also in the eyes of the women who are living in all this poverty."[37]

The racial in-betweenness of Jews and Italians became especially apparent in the context of the notorious black-and-tan resorts located in the slums and red-light districts of New York and Chicago. Perhaps the most socially and racially integrated public amusements in turn-of-the-century America, the black and tan was so named—in opposition to "Negro dives" and "colored resorts"—to designate it as a space for the mixing of the races (figure 13). A wide variety of immigrant and working-class men and women who visited these establishments were racialized as nonwhite simply because of their close and regular association with the resorts' black patrons, even as middle- and upper-class whites saw the black and tan as a "slummers' paradise" in which they could observe all the racialized groups of the slums and red-light districts at the same time. Many of the earliest published descriptions of New York black and tans emphasized the complex racial dynamics of these spaces and their appeal to curious white interlopers. The voluminous 1895 exposé *Darkness and Daylight*, for example, described "The Black and Tan" as a "curious" resort where "most of the customers were negroes, but there were Malays, Chinese, Lascars, and other Asiatics as well." The racial

13   This lantern slide, "A Thompson Street 'Black and Tan Dive,'" photographed during the late
1880s by Richard Hoe Lawrence, provides a glimpse of the resort's racially mixed patronage.
The image is a companion to the Lawrence photograph "A Black-and-Tan Dive in 'Africa,'"
which Jacob A. Riis used in his 1890 exposé *How the Other Half Lives*. (Reprinted with permission from the Collection of The New-York Historical Society, negative 32335.)

diversity of such resorts, however, was hardly restricted to patrons of African and Asian descent. The book's authors reported that visitors to the
dive saw "two American Indians . . . imbibing firewater of a dangerous
character," along with a number of "white m[e]n who had no prejudice
as to color" and "women of all shades from ebony black to the lightest
of tan colors." The resort's Baxter Street location, right in the heart of
the Jewish and Italian immigrant commercial district, suggested an even
more complex racial scenario.[38]

Indeed, in both New York and Chicago, Jews and especially Italians
were not only disproportionately responsible for the operation of the
cities' earliest black and tans, but also comprised a significant portion of
their patronage. New York's Committee of Fourteen documented a "Negro joint run by Italiens [*sic*]" on Macdougal Street, a dive at 29th Street
and Seventh Avenue where two Italians interacted with "white men
with nigger women & white women with nigger men," an Italian-run
"black and tan saloon" at 317 West 41st Street, and a Jewish-operated

Bayard Street resort frequented by whites, Italians, and blacks. Similarly, in Chicago, using a derogatory term for Italians, "reputable property owners" blamed the downslide of South State Street on the "Dago dives" of the Levee, which they insisted were "frequented by disreputable persons of both sexes and *all* colors"—a remark suggesting that Italians constituted a color all their own.[39]

The presence of Italians and Jews in the cities' notorious black and tans raised the concern of urban reformers and municipal authorities who viewed such resorts as spaces that not only *permitted* the mixing of the races but actively *promoted* it. A 1914 letter from the general secretary of New York's Committee of Fourteen, Frederick H. Whitin, to the Progressive reform photographer Lewis Hine demonstrated this particular understanding of the resorts' purpose. Suggesting that Hine might wish to photograph Barron Wilkins's shuttered resort at 255 West 35th Street, Whitin noted that it "was what we call a 'black and tan,' catering not only to whites as well as blacks, but *stimulating* a mixing of the races." This reference to stimulation conveyed a sense of sexual as well as social mixing, while "black and tan" suggested the possibility that this sexual mixing might lead to the production of "tan" offspring. Because Italians and Jews continued to be actively involved in the operation of such resorts well into the 1910s and beyond, their association with such spaces increasingly cast them as sexual threats to the sanctity of white womanhood and the "contamination" of the white race.[40]

As the practice of slumming gave rise to a growing number of racially mixed spaces in the red-light districts of Chicago and New York, the invocation of racialized sexual threats—both to the purity and sanctity of white womanhood and to the virility, physical safety, and financial security of white men—became yet another tool that slummers used to reinforce their racial superiority over the immigrant and working-class residents of these urban districts. In the case of male slummers, the threat usually centered around their interactions with the female prostitutes that they encountered on their rambles through the cities' red-light districts. Although reformers warned that casual interactions with any prostitutes could prove costly—both to one's financial well-being and to one's physical health—the white men who visited immigrant and working-class resorts were more likely to conceive of these potential dangers in racialized terms. In Chicago's West Side Levee, for instance, men "intent upon 'seeing the sights'" in the autumn of 1907 identified an "immediate menace to life and health" in the brothels that housed "heavy-faced, coarse women" who "look[ed] like they had negro blood in their veins" or were "a mixture of Italian, Bohemian, French, Spanish and other foreign races."[41]

Black women constituted by far the most frequently cited menace to white male slummers. In his 1892 guidebook, *Chicago by Day and Night*, Harold R. Vynne counseled readers to be wary of any black woman they encountered on their slumming excursions in the city. He noted that "several dusky female characters of whom the police have wholesome dread" were known to operate out of brothels in the city's South Side red-light district. "They are Amazonian in physique," he warned, "and being thoroughly abandoned, are ready for any hideous devilment which may or may not turn up." An exposé of Chicago moral conditions, published by former police detective Clifton R. Wooldridge in 1901, echoed this warning, profiling a number of black prostitutes and madams who were said to pose a particular threat to the health and financial welfare of white men. Among these were the "African giantess" Emma Ford, a "Levee terror" whom Wooldridge estimated had stolen as much as $100,000 during her career; Hattie Briggs, a six-foot tall, 220-pound madam, "as black as a stick of licorice," whose dives at 388 Clark Street and 120 Custom House Place were said to be the sites of "five to ten cases of robbery or larceny" per day; and Ella Sherwood, "one of the most vicious colored women that ever roamed the street," who had a reputation for "fight[ing] like an infuriated tigress" when "her temper was aroused." Historian Cynthia Blair has argued that such Amazonian representations of black prostitutes and madams reinforced urban whites' conception of black female sexuality as dangerously uncontrollable. Moreover, by exposing white men's sexual encounters with black women, they seemed to erode the boundary that male slummers erected between such activities and more "civilized" leisure pursuits.[42]

Yet the dangers that pleasure-seeking white men associated with black women were not merely representational, nor were they necessarily viewed as disruptions of otherwise "civilized" sexual pursuits. While investigating New York moral conditions and police corruption in 1899, the state-funded Mazet Committee uncovered evidence of black women robbing and assaulting white men, similar to what was documented in Chicago. Consulting the citizens' complaint book for New York's Twentieth Precinct for the period between August 7, 1898, and June 18, 1899, the committee compiled a list of no fewer than twenty-five complaints by white men who claimed that a "colored woman" had robbed them as they walked through the streets of the black Tenderloin or visited a local black and tan. This list was remarkable both because so many crimes were reported within the span of less than a year, especially since they probably accounted for only a fraction of actual crimes committed, and also because the number and diverse background of the complainants suggested that many male slummers considered their interactions with black prostitutes to fall well within the bounds of "civilized" sexual pursuits. The complainants included out-of-town tourists and residents of New York's outer boroughs and other nearby towns, as well as an array of Manhattanites of apparent old-stock, Irish, and German descent. Even more surprisingly, while several of these men claimed to have been unwillingly accosted and mugged on the district's streets, an astonishing number admitted that the robberies had occurred when they "picked up a colored woman for an immoral purpose" or "went to bed with one." The apparent ease with which they reported this fact suggested that, despite the sexual dangers popularly associated with black women, many northern white men considered cross-racial sex to be an acceptable part of their excursions to urban red-light districts.[43]

For white female slummers, however, the sexual dangers associated with racialized immigrant and working-class populations were significantly more pernicious. In turn-of-the-century America, the emerging rhetoric of white slavery cast the male residents of the cities' slums as potential kidnappers and spoilers of white female virtue, lurking in the districts' dance halls and saloons for the chance to ensnare an unwary white woman in a life of permanent prostitution. Although the sexual dangers to white male slummers were usually portrayed in terms of blackness, it is surprising how rarely black men were implicated in the sexual endangerment of white women in northern U.S. cities. Turn-of-the-century exposés of urban moral conditions, produced by both muckrakers and more sincere social reformers, featured only sporadic references to once-reputable white women who fell under the control of black men and found themselves "consorting with the vilest kind of negroes." For the most part, the purported sexual perils that white female slummers faced when they journeyed into the red-light districts of Chicago and New York were associated with recent male immigrants, especially those from southern and eastern Europe.[44]

Not even the threat of the notorious Chinese "white slavers," so prevalent and virulent in San Francisco and other parts of the West, carried much weight in northern U.S. urban centers. Aside from a couple of highly publicized but exceptional murder cases—the 1909 slaying of Elsie Sigel by a Chinese man she had met in New York's Chinatown and the 1913 double murder of Charles Sing and his white wife, Alice Davis Sing, in Chicago's Chinese quarter—there was little suggestion in the popular press that female slummers in the Chinatowns of either city faced anything resembling a "yellow peril." In fact, invoking popular stereotypes of the day, former New York police chief George W. Walling

suggested that, if there were a victim in the social and sexual relationships struck up between Chinese men and white women, it was the
"moon-face, gentle Chinaman" who proved "an easy victim to the wiles
of the immoral white woman."[45]

Rather, the most recent waves of European immigrants were portrayed
as the principal sexual menace to white female visitors to Chicago's Levee districts and New York's Bowery and Tenderloin. In his oft-cited
1907 "study of the great immoralities" of Chicago, muckraker George
Kibbe Turner famously blamed a syndicate of Russian Jews for the down-
fall and ruin of countless "young girls." A number of other journalists
and reformers ardently echoed his assertions. "There are large numbers
of Jews scattered throughout the United States, although mainly located
in New York and Chicago," *McClure's Magazine* reported in 1910, "who
seduce and . . . prey . . . upon young girls whom they find on the street,
in the dance-halls, and similar places." Chicago reformer Ernest A. Bell
extended these allegations to include recent Italian immigrants, noting that while "about a score of resorts" in the city's West Side Levee
were run by Jews, "two or three places are managed by Italian men, although there are few Italian prostitutes in Chicago." On the East Coast,
one of Bell's colleagues likewise claimed that "since 1901 the Sicilian or
Southern Italian has played quite a prominent part in the great traffic of
women in New York City . . . control[ing] from 750 to 1,000 women."
In June 1908, an exposé in the *Chicago Record-Herald* even added "several
'syndicates' made up of . . . Portuguese" to the list of racialized "foreigners" responsible for the proliferation of female prostitution and other
illicit activities in the Windy City.[46]

Despite their diverse geographic origins, the common threads that defined these national groups as potential threats to the sanctity of native-
born white American womanhood were their recent arrival on U.S. shores
in significant numbers, their deviation from Protestant Christianity, and
their similar racial status as in-between people who occupied a racial
position somewhere between old-stock white Americans and the Chinese immigrants and blacks who comprised an expanding proportion of
the population of turn-of-the-century New York and Chicago. Paradoxically, the very foreignness that distinguished these in-between groups
within the United States blurred any differences that might ordinarily
have separated them in their home countries, as Chicago attorney and
anti-vice advocate Clifford G. Roe demonstrated when he recounted his
rescue of a young white woman from the clutches of a potential white
slaver in Chicago: "As I watched him closely I perceived that he was
of foreign parentage," Roe recalled, "probably a Jew, a Frenchman, an

Italian, or perhaps a Greek"—as if the four were indistinguishable and veritably interchangeable.[47]

Sexual Spectacles in the Red-Light Districts and Slums of Chicago and New York

Despite the purported sexual threats that they faced when venturing into the cities' red-light districts and slums, affluent white pleasure seek-ers undertook such slumming excursions in extraordinary numbers from the late 1880s through the mid-1910s. The impact of these trips was clear, at least in economic terms. No matter their moral take on slumming, New Yorkers and Chicagoans alike were forced to admit that the raucous nightlife of the Levee districts of Chicago, the Bowery and Tenderloin of New York, and the Chinatowns of both cities provided a substantial stream of revenue. "I don't know as we ought to let the laws be violated and turn all sorts of immorality loose just to draw a crowd," one observant hotel liveryman remarked during a crackdown on the Tenderloin in 1892. "But it's a fact that every hotel man in New York is perfectly familiar with that strangers don't stay here and hell around much if there ain't no places running where they can see something." Estimating that "not less than 10,000 of [the visitors to New York] are slumming around every night in the year seeing 'the sights,'" the livery-man put the cost of moral reform at nearly $200,000 for every day that the popular "dives" of the Tenderloin, Bowery, and Chinatown were closed. If hotel tabs and other expenditures were added in, he calculated that a "wide open" city netted between $70 and $90 million per year. Though clearly less accepting of the social conditions associated with urban red-light districts, Chicago's municipal Vice Commission arrived at a similar conclusion, estimating in 1911 that Levee prostitution alone generated more than $15 million per year. The money that slummers spent on dancing, drinks, touring cars, trolleys, and cabs surely doubled or even tripled that amount, before hotel rooms and restaurant meals were ever factored in.[48]

The profits, of course, came at a cost. "Slumming," the poet James Clarence Harvey wrote in a popular 1905 sampler of the New York high life, "usually means paying a price to see others do things you wouldn't do yourself for the world, and which perhaps they wouldn't do except for the price you pay." While naive in assuming that slummers were ob-servers of but never participants in illicit activities, Harvey was astutely skeptical of the notion that slum residents were somehow predisposed to indulge in such behavior. Mindful of the cost of exploitation that threatened to compromise both the inhabitants of popular slumming destinations and the women and men who arrived to gaze upon them, he advised readers that, while "the involuntary resident of the slums is blameless, and therefore should be free from prying eyes, . . . the voluntary resident is sure to prepare a fake which does not show you the 'low life' which you are seeking."[49]

Such warnings did little to dissuade affluent white women and men from seeking both to observe and to participate in the easy sensuality to be found in the red-light districts. Of particular interest to slummers was the sexualized "tough dancing" practiced in local resorts in the form of the bunny hug, the turkey trot, the lovers' two-step, and the grizzly bear. Reportedly invented in the brothels of San Francisco's Barbary Coast, these dances became popular mainstays in the dance halls of the Bowery and the Levee—which, in turn, gave rise to an array of new dance steps bearing names related to these locations: the Bowery waltz and the Bowery glide, for instance, as well as the Wabash Avenue whirl, named for one of the principal streets in the Levee. According to one disdainful observer, tough dancing was marked by a pronounced sense of intimacy, as the participants wrapped their arms around each other, cheeks and bodies touching, to "throw aside all restraint and give themselves to unbridled license and indecency." Although unsettling to moral reformers, such dances offered many working-class women a sense of empowerment. In the Wabash Avenue whirl, for example, the female dancer became "the aggressor," choosing her partner from the crowd and "fl[ying] toward him with a plunge almost ferocious." Only then, as the *Chicago Tribune* described the popular Levee dance, did the couple grasp each other in "a vigorous clutch" and "begin a violent whirling motion" like a "gigantic top."[50]

Early short films produced by the Edison Manufacturing Company and the American Mutoscope and Biograph Company allowed audiences to observe exaggerated versions of some of these scandalous dances. In Edison's *Bowery Waltz* (1897), for example, a typical working-class woman appears to initiate the frolic, moving awkwardly toward her partner, only to be jerked roughly into his arms and spun backward over his outstretched leg in a move that sent her airborne, clinging to her partner's shoulders. Equally rough, the action in American Mutoscope and Biograph Company's *A Tough Dance* (1902) more closely resembled the "violent whirling motion" that the *Tribune* attributed to such capers. Dressed in ragged attire, a couple strutted toward each other from opposite sides of the screen, until the man grabbed the woman's arm, pulled her close, slapped her face, and violently twirled her about, in a short scene that ended with the two rolling around with each other on the floor.[51]

No matter how accurately—or fallaciously—these films captured the tough dancing exhibited in the Bowery and the Levee, they remained pale substitutes for an actual visit to the districts' resorts. As silent, black-and-white movies, they necessarily failed to capture the dance halls' raucous sounds and vibrant color, nor did their focus on individual couples give a true impression of the resorts' bustling, crowded environs. Moreover, the films provided no place for amusement seekers to try out the various dance steps they observed. This slummers did with increasing frequency in the early twentieth century, despite warnings that unscrupulous dance hall proprietors, such as the Levee's "Dago" Frank Lewis, "used the 'grizzly bear' dance in his basement dive as a recruiting ground" for local brothels. According to the *Chicago Tribune*, "Many girls who were lured into the district by the strange dance have remained there as 'wards' of the Italian boss."[52]

Even as slummers sometimes participated in the sensual dance-floor antics of Levee and Bowery resorts, they simultaneously clung to notions of social and sexual respectability defined, at least in part, in opposition to the interactions they observed in these spaces. For example, although visitors to the dance halls of New York's Lower East Side often encountered drunken immigrant and working-class women "sitting in the corners of the hall on the laps of their equally intoxicated partners, who were hugging and kissing them," slummers usually refrained from such explicit displays of public affection. They also generally shunned the custom of "breaking," quite popular among working-class women and men, in which two women began dancing together while awaiting the arrival of a pair of men who would "break" them into two separate couples, thereby allowing individuals previously unknown to each other to become better acquainted on the dance floor. Slummers, who usually arrived at such resorts as part of preestablished couples, tended to dance only with each other.[53]

Their relative affluence allowed the white middle- and upper-class patrons of Tenderloin and Levee establishments to eschew other sexual behaviors as well. Slummers could afford to indulge in the newfound intimacy of public leisure without having to resort to the system of sexual exchange that was becoming normative among turn-of-the-century working-class New Yorkers and Chicagoans. Known as "treating" among immigrant and working-class women, this practice involved trading sexual favors (or at least the promise of them) for material goods and cultural amusements—whether a night in a popular dance hall or a new dress or pair of stockings to wear on such an outing—that were otherwise unaffordable on their more limited budgets. Distinctly separated from prostitution in the minds of working-class women and men, who viewed the former strictly in terms of sex exchanged for money, treating constituted an alternative set of sexual norms that, much to their parents' dismay, was increasingly embraced by the Americanized children of late-nineteenth- and early-twentieth-century immigrants. Like the emerging new middle-class norms associated with "dating," treating was part of a uniquely modern sexual framework established in direct relation to the rise of commercialized leisure. Practiced routinely by racialized immigrants and workers in the very dance halls and dives where affluent white pleasure seekers went slumming, the custom provided slummers with an opportune foil against which to define their own shifting standards of social and sexual propriety. Doubtless, some male slummers were the recipients of similar treats from their female peers, but for the most part, well-to-do whites did not engage in casual sexual encounters. Still, the social and sexual practices of the "treating girls" that women observed while slumming surely served as models for their later sexual transformation into emancipated New Women.[54]

In a similar fashion, the cross-racial working-class relations on display in Chinatown provided another opportunity for affluent white pleasure seekers to position themselves in relation to the more casual social and sexual practices of the urban red-light district. The neighborhood's opium dens, in particular, came to be understood as highly sexualized urban locales. Popular exposés routinely characterized them as inordinately intimate places where disheveled smokers lolled about on Chinese matting or low wooden bunks in otherwise dark, subterranean cellars. In their most innocuous formulation, these were spaces of eroticized Chinese homosociability. Two to four Chinese men were typically depicted lying around a tray fitted up with bamboo pipe, lamp, and other utensils required for preparing the opium "pills" for smoking, their heads supported by wooden head rests or "l[ying] on their companions, so that no space is wasted."[55]

More often, however, Chinatown's opium dens were described as spaces that easily rivaled the racial and sexual diversity of local black and tans. In Chicago, for instance, the typical den was said to "hold from ten to sixty people, . . . persons of both sexes, black and white, and Chinese, too." Such descriptions and their increasing incorporation of white women as integral components of the Chinatown spectacle underscored the permeability of the cities' social and racial boundaries, but they also reinforced the notion that Chinese residents posed a particular threat to white female virtue. Whether lying in states of dishabille in local opium dens or walking the district's streets with Chinese men, "disreputable looking and acting white wom[e]n" became symbols of Chinatown's dual perils of opium addiction and cross-racial intimacy, the latter of which—even in cases of legal marriages—both slummers and reformers rallying against white slavery usually interpreted as a form of prostitution.[56]

Despite—or, perhaps, because of—this perception of increasing sexual danger, ever-growing numbers of affluent white women and men flocked to the cities' Chinese quarters from the 1890s through the mid-1910s. Women slummers seemed especially intrigued by the district, even though their enthusiasm for visiting Chinatown was frequently misunderstood during the earliest years of this slumming vogue as a sign of their sexual availability—if not by their white male escorts then by the Chinese men they encountered. Former New York medical student Charles Nesbitt recalled one such occasion when, in the company of a male journalist, he escorted "a couple of quite proper young ladies" to an exclusive Chinatown restaurant. Following a meal consisting of "a lot of presumably edible things," the restaurant's proprietor entered the couples' private dining room to show off "a couple of magnificent jade bracelets." "The girls went into ecstacies [sic]" over them, Nesbitt remembered, "and one of them was indiscreet enough to ask if they were for sale and what price." When the Chinese proprietor "proceeded to tell them in unmistakable language just how each could get a bracelet without the expenditure of any money," the women fled from the room with their embarrassed dates close behind. Only a few weeks later did Nesbitt learn the cause of this confusion as he confronted the restaurant's owner for having "grossly insulted our young lady friends." Expressing great remorse for his impropriety, the Chinese businessman maintained that he "thought they were just a couple of high class whores. I didn't dream that you would bring female members of your own social set to such a place as mine."[57]

By the turn of the century, as respectable white women became more frequent participants in slumming excursions to the Chinatowns of New York and Chicago (figure 14), situations like that described by Nesbitt grew significantly less frequent. No doubt some well-to-do white women continued to be propositioned by Chinese men under the very noses of their husbands and dates, but for the most part, the possibility of such propositions was a figment of the overactive imaginations of white

14   Originally printed as an illustration for William Brown Meloney's article "Slumming in New
      York's Chinatown" in the September 1909 issue of *Munsey's Magazine*, this photograph
      is titled "A Typical Party of Slummers Coming out of a Chinatown Restaurant after a Mid-
      night Banquet of Chop Suey and Chow Mein." Although the magazine likely staged this
      photograph, the demeanor of the group was fairly representative of the pleasure-seeking
      white women and men who visited Chinatown at the turn of the century—pointing and
      staring in apparent amazement at the so-called oddities of New York's Chinese quarter.
      (Reprinted from *Munsey's Magazine*, September 1909. Collection of the Library
      of Congress.)

reformers and pleasure seekers alike. Regardless, some women slummers appeared to use this imagined Chinese menace to justify an increased level of public intimacy with their dates. "Feeling they are on the threshold of a mystery," one journalist reported, when sightseers disembarked from a Chinatown touring car, "the women are clinging timidly to their escorts, or holding one another's hands." By the early 1910s, the district's reputation for providing an excuse for more casual public intimacy had apparently reached national proportions. Arriving in New York after attending a national teachers' conference in Boston, Bessie Casebeer recalled that she and several of her small-town Nebraskan colleagues "started for Chinatown" in a nighttime touring-car excursion, "with each girl in the party endeavoring to 'get a man.'" Whether this man was meant for protection, snuggling, or more, the imagined threats of Chinatown were apparently strong enough to justify such potentially scandalous behavior.[58]

Chinatown was not the only setting for such increased public intimacy. The resorts of the Bowery, the Tenderloin, and the Levee showcased a mélange of so-called sexual perversions and degeneracy against which affluent white pleasure seekers could naturalize their own shifting notions of respectability. In the black-and-tan resorts of the Levee, for instance, observers reported that rowdy, amorous, white slumming parties apparently believed that any social or sexual infraction they might commit would inevitably pale in comparison with the behavior of those "whites and blacks [who] danced together and," in the words of the *Chicago Journal*'s cub reporter Ben Hecht, "wiped out the color line with liquor, music and sex." How else to explain the fact that while "less noisy . . . white men . . . str[uck] up acquaintance with colored girls living in the neighboring 'buffet' flats" and a handful of white women stealthily "associate[d] with colored men," in the district's more popular dives the most "conspicuous" white patrons were almost always "the 'slummers,' largely of the class who kiss on the corner while waiting for street cars and whose terms of endearment would be considered cause for justifiable murder in the far west." Irish American attorney George Francis O'Neill drew a similar distinction between the acceptable shenanigans of white slummers and the supposed depravity of white women who dared to cross the sexual color line. Passing himself off as a "high class vaudeville actor" while assisting the Committee of Fourteen with an investigation of black-owned resorts, O'Neill apparently saw nothing alarming about the presence of "a party of white folks," in which two of the women smoked cigarettes as "the colored entertainers d[id] their stunts." But the white woman in another party, whom O'Neill "ascertained indirectly, of course, was the lover of a rather light colored negro," he immediately pronounced to be "of the degenerate type as far as I can judge."[59]

More surprising was slummers' use of the sexual environs of the cities' high-class brothels to draw a distinction between the willingness of well-to-do white women to participate in the increased intimacy of commercialized leisure and the commercial inclinations of prostitutes to accommodate men's expanding sexual desires, no matter how unconventional. By the late 1890s, critics noted that "slumming parties, composed of respectable men and women . . . , [we]re not infrequently found 'going down the line' dropping into the houses of prostitution," as they made the rounds of the red-light districts' other "all night pest holes." But the practice drew sustained public attention only in 1903, when it resulted in a shooting at the Levee's infamous Everleigh Club. Labeling the incident a "collision of two 'slumming parties,'" the *Chicago Tribune* revealed that the parties in question included a bookmaker and his date, as well as a second party consisting of two young chorus girls and the victim of the shooting, who claimed to be a New York banker named W. H. Robinson "but . . . is understood to be a well known Chicago young man." According to the newspaper, the reason for the shooting remained a bit of a mystery, but the fact that both slumming parties had chosen to spend the night at a high-class brothel appeared to arouse little or no surprise. Though the men had probably patronized the resort's prostitutes on earlier occasions, their decisions to take their dates to the Everleigh sisters' gilded palace likely had less to do with sex than with the availability of late-night victuals and champagne, dispensed within the seeming domesticity of the madams' elaborately decorated parlors. The brothel's highly sexualized setting surely suggested potential pursuits to the women slummers, but such visitors clearly understood that should they choose to become physically intimate with their male companions, their actions would be subjected to even more harsh scrutiny than the prostitutes' paid sexual encounters.[60]

The distinction between women slummers' possible pleasurable pursuits and the services provided by the cities' red-light denizens was made even clearer by the increasing public association of the latter not simply with prostitution but also with the "unnatural practices" that "prevailed in the declining days of Rome and Greece." To many reformers and slummers alike, such descriptions referred primarily to the "circuses" or "so-called 'entertainments' . . . too vile for description" that female prostitutes practiced with each other in an effort to drum up paying male customers. But the "perversions" on display in the Levee and the Tenderloin were not confined to "a renewal of the habits of the Lesbian lovers of the fifth century." They also extended to fellatio, a sexual practice that most Americans considered both "unnatural" and "foreign"—or, more specifically, "French." In at least some cases, the growing association of oral sex with "French girls" seems to have been well founded. Investigators visiting the cities' red-light districts reported that the women who "proposed having intercourse . . . in an unnatural manner" often had French names and spoke with accents. But the designation of fellatio as "frenching"—as the practice came to be known colloquially—became so ubiquitous that allusions to the "French houses" of the Levee and the Tenderloin were at least as likely to refer to brothels where prostitutes were willing to perform oral sex as they were to houses inhabited by women with Gallic ancestry.[61]

Despite the growing association of the "French perversion" with local brothels, most turn-of-the-century female prostitutes refused to perform the practice, because like most other Americans, they considered fellatio to be "unnatural." As one physician noted, prostitutes' general aversion to oral sex did not stop some women "in all our large cities . . . [from] publicly advertis[ing] themselves as devotees of this vice," but it did prompt "regular prostitutes" to ostracize many of the women who did so. In New York, for example, an investigator for the Committee of Fourteen reported that when "the French girls in these houses resort to unnatural practices[,] . . . the other girls will not associate or eat with them." By 1909, however, the stigma attached to these practices seemed sufficiently attenuated for Levee entrepreneurs to begin championing the district's "cunning, brazen, Parisian licentiousness." Reformers reported no fewer than fourteen local resorts that employed the words "'Paris' or 'Parisian' as part of their signs" and at least one high-class house where "pervert methods" were said to be "used almost exclusively"—both for the greater remuneration they garnered and as a prophylactic against pregnancy and venereal disease. The fact that patrons of the latter establishment were "drawn from the ranks of the well-to-do, supposedly substantial and select masculinity" of Chicago evidenced the increasing popularity of oral sex with at least some male slummers, but their decision to satisfy such desires with the denizens of the Levee, rather than with women of their own class, underscored the constraints that continued to shape sexual propriety and respectability—even among the more daring, well-to-do whites who went slumming in the cities' red-light districts.[62]

When white pleasure seekers did choose to push the bounds of respectability, no Bowery or Levee resort provided more cover for their affectionate explorations than one frequented by "degenerate men," whose inversion of traditional gender norms made any woman's social and sexual infractions—whether slummer or prostitute—seem almost conventional by comparison. An investigator for New York's Committee of Fourteen suggested as much when he reported on the presence of "3 male Fruiters" and several female prostitutes at a Chinatown dive "packed with women & men." The fact that "the women sucked, same as men" was enough to prompt the investigator to designate the resort "D— Rotten." But it was the feminine mannerisms and comportment of the joint's fairy entertainer that seemed to unsettle the investigator most, both when he "san[g] the old fruiter song whoops my dear" and especially when he "took out a pow[d]er rag & looking glass & pow[d]ered his face." In the Levee, reformers expressed particular concern about the apparent pride that some men took in upending the established gender order by appearing in public dressed in women's clothing, wearing make-up, and affecting falsetto voices. "Not content with the private and crafty pursuit of their calling," one critic charged, "they must flaunt it in the faces of the public and under the very eyes of the police," apparently taking "an insane pride in their hopeless degradation." Yet no matter how off-putting moral reformers found fairies' public performances to be, they remained astonishingly popular attractions with turn-of-the-century slumming parties, providing a unique foil for slummers' own social and sexual transgressions while simultaneously confirming the normative masculinity and privilege of the men who participated in such activities.[63]

Even as the spectacle of the fairy helped to consolidate normative masculinity and sexuality, it also created opportunities for men to have sex with each other without necessarily undermining their manhood. As historian George Chauncey has documented, many "normal" immigrant and working-class men in turn-of-the-century New York regularly engaged in sex with fairies and female impersonators without thinking that there was anything remotely queer about their actions. Under the then-prevalent gendered framework of sexuality, a man was considered sexually "normal" as long as he maintained his masculinity (at least publicly) and played the "male's role" in sexual encounters with a fairy who in turn expressed his femininity either by wearing women's clothing or by adopting physical mannerisms and affectations typically associated with women. Only the fairy, who inverted his proper gender performance and took on the "woman's role"—or, maybe more accurately, the female prostitute's role—in sexual encounters with other men was considered to be sexually perverse.[64]

White middle-class men, emerging from an era of Victorian sexual restraint, were unlikely to share these immigrant and working-class sexual norms. But given their attendance at the extraordinary number of Bowery resorts that featured fairy entertainers and female impersonators, including at least one—the Palm at 392 Bowery—which had a reputation for being "a place where fancy gentlemen go," it seems likely that at least some male slummers sought out sexual favors from the fairies they encountered. Certainly the resorts attempted to promote such interactions by permitting the fairies to walk around, "soliciting men at the tables." On some evenings, an undercover investigator noted, they even "promised to give a show, as they call it"—apparently a live sexual performance. How successful such shows were in drumming up customers is apparently lost to history, but the prevalence with which they were staged in the slummer-infested Bowery of the 1890s suggests that they met with at least moderate success.[65]

By no means did all the slumming parties who visited such resorts find them entertaining or even acceptable. Arriving in New York in the

1890s when "it was considered very smart to go slumming," Mary Casal recalled that both she and a female friend decided they "wanted to see everything and do as the rest of the people were doing." Engaging "two men friends who knew the ropes" to take them on a tour of the Bowery, they set out for what Casal described as a "night of frightful experiences" and soon resolved that the "one night was all we ever wanted of slumming." Expressing disgust at "the ugliness of the displays we saw as we hurried from one horrid but famous resort to another," she later determined that the tour had at least some redeeming benefits. "In the study of types, it was a good school. Seeing hundreds of male inverts, for instance, gathered together in a group made it easy to recognize them on any occasion where we might meet or see them, and so avoid any contact."[66]

The fact that Casal felt such aversion to the fairies she encountered on her slumming excursion, despite being romantically and sexually involved with the woman who accompanied her, underscores just how different turn-of-the-century conceptions of sexual normalcy were from those delimited in later decades by the increasingly hegemonic hetero/homo sexual dyad. At a time when sexual abnormality was defined not by the expression of one's sexual desire for a person of the same sex but by one's adoption of the mannerisms, public comportment, and even sexual roles commonly associated with members of the so-called opposite sex, Casal and her companion could regard themselves as "normal," properly gendered, middle-class women, even as they considered the flamboyantly feminine men they encountered in the Bowery to be sexual deviants. Other middle- and upper-class whites might have balked at Casal's casual equation of her devotion to another woman with "the very highest type of human love," but they likely would have accepted the notion that these two otherwise respectable, feminine women could hardly be classified as sexual degenerates. That designation was reserved primarily for the fairies and occasional mannish women whom slummers happened upon in the immigrant and working-class resorts of New York and Chicago and who so unabashedly violated the gender norms that demarcated sexual normalcy and respectability in the 1890s.[67]

"We have been pestered to death": Immigrant and Working-Class Resistance to the Slumming Trade

Whether pursuing the promise of sexualized and racialized amusements or motivated by a genuine desire to improve—or at least document—the social conditions in the immigrant and working-class districts of New York and Chicago, by the turn of the century a steady stream of sociologists, urban reformers, and slummers nightly flowed into the cities' red-light districts and slums. Members of each of these groups offered their own justifications for their visits, but to the hard-working women and men on the receiving end of this flood, the distinctions the visitors drew between thrill-seeking and more well-meaning sociological inquiry and benevolent work were nearly meaningless. Some of the cities' immigrant and working-class residents expressed an initial sense of amusement with the craze for slumming, but in time most complained that it was "inconvenient to be intruded upon at all hours by streams of well-dressed people," no matter their intention. As the number of interlopers grew, residents perceived even less disparity among the moral reformer, the social worker, and the fun-loving slummer. At least in part, this was a direct result of the visitors' attempts to blur the characteristics that usually distinguished these different types. Social-purity activists regularly posed as ordinary pleasure seekers in order to gain access to the districts' rowdier resorts, and on occasion, random thrill seekers adopted the guise of social workers to get an even closer look at how the other half lived. Expressing little, if any, hesitation about his participation in the latter practice, the novelist William Dean Howells recalled that, on one occasion during the early 1890s, he barged into the tenement flats of the Lower East Side "without any ceremony but the robust 'Good-morning!' my companion gave them by ways of accounting for our presence." Half-heartedly attempting to view his incursion through the residents' eyes, Howells later acknowledged, "They may have taken us for detectives, or agents of benevolent societies, or journalists in search of copy."[68]

By the late nineteenth century, such incursions into immigrant and working-class districts were increasingly met with rancor and animosity. When candlesticks, religious texts and other heirlooms went missing after their homes were "investigated" by women and men posing to be sociologists, residents of Chicago's West Side Ghetto began organizing to combat the influx of slumming parties in their neighborhoods. "We have been pestered to death," a Russian immigrant typesetter for one of Chicago's Jewish dailies remarked, "and I favor anything that will put a stop to the nuisance." Among the remedies that he suggested was one particularly creative idea: "Next time a party of them comes to my house," he told the *Chicago Tribune*, "I am going to ask each member where he lives and tell them that I am coming, with a party of my friends, to their houses to make an investigation of my own."[69]

Although this declaration might seem more of an exasperated joke than a true plan of action, in 1883 Bowery entrepreneur Billy McGlory invited more than fifty revelers at one of his notorious Armory Hall masquerades to undertake a sort of "reverse-slumming" expedition into elite New York neighborhoods. Never one for subtlety, McGlory chose to thumb his nose at New York society by booking the banquet hall at the high-toned Brunswick Hotel for a late-night supper of unprecedented ribaldry. When he arrived in a "queer, drunken procession, headed by a brass band" and accompanied by more than a dozen prostitutes and at least "three young men in women's costumes," the hotel's upper-class patrons were suitably scandalized. According to one account of the proceedings, they were not only rendered "speechless with astonishment that such goings on could happen at the intensely respectable Brunswick" but were so incensed by this challenge to their propriety that they soon shunned the hotel, lest they be tainted by its association with such disrepute.[70]

But not all reverse-slumming excursions were intended as attacks on the status and pretensions of the urban elite. The Reverend Father Huntington, for instance, had no such objectives in mind when he urged those in attendance at a national convention of shirt makers in 1892 to organize "a delegation from the down-town East Side . . . [to] 'go slumming' among those who 'dwell at ease and revel in luxuries.'" Rather, he hoped that by reversing the geographic and cultural border-crossings of New York's more affluent residents, his followers might "evok[e] the sympathy of the wealthy and the public for the hard lot of the poor." For the most part, however, this strategy not only fell short in its efforts to generate significant compassion and charity for the slum-dwellers of New York but also failed to shame the well-to-do into looking elsewhere for their entertainment and pleasure.[71]

Immigrant and working-class activists who hoped to stem the incursion of affluent thrill seekers into their neighborhoods generally focused their regulatory efforts not on the women and men who visited their communities but on the residents who, whether intentionally or not, contributed to the appeal that these districts had to curious outsiders. Hoping to make their neighborhoods less enticing to slummers, local business and religious leaders urged their fellow residents to minimize the sense of spectacle that encouraged middle- and upper-class whites to tour their neighborhoods in the first place. To avoid "giv[ing] the Americans another point on which to jeer the Italian," the editors of Chicago's Italian daily L'Italia urged their readers to help recent immigrants learn how to comport themselves in an urban environment. In the summer of 1892, the newspaper even decried what it deemed "the shameful spectacle of Italian women with bodice open and breasts exposed, nursing their babies" on the streets of the city's Near West Side. "Neither drunkards' obscene remarks nor the sarcasm of pedestrians serve to awaken in them a feeling of shame for their immodest behavior," the paper reported, ignoring any possibility that such behavior was neither immodest nor shameful.[72]

Jewish leaders in Chicago and New York likewise admonished recent immigrants in their own communities. At the turn of the century, the Ghetto districts of Chicago's West Side and New York's Lower East Side housed many of the cities' most open and prosperous brothels and disreputable resorts—a predicament that, according to many reform-minded middle-class Jews who had generally immigrated years earlier from Germany, was directly attributable to the districts' uneducated eastern European residents. Following investigations of the cities' Jewish neighborhoods, Dr. David Blaustein, superintendent of the Educational Alliance (formerly the Hebrew Institute), reported that "vice was forced upon th[e]se districts by the divekeepers" who took advantage of recent immigrants' ignorance of U.S. anti-vice laws. Hoping to counter this system of exploitation, Blaustein recalled that his organization "began a campaign of education and agitation. We went among the Jews and told them they didn't have to have these dives among them if they didn't want to."[73]

In reality, not all of the illicit activities in the Ghetto districts were imposed from outside, and a significant number of Jewish men and women profited from this trade. In 1907, an investigation of Chicago's West Side requested by Adolf Kraus, president of the Independent Order of B'nai B'rith and former Corporation Counsel for the City of Chicago, "found that of the traffickers in women in that district about twenty per cent were Jews." Two years later, when Julius Frank, the president of Chicago's Congregation Anshe Calvaria, was on trial with his brother Louis for running disorderly houses on the city's West Side, local authorities alleged that "seventy-five per cent of the white slave trade in Chicago is in Jewish hands." While such figures were almost certainly exaggerated, the undeniable involvement of at least some prominent Jews in the commercialized sex industry prompted an unprecedented level of mobilization among reform-minded businessmen, rabbis, and women's club leaders. Recognizing that the presence of even one crime lord in their midst confirmed white Americans' most egregious stereotypes of Jewish avarice and degeneracy, Jewish leaders in Chicago and New York insisted that their communities take a more active role in prosecuting those immigrants involved in prostitution. "The sooner such creatures are cleaned out," one Jewish newspaper editorialized, "the better it will be for the Jews of the world in general and of America in particular."[74]

Following a similar line of logic, black clergy and community leaders in New York and Chicago also worked to curtail the proliferation of prostitution and disreputable resorts in their neighborhoods. Like the cities' Jewish and Italian community leaders, they were motivated by two major objectives. First, they hoped to create habitable neighborhoods for respectable black families within the segregated confines of the black Tenderloin and the Levee. Such was the primary motivation, for instance, of the Reverend Adam Clayton Powell Sr.'s 1909 campaign to convert and baptize the "pimps, prostitutes, [and] keepers of dives and gambling dens" who lived and worked in close proximity to the Abyssinian Baptist Church, then located in the heart of the black Tenderloin on Fortieth Street between Seventh and Eighth avenues. Second, community leaders sought to challenge the increasingly dangerous association in the minds of many white Americans of blacks with sexual licentiousness. In New York, residents of the black Tenderloin learned firsthand about this danger in August 1900 when a full-scale race riot broke out on the city's West Side, following the killing of a white undercover policeman during the arrest of a black woman at the corner of Forty-first Street and Eighth Avenue. Whether one believed the official police story that May Enoch's arrest had been prompted by her alleged "soliciting" on the street or the account of her "husband," Arthur Harris, that the killing was the inadvertent result of his attempt to rescue May from "the grasp of a [white] man in citizen's dress," the message was clear: the interaction of blacks and whites in sex-related settings could prove deadly.[75]

Although many immigrant and working-class activists preferred to establish community-based groups to oversee their reform efforts, others found it more expedient to join forces with preexisting white middle-class reform organizations. Such coalitions helped to curtail the proliferation of commercialized sex in local neighborhoods and provided a more authoritative platform from which to contest the influx of slummers. In the winter of 1901, for instance, several Chinese immigrants served as translators and guides when officers from New York's Committee of Fifteen investigated and raided a number of Chinatown resorts. No doubt some of these men used local authorities to get even with rival tongs, but others, especially those involved in Chinese missionary organizations, seem to have resolved that such cross-racial alliances were the surest means both to protect their fellow countrymen from falling victim to police exploitation and to rout from their midst a "high class" opium den that catered primarily to affluent whites. A decade later, Fred R. Moore, the conservative editor of the black-owned weekly *New York Age*, provided similar assistance to the city's Committee of Fourteen by chairing an auxiliary "Committee of Five" black businessmen who assisted the white anti-vice organization with its investigations of New York's black-and-tan resorts. Employing its own investigators for at least one year, the auxiliary gathered evidence to force black saloon-keepers to sign pledges that they would forfeit their liquor licenses if they "admit[ted] male whites to any part of the license[d] premises to which colored women are admitted" or "admit[ted] at any time any white women." Failure to live up to such agreements resulted either in the committee's pressuring brewers and surety companies to end their support of the offending black and tan or in its urging police to raid and prosecute the venue, permanently terminating its city licenses.[76]

While the Committee of Five thus accepted the equation of cross-racial socializing with immorality and even criminality, other black activists decried this view. In 1908, in the midst of a sustained crackdown on black saloonkeepers, editor and publisher David Elliott Tobias launched a decade-long campaign against the Committee of Fourteen, accusing its leadership of being "most unfair and wholly unjust to colored people." According to Tobias, the committee was much more likely to pressure local officials not to renew the liquor licenses of black-run establishments than to impede the operations of more pernicious all-white saloons, because the former provided public spaces where blacks and whites could interact—the mere existence of which seemed to prove the existence of immorality to the committee's leadership.[77]

Profiting from the Slums

Given the enormous profits to be made, some residents of immigrant and working-class Chicago and New York embraced the lucrative potential of slumming. At the height of Chinatown's popularity among tourists, local businessmen kept their establishments open as late as 3:00 a.m., well beyond the hours kept by their regular patrons, prompting at least one reporter to note that "the liveliest and best times for business there are after midnight." Immigrant and working-class impresarios in Chicago's Levee district and in New York's Tenderloin and Bowery adopted similar hours, capitalizing on the same thrill-seeking crowds. A waiter at one of the Lower East Side's most popular resorts reported that the arrival of the well-to-do almost always translated into an increase in "sales, especially of wine." Another observer noted that sightseers in the concert halls of the Bowery "usually spend something," unlike the resorts' regular patrons, yet they "do not remain long," allowing resort-keepers to usher through several successive waves of curiosity-seekers each evening.[78]

Opportunities for making money from slumming abounded. Some of the more enterprising residents of immigrant and working-class neighborhoods secured jobs as guides on the "rubberneck wagons," or, touring cars, that shepherded the more cautious visitors through the Bowery, Chinatown, and the Levee. But for those who valued their independence and were prone to showmanship, the role of the independent "slumming guide" could prove quite profitable. In the short-lived sporting paper *The Tenderloin*, which was first published in 1898, industrious young men advertised their services in providing introductions to the district's brothels and concert saloons, as well as to the popular resorts of the Bowery and Chinatown. While such ads provoked the wrath of state legislators serving on the Mazet Committee in 1899, within just a few years, similar businesses were so widespread—and slumming so popular—that at least one resident of Chicago's Near West Side felt entirely comfortable seeking police approval to open what he referred to as a "guide system to escort slumming parties and show strangers the 'sights.'" Such professional escorts were especially popular for nighttime visits to Chinatown, creating opportunities for at least some immigrant and working-class men to position themselves as vital bridges between the world of affluent whites and that of the mysterious Chinese.[79]

The most famous of these guides, or, "lobbygows," as they were known in the cities' Chinese quarters, was Chuck Connors. A native-born white working-class character, Connors gave up his work as a bouncer in various Bowery dives in favor of conducting highly orchestrated slumming tours through Chinatown. Dressed in the pearly button-covered attire of the Cockney costermonger, he treated his customers to a series of Chinatown sights: the Mott Street joss house; the popular Chinese theater; the drinking, dancing, and "deviltries" of the Chatham Club; and the horrible "reality" of a staged opium den. "He knew how to stage a convincing show," the not-yet-famous Chatham Club pianist Jimmy Durante recalled. "The tourists were certain they had seen the real thing."[80]

Such performances flourished as the owners of popular slumming resorts in the Bowery, the Tenderloin, and the Levee routinely played up the exoticism of their surroundings to manufacture the very spectacles that slummers hoped to spy. In the black-and-tan dives of the Tenderloin and the Levee, these performances were often blatant, as hyped-up ragtime bands beat out a rhythm that allowed slumming gentlemen to gain a glimpse of black flesh underneath the swirling skirts of the clubs' female dancers. The Yiddish and Italian theaters on the Bowery and similar venues on Chicago's West Side also provided introductions to "authentic" musical and dance performances, as well as stereotypical representations both of Old World types and of misguided immigrant youths, including the "Ghetto Girl," who was lured into decadence by the bright lights and abundant consumer goods of the American city. But in other cases, the performances were more covert. After his Bowery saloon gained a reputation among amusement seekers for being a place where one might rub shoulders with some of the more renowned pugilists of the day, the infamous Steve Brodie was apparently reluctant to disappoint. Neighborhood author Owen Kildare recalled that Brodie often cajoled saloon regulars into impersonating famous boxers if none were present when a gaggle of thrill seekers arrived. On at least one occasion, Kildare himself even joined in the production of this artificial spectacle, portraying the bare-knuckle boxer Jake Kilrain.[81]

The most spectacular performances were staged in Chinatown, drawing unsuspecting visitors on an almost nightly basis. Realizing that slummers visited the district not only to seek out exotic titillation but also to confront their fears of the unknown, local entrepreneurs often deliberately set out to frighten their customers when creating Chinatown's more popular attractions. By arrangement with the larger touring-car companies or with slumming guides such as Connors, visitors to New York's Chinatown were sometimes treated to gunfights on Pell or Mott streets, timed specifically for their arrival and carefully scripted to call to mind the tabloid news coverage of local tong wars. But the most provocative and potentially "dangerous" sight that drew slummers to Chinatown was the renowned opium den. Although many tourists left Chinatown convinced that they had obtained a glimpse of "one of the world's wickedest spots," in most cases, slummers had seen little more than an elaborate stage show. Typical among these was the interracial spectacle produced by Georgie Yee and a "white woman, with hollow cheeks and bare, bony arms," who lay on a platform in his second-story joint, making preparations to smoke opium. Not only was this scenario performed "anywhere from ten to twenty times a night, for pay," one popular magazine reported, but it was actually the product of professional actors. "The Chinaman was a member of a theatrical troupe," the magazine noted, while "his wife had a place in polite vaudeville under a name which has been forgotten." (Ironically, the couple's real-life interracial marriage probably would have unsettled slummers almost as much as the scene they staged.)[82]

Theatricality became so integral to the turn-of-the-century slumming spectacle that it was easily transposed to stage and screen, thereby engaging an even larger audience in the sexual and racial encounters that characterized such urban adventures. In Irish American playwright and producer Edward Harrigan's popular 1894 comedy *Notoriety*, for example, audiences were transported to "a low groggery kept by a negro in the black Tenderloin, where a group of white women from the Atwater Temperance Mission interrupted "a white 'crook,' a shabby boy, and a flashily-attired darky . . . playing poker." The play's use of white actors in blackface to portray the black characters in this scene mitigated the cross-racial peril it implied, even as it perpetuated racist stereotypes and practices that kept black and white actors from sharing the same stage. But other theatrical productions of the day were more faithful to the racial dynamics of slumming. When Brooklyn's Star Theater staged an 1899 sketch entitled "Slumming," the producers employed Chin Yuen Dong, "the original Chinese actor," and "announced that a correct representation of a Chinese opium joint will be given, with every one," including presumably some of the white slummers featured in the scene, "smoking a real pipe."[83]

This penchant for realism in theatrical slumming tours was magnified by productions of Robert Neilson Stephens's comedy *On the Bowery* (1893) and Edmund E. Price's melodrama *In the Tenderloin*, both of which were produced by Lower East Side theaters in the autumn of 1894, before undertaking road tours to other urban locales. Earlier plays had offered glimpses into simulated versions of New York's underworld, but these two were the first to feature actual Bowery and Tenderloin personalities alongside professional actors. At performances of *On the Bowery*, New York theater goers encountered saloonkeeper Steve Brodie, who had risen to fame in 1886 after surviving an alleged stunt-jump off the Brooklyn Bridge. Appearing as himself in a mock-up of his notorious Bowery saloon, Brodie recited a few lines, performed a musical number, and even rescued the show's heroine from the East River after her own dramatic tumble from the city's famed bridge. On the road, the cast was supplemented by other Bowery characters, including renowned Chinatown tour guide Chuck Connors who appeared in an 1897 performance of the play in Charleston, South Carolina. George Washington Lederer's production of *In the Tenderloin* similarly introduced theater-going slummers—both in New York and in localities such as New Haven, Syracuse, Youngstown, and Indianapolis—to what one Cincinnati newspaper approvingly called "a facsimile of occurrences in the heart of New York." The show's professional cast impersonated several notable New Yorkers, but the real stars of the show were Tom Gould and George Appo—the former, the proprietor of the popular Tenderloin resort known as the Sans Souci; the latter, a Chinese Irish American petty criminal, whose celebrity stemmed from his testimony about police corruption and crime before the 1894 Lexow Committee.[84]

Even as these staged spectaculars permitted out-of-towners and timid New Yorkers alike to sample the raucous atmosphere of the Tenderloin and the Bowery without ever setting foot in one of the districts' notorious resorts, the fact that these shows were originally staged in Lower East Side theaters suggests that producers also intended them to provide immigrant and working-class audiences with an opportunity to ridicule affluent white pleasure seekers. This was certainly the case with Loney Haskell's winsome burletta, *Slumming*, which Hurtig & Seamon's Bowery

15   This 1898 poster for Hurtig & Seamon's Bowery Burlesquers advertised the traveling troupe's original burletta, *Slumming*, a musical farce lampooning the "latest New York craze." Performed in working-class theaters on New York's Lower East Side and in similar theaters throughout the country during the late 1890s and early 1900s, this show allowed audiences to laugh at the antics of well-to-do white curiosity seekers. (Reprinted from the collection of the Prints and Photographs Division, Library of Congress.)

Burlesquers performed in working-class theaters across the country for several years beginning around 1898. Described by the popular press, as well as by the company's own advertisements, as a "satire on the latest New York craze" (figure 15), this popular show followed a "slumming party of Fifth Avenue New Yorkers" as they visited a Chinese opium joint, a Bowery concert-saloon, and the Essex Market Police Court—all the while mocking the party's "often ludicrous actions and doings."[85]

Similar portrayals of slumming pervaded early film, inviting immigrant and working-class audiences both to laugh at the discomfiture of amusement seekers and to think up new ways of exploiting their seemingly unremitting gullibility. Never was this focus more obvious than in the D. W. Griffith collaboration, *The Deceived Slumming Party* (American Mutoscope & Biograph, 1908), in which a touring car filled with slummers left 42nd Street for the thrills and perils of Chinatown and the Bowery. At each stop on their excursion, the tourists were jolted by unexpected frights: a police raid and the apparent suicide of a white female addict in a Chinatown opium den, the appearance of a rat in a Chinese restaurant causing one woman slummer to fall into a sausage-making machine, and the fisticuffs in a tough Bowery dive that seemingly led to murder. In each case, the slummers' guide appeared to shepherd them back to safety just in the nick of time, leaving them shaken but sufficiently thrilled. But viewers of the film knew otherwise, and when the tour guide returned to each locale to pay off the actors who had staged these scenes, audiences were prompted to laugh at the slummers' credulity and fright. The film may have warned middle-class viewers about the potential cons awaiting them on slumming expeditions in New York and other cities, but ultimately it glorified the cunning and guile of immigrant and working-class entrepreneurs who profited handsomely from the curiosity and misconceptions of the well-to-do.[86]

While such elaborate performances were by no means uncommon in real life, they were only the most obvious of many ways that immigrant and working-class women and men set out to exploit the slummers who visited local establishments. Levee dance hall proprietor Ike Bloom was among the first to employ attractive working-class "hostesses" both to provide dancing partners for solo male customers and to entice them to purchase round after round of drinks for themselves and their temporary female companions. A number of other Levee, Tenderloin, and Bowery resorts followed suit, using women and wine to bilk their male customers of as much coin as possible. The roughest of them even resorted to adding "knockout drops" to the drinks of particularly gullible patrons who made the crucial mistake of flashing their overstuffed wallets.[87]

Despite the efficiency of the "knockout" approach in lifting excess cash from well-to-do patrons, most dive keepers steered clear of such vicious and obvious tactics—especially as more and more women began to accompany their husbands and boyfriends on slumming excursions. Instead, they adopted the more subtle practice of stacking the check, presenting outrageously inflated bar tabs to men who were either too intoxicated to notice or would likely be too embarrassed to raise a fuss. Another favorite practice among Bowery waiters was to cheat distracted customers as they paid their checks and readied to leave. Counting back the customer's change, the more dexterous of local waitstaff simply employed sleight of hand to slip an extra five- or ten-dollar note into their own pockets. Out-of-town tourists were especially vulnerable to the schemes of underhanded resort keepers and slumming guides. In the summer of 1911, Professor J. W. Shields of Springfield, Illinois, alleged that "he was robbed of $180 by three men after he had engaged one of them to take him 'slumming.'" Muncie, Indiana, resident Carl Andrew Shirk told a similar tale, suing a local broker whom he had met at the Chicago Athletic Club in February 1907, after the latter refused to return the $38 that had been left in his "safe keeping" when Shirk became so intoxicated "on a tour of the 'red light district'" that he had to check in to a Levee hotel for the night.[88]

Even female slummers occasionally found themselves targets of deception and robbery. In January 1906, for example, Mrs. Frank Chamberlain reported the alleged theft of a $400 diamond pendant while on a slumming tour of the Levee with a female friend and two men they had met earlier that night at a local restaurant. Nearly nine years later, the *Chicago Tribune* carried a story reporting the disappearance of "a $500 diamond sunburst brooch," lost by one Addie C. Keiller, a prosperous widow who had gone out to "see the bright lights" with four young men. Unlike the stories of gullible male pleasure seekers, which were usually more factual than didactic, newspaper accounts of swindled women slummers often became morality tales documenting the urban perils that confronted women who played too fast or failed to remain within the patriarchal domain of their protective husbands. Recounting the circumstances of Mrs. Chamberlain's mishap, the local press carefully relayed the fact that her husband was away on business in San Francisco, quoting her in ways that underscored her seeming inability to think for herself. "I did not know there was any harm in it," she allegedly professed. "I had read about slumming parties and I thought it would be great fun. . . . I don't know what my husband will think." The intended message was clear: wives should accede to their husbands' greater knowledge and authority, whether or not they were physically present. Husbandless women like Addie Keiller were subjected to even greater moral chastening if caught in similar situations. Playing up the difference between her age—"her hair is tinged gray"—and the youth of her male companions, the *Tribune* suggested not only that Keiller had stepped well outside the bounds of propriety but also that her financial loss was nothing less than due recompense for such unladylike behavior.[89]

In addition to being targeted by moral reformers and unscrupulous slumming guides, women slummers were also greeted in immigrant and working-class resorts by male patrons and proprietors who offered protection, romance, or some combination of the two. While visiting Barron Wilkins's popular Tenderloin black and tan during the winter of 1910, a woman investigator for New York's Committee of Fourteen became the object of such unsolicited male attention. Almost immediately after she and a female companion entered the resort, the investigator later recalled, they were joined by "two men, well dressed—one with an array of diamond rings and pins—" who "engaged in conversation, and paid for our drinks." Despite the likelihood that the men hoped to spark some intimacy, the investigator noted that they made no untoward advances and appeared genuinely concerned for the women's safety. "When I announced that I was going to leave for Diggs' Place," another nearby black and tan, she reported, "the man looked surprised, and said that was too tough for us." Hoping to discourage the women from their proposed excursion, he added "that he never went there, because he was afraid of getting into trouble."[90]

Protective—and even restrictive—measure were a regular feature of women's slumming experiences. Like pleasure-seeking immigrant and working-class women, female slummers were expected to enter the resorts through their side or rear "ladies' entrances," as mandated by local law, and were often denied entry if not escorted by men. Once inside, however, they were usually granted as much free rein to drink and mix with other patrons as working-class women had already claimed for themselves. But, as the journalist Neith Boyce learned when she accompanied her future husband Hutchins Hapgood to "the backroom of a tough saloon on Eighth Avenue," the freedom that women enjoyed in Tenderloin resorts was by no means unlimited. At a resort "where women were admitted to drink, and where rough conduct was not frowned upon," Hapgood recalled that Boyce's attempt to light up a cigarette provoked an immediate rebuke of her unladylike behavior. "The bartender came over to our table and indignantly said to her: 'Say, where do you think you are? The Ritz?'" suggesting that the female inhabitants of the slum were in some respects held to stricter codes of behavior than middle- and upper-class women faced in elite venues.[91]

Although male slummers enjoyed a good deal more leeway in the resorts of the Bowery, the Tenderloin, and the Levee, they, like their female counterparts, were required to conform to particular codes of behavior. Among the most common restrictions were limitations on their ability to interact with the female immigrant and working-class patrons. Restraints on casual interactions with local women were especially prevalent when they entailed crossing the color line that separated black from white. Because black and tans were subjected to intense scrutiny from moral reformers, the proprietors of such resorts often refused to "serve unaccompanied white men in [the] rear room" where they might socialize with black women, both because they wished to avoid riling local authorities and because they suspected, often correctly, that unfamiliar white male patrons were likely to be anti-vice investigators or undercover policemen. "They would probably serve a white man in rear room if they knew him well," an investigator noted of one Tenderloin black and tan, "but [they] will not take a chance on a stranger."[92]

Whether enforced by proprietors or patrons, the informal rules of conduct that governed interactions at popular slumming venues served several important functions. They helped to maintain a sense of decorum that enabled these resorts to avert potential anti-vice investigations and raids by coaxing—or even compelling—rowdy patrons to modify their behavior. For example, when confronted with a particularly boisterous New York crowd at George Lee's black and tan, the black bartender established order by reminding customers, "You all don't want the white folks to get after us." Resorts also enforced house rules to ensure their reputations as safe destinations for slummers to visit. At McGurk's Sporting House on the Bowery, the management attracted male patrons by discouraging pickpocketing on site. "If a woman robbed a visitor while in this dive, whether caught in the act or afterwards identified by the man whose companion she had been," one observer noted, "she was compelled to disgorge her booty and could not again enter the place. This in part," he aptly acknowledged, "accounted for its popularity." But at most resorts, it appears that house rules were less a part of daily operations than a mechanism invoked by resort keepers and patrons to camouflage the usual goings-on in such establishments when undercover investigators visited. "The young people who attend these balls know immediately when a person different from themselves appears in the hall," one New York investigator noted. "At once the dance becomes modest and sedate and the visitor goes away to report 'that while conditions are not what they should be, yet on the whole there is great improvement.' "[93]

The informal tactics that immigrant and working-class youths employed to protect neighborhood resorts from the regulatory actions of the police and urban reformers often proved sufficient to safeguard the continued operation of such nightspots, as well as their appeal to intrepid slummers. But in the early twentieth century, municipal authorities in both Chicago and New York launched more vigorous and sustained campaigns against the cities' red-light districts and other working-class amusements, which not only resulted in the closure of most of the cities' slumming venues but also fundamentally reshaped the practice of slumming itself. Although slumming had originated as a spatial negotiation by middle- and upper-class whites of the rapidly expanding, racialized immigrant and working-class enclaves of late-nineteenth-century cities, by the early 1910s the practice had largely been detached from the slum itself, becoming focused instead on the tearooms and cafés frequented by artists, writers, and political radicals. These bohemians, like their immigrant and working-class counterparts, occupied parts of the city where ramshackle buildings and commercial amusements made life seem edgier and, therefore, more appealing to well-to-do white thrill seekers. But the geographic location of these districts and the condition of their physical environs ultimately proved less central to their emergence as popular new slumming destinations than the fact that, like the earlier red-light districts of Chicago and New York, the cities' bohemian enclaves gave rise to leisure practices that diverged from white middle- and upper-class social and sexual norms.

Grounded in emerging medical and political discourses, the bohemian emphasis on free love and on women's social and sexual independence provided yet another venue of urban intrigue and escapism for slummers. Even as bohemians themselves were negotiating the complexities of translating theories of sexual identity into the practice of sexual liberation, the increasing presence of thrill seekers in bohemian Towertown and Greenwich Village complicated the dynamics of urban sexual and racial interactions. Participating in the districts' new sexualized and racialized leisure pursuits, bohemians and slummers not only contributed to the further reconfiguration of sexual norms and notions of respectability but also began to challenge the general public's understanding of racial and sexual difference.

FOUR

The Search for Bohemian *Thrillage*

At the turn of the twentieth century, as slummers flocked to the immigrant and working-class amusements of Chicago's Levee and New York's Bowery and Tenderloin, a number of promising young white artists and radicals ventured into these same districts to document their rich cultural traditions. Setting themselves apart from the "well-to-do persons" who visited these neighborhoods "merely from motives of curiosity or philanthropy," this bohemian group insisted that their ventures were motivated instead by either political or aesthetic concerns. "I was led to spend much time in certain poor resorts of Yiddish New York," Hutchins Hapgood noted in his 1902 study *The Spirit of the Ghetto*, "not through motives either philanthropic or sociological, but simply by virtue of the charm I felt in men and things there."[1]

Many of the era's prominent artists and writers—John Sloan, Sherwood Anderson, and Stephen Crane among them—expressed similar sentiments. Despite such assertions, however, bohemian ventures into these neighborhoods had much to do with earliest slumming vogue. Their excursions to the cities' red-light districts and slums often differed little from those undertaken by more obvious slummers. As bohemian writer and journalist Ben Hecht later recalled, he was often much "less purposeful" while visiting Chicago's Levee "and more like my colleagues, drunk and staggering on Saturday nights from saloon to saloon, sitting among bawds and pimps in Colisimo's Café." The effect of bohemians' participation was even more profound, because their books and art depicting immigrant and working-class neighborhoods further stimulated popular interest in slumming.[2]

The relationship between slumming and bohemianism grew even more complicated by the outbreak of the First World War. As aggressive anti-vice campaigns successfully forced the closure of nearly all the slumming destinations of the Bowery, the Tenderloin, and the Levee in the 1910s, affluent whites instead directed their attention toward the very neighborhoods, studios, and tearooms that the cities' white bohemian artists and radicals claimed as their own. Invited to slip "Down the Rabbit Hole" at the Mad Hatter tearoom in New York's Greenwich Village and to "Step high, stoop low, [and] leave your dignity outside" at the Dill Pickle Club in Chicago's Towertown, intrepid pleasure seekers invaded such spaces by the thousands. As they exchanged the rough-and-tumble atmosphere of the cities' working-class amusements for the more fanciful, if still ramshackle, basement and alleyway nightspots of bohemia, slummers discovered an alternate source of amusement and a retreat from the exigencies of everyday life.[3]

The increasingly impersonal character of urban workplaces, cramped residential quarters, and hectic streets discomfited many middle- and upper-class whites. Seeking to satisfy the resulting appetite for escapism, bohemian entrepreneurs transformed their tearooms and cabarets into colorful, imaginary worlds far removed from the realities of city living. Patrons happily left the crush of New York streets to walk the gangplank at Don Dickerman's Pirate's Den, a Christopher Street cabaret rigged up with a cannon, parrots, and monkeys to resemble a pirate's ship. Bucolic haystacks, square dancing, and a few barnyard animals gave Meyer Horowitz's Village Barn a similar air of retreat, while Vincenc Noga's Gold Coast House of Correction and Big John's Coal Scuttle used prison and coal-mining motifs, respectively, to lull affluent Chicagoans into a world far removed from urbanity.[4] But the most distinguishing feature—and the biggest drawing card—of both Towertown and the Village was the growing popular association of these bohemian districts with social and sexual unconventionality. Bohemia's reputation for "free love" proved nearly irresistible to a surprisingly wide variety of visitors. According to poet and novelist Maxwell Bodenheim, "Politely excited groups of men and women in evening clothes" were soon joined in their excursion to bohemian nightspots by "clerks from department stores and offices, who like to visit a less expensive vaudeville show," as well as by "college boys and girls who believe that they are acquiring a risqué and brilliant knowledge of life."[5]

Towertown and Greenwich Village provided well-to-do white pleasure seekers with an important introduction to modern social and sexual norms. Created during the first decade and a half of the twentieth century by white middle-class rebels who had fled Victorian strictures and responsibilities to settle in the lodging-house districts of Chicago's Near North Side and New York's immigrant Ninth Ward (as the Village was then known), these new bohemian districts blurred the physical and cultural boundaries that increasingly separated affluent white urbanites from their working-class neighbors. At the same time, the transformation of these neighborhoods complicated the racial dynamics of the cities. Even as the very designation of *bohemia*—through its historical and linguistic association with the "gypsy" life of Central European Roma—suggested the emergence of new racialized urban places, these districts provided spaces in which Jewish and Italian immigrants began to remake their racial identities, staking more definite claims to whiteness or, at least, becoming absorbed in its bohemian variant.[6]

Such disruptions of the racial and class order of U.S. cities paled in comparison to bohemians' more direct assault on white middle-class notions of sexual propriety and respectability. Bohemians' attention to sexual equality and pleasure fostered increasingly casual attitudes toward public intimacy and nonmarital sex. Moreover, their rejection of the traditional gender roles of the male breadwinner and the female homemaker in favor of more radical self-presentations as carefree "long-haired men" and "short-haired women" undermined the very foundations of gender difference that predominated in nineteenth-century America. Whether affluent visitors to bohemian neighborhoods chose to emulate or to reject these developments, the bohemian spectacle of unconventional sexuality and gender challenged the persistence of separate gendered spheres of domesticity and public activity. In addition, it undermined the continuing relevance of gender performance and presentation as defining markers of sexual normality, signaling the imminent shift from a gendered sexual regime to the now-hegemonic hetero/homo sexual binary. Thus, bohemianism became both a catalyst and a conduit in the emergence of more modern heterosexual norms, providing a strategic counterpoint of "free love" and sexual abandon that helped to normalize well-to-do white youths' increasing participation in the new cultural phenomenon of dating, as well as their more general fascination with urban public amusements.[7]

Remaking Sexuality in Bohemia

Although expeditions to immigrant and working-class amusements had challenged many slummers' assumptions about racial and sexual differences, slumming excursions to bohemian districts augured even more dramatic adjustments, since many of the resident artists and radicals were engaged in a calculated and concerted effort to reconfigure American social and sexual norms. Even as the bohemian spectacle of free love afforded affluent white women and men with an unusually intimate glimpse of alternative sexual practices, Greenwich Village and Towertown provided cover for slummers' own participation in these same practices, allowing unprecedented levels of middle-class sexual exploration and experience.

White bohemian artists and radicals consciously grappled with both the new psychological and sexological discourses of sexuality that emerged at the turn of the century. According to the tramp poet Harry Kemp, the studios of Greenwich Village were often filled with talk about overtly sexual topics, such as "Havelock Ellis; perversion and inversion; the toleration of the Homosexual; the late book of Moll's on the sex-life of the child . . . [and] Freud and his discoveries." Many of the women and men who participated in these conversations likely had little more than passing knowledge of the scholarship in question, but others carefully scrutinized sexological and psychological literature. Accessing these studies, which were marketed almost exclusively to medical professionals and were kept under lock and key in most public libraries, was often a daunting task. But the cognoscenti of Towertown and the Village understood the importance of gaining first-hand knowledge of these new discourses of sexuality, which recognized the existence of female sexual desire and began to challenge the previous emphasis on gender performance in defining sexual identities by focusing on the emerging categories of the heterosexual and the homosexual. Even if one had to get "a doctor's certificate or something of that sort" to view the materials, Chicagoan Margaret Anderson told the readers of the *Little Review* (the literary journal that she founded in 1914 with her lover Jane Heap) it would be "worth your life to get Havelock Ellis's six volumes from a bookstore or a library." Anderson also insisted that the wisdom to be gleaned from German sexologist Otto Weininger's *Sex and Character*, first published in English translation in 1906, fully justified the humiliation of being "taken behind locked doors [and] forced to swear that you want it out of no 'morbid curiosity.'" Far from merely indulging a personal curiosity, writers and radicals began to use the knowledge gained from such material to transform society.[8]

Both in the pages of local literary journals and in the studios and tearooms of Towertown and the Village, bohemians frequently discussed what they saw as the pressing need to change American social policy on sexual issues. In the pages of Chicago's *Little Review*, for example, Margaret Anderson adamantly argued that bohemian thinkers and activists had a particular responsibility to take on a wide variety of sex-related social concerns, ranging from "free love, free divorce, social motherhood, [and] birth-control," to the "social efforts in behalf of the homosexualist." When British sex advocate Edith Ellis, wife of eminent sexologist Havelock Ellis, failed to promote the repeal of laws criminalizing the distribution of birth control and the practice of homosexuality during the Chicago leg of her 1915 lecture tour, Anderson castigated her for disregarding her personal knowledge that "boys and girls, men and women, [were] tortured or crucified every day *for their love*—because it is not expressed according to conventional morality." Noting that "there is so much work to be done," Anderson's readers took up their pens in agreement, as did the writers and readers of *The Quill* in Greenwich Village. In the symposium "The Greatest Need Now in the Sex Life of the Nation," *The Quill* addressed issues like birth control, prostitution, interracial marriage, and the injustice of the "drastic punishments" meted out to "abnormal men and women . . . of the intermediate sex." The symposium also openly challenged social and sexual double standards by asking how women could ever be "assure[d] normal lives" when "the great majority of [them] seldom if ever have their sex needs fully gratified."[9]

Similar concerns led a number of bohemian activists, including Margaret Sanger, Emma Goldman, and Ben Reitman, to take to the streets to disseminate feminist tracts, family-planning literature, and free birth-control devices. But for most Village and Towertown artists and radicals, the process of transforming social and sexual norms began in the privacy of their own homes, as they applied their budding knowledge of sexology and Freudian psychoanalysis to their own lives and began more systematically to explore their sexual desires. For many bohemian intellectuals, this exploration took the form of free love, a practice intended to remove sex from the confines of marriage and reorient it around the pursuit of pleasure and mutual sexual fulfillment. Grounded in the writings of Edward Carpenter and Ellen Key, this new approach to relationships reinforced an emerging recognition of women's social and sexual equality and valorized female sexual desire by freeing sexual activity from the necessities of reproduction. As the increased availability of birth control alleviated concerns about unwanted pregnancies and venereal disease, more Towertown and Village women experimented with free love. One college-educated Towertown resident reported that her discovery of others like herself who felt that "marriage did not legitimate sexual experience" encouraged her to pursue her "desire to be entirely independent" like never before.[10]

Nevertheless, many bohemian women suspected that, despite the promise of social and sexual egalitarianism, free love usually favored male bohemians' prerogatives and desires, thereby diminishing bohemian women's sense of emotional and sexual independence. For more than a decade after her marriage in 1899, Village writer and intellectual Neith Boyce willingly acquiesced to her husband Hutchins Hapgood's passionate obsession with free love. She permitted him to dally as he pleased and, on numerous occasions, even indulged his compulsive desire to share with her the erotic letters that he received from his many paramours. Deriving pleasure from Boyce's permissiveness, Hapgood attempted to reciprocate, articulating his belief in free love as a matter of sexual equality. "Tell me you love me and also tell me about the flirtations you are having," he prodded Boyce when they found themselves in separate cities for an extended period during the mid-1910s. "Have you been unfaithful? Have you sinned? Did you like it[?]" At Hapgood's urging, Boyce engaged in a few affairs of her own. But in 1916, she resolved that the couple's free-love arrangements not only benefited Hapgood disproportionately but also damped her own interest in such extramarital dalliances. "I *know* that your physical infidelities (beginning very early) hurt that instinctive feeling for you in me," Boyce told her husband. "That as time went on I didn't feel it less, but came more and more to feel that you didn't belong completely to me nor I to you—that this gave me a more disengaged feeling to other men."[11]

Historians Leslie Fishbein and Ellen Kay Trimberger argue that most bohemian women's dissatisfaction with free love can be traced to the conflicting priorities of white male intellectuals during this period. While bohemian men often purported to embrace feminism, they frequently found themselves deeply torn between their commitment to sexual equality and their desire to protect and maintain male privilege. Writer Floyd Dell, for example, hoped "to find in woman a comrade and an equal," but he also worried that feminism was encouraging Village women to challenge "the masculine right to boss women around and tell them what they should and should not do." Likewise, editor and Village resident Max Eastman professed a theoretical "liking for women with brains, character and independence," but in practice, he pursued mainly those women whose intellects failed to challenge his own and whose beauty perked his libido. Villager Henrietta Rodman, who noted the persistence of a similar double standard in her troubled relationship with poet Harry Kemp, admonished bohemian men for their hypocrisy. "We choose our partners for their capabilities," Rodman argued on behalf of all Village women, "but, as far as I've been able to observe, it's what you males call 'chickens'—pretty insipid girls that you choose as wives and sweethearts."[12]

Even as the women of bohemia became firmly convinced that free love was often nothing more than, in the words of modernist poet Mina Loy, a "love-racket organized at woman's expense," they continued to settle in the Village and Towertown. For in the cheap apartments of these two neighborhoods, women found spaces where they could afford to live alone and pursue their creative endeavors. Many of these women worked outside of the bohemian districts, but others launched commercial ventures that capitalized on the neighborhoods' reputations as meccas of self-reliant femininity. During the mid-1920s, sociologist Harvey Warren Zorbaugh noted that "young women open most of the studios, run most of the tearooms and restaurants, most of the little art shops and book stalls, manage the exhibits and little theaters, [and] dominate the life of [Towertown]." The same was true in the Village, where women ran many of the district's commercial establishments and also dominated the neighborhood's residences by the early 1930s.[13]

The tendency of bohemian men to define themselves in opposition to the traditional middle-class breadwinner by shunning marriage and stable, lucrative careers complemented the emerging role of women in the local economy. At the same time, bohemians' adoption of nontraditional modes of attire made the gender nonconformity of the Village and Towertown particularly visible to the American public. Bobbing their hair and donning painters' smocks or, in some cases, the tailored suits more often worn by men, the women artists and radicals in these neighborhoods visually set themselves apart from the vast majority of American women. Bohemian men, likewise, distinguished themselves by wearing their hair long and dressing in colorful, often threadbare attire, as seen in one reporter's portrayal of the "nattily dressed" Dill Pickle Club proprietor Jack Jones, smartly decked out "in green beret, last year's haircut, and a green velvet jacket."[14]

Even as bohemian fashion provided a public marker of the transgression of gender norms, its evocation of popular stereotypes of gender inversion and sexual deviance created an atmosphere where lesbians and fairies felt relatively comfortable mingling in public with the districts' artists and radicals. To some extent, this sense of comfort was simply a product of the presence of numerous "third sex" types among the creative women and men of Towertown and the Village. But third-sexers with a less artistic bent also "flocked to bohemia, to the forums, the street meetings, the tearooms, and the hangouts" because, as Towertown regular Ben Reitman noted, bohemians willingly "accepted [them] in full fellowship . . . No one insults them by calling them queer or kids them for being sissies."[15]

Because bohemia's artists and radicals usually steered clear of using derogatory names and engaging in the physical harassment of lesbians and fairies, however, they often found themselves on the receiving end of similar queer-baiting tactics. At a time when sexual identity was still defined by gender performance rather than by the sex of one's object choice (along the now-normative hetero/homo sexual axis), the general public usually failed to distinguish between the gender nonconformity of third-sexers and that of other bohemians. As presumed sexual deviants, long-haired men and short-haired women were subject, along with third-sexers, to waves of indiscriminate persecution, and as a result, many bohemians identified with lesbians and fairies. "We're all a little like that—I mean, queer," Rose-Ann, a fictional version of Floyd Dell's wife Margery Currey, reminded the autobiographical protagonist of Dell's 1921 Towertown novel, *The Briary-Bush*, after he expressed discomfort with the "mincing accent" and "unnatural and 'prissy'" manner of his next-door neighbor. For Rose-Ann, the "queerness" of bohemia referred as much to its general unconventionality as to any particular sexuality.[16]

Even when the intellectuals of Towertown and Greenwich Village adopted the emerging hetero/homo sexual terminology of turn-of-the-century sexologists and psychoanalysts, they usually did so in ways that stressed the sexual similarities rather than the differences between third-sexers and bohemian free-lovers. Following the lead of theorists such as the German sexologist Otto Weininger, they refused to see heterosexuality and homosexuality as mutually exclusive categories. Quoting Weininger in the *Little Review*, Margaret Anderson stressed that "there is no difference between the normal and the inverted type . . . all organisms have both homosexuality and heterosexuality." Other bohemians adopted a more Freudian approach to sexual desire, asserting that "all human beings are capable of making a homosexual object-choice and have in fact made one in their unconscious." Writer Floyd Dell employed this notion to diagnose his own "unconscious homosexuality," well before undergoing professional psychoanalysis. Such amateur psychosexual analyses became a popular, if not always welcome, obsession among the artists and radicals of Chicago and New York. Novelist Sherwood Anderson recalled that, during the early 1910s, Dell and others began "psyching" everyone who visited their studios in Chicago's 57th Street art colony. "In an unfortunate moment, I brought up the subject of homosexuality," Anderson remarked, and they immediately seized upon this mention as "a sure sign of its presence."[17]

Bohemians' appreciation of the embodiment of both homosexuality and heterosexuality in every individual was as likely derived from their personal experiences as from any particular study of sexology or psychoanalysis. Numerous artists, writers, and radicals who participated in the bohemian worlds of Chicago and New York led complicated sexual lives that defied simple categorization as either heterosexual or homosexual. The writer and critic Carl Van Vechten, for example, was for over fifty years a doting, possessive, and sometimes violent husband to actress Fania Marinoff, despite his often hyperactive sexual pursuit of younger men. Chicago sociologist Harvey Warren Zorbaugh documented a similar complexity in the sexual life of a married woman, "indifferent to her husband," who allegedly leased a Towertown studio in order to "pos[e] as a homosexual and hav[e] a succession of violent affairs" with local women. When she ultimately "'fell' for the blond lion of the 'village'" and returned to a long-term relationship with a man, Zorbaugh disparagingly referred to the woman's lesbian relations as a "pose." But her "dramatic farewells featured by long, passionate kisses and embraces" with "former [female] 'flames'" suggest that she was not posing but exploiting the unconventionality of bohemia to negotiate desires that failed to fit neatly into any bifurcated sexual framework.[18]

Not all local residents, however, appreciated the shared sense of queerness that gender nonconformity and unconventionality afforded bohemians and homosexuals. When interviewed by a sociology student from the University of Chicago, several Dill Pickle Club patrons objected to being labeled homosexual simply because they frequented Towertown tearooms. Although "they ha[d] acquired a callous affrontry [sic], an 'I don't care' attitude," the student wrote, "when I untactfully asked one of the Dill Picklians if there was anything 'queer' about any of the members—all who heard me immediately bristled and angrily resented although they tried to laugh off my insinuation." Such insinuations were particularly problematic for the men of Towertown and the Village, whose memoirs are often characterized by recurring efforts to set themselves apart from the districts' "pansipoetical poets." Defending his love for a close male friend, Sherwood Anderson proclaimed that "the whole thing has nothing to do with a man's being, or not being, a fairy."

Yet the possibility that this relationship might have been interpreted as something other than heterosexual friendship prompted Anderson's literary executors to expurgate this entire passage from the posthumous publication of his memoir. Anderson expressed similar discomfort with homosexuality himself; the expurgated passage included an admission that he had "always been afraid of fairies. They sell you out. They are in some queer way outside the life stream. They know it. The male lover of the male is something else."[19]

Such attitudes echoed the ambivalence that many Towertown and Greenwich Village men expressed in relation to women's claims on sexual equality and the public expression of female sexual desire. In both cases, male radicals and artists were frequently torn between bohemian attempts to challenge and transform social norms and practices, including attitudes toward nonnormative sexualities, and the impulse to safeguard their traditional male privileges. But the bohemian discomfort with homosexuality was by no means limited to men. A number of bohemian women also expressed their distaste for the fairies who settled in their neighborhoods. In the wake of several unsuccessful relationships with Towertown men, sculptor Tennessee Mitchell was initially delighted when she stumbled upon "a group of young men who were interested in and intelligent about the arts, with whom I felt free to be friends with a sense of sureness that the element of sex would not be disrupting." But her attitude quickly soured when she learned that her new friends and neighbors preferred sex with men. Following this discovery, "I was only horrified and repelled," she noted in her unpublished autobiography, "and made no attempt to be intelligent."[20]

Fairies were not the only objects of such disdain in the bohemian world. By the mid-1920s, as the presence of "lady lovers" became more visible in the districts' tearooms and cafés, bohemian critics increasingly extended their enumeration of the vices that plagued bohemia to include lesbianism. In a letter to the literary journal that he had once edited, the "most veteran of Villagers," Bobby Edwards, proclaimed that "the *Quill* will be excellent when all such tiresome things as prostitutes, androgynes, gynanders, sex and vers libre are cut out." For Edwards and others, female and male homosexuality, prostitution, and even the bohemian staples of free love and free verse had, by the mid-1920s, become stains on the public perception of serious artistic endeavors in Towertown and the Village. But despite such remonstrations, all means of sexual and gender nonconformity continued to thrive in bohemian districts well into the 1930s, as artists and radicals furthered their challenge to white middle-class norms of social and sexual respectability and as gay men and lesbians took up even more visible residence in the enclaves that serious artists soon began to abandon.[21]

"Not what it seemed, but a composite of many dreams and fantasies": Bohemian Slumming as Social and Sexual Exploration

By the late 1910s, local slummers and out-of-town tourists flocked by the thousands to the tearooms and cabarets of Greenwich Village and Towertown, hoping to get a glimpse of "these people . . . w[h]om they have heard of as free lov[e]rs." Observing their excursions through Chicago's bohemian district, poet and novelist Maxwell Bodenheim noted that a number of these young pleasure seekers remained uneasy about their ventures, "laughing a little too loudly in an effort to simulate a sincere abandon, and trying hard to be reckless without committing themselves to any indecency." Unsure of exactly what they were supposed to see, some of the earliest "rubberneck contingent[s]" to the Village were so intent on spying sexual improprieties that, the *New York Times* reported, they often ended up "rubbering one another in the bland conviction that they were seeing vice in action." The numerous accounts of bohemian *thrillage* that appeared on newsstands across the country in magazines ranging from the *Bookman* and *Literary Digest* to *Vanity Fair* and the *Saturday Evening Post* multiplied such misperceptions. But these publications also generated a steady stream of curiosity seekers who hoped to sample in person the colorful atmosphere they had first encountered on the printed page.[22]

The inclusion of such articles in popular women's magazines had the added benefit of making slumming safe and accessible for women of all ages, even when no male escort was available to accompany them on their excursions. Just days after The Mad Hatter was depicted in a March 1920 feature about the Village, the tearoom's proprietor Helen Criswell noted that the "Lady Slummers who read the *Ladies' Home Journal* are swamping us." On one particular evening, "eleven fair young things came in a bunch & nearly deafened us with their fresh girlish laughter," Criswell later recalled in exasperation; on another, "quartets of old ladies infested [the] front room" of the basement resort. By June the tearoom was proving so popular with women slummers that the staff swore that, on one particularly "profitable . . . but exhausting" night, "forty thousand females from Maine & all points west were here, doing the Village." Safeguarding their reputations against the accusation of impropriety that still attached to women's solo ventures in urban public amusements, nearly all the single women who went slumming to the Mad Hatter and other bohemian resorts did so in groups. To do otherwise was to court potential disaster or at least the disdain of one's friends, as one young woman learned when she confessed to her slumming companions that she had been to the Mad Hatter before. "You don't mean you came here by yourself, do you?" her friends asked in "shoked [sic] tones."[23]

The frequent portrayal of bohemian tearooms and personalities in nationally distributed silent films further accelerated tourist traffic to the Village and Towertown. Cultural historian Jan Seidler Ramirez has noted that light-hearted romps in fictitious Village nightspots began to appear on screen by the mid-1910s and remained a popular motif well into the 1920s. Often shot on location on the streets and in the tearooms of Greenwich Village, features such as *The Trufflers* (1917), *The Broken Melody* (1919), *A Girl in Bohemia* (1919), *Toby's Bow* (1919), *Woman, Woman!* (1919), and *Harriet and the Piper* (1920), gave viewers a lively sample of bohemian unconventionality. Within the safety of their own neighborhood theaters, movie goers were introduced to realistic Village characters, including the fortune-telling Tea-Cup Ann of *Within the Cup* (1918), and they were escorted into imaginary Village cafés, such as the Black Beetle in *The Dangerous Moment* (1921) and the Purple Guinea Pig in *Smiling All the Way* (1920). Although these films often depicted bohemia as a perilous place, especially for unsophisticated single women and newcomers to the city, the spectacle of the cinema not only served to whet viewers' appetites for more bohemian *thrillage* but also encouraged them to extend their interest in such activities beyond mere spectatorship.[24]

Male slummers, in particular, swarmed the districts' tearooms and cafés in hot pursuit of "free-lovers of the Greenwich Village type." Bohemia developed such a reputation for being a spot where men could easily become acquainted with women that traveling businessmen, tourists, and suburbanites increasingly went to sample the district's sexual opportunities. A man who "live[d] up on the Heights" told an undercover investigator for New York's Committee of Fourteen that he had finally decided to "come down and take it in" for himself after some of his friends had "picked up a couple of girls and had a good time" in the Village. Likewise, in the spring of 1919, a member of the Secret Service escorted an unnamed U.S. senator and three of his male friends to look for female companionship at one of Webster Hall's famed masquerade balls. A recent crackdown on Village revelry had left the place "dead," however, prompting the officer to admit regretfully "that thanks to the Committee of Fourteen they would probably all depart without partners."[25]

Despite such occasional suppression, the tearooms and cafés of Towertown and Greenwich Village were favored cruising sites during the late 1910s and 1920s. Although some male slummers continued to frequent working-class venues to pick up charity girls and prostitutes for sexual encounters, the changing social and cultural landscape of U.S. cities shifted their attention to bohemia during this period. The closure of urban red-light districts in the mid-1910s and municipal authorities' subsequently intensified policing of working-class dance halls, especially "taxi-dance" halls where hostesses were paid by the dance, forced well-to-do white men to redirect their search for both paid and unpaid female sexual partners primarily toward either streetwalkers or the covert prostitutes and other sexually available women who frequented local cabarets. Under these conditions, the casual, often communal, atmosphere of bohemian tearooms and cabarets made them particularly useful places for meeting women. In these spaces, neither the management nor fellow patrons ordinarily objected if men and women moved from table to table, meeting new acquaintances. Moreover, at a time when working-class taxi dancers and charity girls were earning reputations, in the words of one disgruntled dance hall patron, as "gold-diggers, out to exploit the men as much as possible," the perceived willingness of bohemian women to have sex with little or no expectation of receiving money or gifts in exchange made them particularly appealing companions. Attributing the popularity of free love as much to its lack of cost as to its practice outside formal relationships, one Committee of Fourteen investigator noted, "There is much so-called free love down here. There are some girls in the Village who are as much women of the usual cabaret type only they do not receive money for the sexual act, differing only in this respect from an ordinary prostitute."[26]

The advantages of pursuing sexual encounters in bohemia extended far beyond matters of cost and convenience. White middle- and upper-class men perceived such encounters to be both socially and physically safer than those available in working-class resorts. This perception was due, in part, to the veneer of respectability that local nightspots lent to the men's sexual endeavors. Although visitors to Village tearooms might sense "something mysterious about [them]," as guidebook author Anna Alice Chapin did when stepping into the Purple Pup on Washington Square (figure 16), they generally agreed that the district's venues were "quite well conducted." But the greater sense of safety that male slummers associated with bohemian sexual pursuits likely owed even more to local women's reputed familiarity with birth control.[27]

16   This photograph by Jessie Tarbox Beals, "Dancing at Charley Reed's Purple Pup," shows
      bohemians and slummers in Greenwich Village. Located "in the basement of one of the
      really handsome houses" on Washington Square, the Purple Pup was described by guide-
      book author Anna Alice Chapin as "a queer little place" that was "quite well conducted,
      yet there is something mysterious about it." (Reprinted with permission from the Collec-
      tion of the New-York Historical Society, negative 41429.)

During the First World War, public health campaigns designed to
protect the country's soldiers and sailors routinely equated working-
class prostitutes and charity girls with the dangers of venereal disease.
Pamphlets and other educational materials urged men to avoid sexual
contact with such women or, at least, to protect themselves from infec-
tion by using condoms when engaging in sexual intercourse. In this
climate, bohemian women almost certainly seemed to be safer sexual
partners. The public sex forums and discussions in Village and Towertown
tearooms had so familiarized bohemian women with the benefits of
condoms and other birth-control devices that, as one social investigator
noted in 1917, "Any of the women of the Village will discuss sex and
birth control quite readily with her male escort." While reformers interpreted this behavior as a woman's misguided attempt to prove herself "a
modern girl or feminist or what not," in the minds of male slummers,

such actions established her as a safety-conscious sexual partner. A free-lover who discussed birth control, these men reasoned, was much less likely to harbor venereal disease than the prostitutes and charity girls who seemed less educated or concerned about such matters. Coupled with free-lovers' usually higher class status (as daughters of the white middle and upper classes), this presumption of greater sexual hygiene positioned bohemian women as some of the most desirable—and sexually available—women in Chicago and New York.[28]

The growing popularity of bohemian nightspots and male slummers' increasing fondness for the free-loving women who frequented them actually resulted in an influx of white working-class prostitutes into these spaces. In Chicago, well-known ladies of the evening were regular patrons at the famous Dill Pickle Club and other Towertown resorts. At the 606 Cabaret on North Clark Street, anti-vice investigators often spotted such women soliciting the nightspot's unaccompanied male patrons. Similar behavior was observed in the tearooms and cabarets of Greenwich Village. In fact, one investigator from New York's Committee of Fourteen suggested that savvy working-class prostitutes exploited the district's reputation for free love as a conscious cover for more illicit activities. "Some of the women, after dancing were sitting on tables, smok[ing] cigarettes and act[ing] as they would be real Bohemians," he noted in 1919, while attending the Black Parrot at 133 Washington Place, "but in fact they appeared to be professional prostitutes." What was apparent to the investigator was less clear to some unsuspecting patrons. Many of these women proved so successful in passing themselves off as bohemians that Village notables, such as the "soul candy" peddler "Tiny Tim" Felter, sometimes took it upon themselves to warn male pleasure seekers that the women they met in local tearooms were more likely to be "prostitutes who came from Broadway and the Times Square district" than the Village's famed free-lovers.[29]

Middle- and upper-class whites also consciously exploited this blurring of social types in the Village and Towertown, using a feigned interest in free love to conceal their more pressing desires for paid sexual companionship. In the popular tearoom located in the basement of the Brevoort hotel, at least one clever Village entrepreneur expertly exploited slummers' deceptions, serving as "a procurer, both for men and women" who visited the nightspot intending to purchase sex. In a similar fashion, slummers also manipulated the free-love reputation of bohemia to mask their extramarital affairs. In a statement echoed by many others in Chicago and New York, an informant told Zorbaugh that "business and professional men use [Towertown's] studio apartments to keep their mistresses." Moreover, the "anything goes" atmosphere of these districts provided effective cover for the May-December relationships that blossomed among middle- and upper-class women and men during the cabaret era. Author Maxwell Bodenheim noted that bohemia drew both "the business-man who sees an opportunity to capture young women by pretending to be overawed at the mention of art, [and] the lady of advanced years who is hunting for a gaudy Indian-Summer of the senses." Indeed, "many men of fourty [*sic*] and over who came stag" could be found at Village and Towertown masquerades and tearooms "picking out the younger girls to dance with."[30]

But the bohemian sensibility was, perhaps, even more successfully exploited by female slummers who desired younger, often paid, male escorts. From the late 1910s, hordes of "young men with thirty-five-year-old women" were a staple of the bohemian tearooms of Chicago's Near North Side, and this trend was soon replicated in New York. At a popular Village hideaway, British author Stephen Graham recalled meeting a middle-aged woman from Kansas City who "asked us to realise that she was risking a home and husband for this one night" on the town—a night that would have been far from complete in her estimation had she not "danc[ed] with all the Italians" in the club, while "twiddling her gartered knee, and shewing the undulatory elegancies of her person."[31]

The public toleration of such relationships in Greenwich Village and Towertown was due, in large part, to the growing expectation that women visited these neighborhoods specifically to challenge social and sexual mores. Novels and short stories by resident writers popularized the notion that, in the Village, according to the heroine of Dorothy Day's *The Eleventh Virgin* (1924), "anything short of absolute promiscuity is disregarded, as long as you can speak of sexual relationships as love affairs." The increased sexual freedom that this formulation afforded to women opened a unique space in bohemian resorts where female slummers could approach unknown men without damaging their reputations. James A. Seaman, a medical student who moonlighted as an investigator for New York's Committee of Fourteen, reported that a large number of respectable "girls living with their families" attended a Liberal Club masquerade in early 1917, "danc[ing] with anyone, for every one was there for a good time." Despite their unusually forward social and sexual behavior, however, Seaman chose to ignore the requests of "at least a half dozen of them [who] asked me to call on them sometime," not because he considered them any less respectable than more subdued and chaste middle-class women, but because "they seemed so much the silly N.Y. type that goes to the theatre and pink teas."[32]

Other well-to-do white women went slumming in bohemia for expressly sexual purposes. Like their male counterparts, these women were often drawn by a desire to participate in free love or, at the very least, to share some level of physical intimacy with the writers and artists who called bohemia home. One such woman was Eve Blue, a University of Chicago undergraduate from nearby suburban Flossmoor who eventually married the renowned psychologist B. F. Skinner. As a high school student, Blue was fascinated by the daringness of Towertown's "Bohemian restaurants" where "the motley crowds all reek of adventure," but by the time she enrolled in college, her fascination with bohemia had become thoroughly sexualized. Gaining entrée to Chicago's 57th Street art colony, she quickly set out to meet the district's male artists, kissing the first painter of her acquaintance. While her easy physical intimacy with the colony's men initially made Blue feel she was "a lousy person," she resolved that she "was interested in seeing real Bohemian life" and that doing so demanded her participation in "the greatest American sport." On her next visit to the colony, she recalled that she "let six men kiss me—and so forth." And Blue was not unique in her pursuits. While living in Chicago's Towertown during the early 1920s, poet Kenneth Rexroth met "two stenographers from Milwaukee" who had moved to bohemia with the express purpose of losing their virginity. Failing in their initial attempts to accomplish this goal, they decided to make one last, concerted effort. After downing an aphrodisiac that they had acquired from a local druggist, the women set off "all around bohemia [to] see if somebody real nice wouldn't pick us up."[33]

In the eyes of local reformers, such behavior provided evidence that one of their worst fears was actually coming to pass: the bohemian challenge to social and sexual norms was transforming the behavior of white middle- and upper-class young women, as well as that of young men. One of the most visible signs of this transformation was the adoption of bohemian fashions by young women around the country who bobbed their hair, donned shorter skirts, and began wearing cosmetics on a regular basis. These women further unsettled local authorities by following their bohemian counterparts in demanding equal rights with men, including the right, as historian Paula Fass notes, to "enjoy the same vulgar habits and ultimately . . . the same vices as men." One undercover anti-vice investigator complained, "Many of the girls [in the Village] smoke cigarettes because they have a right to . . . [and they] boast of being unconventional." For such women, the act of sipping a cocktail or lighting up a tightly rolled cigarette were conscious assertions of both their social equality and their sexual allure.[34]

Local authorities were even more alarmed by the presence of collegiate and even some high school–age slummers who ventured into the dark, often candle-lit nightspots of Towertown and the Village in hopes of imitating the public intimacy they associated with bohemian free love. At Towertown's Wind Blew Inn, located in a building that was not even wired for electricity (figure 17), the police spotted "numerous 'petting parties' in progress . . . most of whom were students of Northwestern university on a 'slumming party.'" New York authorities reported similar activities at the Black Cat in Greenwich Village, where "uptowners who came down there for a good time" apparently "felt that they could do anything they pleased." "There was general singing by the entire crowd," Committee of Fourteen investigator Florence Rose reported. "Men were changing tables. Women were leaning all over men and there was a general mix-up with kissing, etc."[35]

Local press reports that such experimentation with free love was rapidly eroding youthful innocence spurred vigorous campaigns to clean up the Village and Towertown. Police raids and the padlocking of nightspots violating Prohibition became a recurring feature of bohemian nightlife during the early 1920s. If legal loopholes allowed resorts to survive concerted efforts at regulation, local authorities sometimes adopted more imaginative tactics to discourage respectable white youths and adults from pursuing their search for bohemian *thrillage*. In New York, the police routinely ticketed the automobiles that slummers parked outside popular resorts, providing judges with an opportunity to call the cars' owners into traffic court to chastise them for attending such places. "Didn't you feel ashamed of yourself for [visiting the cabaret]?" magistrate Frederick B. House asked one young man who had been hauled into his court during the summer of 1921 to settle a parking violation he received just outside the Village's famed Pirate's Den. "I sure did Your Honor," the man obligingly replied, "it was long enough for me."[36]

In Chicago, authorities sometimes resorted to even more radical techniques, arresting every person present in the offending cabaret and releasing their names for publication in the *Chicago Tribune* and other local newspapers. In the most dramatic example of this particular practice, local authorities apprehended 122 "fashionably garbed . . . society folk, artists' models, actresses, prominent business men and club fellows" during a July 1923 raid on the Tent, located at 1021 North State Street. Police chief Morgan A. Collins later apologized to society matrons and their children for any embarrassment they might have suffered as a result of the raid. But the publicity that it generated, including courtroom photographs and stories documenting the long night

17   The Wind Blew Inn was located in this ramshackle wood frame house at 116 East Ohio
      Street in Chicago during the early 1920s. Lacking electricity, proprietor Lillian Colley lit
      this cozy tearoom with candles—a practice that made the darkened nightspot popular
      with slummers and "petting parties," but ultimately spelled its demise. After closing one
      night in April 1922, the building burned to the ground. (Reprinted with permission of the
      Chicago History Museum Archives, ICHi-38689.)

these fashionable detainees spent in an East Chicago Avenue court, provided dramatic, if only temporarily effective, deterrents to such slumming
expeditions.[37]

In truth, the dangers that slummers allegedly faced on their visits to
the Village and Towertown proved largely illusory. After conducting an

undercover study of the Village during the late 1910s, Dr. I. L. Nascher told the general secretary of New York's Committee of Fourteen that there was "a lot of sham and fake in the village for the benefit of the uptown slummer crowd," but it was largely harmless—"about as dangerous as a Sunday school side show." While diagnosing "real Bohemians" with a "form of insanity" called esthesiomania, Nascher found little to suggest that slummers, or even the "shambos who imitate and exaggerate [their] eccentricities . . . to gain notoriety," were in danger of catching the malaise that stripped "real Bohemians" of their sense of ambition and their ability to "adjust themselves to the restrictions upon behavior imposed by society." Writing for the *New York Times*, Charles J. Rosebault came to a similar conclusion about "the rumpus in Greenwich Village." Watching a young woman in her twenties "moving from one garish dive to the other—under safe escort, of course—and revealing in her glistening eyes her faith that this incursion into a flamboyant world was 'seeing life,'" Rosebault became convinced that bohemia and free love constituted a relatively harmless amusement for slummers. "The Village was not what it seemed," he reported, "but a composite of many dreams and fantasies."[38]

Some well-to-do white women and men clearly used their bohemian excursions to experiment sexually with free-lovers and prostitutes, but for the most part, slumming reified bohemianism and free love as exotic, undesirable extremes. During the late 1910s and early 1920s, when the new urban phenomenon of dating began to replace chaperoned socializing among white middle-class youths, the quest for bohemian *thrillage* provided the perfect counterpoint for establishing new social and sexual norms. In direct contrast with the casual promiscuity of the free-loving bohemians, slummers usually made their visits in discrete couples as part of a "private act" of courtship—to borrow historian Beth Bailey's formulation—"conducted in the public world." Although this tendency toward public intimacy may have unsettled middle-class parents and social reformers, when juxtaposed with the bohemian stereotype of promiscuous free love, it seemed decidedly tame.[39]

Well-to-do white youths challenged traditional conceptions of proper social and sexual behavior, but they did so in ways that constructed new boundaries of propriety separating respectable young women and men from free-loving bohemians. For instance, although parents and reformers usually assumed that petting necessarily led to sexual intercourse, sociological studies conducted during the 1920s suggest that youths often thought of the practice as a sort of safety valve. "Very many girls draw a distinct line between the exploratory activities of the petting party and complete yielding of sexual favors to men," sociologists Phyllis Blanchard and Carlyn Manasses concluded from their survey of 252 female college students and working girls. Even when affluent white youths did indulge in premarital sexual intercourse, free love still provided a useful contrast for their activities. Unlike bohemian women and men who were assumed to hop from one bed to another, the so-called respectable women who went slumming usually restricted sexual intercourse to their most serious relationships, often only after they had become officially engaged. Even then, middle-class women remained acutely aware of the double standard which penalized them for premarital sexual involvement. Blanchard and Manasses found that only "seven per cent were willing to permit themselves indulgence in extra-marital intercourse."[40]

Young men might take their girlfriends on bohemian slumming expeditions in hopes that the sexually charged atmosphere would excite their companions, while simultaneously naturalizing their romantic exploits in contrast to the supposed licentiousness of bohemia. Certainly, Eve Blue's experiences made the desire to participate in premarital sexual intercourse seem more natural to her. After engaging in heavy petting with several writers and painters in Chicago's 57th Street art colony, Blue became intent on experiencing sexual intercourse. Nevertheless, she distinguished her own sexual experiences from free love, turning down several offers to sleep with bohemian men, some of them already married and all of them apparently quite sexually active, in favor of losing her virginity with a fellow college student. Although she was "not at all in love with him nor he with me," the fact that both were outsiders on a pleasure-hunting lark in Chicago's bohemian studios placed them on more equal ground, rendering the young scholar a much safer sexual prospect than the free-love-them-and-leave-them Lotharios of the art colony.[41]

The cumulative result of thousands of such slumming experiences in bohemia effected the broadening acceptance of the new middle- and upper-class social phenomenon of dating, which increasingly included petting and even occasional premarital sex. Moreover, as popular conceptions of sex were further detached from reproduction, more middle-class couples acknowledged and explored female sexuality and sexual pleasure. Although these emerging practices established the foundation of what has come to be known as heterosexuality, during the bohemian slumming craze of the late 1910s and early 1920s, people did not yet identify themselves or their sexual desires along a hetero/homo sexual axis. Most people, including those who participated in bohemian slumming expeditions, remained largely unaware of such terms and what they represented: mutually exclusive sexual categories that were organized around the sex of one's desired sexual object. Rather, sexuality continued to be marked primarily by an individual's gender performance and by the gendered role one played in particular sexual acts—especially among men.

The interactions of male slummers with the fairies who frequented the tearooms and masquerade balls of Greenwich Village and Towertown provided a vivid display of this continuing gendered sexual hierarchy, thereby reinforcing its cultural dominance. An undercover investigator from New York's Committee of Fourteen noted that the fairies who attended Webster Hall dances were "looked upon as a disgusting laughing stock by those other guests," but it was their gender—particularly in relation to so-called normal men—rather than their sexuality which made them the center of attention. While some female slummers thought "it was silly" that fairies arrived at these balls in "female attire" and danced with each other, the male slummers who attended these events often did so specifically to emphasize the gendered differences that distinguished them from bohemia's feminized third-sexers. According to one anti-vice investigator, at every Village ball, "groups of younger men" could be found who "pick[ed] out these perverts and ma[d]e them goats all the evening," drawing attention to their femininity by "calling them girl's names" and mocking them, "affecting an air of effeminacy," and "making all kinds of feminine appeals to them." On occasion, slummers—including undercover anti-vice investigators—even resorted to violence to draw a gendered distinction between their "normal" masculinity and the feminine "perversion" of third-sexers. At the Golden Ball of Isis in February 1917, when one particularly aggressive fairy "began rubbing his hand up my leg . . . doing the same with anyone who came near him," James A. Seaman reported, "I gave him a shove which sent him over against the other wall," thus making the boundary between men and fairies quite explicit.[42]

Similar harassment and violence directed toward fairies and cross-dressed men had been commonplace for years, but in the Bowery and the Levee, it took place primarily on the streets and only more rarely inside those venues where third-sexers performed for thrill-seeking patrons. During the popular search for bohemian *thrillage*, however, young male slummers mistreated fairies much more publicly, harassing them as they entertained in Village and Towertown nightspots and as they attempted to enjoy themselves within the relatively tolerant confines of bohemian masquerades. In part, this change in treatment served to reinforce the normalcy of those men who continued to accept sexual favors from fairies in an era when such exchanges became increasingly suspect. For in the midst of the "catcalling and imitation female calling," one Committee of Fourteen investigator noted, a "few young men in evening clothes" danced with fairies at every Village ball, hoping that their partners would ask them "down stairs that very evening [to] practice their homosexuality." At a time when few female prostitutes—and almost no respectable women—willingly performed fellatio, fairies remained a rare treat for men desiring oral service. For this reason, the men who went slumming in Towertown and the Village, including soldiers and sailors warned away from working-class women by the government's World War I campaigns against venereal disease, often referred to fairies—sometimes even affectionately—as "blowers."[43]

In fact, fairies often found their encounters with male slummers and bohemians to be both sexually and financially lucrative. During the early 1920s, sociologist Nels Anderson watched a "well-dressed young fellow" wander through the crowd at Towertown's Grey Cottage, "talk[ing] only with the men." For the going rate of $2, this young man later informed Anderson, he plied his trade according to the gendered dynamic which shaped popular conceptions of sex, "play[ing] either the active or the passive role . . . cater[ing] to trade that might be one way or the other." Soliciting in bohemian dives, "along the lake front, in the parks, along Michigan Boulevard, and in the art gallery," this hustler claimed that he was able to support himself quite readily, noting that "You'd be surprised how many of these artists are fagging." Male prostitutes also engaged in the risky business of cruising the streets and cabarets of Greenwich Village, searching for male slummers and bohemians willing to pay for their sexual favors. In late June 1924, while masquerading as an Uptown pleasure seeker, police detective Edgar X. Frost stumbled upon one such gentleman who invited him to visit a tearoom at 41 Greenwich Avenue for the purpose of having sex. Finding all the upstairs rooms occupied, the hustler allegedly paid the tearoom's manager Leon Mirabeau for the use of his toilet, an act that prompted the arrest of both Mirabeau and the male prostitute for "lewdness and assignation."[44]

"There is a fine distinction between slummers and visitors": Bohemians Respond to the Tourist Trade

Residents of Towertown and the Village astutely played to middle- and upper-class visitors' expectations about free love. "I give them the high brow stuff until the crowd begins to grow thin," Dill Pickle Club proprietor

Jack Jones remarked during the late 1910s, "and then I turn on the sex." Jones advertised lectures and debates on topics such as "Women That I Have Trifled With," "Men Who Have Approached Us," and a discussion by "Bohemia's Noted Man-Killers" to entice Chicago's wealthier residents to visit his resort. "That," bouncer Slim Brundage later remarked, "was to pay the rent. Back then, you couldn't get sex at any newsstand or movie house so you stepped high, stooped and squeezed into the Dil [*sic*] Pickle, to catch up on it." According to the Committee of Fourteen, similar motives prompted several "Greenwich Villagers" to begin "exploiting the Bohemianism of the neighborhood" after they realized that their occasional masquerades at Webster Hall were becoming quite popular with uptown slummers. Throwing balls almost every weekend, the organizers of these events were soon clearing profits as high as $600 per dance.[45]

Bohemia's female entrepreneurs also attempted to cash in on the district's reputation for unconventionality. In Towertown, a "group of young women writers" led tours of curious slummers through the area's resorts and "studios bizarrely decorated for the occasion" at a cost of "seventy-five cents a head." Tearoom hostess Adele Kennedy (figure 18) and a woman calling herself "Mademoiselle de Maupassant" conducted similar excursions in the Village, advertising their services in local publications, such as *The Quill*, or with flyers distributed at area cabarets. While these women focused on the general oddities of bohemia, introducing slummers to more trinket shops than scandalous nightspots, others promoted the sexual freedom of the neighborhood for their personal gain. At the Black Parrot Tea Shoppe Hobo-Hemia on Charles Street, for instance, Lucy Smith and Patricia Rogers attempted to boost the slumming trade by offering a sexual circus of women and men, including a female impersonator "familiarly known in the village as 'Ruby.'" Before the performance could get underway, however, it was interrupted by two undercover detectives who arrested the women proprietors and Ruby, as well as ten other male and female participants, on charges of disorderly conduct and incorrigibility.[46]

Clearly, women balanced such risks against the relative freedom they enjoyed in bohemia. Betty Seldes and Réné LaCoste, whom one Committee of Fourteen investigator labeled "regular village prostitutes high brow supposedly; but very low brow," sponsored a number of commercial masquerades at Webster Hall. Positioning themselves as the center of male attention at these events, they claimed first dibs on any free or paid sexual encounters that they desired. Still other women artists and performers exploited the desires of slummers in Towertown and the Village by becoming charity girls, putting the price of small gifts on the "free"

ADELE KENNEDY
THE ONLY GUIDE TO GREENWICH VILLAGE _ NEW YORK.

18   Adele Kennedy was one of the most popular slumming guides in Greenwich Village, where she conducted curiosity seekers on tours of local tearooms, studios, and craft shops during the late 1910s and early 1920s. She is pictured here in one of the postcards of popular Village personalities and tearooms that were produced by photographer Jessie Tarbox Beals for sale to tourists and other slummers who longed to share their adventures with the folks back home. (Reprinted with permission from the Collection of the New-York Historical Society, 78886d.)

love they shared with acquaintances. Bobby Edwards parodied such women in *The Quill*: "Because I love pretty things and nice underwear," the fictional dancer Zippy Flynn was made to remark, "I have to depend on the slummers in the Brevoort for my needs." In reality, as slummers moved into bohemia, they pushed up the rents on local studios, thus increasing the financial pressure on women residents who thereby became more reliant on "charity" for their necessities.[47]

Edwards intended his portrayal of Zippy Flynn primarily as entertainment, but it provided a more authentic description of the social conditions facing bohemian women than the author realized. For in its parodic and even moralistic tone, it gave a pitch-perfect representation of the double standard that most free-loving women encountered from bohemian men. Although male residents often chastised their female counterparts for being too quick to succumb to the sexual advances of male slummers, many of these same men gladly seized every opportunity to exploit the women who visited bohemia. William Targ readily accepted the offer of a beautiful "Eurasian girl" who asked him to "make love" in his Towertown bookstore, while Villager Harry Kemp confessed to being "always on the quest," landing "numerous erotic adventures . . . most of them not outlasting three revolutions of the hour-hand of the clock." Should they encounter resistance from their prey, bohemian men usually had at the ready well-rehearsed lines that played on the stereotype of free love. When Chicagoan Eve Blue expressed her discomfort at making out with a married painter in his 57th Street studio, the artist promptly countered that his wife was not an issue. "We're not domesticated," he insisted.[48]

To lure women into their beds, bohemian men also exploited their exotic reputation as artists and writers. One Village character, referred to pseudonymously as "Peter Pan," claimed to have employed this method in seducing nearly "1,000 different women," many of them well-to-do slummers. "His technique was simple," Dr. Ben L. Reitman recalled. "He would dance with a strange wom[a]n, have a few drinks with her and say, 'I have a wonderful studio around the corner and some pictures you'd like to see.' That was all there was to it." In fact, the men of the Village and Towertown claimed that female slummers were so gullible that they could be easily convinced to provide financial support to amorous artists and writers. According to Floyd Dell, "any tenth-rate free-verse poet" in Towertown or Greenwich Village "could find a capable and efficient stenographer to type his manuscripts, buy his clothes, pay his rent, and sleep with him." Unbothered by assuming a position analogous to the charity girls they often scorned, bohemian men proudly accepted such domestic and financial support. In his memoirs, the writer Harold Stearns recalled that, while living in the Village during the 1920s, a female fashion designer paid his bills, cooked his meals, and occasionally bought him clothes, "as if it were the most natural thing in the world."[49]

The positioning of bohemia as a sexualized space inevitably took a toll on the neighborhood. Female residents were subject to frequent, and often unwelcome, sexual propositions from both slummers and local men. As independent women, they became practiced at fending for themselves, repulsing unwanted advances or, at the very least, controlling the situations under which they agreed to meet potential suitors. An undercover investigator at a Webster Hall masquerade reported that the woman he was trying to "date up" adamantly "refused to give me her home address," telling him instead that "she comes into the Black Cat restaurant almost every night" and could meet him there if he wanted to pursue things further. On other occasions, however, bohemian women were clearly imperiled by their neighborhood's free-love reputation—a reputation that, some men believed, rendered the women of Towertown and Greenwich Village fair game for any sexual exploit. While escorting the proprietor of Zina's Restaurant on her way home from the MacDougal Street resort, Committee of Fourteen investigator Harry Kahan was approached by five local Italian men "inten[ding] to 'line her up'" for a gang rape. Quick maneuvering allowed Zina and Kahan to escape physical harm, but the incident reflected the risk of sexual violence female bohemians faced.[50]

As hordes of white pleasure seekers poured into bohemia looking for sexualized entertainment, the women and men who lived in Greenwich Village and Towertown greeted them with conflicting messages. To the districts' most serious artists and radicals, the appearance of slumming parties—and the crass commercialization and rising rents they brought with them—spelled the death of bohemia. These disillusioned writers, painters, and intellectuals abandoned the studios of Towertown and the Village by the scores, heading off for Paris and Hollywood or disappearing into the quieter (even suburban) neighborhoods of Chicago and New York to pursue their work. Writer Charles Hanson Towne noted that the "gay little restaurants, filled with struggling artists and poets," quickly lost their appeal with serious bohemians as they were "spoiled by trippers and became nothing but professional show-places," marked by "a drab attempt to be naughty and wicked." By the mid-1920s, editor Samuel Putnam recalled, few major literary or artistic figures could be found in these districts. "The essentially bourgeois-escapist character [they] had always had was now visible and becoming all the more accentuated," he remarked. "The creative atmosphere of the old . . . days was gone forever."[51]

But other bohemians welcomed at least some visitors to Towertown and the Village. Both neighborhoods were filled with male and female entrepreneurs who depended upon the patronage of outsiders to support their literary and artistic enterprises, as well as their restaurants and tearooms. "There is a fine distinction between slummers and visitors," the editor of one Greenwich Village literary journal noted. "We welcome visitors. We have much that they will appreciate: Our quaint streets and old houses, our charming theatre, our gift shops and our really distinctive restaurants and coffee houses." But the "slummers [who] demanded showplaces, 'atmosphere,' local color, etc." were decidedly less welcome. The proprietors of the Wine Cellar at MacDougal and Third streets in the Village admitted "the ultra-Ritz from Pawk Avenoon [*sic*]," Villager Harry Kemp recalled, but when "one fellow climbed unsteadily onto a table and began shouting a toast . . . up came Tony waving a towel as if it were a horsewhip. 'You shut up—you get out!' he growled," hustling "those spats-and-canes" out the door while they "begged him for permission to buy another round of drinks."[52]

Even Jack Jones, the usually gregarious proprietor of the Dill Pickle Club, sometimes lost his patience with the antics of Chicago's wealthy Gold Coast crowd, especially when they became more explicitly sexual. Referring to the 1920s fad of transplanting "monkey glands" into men to increase their sexual potency, Jones complained that "since the gland craze has struck the rich, they are turning bohemia into a madhouse." Arriving at the Dill Pickle Club (figure 19) loud, drunk, and lecherous, these well-to-do slummers increasingly upset the club's regular patrons with sexual advances and displays far more crude than any exhibited by Towertown's free-lovers. "The actions of the flapper and the jelly bean scions of our social and industrial kings," one local tabloid reported, "are shocking the aesthetic souls of our budding artists, poets, authors and other members of the intellectual mob." Responding to patrons' complaints, Jones adopted a temporarily hard-line stance against such rowdy behavior, demanding that slummers cease using bohemia as a playground for their own sexual pleasure. "Let them pull their stunts at the Casino or some other joint," he insisted, directing slummers back to the mainstream cabarets of the Loop. "I'll have no monkeyshines in this place."[53]

Occasionally, bohemians became so desperate to mute the social and sexual excesses of the slumming trade that they were even willing to put aside their general disdain for local authorities. In September 1920, Village resident Dolly Lewis agreed to cooperate with the New York Police Department and the Committee of Fourteen when they launched a joint crackdown on local prostitution. Despite the fact that she called herself "Bohemian and has no objection, that girls and boys have intercourse, because every girl must be ruined once in her life," Lewis's

19 The Dill Pickle Club, owned and operated by former IWW radical Jack Jones, was easily the most popular bohemian tearoom in Towertown. It attracted hordes of curious slummers from its founding in 1915 until its closure in 1932. This slang-ridden original watercolor poster by an unknown artist played up the tearoom's popularity with pleasure-seeking flappers and their dandified beaux, while subtly mocking the nightspot's manufactured atmosphere of poverty through its depiction of discarded tin cans on the dance floor. (Reprinted with permission from the collection of the Newberry Library.)

toleration for unconventionality had its limits. If slummers and prostitutes insisted on "hav[ing] intercourse in [the] yard right in front of her eyes," she resolved that she had no alternative but to offer her second-floor apartment as a lookout for investigators working to terminate such activities. Residents at Towertown's famed Tree Studio Building sought similar intervention at the Classic Café, located across Ohio Street from their apartments. In letters to the police superintendent and Chicago's reform-minded mayor William E. Dever during the autumn of 1923, they complained that "people are coming and going from this café every night until two or three o'clock," talking and laughing loudly, and occasionally breaking into "fist fights, calling and screaming" and generally making it impossible for area residents to get a good night's sleep. Coming in the midst of Dever's campaign to clean up Chicago's illicit nightlife, the letters provided the very excuse the mayor needed to order an investigation of yet another Near North Side cabaret. Within a day of receiving the residents' letters, police investigators seized "six quart bottles of whiskey, gin and wine" at the Classic Café and issued an immediate request to revoke the cabaret's license.[54]

Race in Bohemia

Although bohemia served primarily as a space in which sexual mores were challenged and new constructions of sexual normativity and deviance emerged, the tearooms and studios of Towertown and Greenwich Village also provided places where racial difference was contested and reformulated. Bohemians' involvement in radical politics and artistic pursuits prompted them to traduce the boundaries of racial otherness that permeated U.S. culture. While nativist urban workers and progressivists perpetuated the racialization of southern and eastern Europeans both by campaigning for immigration quotas and by encouraging the physical segregation of those immigrants who settled in American cities, bohemian artists and radicals generally rebuffed such racist tactics. Living in or near predominantly Italian neighborhoods in New York's Greenwich Village and on Chicago's Near North Side, they became frequent patrons at many of the districts' Italian-run resorts, fraternizing with the very immigrants who drew nativist ire. Moreover, bohemians heartily welcomed eastern and southern European writers, musicians, socialists, and anarchists into their inner circles. Harvard-educated intellectuals, including the bookseller and publisher Albert Boni and writers John Reed and Hutchins Hapgood, frequently dined with Jewish immigrant radicals, such as Emma Goldman, Alexander Berkman, and Hippolyte Havel, at the renowned Liberal Club and other popular Village resorts. In Chicago, bohemian and immigrant intellectuals and artists also socialized together, many of them gathering at the Thursday night salons of Jacob Loeb, a prominent Jewish insurance broker (and uncle of Richard Loeb who, along with Nathan Leopold, became national criminal-celebrities in the spring of 1924), or in Towertown tearooms, including the Dill Pickle Club and the Green Mask. Focusing on shared artistic and political pursuits, such interactions subverted the segregation faced by most Italian and Jewish immigrants in early-twentieth-century New York and Chicago.[55]

Bohemian artists and radicals sometimes employed similar tactics to challenge the segregation of urban blacks. Although blacks were actively excluded from many of the studios and tearooms of Towertown and the Village, several enterprising white bohemians created spaces where black artists, musicians, and radicals could meet freely with their white counterparts. Throughout the 1920s, Harlem Renaissance artist and writer Richard Bruce Nugent continuously migrated between Harlem and the Village, living and socializing with a variety of artists in both communities, while Jamaican-born author Claude McKay received a similar welcome in New York's radical political circles, joining *The Liberator*, a Village journal of revolutionary art and protest, as associate editor and striking up important, long-lasting friendships with Crystal and Max Eastman and Louise Bryant, among others.[56]

In the Windy City, Kenneth Rexroth recalled that the black and white mistresses of "Chicago's leading Negro banker" were responsible for bringing "a lot of South Side high society, music, and underworld" to Towertown's Green Mask, a tearoom that was also frequented by notable black talents, such as Bert Williams, Lil Hardin Armstrong, Alberta Hunter, Fenton Johnson, Langston Hughes, and Countée Cullen. Jack Jones also used art and politics to promote racial mixing at his Dill Pickle Club. On the September night in 1921 when the club hosted Reformed Episcopal Bishop Samuel Fallows's public denunciation of the Ku Klux Klan, the *Chicago Tribune* reported that a "third of the audience were Negro men and women." Likely among them was the black communist leader Harry Haywood, who recalled meeting both black and white radicals among the speakers and patrons in Tooker Alley when he attended the Dill Pickle's "radical forums and lectures" accompanied by members of his "discussion circle" of fellow black postal employees.[57]

The interracial environment created in bohemian studios and resorts spawned a number of cross-racial political and artistic collaborations, even encouraging the flowering of several cross-racial romances. Chicago bohemian Edna Dexter Fine recalled that a "brilliant Negro" named Claude, who often entertained the patrons of the Dill Pickle Club with "his pyrotechnics in mathematics and logic," took up with "a Russian girl" whom he met in the nightspot's audience. Likewise, in 1924, a Jewish waitress at this same tearoom was said to have leased a Towertown studio to share with Bob Crenshaw, a black activist in the Industrial Workers of the World and a regular Dill Pickler to boot. Following the lead of bohemian artists and radicals, middle- and upper-class white slummers also romanced the black, Jewish, and Italian Americans whom they met in the tearooms of bohemia. Jewish poet Lester Cohen, for instance, first became acquainted with "the North Shore society girl who married him" at Towertown's Dill Pickle. "My, how her relatives carried on," Edna Dexter Fine recalled, "and what capital the newspapers made of the story." Even as the local press cited Cohen's relationship as an example of the perils of racial mixing that awaited slummers in Towertown tearooms, Fine suggested that such stories served mainly to boost the popularity of bohemian resorts. "What publicity we got!" she joyfully remembered.[58]

Indeed, far from detracting from the appeal of bohemia, the racial mixing in Towertown and Village resorts—especially that between native-born whites and Italian and Jewish immigrants—seemed more often to heighten their appeal by combining the allure of bohemian sexual nonconformity with slummers' earlier fascination with immigrant working-class spaces and cultures. In Chicago and New York, several tearoom proprietors sought to capitalize on this combination, infusing their resorts with a racialized flavor. Along North Clark Street in Towertown, Turkish, Greek, and Syrian entrepreneurs marketed their coffeehouses to both bohemians and slummers by featuring strong Turkish coffee, narghiles, and belly dancers, while in the Village, a Native American man opened the "Sioux T. Room" in a basement at 72 Sixth Avenue. Russian waitresses and dancers also became prominent fixtures in several resorts, including the Village's Band Box, located in a basement at the corner of Sixth Avenue and West Third Street in New York, and Towertown's Dill Pickle Club. Middle- and upper-class whites' enchantment with the exotic, racialized elements of bohemia became so pronounced that by the late 1910s, at least some Villagers chose to exaggerate their racial identities—or even created new ones from whole cloth—to market their wares more successfully to thrill-seeking tourists. When Ella Breistein (also known as Eleanor Brandt) opened a cigarette shop at 174 West 4th Street, for example, she became "Sonia, the Russian 'Cigarette Girl,'" gaining renown for her bobbed hair and hand-rolled smokes, despite her inability to speak a single word of Russian. Similarly, Romanian Jewish immigrant Marie Marchand exchanged the Yiddish of her childhood for a heavier accent and large hoop earrings, dubbing herself "Romany Marie" and employing "colorful trappings, fortune-telling, and Gypsy music" to enhance the popularity of her Village tearoom.[59]

Although Romany Marie reportedly adopted her new persona, in part, to escape the Red Scare tactics that resulted in the December 1919 deportation of her political mentor Emma Goldman, her bohemian performance of racial otherness served only to solidify the growing public perception of Greenwich Village and Towertown as un-American caldrons of radicalism and iniquity. In the aftermath of the First World War, as U.S. attorney general A. Mitchell Palmer fanned the flames of a national anti-radical panic, native-born white bohemians increasingly found themselves facing the same local and federal surveillance that threatened to overwhelm entire communities of southern and eastern European immigrants in Chicago and New York. In fact, the popular linkage of such immigrant groups with bohemians became so potent that critics of the Village and Towertown began to regard these neighborhoods as thoroughly foreign districts. In September 1919, Bronx Supreme Court justice John M. Tierney insisted that the so-called moral deterioration of Greenwich Village was due entirely to suspect alien influences. "I am astonished at the people and the change of character that the neighborhood has undergone," he told spectators in his courtroom. "These disgusting and debauching conditions cannot be traced to native New Yorkers. They have been introduced by people who came over from the old world."[60]

Although native-born white artists and radicals usually minimized the importance of racial differences in Towertown and the Village, in this era of rising nativism, more recent arrivals often felt compelled to obscure their immigrant status before bohemians and slummers alike. June Wiener, the Jewish proprietor of Chicago's Green Mask and, later, New York's Wind Blew Inn (which she named after the Towertown establishment), adopted the anglicized name June Carter to downplay her ethnicity among patrons and friends. Likewise, the Polish immigrant proprietor of the Grey Cottage in Towertown and Eve's Hangout in the Village transformed her given name, Eva Kotchever (or Eve Czlotcheber), into Eve Addams. Other immigrants adopted similar strategies in an effort to blend into the white American middle-class fabric of bohemia, severing ties with their own cultural traditions. After moving to Towertown, the American-born daughter of an Orthodox Russian immigrant couple, for instance, "discarded her Jewish name," Natalie Feinberg, in favor of the more American-sounding moniker Jean Farway. Yet finding that a simple name change was insufficient to win full acceptance among the native-born residents of the district, she further ingratiated herself into bohemian life by working at a radical bookstore, waiting tables at a Towertown café, and modeling for a local art class. "Attempting to outdo the older members in unconventionality," an observer from the University of Chicago noted, Feinberg/Farway even "began to talk of 'free love'" and to have "free relationships with several different men," using sex to prove her bohemianism, and thus her Americanness, in the face of persistent nativist sentiments.[61]

By the mid-1920s, however, such attempts to blend in with bohemians were increasingly unnecessary for many eastern and southern European immigrants. Although they were still not accepted as equals among most native-born white bohemians and slummers, their own growing presence *as* slummers in the bohemian districts of New York and Chicago worked against their designation as racialized others. The swelling crowds of women and men coming "from Brooklyn and the Bronx to cut up among the neo-Murgeroids" of the Village recast immigrant New Yorkers in the role of spectators instead of spectacles. Following the lead of white middle- and upper-class slummers, these Jewish and Italian youths became enthusiastic fans of the exotic entertainment and sexually permissive atmosphere that bohemia offered. And, like the native-born white slummers before them, they exploited this exoticism. For some, this meant using their slumming excursions as cover for casual sexual encounters with bohemian free-lovers. One young Russian, for example, told an investigator from the Committee of Fourteen that he frequented the Band Box and other Village resorts "quiet [*sic*] often purposely to pick up girls, which are easy to be gotten in Greenich [*sic*] Village." For others, bohemian slumming provided an opportunity to try the new style of dating. These immigrant youths joined white slummers in juxtaposing their own public couplings against the supposedly promiscuous mingling of free-loving bohemians. Visiting a dive known as the Second Half of the Night, British writer Stephen Graham encountered several such couples from the Bronx and Brooklyn among the crowd of tourists and celebrities taking in the Village sights.[62]

By pouring into Greenwich Village and Towertown during the early and mid-1920s, these slumming parties of immigrant and first-generation southern and eastern Europeans accelerated the redrawing of racial boundaries in New York and Chicago. They used their position as slummers to start integrating themselves with native-born whites, contributing to the creation of the modern white/black racial dichotomy that came to pit a more inclusive construction of whiteness against the increasingly visible blackness of the tens of thousands of Southern African American migrants and the smaller but still substantial number of West Indian immigrants who arrived in northern U.S. cities during the late 1910s and early 1920s. Bohemian entrepreneurs further expedited this process by hiring substantial numbers of black jazz musicians and performers to entertain their slumming patronage. By early 1923, both immigrant and native-born white youths sat around Robert Cushman's popular Village restaurant, located at Fourth and Cornelia streets, eating "sandwiches, and listen[ing] to the music provided by some negroes in high collars and shell-rimmed spectacles," and similar performances became popular attractions at the Dill Pickle Club and several other resorts. While catering to a growing public fascination with black music and culture, this introduction of black performers into bohemian resorts also made the shifting boundaries of whiteness all the more discernible to bohemia's visitors. In tearooms and cabarets, the contrast of black entertainers and their lighter-skinned audiences provided a striking visual display of the new urban racial order which was then taking shape, one that became even more perceptible as the vogue for black-and-tan cabarets succeeded the search for bohemian *thrillage*.[63]

FIVE

The Negro Vogue: Excursions into a "Mysterious Dark World"

As the search for bohemian *thrillage* drew to a close, well-to-do whites launched a new slumming craze centered around black nightlife. Participating in what was perhaps the most popular slumming vogue of the early twentieth century, throngs of curious white interlopers began to venture into the bustling black nightspots of Prohibition-era New York. "Harlem was runnin' twenty-four hours a day," African American jazz saxophonist Eddie Barefield recalled. "When downtown closed, all of the people came up to Harlem in busloads to the Cotton Club, Connie's Inn, [and] Small's Paradise." Whether in limousines full of ermine and tails or in more modestly attired clusters on subways and in taxis, by the early 1920s, thousands of white slummers were trekking to Harlem's interracial black-and-tan cabarets on a nightly basis. "To call yourself a New Yorker," Harlem Renaissance author Wallace Thurman once noted, "you must have been to Harlem at least once. Every up-to-date person knows Harlem, and knowing Harlem generally means that one has visited a night club or two."[1]

While closely associated with Harlem, the slumming vogue for black nightlife was hardly unique to New York. At a time when tens of thousands of African American migrants from the rural South—and smaller but significant numbers of West Indian immigrants—were making their way to major cities throughout the North and West, this phenomenon captivated urban residents all across the country. In Philadelphia, Pittsburgh, Cleveland, Detroit, Atlantic City, Baltimore, Los Angeles, and San Francisco, black jazz entertainment and cabarets became a mainstay in the nighttime diversions of affluent whites.[2] Outside New York, however, the most thriving center of black nightlife was Chicago. On the city's South Side, in a district that came to be known as Bronzeville, several large cabarets and scores of smaller, more difficult-to-locate drinking spots drew almost as many late-night white revelers as the hotspots of Harlem. According to one local black columnist, by the late 1920s, these "bizarre and gaudy night clubs" were "about the only real live oasis that the prohibition authorities have left in this torrid desert of temperance."As in Harlem, thousands of middle- and upper-class whites journeyed to Bronzeville each night to indulge in the freest flowing bootlegged liquor in the city, not to mention the hottest jazz. But music and booze were not the only attractions that drew white pleasure seekers to the cities' black neighborhoods. Slummers also visited Harlem and Bronzeville to savor—and, on occasion, even wallow in—the "primitive," libidinous atmosphere that they had come to associate with black urban life.[3]

For these reasons, although intended as little more than an amusement, black-and-tan slumming excursions assumed a crucial role in the process of reformulating white middle-class sexual propriety. Removed from the eyes of nosey neighbors and parents, thousands of young white women and men used their journeys into black neighborhoods to challenge the bounds of sexual respectability and to contest the popular notions of racial difference that separated early-twentieth-century Americans. In the darkness and relative anonymity of local black and tans, they became even more sensual and publicly affectionate with each other and, more striking still, began to undermine the very notion of the color line. As one black Chicago journalist noted upon entering a 35th Street cabaret, when "ebony and white savagely sway in the semi-darkness, their bodies writhing and contorting to the rhythm of jungle blues, . . . there are no social or color lines." Whether "social mentors and vibrant pulsating debutantes" or "racketeers and harlots," they "all look and are the same in these soft suggestive lights." Many slummers experienced a similar feeling of commonality with the blacks they met in the nightspots of Harlem and Bronzeville—a connection that sometimes carried over into temporary or even more significant cross-racial friendships and sexual relationships.[4]

Despite the possibilities that black-and-tan cabarets presented for bridging racial differences, however, sluming usually served primarily to redefine and reinscribe them. While some whites viewed their journeys to Harlem and Bronzeville as conscious opportunities to break down the color barriers separating urban Americans, most were immediately aware that they were—as former Cotton Club dancer Howard "Stretch" Johnson described the process—"entering into a segregated community." For these men and women, a slumming excursion to Harlem or Bronzeville was "like taking a trip from their white world into another mysterious dark world," a trip that offered numerous occasions to take advantage of the supposed freedoms of black nightlife while simultaneously reinforcing a sense of white superiority. That is, slumming created a space where middle-class whites could normalize their own increasingly public sexual behavior by contrasting it with the spectacle of cross-racial and black sexuality presented in local black and tans. Engaging in such activities allowed slummers not only to redefine the contours of early-twentieth-century race and sexuality but also to put this process, including the black resistance to it, on astonishingly public display.[5]

"The grossness of primitive sensuality with the gilded refinement of modern licentiousness": Sexualizing Racial Difference

During the 1920s, the nightlife of Harlem and Bronzeville preoccupied white Americans more than any other slumming vogue ever had. Whether visitors to New York and Chicago or longtime residents of these cities, they longed to gain a glimpse both of the thousands of Southern blacks who had only recently settled in the area and of the flourishing jazz culture they brought with them as part of the Great Migration. But night after night, hordes of affluent white slummers came no closer to encountering black urban life than the elaborate floorshows they observed in popular cabarets like Harlem's Cotton Club (figure 20) and Bronzeville's Plantation Café. Replete with romantic fantasies of the antebellum South, as indicated by their names, these largely segregated nightspots provided white patrons with the very performances of blackness that they expected to see: jazzed-up versions of the jocular mammies, shiftless urban dandies, and alluring jezebels that peopled the most problematic minstrel performances of the nineteenth century. Only when white amusement seekers ventured off the beaten path to visit black-owned or managed nightspots, such as Bronzeville's Dreamland Café, Small's Paradise in Harlem, or one of the hundreds of smaller speakeasies or buffet flats strewn across the backstreets of these black

20　This 1925 broadside advertising Harlem's famed Cotton Club conveys a relatively accurate picture of the upscale cabaret's preferred clientele. Controlled by Welsh American gangster Owney Madden, the Cotton Club provided black jazz entertainment, dance revues, and wait service for an almost-exclusively white after-theater crowd in New York's preeminent black neighborhood from 1923 to 1936, when the club moved downtown. This cabaret proved so popular with slummers that reservations for one of its approximately seven hundred seats were strongly recommended. (Reprinted with permission from the Photographs and Prints Division, Schomburg Center for Research in Black Culture, The New York Public Library, Astor, Lenox and Tilden Foundations, image #SC-CN-93-0689.)

neighborhoods, did they come anywhere close to participating in authentic black urban culture. Despite all of this, throughout the Prohibition era, white Americans' popular obsession with the pulsating rhythms
of black jazz prompted them to beat a continuous path to the late-night
amusements of Harlem and Bronzeville.

The popularity of black-and-tan slumming was so widespread that
it permeated the very fabric of 1920s popular culture. Beginning with
the 1926 publication of Carl Van Vechten's *Nigger Heaven,* which many
reformers incorrectly credited with prompting the initial white fascination with Harlem, black-and-tan cabarets became integral settings
for popular literature set in northern U.S. cities. They provided back-
drops in the novels of Harlem Renaissance writers, including Claude
McKay's *Home to Harlem* (1928), Rudolph Fisher's *The Walls of Jericho*
(1928), Nella Larsen's *Passing* (1929), and Wallace Thurman's *Infants of
the Spring* (1932), and were also featured in popular novels written by
white Americans, such as Thomas Beer's *The Road to Heaven* (1928) and
Katherine Brush's *Young Man of Manhattan* (1930). With the advent of
"talkies," black and tans even became featured locales in American film,
usually as part of a jazz interlude prompted by a white character's participation in a slumming excursion to the studio version of a Harlem
nightspot. But in a handful of early motion pictures, including the 1931
Tallulah Bankhead vehicle, *Tarnished Lady,* directed by George Cukor,
the boundary between reality and fiction was blurred by taking the film
cast and crew on location to actual Harlem cabarets.[6]

Yet even as such novels and films whetted the public appetite for
black-and-tan slumming by transporting thousands of urban and rural
Americans to a world of imaginary cabarets, the recordings of prominent black jazz musicians and blues singers brought those spaces to life
in living rooms across the nation. On the "race records" produced by
General Phonograph's OKeh label, as well as by Victor, Columbia, and
Vocalion Dance Records, listeners could hear some of the most popular
Harlem and Bronzeville performers of the 1920s. Recordings of Bessie
Smith, Gertrude "Ma" Rainey, Joe "King" Oliver, Sidney Bechet, and
others so closely captured the sound of local black and tans that, according to the owner of one Bronzeville record store, "Colored people would
form a line twice around the block when the latest record of Bessie or Ma
or Clara or Mamie came in." In short order, they were joined by thousands of well-to-do white women and men, ranging from novelist Carl
Van Vechten and his bohemian friends to ordinary middle-class cabaret
goers who sought to recapture some semblance of their slumming experiences within the privacy of their own homes.[7]

But no development in popular culture helped reinforce the popularity of black-and-tan slumming as much as radio. In 1925, less than four years after local broadcasts had first begun in Chicago, WBBM began experimenting with remote transmissions from Bronzeville black and tans. Simply by turning a knob on their radio, listeners could nestle into the clamorous surroundings of the Sunset Café, the Regal, the Apex, or the Grand Terrace Ballroom, where Louis Armstrong, Jimmie Noone, and Earl Hines sported their best for racially mixed audiences. In New York, the situation was much the same, with several small radio stations broadcasting remote shows from Harlem cabarets. By 1927, listeners could tune in WHW to hear the nightly broadcasts of Duke Ellington from the stage of Harlem's renowned Cotton Club, a pleasure that was available soon thereafter to listeners nationwide, courtesy of the Columbia Broadcasting System.[8]

Despite the proliferation of these increasingly lifelike surrogates, nothing could compare to the firsthand experience of a black and tan. Opting for live-action performances over remote radio broadcasts, well-to-do white pleasure seekers flocked to Harlem and Bronzeville cabarets with resounding frequency. In doing so, they not only ignored white reformers' warnings that such nightspots were spaces of impending racial and sexual conflict but also demonstrated a decided resolve to portray themselves as worldly urbanites who challenged conventional social boundaries while indulging a voyeuristic fascination with black culture. One female college student told Chicago sociologist Walter Reckless that she understood her recent slumming expedition in Bronzeville both as an expression of her "desire to be sophisticated concerning the ways of the large city" and as a chance to sample jazz and black nightlife up close. For many middle-class whites, participation in this latest vogue was simply another experience—like smoking, drinking, and petting—to be added to the repertoire of the modern cosmopolitan. "I danced with the Negroes at the Speak-easy," University of Chicago undergraduate Eve Blue confided to her diary, "simply because I was a little binged [drunk] and because I wanted the experience."[9]

Still other middle-class slummers were drawn to black nightlife as part of a desire to escape, however temporarily, the restrictive confines of their daily lives. Under cover of darkness, one Chicago guidebook noted, whites arrived at black-and-tan cabarets "to partake of the happy-go-lucky and joyous spirit supposed to be inherent in the Negro soul." Amid such allegedly primitive sensuality, white middle-class men were said to seek relief from the bureaucratic routine of modern-day work. That is, having been allegedly unmanned by professions such as advertising, engineering, and corporate management that placed them in positions where they had control over neither their labor nor the products of that labor, men in this new class of salaried managers and professionals supposedly sought release and inspiration in the "uncivilized" nightlife of black New York and Chicago. "The business man lives a strenuous life and expends on his work all that overflowing energy which an idler species is tempted to throw into a bout of sensual pleasure," British travel writer Stephen Graham remarked in 1927, suggesting—through a typically racist formulation of newly popularized Freudian psychology—that white businessmen might temporarily reclaim their sensuality by embracing the so-called primitivism of black cabaret patrons.[10]

By and large, white middle- and upper-class women were not subject to the routine labor of the modern workplace; even so, they also sought to escape the perceived sterility of modern life. Writing in *The Rogue,* a literary journal that she coedited with her husband, Louise Norton remarked that she returned time and again to a particular New York black and tan because the atmosphere allowed her to "forget, *forget, forget!*" To forget what, she did not say, but one might safely surmise that she went to forget convention, if not the very racial and sexual boundaries that separated her from others—and that in forgetting, she intended to give herself over to the basic human urges and desires that she associated with the supposed primitivism of black culture.[11] One female undergraduate told sociologist Walter Reckless that she felt all her reservations dissolve when she visited her first Chicago black and tan. At first, she "wished [she] might look in, unseen, untouched by its actual contact," but after a few drinks, when the strains of a familiar tune came wafting from the jazz orchestra, she longed to join the "joyous, mongrel horde." Dancing with her white male companion, she recalled:

I lost my old self in the delight of perfect freedom and movement. A Jewish boy with a nice face pressed his lips to those of a mulatto girl who was his partner. They danced on and on, their lips and bodies pressed together. The girls' [*sic*] drunken eyes closed. I shut mine too. With the last strains of the music, Tom gave me an added pressure and kissed my forehead, I was like the rest now.[12]

For one brief moment, liquor, jazz, and the "perfect freedom" of dancing not only dissolved the racial and sexual boundaries that ordinarily separated this young white woman from "Jewish boys" and "mulatto girls" but also allowed her to escape the social constraints that usually proscribed public expressions of affection and sexual desire by respectable white women and men.

During the 1910s and early 1920s, white middle-class youths challenged the boundaries of sexual respectability with public displays of affection and "petting parties" on college campuses and in the bohemian tearooms of Towertown and Greenwich Village. But in the sexual primitivism that they identified with the pulsing rhythms and unfamiliar sounds of black jazz, slummers found a ready-made excuse for their further escape from social convention and sexual propriety. "You go sort of primitive up there," Jimmy Durante wrote of Harlem in 1931, "with the bands moaning blues like nobody's business, slim, bare-thighed brown-skin gals tossing their torsos, and the Negro melody artists bearing down something terrible on the minor notes."[13] Indeed, the "evil genius" of black-and-tan cabarets, one Chicago official insisted, was their use of black culture to promote intimacy among middle-class whites. Ordering the closure of the Entertainers' Café in 1922, judge Arnold Heap denounced its ability to "artfully" combine "the grossness of primitive sensuality with the gilded refinement of modern licentiousness." It was not the mixing of blacks and whites in this Bronzeville cabaret that most disturbed him, but the intimate contact its popularity and close quarters promoted among the white couples who visited the establishment. While dancing to the "loud and discordant noises" of the cabaret's jazz orchestra, Judge Heap observed with disgust, "each couple scarcely moved from their original positions. To do otherwise was impossible."[14] Observing similar conditions at Barron Wilkins's Harlem cabaret, an investigator from New York's Committee of Fourteen claimed that the close personal contact on the cabaret's dance floor actually allowed slummers to transform their dancing into sexual acts. While dancing "an improper dance," the investigator reported, a young white woman told her male partner "that he was bound to get a dry f. . . . if she'll keep on rubbing her abdomen against [him]."[15]

Anti-vice investigations of several fashionable slumming destinations in the black neighborhoods of Chicago and New York revealed that the white patrons of black and tans often behaved more freely and sexually than the cabarets' black patrons and performers. "According [to] my observation," Committee of Fourteen investigator Harry Kahan reported after visiting one popular Harlem resort, "the colored patrons in here behaved better th[a]n the white and frankly said the white patrons were running wild in here (both, men and women)." German sexologist Magnus Hirschfeld reached a similar conclusion during a visit to Harlem's Savoy Ballroom in the early 1930s. "White men and white women have lost, to a large extent, the sense of play which animates . . . colored dancers," he insisted. "They are too sex-conscious and self-conscious.

Hugging each other closely, dancing cheek to cheek," in a more obvious "manifestation of eroticism."[16]

Although Hirschfeld's comparison of black and white dance styles relied on racist notions of black "primitivism" and "immaturity" to draw a clear distinction between the conscious behavior of whites and the supposedly unconscious behavior of blacks, his characterization of white dancing in Harlem black and tans accurately captured the sexual permissiveness that white slummers often exhibited in black spaces. For many white women and men, a trip to Harlem or Bronzeville offered a chance to indulge their sexual desires for each other while maintaining a sense of respectability in their own neighborhoods. On occasion, white women even expressed their sexual availability to white men simply by suggesting that they go slumming in a black cabaret. For instance, when an undercover investigator propositioned a Lower East Side dance-hall hostess by asking where she went "when you go out for a good time," she remarked, "I've been up to the Cotton Club in Harlem and have danced there all night." Only later did she acknowledge that the investigator was asking where she usually went to have sex, noting that her suggestion of a trip to the Cotton Club was intended as an indirect confirmation of her sexual availability.[17]

While some white women used slumming as an excuse to give white men easier sexual access to their bodies, most middle-class women accompanied their suitors and husbands to black-and-tan cabarets just as they would on any other date—to solidify their relationships with these men and simultaneously proclaim their "emancipation" as New Women. Like their attempts to partake of the bohemian *thrillage* of Greenwich Village and Towertown, these jaunts to black neighborhoods generated new norms of white sexual propriety, encompassing both the acceptance of more casual sexual familiarity among respectable white couples and the increasingly public display of such familiarity. But unlike other white middle-class forays into sexualized urban spaces, black-and-tan slumming expeditions provided an opportunity to contain the emancipation of the New Woman by reinforcing her dependence upon and subservience to white men. In a twist on the ideology that struck fear into the hearts of Southern white women and motivated the lynching of numerous Southern black men during the late nineteenth and early twentieth centuries, northern white men sometimes exploited the myth of the black male sexual predator who lurked in the black-and-tan cabarets of the urban North, waiting to prey on unsuspecting female slummers, in order to discourage white women's increased independence.[18]

One white female undergraduate reported experiencing precisely this dynamic when she attended a Bronzeville cabaret with a group of college friends. Imagining herself the object of a black man's desire, she literally threw herself into the arms of her white male companion, whom she had met only hours before and "scarcely knew." "From our table," she recalled, "I saw a shiny, black male negro with a wide teethy smile watching me. I dug my fingers into Tom's arm. I had heard that these creatures asked white girls to dance with them." Initially, the undergraduate averted her gaze to avoid encouraging the black man's desire, but ultimately she accepted her date's invitation to dance in an effort to deter any further advances. The bestial danger that she associated with the black man not only rendered her dependent upon Tom, reinforcing her subservience as a white woman, but also drove her into increased physical intimacy with him. Moreover, it helped to normalize the casualness with which she accepted this intimacy, shoring up new norms of white sexual propriety by contrasting her same-race relationship with the perversity that whites assigned to cross-racial sex in particular and blackness more generally.[19]

"I simply can't get any kick from a white skin any more": Cross-Racial Spectacles and Desires

"The night-life [in Harlem] has a great deal of . . . sex perversion," a popular 1920s travelogue remarked, more than accurately capturing the popular representation of local black and tans. "I am bound to say that there was much that was vicious and nasty which if described plainly might cause my book to be banned," its author continued, "[but] I dare say many people would have given their eyes to see [it]." Indeed, many white women and men flocked to Harlem and Bronzeville cabarets expressly to witness their risqué entertainments, thrilled by the thought that they were participating in something dirty even as they carefully distanced themselves from it. Watching dancers "as sinuous as serpents" and "marvellous incredible waiters" with "doglike heads [that] came out of their collars on sinuous doggy necks," white amusement seekers juxtaposed their supposedly respectable behavior with the primal, animalistic demeanor they perceived in blacks. To more sharply define the distinction between white respectability and black licentiousness, slummers even encouraged the cabarets' black entertainers to jazz up the sensuality of their performances. In a fairly typical example of such conduct, a "party of four young white boys" at a Bronzeville black and

tan reportedly "shout[ed] encouragement to the dancers to more obscene movements with their bodies." White patrons also reveled in the
suggestiveness of blues lyrics, urging performers to sing more and more
racy numbers. At Chicago's Pioneer Cabaret, for instance, they greeted
a young black male performer with appreciative howls when he sang
about "screw[ing] her with his sweet little thing," becoming "so boisterous" that an anti-vice investigator regretfully reported that he "could
not catch all the words."[20]

For the most part, the so-called lewdness of black-and-tan performances was fairly tame by today's standards. In the early 1920s, anti-
vice investigations in New York and Chicago most often cited black
female dancers for lifting their skirts above their knees, flashing glimpses
of their undergarments, or moving their bodies in a suggestive manner.
Nudity was rarely observed at the cities' most popular black and tans.
Yet because the black performers' perceived vulgarity provided a useful
counterpoint against which slummers could establish new boundaries
of white sexual propriety, municipal authorities often sought to eliminate such displays with the same fervor they usually reserved for public
sexual acts and indecent exposure. In a 1922 case initiated by Chicago's
Committee of Fifteen, municipal judge Arnold Heap even suggested that
a fully clothed black female dancer at the popular Entertainers' Café
was more "indecent and obscene" than a naked one would have been.
"Counsel for defendant seems to try to make a point that defendant
did not expose her flesh to the gaze of the patrons of the show," Heap
rebuffed the performer's attorney, insisting that "The point is insignifi-
cant and will not stand the test of analysis. Experience teaches that too
gross an exhibition of immodesty frequently shocks the sensibilities of
the gazer since nothing is left for the imagination whereas the fascination lies in obtaining but a half view of what is desired to be seen."[21]

By the mid-1920s, however, anti-vice organizations largely accepted
such performances despite their continued disdain for them. Chorus
lines of "tall, tan, and terrific" women became regular features at the
most popular black and tans, especially those that catered primarily to a
white patronage. Appearing in "nothing but small jock straps over their
buttocks and private parts and scanty brassieres" at the famed Lenox Avenue Club and elsewhere, these entertainers mirrored the white chorus
girls who appeared nightly in Broadway and Rush Street cabarets and in
stage revues, such as the Ziegfeld Follies. Yet unlike white chorus lines,
these black female dancers—no matter how light-skinned (or, perhaps,
precisely because they were light-skinned)—served as potent reminders
of the cross-racial sexual desires and taboos that circulated in black and

tans, stimulating and frightening the cabarets' white patrons while supplying a foil for their increased sexual intimacy with each other.[22]

"The South Side cabarets still attract large crowds of slumming parties who are apparently pleased with the atmosphere of sensuality and find delight in seeing the intermingling of races," a New York social reformer, Paul M. Kinsie, told Chicago's JPA in late 1923, after completing a series of investigations commissioned by the organization. In fact, Kinsie noted, the cross-racial sexuality on display at Bronzeville black and tans so fascinated some middle-class whites that they simply could not keep their hands off it. At the popular Paradise Cabaret, located at Prairie Avenue and 35th Street, he watched as one particularly adventuresome white couple transformed the common voyeurism of slumming into a tactile sport that simultaneously made a spectacle of the seeming perversity of cross-racial sexuality, while reinforcing the sexual respectability of the couple's own racially homogeneous relationship. The "young [white] couple who were seated near the dance floor," Kinsie reported, "continually plac[ed] their hands upon the person of a white man and a colored woman who were dancing. Each time this couple would pass, the [white couple] seated at the table would slap them on the back and in one instance the man was seen to put his hand under the colored woman's clothes." Yet despite their unruly behavior, by remaining seated at their table, the white couple assumed a position of relative respectability—a position gained at the expense of unwitting dancers whose cross-racial coupling they cast both as entertainment and as an oddity requiring hands-on examination.[23]

Although the majority of white visitors to Harlem and Bronzeville never ventured beyond the showplace cabarets designed for white audiences, those who dared to explore the neighborhoods' basement speakeasies and buffet flats uncovered even more explicitly sexual spectacles against which they could define themselves. In Harlem's buffet flats, such as the one on 131st Street that New York detectives raided during the summer of 1925, slummers might stumble upon a "rainbow party" where "white and colored women and men" cavorted together, "clad in less than nothing." Or, at Chicago's Pioneer Cabaret they might watch—as one social investigator claimed to have done—the black male dance partner of a white woman "r[u]n his fingers into her anal cavities while they were dancing and she laughed through it all," taking pleasure in "being the center of attraction." At times, the black-and-tan spectacle in local nightspots became so graphic that any indiscretion committed by white couples simply paled in comparison. Such was certainly the case at Harlem's white-owned Elks Café, where the public petting of white pleasure seekers seemed the very image of sexual restraint, compared with cross-racial couples regularly "going through the act of sexual intercourse in view of the others."[24]

Several buffet flats in Harlem and Bronzeville actually specialized in presenting live sexual performances that paying audiences might easily co-opt as exemplary counterpoints to their own social and sexual respectability—despite the fact that slummers' mere observance of such activities should have called their respectability into question. Originally attended primarily by black and white working-class men, the most popular of these flats featured black women "performing indecent acts on each other." But when white middle-class women and men began to frequent these performances as part of their slumming expeditions to black neighborhoods, the sex circuses or "freak shows," as such performances were known, also incorporated displays of cross-racial sex. Anthropologist J. A. Rogers recalled that "orgies á la gai Paris and Berlin" were often "staged between Negroes and white women for the benefit of white slummers" in Prohibition-era Harlem. Similar events became popular among Chicago slummers at about this same time, reaching peak concentration during the 1933–34 Century of Progress World's Fair. In the first months of the exposition, Chicago's JPA turned up numerous locations in Bronzeville where, as one Jewish taxi driver told the organization's undercover investigator, "you can see colored and white men and women together" who were "putting on REAL things for the World's Fair." In language apparently too explicit even for the JPA's internal consumption, another driver suggested a live performance that incorporated three separate "perversions"—cross-racial sexuality, cunnilingus, and fellatio—asking, "Have you ever heard of a dark man (Negro), going ____, ____ on a white woman? And then she goes ____, ____ on him?"[25]

Some slummers, however, were less interested in establishing their own sexual respectability vis-à-vis cross-racial sexual spectacles than they were in participating in the opportunities for cross-racial intimacy that flourished in these public amusements. Indeed, many affluent whites relished the thought of even the most casual cross-racial contact, including the close physical intimacy associated with simply dancing. Although white middle-class men had cultivated such cross-racial encounters at least since the first slumming crazes hit New York and Chicago, it was not until the Negro vogue of the 1920s that substantial numbers of white middle-class women began to follow their lead, taking to the dance floors of Harlem and Bronzeville with their black male escorts. Whether at Small's Paradise (figure 21) or another popular black

21   In this 1929 photograph, a crowd of black and white patrons looks on as an entertainer
     dances the shimmy to the accompaniment of a jazz band at Small's Paradise in Harlem.
     Owned and operated by African American entrepreneur Edwin Smalls at 2294½ Seventh
     Avenue near 135th Street, Small's Paradise was the only upscale Harlem black and tan that
     actively solicited black patrons. The number of turned heads and hands covering faces in
     this photograph demonstrates that slumming remained a somewhat controversial pastime
     even in the late 1920s. (Reprinted with permission, © Bettmann/Corbis.)

and tan, during Prohibition, a correspondent for the *New York Graphic*
reported, one was as likely to encounter white "women short story writers, [or] the wife of an eminent Wall street lawyer dancing with a Negro
man" as the more stereotypical couplings of black women and white
men. For many female slummers, the cross-racial adventure terminated
at the end of one relatively restrained—and often awkward—dance, but
others carried the erotic charge of slumming one step further by indulging in cross-racial necking and petting both on and off the dance floor.
According to investigators working for the JPA, the daring entailed in
such public displays apparently heightened the thrill that white women
and men achieved by "hugging and kissing their colored companions"
or by dancing "the most obscene and degrading movements to the limit
of sensuality."[26]

By the 1920s, white middle-class social commentators had come to
expect such behavior from working-class whites, but they still bristled
at the thought that the well-to-do participated in public displays of

cross-racial intimacy. "Gorgeous looking white girls unashamedly neck with dapper sepias" in Harlem cabarets, the nationally syndicated columnist Walter Winchell noted in 1929.

What amazes the newcomer to these black and tan rendezvous is that the women who Go In For Such Things are not the types you expect to find; the coarse and tough sort. The women who enjoy the companionship of a colored man appear to be the class sort, the lorgnette-juggling "ladies," who make you self-conscious about your inferiority with their broad A's, and who attire themselves in the most costly finery.[27]

Yet if the public cross-racial intimacies of such "class" women disturbed commentators like Winchell, the forthrightness with which some of these same "ladies" arranged private cross-racial assignations almost certainly appalled them. To express their "fascination for Negro men," the jazz entertainer Bricktop recalled, at Bronzeville's Panama Inn a number of white women began using "a thing . . . called 'grenades.' These were notes that usually read something like 'Call me at such-and-such a number,'" which they "would pass . . . to a waiter or entertainer, who in turn would deliver the note to the intended party." And if these women wanted the man badly enough, Bricktop insisted that there was little that could get in their way; the boldest among them distributing such grenades even while in the company of their white male escorts.[28]

One Southern white woman explained such liberated behavior to anthropologist J. A. Rogers by insisting that as the New Woman "t[ook] over all the habits of the white male, . . . she certainly is not going to miss the most delectable one." Although the average middle-class white woman might "come up to Harlem, have a good time there, and then go back downtown and talk against Negroes," Rogers's informant insisted that a growing number of these women were beginning to indulge their sexual desires for black men, no matter how racist their foundation. Indeed, some white women visited Harlem and Bronzeville for the express purpose of having sex with black men, becoming quite upset when their dates failed to fulfill their sexual expectations. "A young Jewess on the staff of the . . . magazine grew angry at me," one well-known black man recalled, "because I spent an evening with her in Harlem and did not suggest taking her to my room." But for most of the female slummers who were so inclined, finding a black man who was willing to have sex with them posed little problem. This ease even encouraged some of them to develop a decided preference for black sexual partners. "I simply can't get any kick from a white skin any more," one such woman remarked, while another, questioned at Harlem's Green Leaf Melody Club, expressed a partiality for "the colored man's technique." She "comes to Harlem just to have a fling and learn some new tricks," the latter woman told the Committee of Fourteen's black undercover investigator, "because the people (of the [black] night life) do more tricky things than they do downtown."[29]

Like the white male slummers who kept black mistresses or hired black prostitutes when they visited Bronzeville or Harlem, wealthy white women sometimes paid for the sexual favors of their black paramours. Challenging the social dictates which both delimited respectable white women's sexual involvement with black men and placed their sexuality under the control of white men, these women used money to assert their sexual independence and their right to pursue cross-racial desire. As early as 1915, New York's Committee of Fourteen noted that "From time to time reports have been received that there are a certain number of white women who have colored lovers, the lover being a male with whom they consort for the satisfaction of their sex passions. Less frequently reports are heard of resorts where white women go for the purpose of having these passions satisfied by a colored man." At the height of the Negro vogue, however, this trend seems to have increased. According to the *New York Amsterdam News*, "A group of Park avenue girls anxious for a thrill" were even rumored to be covering the rent on a basement dive known as the Club Anna—not because they wanted to show a "particular interest in any one man," but because the club's manager, Hillis Waters, "pick[ed] out" a few desirable black male partners "for the occasion" every time the women came uptown.[30]

While such arrangements between white women and black men challenged the dominant power structure by removing white women's bodies and sexuality at least temporarily from white male control, the brothels that provided black women for white men reconfirmed it. Treating these women as mere outlets for white male sexual desire, local buffet flats contributed to the confirmation and maintenance of white manhood, as well as to the reinforcement of white men's racial domination over the nonwhite residents of Harlem and Bronzeville. The story was a familiar one. At least since the era of slavery, Southern white men had affirmed their position of racial and sexual dominance by using black women as their primary extra- and premarital sexual partners. Supposedly intended to protect the respectability and marriageablity of white women by diverting white male sexual aggression onto blacks, this practice not only confirmed white male power over white women by prescribing the boundaries of proper white female sexuality, but also asserted white men's racial privilege over slaves and emancipated blacks by compelling them, either for reasons of ownership or economics, to bow to white men's wishes.[31]

During the early twentieth century, similar practices became common in the urban North, as the Great Migration brought thousands of unemployed black women to northern U.S. cities where they became easy targets for white men's attempts to secure their public status and racial privilege. By the early 1930s, for instance, male students at the City College of New York regularly encouraged each other to prove their manhood and their acceptability for fraternity membership by having sex with black women in Harlem's brothels. As one freshman reported, "sophomores had told them that 'one does not become a man until he had had a black woman,' and that they could not be considered for membership in a fraternity until they became 'men.'" Municipal authorities, charged with eliminating both white and black female prostitution, often seemed to support this position by choosing to focus their attention on preserving the sanctity of white womanhood at the expense of the black women who worked in the buffet flats of Harlem and Bronzeville. "They ought to let those places run," a white Chicago police officer told an undercover investigator from the JPA following a temporary crackdown on Bronzeville prostitution in 1923. "Young fellows have got to go out and if they close them up wait till you see all the rapes that'll be taking place. Why your sister and my sister won't be safe on the streets."[32]

This permissive attitude toward female prostitution marked a decided shift from the white slavery panic of the previous decade, but it was a shift made possible only because white urbanites began to associate illicit sexual activity primarily with blacks. Where once reformers had labored to prevent the commercial exploitation of seemingly innocent white women, by the late 1910s they were coming to think of urban prostitution as an almost natural outgrowth of the supposed pathologies of black female sexuality. The greater visibility of black prostitutes on the streets of New York and Chicago and their disproportionate representation among the women charged with sexual offenses appeared to confirm this assessment with the majority of the cities' white residents. Few, if any, gave serious consideration to the role that employment discrimination and poverty played in encouraging black women to enter the sex trade at higher rates than their white counterparts. Nor did many whites stop to ponder how their fascination with black urban culture and sexuality almost certainly contributed to the increased viability and profitability of prostitution in Bronzeville and Harlem. Yet as the correlation of black women and prostitution became fixed in the minds of slummers and other white urbanites, it not only reinforced the racial privilege of white men who used black women to satisfy their illicit sexual desires but also facilitated the expansion of the bounds of white female sexual propriety. At a time when "slumming, night life, exaggerations in dress, [and] an unchaperoned life outside the home" had begun—in sociologist Walter Reckless's famed formulation—to blur "the outward distinction between the painted sport and the paler protected lady," the figure of the black prostitute provided a useful foil for white women's increasingly public sexual behavior and helped secure a certain level of social status and sexual respectability for even the least reputable of modern white women.[33]

"Merely side shows staged for sensation-seeking whites?" Black Resistance to the Negro Vogue

By the early 1920s, the black residents of both Chicago and New York began to recognize that their neighborhoods were becoming havens for a range of so-called sexual perversions, including prostitution, cross-racial sexuality, and other public sexual expressions and performances. Responding to this discovery, the communities' newspapers, churches, and social reform organizations launched a series of sustained protests against this unsavory development. They objected not only to the virtual segregation of illicit sexual activity to black residential and commercial districts but also to its fertilization and growth under local police protection. Writing about the "'wide open' conditions" in Harlem during the fall of 1922, editors of the black-owned *New York Age* complained that "the city administration seems to have given over this section of the town for the exploitation of vicious practices . . . without the slightest effort at restraint or concealment." The *Chicago Whip,* another black-owned newspaper, described similar conditions in Bronzeville as "a direct slap in the face" of a black electorate that had supported the administration of the Republican mayor "Big Bill" Thompson. "If the people want open prostitution and gambling and it is compelled to exist because the politicians profit from it," the editors of the *Whip* lamented, "we can only hope that it will be segregated and removed from residential sections where people make the pretense of decency."[34]

What made this situation particularly objectionable to black reformers was the fact that most of the illicit amusements in these districts were white owned and catered to increasingly white audiences. "The vice and corruption which infests Chicago's black belt is not to be attributed to the black people," the *Chicago Whip* insisted in 1922. "In every investigated case it is always discernible that some white wretch is the profiteer and protector." The editors of the *New York Age* agreed, noting that "most of the proprietors" of Harlem cabarets "are white, and the immunity which they enjoy is but another example of the exploitation of the darker race." This exploitation only increased during the mid- to late 1920s, as the growing "invasion" of white slummers, in the words of Harlem Renaissance author Wallace Thurman, rendered most black public amusements "merely side shows staged for sensation-seeking whites."[35] Capitalizing on the Negro vogue, white entrepreneurs opened an increasing number of black and tans to cater to the slumming trade that had descended upon black urban communities and expanded their commercial enterprises to include the operation of buffet flats that specialized in the procurement of black and white female prostitutes for a high-scale white clientele.[36]

Occasional crackdowns on the public amusements of Harlem and Bronzeville did little to end this system of white exploitation. When municipal authorities chose to rein in the illicit sex, drinking, and gambling that flourished in black neighborhoods, several black social commentators noted, they usually focused their efforts on black-owned establishments. Venues owned and frequented by whites were allowed to operate largely unimpeded. By 1922, this tendency had become so pronounced that Virgil Williams, the black proprietor of several different Bronzeville cabarets, publicly contended that "a color line . . . has been drawn so firmly that only white people, mostly Jews, are permitted to operate" buffet flats and black and tans in Chicago's black community.[37] As the bias of white anti-vice organizations and municipal authorities became even more conspicuous throughout the 1920s, black newspapers protested such selective closings with significant verve. In one sharply worded complaint, the *Chicago Whip* drew its readers' attention to the moral hypocrisy of white regulatory actions that closed down black-owned Bronzeville cabarets while overlooking "the most brazen [white-owned] dives in the community." Adopting the language of social and religious reformers, the newspaper's editors remarked, "The purification of the black man's morals will not save the white sinner's souls [*sic*]."[38]

While black reformers agreed with their white counterparts that the sexual excesses exhibited in black entertainment districts required immediate and strict policing, they usually disagreed on who and what should be policed. White municipal authorities blamed the immorality of these spaces on black sexual practices and enticements to cross-racial encounters, but black observers attributed the deteriorating moral conditions to the "white sinners" who flocked to Bronzeville and Harlem by the thousands. Reversing the rhetoric of primitivism and perversity that whites often used to depict black sexuality, African American social critics ascribed uncontrollable desires and animalistic urges to the white patrons of buffet flats and black and tans. In the winter of 1922, the *Chicago Whip* warned its black readership that "sexual perversion of the worst kind" was being "encouraged and advertised" by a local "prostitution syndicate of white reprobates," and it insisted that neighborhood residents mobilize to protect their "wives, daughters and little children" from being "intimidated and corrupted by these terrible creatures." The *New York Age* similarly indicted the white proprietors of local amusements for promoting the proliferation of white sexual perversity in a black residential district. By "cater[ing] to the demands of their perverted [white] patrons," the paper's editors asserted, white cabaret owners were, as the title of the editorial exclaimed, "giving Harlem a bad name."[39]

Although most black observers focused their wrath on the white proprietors of local black and tans, they reserved at least some scorn for those blacks who facilitated white sexual antics. Reform-minded reporters and ministers often lashed out at black politicians who appeared to profit personally from the slumming trade, and even an occasional neighborhood church or two found itself under attack for turning a blind eye to the situation in order to "get money from the white dive-keepers when a new organ is needed for the worship of the Lord."[40] But particular opprobrium was levied on the ordinary black women and men who aided and abetted white displays of illicit sexuality. As early as 1917, the *Chicago Defender* railed against the scores of black male "fixers" who "f[ou]nd a profitable field in acting as escorts to young white men slumming through the south side," while the *New York Age* launched a similar campaign in 1926 against local "slumming hostesses" who offered to show "inquisitive Nordics . . . the real inside of the New Negro Race of Harlem." Local commentators were especially enraged by the black bartenders, taxi drivers, and pimps who arranged liaisons between white men and black women in an effort to line their own pockets. Insisting that the protection of black womanhood formed the cornerstone of racial respectability, the *Defender*'s editors lambasted "this slimiest of all creatures" for betraying his responsibility as a "Race man" by selling local women to "some slumming white rogue." Moreover, they urged readers to chase such men "out of town or put him in the [B]ridewell [prison], where he belongs."[41]

The rhetoric employed by black social critics was a photographic negative of that adopted by white reformers, for it condemned the cross-racial sexual interactions of white men and black women, rather than white women and black men. In an attempt to rehabilitate the sexual image of black men, some observers even contrasted the myth of the black male sexual predator with the reality of the white one. "We hear that word 'moron' used quite frequently now," the *Chicago Whip* noted in 1922,

and in many instances we read that these morons, most of them white, have raped and despoiled young girls. . . . We venture to say that the white morons of Chicago have defiled and seduced more women and girls in the city of Chicago than black men have in the whole United States during the last ten years.[42]

According to such critics, white men were particularly guilty of exploiting the economic vulnerabilities of Southern black migrants, nudging them into lives of prostitution shortly after their arrival in northern cities or, at the very least, into casual encounters that encouraged them to treat white men with sexual favors in return for dinner, entertainment, or gifts of clothing. African American composer Will Marion Cook noted that "this degrading of colored girls by white people" occurred even at upscale nightclubs like Connie's Inn, where management not only exhibited scantily clad black women in its famous Harlem revues, but also arranged "drinking parties and dates . . . with the colored show girls . . . as extra attractions."[43]

In the districts' less prominent black and tans, the white male exploitation of black women often assumed even more shockingly public dimensions. At Harlem's Sheep Club, a basement speakeasy frequented in 1928 by such prominent whites as "the warden of Welfare Island, the physician of [New York mayor] Jimmie Walker's family, and a man who is the brother of the runner-up for the next mayor," the Committee of Fourteen's black investigator observed white male patrons "seiz[ing] a colored girl who was entertaining" in order to bite her on the "bare buttocks" and pat her "private parts"—all under the permitting gaze of the dive's black manager.[44] Financial incentives no doubt prompted the employees of such venues to tolerate slummers' unruly behavior, but disgust with such exploitation was clearly not limited to the black middle class. An African American prostitute at Chicago's Schiller Cabaret drew a white undercover investigator's attention to a "drunken white man" who seemed to be "amusing himself" by tickling a fourteen-year-old black girl until she grew "so uncomfortable" that she began struggling to escape him. "I am 18 and am old enough to know the difference between right and wrong," the prostitute told the investigator, "but I want to tell you its [*sic*] all wrong for a kid like that to be permitted in here. . . . These cabarets are the ruination of many a girl."[45]

While local black critics attacked white male slummers' exploitation of black women and spaces, they had few complaints about white women's incursions into these same cabarets. Unlike the white male slummer, his female counterpart was not understood to be a carrier of sexual perversity poised to infect black society. As a result, only occasional protestations appeared in the black press contesting her presence. In one such case, using a black slang word for "white," a columnist for the *New York Amsterdam News* complained that "ofay women slowly but surely are moving in on our local femmes and are making efforts to displace them as social accoutrements." But ultimately, even this criticism referred more to black men's disinterest in and disrespect for local women than to any perceived corruption of black men by white women. On occasion, the black press and other agents of social reform did rail against the presence of white prostitutes in black neighborhoods, but in a reversal of the concerns of most white reformers, these protests usually focused on the threat that white prostitutes and their customers posed to respectable black women and children, not on their enticement of black male patrons. A letter that one Harlem woman sent to the Committee of Fourteen further suggests both the willingness of the black middle class to overlook black men's cross-racial shenanigans and their relative inability to stop them. Signing herself a "Broken Hearted Wife," this mother of three small children turned to the powerful white anti-vice organization to close two Harlem dives where her husband "goes and . . . spends his money on white women," apparently having resolved that the Committee of Fourteen could be more effective in this regard than local black newspapers and churches.[46]

For the most part, however, black social commentators—especially male journalists—simply overlooked the sexual and romantic relationships that white women carried on with local black men. At times, they seemed even to promote such liaisons, believing that female slummers' interactions with the men of Harlem and Bronzeville would ultimately undercut the persistent stereotype of black men as dangerous sexual predators. Writing in the *Inter-State Tattler*, Bennie Butler maintained that "the white woman [who] found Harlem a pleasant or 'Happy Hunting Ground'" soon learned to disregard the "vicious creature pictured in the papers. . . . As a matter of fact, the stereotyped, offensive journalistic phrase 'Black Brute' was found to be a 'Handsome Black Brute' with engaging personality, a ready smile and an infectuous [*sic*], jovial disposition." Charmed by these unexpected qualities, a number of female slummers set aside their initial prejudices to embrace the amorous advances of the black men they met in Harlem and Bronzeville cabarets. But the willingness of these women to cross the color line for friendship or romance was hardly sufficient to dispel popular prejudices. As more than a few black men could attest, the simplest interactions with white women remained dangerous propositions—when white men took it upon themselves to defend the women's honor or to protect them physically from perceived sexual threats. Even at Harlem's most racially integrated and popular black and tans, black men faced violence if their flirtations were deemed offensive. On one such occasion, the *New York Amsterdam News* reported, when two black men asked one of the women in a white party at Small's Paradise to dance, her white male companion not only decked one of the potential suitors but also successfully demanded that the cabaret's black management expel the "offending" men from the club's premises.[47]

Jazz, Parties, and Cabaret Dancing: Popular Incursions across the Color Line

The white middle-class fascination with black-and-tan slumming undoubtedly led to increased levels of cross-racial social and sexual interaction, both on the dance floors and in the bedrooms and hallways of Harlem and Bronzeville. But it rarely secured the "wholesome democratic life" devoid of racial animosity and prejudice that African American journalist Floyd Snelson imagined when he "danced with a white girl in a Harlem cafe." Among ordinary slummers, in fact, the Negro vogue depended upon the maintenance of racial boundaries; the thrill was derived from their temporary relaxation. Middle-class whites crossed over to the "black side" for the night, but almost all of them returned to the safe confines of whiteness and secure, segregated urban and suburban neighborhoods by morning. This said, however, at least some small portion of the white visitors to black-and-tan cabarets was committed to the ideal of racial equality. Traveling to Harlem and Bronzeville like other slummers to partake of jazz, liquor, and other forbidden pleasures, these musicians, literati, and socialites struck up significant cross-racial relationships with the black women and men they met on their visits. While such relationships often remained fraught with racialist, and sometimes even racist, implications, they far exceeded the exoticism that motivated most whites to visit black neighborhoods. Moreover, they provided the hope that racial and urban boundaries could be not only temporarily transgressed but ultimately eradicated.[48]

Numerous jazz historians have written about the friendships that developed between black and white musicians, especially the Chicago-based players who rose to national prominence during the 1920s and 1930s. Eddie Condon, Art Hodes, Benny Goodman, and many other young white musicians made repeated trips to Bronzeville to take in the jazz stylings of Earl Hines, Joe "King" Oliver, Bessie Smith, and others, often striking up personal relationships and, on rare occasions, jamming with them at some of Chicago's more prominent black and tans. Noting the growing presence of these white musicians in Bronzeville during the mid-1920s, the *Chicago Defender*'s music critic Dave Peyton remarked that "Louis Armstrong . . . is drawing many Ofay musicians to Dreamland nightly to hear him blast out those weird jazzy figures." Indeed, after learning about Bronzeville clubs from students at North-western and the University of Chicago, Jimmy McPartland, Lawrence "Bud" Freeman, and the rest of the famed Austin High School Gang dropped by the black and tans almost every night to study the experts' techniques.[49]

The white clarinetist Milton "Mezz" Mezzrow understood that he and his fellow musicians were joining a "revolution simmering in Chicago" in their quest, with other white slummers, to partake of black nightlife and music. But taking pride in the friendships he made with black musicians, he suggested that white jazz performers had done slummers one better. In his best-selling 1946 autobiography *Really the Blues*, Mezzrow wrote:

Making friends with Jimmy [*sic*] Noone, and Sidney Bechet and Joe Oliver and Clarence Williams, I began to feel like I owned the South Side. When I stood around outside the Pekin, beating up my chops with Big Buster, and he put his arm around my shoulder in a friendly way, I almost busted the buttons off my vest, my chest swole up so much. Any time I breezed down the street, cats would flash me friendly grins and hands would wave at me from all sides, and I felt like I was king of the tribe.[50]

In remarking that he felt like he "owned the South Side" and was "king of the tribe," Mezzrow claimed black jazz culture as his own—an act that suggests some of the proprietary issues that complicated relationships between black and white musicians and simultaneously confirms the genuine sense of welcomeness that Mezzrow felt from black members of the Chicago jazz scene. For musicians like Mezzrow, race became un-important. Adopting jazz as their profession, these young white Chica-goans learned to value the musicianship of their colleagues irrespective of skin color. As jazz historian Burton W. Peretti argues, "No other identifiable group of white Americans of this era approached black culture with such openness and repaid it with comparable gratitude, praise, and emulation" as these white jazz artists did.[51]

Many black musicians and entertainers apparently welcomed the friendship that their white counterparts extended to them, greeting them warmly when they visited Bronzeville. Russian immigrant pianist Art Hodes recalled that whenever he and Joseph "Wingy" Manone dropped in to hear Louis Armstrong at Chicago's Savoy Ballroom, "Louis would see us at once, and his face would light up—and we'd feel warm inside." Mezz Mezzrow experienced a similar camaraderie with numerous black jazz personalities in Bronzeville and, later, in Harlem where he supplied "tea" (marijuana) to Armstrong and many other performers throughout the 1930s. Such relationships existed not only in the minds of white musicians, but also in the hearts of numerous black performers. Speaking of a slightly older group of white jazz players, including Bix Beiderbecke, Pee Wee Russell, and Frank Trumbauer, African American bassist George "Pops" Foster remembered, "We just got together for kicks. The colored and white musicians were just one" in early 1920s Chicago. In fact, Foster remarked, the relationships were so close that black and white jazz musicians would even "go out with the same girls." Louis Metcalf, a trumpeter with Duke Ellington's band, confirmed that similar relationships existed between the black musicians who played in Harlem's cabarets and the white musicians who came to listen. As in Chicago, Beiderbecke was a particularly welcome figure. "Why, Bix would come uptown and blow with us, eat with us, sleep with us," Metcalf later recalled. "He was one of us."[52]

But not all black musicians recalled having such close relationships with whites, nor did they always speak fondly of their interactions in black and tans. They were well aware of their position in the social power structure and of how that position constrained their friendships with white musicians, despite everyone's best intentions. Referring both to the faddishness of the Negro vogue and to the racially discriminatory policies that banned black patrons—and, often, musicians—from white cabarets and dance halls, Milt Hinton sarcastically recalled that Chicago's black jazz artists "didn't fraternize with white guys. . . . We didn't go downtown to the College Inn to hear Ben Bernie, you see. It wasn't chic."[53] Years after the fact, black jazz pianist Lil Hardin Armstrong told Bud Freeman that Bronzeville musicians had often felt uncomfortable under the gaze of white musicians. "We used to look out at you all and say, 'What are they staring at? Why are they all here?'"—a remark that suggests that Chicago's black musicians, at least in the early years, did not always consider their white counterparts' presence at Bronzeville cabarets to be particularly friendly.[54]

Black musicians had good reason to be skeptical of their white colleagues' participation in the nightlife of Bronzeville and Harlem. According to one Bronzeville resident, when white musicians arrived at the Lincoln Gardens to hear Louis Armstrong and King Oliver play, they "literally muscled their way through the throngs of black dancers to get near the bandstands" and, once there, "hog[ged] that area until just before dawn." Even more problematically, as jazz historians Berton Peretti and William Kenney have demonstrated, white musicians often viewed black jazz through the very same prism of primitivism that attracted other white slummers. Like Mezz Mezzrow, many of them praised the "simple and natural" bearing of black jazz musicians, believing that "everything the Negro did . . . had a swing to it," and they expressed little or no misgivings about asking prominent black entertainers to set aside their studied performances of popular tunes, in favor of some "real lowdown New Orleans gutbucket" blues.[55] When white musicians memorized and appropriated the improvisations they heard on such occasions, only to repeat them in the higher-paying, segregated white nightspots where black performers were banned, they gave their black colleagues still more reason to doubt their sincerity and friendship. Calling attention to this complicated combination of "love and theft," the black doorman at the Sunset Café reportedly welcomed white musicians to his club by noting that they had "c[o]me for another music lesson, didn't you?" But Lil Hardin Armstrong was even more blunt in her assessment of the white musicians' actions: "Many famous white performers came out to seek inspiration at the Dreamland, or so they said," she told one longtime Bronzeville resident. "Actually, they were stealing our material."[56]

Jazz musicians were not the only ones who struck up congenial, if complicated, relationships with the black women and men they met in Bronzeville and Harlem. A substantial group of New York socialites and literary figures also used their slumming excursions to black and tans to expand their circle of friends and acquaintances. Writer and photographer Carl Van Vechten, his actress-wife Fania Marinoff, and many of their white friends and social acquaintances—among them, publishers Alfred and Blanche Knopf, socialites Rita Romilly and Muriel Draper, Wall Street banker Edward Wassermann, and Greenwich Village artist Robert Winthrop Chanler—developed significant cross-racial friendships, regularly inviting their black friends to dinner and cocktail parties in their homes. "What was at first an innovation and a novelty soon became commonplace, an institution," African American journalist George Schuyler wrote of the Van Vechtens' "revolutionary" parties and the challenge they posed to 1920s racial norms. Not only did these occasions cement the hosts' developing friendships with their black guests, but they also introduced black performers and intellectuals into the usually segregated social lives of numerous other white socialites and celebrities, ranging from the cosmetics mogul Helena Rubinstein, actress Tallulah Bankhead, and artist Salvador Dali to writers such as Theodore Dreiser, Somerset Maugham, Noël Coward, and Elinor Wylie. At a time when such cross-racial interactions were still quite rare, they provided hope for at least some black activists. "If those of the upper crust could be weaned over to such social acceptance," George Schuyler argued, "it was likely that a trend would be started which would eventually embrace the majority of those whites who shaped public opinion and set the social pace."[57]

Scores of prominent blacks contributed to this noble project simply by spending an evening amid the comfortable interracial atmosphere that the Van Vechtens labored to create in their lavish West 55th Street apartment. The guest list often included the writers Zora Neale Hurston, Eric Walrond, and Nella Larsen Imes, activist-actor Paul Robeson, NAACP officers and authors Walter White and James Weldon Johnson, and popular performers such as Nora Holt and Jules Bledsoe. The Van Vechtens' parties "were so Negro," according to Langston Hughes, "that they were reported as a matter of course in the colored society columns, just as though they occurred in Harlem." Here, blacks and whites alike partook of scintillating conversation, premium bootlegged liquor, and live entertainment from some of the nation's most prominent performers. Like their white counterparts, the Van Vechtens' black friends were often asked to perform at these gatherings. As a result, their guests were as likely to be treated to the musical stylings of Ethel Waters and Bessie Smith or the Charleston dancing of poet Countée Cullen, as they were to be entertained by Marguerite d'Alvarez's arias, George Gershwin's latest compositions, or Adele Astaire's fancy footwork.[58]

Those Harlemites who were invited downtown returned the favor by hosting dinners and parties for their new white friends and acquaintances. Wallace Thurman's parties drew bohemians from both the Village and Harlem, while Walter White and James Weldon Johnson welcomed such prominent downtown celebrities as *Vanity Fair* caricaturist Miguel Covarrubias, attorney Clarence Darrow, and the Theatre Guild's Lawrence Langner and Armina Marshall. "All classes and colors met face to face" at Taylor Gordon's ritzy rent parties, according to

African American society columnist Geraldyn Dismond, "ultra aristocrats, bourgeoise [sic], communists, Park Avenuers galore, brokers, publishers, Broadway celebs, red comrades and Harlemites." But Harlem's
most spectacular interracial parties were presented by A'Lelia Walker,
the heiress to Madame C. J. Walker's beauty products fortune. At both
her Harlem apartment and her townhouse, the ground floor of which
she opened for most of the late 1920s as an exclusive tearoom called the
Dark Tower, Walker produced elaborate parties which were, in Langston
Hughes's estimation, "as crowded as the New York subway at the rush
hour—entrance, lobby, steps, hallway, and apartment a milling crush
of guests, with everybody seeming to enjoy the crowding." Attended by
visiting European dignitaries, numbers runners, and racketeers, as well
as New York's most fashionable black and white entertainers, literati,
and socialites, Walker's parties were the height of Harlem's interracial
mixing. "Wherever else one is invited or expected," the young white
novelist Max Ewing wrote his parents in Ohio, "one must cancel all
other plans if invited to A'Lelia's! She is the Great Black Empress, She
Who Must Be Obeyed!"[59]

Although such parties provided much drunken entertainment for
both whites and blacks, many of the cross-racial friendships that were
established through these networks far exceeded the party circuit. Carl
Van Vechten, for instance, provided literary advice to several writers,
including Rudolph Fisher and Nella Larsen Imes, loaned money to Paul
Robeson and Langston Hughes, funded European trips for Ethel Waters
and others, and helped popularize the recordings of blues musicians,
including Bessie Smith, with published reviews in Vanity Fair. As one
of the so-called Negrotarians, a word that Zora Neale Hurston coined to
refer to the white women and men who specialized in "Negro uplift," he
joined with Fania Marinoff, Muriel Draper, journalist Heywood Broun,
and novelist Fannie Hurst, as well as a host of business liberals including
Alfred A. Knopf, Albert Barnes, Otto Kahn, Julius Rosenwald, and Horace
Liveright, to support the NAACP and the Urban League with generous
contributions and rousing turnouts at the organizations' annual dinners
and balls. At other times, the cross-racial friendships of the Van Vechtens
and others took on more radically political dimensions. When urged by
Langston Hughes to become involved in the infamous Scottsboro case
of 1931, in which nine itinerant black men were unjustly sentenced to
death for the rape of two white women near Scottsboro, Alabama, Van
Vechten, Draper, the artist Prentiss Taylor, and others helped publicize
the racist inequities of the trial, donating time, creative work, and funds
to the effort to overturn the men's convictions.[60]

These involvements confirmed Fania Marinoff's claim, published in the London *Sunday Herald* in 1927, that she and her husband were "engaged in a crusade to break down the colour bar," but their crusade, of course, had its limitations. Like other white New Yorkers, Van Vechten and Marinoff sometimes found themselves constrained by social convention. Holding their May 1929 bon voyage party at the Algonquin Hotel, for example, the couple acquiesced to the unspoken rule that blacks were not allowed in this all-white space by excluding the black friends who would ordinarily have attended such a function. On occasion, even those who had become accustomed to hosting interracial gatherings in their private apartments resegregated their invitation lists, giving in to outside pressure from disapproving whites. Such was the case when the novelist Max Ewing hosted a soiree in his studio apartment to which Emily Vanderbilt had been invited. "At the party we were all sorry not to have Taylor Gordon and the other Negro friends," Ewing told his parents, "but their absence was due to Emily, who is in the throes of her divorce suit, and as Bill Vanderbilt is very conventional, he could never understand the toleration of Negroes as guests, and could only see some scandalous aspect of their being there, and Emily is afraid he would cut down her alimony on the grounds of her being too wild a woman, who entertains black men, and so forth." Yet even when blacks were included in the guest list, such easy concessions to racist convention raise serious questions about both the level of and the desire for social equality between New York's sophisticated whites and blacks. For although the cover of darkness promoted toleration, equality, and fraternization, the harshness of day often revealed the stark inequalities and prejudices that continued to separate these two racialized groups in urban America.[61]

"Colored and white people mix together": The Remarking of Race in the Negro Vogue

Whether participants used the Negro vogue to bridge some of the differences that separated their urban communities and cultures or to reinforce those differences, its cultural legibility and popularity depended upon the existence of easily recognizable definitions of race. The lines between blackness and whiteness had to be clearly drawn—even inscribed—on the urban landscape, before they could be traversed. Slumming expeditions to Harlem and Bronzeville accomplished this task by reifying the geographic boundaries that segregated blacks from other groups in the city. And in doing so, these seemingly innocuous night-time excursions helped to reshape the popular conceptualization of racial difference, shoring up a new hegemonic social order that insisted upon a polarized racial distinction between black and white.

In early-twentieth-century New York and Chicago, the boundaries between blackness and whiteness were anything but clear. Not only had the migration of tens of thousands of blacks, the vast majority from the U.S. South but some from the West Indies, produced a black urban population scored by significant class and color distinctions, but the arrival of huge waves of darker-skinned, "in-between" southern and eastern European immigrants had further complicated the urban racial schema. Indeed, the investigative reports of the major anti-vice organizations of both Chicago and New York are replete with instances in which white investigators professed confusion about the racial identities of the individuals they encountered in black-and-tan spaces. Not even blackness could be determined with any particular degree of certainty. In the winter of 1921, for instance, when white investigators from Chicago's Committee of Fifteen visited a buffet flat in Bronzeville, they reported their confusion about the racial identity of one of the women they encountered. "In all appearance," they noted, she "appears to be a white girl, inasmuch she told us that she was of negro descent." The white staff of New York's Committee of Fourteen expressed similar difficulties in discerning race during their investigations of Harlem, admitting at one point that the chorus girls at Connie's Inn, "while colored, are so white that the true facts of their color can be known only to colored people." Yet even the black proprietors and employees of Harlem and Bronzeville establishments sometimes had trouble determining the racial identities of their paler patrons. When a light-skinned African American Philadelphian, whom New York's Committee of Fourteen had hired as a temporary investigator, visited a black-run Harlem cabaret with members of his family, he recalled that the staff "started at first not to serve us thinking we were white," until "some one in the place recognized me [and] came to my table and spoke so every thing passed off O.K."[62]

Amid such confusion over the color of blackness, however, municipal authorities in both Chicago and New York frequently acted as if they had the ability to accurately determine race on sight. This was especially true when they encountered light-skinned black women in the company of darker men. In such cases, even when the individuals involved protested to the contrary, local police and anti-vice investigators almost always assumed that such women were merely pretending to be African American in order to camouflage their relationships with black pimps or to profit in some other way. Doubtless this was sometimes the case. When jobs were scarce during the early years of the Depression, for example, a black Chicago newspaper reported that at least "two beautiful [white] Broadway chorines . . . executed affidavits to the effect that the tinge of Sepian blood runs through their veins" in order to obtain employment as dancers in a Harlem cabaret. But the certainty with which local white officials approached such situations was as likely as not to miss the mark.[63]

The fact that some whites did successfully exploit the troublesome connection between racial identity and skin color should have alerted white authorities to their flawed thinking in this matter. After all, even an occasional white undercover anti-vice investigator sometimes utilized the disjunction between racial identity and skin color in an attempt to gain entry to black nightspots. Told by the management of Harlem's Snug Café that, on orders of local police, they no longer admitted whites to their establishment, the Committee of Fourteen's David Oppenheim cunningly suggested that if they were willing to admit him, he would promise to "pass" as Cuban should the police question his presence in the cabaret.[64] As useful as such tactics often proved when white reformers investigated otherwise inaccessible black and tans, the possibility of their flip side deeply disturbed white municipal authorities. They shuddered to contemplate the fact that numerous light-skinned blacks, often passing as Spanish, Jewish, or Italian, were also able to manipulate the disjunction between color and race, not only gaining access to white restaurants and public amusements, but also sometimes disappearing permanently into the white world.[65]

In most situations, however, rather than confusing the definition of race, the Negro vogue contributed to the solidification of the social and physical boundaries that separated urban blacks from whites. Because their attraction revolved around reified notions of racial difference, the success of black-and-tan cabarets required the drawing of a sharp dichotomy between black and white—a contrast that provided little room for recognizing ethnic or class differences. As a result, when first- and second-generation Italian and Jewish immigrants visited the cabarets of Harlem and Bronzeville, they were able to stake out a claim to whiteness simply by contrasting themselves with the black objects of their slumming expeditions. "Stepp[ing] outside many of their cultural definitions of the past, but . . . refus[ing] to step across the barrier of race," historian Lewis A. Erenberg has noted, "whites of all ethnic backgrounds [became] white and hence American" when they ventured into black and tans. The participation of Jewish and Italian Americans in the Negro vogue, then, facilitated their absorption into a broader conception of American whiteness that was secured only through the continued subjugation of blacks.[66]

Perhaps because of this newfound ability to "whiten" themselves in the cabarets of Harlem and Bronzeville, the craze for black-and-tan slumming proved extraordinarily popular with Jewish and Italian immigrants and their descendants. As early as 1914, investigators from New York's Committee of Fourteen began to note their growing presence at many of the highest-caliber slumming venues in Harlem, including Barron Wilkins's Astoria Café. In Bronzeville, Jews and Italians were likewise discerned among the thousands of patrons in the district's most popular nightspots, where they comported themselves much like any other slummer. Indeed, when visiting local black and tans, many Jewish and Italian couples exploited the primitivism associated with the Negro vogue to indulge their most primal desires, copying the carefree behavior that had come to signify whites' racial privilege in such spaces. At Bronzeville's renowned Entertainers' Café, the antics of one particular set of Jewish slummers grew so extreme that a columnist for the *Chicago Whip* remarked that it constituted the "best free side-show [he] had ever witnessed." Recounting the incident for the newspaper's black readership, "Nosey" reported that "Two friends from the Jewish colony had interlocked and entwined their bodies so successfully that it was difficult to tell one from the other. According to a speedometer held in the hands of the floor-walker, they were shaking the shimmy at the terrific rate of 70 miles per hour." But just as they reached the climax of their dance, "Nosey" recalled, "two policewomen intervened," arresting them for disorderly conduct.[67]

Accused of engaging in the sensual, "primitive" behavior popularly associated with blacks, this young Jewish couple joined scores of similarly apprehended affluent white slummers who were hauled before city magistrates during the early 1920s. Yet no matter how embarrassing the circumstances of their arrest, the very fact that this couple found themselves subjected to such moral policing suggested that they had moved one step closer to the solidification of otherwise tentative white identities. For the arrest, like those of other white slummers, was intended to penalize them for making a conscious decision to engage in conduct that supposedly came naturally to black women and men.

Still, the very fact that Italians and Jews were identified as such in contemporaneous accounts of the Negro vogue confirms that the assimilation of these recent immigrant groups into the ranks of whiteness was far from complete. In fact, anti-vice investigators carefully distinguished between Jews and whites. When an agent from the U.S. Interdepartmental Social Hygiene Board investigated a Bronzeville cabaret where "colored and white people mix together," he described the cabaret's owners not as "white" and "colored" but as "a Jew and Negro," as if to suggest that a Jewish man could not be included in the category of "white." At times, the investigators seemed even to believe that Jews were more closely associated with blacks than with whites, especially when they were in business in the cities' black neighborhoods. An investigator from Chicago's JPA described the appearance of Joe Gorman, the Jewish proprietor of the Paradise Gardens, as having a "rather wide face, wide nose, typical negro in appearance," before crossing out the word "negro" and replacing it with "Hebrew."[68] Indeed, several Jewish and Italian men found themselves positioned, both literally and figuratively, in between blackness and whiteness. As proprietors of the majority of Bronzeville and Harlem black and tans, they actually mediated much of the racial interplay that characterized the Negro vogue. By 1926, Baltimore's *Afro-American* noted that of fifty-six Harlem cabarets registered with the bartenders' union, forty-two were owned by Italians, ten by Jews, and only four by local blacks. In Chicago, the bulk of Bronzeville's cabarets were controlled by Al Capone's Italian syndicate, although most of them, including the Entertainers', the Plantation (figure 22), and the Sunset cafés, had Jewish front men or, like the Paradise Gardens and Dreamland Café, had both black and Jewish managers.[69]

While their skin color and recent immigrant status continued to render Italians and Jews "in-between" peoples in the eyes of many native-born whites, their simultaneous positioning as both slummers and neighborhood business owners complicated their relationships with urban blacks. In a reference to Carl Van Vechten's novel, *Nigger Heaven* (1926), a columnist for Harlem's *Inter-State Tattler* called attention to local Italian and Jewish entrepreneurs' alleged economic exploitation of their black customers and employees by asserting that "Harlem might have had the better suited pseudonyms of 'Wop or Kike Heaven.'" In Bronzeville, a group of African American cabaret performers gave vent to equally racist suspicions, "convinced . . . that they [we]re the victims of a wilful [sic] Jew" when their wages were unexpectedly reduced. But, even as such characterizations of Jewish and Italian business practices resonated with many urban blacks, they were at least partially offset by the praise that others lavished on many of these same proprietors for their equitable treatment of local residents. In Bronzeville, when Jewish cabaret owner Joe Gorman died shortly after serving prison time for liquor violations in 1924, the *Chicago Defender* sought to

22   The Plantation Café, located at 338 East 35th Street near Calumet Avenue, was one of
Bronzeville's most renowned black-and-tan cabarets. It operated from 1924 until early
1928, when federal officials shut it down permanently for Volstead Act violations.
(Reprinted with permission from the Chicago History Museum Archives, ICHi-14428.)

repair his reputation by heralding his "popular[ity] among our people"
and insisting that he was "absolutely unprejudiced." Harlem Renaissance author Claude McKay expressed similar sentiments about local
Italian impresarios, noting that they "were more engaging, freer and
more intimate in their relationship with the Negroes than were the
Irish" saloon owners who preceded them in the district. Even George
Immerman, one of two Jewish brothers who ran Harlem's relatively

segregated Connie's Inn, was proclaimed "one of New York's good fellows without a peer" by the *Inter-State Tattler* for providing financial assistance to a number of local black families, "paying their rents without any thought of returns."[70]

Despite such complicated relationships with the residents of Harlem and Bronzeville, Italians and Jews who visited these districts increasingly positioned themselves as white consumers of a black spectacle. By the late 1920s, they comprised a substantial and visible segment of the white slumming trade that patronized local black and tans. When the attendance of "villagers and the midtown dilettantes" began to fall off at Harlem cabarets in late 1927, local columnist Geraldyn Dismond remarked that their absence was more than compensated by an influx of "tourists and non-gent[il]es from the wilds of the Bronx." In fact, Harlem's nightspots became so popular with recent immigrant groups that the *New York Amsterdam News* reported a noticeable drop in "business at the Savoy . . . during the Jewish holidays."[71]

This extraordinary rate of participation in slumming signaled the upward economic mobility of local Jews and Italians, but it also generated significant concern among the more traditional members of these communities. According to historian Hasia R. Diner, during the late 1920s and early 1930s, the editors of the *Jewish Daily Forward* regularly warned their readers about the alleged dangers of Harlem nightspots and discouraged them from participating in a practice that might implicate them in "a larger pattern of white economic exploitation of blacks." Yet the fact that these warnings appeared under headlines announcing that "the gay night places in Harlem are for whites, not for blacks," subtly undermined the *Forward*'s admonition to avoid such cabarets by casting the racial landscape of the city along a distinct white/black axis and suggesting that the nightspots' Jewish patrons necessarily fell on the white side of this line. At a time when nativist sentiments had prompted the recent imposition of strict quotas on southern and eastern European immigration, slumming provided Jewish and Italian New Yorkers and Chicagoans with an opportunity not only to differentiate themselves from local blacks but also to contribute to the production of a new definition of whiteness that encompassed, rather than excluded, their ethnic particularities.[72]

The power of slumming to redefine the boundaries of whiteness was not, however, without its limitations. Failing to fit neatly on either side of the prevailing white/black divide, men and women of Asian descent generally remained situated somewhere in between. For men of Filipino,

Chinese, and Japanese ancestry, who greatly outnumbered female immigrants from their home countries in the United States, this in-between status made life in Chicago and New York particularly perplexing. Although Asian men generally experienced more freedom than blacks to traverse the cities' streets and to frequent public amusements, they were still marked as nonwhite outsiders in mainstream popular culture. In midtown Manhattan and on Chicago's Near North Side, where a number of so-called Oriental dancehalls specialized in providing white female partners at a dime a dance, Chinese, Japanese, and Filipino men even found themselves equated with blacks. White taxi-dancers routinely referred to their Asian clientele as "monkeys" and "niggers," even though the men's willingness to purchase multiple dances in order to gain access to female companionship usually made them more lucrative customers than working-class whites. The racial divide between these women and their Asian customers was further reinforced when the former rejected the romantic advances of the latter, insisting that they were "staying white"—that is, that they were "accepting dates from only white men."[73]

Despite the risk of being branded "nigger lovers," however, not all white women ignored the amorous entreaties of Asian men, and those who accepted found the cabarets of Harlem and Bronzeville to be a welcome retreat from the racial prejudices and public scrutiny of fellow whites. The restaurants of Chinatown provided a similar haven for white/Asian couples, but the cities' popular black and tans were uniquely positioned both to promote cross-racial encounters and to allow Chinese, Japanese, and Filipino men to avoid community supervision of their social and sexual lives. Capitalizing on the nightspots' well-established reputations for race mixing, Asian men frequently invited white dates to accompany them on late-night excursions through the black entertainment districts of Chicago and New York—hoping above all else to escape the name-calling and occasional violence that attended their recurrent patronage at the cities' Asian-oriented taxi-dance halls. More often than not, they achieved their goal: The management and patrons of local black and tans welcomed these white/Asian couples in the very same way that they greeted every other slumming party.[74]

Yet just as the presence of white women in the company of black men sometimes stirred animosities among white pleasure seekers, Asian men who escorted white women to Harlem and Bronzeville occasionally encountered resistance from fellow slummers. In one particularly violent incident at Chicago's Sunset Café, when a young Filipino man named John Suarrez confronted two separate slumming parties who insulted his white wife, he was challenged to "come on outside" if he wanted to defend her honor. Accepting the men's invitation, he accompanied them to an alleyway behind the cabaret and, while doffing his coat to prepare for the fight, was gunned down by one of his white hecklers. Most Asian men eluded such brutal responses to their cross-racial liaisons with white women, but the publicity generated by the Suarrez incident and others like it served as a not-so-subtle reminder of Asian immigrants' continued nonwhite status in the urban racial hierarchy. Black-and-tan slumming might have been able to extend the boundaries of whiteness to incorporate Jews and Italians, but its power to "whiten" never extended to immigrant groups originating outside Europe.[75]

Accounting for these limitations on slumming's ability to reformulate whiteness, however, fails to capture the full effects of this popular pastime on the reconfiguration of popular conceptualizations of race at the height of the Negro vogue. Because the mechanics of slumming contributed to the re-marking of the boundaries of whiteness, they necessarily redefined the contours of American blackness. Although urban blacks recognized significant differences among themselves, the droves of white pleasure seekers who flocked to local black and tans saw them all as equal components in the spectacles that comprised the Negro vogue. Flattening out distinctions of class and national and regional origin, slumming marked all dark-skinned people as racial others, whether they were longtime urban residents or more recent arrivals from the Caribbean or the rural South. In fact, the white perception of blackness became so homogeneous that private detectives hired by New York's Committee of Fourteen actually seemed befuddled when an African American entertainer at Harlem's Shuffle Inn referred to some of her fellow performers as foreigners. "She said that the band that was there that night she did not like as they were foreigners," the detectives reported with apparent surprise, since the performers clearly appeared to be black. Only later did the investigators realize that the entertainer had "mean[t] they were West Indians."[76]

Among the black residents of Harlem and Bronzeville, however, differences of class, color, and national and regional origin retained their currency well into the 1920s. Primary among these were the class and regional distinctions that separated the cities' "Old Settlers" from the recent arrivals. Historians James R. Grossman, Gilbert Osofsky, and others have shown that the Old Settlers of Chicago and New York adopted rather paternalistic attitudes toward Southern migrants who participated in the Great Migration. Having experienced a relatively congenial relationship with urban whites during the late nineteenth and early twentieth centuries, they blamed the "backward," rural ways of these newcomers for the rising level of racial animosity in both cities. Through community newspapers, churches, and social reform organizations, the Old Settlers undertook extended campaigns to educate the new arrivals on the proper behavior expected of blacks in northern urban centers. They discouraged migrants from wearing work clothes in public, gathering on street corners, talking loudly and in "vile language," and living in "unsanitary houses."[77]

For the most part, the behaviors that rankled middle-class urban blacks were attributed to two cultural factors: the migrants' Southern identity, including rural customs and mores, and their overwhelming youth. Just as the Old Settlers urged newcomers to reject such Southern traditions as eating pigs' feet and watermelon and wearing head rags and overalls in public, they protested against the singing of "plantation melodies" and the proliferation of jazz and blues which arrived in Chicago and New York via New Orleans and rural Southern honky-tonks. Quoting stride pianist Willie "the Lion" Smith, jazz historian Kathy J. Ogren has argued, that "the 'average [northern] Negro family did not allow the blues' precisely because they wanted to distance themselves from the South." Yet the blues and jazz were so popular with the young women and men who made up the bulk of the migrants that some longtime urban residents began to blame them for creating the very spectacle that white slummers came to see. In the *Chicago Defender*, for instance, YWCA member Mrs. B. S. Gaten railed against young black women "dancing in a rareback fashion entirely too close to her partner to be anything other than VULGAR," while reporters at the *Whip* rebuked "people who have recently arrived from the South, and who have not learned that better accommodations and shows can be found elsewhere," for encouraging the perpetuation of "lewd" performances at several white-owned nightspots. As literary historian Hazel Carby has noted, urban middle-class blacks were particularly vigilant in their efforts to police the social and sexual behavior of migrant women—both because they believed women could temper the sexual desires of men, and because the figure of the sensuous black seductress was frequently mobilized by racist ideology to portray black neighborhoods as spaces of social disintegration and their inhabitants as morally inferior, uncivilized subhumans.[78]

West Indian immigrants were also subject to intraracial scorn, especially in Harlem, where they numbered, according to historian Jervis Anderson, more than twenty percent of the black population by the early 1930s. Unlike Southern migrants, West Indians were not censured for lewd and immoral behavior; on the contrary, native-born blacks often thought them particularly moral, straitlaced, and religiously strict. Instead, because of their tendency to open small businesses like those run by Jews in Harlem and Bronzeville, Caribbean immigrants became targets of a black nativist rhetoric that cast them as foreign, frugal "black Jews." This distinction, however, did not protect them from being accused of contributing to the primitive, jungle-like atmosphere that attracted white slummers to Harlem. In the eyes of longtime residents, wearing "tropical clothing" and speaking in unfamiliar accents made West Indians especially vulnerable to such accusations. Ironically, however, when Harlem's native-born residents expressed their disdain for such practices, they often invoked the very rhetoric of primitivism that white slummers used to refer to blacks more generally. Calling the West Indians "monkey-chasers," "monks," "ringtails," and "monkey-hip eaters" (the last derived from the legend that Barbadians's favorite meal was monkey hips and dumplings), they copied the worst practices of white slummers, suggesting that their own humanity could be assured only by rendering others inferior African animals.[79]

On occasion, affluent blacks also employed the rhetoric of white slummers to shore up their class position within the black community. As the rising popularity of jazz drew more and more of them to the cabarets of Harlem and Bronzeville, many of these women and men claimed that, like white slummers, they were visiting local black and tans simply to observe the behavior of the resorts' black working-class patrons. "Many more of the 'elite society' folks," a gossip columnist for the *Chicago Whip* noted in 1921, "ha[ve] taken to 'slumming' as they call it when they want to go to a cabaret and have some excuse afterwards to tell their friends."[80] Black jazz singer Alberta Hunter recalled that at Chicago's Panama Club, the proprietors actually split the cabaret into two separate, morally differentiated, class-marked sections to protect their patrons' social position. "Bricktop, Cora Green . . . and Florence Mills were downstairs," Hunter recounted. "Now, they were like the nice, quiet girls, you know, that sang the nice, sophisticated stuff and like that. But upstairs, they called us barrel-housers. . . . That means you were kind of rough and ready." Along with the other upstairs entertainers, Hunter's job was to belt out the ribald blues that were popular with the club's working-class patrons.[81]

Yet as middle-class blacks flocked to cabarets in expanding numbers, their mimicking of white slummers and their attempts to distance themselves from the black working class often gave way to a greater sense of black community. In part, this was a byproduct of the fact that whites usually failed to recognize any class distinctions among urban blacks, objectifying them all, as dictated by the Negro vogue. But middle-class blacks' increasingly sexual comportment in local nightspots also contributed to the blurring of any remaining social or moral distinctions between the Old Settlers and newcomers. In 1920, the editors of the *Chicago Whip* still recognized a class distinction among black cabaret patrons, chastising members of "one of the leading social clubs in Chicago, morally, socially and economically," for allowing "lewd women of the street" to mix "freely on the same social plane with the best girls of the race" at their New Year's Eve cabaret festivities.[82] But during succeeding years, reporters at this same newspaper became increasingly skeptical that such a difference actually existed. Noting the presence of "three of Chicago's nicest and most refined young ladies" in a crowd waiting to enter a popular Bronzeville cabaret in late 1922, the paper's gossip columnist remarked that "They were laughing in their modest way, talking about the fun there was in 'slumming,' as they called it." Once inside, however, the young women's claims to the supposedly superior status of the slummer quickly gave way to a more complicated reality. The *Whip*'s professional magpie reported that they "danc[ed] with some of the sleek-haired 'sheiks' who make their living off women" and engaged in a range of other behaviors that middle-class blacks ordinarily condemned among their working-class counterparts. "Funny how some people like to make things seem better than what they really are," the columnist chided. "They were not slumming. They were 'doing their stuff.'"[83]

Not only did black middle-class women and men redefine their sexual mores and public behavior in the cabarets of Harlem and Bronzeville, but they also increasingly embraced jazz as a valuable black art form—a development which, as jazz historian Burton W. Peretti has argued, played an important role in "forging . . . [more unified] North black communities."[84] While many black intellectuals advocated the production of a black "high culture," a number of middle-class Harlem Renaissance writers, artists, and scholars, including Langston Hughes, Aaron Douglas, Zora Neale Hurston, and Richard Bruce Nugent, insisted upon the power of jazz to bridge class differences by incorporating its rhythms and techniques into their fiction, poetry, drawings, and criticism. By 1927, even W. E. B. Du Bois began to appreciate the role of jazz and black-and-tan cabarets as cornerstones of a unifying African American culture. Putting aside his skepticism about the primitivism of the performances staged in local nightspots, he joined a host of black and white luminaries to attend the opening of Harlem's black-owned Club Ebony. Surrounded by "the startling blues, reds, yellows and blacks" of the "jungle and jazz-boes" that Aaron Douglas had painted on the nightclub's walls, Du Bois resolved to participate, for this particular evening at least, in a jazz communion that, one local reporter suggested, was capable of "lead[ing] the imagination from Africa to Van Vechten's Heaven and into the wide open spaces."[85]

Even as middle-class blacks stepped up their participation in the black-and-tan nightlife of New York and Chicago, the lights were starting to dim on the Negro vogue. Among fickle white thrill seekers always on the lookout for exciting new urban adventures, the novelty of heading up to Harlem or down to Bronzeville had already begun to wear thin before the stock market crashed in October 1929. But the worsening economy and consequent belt-tightening among middle- and upper-class whites contributed to a further curtailment of the black-and-tan slumming trade. So, too, did the growing competition for slummers' limited entertainment budgets.

When the lingering economic crisis forced white cabaret proprietors in New York's Times Square and Chicago's Loop to look for new ways to attract customers, it did not take them long to arrive at the idea of employing considerable numbers of black jazz performers in their otherwise all-white nightspots. In fact, at least two entrepreneurs were so taken by this concept that they meticulously recreated and repackaged the racy atmosphere of the black and tan within the safer confines of the cities' mainstream entertainment districts. In late 1929, *Variety* reported that Harold Mayberry took over a cellar on West 40th Street, near Seventh Avenue, with the express intention of staging an all-black floorshow that would transport the "lowdown black and tan joint within Times Square precincts." In Chicago, a former manager of the padlocked Plantation Café did much the same in 1932, opening a new Plantation in the Loop at Clark and Lake streets, featuring "a colored show, colored band, and colored waiters together" for the first time in Chicago's principal white entertainment district. A handful of Greenwich Village nightspots even made short-lived attempts at converting themselves into black and tans during the early 1930s. Although these amusements failed to take root among the vestiges of New York's bohemia, they still served to underscore the reorganization of the urban landscape along an increasingly white/black racial axis. This development became even more apparent as the decade progressed and two of Harlem's premier cabarets relocated along Broadway in midtown Manhattan—first, Connie's Inn (in 1933) and later the famed Cotton Club (in 1936). Their move allowed affluent whites to sample the choicest of jazz stylings and black entertainment without ever having to set foot in the segregated black neighborhoods of New York and Chicago.[86]

The decline of the Negro vogue was also fueled by the rising popularity of a new slumming craze focused on the increasingly visible presence of lesbians and homosexual men in Depression-era U.S. cities. Known as the pansy and lesbian craze, this latest in nightlife trends highlighted the entertainment of female impersonators and mannish women, reinforcing the ongoing shift in white urban thrill seeking from the black and tans of Harlem and Bronzeville to the cabarets of Times Square, Greenwich Village, and Towertown. Yet this new vogue not only transformed the terrain of urban exploration in New York and Chicago temporarily but also redirected slummers' attentions away from the racial reorganization of American culture and urban space toward the emergence and codification of a new hetero/homo sexual order. The cities' black-and-tan cabarets quickly capitalized on this development, presenting homegrown lesbian and drag entertainers in elaborate floorshows reminiscent of the Cotton Club's tall, tan, and terrific chorus lines. But by the early 1930s, the mere promise of race mixing was no longer enough to attract the high-dollar crowd; slummers had come to expect their entertainment to be more queer than that.

SIX

The Pansy and Lesbian Craze in White and Black

With the waning of the Negro vogue in the late 1920s, affluent white pleasure seekers increasingly turned their attention to the spectacle of homosexuality emerging in the mainstream amusement districts of New York's Times Square and Chicago's Near North Side. Like earlier generations of slummers, who had ventured into racialized and sexualized neighborhoods inhabited by immigrants, prostitutes, blacks, and bohemian free-lovers, participants in this new slumming craze sought out urban districts where they could indulge a similar fascination with sexual and racial difference. Since the late nineteenth century, three successive slumming vogues had created spaces where the interactions of middle- and upper-class whites with a variety of racial and sexual others had subtly but surely reconfigured the contours of whiteness and sexual normality. This final slumming craze was no exception, spurring a process through which modern notions of heterosexuality and homosexuality became clearly established within the highly racialized contexts of urban commercial leisure. In addition to visiting the white mainstream cabarets at the center of this new nightlife fad, slummers also returned to the nightspots of Greenwich Village and Towertown where white lesbians and pansies replaced the bohemian artists, writers, and political radicals who had previously dominated the districts' tearooms and cabarets. During the late 1920s and early 1930s, New York tabloids reported a "tremendous nocturnal influx of innocent slummers from Brooklyn, The Bronx, Staten

Island and the Jersey cities" attempting to partake of this new source of urban entertainment—efforts that were mirrored in Towertown by frolicsome adventurers from suburban Chicago and other outlying areas.[1]

By 1930, this growing fascination had become a definitive "pansy and lesbian craze," signaled in part by the sudden appearance of the term *pansy* in the headlines of New York tabloids and trade publications such as *Variety* and *Zit's Theatrical Newspaper*. Although akin to the term *fairy* and likewise associated with male femininity, *pansy* hinted at the development of a new urban type—one that implied something closer to our present-day understanding of homosexuality as defined by same-sex sexual desire rather than by the adoption of a particular gendered role in male-male sexual activity. The representation of pansies as closely linked to lesbians underscored their shared state of queerness. Writing of a public that was becoming increasingly "pansy conscious," *Variety* and other publications described entertainments that incorporated male and female impersonators, lesbians, and "nances"—all part of a related phenomenon that was captivating audiences in the racially homogeneous cabarets of New York's Times Square and Chicago's Near North Side during the first half of the 1930s. Male entertainers and patrons predominated in these nightspots, but lesbians formed a significant part of the entertainment and patronage as well, so much so that individuals critical of this development attacked both the "male [and] female impersonators—tribadists and homosexuals—[who] were paid unheard-of salaries in night clubs and cabarets, to pander to the sex-drunk senses of susceptible patrons of these palaces of gin."[2]

Against this emerging understanding of urban homosexuality, white middle- and upper-class slummers began to think of themselves as heterosexuals—that is, as women and men who publicly pursued sexual relations exclusively with members of the opposite sex for reasons other than reproduction or marital obligation. Describing this shift in the popular conceptualization of male-female relations, the once-notorious "girl in the red velvet swing," Evelyn Nesbit, remarked that "love has changed so much," since she rose to fame in the early 1900s, "that nowadays it's usually referred to as 'sex' . . . [and] if you lack sex-appeal—male or female—you are out of the running." Nesbit specifically linked the development of society's new non-reproductive and increasingly public heterosexual norms with the popularization of homosexual entertainments in urban America: "Twenty years ago 'queers' were a rarity," she insisted, "[but] today they are quite the fashion. They are undoubtedly the heaviest drawing cards in the night clubs of today. As for the Lesbian—a decade ago one had to dash for the nearest book of reference to learn the term's meaning. Today they are accepted with a cynical shoulder-shrug and the casual remark that many of them are to be found in the best social circles and that many stars of the theatre and screen are 'that way.' In fact, all the unusual sex sins of this period have now become exceedingly 'common or garden.'"[3]

Just as entering racialized immigrant and black neighborhoods had previously reified the racial singularity of native-born whites, exploring the queer spaces of New York and Chicago allowed slummers to delineate their own sexual identification within the emerging category of the heterosexual. But the reciprocal relationship through which heterosexuality and homosexuality were defined also created opportunities for white lesbians and pansies to establish a more public sense of community—one that could be located with relative ease by those women and men who came to identify as homosexual. With "homosexual 'joints,' 'queer' clubs, pervert 'drags,' or homosexual plays in practically every considerable American city," according to one critic, this temporarily vibrant urban community—and the growing dichotomization of American society along a hetero/homo sexual axis—was almost impossible to miss.[4]

Race complicated the process of sexual identification and categorization in this period, with black nightspots providing even more room for experimentation than white venues did. Even as the distinctive identities of modern heterosexuality and homosexuality were emerging in Times Square and on the Near North Side, black leisure spaces remained arenas in which sexual identities were less fixed and sexual encounters, less regulated. When post-Prohibition crackdowns restricted slummers' access to the spaces initially associated with the pansy and lesbian craze, white curiosity seekers returned once again to Harlem and Bronzeville. In a black-and-tan adaptation of the latest slumming vogue, they ventured out to the districts' dance halls, attending interracial masquerades that put fashionable, cross-dressing lesbians and drag queens on prominent display. Well-to-do white slummers also frequented floorshows in out-of-the-way cabarets where entertainers such as Gladys Bentley and the Sepia Gloria Swanson made careers out of their same-sex desires. While some of the queer performances in Harlem and Bronzeville were similar to the white lesbian and pansy entertainments that slummers had earlier encountered, the contrast between heterosexuality and homosexuality so newly constructed in all-white contexts remained less distinct—and often actually grew more complicated—in the performances and daily practices that flourished in black neighborhoods.

White Mainstream Venues: The Spectacle of Homosexuality and the Making of Heterosexuals

From their earliest pleasure trips to the immigrant and working-class resorts of the Levee and the Bowery, affluent whites sought out sexual spectacles in which male performers embraced female roles by wearing makeup and women's clothing. As the vogue for red-light districts gave way to the search for bohemian *thrillage* in the mid-1910s, interest in these performances persisted. In the tearooms and masquerade balls of Towertown and Greenwich Village, fairies and female impersonators, joined for the first time by substantial numbers of "lady lovers," or, lesbians, were an integral part of the free-love atmosphere. But it was not until the emergence of the pansy and lesbian craze of the late 1920s and 1930s that a slumming vogue focused primarily on such women and men and the spaces they dominated. Centered on the increasingly visible concentration of white lesbians and homosexual men in urban districts, such as Towertown, Times Square, and the Village, this popular new craze called attention to the shared sense of community and homosexual identity that defined this vibrant new urban population. And it provided white urban thrill seekers with an opportunity to explore firsthand the homosexual world that they were already beginning to discover in popular stage shows of the day.

During the latter half of the 1920s, a handful of highly publicized theatrical productions stoked the public fascination with homosexuality in New York and Chicago. In the most celebrated of these plays, *The Captive* (an American adaptation of French playwright Edouard Bourdet's *La Prisonniere*), Broadway audiences encountered a young French woman whose marriage to a male friend never managed to quell her intense sexual desires for the mysterious Madame d'Aiguines. *The Captive* opened in late September 1926 and met with immediate success, netting weekly box-office receipts of $21,000 to $23,000 during its four-and-a-half month run. Within weeks, several Chicago and New York producers maneuvered to capitalize on the show's popularity. Chicago's Adelphi Theater introduced drama enthusiasts to lesbian characters in William Hurlbut's *Sin of Sins*, a play nearly identical in plot to *The Captive*, while producers in both New York and Chicago offered theater devotees a play known as *New York Exchange*, which was said to have "a counter plot of a sort of male 'captive.'" By early 1927, Broadway was atwitter over forthcoming productions of Lester Cohen's *Oscar Wilde* and Mae West's *The Drag*; the former was to document the exploits of its title character, and the latter, to feature "some 30 young men . . . half tricked out in women's clothes and half in tuxedos" in a twenty-minute recreation of the drag party referenced by the play's title. But neither of these plays ever managed to open in New York, falling victim to William Randolph Hearst's campaign for a statewide stage censorship law—the same campaign that prompted local police to close *The Captive* and two other "dirt shows," including Mae West's play *Sex*, in early February 1927.[5]

Despite New York's sudden crackdown on such theatrical productions, the reviews of these shows directed the attention of curiosity seekers to the speakeasies and cabarets that would come to form the core of the city's emerging pansy and lesbian craze. *Variety*'s opening-night review of *The Captive* noted that "'Ladies' of this character are commonly referred to as Lesbians," advising curious theater goers that "Greenwich Village is full of them." The magazine's review of the Bridgeport, Connecticut, premiere of *The Drag* proclaimed that the show played "exactly like a revue number, or the floor show of a night club," including one performer who "sings after the manner of female impersonators." This resemblance to a nightclub floorshow was hardly surprising, given the fact that playwright and producer West had apparently visited "a dim-lit Greenwich Village hangout for chorus boys and girls" to audition more than fifty Villagers for the play's largely ad-libbed drag ball scenes. The review publicized a world that was little known to most readers. During the mid-1920s, the female impersonators and lesbian performers at Jack Mason's Red Mask on Charles Street, Jackie Law's Studio on Fifteenth Street, and several other Village speakeasies catered primarily to a homosexual following.[6]

Only around the autumn of 1928 were pansy and lesbian entertainers of the Village first marketed to an uptown clientele, when Meyer Horowitz hired the campy Scottish drag queen La Belle Rose to headline his popular Village Nut Club at 72 Grove Street. Attired in "bizarre costumes (of her own creation), fantastic make-up," and a "wicked peroxide blonde" wig, La Belle Rose attracted a growing patronage with his "high-soprano" singing and sexy fandango dancing. By the close of the year, he had become a local radio celebrity, and *Variety* estimated that an audience the size of "a small city stayed up two hours past the witching hour" to tune in to his live performances on WMSG and WMCA. Such unprecedented access to drag entertainment fueled the public's growing fascination with these acts. By the end of the decade, slummers were becoming frequent visitors at a number of Village cabarets that previously catered primarily to lesbians and homosexual men. Times Square nightspots even added their own queer entertainment as a way of boosting sagging, Depression-era revenues.[7]

Towertown's speakeasies began to warm up to the pansy and lesbian craze at about the same time, giving rise to several extravagant queer personalities. The flamboyant Ed Clasby drew overflowing crowds of "widows and old maids" to his Seven Arts Club, a roving lecture forum that took up temporary residence in a variety of "alley garages and hotels in the Near North Side." Enticing slummers with sexually explicit lectures by "Prostitutes and Queens as well as scholars," Clasby fashioned himself into the club's main attraction, peppering each night's scheduled entertainment with his own Wildean witticisms and risqué jokes. At nearby Diamond Lil's, located at 909 Rush Street, Roy Spencer Bartlett employed similar tactics in late 1928 to boost his club's popularity with the "college boys" and other curious thrill seekers. Making a spectacle of his fey personality and attire, including a "red tie with a huge imitation diamond stick pin," Bartlett adopted the name of Mae West's controversial play for both himself and his nightspot. He soon became a "huge success" as "Diamond Lil," and on Saturday nights was routinely required to turn away scores of disappointed patrons from his overcrowded establishment.[8]

The popularity of these smaller queer speakeasies paled in comparison to the more mainstream cabarets, even though both types of venues shared a racial exclusivity in terms of audience. Foremost among the larger nightspots that sought to capitalize on the latest slumming craze was New York's swank Club Abbey, a popular West 54th Street nightspot, where, according to Broadway columnist Mark Hellinger, Jean Malin (figure 23) gave up his Village drag act in the spring of 1930 to become "a professional pansy." Malin's act met with such "tremendous success," another local journalist recalled, that several more club owners soon followed his lead, and "before the main stem knew what had happened, there was a hand on a hip for every light on Broadway." But it was the district's original pansy act that remained its most popular and most highly promoted. By the fall of 1930, even the trend-setting *New Yorker* indirectly endorsed Malin's performance by including the Club Abbey in its weekly column "Goings On about Town," which suggested that readers might enjoy mingling with the "Broadway celebrities, rowdies, and others" who nightly gathered at the renowned cabaret. Likewise, in Chicago, where the popular K-9 Club launched that city's "professional" pansy and lesbian craze in the summer of 1930, the cabaret's sophisticated revue of female impersonators was copied by local nightlife impresarios and even promoted, albeit somewhat obliquely, by one of the city's toniest entertainment guidebooks. In his 1931 "intimate guide" titled *Dining in Chicago,* John Drury slyly encouraged amusement seekers

23   Pansy entertainer Jean Malin poses between film actresses Harriet Parsons and Sally Eilers
      at Hollywood's Club New Yorker, where Malin became master of ceremonies in the fall of
      1932 after leaving New York. (Photograph from Modern Screen, March 1933. Reprinted
      with permission from the collection of JD Doyle.)

to join the after-theater crowd at the K-9 Club, a popular but "odd sort
of place," located in the former quarters of a "dog club . . . hence the
name" in the basement at 105 East Walton Place.[9]

   The clubs' almost immediate inclusion in the cities' more upscale magazines and entertainment guides confirmed their centrality in urban
nightlife. By the early 1930s, slummers' participation in the pansy and
lesbian craze was becoming the ultimate mark of cosmopolitan sophistication. This notion clearly resonated with a young University of Chicago
student who insisted on using the term *cognoscenti* to describe the well-
to-do white women and men who visited one Towertown nightspot to
watch the "queens display the latest Parish [Paris?] gowns in 'Drag.'" But
she was hardly the only observer to draw this connection. In early 1931,
Vanity Fair reported that the New Yorkers who attended "Jean Malin's
'smart' Club Abbey" were the very embodiment of urbanity. "Through
a lavender mist," the magazine noted, the cabaret's "somewhat bewil-
dered clientéle" stifled any remaining reservations they had about the

evening's entertainment, choosing instead to "smirk with self-conscious sophistication at the delicate antics of their host."[10]

Despite the singularity that such slumming excursions provided for expressing one's sense of urbanity amid the upheaval of the Depression, not all the women and men who participated in this popular pastime had such particular outcomes in mind. Rather, as with preceding slumming vogues, they sometimes saw their participation in the pansy and lesbian craze merely as a means to gain access to the unique social and sexual opportunities fostered in such racially exclusive, white nightspots. Anti-vice investigators from Chicago's JPA certainly suspected as much when they noted that the Picardy Club, located near the Century of Progress fairgrounds on the city's South Side, employed "several [male] performers, attired as women," and a young male "hostess" with "eyelids colored and lips rouged" who was "supposed to entertain the men patrons." Calling to mind the female nightclub hostesses whom urban reformers insisted were little more than covert prostitutes, this reference to the Picardy's pansy host was clearly intended to imply his sexual availability to the cabaret's male clientele. At Times Square's popular Coffee Cliff cabaret, one of the club's wisecracking entertainers employed more surreptitious tactics to inform his audience about the sexual favors that could be obtained from the cabaret's resident female impersonator. As the begowned entertainer danced with several male patrons, an undercover investigator later reported, the comedian "cracked the following joke 'How does she look? Don't she look like Polly Adler?'" Audience members would have instantly recognized the object of this comparison, one of New York's most notorious madams.[11]

During the pansy and lesbian craze, well-to-do white men were not the only ones to exploit the cover that slumming provided for homosexual experimentation. Their female counterparts also used this vogue to gain easy access to casual same-sex encounters. In part, this development was a direct result of white middle-class women's growing sense of independence and their increased participation in urban public amusements, but it was also a product of the rapid proliferation of specifically lesbian-oriented cabarets during the late 1920s and early 1930s. With destinations catering specifically to their interests, white female slummers professed their fascination with "perversity" as easily as they had begun to speak of sex in general. A nineteen-year-old bleached blonde told a social worker at one Chicago venereal disease clinic that "as soon as she got rid of [the] gonorrhea" she had acquired during a blind date with a local fellow, "she intended to go to a night club called the 'Canine Club'" (actually, the K-9 Club). "She told me that she had heard that you couldn't go to a toilet there without some man or woman following you in," the social worker reported, and her "idea was to meet a pervert and have a sexual experience with one of them." In New York, so many female slummers were believed to be involved in such sexual experimentation that critics, including sociologist Caroline Ware and bohemian journalist Bobby Edwards, suggested that these "pseudo-Lesbians" significantly outnumbered the "real lesbians" who frequented Village cabarets during the early 1930s.[12]

Such references to pseudolesbianism, however, were intended less to acknowledge female slummers' increasing sexual experimentation, than to portray lesbians as dangerous sexual predators, preying upon the innocent young women who visited the queer nightspots of New York and Chicago. Just as immigrant and black working-class men were often construed as predatory threats to white women's sexual purity, white lesbians were similarly perceived as hypersexual beings who might take advantage of otherwise "normal" women. Sounding the alarm against these dangers in the summer of 1932, one tabloid columnist suggested that slumming had turned Greenwich Village into a "Lesbians' Paradise," where "Lesbos, filthy with erotomania," frequently went "on the make for sweet high school kiddies down for a thrill." Hardly unique to sensationalistic tabloids, such accusations gave popular expression to the fears held by a number of observers who believed that the pansy and lesbian craze had the potential to lure their friends and relatives into a life of homosexuality. In Chicago, a young woman consulted a psychiatrist when a female friend expressed a desire "to rent a tuxedo to go to a drag party," shortly after the two had undertaken a "slumming party" to Towertown's Ballyhoo Café. Advised that the only way to protect her friend from the potential hazards of homosexuality "was to stop her from going to that drag party in male costume," the young woman attempted to intervene. But her friend went anyway and, within only a matter of weeks, announced that she had "fallen in love with another girl." This unprecedented expression of lesbian desire confirmed the young woman's fears concerns about the perils of slumming, but it also provided clear evidence that one woman's temporary nighttime diversion could prove to be another's lifelong awakening.[13]

Even as the sexual experimentation afforded by the pansy and lesbian craze provided inexperienced homosexuals with an effective entrée into queer New York and Chicago, the interactions that took place in these nightspots hardly resulted in the display of homosexuality run amok that critics seemed to fear. Just as the preceding slumming vogue for black-and-tan cabarets reified racial hierarchies, this new craze for things homosexual provided well-to-do white amusement seekers with an opportunity for defining and policing the newly emergent boundaries of acceptable heterosexual behavior. As they clung, in the words of *Vanity Fair*, "with one hand . . . to the linsey-woolsey skirts of respectability (that eternal ideal of the bourgeois) and with the other timidly pat[ted] the silken knee of Pleasure," white middle- and upper-class slummers naturalized their own social and sexual transgressions by juxtaposing them with "the wilted postures and tense warbling" of the cities' extensive chorus of pansy and lesbian entertainers. The spectacle of lesbians, pansies, and male and female impersonators provided a useful foil for the shifts in normative sexual practices and gender identities that came to define heterosexuality in Depression-era America.[14]

By the late 1920s, U.S. gender norms had undergone rapid modification. The passage of women's suffrage in 1920 and the increasing social and sexual adventurousness of well-to-do white urban women significantly undermined the nineteenth-century notion that a woman's place lay primarily within the domestic confines of the home. Women ventured, instead, into the cities' public spaces—its department stores, movie theaters, dance halls, and cabarets—spurred by the country's burgeoning urban consumer culture. Concomitantly, the turn-of-the-century masculine ideal of Theodore Roosevelt's "strenuous life" gave way to a more consumption-oriented model of masculinity, as advertisers encouraged white middle-class men to pay closer attention to their appearances. According to historian Kevin White, "sex appeal" became the masculine catchphrase of the 1920s, and whatever anxiety men felt about their gradual shift away from rugged masculinity was largely allayed by advertising campaigns that insisted that male consumers were still "real" men, despite their use of mouthwash, hair pomade, and the like.[15]

But as the economic crisis of the early 1930s deprived many men of the remaining cornerstone of their middle-class masculinity—their ability to serve as the family breadwinners—the consumer-oriented model of modern American manhood required some reinforcement. The commercialized spectacle of homosexuality that formed the centerpiece of the new pansy and lesbian craze proved effective. When well-to-do white men took their female companions slumming, they encountered the perfect counterpoint to highlight their own masculinity. Whatever complaints critics had about the appearance-obsessed American male, he was undeniably masculine, even gruff, in comparison to the stereotypically slim-waisted, limp-wristed, and often-lisping pansies who peopled the stages and audiences of queer nightspots. The distinction became even more stark in early 1933, when New York authorities enforced a ban against male performers appearing in women's clothing, forcing the long-haired Jackie Maye to become, in the words of *Zit's Theatrical Newspaper*, "the first female impersonator to imitate the dames in male attire" when he appeared at the popular Lido Cabaret.[16]

As pansy performers reinforced the masculinity of the cabarets' "normal" male spectators, however, they simultaneously threatened to undermine male slummers' fledgling heterosexual identities by positioning themselves as feminized objects of male patrons' desires. Unlike the earliest slumming vogue, during which the dominant gendered system of sexual classification permitted masculine male patrons in immigrant and working-class resorts to couple with fairy entertainers and other feminine men without calling the slummers' sexual normalcy into question, the pansy and lesbian craze operated within a newly emergent hetero/homo sexual dichotomy that rendered such same-sex encounters undeniably queer. This new sexual paradigm was underscored by cabarets such as Chicago's Ballyhoo Café that employed both lesbian and pansy entertainers, for the performers' joint appearance called attention to their shared identities as homosexuals—identities that clearly set them apart from heterosexual audience members.[17]

Notably, the reorganization of slumming along a hetero/homo sexual axis first developed within largely all-white venues, where racial exclusivity provided a space in which sexual difference, rather than racial difference, became the key marker of identity. Managers of the cities' more mainstream white cabarets further reinforced this hetero/homo sexual distinction by pairing female impersonators and pansy entertainers with fan dancers or other scantily clad female performers who would appeal to male slummers, thereby clearly establishing those men as heterosexuals. Arkie Schwartz, the owner of New York's Club Richman, made this ploy especially clear in the spring of 1932, when he changed the name of his West 56th Street cabaret to the Café Folies Bergére and began billing headliner Jean Malin in conjunction with a "continental revue" of beautiful chorus girls. At Chicago's "flamboyant club" The Pit, one writer recalled, female strippers were similarly employed to offset "that mélange of middle sex which nature started but never finished." The pairing of pansy entertainers and fan dancers—and the overwhelming popularity of the latter with male slummers—became so prevalent in the slumming hotspots of New York and Chicago that queer entertainers even began to lampoon the flimsily dressed women. "A couple of pansy comics," Art West and Lena Rivers, "do THEIR fan-dance at the Club Le Masque in long underwear," a special Chicago correspondent for the *Broadway Tattler* reported in September 1933. "More fanny than fan, though, in . . . [this] case." Such joking should not obscure the crucial role that fan dancers played in popularizing the pansy and lesbian craze. Their sexualized performances, directed specifically at male patrons, helped to shore up an emergent system of sexual classification that privileged heterosexual object choice over gendered sexual desire, as the half-naked heterosexual woman emerged the clear winner in an onstage rivalry that pitted her against the professional pansy of the early 1930s.[18]

Slumming excursions into the lesbian-oriented cabarets of Chicago and New York provided even more tactile means of constructing and reinforcing the new categories of sexual identity. In the early 1930s, two Chicago men known to be "sophisticated as to some of the aspects of queer life" invited their unsuspecting girlfriends to spend the evening at the lesbian-oriented Roselle Inn on Chicago's Near North Side. Shortly after they arrived at the cabaret, one of the men noted:

A girl . . . came over to our table and asked one of the girls in our party to dance with her. After the first dance was over, this girl came over to our table again and asked for another dance with my girl friend. The girl who asked for the dance kissed my girl friend and my girl friend said, "Is that girl drunk—is she crazy?" I then let my [male] friend explain to these girls what it was all about. . . . At first the girls in our party thought these queer girls were clowning and then after being told, they became disgusted. These girls would not have gone down there in the beginning if they were told about this place beforehand. This was merely a way to spend an evening.[19]

The account of this slumming expedition seemingly provides striking evidence of male heterosexual privilege: the men consciously manipulated female sexuality, depriving their girlfriends of information and forcing them to participate in a public enactment of lesbian behavior. But the female slummers may not have been so ignorant of the sexual dynamics of this nightspot as their boyfriends would have liked to believe. If this were the case, the women may have intentionally exploited the heterosexual cover that slumming provided to enjoy somewhat sanctioned same-sex intimacy. The women's professed "disgust" with the homosexual interpretation of their encounters thus served to naturalize their heterosexuality even as it may have obscured their enjoyment of lesbian activity.[20]

Although the queer behavior on display in lesbian and pansy resorts usually reinforced the heterosexual identity of slummers, slumming also contributed to the incorporation of purportedly queer sex acts into the pantheon of acceptable heterosexual behavior. Historian Elizabeth Clement has suggested that middle-class whites' enraptured attendance at the live sex circuses of New York call houses—where female prostitutes performed oral sex on each other for the amusement of paying customers—likely contributed to the increasing acceptance of oral sex within heterosexual relations. In Chicago, where the proliferation of such shows coincided with the rising popularity of the lesbian and pansy craze during the 1933–34 Century of Progress World's Fair, authorities expressed concern that respectable middle-class slummers might emulate the activities on display. Chastising a couple of Chicago "playgirls" for putting on lesbian performances, Dr. Ben L. Reitman argued that "the things that you do in private and public to amuse men are bad for the community." Eliding the difference between same-sex cunnilingus and opposite-sex fellatio, he admonished, "You not only make it easy for men to have extramarital sex but you make perversion and degeneracy funny and delightful to others, and the things that you demonstrate to men they demand from their sweethearts and wives."[21]

While Reitman characterized heterosexual women as the passive audience to their male partners' allegedly perverse requests, in reality many such women actively sought opportunities to expand their sexual repertoire. The pansy and lesbian craze provided them with one means to develop new forms of sexual expertise, as they adapted ostensibly queer sexual practices for use in heterosexual contexts. *Vanity Fair* editor Helen Lawrenson attested that she and her female friends eagerly sought to learn how to perform fellatio, asking "a homosexual friend" for "practical hints on the procedure." In a booth at a local luncheonette, Lawrenson shared his advice with a female friend, using a salt cellar to demonstrate the technique. The lesson proved so valuable that they "became aware that the women at the next table were listening, mesmerized to the point of forgetting their fudge sundaes." For Lawrenson, her friend, and the women eavesdroppers, successfully participating in new heterosexual behaviors depended on access to—although not direct participation in—homosexual practices. Responding to a letter in which a former college classmate wrote about her own struggle to master oral sex, Lawrenson urged, "As to cocksucking, you really should come to New York and join our class." Reitman and other crusaders might have been shocked at such frankness, but Lawrenson glibly noted, "we are practicing like mad. . . . We are such nice girls and we have such an innocent, worthwhile attitude toward it"—testimony that indicated the new practice hardly seemed immoral to the women who sought to engage in it.[22]

The opportunity slumming offered for heterosexuals to indulge in or adopt queer behavior ultimately resulted in intense policing of the boundary between heterosexual and homosexual identities. Lesbian flirtations like those observed at the Roselle Inn provided a titillating, yet relatively harmless, counterpoint for newly developing heterosexual norms. But if the lesbian patrons or entertainers in such cabarets appeared to challenge heterosexual men's control over their dates, they were sometimes greeted with violence akin to what white male slummers used to thwart the advances of black men toward white women in the cities' black-and-tan cabarets. During the winter of 1931, the male impersonator Edna "Eddye" Adams flirted with a young woman in the audience at one of her performances at New York's Club D'Orsay. The woman's boyfriend, New York gangster Dutch Schultz, took Adams's flirtations as a sexual challenge and beat the performer so savagely that she suffered a black eye, a cut lip, and some missing teeth. "There ain't no one going [to] cut in on my gal," Schultz told one newspaper reporter who covered the incident, not "man or dame!" Schultz's response to Adams's supposed lesbian menace also included persuading the cabaret's manager to fire the performer, thus bringing an end to queer entertainment at the D'Orsay and concluding its days as a public haven for local homosexuals.[23]

"Queer people despise Jam people": Resistance and Community Building in the White Mainstream Venues of the Pansy and Lesbian Craze

In the face of such hostile endeavors to separate heterosexuality from homosexuality, it is important to remember that the pansy and lesbian craze, like all preceding slumming vogues, was a product of the social interaction between distinct urban communities. The craze's primary nightspots operated not only for the amusement of white heterosexual pleasure seekers but also as vital meeting places where white lesbians and gay men established a sense of community within the vast physical spaces and anonymity of Prohibition-era Chicago and New York. The social networks that took shape in the private spaces of lodging houses and studio apartments in Towertown, Times Square, and Greenwich Village served as the core of these cities' homosexual worlds, but the connections that provided entrée into these communities were often secured in public spaces. At the height of the pansy and lesbian craze, the sheer proliferation of queer-oriented nightspots meant that such places inevitably became nodes in the process of building a community, albeit a racially homogeneous one, since it developed largely in venues that excluded queers of color. "Queens, fairies, fags," one white New York lesbian commented, "they all flock when they hear of a restaurant or some other place" that seemed to welcome queer patrons—regardless of whether the proprietor's congenial reception was simply part of a ploy to attract a more profitable slumming trade. While claiming that lesbians usually "get acquainted through friends," the woman reported that they, too, sometimes used the cities' queer cabarets to make social and sexual acquaintances. "In the Village you can go cruising," she candidly observed, "and a lot of dykes go to some of the midtown clubs" with similar intentions.[24]

If this observer seemed unmindful of the exclusion of lesbians of color from the nightspots she described, her attitude reflects the larger reality that racial exclusivity was a defining fact in the development of urban homosexual communities. Even as white lesbians and gay men began to establish a unified identity in contrast to the heterosexuality of slummers, the homosexual world they were creating in Towertown, Greenwich Village, and Times Square was riven by race. The spatial reconfiguration of northern urban centers along an increasingly white/black racial axis, in response to the Great Migration, permeated the cities' emerging queer communities—especially within the relatively segregated confines of popular entertainment districts. White mainstream cabarets, including Towertown's Monte Carlo or the King's Terrace near Times Square, might make room for black queer entertainers, such as the Sepia Gloria Swanson and the "smart-smut-songstress" Gladys Bentley, but these performances were intended for the nightspots' usual white audiences of heterosexual slummers, lesbians, and gay men. The inclusion of blacks among the cabarets' vast patronage—whether as slummers or as part of the homosexual audience—would have challenged local Jim Crow practices and thus was extremely rare.[25]

Immersed in the prevailing racial ideologies of the day, white lesbians and gay men usually greeted the presence of blacks in mainstream cabarets with a sense of bemusement, fear, hostility, or some combination of the three. For instance, when Jean Malin challenged the color line by arriving in the company of a large black man at New York's Depression Club, he was "immediately surrounded by a twittering circle of flowers." In this cabaret, which was "devoted to the third sex and interested onlookers," the mere presence of a dark-skinned man was unusual enough to cause a sense of consternation—although at least one New York tabloid offered a more hyperbolic explanation for the scene that allegedly ensued. Claiming that Malin's date was "one of the huge black Ubangi savages left over from the circus at the Garden" and that he had arrived at the cabaret "dressed in a purple blanket and a none too secure looking loin cloth," a journalist for *Brevities* conjured a rather unbelievable spectacle of black primitivism run amok in the city's white pansy resorts. The reporter insisted that, after playfully manhandling Malin to everyone's general amusement, this "seven foot two [inch] . . . savage specimen of the animal world" caused a sudden uproar by attempting to hold a young white baby who, according to the tabloid's increasingly unlikely scenario, had unexpectedly arrived at the late-night cabaret in the arms of her mother, "Nellie, the coatroom girl." No doubt there was some morsel of truth to this story—maybe Malin's companion really was a visiting African entertainer. But the scene that *Brevities* painted for the amusement of its readers was so embellished with racist fantasies of sexual savagery that it evidences the rarity with which such cross-racial encounters occurred in white queer spaces and the potential—if exaggerated—responses that blacks might expect to encounter in similar situations.[26]

The diary of a student from Chicago's Near North Side, procured by sociologist Harvey Warren Zorbaugh during his intensive study of Towertown, provides a more reliable account of the response that likely greeted most black homosexuals when they ventured into white pansy and lesbian cabarets. Recounting an evening spent in a popular Towertown resort, the student recalled that "a group of 'homos' from the South Side also came in," taking seats at a nearby table where they "drank tea and talked loudly of labor." Among the group was one particularly "beautiful boy with red hair and a dead white skin," who apparently piqued the romantic and sexual interests of his observers. But the group also included another gentleman who "claim[ed] to be a Spaniard" and called himself "'Alonzo,'" the student skeptically reported. Unlike his fairer-skinned companion, this darker-skinned man was clearly marked as an outsider in Towertown's white homosexual world. "The village suspects him of being an octoroon," the student recorded in his diary, "and will have nothing to do with him." Although the patrons at this white pansy resort were willing to tolerate the presence of "a group of college boys who had been to the Dill Pickle and were slumming," the mere suspicion that a gay man in their midst might have a single great-grandparent of African descent was sufficient to warrant his exclusion. The ideologies of race and racism ran strong, even within marginalized communities.[27]

Yet the shared racial identity of white lesbians and pansies proved an insufficient foundation for establishing a sense of community. Unlike other recently emergent urban populations (namely, the southern and eastern European and Chinese immigrants and black migrants who had been the focus of earlier slumming vogues), white urban homosexuals shared no ancestral lineage or geographic origin. As a result, the group lacked the traditional public centers of urban community, such as benevolent organizations, mutual benefit societies, synagogues, and churches, that other groups enjoyed. The lesbian and gay community did not even have its own newspaper, although evidence suggests that enterprising individuals exploited the public fascination with the pansy and lesbian craze to make at least a couple of unsuccessful attempts at establishing just such a community mouthpiece in Chicago during the 1920s and early 1930s. Instead, like the bohemian radicals and artists before them, the white lesbians and gay men of Chicago and New York established connections to one another through their interactions in a series of informal tearooms, restaurants, and posh cabarets.[28]

Given the important role that these nightspots played in the formation of a sense of community among the white lesbians and gay men who frequented Towertown, Times Square, and Greenwich Village, they did not always welcome the influx of curious heterosexual pleasure seekers, whose presence disrupted their own queer socializing. While some homosexual women and men sought to exploit slummers' naiveté, pressuring visitors to dance or flirting with them mercilessly until their discomfort with the situation prompted their departure, many of the lesbians and gay men who daily struggled to carve out a space for themselves in the public urban landscape offered significant displays of resistance to slummers. In particular, when the interactions between heterosexual slummers and homosexuals occasioned the foreclosure of queer-friendly spaces—as the confrontation between Dutch Schultz and Eddye Adams did—lesbians and gay men openly expressed their displeasure. As the rising popularity of the pansy and lesbian craze boosted the traffic of white curiosity seekers, the mere presence of heterosexual outsiders in the cities' pansy and lesbian resorts provoked vocal opposition. "One of the queer girls" among the patrons at Towertown's Ballyhoo Café, for example, warned an inquisitive observer that "queer people despise Jam people" (queer slang for heterosexuals) who invade their cabarets.[29]

Despite the disruptions that slumming wrought, the pansy and lesbian craze actually played a pivotal role in introducing otherwise uninitiated white lesbians and gay men to the urban homosexual world. A young woman named Marian, for instance, first discovered the existence

Prof. Magnus Hirschfeld
Europe's Greatest Sex Authority
"HOMOSEXUALITY"
Beautiful Revealing Pictures
Postponed to SUN., JAN. 18, DIL-PICKLE CLUB, 858 N. State St.

24   This placard announced the rescheduled appearance of Dr. Magnus Hirschfeld at Tower-
      town's Dill Pickle Club in January 1931. Hirschfeld, a pioneering Jewish sexologist and early
      advocate for homosexual emancipation, visited Chicago as part of a lengthy international
      tour on behalf of the World League for Sexual Reform. (Reprinted with permission from
      the collection of the Newberry Library.)

of Chicago's lesbian nightspots when she attended a lecture presented
by the infamous clap doctor and slumming tour guide Ben L. Reitman.
"Desirous of making friends of [her] own kind," Marian quickly dashed
off a letter to the congenial speaker, asking for the addresses of some of
the clubs that he had mentioned so that she could set out to explore
their social and sexual possibilities. While enrolled as an undergraduate
at Northwestern University during the early 1930s, pioneering gay activist Bruce Scott experienced a similar introduction to Towertown's queer
venues—acquired through the very advertisements that local nightspots
placed to appeal to heterosexual slummers. "I arrived on campus one
morning," Scott later recalled, "and there were placards all over the
picket fence advertising a lecture by Magnus Hirschfeld on homosexuality at the Dill Pickle Club" (figure 24). Having already recognized his
own homosexuality and hoping to meet others like himself, Scott resolved to take the train down from Evanston on the appointed night.
Although the promised lecture was canceled, the Dill Pickle Club's active promotion of the city's latest slumming craze provided Scott with
a means to bond with campus residents familiar with Chicago's popular pansy cabarets. Hearing of Scott's failed expedition, a counselor in
his college dormitory soon recommended that he make another trip to

Towertown—this time to visit the district's famed K-9 Club and its re-nowned chorus of female impersonators.[30]

For those who were less willing to identify publicly as homosexuals, slumming provided a convenient cover for their presence in popular pansy and lesbian resorts. These women and men could simply position themselves as part of the more general slumming audience—that is, as people drawn to the novelty of the districts' nightspots. Such was the case when a queer man named Clarence bumped into his heterosexual cousin at Chicago's Ballyhoo Café. "Why, Clarence what are you do-ing here?" the cousin inquired, prompting Clarence to lob the same question back at his inquisitive relative. "The cousin said that he was merely visiting this place with friends," a written account of the inci-dent later noted. "Clarence said that he was also," despite the fact that he was known to "frequent the Ballyhoo quite often." "Why, if [my cousin] should only know!" Clarence ultimately admitted—a statement that dramatically underscored the invaluable protection that slumming accorded to fledgling homosexuals.[31]

Whether they chose to flaunt or to camouflage their participation in the urban homosexual world, the lesbians and gay men who gathered in the queer cabarets of New York and Chicago constructed an identifiable white homosexual community in which both women and men were welcome. The repeal of Prohibition in 1933 would usher in an era of more sex-segregated gay and lesbian bars, along with a series of new laws and regulations that prompted increased crackdowns on queer nightlife more generally. But at the height of the pansy and lesbian craze in the early 1930s, the mixed character of the cities' most popular slumming venues promoted a shared sense of identity among female and male ho-mosexual patrons. At Chicago's Ballyhoo Café, for example, the pansies and "mantees," as lesbians were sometimes called during this era, devel-oped a strong common bond, setting themselves apart from the "jam" who came to observe their interactions. Journalist Paul Yawitz observed a similar dynamic in 1931 at a Village cabaret known as The Bungalow, where the "patronage is composed almost entirely of lisping boys and deep-voiced girls."[32]

A significant number of cabarets catered to a mixed, though racially homogenous, homosexual crowd during the early 1930s. On Chicago's Near North Side, Jack Ryan's Phalanstery, the K-9 Club, and the Dill Pickle Club were but a few of the many nightspots that played host to white lesbians and gay men, as well as to substantial crowds of slummers. In New York, Times Square hotspots, including the Club D'Orsay, Louis' on 49th Street, the Jewel Restaurant, and Jack's, provided slummers with a display of "fairies and lady lovers," as did such notable Village cabarets as The Camp, Paul's, and the Greenwich Village Casino. Lesbian entrepreneurs appear to have played a particularly active role in creating mixed spaces and in promoting the shared sense of white homosexual community that they facilitated. After launching her career as the producer of a female impersonator revue at Chicago's Club Piccardy, for instance, lesbian Billie LeRoy actively endeavored to bring lesbians and gay men together in the string of relatively mixed cabarets that she opened on the city's Near North Side during the 1930s. In similar fashion, the Duchess, the mannish proprietor of a colorful Village nightspot, hired a wait staff of "four young 'men' with painted lips and rouged cheeks," apparently hoping to expand her patronage of lesbians and heterosexual slummers to include pansies as well.[33]

In the midst of the pansy and lesbian craze, these cabarets undeniably contributed to the codification of the now-dominant hetero/homo sexual binary by allowing white lesbians and pansies to construct a shared communal identity in opposition to slumming heterosexuals (and vice versa). But they also created spaces in which lesbians and gay men could begin to challenge both the presumed normalcy of heterosexuality and the social privileges that accompanied it. Flirting openly with the heterosexual men in his audience, for instance, pansy entertainer Jean Malin cast public doubt on their sexual normalcy by insinuating that they were not only the objects of homosexual desire but also the possessors of such desires themselves. Just as he challenged the color line by bringing a black guest into a normatively white club, Malin further undermined the foundations of normative masculinity by appropriating the very acts of violence that many "normal" men used to secure their heterosexuality, on occasion greeting the insults of his rowdiest male hecklers with raised fists and, in at least one instance, with a beer bottle broken across a heckler's brow. Gay men and lesbians also disrupted the equation of heterosexuality with respectability and propriety. Painting slummers as socially aberrant interlopers whose "uncouth manner" and loud vulgar antics increasingly warranted, in the words of one disgruntled pansy, "a good, hard slap," queers disclosed the disreputable public behavior that often lay at the very heart of supposed sexual normalcy.[34]

Other lesbians and gay men extended this critique to include fellow homosexuals. Many white middle-class queers preferred the class status and supposed respectability of heterosexual slummers to the unrestrained public behavior of pansy and lesbian performers. "I think a good deal of harm has been done on the stage by talking about pansies," one white middle-class New Yorker remarked in the mid-1930s, adding that he didn't "begrudge normal people their feeling against homosexuals." "I don't object to being known as a homosexual," he later clarified, "but I detest the obvious, blatant, made-up boys whose public appearance and behavior provoke onerous criticism. . . . I don't think it's too good a plan to have homosexuality too much accepted because it gives pansies too much chance. I think the police should stamp it out." A native Californian who had relocated to New York in the early 1930s vociferously agreed, expressing particular contempt for the pansies who entertained in local nightclubs: "Queens prancing around on the street was bad enough, I always thought. No discretion. No dignity. Before a crowd of straight men in a cabaret, being laughed at—I mean, what good did that do us?"[35]

At its most basic, such hostility against "blatant, made-up boys" was an expression of the class divisions that, like race, marked the homosexual world of 1930s New York and Chicago—divisions that simultaneously reinforced the historical shift away from a gendered system of marginalized fairies and mannish women to the privileging of heterosexual object choice over same-sex attraction. Historian George Chauncey argues that homosexual men's decision to eschew the feminine role of the fairy was largely a function of age and rising social status. As white men grew older or assumed work responsibilities in a business world where success was premised on conventionally masculine comportment, they became increasingly likely to distance themselves from the flamboyant public behavior of white working-class homosexuals. Calling themselves "queers," in contradistinction to fairies, white middle-class homosexual men developed a more conservative and covert public style that allowed them to pass in the world of middle-class heterosexuality. They restricted open displays of their sexuality primarily to private spaces and created less recognizable public expressions of their sexual identity and desires, including the use of coded language and the adoption of more normatively masculine behaviors and fashions.[36]

Despite their insistence on distancing themselves from the cities' more visible working-class homosexuals, however, not all white middle-class queer men shunned the popular nightspots of the pansy and lesbian craze. In fact, they sometimes used queer resorts as spaces in which to consciously construct more masculine homosexual identities in juxtaposition with the public personae of both pansy entertainers and heterosexual male slummers. Thus, in his endeavor to "set about to try and invent a new sex" in late 1933, one young queer told a friend that he had purchased a new tuxedo to wear to New York's toniest queer resorts. Apparently hoping to distinguish himself from the berouged, femininely attired pansies he expected to encounter, he placed great faith both in his own masculine comportment and in the notion that the clothes always make the man.[37]

In a similar fashion, some white middle-class homosexual women used their participation in urban nightlife as a means to challenge the gendered conception of lesbians as mannish women in coats and ties. Although they remained much less visible than the highly gendered working-class lesbians—both butches and femmes—who formed the core female clientele of most queer cabarets, growing numbers of middle- and upper-class homosexual women ventured outside their private social networks to assume more public roles. "Gradually a revolution broke out in Lesbian ranks," one New York tabloid remarked in a lighthearted effort to document this trend. "The uptown crowd suddenly went swank. Masculine[ly] attired girls were prohibited in any of the well-known uptown clubs with the exception of Helen Lambert's Club and the Attic Club at 58th Street. . . . No longer did they boast of their masculinity or show off their physical attractiveness through the medium of bobbed hair and collar and tie." Instead, "Lesbians had gone effeminate," the reporter noted, literally refashioning themselves as normatively gendered homosexuals whose common link resided in their attraction to sexual partners of the same sex.[38]

Even as the emergence of significant numbers of self-identified white middle-class masculine queer men and feminine lesbians seemed to herald the historical shift toward the now-dominant hetero/homo binary of sexual classification, their increasing presence in urban public culture had unexpected consequences. First, as these women and men remade the upscale queer nightlife of New York and Chicago in their own image, they rendered it increasingly invisible to prospective heterosexual slummers who failed to recognize any significant difference between the cabarets' normatively gendered heterosexual and homosexual patrons. This was especially true when the latter took the added precaution of going out in complementary pairs of women and men, as white middle-class lesbians and queer men often did by the mid-1930s. No doubt this increasing ability to blend in with their heterosexual compatriots pleased many conservative middle-class homosexuals—both because it allowed them to lay claim to a sense of white bourgeois respectability and because the social privilege associated with this status gave them access to a wider range of public urban spaces. But as respectable, white middle-class queers became less visible in the popular pansy and lesbian cabarets of

New York and Chicago, they drew added attention to the more flamboyant working-class men and women that they left behind. This move
rendered the cities' remaining pansy and lesbian cabarets even more vulnerable to increased regulation in the post-Prohibition era and intensified
the social stigma that working-class lesbians and homosexual men were
forced to shoulder because of their greater visibility. By the mid-1930s,
when local authorities essentially eradicated the pansy and lesbian craze
from the white mainstream cabarets of New York and Chicago, this ever-
present class divide began to challenge any sense of shared homosexual
community that might have emerged across class lines among white
queers at the height of the popular slumming vogue.[39]

In Search of Something New: White Heterosexual Slummers Return to the Black and Tans

During the early 1930s, as local authorities foreclosed on queer-oriented
resorts in the white entertainment districts of New York and Chicago,
the police seemed content to allow the pansy and lesbian craze to reestablish itself in black urban spaces, much as they had quietly con-
sented years earlier to the relocation of white prostitution to Harlem and
Bronzeville upon the closing of the cities' red-light districts. As a result,
a number of white queer entertainers and impresarios transferred their
professional activities from the Village, Towertown, and Times Square
to the cities' less closely policed black neighborhoods. When local authorities closed the Sixth Avenue nightspot where he was working in
drag, Robert Brennan recalled that his employer simply informed the
club's white entertainers that "we've opened up another place." Soon
he was "work[ing] in Harlem where we went to work at midnight and
got through at eight o'clock in the morning." George Burns, an organizer of Greenwich Village masquerades during the 1920s, also shifted
his attention to the less regulated environs of black New York, promoting at least one ball at the Rockland Palace during the summer of 1930.
Even the owners of Harlem's Renaissance Casino were rumored to have
solicited white drag impresario Jack Mason to "host that dainty costume ball they're staging" in the spring of 1932, after his latest Madison
Square Garden extravaganza had been canned by the police. But the
queer attractions of Harlem and Bronzeville that became central to the
continued popularity of the pansy and lesbian craze were by no means
limited to the productions of white entrepreneurs. Rather, they included
the black queer performers and patrons of local speakeasies, who had

developed their own vibrant communities in response to their exclusion from the cities' white homosexual worlds.[40]

Although the de facto racial segregation of New York and Chicago prevented black queers from establishing a residential enclave separate from the rest of the cities' black inhabitants, the boarding houses and kitchenette apartments of Harlem and Bronzeville accommodated a burgeoning—and increasingly visible—population of lesbians and gay men. Like most of the cities' other black residents, a significant number of black queers had moved to New York and Chicago as part of the Great Migration, seeking industrial and service-oriented jobs, including work in local black and tans, as well as a greater sense of freedom. But for black homosexuals, Chicago and New York offered more than the promise of racial equality and decreased poverty. The relative anonymity afforded by the cities' rapidly expanding black populations provided black women and men with an opportunity to engage in unsupervised and often unremarked homosexual relations with each other. Even before the Great Migration, black lesbians and fairies had begun to associate northern cities with increased sexual freedom and tolerance. According to Ferdinand "Jelly Roll" Morton, blues pianist Tony Jackson "happened to be one of those gentlemens [sic] that a lot of people call them lady or sissy . . . and that was the cause of him going to Chicago [from New Orleans] about 1906. He liked the freedom there"—a freedom that included the ease of meeting others who shared his sexual and social interests.[41]

During the Great Migration, this same desire for freedom motivated the journeys of many similar black men and women to Chicago and New York. By the late 1910s, the population of black fairies and lesbians in both cities was ample enough to merit regular mention in the news and gossip columns of the black press, and the association between homosexuality and black-and-tan cabarets was already well established among local residents. Just as white homosexuals had carved out a public space for themselves in the tearooms and cabarets of Towertown, Times Square, and Greenwich Village, black queers exploited the social and sexual possibilities of similar spaces in Bronzeville and Harlem. As centers of other nonnormative sexual practices, including cross-racial sexuality and prostitution, black and tans easily accommodated same-sex sexual desire. As early as 1916, at "certain cafés patronized by both negroes and whites," one Chicago physician reported observing "negro perverts" soliciting white men, and only a decade later, the presence of black lesbians and fairies became so common in Harlem and Bronzeville that slummers began to encounter them even in the districts' more high-toned cabarets. When the director of Chicago's JPA, Jessie Binford, visited the popular Plantation Café in the autumn of 1926, she spotted "groups of negro men . . . who dress as women and with whom groups of white boys associate," while in Harlem, a columnist for the *New York Evening Graphic* reported that "two mannish faced, heavy jawed gals . . . remained absorbed in each other, holding hands in lover fashion," when he visited Tillie's, a popular local restaurant and cabaret. By the early 1930s, when black observers avowed that "sissies in drag [held up] the corners" of Harlem and "lady-lovers cluster[ed] along the curb," it was hardly surprising that one particularly brazen local resort called itself simply the Sissy Club.[42]

Into this robust atmosphere of black queer amusements the slumming trade quickly moved, hoping to skirt the post-Prohibition regulations that had halted the proceedings of the pansy and lesbian craze in the white entertainment districts of Chicago and New York. This virtual segregation of the slumming vogue at the very height of its popularity created a situation rife for social and financial exploitation that extended well beyond the cities' queer communities. In the midst of the Great Depression, this development bolstered the waning black nightlife of New York and Chicago while providing local entrepreneurs with a means to lure affluent white pleasure seekers back to the cities' black neighborhoods. Sensing an opportunity for profit, the districts' nightlife impresarios soon created a distinctively black version of the pansy and lesbian craze that simultaneously indulged slummers' latest fascination with homosexuality and reinvigorated the Negro vogue. Whether in spectacular new black and tans that featured black queer entertainers or in more explicitly sexualized venues where live performances of queer sex acts became part of the draw, the pansy and lesbian craze fueled a new run on Harlem and Bronzeville by thousands of jaded white heterosexual thrill seekers who longed for the latest in urban adventure.

Having grown tired of the plantation décor and near-minstrel performances of popular black and tans, such as Harlem's Cotton Club and Bronzeville's Sunset Café, by the late 1920s, well-to-do whites expressed an increasing desire for more "authentic" black nightlife—by which they usually meant more informal and explicitly sexualized entertainment that drew on stereotypes of black primitivism and sensuality. This thrill seeking was reflected in popular fiction. "I want to see the other Harlem," June Westbrook, the semi-autobiographical character of Blair Niles's 1931 novel *Strange Brother*, told a white male acquaintance at the fictional Magnolia Club, a cabaret much like Harlem's Cotton Club. "I've never been anywhere but these regulation places, fixed up for white people. Let's explore!" In John Dos Passos's *The Big Money* (1936), a novel filled with actual New York locations and overly symbolic character names, Pat Doolittle asked her date, Dick Savage, to leave Small's Paradise and "take me some place low." In both novels, the seemingly real Harlem turned out to be the world of queer-oriented basement speakeasies. In *Strange Brother*, June's new friend took her to the Lobster Pot (a fictionalized representation of the Clam House), where she was surrounded by lesbians and pansies, many of them white, listening to a large, mannish black singer named Sybil (a character styled after Gladys Bentley). In *The Big Money*, Dick escorted Pat to an unnamed, all-black dive where she was soon "dancing with a pale pretty mulatto girl in a yellow dress" while Dick cozied up with "a softhanded brown boy," who called himself "Gloria Swanson."[43]

These commercially successful novels confirmed the growing queer reputation of black nightlife in 1930s Harlem and Bronzeville, encouraging readers to venture out to similar spaces. And venture out they did—first to short-lived basement clubs, and by 1934 to elaborately decorated, queer-oriented black and tans that rivaled the best cabarets of Towertown and Times Square. Given their location off the beaten path, the earlier basement speakeasies had the advantage of being able to offer more ribald entertainments and to operate well beyond the cities' appointed closing hours. When the Sepia Gloria Swanson launched his career in Bronzeville's after-hours resorts, for instance, he literally entertained all night, entrancing patrons with a "whiskey voice," "his every gesture and mannerism more feminine than those of any female, his corsets pushing his plumpness into a swelling and well-modeled bosom." African American jazz guitarist Danny Barker recalled that Swanson kept the slummers so enthralled that they left "stumbling up the stairs in the morning, when the sun would hurt their eyes." Even the colorful performances of the "plump, jolly and bawdy" Swanson fell short of the ribaldry on display at Harlem's short-lived Jitter Bug Club, located in the basement of a private house on West 138th Street. With its "claim to fame . . . vested in its parade of she-men and a chap who could do tricky things with an alleged piano," according to the *New York Amsterdam News*, this resort soon became "a popular night-easy for jaded men and women who wanted to see something different"—something so different, in fact, that it prompted one of the few black cops on the Harlem beat to undertake a one-man "Carrie Nation"–type mission to shut the place down.[44]

By the mid-1930s, the pansy and lesbian craze was so pervasive in Harlem and Bronzeville that even the most timid white heterosexual amusement seekers could comfortably experience this popular slumming vogue. When the Ubangi Club, a venue named to emphasize the

25 Lesbian entertainer and "male impersonator" Gladys Bentley appears in her trademark top
hat and tuxedo in this promotional photograph. (Reprinted with permission from the collection of the Prints and Photographs Department, Moorland-Spingarn Research Center,
Howard University.)

purportedly inherent primitivism of American blacks, opened in the
spring of 1934 on the former premises of the once-popular Connie's
Inn, "Broadway's kings and queens" and an assortment of other white
slummers received a queer version of the same white-glove treatment to
which they had become accustomed at such upscale nightspots as the
Cotton Club (whose management was said to have a hand in the operation of this latest Seventh Avenue rival). Featuring "a chorus of singing,
dancing, be-ribboned and be-rouged 'pansies,' and Gladys Bentley [fig-
ure 25], who dressed in male evening attire, sang and accompanied

herself on the piano," the Ubangi Club was the latest in a long trend of black nightspots designed specifically for white patronage. In Bronzeville, the Cabin Inn and the Annex Buffet shared similar prestige, usually headlined by the Sepia Mae West or Valda Gray and drawing large crowds, which the *Chicago Defender* reported, "appeared to be comfortable . . . and . . . enjoying themselves."[45]

These cabarets became such an integral part of upscale black nightlife that, following the tradition of earlier Bronzeville entertainers, including Louis Armstrong and Jimmie Noone, Dick Barrow (who performed as the Sepia Mae West) recorded what amounted to a promotional number for the Cabin Inn. Backed by Dott Scott's Rhythm Band, Barrow's Decca recording of "Down at the Cabin Inn" gave listeners a sample of what they could expect at Bronzeville's "oddest night club":

There's Jimmy singing his jazzy jazz;
Impersonators do the rest.
You buy whiskey any blend.
You don't need much dough to spend.
There's the best of class and brand new friends
Down at the Cabin Inn.

By the summer of 1935, local jazz aficionados in New York could even tune in Gladys Bentley's Ubangi Club proceedings in nightly broadcasts on WMCA, until "that buxum [*sic*] lass singing there" became too much for the local station and the show was picked up by CBS for a short-lived national broadcast in February 1936.[46]

For those slummers who preferred more intimate settings, however, the buffet flats and upscale apartment-clubs of Harlem and Bronzeville recast the pansy and lesbian craze within the context of the private residence, accompanied by all the amenities such venues implied. Some, like the dapper Clinton Moore's "dimly lit" Harlem flat, acquired an international reputation for "cater[ing] to an epicene coterie." According to *Vanity Fair* editor Helen Lawrenson, who was often assigned the task of escorting Condé Nast's European visitors around Harlem, the "titled male Britons flew there like homing pigeons almost the moment they hit New York." With a guest list that included Cole Porter, Cary Grant, Helen Morgan, Harry Richman, Gloria Morgan Vanderbilt, Mademoiselle Cartier, and at least one governor of Tennessee, Moore's became one of Harlem's most exclusive attractions during the 1930s. A former cabaret proprietor turned queer man-about-town, Moore knew exactly how to entertain his patrons and provided them with bawdy amusements that included a "young black entertainer named Joey, who played piano and sang but whose *spécialité* was to remove his clothes and extinguish a lighted candle by sitting on it until it disappeared." At Moore's and at other such private apartment-clubs in Harlem and Bronzeville, the homosexual spectacle was not limited to staged performances; slummers could also participate if they wished. During the early 1930s, for instance, Bronzeville spiritualist Madame Block opened her huge, three-story house at the corner of 55th Street and Drexel Boulevard every weekend to a swarm of black and white men. For a $2 cover charge, one of her gay white patrons recalled, one could "stay all night and drink all you wanted," having sex with newfound acquaintances in one or several of the house's many rooms.[47]

White heterosexual slummers also continued to beat a path to the sex circuses and freak shows that were staged in the buffet flats of Harlem and Bronzeville. Such live sexual entertainment had long been popular with white men as a prelude to sexual encounters with the performers, but during the pansy and lesbian craze, these performances began to attract substantial numbers of affluent white female spectators even as they took on a queerer cast. At one popular Harlem flat which featured a performance that "Sappho in her most daring moments never imagined," one New York tabloid reported that the sound of "high laughter, strangled ere it completes its hysterical peal, reveal[ed] the presence of women" slummers, who seemed simultaneously horrified and aroused by the spectacle they observed: "Little yellow girls, little black girls, little white girls . . . all writhing together on the dark blue velvet carpet under the white glare of the spot light." During the 1930s, homosexual performances by black men increasingly supplemented these lesbian spectacles. At Hazel Valentine's "Daisy Chain" on 140th Street in Harlem, "an enormous transvestite" was an integral part of the evening's entertainment. And such spectacles were not limited to buffet flats; cabaret proprietors and performers sometimes offered to stage similar shows on the premises of their nightspots after closing. In New York, an investigator for the Committee of Fourteen reported that Johnny Carr, the black proprietor of the Lenox Avenue Club, offered to "give a 'circus' with either white or colored participants or both in which pervert practices would be offered." In Bronzeville, the Cabin Inn's female impersonators were, according to one observer, "notorious varietarists [*sic*]. . . . continually on the make for trade," and were willing to arrange sexual performances on occasion for a "select few."[48]

With such an abundance of queer attractions, Harlem and Bronzeville entrepreneurs continued to draw large crowds of affluent white slummers throughout the 1930s. At a time when Americans were just beginning to think of themselves as heterosexual or homosexual, such spectacles offered white pleasure seekers yet another opportunity to affirm both their newly defined heterosexuality and their increasingly privileged status as white. At a Bronzeville cabaret featuring a "huge mulatto" drag entertainer accompanied by a chorus of "sexual indeterminants," University of Chicago graduate student Conrad Bentzen reported observing precisely this dynamic. Contrasting themselves with a "very noisy and quite animated" group of young "homos" in the club's audience, several white couples established themselves as heterosexuals simply by sitting "dour and unresponsive, watching the proceedings with morbid interest." Others reinforced the distinction between themselves and club's queer patrons and performers by "watch[ing] and ridicul[ing] the homos." "They talk to them and ask them where their girls are meaning other homos," Bentzen noted, "which all seems quite agreeable to these peculiar people."[49]

The Persistence of Mannish Women and Fairies in Harlem and Bronzeville

The relocation of lesbian- and pansy-inspired slumming to the black neighborhoods of Chicago and New York was complicated by the different attitudes blacks maintained toward sexual identity and activity. In Bronzeville and Harlem cabarets, drag balls, and other queer venues, the diversity of social and sexual interactions on display demonstrated that the hetero/homo sexual distinctions taking hold among whites in the early 1930s were hardly universal. Like their white counterparts, many middle-class blacks shunned the highly gendered performances of the mannish woman and the fairy—or, the "bulldagger" and the "faggot," as these two types were more commonly known in black urban culture—by refashioning themselves as normatively gendered homosexuals, whose conservative comportment and public discretion won them a level of respect and toleration among their heterosexual peers. But among the working-class blacks of Harlem and Bronzeville, the earlier sexual framework of marginalized fairies and mannish women continued to predominate, as was easily seen when such women and men interacted with prospective sexual partners on the streets and in the queer resorts of the cities' black entertainment districts.[50]

Under the gendered framework of sexual norms still in place in black working-class culture, faggots and bulldaggers felt free to solicit any "normal" man or woman who caught their fancy at local drag balls—and they frequently discovered that their solicitations were welcomed. "Open, and often encouraged, flirtations were carried on; telephone numbers were passed; and broad shouldered bodies which would grace any football player or truck driver were rubbed suggestively against any man who happened to be standing near," one account of Harlem's famed Hamilton Lodge ball noted in 1932. "In the same way," and apparently meeting with similar success, the *New York Amsterdam News* reported, "scores of masculine-looking women sought to touch the few unattached feminine spectators." No doubt many such interactions terminated at the level of mere flirtation, but others almost certainly led to more intimate sexual activities.[51]

Black working-class men, in particular, appear to have moved quite freely between female and male sexual companions, usually relying on the feminine gender performance and mannerisms of their partners to secure their own masculinity and status as "normal" men. For this reason, the black female impersonators who competed at drag balls or entertained in local cabarets became favorites among black men seeking same-sex encounters. Chicago drag entertainer Nancy Kelly (née Lorenzo Banyard) remembered that the first drag queen he ever saw—Joanne, a performer at the Cabin Inn—was quite popular with the black men who gathered at the corner of 31st and State streets. Although the men laughed at Joanne as she stood "on the corner with her hand on her hip, her hair drawn to the back into the ponytail like," Kelly later recalled, "they wasn't botherin' her or nothin'. . . . They'd do her, you know."[52]

Black newspapers and blues recordings of the era reinforced this gender dynamic by suggesting that faggots presented a socially acceptable alternative to women who did not treat their men right. When one "'hard-to-vamp' man" said he was "thru [*sic*] with deceitful women," a gossip columnist for Harlem's *Inter-State Tattler* casually remarked, "Guess he'll be a prosperous star at the next Faggots Ball." Notably, the writer directed contempt not at the man in question or even his prospective pansy partners but at the woman on "138th St. [who] seems to be the cause of it all." The lyrics of "Sissy Blues" and a number of other queer-oriented black recordings conveyed a similar sentiment, warning black women that if they failed to make their men feel manly, a feminine man would. "Now all the people ask me why I'm all alone," Gertrude "Ma" Rainey declared in her rendition of the popular song, proclaiming, "a sissy shook that thing and took my man from home."[53]

Rather than embracing a notion of sexual normalcy that privileged heterosexual object choice, many working-class blacks continued to believe that sexual normalcy and "deviance" were defined primarily by gender performance. In fact, most of the harassment of black faggots focused on their feminine mannerisms and public comportment, rather than on any particular sexual activities they may or may not have engaged in. This focus on gender performance provided a highly visible contrast for Depression-era black masculinity. At a time when many black men had lost their jobs, one of the few ways they could still secure their status was by ridiculing the displays of feminine males, which they cast as "deviant." Thus, black men greeted sissies with derisive comments and catcalls on the streets and dance floors of Harlem and Bronzeville. When the "truck," a swing dance of the 1930s, reached the height of its popularity, black men even developed a variation known as the "fairy truck," in which they adopted "very effeminate" gestures to mock the black and white faggots who patronized local cabarets.[54]

Although such gender dynamics continued to create opportunities for masculine black men to pursue same-sex relations without necessarily being labeled queer, during the Depression, these same dynamics increasingly foreclosed similar options for black women. Black men, deprived by economic circumstances of the means to support their families, perceived the increasing boldness and visibility of mannish women in Harlem and Bronzeville as a direct threat to their manhood. These bulldaggers presumably had the power to undermine black men's strongest remaining claims to masculinity—their sexual prowess and ability to pleasure women. As a result, while black popular culture portrayed faggots as abnormal but relatively harmless buffoons, it generally presented mannish women as dangerous interlopers. In George Hannah's blues recording, "The Boy in the Boat," he warned black men that mannish women like "Tack Ann / took many a broad from many a man." *New York Age* columnist Marcus Wright laid out the lesbian peril in even more personalized terms. "Seventh avenue is still as popular as ever with the sophisticated ladies and their boyish bobs," he reported in May 1934, "and women strolling down the avenue [are] serving death warrants on all women lovers . . . . The fellows had better keep their eyes open and watch their women. If you don't, you might lose Susie."[55]

The persistence of gendered sexual norms among working-class blacks demonstrates that the transition from marginalized fairies and mannish women to a cultural dyad privileging heterosexual object choice was by no means a natural or certain progression—especially when the construction of sexual identities and desires intersected with ideologies of race. Surprisingly, however, a number of black working-class bulldaggers and faggots also exploited the intermediary space created by the pansy and lesbian craze of Harlem and Bronzeville to coax middle-class whites away from the increasingly hegemonic hetero/homo sexual classification. Invoking eroticized notions of racial difference, they created situations in which otherwise heterosexual white women and men could once again indulge in same-sex relations without calling their sexual normalcy into question.[56]

Most black working-class men recognized that the adoption of the faggot's feminine persona or women's clothing was the surest way to get a "normal" black man to consent to have sex. But when it came to attracting white middle-class heterosexual partners, who were seemingly uninfluenced by the gender play of the earlier sexual regime, black working-class men had to resort to other tactics. Rather than play up their femininity, they emphasized their racial difference, attempting to offset white heterosexual men's anxieties about same-sex encounters by reinforcing the white men's sense of sexual normalcy via subtle invocations of white male supremacy. A black pansy named Norman employed just such a strategy when soliciting an undercover white antivice investigator at the corner of 31st and State streets in Chicago, the very heart of Bronzeville's black-and-tan district. According to the investigator, after Norman learned that the "girl that I had a date with" had failed to show, he "asked if I am particular, who I am getting my satisfaction [from], and remarked WOULDN'T A BOY DO? . . . I have 2 others besides myself, and we'll entertain you better than any women would." Fairies had long used similar lines to convince "normal" men to have sex with them, but the fact that Norman was black and the investigator was white gave his words a particular spin. One of Norman's male companions added that "a lot of white fellows come to [our] apartment for 'pleasure.'" These black men thus played both explicitly and implicitly on their racial difference, suggesting that they could take the woman's place in the proposed sexual encounter, thereby rendering it normal for the white investigator, while implying that the encounter would enhance the investigator's status as a sexually dominant *white* man, by confirming his ability to procure the sexual services of a black "boy."[57]

Like the black working-class faggots who solicited white heterosexual partners, black lesbians sometimes played up their racial difference to establish sexual relationships with otherwise heterosexual white women. Black working-class bulldaggers engaged in highly gendered, cross-racial relationships in which their blackness was equated with masculinity and their "mannish" behavior reinforced the normative sexual and gender roles of their more feminine white partners. Most often this meant assuming a dominant role in sex with a more passive womanly partner, but the exact parameters of sexual activity varied from couple to couple. For Marian J., a black, middle-aged cabaret singer, a typical encounter entailed performing oral sex on a passive but passionate white woman. Professional comedian and male impersonator Myrtle K. adopted an even more aggressive role. Expressing a decided "attract[ion] . . . to white women," she reported that she usually lay on top of her partners, penetrating the compliant women with her clitoris—a practice that Marian also claimed to have performed at a younger age, until she "grew heavier [and] decided that [she] should develop a less hazardous technique."[58]

Emphasizing racial difference over same-sex sexual desire, black bulldaggers such as Marian and Myrtle embraced male sexual roles that reframed their white partners' sexual experiences in terms implying, rather than disrupting, heterosexuality. On its face, this move appeared to confirm the speculations of social reformers who blamed the presence of similar cross-racial relations in women's prisons and reformatories on black lesbians' masculine aggression toward otherwise "normal" white women. But the experiences of Harlem and Bronzeville lesbians like Marian, who reported receiving propositions from married women who attended her cabaret performances, proved that female slummers were hardly the victims of manipulative bulldaggers. Nevertheless, the gendered dynamics of sex often remained central to the sexual identities and practices of women who sought out lesbian encounters across the color line. "While a woman is going down on me," Myrtle K. remarked, "I visualize myself as a man and I talk as if I was a man. I say, 'Ain't that a good dick? O baby, ain't that good.'" Her impersonation was so effective, according to Myrtle, that "some women think I have an emission, but I don't think so."[59]

"Solid Colored Citizens" Respond to the Pansy and Lesbian Craze

While the cross-racial encounters of bulldaggers and faggots embodied some of the most explicit sexual interactions between local blacks and white slummers, the response of Harlem and Bronzeville residents to the districts' pansy and lesbian entertainments was quite varied. Members of the local community who frequented these venues ran the gamut of black culture from working class to high society. Among the perennially popular events were the drag balls, at which the line between observers and participants was often difficult to discern. By the late 1920s, black businessmen, doctors, artists, prostitutes, socialites, and secretaries crowded into the annual Hamilton Lodge balls by the thousands to watch, as one Harlem newspaper headline put it, the "Feministic Males Turn Out in Gorgeous Costumes." Several "colored people with their families brought their suppers and ate" at the drags, one participant recalled, while the more well-to-do settled into private boxes to watch the festivities in relative luxury.[60]

While the distinction between heterosexuality and homosexuality had initially been drawn in the all-white venues of de facto Jim Crow entertainments in the Village, Towertown, and Times Square, at Harlem and Bronzeville drag balls, spatial segregation conformed to lines of sexuality more than of race. Outside the dance halls, black and white heterosexual spectators lined the sidewalks, "joking at the arrival of each newcomer in costume," while, inside, the physical structure of the buildings created visible boundaries between these two sexual factions. At Harlem's Rockland Palace and at Chicago's Coliseum Annex, where the cities' largest annual masquerades were held, the layout of the auditoriums made the distinction between heterosexuality and homosexuality uniquely visible, displaying the former above the latter in a two-tiered exhibition. At Harlem's famed Hamilton Lodge Ball, middle-class heterosexual slummers and society folk crowded into the boxes of Rockland Palace to "look down from above at the queerly assorted throng on the dancing floor, males in flowing gowns and feathered headdresses and females in tuxedos and box-back suits." As George Chauncey has noted, such arrangements even allowed for a momentary mediation of racial difference through sexual hierarchy, as black and white heterosexuals united spatially—if not always socially—to contrast their shared sense of sexual normalcy and respectability with the homosexual antics on the dance floor below. The extent to which the balls' heterosexual observers used the spatial configuration of the dance halls to distance themselves from the queer spectacle they had come to see was made especially clear to one young white man when he ventured to join the cheering crowds in the balcony. "Assuming that they too were open to racial [sic] and variant sexual behavior," he later recalled, "I guilelessly went up there and soon discovered how wrong I was! These were Romans come to the Coliseum to see the spectacle, but keeping a wall well between themselves and the arena."[61]

Nevertheless, some blacks in attendance experimented with the thrill of crossing the line between observer and participant. According to the black-owned *New York Amsterdam News*, some ostensibly heterosexual blacks at the Hamilton Lodge ball "joined in the unorthodox orgies," interacting with the "impersonators" as they "started making promiscuous 'passes.'" More than a few black spectators appeared to revel in the gender play that permeated these events. While generally dismissive of the balls' "girls," some black male spectators complimented the drags' femininely costumed participants on "'her' beautiful calves, 'her' shapely hips, 'her' well proportioned breasts, [or] 'her' sensuous lips." Still others enjoyed creating a little gender confusion of their own. One of the daughters of Fred R. Moore, the conservative black publisher of the *New York Age*, recalled that when she and her sister attended the "faggots' ball," they "always had short haircuts." "We'd go in our sequin dresses, and you couldn't tell the men from the women," she later remarked. "They were dancing and having a good time, and they would come up to us. We'd say, 'We're women, no, no.' . . . [but] they didn't know whether we were the real thing or not."[62]

For those who preferred to watch rather than participate in such queer interactions, there were always the local black and tans which, like the famed drag balls of Harlem and Bronzeville, attracted a wide cross-section of the districts' black residents and tourists. When the Sepia Mae West took to the garden stage of Bronzeville's Annex Buffet in the late summer of 1934, the *Chicago Defender* reported, "The house was packed to capacity" with the best of black society. The crowd included composer William C. Handy and "the world's greatest fighter," Jack Johnson, as well as a host of "other well known celebrities and visitors from all points of the United States." Some upper-crust Harlemites became so enchanted by this popular slumming craze that one local gossip columnist overheard members of a prominent black social club discussing the "relative . . . merits of the well known female impersonators," with one group favoring the Hot Tamale "Daisy Navarro," "while the other side was loud in voicing the praises of 'Gloria Swanson.'" But the public fascination with pansies and lesbians was hardly limited to elite blacks. Although the most famous and lavish queer black and tans remained far too expensive for most working-class blacks in the midst of the Depression, a number of smaller Harlem and Bronzeville cabarets managed to provide more economical versions of such entertainment. At Harlem's Log Cabin, located in the midst of Jungle Alley on West 133rd Street, a "whiskey-voiced blues singer and a chap of indifferent sex" entertained an audience of local workers, while at Rocco's Grill on Lenox Avenue, black working-class toughs mingled with "Magdalenes of the downtown area and men with a dash of lavender."[63]

During the mid-1930s, one of Harlem's hottest queer-oriented cabarets—the 101 Ranch, located at 101 West 139th Street—appeared to make room for all types of patrons, albeit on seemingly separate nights. "On Friday nights the Coal Bin's dicties jam the club," local columnist Roi Ottley reported, "Saturday the rug-cutters romp to their hearts' content, and on Sunday nights the ofays find their way to this sin spot for frolicking." That is, Harlem's high-class snobs, rabble-rousers, and slumming whites were each said to arrive on separate nights to witness the "clever performances, spritely humor, infectious gaiety, and. . . . dazzling gowns" of "Clarenz" (née Clarence Henderson), the black and tan's popular black mistress of ceremonies. For nearly two years, this young former Chicagoan ruled the roost at Harlem's 101 Ranch, rising from local favorite to the "Toast of the Night Flight" and rivaling Gladys Bentley and the Sepia Gloria Swanson for popularity among the district's many pleasure seekers. "In 'drag,' it was next to impossible to detect that Clarenz was a man," one reporter for the *New York Amsterdam News* recalled. "One gown in particular, of sophisticated black velvet, hugged his svelte figure like a glove, revealing unsuspected curves." In the midst of Harlem's pansy and lesbian craze, however, Clarenz's queer male identity was hardly a secret. Rather, it was a highly marketable and profitable asset.[64]

Not all residents of Harlem and Bronzeville welcomed the growing popularity of the pansy and lesbian craze in their neighborhoods. By 1930, the Hamilton Lodge ball had become so popular that the founder and pastor of Harlem's Refuge Church of Christ decided to address the phenomenon directly. After attending the ball with two parishioners, Bishop R. C. Lawson offered a sermon titled "The 'Faggots' Ball, and What It Means in the Light of the Scriptures." Publicizing the sermon with posters and an advertisement in the *New York Age*, he drew an overflowing crowd to hear him preach about both the alleged sinfulness of homosexuality and the need to "save" the men and women who succumbed to this sin. But halfway through his address, Lawson's focus shifted from the ball's queer participants toward his own supposedly pious and heterosexual congregants. "As this is becoming a fad and is wide-spread," Lawson admonished his parishioners, "I think it high time for the ministry of our city to raise their voice against this iniquitous traffic in degeneracy." In Lawson's view, the moral issue posed by the Hamilton Lodge ball was not simply that "five hundred men cavorted, squirmed and wiggled around with each other," but that "hundreds of other people look[ed] down from balcony and side lines, while they held their high carnival of sin, unabashed, yea, brazenly, drinking and flirting, blaspheming and making mock of themselves and God." The spectators, the bishop noted, were just as guilty as the participants, both for promoting an event that "out-Sodoms Sodom" and for risking their own salvation merely for the sake of "a new diversion." If godly people continued to flock to such entertainments, Lawson warned, they were likely to find themselves pressured to "indulge in these abnormalities in the spirit of bravado, simply because they do not wish to appear green."[65]

Other criticisms of the latest slumming craze centered on the relationship between race and profit. Rightly noting that whites not only patronized but also owned a number of the districts' more popular queer-oriented resorts, some blacks accused these outsiders of perverting black urban space for their own capital gain. "Owned and controlled by white racketeers for the patronage of slumming whites and petty gangsters," Harlem's most spectacular sex circuses were the subject of particular opprobrium among local residents. These businesses offended "the solid colored citizens who are forced to live near the joints," one New York tabloid reported, and "dr[e]w nothing but contempt from the Negroes who make a living in them." Even the upscale Ubangi Club elicited the wrath of some Harlem residents, who assailed the nightspot's black performers along with its white owners and management. One particularly aggrieved local columnist described the popular cabaret as a "canker" growing on New York's black community, "produced and fostered by and for low-minded white[s] and performed by cheap, grasping Moses"—a description that equated black queer performers with the "Mose" character common in minstrel shows. The writer further implicated municipal authorities in the promotion of Harlem's pansy and lesbian craze, noting that the intensified regulation of white entertainment districts encouraged the segregation of queer amusements to the city's preeminent black neighborhood. Although Gladys Bentley's act at the King's Terrace in midtown Manhattan had been "raided in short order when commissioner John F. O'Ryan took charge," the columnist noted, less than two months later, both she and her "effeminate retinue" were permitted to headline Harlem's Ubangi Club "under the very eyes of the local police."[66]

A number of black commentators attributed the very presence of homosexuality in Harlem and Bronzeville to the frequent slumming of white bohemians. Drawing on a stereotype of bohemianism that blurred the boundaries between *bohemian* and *queer*, they chastised black women and men for socializing with disreputable Nordics. "Here is a group of mortals," Terence E. Williams wrote in the *Pittsburgh Courier*, "who seem to be different in more ways than one, than all the rest of the people in New York—in the world. They dress differently, act differently, and really are—well 'queer' is the word, it seems." Other commentators, referring to firsthand observations of the substantial numbers of gay men and lesbians who cavorted in black nightspots, were more explicit about the white homosexual threat. The criticism surrounding Harlem society's April 1927 benefit ball for the all-black Fort Valley Industrial School was especially direct. Writing in Baltimore's *Afro-American*, Harry B. Webber reported, "Objection to the party came from two sources, first, that 60 per cent of the attendance was white and some of them habitués of Bohemian Greenwich Village, and second, that a group of abnormal men came dressed in women's garb." On another occasion, the *Chicago Whip* adamantly suggested that "the black people of New York should politely hang the unwelcome sign," directing white slummers "back to Greenwich Village where the New York neurotics revel."[67]

Such assessments inverted traditional white narratives of the origins of illicit urban sex districts. While white reformers contended that black neighborhoods were factories of prostitution and other forms of sexual "deviance," black critics insisted that it was whites who brought such unwelcome practices into their neighborhoods. Far from expressing supposedly innate sexual urges, these observers argued, urban blacks were merely copying the behavior of the white pleasure seekers who gamboled in their midst. Homosexuality, like prostitution and bohemian free love, was seen as a white cultural import, now embraced by members of the black elite as well as the working class. "With the abolition of the red light districts, one would have supposed that the underworld would adopt the manners of Society," African American writer George S. Schuyler remarked in 1929, "but it's been the other way around. Our 'best people' too often have descended from the seemly to the seamy." With "modesty, simplicity and dignity . . . quite on the wane," he suggested, maybe this was simply a sign of the times. "When smart [white] society is a curious mixture of refinement and bawdiness, crudity and culture, Bulls and Faggots, gentlemen and gangsters, the upper and netherworlds," Schuyler asked, "should we expect too much from their apt pupils, the Negroes?"[68]

The association of white slumming parties with social and sexual disrepute became so pervasive among urban blacks that one Harlem newspaper suggested that a visit to the district's popular queer-oriented cabarets offered blacks a chance to engage in a little "reverse slumming." The "frolicking" of white pleasure seekers was often "crude, coarse and boring," the *New York Amsterdam News* acknowledged, but "Dickie Wells' basement speak is the spot to visit if you desire to see the ofay go native." As slummers gathered at Wells' Theatrical Grill to hear the Sepia Gloria Swanson belt out his bawdy tunes, their unruly behavior provided local black residents with a means to challenge whites' presumptions of social and moral superiority by comporting themselves with greater dignity and social reserve.[69]

Because such cabarets attracted a sizable homosexual following, they afforded blacks and whites with an opportunity to establish a sense of common ground as heterosexuals in opposition to the public flamboyance of queer entertainers, such as the Sepia Gloria Swanson, and the many pansy and lesbian fans of this type of entertainment. This interracial contrast between heterosexuality and homosexuality reinforced the shift away from the earlier gendered system of marginalized fairies and mannish women and also helped to naturalize cross-racial heterosexual relations by rendering them less deviant in comparison with homosexuality. During the mid-1930s, African American journalist Frank Marshall Davis recalled that he spent many evenings with his white mistress "at the little [Bronzeville] cabarets between 22nd and 35th, particularly a cozy spot featuring . . . a female impersonator who called himself 'The Sepia Mae West.'" It was no accident that Davis found this particular cabaret so cozy, because here the "unquestionably spectacular" performance of Dick Barrow as a "transvestite king-size version of the movie queen" detracted attention from the racial differences among the nightspot's heterosexual patrons. Barrow and his homosexual fans became the foil against which the norm of heterosexuality was secured, even when it dared to cross the color line.[70]

"We carry on till de-*mented*": Race, Queer Community–Building, and Slumming in the Nightlife of Harlem and Bronzeville

The same Harlem and Bronzeville venues that provided cover for cross-racial heterosexual pairings also afforded opportunities for cross-racial interactions among lesbians and gay men. Indeed, whatever limited degree of interracial collegiality emerged in the homosexual worlds of New York and Chicago during the 1920s and 1930s was primarily a product of the social and sexual interactions that took shape in black urban spaces. The popular masquerade balls of Harlem and Bronzeville and a significant number of the districts' clandestine buffet flats and smaller black and tans served as places where lesbians and gay men could freely cross the color line to establish some broader sense of queer community. The drag balls, in particular, provided a uniquely visible and sizable space where first hundreds and then thousands of black and white homosexuals interacted on relatively equal terms. Although the white queers of New York and Chicago supported a range of segregated, white-only drag balls during the late 1920s and early 1930s, held at Madison Square Garden, Webster Hall near the Village, and a number of public dance halls on Chicago's North Side, it was the interracial balls of Harlem and Chicago's South Side that proved most popular with local lesbians and gay men. At the annual Halloween and New Year's Eve drags held at the Coliseum Annex on Chicago's Near South Side, at Harlem's annual springtime Hamilton Lodge masquerade, and at any number of smaller drags held in the dance halls of Harlem and Bronzeville, thousands of tuxedoed lesbians and glamorous pansies in sequins and "billowing clouds of feathers" paraded across the dance floors, indifferent to any purported racial divide.[71]

Some white middle-class queers disdained such flamboyant cavorting, even as they admitted to having attended such balls and experiencing some sense of pleasure in the interracial atmosphere. "I went to a drag in Harlem once," one white gay male artist recalled in the late 1930s, "but it made me sick. I don't like people who are so flagrant." Despite this seemingly visceral reaction, however, the young man later admitted that he "was fascinated by the boys in drag" whom he encountered on his visit uptown and, one suspects, he was a little titillated as well. Indeed, a number of white homosexuals remarked that interracial drags were useful for arranging cross-racial sexual encounters, which were sometimes even consummated on site. At one of Chicago's annual Halloween balls in the late 1920s, a white participant recalled, "The washroom was so popular all evening you couldn't go in to do your business legitimately." Entering the restroom on his very first visit to a formal drag ball, this young man "couldn't believe it. . . . There was a man hanging over the washbasin and there was a line-up of hard-ons waiting to penetrate him. I never saw anything like it in my life. Of course, the blowjobs were going on," he noted more casually, as if having expected as much. But the "public exhibition" of anal sex that he witnessed that night made an indelible impression. "Oh, my God! I didn't think I would recover," he told an interviewer some fifty years after the fact.[72]

For other white homosexuals, the cross-racial interactions that the drag balls of Harlem and Bronzeville promoted extended well beyond any particular evening's sexual shenanigans. Having launched his career as a prize-winner at Harlem's Hamilton Lodge ball in the late 1920s,

Jean Malin maintained a special affinity with the local black community. Even at the height of New York's pansy and lesbian craze, when the white Malin was the toast of midtown nightlife, he made frequent trips uptown to visit friends and fellow entertainers at popular black and tans. In fact, Malin felt so closely connected to Harlem nightlife that when the *Inter-State Tattler* began to feature drawings of popular black performers on its front page in early 1932, Malin sent word, the newspaper's nightlife columnist reported, that "he would like his (girlish) face to adorn our cover in caricature." The sense of affinity with blacks displayed by Malin and other white homosexuals constituted an attempt to identify with them based on perceived similarities in their experiences living under oppression. Historian Eric Garber has argued that this shared "identification and feeling of kinship" may have provided "the beginnings of [a] homosexual 'minority consciousness,'" a theory supported by the testimony of homophile activist W. Dorr Legg. An early member of the Los Angeles Mattachine Society and a founder of the homophile organization ONE, Inc., which began to publish the nation's first gay rights–oriented monthly, *ONE Magazine*, in 1953, Legg claimed that his "Harlem experience made more of an impression on me than I had realized. I made new Negro friends . . . and found the earthy pragmatism of many of them and their psychological insights delightful." From these friends, he later recalled, "I was discovering what the day-by-day effects of prejudice and minority stigmatization were like."[73]

For many other white lesbians and gay men, however, the main attraction in Harlem and Bronzeville was the sense of escape that these districts offered to outsiders, especially when the white-oriented pansy and lesbian cabarets of New York and Chicago came under closer police surveillance and were routinely raided in the early 1930s. "Harlem was wide open," the white female impersonator Robert Brennan recalled, noting that many of the clubs did not close until dawn. Taking advantage of these late-night hours, white lesbians and pansies increasingly ventured to Harlem and Bronzeville where the cover of darkness—both literal and figurative—provided them with a safer place to frolic. Here they could flirt, socialize, and arrange sexual encounters well beyond the watchful eyes of family, friends, and colleagues. "Uptown we carry on till de-*mented*," the writer Parker Tyler told a friend in 1929, suggesting that, although they rarely spoke of going slumming, white homosexuals did just that. A "young 'phay queer," recently arrived from Hollywood, confirmed as much in 1935 when he told a black newspaper columnist that "Harlem is the only place in which to live." Even the usually well-meaning and socially engaged Carl Van Vechten went to black and tans in part for the cross-racial homosexual opportunities they provided. Indeed, he was renowned for chasing black men around Harlem.[74]

White lesbians and gay men echoed earlier white heterosexual slummers from the Negro vogue in equating blackness with primitivism, sensuality, and hypersexuality. Many of these slumming queers believed that black men and women possessed innate, almost uncontrollable sexual urges, and thought the atmosphere created in black jazz cabarets actively encouraged public sexual display. Acting upon these racist assumptions, white homosexuals often engaged in much more sexually explicit behavior in black nightspots than they did in any white cabaret. This was especially true when the black nightspot in question was one of the more obscure buffet flats. A case in point can be found among Carl Van Vechten's many slumming expeditions to Harlem. Never especially reserved, even in Harlem's more upscale black and tans, Van Vechten felt particularly uninhibited when the black entertainer Louis Cole escorted him and a group of his white homosexual friends, including the actor Clifton Webb, to an all-black basement speakeasy where they were able to "see & do some strange dancing." Because he provided no further details of this occasion in his daily diary, it is difficult to know exactly what Van Vechten meant by this notation, but the investigative reports of the Committee of Fourteen suggest that the dancing was probably quite sexual in character. Visiting this same hole-in-the-wall less than a year earlier, the Committee's black male investigator had observed two women who "were dancing with one another going through the motions of copulation," as well as "two men who were dancing with one another kiss[ing] each other," while "one sucked the other's tongue."[75]

Even outside the buffet flats and black and tans, white lesbians and gay men increasingly identified black jazz culture with a sense of sexual permissiveness and release from social constraint. Purchasing "race records," such as Gertrude "Ma" Rainey's 1928 rendition of "Prove It on Me Blues" or George Hannah's 1930 "Freakish Man Blues" (both of which were recorded in Chicago), white homosexuals reveled in the sexual frankness of African American performers. Playing "a number of pornographic records sung by some negro entertainers," for example, a group of five young, white gay men recreated the sensual atmosphere they might have found in Bronzeville's black and tans within the privacy of a small Towertown apartment. Observed by University of Chicago sociology student Earle W. Bruce, these men "did not seem to get tired but danced on and on," as "a homosexual theme ran through the lyrics," seemingly giving expression to their deepest desires and prompting one of the group to shout out, "Come on, girls, and do your stuff!" Still others exploited the double entendre of African American music to convey more surreptitious messages to one another under the noses of less knowledgeable neighbors. According to physician Maurice Chideckel, "two tribadists living next door to each other" regularly played their phonographic recordings of the "Negro blues" in order to set up appointments with each other or to express the pleasure they had "derived from the tribadistic practices." "Mamma's got something sho' gonna surprise you," the lyrics of one of the women's chosen records reportedly sang out, "Mamma's got something I know you want."[76]

In Depression-era Chicago and New York, the 78s that white lesbians and gay men purchased from local record stores were little more than pale reminders of the supposed sexual permissiveness and possibilities that they routinely exploited in the cabarets of Bronzeville and Harlem. After the post-Prohibition crackdown on white pansy and lesbian entertainments, queer black and tans provided the most prominent and, in many respects, the most protected public spaces where white lesbians and gay men could socialize openly. At one popular Bronzeville cabaret, an observer noted that the young white pansies in attendance seemed much more interested in each other than in the club's spectacular revue of black female impersonators (figure 26). Excited by the "de[e]p husky voice" of the cabaret's begowned master of ceremonies and by the "sensuous and r[h]ythmic" music that accompanied the floorshow, these young men "g[a]ve vent to their feeling by shrill stacatto [sic] shouts." But between numbers, they largely ignored the nightspot's black patrons and entertainers, as well as the white heterosexual slummers who had come in search of a thrill. Instead, they walked from table to table, "placing their hands on their hips and fluttering handkerchiefs," while they chatted with their fellow white pansies to arrange sexual encounters.[77]

The members of this particular slumming party may not have realized it, but when they "gave vent to their feelings" in the racialized environs of the queer black and tan, they embodied the latest rendition of a decades-long phenomenon through which well-to-do urban whites negotiated the shifting social and spatial contours of race and sexuality from the mid-1880s to the outbreak of the Second World War. By the late 1930s, Americans were well practiced at the commercialized boundary-crossings that slumming entailed, routinely charting a course into the urban spaces associated with populations whom they perceived to be racially and sexually exotic and, therefore, distinct from themselves. But

26 These unidentified black men provide an example of the drag entertainment that became popular in Bronzeville cabarets, such as the Cabin Inn and the Annex Buffet, during the mid- to late 1930s. (Reprinted with permission from the Chicago History Museum Archives, ICHi-24648.)

as slummers crossed into the neighborhoods and nightlife venues populated by the objects of their fascination and fears, they discovered that
the distinctions they drew between themselves and these groups often
proved highly permeable and even permutable.

The four successive slumming vogues that preoccupied Americans
during the late nineteenth and early twentieth centuries may have

seemed to have little more in common than frivolous thrill seeking. But, in fact, the cumulative effect of these boundary crossings far exceeded mere titillation. From immigrant dance halls and Chinatown opium dens to bohemian tearooms and interracial drag balls, slumming hot spots offered a series of compelling and complicating venues where Americans could come to terms with the demographic changes that were reshaping the nation and its cities and where the shifting popular conceptualization of race and sexuality was made more visible—and tangible—than ever before.

Epilogue

While the practice of slumming never faded entirely from U.S. urban culture, this once-popular pastime dwindled into near-obscurity in the years following World War II. No longer did well-to-do white Chicagoans and New Yorkers make nightly forays across the social and spatial boundaries that separated their neighborhoods and lives from expanding populations of Jewish, Italian, and Chinese immigrants; free-loving bohemians; blacks; and homosexuals. Nor did they routinely attempt to use their participation in the nightlife associated with these groups to reinforce some sense of racial and sexual normativity—or even superiority—by first sampling and then distancing themselves from the groups' purported primitivism and perversity. Rather, to shore up their position atop American racial and sexual hierarchies and to distance themselves from the dangers increasingly associated with postwar U.S. cities, middle- and upper-class whites redirected their leisure pursuits inward—toward their own increasingly suburban, racially homogeneous, heterosexually oriented communities and homes. And in doing so, they more firmly grounded the incipient dichotomies of blackness and whiteness and of heterosexuality and homosexuality in the physical and cultural landscapes of urban America.

The diminution of slumming in postwar Chicago and New York, like its advent in the late nineteenth century, was a byproduct of several significant developments, including the spatial and demographic reorganization of U.S. cities, the continuing reconfiguration of popular conceptions of race and sexuality, and the emergence of new forms of commercialized leisure. Each of these developments took shape in reciprocal relation to the others, but perhaps none played a more pivotal role in suppressing the popularity of slumming than the rampant suburbanization of the immediate postwar period. Fueled by the growth of the interstate highway system, the deindustrialization of cities, and the increasing availability of mortgage assistance through the Federal Housing Administration and the Servicemen's Readjustment Act of 1944 (more commonly known as the G. I. Bill), thousands of young urban whites left the cities of their youth to take up residence in new, mass-produced suburbs. This exodus not only removed most white amusement seekers from the cabarets and other public amusements around which slumming was usually organized but also contributed to whites' increasing perception of urban America as racialized "inner cities" filled with potentially dangerous, darker-skinned people.[1]

Postwar suburbanization initially replicated many of the class and racial divisions that characterized turn-of-the-century cities. As middle- and upper-class whites settled in exclusive new subdivisions, more often than not they continued to separate themselves from their working-class counterparts. Longstanding prejudices against Catholics and Jews also persisted, prompting their exclusion from a number of postwar suburbs, as well as the establishment of identifiably Italian and Jewish American communities on the outskirts of Chicago and New York. Yet whatever cultural divisions these suburban populations insisted on preserving, they paled in comparison to the geographic and cultural divide that came to unify them racially in opposition to urban blacks. Because a host of racially discriminatory practices prevented nearly all blacks from gaining access to suburban housing, residency in postwar suburbia became an undeniable marker of whiteness, overriding nearly all perceived differences between old-stock white Americans and the descendants of southern and eastern European immigrants.[2]

The reconfiguration of urban and suburban space along a black/white axis was made even clearer—and rendered even more threatening to many white Americans—by the unprecedented influx of Southern blacks to northern and western cities during and after World War II. Between 1940 and 1970, the black population of Chicago nearly quadrupled from 277,731 to 1,102,620—a rate which only slightly exceeded that experienced by New York, where the number of black residents rose from 458,444 to 1,668,115. This Second Great Migration of Southern blacks, fueled initially by wartime industrial needs and sustained by the diminishing promise of skilled urban employment, offset much of the population decrease associated with the purported white flight from Chicago and New York. In the process, it also dramatically darkened the complexion of these two cities. In Chicago, blacks quickly overflowed the traditional bounds of Bronzeville, occupying broad swaths of the city's south and west sides, while in New York, they expanded their residential turf to encompass not only Harlem but also portions of the South Bronx and Brooklyn, especially Bedford-Stuyvesant.[3]

The postwar migration of Puerto Ricans—many of whom claimed African as well as Spanish and Taino Indian ancestry—further intensified the racialization of New York and Chicago as thousands of island residents moved to the mainland in search of jobs. In New York, where the Puerto Rican population mushroomed from 61,463 in 1940 to 860,584 in 1970, many whites viewed the emergence of substantial Puerto Rican barrios in East (or Spanish) Harlem, the South Bronx, Manhattan's Lower East Side, and Brooklyn's Columbia Street district as impending threats to the social and racial order of the city. Likewise, the dramatic growth of Chicago's Puerto Rican population, though much smaller in absolute numbers (having increased from 259 residents in the entire state of Illinois in 1940 to approximately 79,000 in Chicago alone by 1970), was perceived as a potential tinderbox by many white observers, especially on the city's northwest side, the site of its largest Puerto Rican barrio.[4]

Yet white Americans' growing fears of urban racial conflict and their increasing unwillingness to venture into neighborhoods associated with nonwhite populations were not simply irrational responses to the darkening complexions New York and Chicago. They were also products of the sporadic violence that erupted between blacks and whites in and around Harlem and Bronzeville. As early as 1935, when the rumored murder of a young Puerto Rican shoplifter in a white-owned Harlem store prompted protests and looting by black residents and the violent reaction of local police, white slumming expeditions to Harlem began to fall off precipitously. In Chicago, working-class whites' occasional neighborhood skirmishes with the black migrants who spilled out of Bronzeville had a similarly damping effect on white participation in black nightlife.[5]

Rising concerns about race riots during World War II marked a distinct turning point both in the policing of slumming venues and in the readiness of white amusement seekers to cross the urban color line. When the shore patrol declared Bronzeville's nightlife district off limits to white sailors in the summer of 1942, the order had the effect of simultaneously reinscribing the racialized boundaries of Chicago's neighborhoods and rendering all cross-racial interactions potentially hazardous. U.S. naval authorities claimed they were "trying to protect Negro womanhood from approaches of white sailors," but black residents were skeptical of their motives and worried that "this order will serve only to emphasize racial differences." The following June, when municipal and military authorities followed suit in Harlem by shuttering the Savoy Ballroom, the district's last remaining bastion of cross-racial socializing, locals took particular umbrage. The military insisted the closure was intended to combat venereal disease among white servicemen who claimed to have contracted the malady from prostitutes they met at the Savoy, but Harlemites, including Malcolm X, believed "the real reason was to stop Negroes from dancing with white women." Ironically, the perceived insult associated with the ballroom's closure likely contributed to the very rioting that authorities hoped to prevent. In August 1943, Harlem followed such cities as Detroit, Los Angeles, and Mobile, Alabama, in experiencing severe racial conflict, as a series of wartime riots rendered the country's black urban districts and their residents particularly ominous threats to white America.[6]

Mounting racial animosities and fears were not the only barriers to whites' continued interest in slumming; thrill seekers were also confounded by the perceived homosexual dangers that came to be associated with mid-twentieth-century U.S. cities. In the late 1930s and again in the early 1950s, a series of local and national sex crime panics increasingly equated urban gay men with sexual psychopaths and child molesters. Fueled by the sensationalistic press coverage of a series of unrelated child murders and rapes, these panics generated a public outcry against "sex morons" and other "sex criminals" and prompted sustained drives throughout the country both to control the sexual activities of gay men and to police the urban spaces they frequented. During the first Chicago panic in early 1937, police stepped up their surveillance of the city's theaters and public cruising areas, including a popular stretch of South State Street, routinely arresting the men who used such spaces to search for sexual partners. In New York, the response was much the same. Local law enforcement carefully scrutinized the queer goings-on around Times Square and other gay neighborhoods, accosting men in local nightspots or even concealing themselves in public toilets in order to catch men engaging in homosexual acts.[7]

Americans' escalating fear of homosexuality extended even to the drag performers who had proved so popular during the pansy and lesbian craze. As early as the spring of 1937, when the Michigan state legislature began to debate passage of the country's first "sexual psychopath law," the press carried stories linking queer entertainments to recent sex crimes. Citing the presence of pansy revues "in about a score of local niteries," *Variety* reported that Dr. Thomas K. Gruber, head of a Detroit mental sanitarium, recommended a twofold approach "to stamp

out [the] rising wave of sex killers." The first step was to "establish special clinics" where such "criminals" could be incarcerated until psychia-
trists could "cure" them of their psychopathy. The second was to put a
stop to the "floating population of female impersonators." "No one can
convince me it is safe to allow such groups to roam at liberty," Gruber
told the media, "though I cannot go so far as to say all members of
such troupes are potential murderers." While it appears that Chicago
and New York authorities never embraced Gruber's wilder speculations
about gay entertainers, the mere circulation of such ideas at a time when
these localities were considering their own sexual psychopath laws only
served to reinforce the already mounting public perception of these cities and their queer nightspots as sexually dangerous places.[8]

Combined with the postwar relocation of thousands of white heterosexual couples to suburban neighborhoods, the growing association of
U.S. cities with a presumed homosexual menace recast sexual identities
and communities in geographic terms every bit as stark as the color line
that separated white American suburbs from progressively nonwhite inner cities. Although urban marriage rates rose in the immediate postwar
period, suburban developments housed so few unmarried adults and became so closely identified with single-family homes that the increasingly
predominant hetero/homo sexual binary began to equate with the new
suburban/urban divide. The public's conception of suburbs as exclusive,
family-oriented, white, heterosexual spaces was further reinforced by
emerging ideologies of containment that reinscribed traditional racial
and gender norms and encouraged parents—especially stay-at-home
mothers—to protect their homes and children from a host of outside
threats, ranging from communism to urban blight and homosexuality.
Underscoring the heightened importance of domesticity in cold war
America, this sense of containment extended even to suburbanites' leisure activities, prompting the vast majority to eschew the public amusements of the city in favor of more local diversions.[9]

Still, the sudden departure of most white heterosexuals from the
nightlife of Chicago and New York—and the near-elimination of slumming—was not simply a product of suburbanites' growing fear of cities.
As Americans married and started families at younger ages, they also
had less time and energy to devote to urban nightclubs, movie palaces,
and amusement parks that were now located a considerable distance
from their suburban homes. Moreover, just as the emergence of such
turn-of-the-century amusements had first fueled the public's interest in
slumming, the development of new forms of mass-cultural entertainment—especially the television—spurred the reorientation of Americans'

leisure pursuits around the home. With national television ownership rates escalating from only 2 percent of all households in 1949 to 64 percent just six years later (and 90 percent by 1962), white suburbanites quickly became preoccupied with these innovative "home theaters" and distanced themselves even farther from the nightspots and other urban spaces they associated with blacks and homosexuals—a move that effectively divided racial and sexual identities and communities along an urban/suburban axis.[10]

Although the practice of slumming never completely disappeared, the suburban ethos of containment remained so strong that well into the last quarter of the twentieth century, white suburbanites sought their entertainment primarily within the privacy of their own homes (facilitated by the advent of the VCR) or in the semipublic spaces of shopping malls and multiplex cinemas. Only in the past decade or so, as an intensifying wave of gentrification has reshaped the demographic and spatial characteristics of Chicago and New York, have white heterosexuals returned to the cities' more marginalized neighborhoods and nightlife in substantial numbers. Giving rise to what might be viewed as a second wave of slumming—although the term itself is no longer in vogue—these ventures have provided opportunities for suburban-reared whites to reacquaint themselves with urban entertainment and with the queer and black communities that once seemed so forbidding and undesirable.[11]

In the mid-1990s, drag artists and transgender entertainers once more became feature attractions, constituting what columnist Michael Musto called "the drag queen explosion." During this period, suburban and urban revelers encountered over-the-top performers at some of the trendiest night clubs in New York and Chicago and also hired popular drag queens "to give attitude" at private parties. A number of drag-oriented restaurants also began to draw a steady stream of heterosexual patrons to queer urban spaces. After Lucky Cheng's employed transgender Asian waitresses and flamboyant queens at its East Village locale in 1993, several New York and Chicago establishments followed suit, including the West Village's Lips and Lakeview's Kit Kat Lounge and Supper Club. In short order, a group of lesbian entertainers and transgender men augmented the feminine focus of this nightlife trend with an array of more masculine performances. Transforming the East Village lounge Velvet into the Club Casanova in 1996, they launched the country's first weekly drag king revue, attracting "a mostly white, punk, alternative crowd," as well as a sizable number of photographers, filmmakers, and reporters, who helped popularize their activities with more mainstream heterosexual audiences. As the kinging phenomenon grew, troupes like the Chicago Kings became regular features at both queer and straight nightspots, building loyal lesbian, gay, and transgender fan bases while eliciting praise and occasional flirtation from heterosexual women and men.[12]

Tempting as it might be to view this nightlife trend as a nostalgic return to the earlier pansy and lesbian craze, this recent vogue is a product of its own historical era, reflecting current urban spatial and demographic changes. While signaling the growing integration of lesbians and gay men in mainstream American culture, it also reveals a willingness, on the part of at least some heterosexuals, to grapple with the challenges that an increasingly visible population of transgender women and men are posing to the very concept of fixed sexual and gender identities. Whether in the guise of drag kings and queens who parody traditional gender norms in order to reveal their performative construction or in the form of transsexuals whose hormonal and/or surgical interventions seek to correct discrepancies between biology and gender identity, transgender individuals routinely expose the fictiveness and fluidity of both femininity and masculinity. Yet even as heterosexual spectators appear to acknowledge this notion within the context of popular drag clubs, the fact that these nightspots have become favored venues for bachelorette parties belies their power to disrupt traditional gender and sexual norms. Not only do such pre-wedding rituals subordinate public expressions of queer identity to heterosexual marriage, they also implicate these nightspots in the gentrification of lesbian and gay communities, as more and more straight white newlyweds move back into cities.[13]

Gentrification—and the related reconfiguration of urban racial dynamics—has also fueled a renewed interest in black residential districts. But unlike the latest drag craze, this new fascination with black Chicago and New York has not prompted any significant white influx into the cities' black nightspots. Rather, since the mid-1990s, busloads of white American and foreign tourists have streamed into Harlem on so-called gospel tours. While local churchgoers have bristled at the presence of such Sunday morning slummers, at least some congregants have been forced to acknowledge the economic benefits these tours bring to their financially strapped institutions. Yet as black community leaders collect commissions from commercial tour companies and donations from white visitors, they are also finding ways to channel this newfound interest in their communities into valuable critiques of urban redevelopment. In Chicago, where gentrification has proceeded in tandem with the Chicago Housing Authority's $1.6 billion plan to demolish public housing high-rises and replace them with mixed-income units, local black activists have created a new type of slumming excursion to call attention to the venture's ill effects. On these "Ghetto Bus Tours," former Robert Taylor Homes resident Beauty Turner leads groups of mostly white professionals through the vacant lots where Chicago's largest housing projects once stood and into the unrenovated residences of one of the city's last remaining public housing complexes. While acknowledging the benefits that have accrued from the city's new, mixed-income developments, Turner rues the sense of community lost by poor blacks who were displaced from the only homes they had ever known. Moreover, she cautions against the potential of gentrification and redevelopment to further rend the cultural fabric of long-standing black urban districts, noting that when white people move into the neighborhood, they "don't want to look across the street and see seven little black churches in a three-block radius. What they want to see is a Dominick's and sushi joints and a Starbucks"—national franchises and commercial food fads that threaten to erase any remaining remnants of the neighborhoods' proud black history.[14]

This increasing cultural homogeneity in U.S. cities is probably one reason why slumming has become more transnational in recent years. As global capitalism and technological advances have fueled a dramatic upsurge in international travel, Americans—whether white or black, straight or gay—have begun to focus their search for racialized and sexualized amusements on the people and spaces of the developing world. Joined by a host of European, Canadian, Australian, and Japanese tourists, these jet-setting travelers have usually been content to confirm their social and economic privilege simply by exploiting the relatively low-cost cultural attractions and other amenities that the world's poorest nations routinely offer to cash-rich foreigners. But a growing number of international travelers have begun to imitate the behavior of late-nineteenth- and early-twentieth-century slummers, undertaking visits to the countries' most impoverished urban districts.

Since 1992, a company called Favela Tour has endeavored to "put people in touch with reality" by conducting sightseers through Rio de Janeiro's crowded mountainside slums. These tours have proved so popular that in recent years they spawned a number of imitators both in Rio's *favelas* and in similar locations around the world, ranging from South Africa's black townships and the slums of Mumbai to the "railway underworld" of New Delhi and the garbage dumps outside Mazatlán, Mexico. While most of these touring companies have embraced Favela Tour's model of donating part of their proceeds to neighborhood schools and clinics, the tension between the tours' charitable aims and their voyeuristic tendencies never lies far below the surface. Promotional materials for Victoria Safaris's "Nairobi City Slum Tours" provide a troublesome case in point. Calling its activities "Pro-Poor Tourism Adventures," the company's Web site cultivates a sense of economic, and even racial, superiority among potential customers by portraying local slum dwellers in almost animalistic terms. "You will be amazed with the number of roaming children in the slum," a description of its tour proclaims, "the type of housing, . . . lack of normal feeding timetable, [and] the flowing sewage." The company's offer to combine such tours "with the other regular Safaris to the wildlife lodges" only reinforces the notion that slum-dwellers are little more than beasts to be observed on African safari, echoing a similarly racist rhetoric that circulated widely as part of earlier U.S. slumming vogues.[15]

Yet even as present-day slumming excursions hark back to American exemplars, they also differ in important respects. Except for an extended version of Reality Tours and Travel's "Dharavi Slum Tours," which incorporates a drive through Mumbai's "red light area," slumming today rarely combines sexualized spectacles with explorations of poverty. This is not to say that sexual slumming no longer exists, just that most of the participants in sex tourism apparently choose to separate their erotic encounters from tours of local slums. In the sex tourism guide *Lusty Traveler* (2008), Wiley Cooper expresses his disbelief that "wealthy tourists [would] shell out good money to ride a bus" through Rio's "most horrid slums," when they could "watch beautiful women stroll the beach" instead. "Girls . . . [who] live in favelas and skirt the razor's edge" might seem appealing to straight male tourists seeking sexual adventure, but the author encouraged readers to patronize more upscale brothels and nightclubs instead, insisting that no matter "what people say, fear is not an aphrodisiac." Apparently reaching the same conclusion, operators of the developing world's sex tourism industry—a significant portion of which is now directed at straight women and gay men—have moved much of their traffic from the cities' dilapidated slums and red-light districts to beach resorts popular with foreign travelers. Sex workers are still likely to be from urban slums, but sex tourists no longer have to venture into such districts to procure their services.[16]

Despite these geographic reconfigurations, slumming's renewed popularity in the developing world only confirms its productiveness in negotiating the spatial and demographic changes that regularly restructure daily life. Just as earlier generations of slummers used this unique cultural practice to make sense of the reorganization of urban space associated with newly arrived populations in the late nineteenth and early twentieth centuries, so present-day participants in the transnational phenomenon employ it as a means to make sense of the compression of geographical distances and the blurring of national cultures associated with globalization. While the cross-cultural encounters this activity promotes are likely to reify the borders of current nation-states, as they previously reified the bounds separating white residential districts from the racialized and sexualized slums of urban America, it seems probable that slumming will once more facilitate the proliferation of new identity categories—including but not limited to those associated with nation, race, and sexuality—while simultaneously contributing to the emergence and codification of a new twenty-first-century social order. More than a century since slumming first captured Americans' imagination, this distinctive cultural practice is now poised to help both Americans and others to better understand the new global economy and transnational culture in which we live. The challenge will be to minimize slumming's more exploitative effects, while capitalizing on its ability to foster mutually beneficial, cross-cultural interactions.

Notes

INTRODUCTION

1.   Bricktop [Ada Smith Ducongé] with James Haskins, *Bricktop* (New York: Atheneum, 1983), 75.
2.   Although no other scholar has addressed the sexual and racial dynamics of the full range of slumming vogues that swept U.S. cities, my understanding of these trends has been shaped by the following meticulous scholarship: Nathan Huggins, *Harlem Renaissance* (New York: Oxford University Press, 1971); David Levering Lewis, *When Harlem Was in Vogue* (New York: Oxford University Press, 1981); Lewis A. Erenberg, *Steppin' Out: New York Nightlife and the Transformation of American Culture, 1890–1930* (1981; repr., Chicago: University of Chicago Press, 1984); Eric Garber, "A Spectacle in Color: The Lesbian and Gay Subculture of Jazz Age Harlem," in Martin Duberman, Martha Vicinus, and George Chauncey, eds., *Hidden from History: Reclaiming the Gay and Lesbian Past* (New York: New American Library, 1989), 318–33; Kathy J. Ogren, *The Jazz Revolution: Twenties America and the Meaning of Jazz* (New York: Oxford University Press, 1989); Luc Sante, *Low Life: Lures and Snares of Old New York* (New York: Farrar Straus Giroux, 1991); Lillian Faderman, *Odd Girls and Twilight Lovers: A History of Lesbian Life in Twentieth-Century America* (1991; repr., New York: Penguin Books, 1992), 67–79; Burton W. Peretti, *The Creation of Jazz: Music, Race, and Culture in Urban America* (Urbana: University of Illinois Press, 1992); William Howland Kenney, *Chicago Jazz: A Cultural History, 1904–1930* (New York: Oxford University Press, 1993); David Nasaw, *Going Out: The Rise and Fall of Public Amusements* (New York: Basic Books, 1993); George Chauncey, *Gay New York: Gender, Urban Culture, and the Making of the Gay Male World, 1890–*

1940 (New York: Basic Books, 1994), 33–45, 227–354; Ann Douglas, *Terrible Honesty: Mongrel Manhattan in the 1920s* (New York: Farrar, Straus and Giroux, 1994); Marybeth Hamilton, *When I'm Bad, I'm Better: Mae West, Sex, and American Entertainment* (New York: HarperCollins, 1995), esp. 70–103; Donald L. Miller, *City of the Century: The Epic of Chicago and the Making of America* (New York: Simon & Schuster, 1996), 488–551; Kevin J. Mumford, "Homosex Changes: Race, Cultural Geography, and the Emergence of the Gay," *American Quarterly* 48.3 (September 1996): 395–414; idem, *Interzones: Black/White Sex Districts in Chicago and New York in the Early Twentieth Century* (New York: Columbia University Press, 1997), esp. 133–56; David K. Johnson, "The Kids of Fairytown: Gay Male Culture on Chicago's Near North Side in the 1930s," in Brett Beemyn, ed., *Creating a Place for Ourselves: Lesbian, Gay, and Bisexual Community Histories* (New York: Routledge, 1997), 97–118; Allen Drexel, "Before Paris Burned: Race, Class, and Male Homosexuality on the Chicago South Side, 1935–1960," in Beemyn, ed., *Creating a Place for Ourselves*, 119–44; M. H. Dunlop, *Gilded City: Scandal and Sensation in Turn-of-the-Century New York* (New York: William Morrow, 2000), 113–99; Christine Stansell, *American Moderns: Bohemian New York and the Creation of a New Century* (New York: Metropolitan Books, 2000); Catherine Cocks, *Doing the Town: The Rise of Urban Tourism in the United States, 1850–1915* (Berkeley: University of California Press, 2001), 186–203; Nayan Shah, *Contagious Divides: Epidemics and Race in San Francisco's Chinatown* (Berkeley: University of California Press, 2001), esp. 45–104; Mark Caldwell, *New York Night: The Mystique and Its History* (New York: Scribner, 2005; Mary Ting Yi Lui, *The Chinatown Trunk Mystery: Murder, Miscegenation, and Other Dangerous Encounters in Turn-of-the-Century New York City* (Princeton: Princeton University Press, 2005), 17–51; and *Slumming It: Myth and Culture on the Bowery*, directed by Scott Elliott (Greenhouse Pictures, 2005).

3. On the transformation of racial ideologies in the United States from late-nineteenth-century formations that characterized southern and eastern Europeans as nonwhites or "in-between" peoples to an increasingly polarized white/black axis, see especially Robert Orsi, "The Religious Boundaries of an Inbetween People: Street *Feste* and the Problem of the Dark-Skinned Other in Italian Harlem, 1920–1990," *American Quarterly* 44.3 (September 1992): 313–47; James R. Barrett and David Roediger, "In Between Peoples: Race, Nationality and the 'New Immigrant' Working Class," *Journal of American Ethnic History* 16 (1997): 3–44; Matthew Frye Jacobson, *Whiteness of a Different Color: European Immigration and the Alchemy of Race* (Cambridge, MA: Harvard University Press, 1998); and David R. Roediger, *Working Toward Whiteness: How America's Immigrants Became White; The Strange Journey from Ellis Island to the Suburbs* (New York: Basic Books, 2005). On the transition from gendered regimes of sexuality to the now-dominant hetero/homo sexual binary, see esp. Chauncey, *Gay New York*.

4. On the Five Points region of New York and the visits of affluent white
    New Yorkers and tourists to this area during the mid-nineteenth century,
    see especially Sean Wilentz, *Chants Democratic: New York City and the Rise
    of the American Working Class, 1788–1850* (New York: Oxford University
    Press, 1984); Christine Stansell, *City of Women: Sex and Class in New York,
    1789–1860* (New York: Alfred A. Knopf, 1986); Timothy J. Gilfoyle, *City of
    Eros: New York City, Prostitution, and the Commercialization of Sex, 1790–1920*
    (New York: W. W. Norton & Company, 1992); and Tyler Anbinder, *Five
    Points: The 19th-Century New York City Neighborhood That Invented Tap
    Dance, Stole Elections, and Became the World's Most Notorious Slum* (New
    York: The Free Press, 2001).
5. On the mixed commercial and residential geography of antebellum walk-
    ing cities, see Sam Bass Warner Jr., *The Urban Wilderness: A History of the
    American City* (New York: Harper and Row, 1972), 81–82; and David Ward,
    Cities and Immigrants: A Geography of Change in Nineteenth-Century America
    (New York: Oxford University Press, 1971), 88–93. On the spatial reorgani-
    zation of Gilded Age New York, see especially David Ward, *Poverty, Ethnic-
    ity, and the American City, 1840–1925: Changing Conceptions of the Slum and
    the Ghetto* (New York: Cambridge University Press, 1989); Elizabeth Collins
    Cromley, *Alone Together: A History of New York's Early Apartments* (Ithaca,
    NY: Cornell University Press, 1990); and David Scobey, *Empire City: The
    Making and Meaning of the New York City Landscape* (Philadelphia: Temple
    University Press, 2002). On the reorganization of urban space following Chi-
    cago's Great Fire, see Daniel Bluestone, *Constructing Chicago* (New Haven,
    CT: Yale University Press, 1991); Karen Sawislak, *Smoldering City: Chicagoans
    and the Great Fire, 1871–1874* (Chicago: University of Chicago Press, 1995);
    Carl Smith, *Urban Disorder and the Shape of Belief: The Great Chicago Fire,
    the Haymarket Bomb, and the Model Town of Pullman* (Chicago: University
    of Chicago Press, 1995); and Ross Miller, *The Great Chicago Fire* (Urbana:
    University of Illinois Press, 2000).
6. On the ideology of separate spheres and the distinction drawn between
    "public women" and those who conformed to the dictates of this ideology,
    see especially Stansell, *City of Women*; Linda K. Kerber, "Separate Spheres,
    Female Worlds, Woman's Place: The Rhetoric of Women's History," *Journal
    of American History* 75.1 (June 1988): 9–39; and Mary P. Ryan, *Women in
    Public: Between Banners and Ballots, 1825–1880* (Baltimore: Johns Hopkins
    University Press, 1990). On the mid-nineteenth-century moral reform
    work of evangelical Protestant women, see Ladies of the Mission, *The Old
    Brewery and the New Mission House at Five Points* (New York: Stringer &
    Townsend, 1854); Carroll Smith-Rosenberg, "Beauty, the Beast, and the
    Militant Woman: A Case Study in Sex Roles and Social Stress in Jackso-
    nian America," [1971], in *Disorderly Conduct: Visions of Gender in Victorian
    America* (New York: Oxford University Press, 1986), 113–15; and Mary P.

Ryan, *Cradle of the Middle Class: The Family in Oneida County, New York, 1790–1865* (New York: Cambridge University Press, 1981).

7. On sporting-male culture, see Elliott J. Gorn, *The Manly Art: Bare-Knuckle Prize Fighting in America* (Ithaca, NY: Cornell University Press, 1986); idem, "'Good-Bye Boys, I Die a True American': Homicide, Nativism, and Working-Class Culture in Antebellum New York City," *Journal of American History* 74.2 (September 1987): 388–410; Richard B. Stott, *Workers in the Metropolis: Class, Ethnicity, and Youth in Antebellum New York City* (Ithaca, NY: Cornell University Press, 1990); Gilfoyle, *City of Eros*, esp. 76–160; Patricia Cline Cohen, "Unregulated Youth: Masculinity and Murder in the 1830s City," *Radical History Review* 52 (Winter 1992): 33–53; idem, *The Murder of Helen Jewett* (New York: Alfred A. Knopf, 1998); and Helen Lefkowitz Horowitz, *Rereading Sex: Battles over Sexual Knowledge and Repression in Nineteenth-Century America* (New York: Alfred A. Knopf, 2002), 45–69, 125–248.

8. On the heterosocialization of public leisure during the late nineteenth and early twentieth centuries, see especially John F. Kasson, *Amusing the Million: Coney Island at the Turn of the Century* (New York: Hill & Wang, 1978); Erenberg, *Steppin' Out*; Kathy Peiss, *Cheap Amusements: Working Women and Leisure in Turn-of-the-Century New York* (Philadelphia: Temple University Press, 1986); idem, "Commercial Leisure and the 'Woman Question,'" in Richard Butsch, ed., *For Fun and Profit: The Transformation of Leisure into Consumption* (Philadelphia: Temple University Press, 1990), 105–17; Nasaw, *Going Out*; and Randy D. McBee, *Dance Hall Days: Intimacy and Leisure among Working-Class Immigrants in the United States* (New York: New York University Press, 2000).

9. See James L. Ford, *The Literary Shop and Other Tales* (New York: Geo. H. Richmond & Co., 1894), 129–31; Albert Parry, *Garrets and Pretenders: A History of Bohemianism in America*, rev. ed. (1933; repr., New York: Dover Publications, 1960), 14–37; and Timothy J. Gilfoyle, *A Pickpocket's Tale: The Underworld of Nineteenth-Century New York* (New York: W. W. Norton & Company, 2006), 81–94, 110–24.

10. On the benevolent origins of slumming in nineteenth-century London, where the term and practice apparently first emerged, see "Slumming in This Town," *NYT*, September 14, 1884, 4; and Seth Koven, *Slumming: Sexual and Social Politics in Victorian London* (Princeton, NJ: Princeton University Press, 2004), esp. 6–10. On the various historical meanings and uses of *slumming*, see also Peter Hitchcock, "Slumming," in María Carla Sánchez and Linda Schlossberg, eds., *Passing: Identity and Interpretation in Sexuality, Race and Religion* (New York: New York University Press, 2001), 160–86.

11. John T. McEnnis, *The White Slaves of Free America; Being an Account of the Sufferings, Privations and Hardships of the Weary Toilers in Our Great Cities as Recently Exposed by Nell Nelson, of the* Chicago Times (Chicago: R. S. Peale & Company, 1888), 69–70.

12. See especially Robert H. Wiebe, *The Search for Order, 1877–1920* (New York: Hill & Wang, 1967); Paul S. Boyer, *Urban Masses and Moral Order in America, 1820–1920* (Cambridge, MA: Harvard University Press, 1978); Joanne J. Meyerowitz, *Women Adrift: Independent Wage Earners in Chicago* (Chicago: University of Chicago Press, 1988); Mary E. Odem, *Delinquent Daughters: Protecting and Policing Adolescent Female Sexuality in the United States, 1885–1920* (Chapel Hill: University of North Carolina Press, 1995); Ruth M. Alexander, *The "Girl Problem": Female Sexual Delinquency in New York, 1900–1930* (Ithaca, NY: Cornell University Press, 1995); Michael Willrich, *City of Courts: Socializing Justice in Progressive Era Chicago* (New York: Cambridge University Press, 2003); and Derek Vaillant, *Sounds of Reform: Progressivism and Music in Chicago, 1873–1935* (Chapel Hill: University of North Carolina Press, 2003).
13. On red-baiting and nativism, see especially John Higham, *Strangers in the Land: Patterns of American Nativism, 1860–1925* (New Brunswick, NJ: Rutgers University Press, 1955); Dale T. Knobel, *"America for the Americans": The Nativist Movement in the United States* (New York: Twayne Publishers, 1996); and Jacobson, *Whiteness of a Different Color*. On the legislative exclusion of Asian immigrants and the passage of quotas regulating southern and eastern European immigration, see especially Sucheng Chan, ed., *Entry Denied: Exclusion and the Chinese Community in America, 1882–1943* (Philadelphia: Temple University Press, 1991); Mae M. Ngai, *Impossible Subjects: Illegal Aliens and the Making of Modern America* (Princeton, NJ: Princeton University Press, 2003); and Roger Daniels, *Guarding the Golden Door: American Immigration Policy and Immigrants Since 1882* (New York: Hill and Wang, 2004).
14. On the Klan, see Kenneth Jackson, *The Ku Klux Klan in the City, 1915–1930*, rev. ed. (1967; repr., Chicago: Ivan R. Dee, 1992); and Nancy MacLean, *Behind the Mask of Chivalry: The Making of the Second Ku Klux Klan* (New York: Oxford University Press, 1994). Important studies on the complex dynamics of lynching include Gail Bederman, "'Civilization,' the Decline of Middle-Class Manliness, and Ida B. Wells's Antilynching Campaign (1892–94)," *Radical History Review* 52 (Winter 1992): 5–30; Nancy MacLean, "The Leo Frank Case Reconsidered: Gender and Sexual Politics in the Making of Reactionary Populism," *Journal of American History* 78.3 (December 1991): 917–48; Jacquelyn Dowd Hall, "'The Mind That Burns in Each Body': Women, Rape, and Racial Violence," in Ann Snitow, Christine Stansell, and Sharon Thompson, eds., *Powers of Desire: The Politics of Sexuality* (New York: Monthly Review Press, 1983), 328–49; and Joel Williamson, *A Rage for Order: Black-White Relations in the American South Since Emancipation* (New York: Oxford University Press, 1986).

On the migration of Southern blacks to Chicago and New York and the conflicts they encountered there, see especially The Chicago Commission on Race Relations, *The Negro in Chicago: A Study of Race Relations and a Race Riot* (Chicago: University of Chicago Press, 1922); James Weldon Johnson,

Black Manhattan (New York: Knopf, 1930); St. Clair Drake and Horace R. Cayton, *Black Metropolis: A Study of Negro Life in a Northern City* (Chicago: University of Chicago Press, 1945); Gilbert Osofsky, *Harlem: The Making of a Ghetto; Negro New York, 1890–1930* (New York: Harper and Row, 1966); Allen Spear, *Black Chicago: The Making of a Ghetto, 1890–1920* (Chicago: University of Chicago Press, 1969); William Tuttle, *Race Riot: Chicago and the Red Summer of 1919* (New York: Athenaeum, 1982); James Grossman, *Land of Hope: Chicago, Black Southerners, and the Great Migration* (Chicago: University of Chicago Press, 1989); Cheryl Greenberg, *"Or Does It Explode?" Black Harlem in the Great Depression* (New York: Oxford University Press, 1991); James M. Gregory, *The Southern Diaspora: How the Great Migrations of Black and White Southerners Transformed America* (Chapel Hill: University of North Carolina Press, 2005); and Davarian L. Baldwin, *Chicago's Negroes: Modernity, The Great Migration, and Black Urban Life* (Chapel Hill: University of North Carolina Press, 2007).

15. On the women's suffrage movement, see Nancy Cott, *The Grounding of Modern Feminism* (New Haven, CT: Yale University Press, 1987). On the influx of single women and men—including a substantial number of bohemian artists and radicals—into early-twentieth-century New York and Chicago, see (among others): June Sochen, *The New Woman: Feminism in Greenwich Village, 1910–1920* (New York: Quadrangle Books, 1972); Robert E. Humphrey, *Children of Fantasy: The First Rebels of Greenwich Village* (New York: John Wiley & Sons, 1978); Leslie Fishbein, *Rebels in Bohemia: The Radicals of* The Masses*, 1911–1917* (Chapel Hill: University of North Carolina Press, 1982); Peiss, *Cheap Amusements*; Meyerowitz, *Women Adrift*; Kevin White, *The First Sexual Revolution: The Emergence of Male Heterosexuality in Modern America* (New York: New York University Press, 1993); Chauncey, *Gay New York*; Howard P. Chudacoff, *The Age of the Bachelor: Creating an American Subculture* (Princeton, NJ: Princeton University Press, 1999); and Stansell, *American Moderns*.

16. Thomas C. Holt, "Marking: Race, Race-making, and the Writing of History," *American Historical Review* 100.1 (February 1995): 1–20. Holt argues that "'race' inheres neither in biology nor in culture but must be summoned to consciousness by . . . encounters in social space and historical time" (1). I suggest that the same concept applies to sexuality and that slumming played a pivotal role in "marking" both race and sexuality in American culture during the late nineteenth and early twentieth centuries.

17. Jacobson, *Whiteness of a Different Color*; idem, *Barbarian Virtues: The United States Encounters Foreign Peoples at Home and Abroad, 1876–1917* (New York: Hill & Wang, 2000); Orsi, "The Religious Boundaries of an Inbetween People"; and Roediger, *Working Toward Whiteness*. See also Barrett and Roediger, "In Between Peoples"; Michael Rogin, "Making America Home: Racial Masquerade and Ethnic Assimilation in the Transition to Talking Pictures," *Journal of American History* 79.3 (December 1992): 1050–77; idem, *Black-*

face, White Noise: Jewish Immigrants in the Hollywood Melting Pot (Berkeley: University of California Press, 1996); Joseph P. Cosco, *Imagining Italians: The Clash of Romance and Race in American Perceptions, 1880–1910* (Albany: State University of New York Press, 2003); Jennifer Guglielmo and Salvatore Salerno, eds., *Are Italians White? How Race Is Made in America* (New York: Routledge, 2003); and Thomas A. Guglielmo, *White on Arrival: Italians, Race, Color, and Power in Chicago, 1890–1945* (New York: Oxford University Press, 2003). In a slightly different take on this subject, Thomas Guglielmo separates "color" from "race," insisting that although many turn-of-the-century Americans may have thought Italian immigrants were *racially* distinct from old-stock Americans of northwestern European descent, they believed that even the most recently arrived Italians were *white*. After all, Guglielmo argues, U.S. immigration authorities and other government officials classified all Italians as "white on arrival," making them eligible for naturalization and other legal privileges and protections typically denied to Asians and blacks.

18. Chauncey, *Gay New York*, esp. 12–23; idem, "Christian Brotherhood or Sexual Perversion? Homosexual Identities and the Construction of Sexual Boundaries in the World War I Era," *Journal of Social History* 19.2 (Winter 1985): 189–211; idem, "From Sexual Inversion to Homosexuality: Medicine and the Changing Conception of Female Deviance," *Salmagundi* 58–59 (Fall 1982–Winter 1983): 114–46; Lisa Duggan, "The Trials of Alice Mitchell: Sensationalism, Sexology, and the Lesbian Subject in Turn-of-the-Century America," *Signs* 18.4 (Summer 1993): 791–814; idem, *Sapphic Slashers: Sex, Violence, and American Modernity* (Durham, NC: Duke University Press, 2000); Jonathan Ned Katz, *The Invention of Heterosexuality* (New York: Dutton, 1995); and idem, *Love Stories: Sex between Men before Homosexuality* (Chicago: University of Chicago Press, 2001). On the gradual and often incomplete emergence of heterosexuality and homosexuality as hegemonic categories of social experience, see also Michel Foucault, *The History of Sexuality, Volume 1: An Introduction*, trans. Robert Hurley (1978; repr., New York: Vintage, 1980); John D'Emilio and Estelle Freedman, *Intimate Matters: A History of Sexuality in America* (New York: Harper & Row, 1988); Faderman, *Odd Girls and Twilight Lovers*; White, *The First Sexual Revolution*; Elizabeth Lapovsky Kennedy, "'But we would never talk about it': The Structures of Lesbian Discretion in South Dakota, 1928–1933," in Ellen Lewin, ed., *Inventing Lesbian Cultures in America* (Boston: Beacon Press, 1996), 15–40; and Sharon R. Ullman, *Sex Seen: The Emergence of Modern Sexuality in America* (Berkeley: University of California Press, 1997).

19. Only a handful of recent studies have investigated the reciprocal relationship between transformations in sexual and racial regimes. See, for instance, Kevin J. Mumford, "Homosex Changes"; idem, *Interzones*; Siobhan B. Somerville, *Queering the Color Line: Race and the Invention of Homosexuality in American Culture* (Durham, NC: Duke University Press, 2000); Eithne

Luibhéid, *Entry Denied: Controlling Sexuality at the Border* (Minneapolis: University of Minnesota Press, 2002); Nayan Shah, "Between 'Oriental Depravity' and 'Natural Degenerates': Spatial Borderlands and the Making of Ordinary Americans," *American Quarterly* 57.3 (September 2005): 703–26; and Pablo Mitchell, *Coyote Nation: Sexuality, Race, and Conquest in Modernizing New Mexico, 1880–1920* (Chicago: University of Chicago Press, 2005). The process of emulation and differentiation encompassed by slumming closely resembles the racial and sexual dynamics that historian Eric Lott has ascribed to the popular fascination with minstrelsy among nineteenth-century Americans (*Love and Theft: Blackface Minstrelsy and the American Working Class* [New York: Oxford University Press, 1993], esp. 3–12).

20. On the British origins of slumming, see Koven, *Slumming*, esp. 1–14.

21. Recent historical studies have suggested that even settlement house workers shared more in common with the average slummer than has previously been acknowledged. This new scholarship argues that reformers, such as Chicago's Jane Addams and New York's Charles B. Stover and John Lovejoy Elliott, took up residence in the cities' immigrant neighborhoods not only to provide aid to local residents but also to exploit the cover that such living arrangements provided for their same-sex relationships with other settlement house workers and, in some cases, neighborhood youths. See especially Kevin P. Murphy, *Political Manhood: Red Bloods, Mollycoddles, and the Politics of Progressive Era Reform* (New York: Columbia University Press, 2008), 104–24; and Scott Herring, *Queering the Underworld: Slumming, Literature, and the Undoing of Lesbian and Gay History* (Chicago: University of Chicago Press, 2007), 25–66. In *Slumming*, Seth Koven discusses similar dynamics among the settlement house workers of Victorian London (181–281).

22. According to U.S. census figures, Chicago became the nation's second largest city sometime between 1880 and 1890, outstripping Philadelphia by more than 50,000 inhabitants by the early 1890s. Chicago would retain its spot behind New York as the second most populous city in the United States until the 1980s, when Los Angeles finally surpassed it in size (Campbell Gibson, "Population of the 100 Largest Cities and Other Urban Places in the United States: 1970 to 1990," Population Division Working Paper No. 27 [Washington, DC: Population Division, U.S. Bureau of the Census, 1998], available at http://www.census.gov/population/www/documentation/twps0027.html; accessed August 13, 2006).

CHAPTER 1

1. "Life in New York City," *BDE*, February 24, 1884, 3; "Slumming in This Town," *NYT*, September 14, 1884, 4; and "The Talk of New York," *BDE*, September 30, 1888, 10.

2. "Slumming in This Town," *NYT*, September 14, 1884, 4.

3. On the heterosocialization of public leisure in the working-class districts of late-nineteenth-century U.S. cities, see especially Peiss, *Cheap Amusements*, esp. 34–55, 88–162; Nasaw, *Going Out*, esp. 19–33, 80–95, 104–19; and McBee, *Dance Hall Days*, esp. 51–156.

4. On the emergence of the "slum" as an identifiable space and an ideological concept, see especially Sam Bass Warner Jr. and Colin B. Burke, "Cultural Change and the Ghetto," *Journal of Contemporary History* 4.4 (October 1969): 173–87; David Ward, "The Emergence of Central Immigrant Ghettoes in American Cities: 1840–1920," *Annals of the Association of American Geographers* 58.2 (June 1968): 343–59; idem, "The Victorian Slum: An Enduring Myth?" *Annals of the Association of American Geographers* 66.2 (June 1976): 323–36; idem, *Poverty, Ethnicity, and the American City, 1840–1925*; Kathleen Neils Conzen, "Immigrants, Immigrant Neighborhoods, and Ethnic Identity: Historical Issues," *Journal of American History* 66.3 (December 1979): 603–15; and Alan Mayne, *The Imagined Slum: Newspaper Representation in Three Cities, 1870–1914* (Leicester: Leicester University Press, 1993).

5. On the spatial reorganization of Gilded Age New York and Chicago, see especially Ward, *Poverty, Ethnicity, and the American City, 1840–1925*; Cromley, *Alone Together*; Bluestone, *Constructing Chicago*; Sawislak, *Smoldering City*; and Scobey, *Empire City*.

6. Robert Lewis, "The Industrial Suburb Is Dead, Long Live the Industrial Slum: Suburbs and Slums in Chicago and Montreal, 1850–1950," *Planning Perspectives* 17.2 (April 2002): 127–28, 135–37.

7. Ward, *Poverty, Ethnicity, and the American City, 1840–1925*, 107–8; Scobey, *Empire City*, 71–72, 144–46; and Thomas Lee Philpott, *The Slum and the Ghetto: Neighborhood Deterioration and Middle-Class Reform, Chicago, 1880–1930* (New York: Oxford University Press, 1978), 15–37.

8. Robert W. DeForest and Lawrence Veiller, "The Tenement House Problem," in Robert DeForest and Lawrence Veiller, eds., *The Tenement House Problem; Including the Report of the New York State Tenement House Commission of 1900*, vol. 1 (New York: Macmillan Company, 1903), 4, 7–8; and Lawrence Veiller, "Housing Conditions and Tenement Laws in Leading American Cities," in ibid., 131. For additional contemporaneous descriptions of the social conditions of the tenement districts of New York and Chicago, see also Jacob A. Riis, *How the Other Half Lives: Studies Among the Tenements of New York* (New York: Charles Scribner's Sons, 1890); Robert Hunter, *Tenement Conditions in Chicago: Report by the Investigating Committee of the City Homes Association* (Chicago: City Homes Association, 1901); Milton B. Hunt, "The Housing of Non-Family Groups of Men in Chicago," *American Journal of Sociology* 16.2 (September 1910): 145–70; Alzada P. Comstock, "Chicago Housing Conditions, VI: The Problem of the Negro," *American Journal of Sociology* 18.2 (September 1912): 241–57; Grace Peloubet Norton, "Chicago Housing Conditions, VII: Two Italian Districts," *American Journal of Sociology* 18.4 (January 1913): 509–42; Raymond Calkins, *Substitutes for the*

Saloon: An Investigation Originally Made for the Committee of Fifty, introduction by Francis G. Peabody, 2nd rev. ed. (Boston: Houghton Mifflin Company, 1919), 267–301; and Edith Abbott and Sophonisba P. Breckinridge, *The Tenements of Chicago, 1908–1935* (Chicago: University of Chicago Press, 1936); among others.

9. "Slumming Parties," editorial, *CT*, June 4, 1907, 8; "Prof. Bailey's Class Here Again to See Us," *NYT*, May 4, 1906, 5; "Limitations of 'Sociology,'" editorial included in "Topics of the Times," *NYT*, May 5, 1906, 8; and McEnnis, *The White Slaves of Free America*, 69–70. The popular conflation of slumming and urban sociology was so widespread that turn-of-the-century scholars directly addressed this issue in print, lest their nascent academic discipline be dismissed as mere entertainment. See Albion W. Small, "What Is a Sociologist?" *American Journal of Sociology* 8.4 (January 1903): 471.

Prominent examples of muckrakers' "armchair slumming" tracts include Riis, *How the Other Half Lives*; idem, *The Battle with the Slum* (New York: The Macmillan Company, 1902); Lincoln Steffens, *The Shame of the Cities* (New York: McClure, Phillips & Co., 1904); George Kibbe Turner, "The City of Chicago: A Study of the Great Immoralities," *McClure's Magazine*, April 1907, 575–92; idem, "Tammany's Control of New York by Professional Criminals," *McClure's Magazine*, June 1909, 117–34; idem, "Beer and the City Liquor Problem," *McClure's Magazine*, September 1909, 528–43; and idem, "Daughters of the Poor: A Plain Story of the Development of New York City as a Leading Center of the White Slave Trade of the World, under Tammany Hall," *McClure's Magazine*, November 1909, 45–61. See also Keith Gandal, *The Virtues of the Vicious: Jacob Riis, Stephen Crane, and the Spectacle of the Slum* (New York: Oxford University Press, 1997).

10. "Slumming Parties," editorial, *CT*, June 4, 1907, 8.

11. Leonard Covello, *The Heart Is the Teacher* (New York: McGraw-Hill, 1958), 19–27, repr. in Ronald H. Bayor, ed., *The Columbia Documentary History of Race and Ethnicity in America* (New York: Columbia University Press, 2004), 465; Ward, "The Emergence of Central Immigrant Ghettoes," 345–46; and E. A. Goldenweiser, "Immigrants in Cities," *The Survey*, January 7, 1911, 598, 600, 602.

12. Mayne, *The Imagined Slum*, 2.

13. The centrality of blacks and of Chinese, Italian, and Jewish immigrants to the emergence of slumming reveals that it was a practice defined more by racial than by class boundaries. Notably, not all slums became focal points of the increasingly popular pastime of slumming. Turn-of-the-century New York reformers and amusement seekers developed a near-obsession with the tenement districts of the Lower East Side of Manhattan, while largely ignoring similarly dilapidated and older neighborhoods on the city's Lower West Side. Likewise, although well-to-do white residents and tourists routinely flocked to the Union Stock Yards and slaughterhouses on Chicago's southwest side to get a glimpse of mass production at it rawest, the shabby

wood-frame tenements and saloons of the surrounding working-class district rarely attracted their attention. One key factor that distinguished these particular slum districts from more popular slumming destinations was the composition of their population. As late as 1900, both New York's Lower West Side and Chicago's Packingtown were inhabited primarily by native-born whites and members of "old" immigrant groups, such as the Irish, Germans, and Canadians, rather than the blacks, Chinese immigrants, and "new" immigrant groups from southern and eastern Europe who populated the areas favored by slumming parties. See Lawrence Veiller, "A Statistical Study of New York's Tenement Houses," in DeForest and Veiller, eds., *The Tenement House Problem*, vol. 1, 194; *A West Side Rookery* (New York: Greenwich House Publications, 1906), 8; L[ouis] Schick, *Chicago and Its Environs: A Handbook for the Traveler* (Chicago: L. Schick, 1891), 119–21; Hunter, *Tenement Conditions in Chicago*, 12; and James R. Barrett, *Work and Community in the Jungle: Chicago's Packinghouse Workers, 1894–1922* (Urbana: University of Illinois Press, 1987), 64–117.

14. *Compendium of the Tenth Census (June 1, 1880), Compiled Pursuant to an Act of Congress Approved August 7, 1882*, Part I (Washington, DC: Government Printing Office, 1883), 382–83, 396–97; and *Thirteenth Census of the United States Taken in the Year 1910*, vol. I, *Population 1910: General Report and Analysis* (Washington, DC: Government Printing Office, 1913), 178. Because the present-day, five-borough City of New York was not created until 1898, statistics from the 1880 and 1910 censuses cannot be easily equated. For 1880, I have used the figures for New York, NY, a designation that included present-day Manhattan and large sections, but not all, of the Bronx. For 1910, I have used the figures for Manhattan only.

15. *Reports of the Immigration Commission*, vol. 3, *Statistical Review of Immigration 1820–1910; Distribution of Immigrants, 1850–1900* (Washington, DC: Government Printing Office, 1911), 8; *Report on Population of the United States at the Eleventh Census: 1890*, Part I (Washington, DC: Government Printing Office, 1895), 672; and *Thirteenth Census of the United States Taken in the Year 1910*, vol. I, *Population 1910: General Report and Analysis* (Washington, DC: Government Printing Office, 1913), 829. Again, the comparative census figures available for New York are somewhat uneven. For 1890, I have employed statistics pertaining to New York, NY, including all of present-day Manhattan and large sections of the Bronx. For 1910, however, I have had to use figures for New York City in its entirety, including all five modern-day boroughs.

The difficulty of discerning Jewish rates of immigration is made clear in reports of the day. In DeForest and Veiller's *The Tenement House Problem*, Kate Holladay Claghorn writes: "The real race composition of the newer immigrants . . . is more or less concealed under the nomenclature formerly used in the statistics of immigration, and still used in the United States Census, which shows country of birth only. The terms 'Russian' and 'Pole,' for example, cover Hebrews and Slavs indiscriminately. 'Austrian' and 'Hungarian' may indicate any one of many races of the most diverse social affinities—Slavs, Magyars, Hebrews, and Germans." She goes on to state, "from the immigration statistics and general observation, however, it is certain that a considerable proportion [of the Austro-Hungarians in New York] are Hebrews, and in like manner that practically all of the 'Russians' in the city are of the Hebrew race" (Claghorn, "Foreign Immigration and the Tenement House in New York City," in DeForest and Veiller, eds., *The Tenement House Problem*, vol. 2, 81, 84).

16. Schick, *Chicago and Its Environs*, 106; Ernest Ingersoll, *A Week in New York* (Chicago and New York: Rand, McNally & Co., 1891), 202–13; and *Rand, McNally & Co.'s Handy Guide to Chicago and the World's Columbian Exposition* (Chicago and New York: Rand, McNally & Co., 1893), 104–11. On "Niggertown" and "Little Africa," see Allan Forman, "New York Niggertown," *WP*, August 15, 1886, 6; John J. Coughlin, "The Kings and Queens of the First Ward," *CT*, December 2, 1906, F4; and Eleanor Harvier, "Walking Abroad in Old New York," *NYT*, November 28, 1920, 27. On "Chinatown," see especially Allan Forman, "Celestial Gotham," *The Arena*, April 1893, 620–28; "Seitz in Chinatown," *Frank Leslie's Popular Monthly*, May 1893, 612–18; Helen F. Clark, "The Chinese of New York: Contrasted with Their Foreign Neighbors," *Century Illustrated Magazine*, November 1896, 104–13; and "The Spectator," *The Outlook*, August 20, 1898, 960–63. On the Jewish "Ghetto," consult Francis J. Douglas, "The Hebrew Quarter of New York," *Christian Union*, January 17, 1889, 71–72; Henry Hoyt Moore, "City Sketches, III: East Side Shoppers and Shopping," *Christian Union*, December 26, 1891, 1274–75; Richard Wheatley, "The Jews in New York," *Century Illustrated Magazine*, January 1892, 323–42; and Katherine Hoffman, "In the New York Ghetto," *Munsey's Magazine*, August 1900, 608–19. And on "Little Italy," see "Low Life," *NPG*, July 23, 1887, 7; and Charles Henry White, "Chicago," *Harper's Monthly Magazine*, April 1909, 729–38. The following articles and books address some combination of these racialized working-class communities: "The Spectator," *Christian Union*, November 14, 1891, 919; Allan Forman, "Some Adopted Americans," *Arthur's Home Magazine*, September 1893, 710–17; "The Spectator," *The Outlook*, August 25, 1894, 306; "The Spectator on the East Side," *The Outlook*, August 29, 1896, 364; M. G. Van Rensselaer, "Places in New York," *Century Illustrated Magazine*, February 1897, 501–16; "Bowery as It Is To-Day," orig. pub. *New York Mail and Express*, repr. *WP*, March 2, 1900, 8; and Edward A. Stein, *On the Trail of the Immigrant* (New York: Fleming H. Revell Company, 1906).

17. On the history of "Little Italy" in New York's East Harlem, see Thomas Kessner, *The Golden Door: Italian and Jewish Immigrant Mobility in New York City, 1880–1915* (New York: Oxford University Press, 1977); and Robert Orsi, *The Madonna of 115th Street: Faith and Community in Italian Harlem, 1880–1950*

(New Haven, CT: Yale University Press, 1985). On Chicago's "Little Sicily" and "Little Hell," see Hunter, *Tenement Conditions in Chicago;* Harvey Warren Zorbaugh, *The Gold Coast and the Slum: A Sociological Study of Chicago's Near North Side* (Chicago: University of Chicago Press, 1929); Philpott, *The Slum and the Ghetto;* and Rudolph J. Vecoli, "The Formation of Chicago's 'Little Italies,'" *Journal of American Ethnic History* 2.2 (Spring 1983): 5–20.

18. On the origin of the notion of "red-light districts," see I. L. Nascher, *The Wretches of Povertyville: A Sociological Study of the Bowery* (Chicago: J. J. Lanzit, 1909), 89. The alleged "memoirs" of the madam Nell Kimball (which were almost certainly a product of the historically grounded imagination of their "editor," Stephen Longstreet [pseud. Chauncey Weiner]) suggest an alternative etymology of the term. Tracing its origin to the railyards of the American Midwest, the memoirs assert that the "red light" in question was the lantern that train conductors and brakemen hung outside the local brothels where they repaired while the train was being loaded and refueled, enabling railyard workers to easily relocate them when the train was ready for departure. (*Nell Kimball: Her Life as an American Madam, by Herself*, ed. Stephen Longstreet [New York: Macmillan, 1970], 90–91.)

19. On the establishment of legally sanctioned sex districts in New Orleans, see Herbert Asbury, *The French Quarter: An Informal History of the New Orleans Underworld* (New York: A. A. Knopf, 1936), 424–55; Al Rose, *Storyville, New Orleans: Being an Authentic, Illustrated Account of the Notorious Red-light District* (Tuscaloosa, AL: University of Alabama Press, 1974); and Alecia P. Long, *The Great Southern Babylon: Sex, Race, and Respectability in New Orleans, 1865–1920* (Baton Rouge: Louisiana State University Press, 2004), 102–47. On the existence of well-accepted, relatively segregated, extralegal red-light districts in turn-of-the-century Chicago and New York, see especially Vice Commission of Chicago, *The Social Evil in Chicago: A Study of Existing Conditions with Recommendations by the Vice Commission of Chicago* (Chicago: Gunthorp-Warren Printing Company, 1911), 143–46; Howard B. Woolston, *Prostitution in the United States*, vol. 1 (New York: The Century Co., 1921), 102–30; Walter Cade Reckless, "The Natural History of Vice Areas in Chicago" (PhD diss., University of Chicago, 1925), 39–81; Willoughby Cyrus Waterman, *Prostitution and Its Repression in New York City, 1900–1931* (1932; repr., New York: AMS Press, 1968), 11–15; and James Lincoln Collier, *The Rise of Selfishness in America* (New York: Oxford University Press, 1991), 49–66.

Although legally segregated sex districts did not exist in Chicago, the city's Vice Commission noted in 1911 that "for years the people have seen develop under their very eyes a system of restricted districts under police regulation, the result of which has been to nullify the law, and render it inoperative" (Vice Commission of Chicago, *The Social Evil in Chicago*, 144).

This does not mean that the city's brothels and other commercialized, sex-related enterprises were all confined to these districts, but they were concentrated enough in the South, West, and North Side levees that many Chicagoans wished to maintain these "segregated," or, "restricted," districts in hopes of containing illicit sex in particular geographic locales. To this end, debates over the proper boundaries of these districts surfaced from time to time in the local government and popular press (see, for example, "Another Jolt for Levee," *CT*, August 24, 1901, 2; "To Clean Wabash Avenue," *CT*, May 6, 1903, 3; and "Wants Vice in Bounds," *CRH*, May 31, 1905, 7).

In New York, public discussion of "segregated," or, "restricted," sex districts was never as pronounced as in Chicago, but municipal authorities did raise the possibility of establishing an officially segregated vice district in the Tenderloin on more than one occasion (see "Two Tammany Measures," *NYT*, January 8, 1898, 3; and "Only One System for Control of Vice," *NYT*, February 28, 1909, 4). Artfully and systematically demonstrating that prostitution flourished in nearly every turn-of-the-century Manhattan neighborhood, historian Timothy Gilfoyle questions the applicability of the very concept of segregated vice districts to a New York context. Yet as Gilfoyle's own extensive research demonstrates, among the general public of the day, the commercial sex trade and other illicit activities were associated with only a handful of entertainment districts—the Tenderloin and the Bowery (and its neighboring "Rialto") foremost among them (see Gilfoyle, *City of Eros*, esp. 197–223).

20. On the geographic "coincidence" of the isolation of vice and the segregation of blacks and of Chinese and other immigrant groups, see especially Ivan Light, "From Vice District to Tourist Attraction: The Moral Career of American Chinatowns, 1880–1940," *Pacific Historical Review* 43.3 (August 1974): 367–94; idem, "From Racketeers to Restaurateurs," *Mankind* 5.10 (1976): 8–10, 52–53; idem, "The Ethnic Vice Industry, 1880–1944," *American Sociological Review* 42.3 (June 1977): 464–79; Neil Larry Shumsky, "Tacit Acceptance: Respectable Americans and Segregated Prostitution, 1870–1910," *Journal of Social History* 19.4 (Summer 1986): 665–79; Cynthia Marie Blair, "Vicious Commerce: African American Women's Sex Work and the Transformation of Urban Space in Chicago, 1850–1915" (PhD diss., Harvard University, 1999), 277–90; Mara L. Keire, "The Vice Trust: A Reinterpretation of the White Slavery Scare in the United States, 1907–1917," *Journal of Social History* 35.1 (Fall 2001): 5–41; and Baldwin, *Chicago's New Negroes*, 22–26.

21. Vice Commission of Chicago, *The Social Evil in Chicago*, 38; and "An Appeal for Funds," *NYT*, October 16, 1898, 18; Marcy S. Sacks, *Before Harlem: The Black Experience in New York City Before World War I* (Philadelphia: University of Pennsylvania Press, 2006), 72–76. By the spring of 1901, knowledgeable observers of the city's black population estimated that "fully one-half

of the colored people in New York" had been forced to seek shelter in the
Tenderloin (P. Butler Thompkins, "Colored Mission's Needs," letter to the
editor, *NYT*, March 31, 1901, 23).

22. Hutchins Hapgood, *The Spirit of the Ghetto: Studies of the Jewish Quarter in
New York*, rev. ed., with a new introd. by Irving Howe (1902; repr., New
York: Schocken Books, 1976), 5; and Claghorn, "Foreign Immigration and
the Tenement House in New York City," 88–89. On the spatial conflation of
Chicago's Jewish Ghetto and its Near West Side red-light district, see Hunter,
Tenement Conditions in Chicago. In a notable turn of phrase, Hunter referred
to this phenomenon as the "double curse of the slum and the ghetto" (189).

23. United States Immigration Commission, *Reports*, Vol. III, *Statistical Review
of Immigration, 1819–1910—Distribution of Immigrants*, 1850–1900 (Washington, DC: Government Printing Office, 1911), 34–44, 88–91; and
Kessner, *The Golden Door*, 26–32. On the Page Law, see, among others,
Sucheng Chan, "The Exclusion of Chinese Women, 1870–1943," in Chan,
ed., *Entry Denied*, 94–146; and Bill Ong Hing, *Making and Remaking Asian
America through Immigration Policy, 1850–1990* (Stanford, CA: Stanford University Press, 1993), 23–36.

24. Ike Swift, "Sketches of Gay New York, Written Specially for the Police
Gazette; No. 9: On the Bowery," *NPG*, May 13, 1899, 3. On late-nineteenth-
and early-twentieth-century male homosocial public leisure, see Jon Kings-
dale, "The 'Poor Man's Club': Social Functions of the Urban Working-Class
Saloon," in Elizabeth H. Pleck and Joseph H. Pleck, eds., *The American Man*
(Englewood Cliffs, NJ: Prentice-Hall, 1980), 255–83; Perry R. Duis, *The Saloon: Public Drinking in Chicago and Boston, 1880–1920* (Urbana: University
of Illinois Press, 1983); Peiss, *Cheap Amusements*, 11–33; Robert C. Allen,
Horrible Prettiness: Burlesque and American Culture (Chapel Hill: University of
North Carolina Press, 1991), 197–240; Madelon Powers, *Faces along the Bar:
Lore and Order in the Workingman's Saloon, 1870–1920* (Chicago: University
of Chicago Press, 1998); and Brooks McNamara, *The New York Concert Saloon: The Devil's Own Nights* (New York: Cambridge University Press, 2002).

On the emergence of fairy resorts in the slums of New York and Chicago, see Chauncey, *Gay New York*, 33–45; *Mazet*, 173–77, 277–78, 1382–83,
1394–95, 1429–32, 5130; L. O. Curon, *Chicago, Satan's Sanctum* (Chicago:
C. D. Phillips & Co., 1899), 144–48; G. Frank Lydston, *The Diseases of Society:
The Vice and Crime Problem* (Philadelphia: J. B. Lippincott Company, 1904),
308–9; and Vice Commission of Chicago, *The Social Evil in Chicago*, 295–98.

On the establishment of heterosocial leisure spaces in the immigrant
and working-class districts of New York and Chicago, see especially Peiss,
Cheap Amusements, 34–55, 88–162; Nasaw, *Going Out*, 19–33, 80–95,
104–19; McBee, *Dance Hall Days*, 51–156; and Elizabeth Clement, "From
Sociability to Spectacle: Interracial Sexuality and the Ideological Uses of
Space in New York City, 1900–1930," *Journal of International Women's*

Studies 6.2 (June 2005): 24–43, available at http://www.bridgew.edu/soas/ jiws/Jun05/Clements.pdf; accessed April 22, 2006.

25. H. C. Bunner, "The Bowery and Bohemia," *Scribner's*, April 1894, 458. A similar description of the cosmopolitan Bowery, "the western boundary of the great Hebrew section and the eastern boundary of the land of the Italians," can be found in the 1899 annual report of the University Settlement Society of New York. According to one member of the society, Bowery amusements attracted an "unending stream of the curious minded out for a good time; soldiers and sailors, boys showing the town to their guests, occasional slum parties, and other flotsam and jetsam of that sort," plus the "Irish, German, and Hebrew contingents" (F. H. McLean, "Bowery Amusements," *Yearbook of the University Settlement Society of New York* [New York, 1899], 14).

26. Bunner, "The Bowery and Bohemia," 458–59; Forman, "Some Adopted Americans," 712; "The Spectator," *Outlook*, August 25, 1894, 306; "The Spectator on the East Side," *Outlook*, August 29, 1896, 364; and Richard Wheatley, "The Jews in New York," *Century Illustrated Magazine*, January 1892, 326.

27. W. D. Howells, *Impressions and Experiences* (New York: Harper & Brothers, 1896), 138, 141, 145.

28. "New York Society's Hungarian Fad," orig. pub. in *New York Press*, repr. in *Current Literature*, May 1899, 434.

29. Bunner, "The Bowery and Bohemia," 458.

30. *Mazet*, 1307–8; and Julian Ralph, "Coney Island," *Scribner's*, July 1896, 18. See also Peiss, *Cheap Amusements*, esp. 100–4. A description of similar goings-on in the concert hall known as The Windsor, 27 Bowery, can be found in Charles W. Gardner, *The Doctor and the Devil; or, Midnight Adventures of Dr. Parkhurst* (New York: Gardner & Co., 1894), 46–49.

31. Gardner, *The Doctor and the Devil*, 49–50; and *Lexow*, 1665–66, 1778–81, 1835–37, 2752–55 (quote from 1780). See also Harry Collins Brown, *In the Golden Nineties* (Hastings-on-Hudson, NY: Valentine's Manual, Inc., 1928), 348.

32. Clement, "From Sociability to Spectacle," 24–43; and Forman, "New York Niggertown," 6 (here and throughout the book, capitalization—or lack thereof—of the word "Negro" is shown as it is in the original source). The district's most popular establishments included Frank Stephenson's Black and Tan (located at 153 Bleecker Street), the nearby House of Blazes, Niggar [*sic*] Alley, an unnamed black and tan on Baxter Street, and Bleecker Street's Burnt Rag. While former New York police chief George W. Walling attributes ownership of the eponymous resort at 153 Bleecker Street to Frank Stephenson in his 1887 memoir, the *New York Times* report of its closure in July 1885 lists the proprietor as Patrick Mee. (See "The 'Black and Tan' Closed," *NYT*, July 28, 1885, 2; George W. Walling, *Recollections of a*

New York Chief of Police [New York: Caxton Book Concern, Limited, 1887], 485–87; Riis, *How the Other Half Lives*, 119; Helen Campbell, Thomas W. Knox, and Thomas Byrnes, *Darkness and Daylight; or, Lights and Shadows of New York Life; A Pictorial Record of Personal Experiences by Day and Night in the Great Metropolis* [Hartford, CT: The Hartford Publishing Company, 1895], 471–74; Gustav Kobbé, *New York and Its Environs* [New York: Harper & Brothers, 1891], 143–44; and Brown, *In the Golden Nineties*, 348.)

33. On the brothels and opium dens of New York's Chinatown, see Louis J. Beck, *New York's Chinatown: An Historical Presentation of Its People and Places* (New York: Bohemia Publishing Co., 1898), 107–21, 146–64; *Lexow*, 2244–46; *Mazet*, 4778; Investigator's Report on 17 Mott St., Disorderly House, March 1, 1901, box 4, CFP; Arthur E. Wilson, Investigator's Report on 11 Pell St., Prostitution, March 1, 1901, box 5, CFP; John Stewart Burgess, "A Study of the Characteristics of the Cantonese Merchants in Chinatown, New York, as Shown by Their Use of Leisure Time" (MA thesis, Columbia University, 1909), 25; and Lui, *The Chinatown Trunk Mystery*, 27–37, 46–48. On opium dens and smoking performances staged strictly for slummers, see, among others: Campbell, Knox, and Byrnes, *Darkness and Daylight*, 558; William Brown Meloney, "Slumming in New York's China-town," *Munsey's Magazine*, September 1909, 822; James L. Ford, *Forty-Odd Years in the Literary Shop* (New York: E. P. Dutton & Company, 1921), 239; and Jimmy Durante and Jack Kofoed, *Night Clubs* (New York: A. A. Knopf, 1931), 95–96.

34. Beck, *New York's Chinatown*, 317, 326. See also "Seitz in Chinatown," 612–18; Ford, *The Literary Shop and Other Tales*, 129–30; and Clark, "The Chinese of New York," 104–13.

35. "Tenderloin as It Was," *NYT*, July 12, 1896, 16; and *Mazet*, 2004, 1582. My description of the Tenderloin here and throughout the text is further informed by my reading of Gilfoyle, *City of Eros*, esp. 203–10; and Richard O'Connor, *Hell's Kitchen: The Roaring Days of New York's Wild West Side* (Philadelphia: J. B. Lippincott Company, 1958), esp. 81–98; and by an examination of the extant run of *The Tenderloin*, 1898–1899, available on microfilm at the Library of Congress.

36. *Mazet*, 2004, 1582; and "Wicked Streets Are Scarce in the New York of Today," *NYT*, September 20, 1925, X20.

37. *Mazet*, 1551, 2437; Gilfoyle, *City of Eros*, 205, 209–10; James Weldon Johnson, *Along This Way* (1933), repr. in James Weldon Johnson, *Writings* (New York: The Library of America, 2004), 296–300, 318–25; "Popular Resorts," n.d. [March 1910], 1910–12 folder, box 28, C14P; S.W.L., Report on Baron Wilkins' Café, (331 West 37th Street) 253 W. 35th Street, March 16, 1910, 1910–12 folder, box 28, C14P; Edward S. Ford, Investigator's Report (on U.S. House of Representatives letterhead), n.d., 1910–12 folder, box 28, C14P; Wm. F. Pogue, "Report of Investigations," June 21, 1913,

June–July 1913 folder, box 28, C14P; and "Report for Saturday Night Aug. 30, [1913],"August–September 1913 folder, box 28, C14P.

38. *A Guide to the City of Chicago* (Chicago: Chicago Association of Commerce, 1909), 26–27, 125 (quote from 125); *Chicago for the Tourist* (Chicago: Illinois Central Railroad, 1908), 36–37; Charles Henry White, "Chicago," *Harper's Monthly Magazine*, April 1909, 729–38; Edmund J. James, Oscar R. Flynn, J. R. Paulding, Mrs. Simon N. Patton (Charlotte Kimball), and Walter Scott Andrews, *The Immigrant Jew in America* (New York: B. F. Buck & Company, 1906), 56–60, 249–54; Philip P. Bregstone, *Chicago and Its Jews: A Cultural History*, introduction by Julian W. Mack ([Chicago]: Privately Published, 1933), 344, 355–58; *Sporting Club House Directory; Containing a Full and Complete List of All Strictly First-Class Club and Sporting Houses* (Chicago: Ross and St. Clair, 1889), 25, 45–46; "Chicago as Seen by Herself," *McClure's Magazine*, May 1907, 69; and Cocks, *Doing the Town*, 186–203. Cocks notes, with considerable accuracy, that "Chicago's sprawling immigrant settlements, curiously, did not much attract travel and guidebook writers" (188). But she errs somewhat in interpreting this evidence as proof that Chicago did not "seem to have supported ethnic slumming to a[ny] great extent" (203).

39. "Chicago as Seen by Herself," 69; Herbert Asbury, *Gem of the Prairie: An Informal History of the Chicago Underworld* (New York: A. A. Knopf, 1940), 106–24, 243–80; unnamed Chicago newspaper article, 1891, quoted in V. H. D. [Vivia H. Divers], *The 'Black Hole'; or, the Missionary Experience of a Girl in the Slums of Chicago, 1891–1892* (n. p., 1893), 8; Reckless, "The Natural History of Vice Areas in Chicago," 39–81; and Blair, "Vicious Commerce," 277–87. In addition to the South and West Side levee districts, Chicago also had a small North Side Levee that consisted primarily of a string of brothels and saloons located along and immediately to the west of Clark Street, north of the Chicago River. See "Wants Vice in Bounds," *CRH*, May 31, 1905, 7; and Reckless, "The Natural History of Vice Areas in Chicago," 31–36.

40. *Sporting Club House Directory*, 7–45; Harold R. Vynne, *Chicago by Day and Night: The Pleasure Seeker's Guide to the Paris of America* (Chicago: Thomson and Zimmerman, 1892), 40, 49–52; *Rand, McNally & Co.'s Handy Guide to Chicago and the World's Columbian Exposition*, esp. 68–72, 104–11; *Chicago By Night* (Chicago: Rand McNally, 1893); Asbury, *Gem of the Prairie*, 135–41; Reckless, "The Natural History of Vice Areas in Chicago," 53–57; *Madeleine: An Autobiography*, introduction by Judge Ben B. Lindsey (New York: Harper & Brothers, 1919), 120–21 (quotes from 120); and Lauren Rabinovitz, *For the Love of Pleasure: Women, Movies and Culture in Turn-of-the-Century Chicago* (New Brunswick, NJ: Rutgers University Press, 1998), 15–46.

41. Asbury, *Gem of the Prairie*, 243–80 (quote from 243); Franklin Matthews, "'Wide-Open' Chicago," *Harper's Weekly*, February 12, 1898, 89; and "Judge Uhlir Tours 'White Lights,'" *CRH*, January 30, 1916, 1, 8. On the

relocation of Chicago's South Side Levee, see also R. B. P., "Chicago's Reform Wave," *NYT*, December 2, 1900, 15; "Another Jolt for Levee," *CT*, August 24, 1901, 2; "Another 'Levee' Must Go," *CT*, December 28, 1904, 5; and Blair, "Vicious Commerce," 277–87. On the Everleigh Club, Freiberg's, and other Levee resorts, see also H. W. Lytle and John Dillon, *From Dance Hall to White Slavery: The World's Greatest Tragedy* (Charles C. Thompson Co., 1912), 163–90; Charles Washburn, *Come into My Parlor: A Biography of the Aristocratic Everleigh Sisters of Chicago* (New York: Knickerbocker Press, 1934); and Karen Abbott, *Sin in the Second City: Madams, Ministers, Playboys, and the Battle for America's Soul* (New York: Random House, 2007).

42. V. H. D., *The 'Black Hole,'* 15–16; Ernest A. Bell, "Chicago's White Slave Market," in Ernest A. Bell, ed., *Fighting the Traffic in Young Girls, or War on the White Slave Trade* (G. S. Ball, 1910), 261–62. British editor and publisher William T. Stead noted a similarly diverse population when visiting the region during the 1893 Columbian Exposition. Focusing on the nineteenth precinct of the First Ward (the area bounded by Harrison and Polk streets to the north and south, and Dearborn and Clark streets to the east and west) he enumerated a population of 263. Of these residents, sixty (or nearly a quarter) were found to be foreign-born—primarily of German, Russian, or Italian descent, but also French, Austrian, Irish, Canadian, English, Norwegian, Scotch, Swedish, Danish and Polish—while 203 (or 77 percent) were native-born, 74 of whom originally hailed from the "Southern States," by which Stead meant they were "men of color" (William T. Stead, *If Christ Came to Chicago! A Plea for the Union of All Who Love in the Service of All Who Suffer* [Chicago: Laird and Lee, 1894],124–25).

43. Adam McKeown, *Chinese Migrant Networks and Cultural Change: Peru, Chicago, Hawaii, 1900–1936* (Chicago: University of Chicago Press, 2001), 193–98; Curon, *Chicago, Satan's Sanctum*, 151; John Curry, "The First Chinese Restaurant," *CT*, March 27, 1943, included in the "Restaurant" clippings files, CHM; A Looper, "According to the Telephone Book—," *CT*, March 31, 1943, included in the "Restaurant" clippings files, CHM; and *CT*, September 7, 1926, quoted in McKeown, *Chinese Migrant Networks and Cultural Change*, 196.

44. History of Near South Side Document #5: "Informant: Of Scotch-Irish stock, born in north Ireland, arrived in Chicago the day of the Haymarket Riot, 1886," October 1927, vol. 4, pt. 1, CNS; Qingchao Wu, "Chinatowns: A Study of Symbiosis and Assimilation" (PhD diss., University of Chicago, 1928); "Building Report Alarms Hinky Dink and Chinatown," *CT*, January 18, 1911, 1; "Chinatown Plans to Move Two Miles to the South," *CT*, November 24, 1911, 2; "Breakup of Old Chinatown in Clark Street Has Begun," *CT*, April 28, 1912, 3; "Chinese Merchants Move to New South Side Colony," *CT*, April 30, 1912, 3; and McKeown, *Chinese Migrant Networks and Cultural Change*, esp. 209–12 (McKeown provides a lengthier and far

more nuanced account of the tensions between the Hip Sing and On Leong Tongs).

45. Spear, *Black Chicago*, 12; Clifton R. Wooldridge, *Hands Up! In the World of Crime* (Chicago: Police Publishing Company, 1901), 322–28; Asbury, *Gem of the Prairie*, 140–41, 167–68, 257–58, 264 (the last page being the source of the quote about Black May's); and Stead, *If Christ Came to Chicago!*, 247 (on Vina Fields's house).

46. Reckless, "The Natural History of Vice Areas in Chicago," 53–54n3 (quote from 54); George J. Kneeland, *Commercialized Prostitution in New York City* (New York: The Century Co., 1913), 15; and Rosen, *The Lost Sisterhood: Prostitution in America, 1900–1918* (Baltimore: The Johns Hopkins University Press, 1982), 89.

47. Curon, *Chicago, Satan's Sanctum*, 144; and P. J. Duff, *Side Lights on Darkest Chicago* (Chicago: M. Hayes, 1899), 64. For a description of after-hours performances at the Park Theater, see *Chicago's Dark Places: Investigations by a Corps of Specially Appointed Commissioners, Edited and arranged by the Chief Commissioner* (Chicago: The Craig Press and the Women's Temperance Publishing Association, 1891), 61; and Stead, *If Christ Came to Chicago!*, 258–59.

48. *Mazet*, 5125–26, 1394, 173–76, 1431, 1429.

49. Ibid., 1382–83; and Vice Commission of Chicago, *The Social Evil in Chicago*, 295–98.

50. Charles Torrence Nesbitt, unpublished autobiographical manuscript, 1938, 105, folder 1, box 1, CTNP; and Curon, *Chicago, Satan's Sanctum*, 146. For more on Nesbitt's adventures in Walhalla Hall and elsewhere in the Bowery, see Jonathan Ned Katz, *Gay/Lesbian Almanac: A New Documentary* (New York: Harper & Row, 1983), 218–22; and Chauncey, *Gay New York*, 40–41.

51. Nesbitt, unpublished manuscript, 106, folder 1, box 1, CTNP; Katz, *Gay/Lesbian Almanac*, 218–22; Chauncey, *Gay New York*, 41; and Curon, *Chicago, Satan's Sanctum*, 146–47. While Curon's reference to "fruits" (147) is clearly intended to call to mind fairies, his mention of "cabmen" (ibid.) is more ambiguous. He may be referring to the fairies' masculine partners. More likely, though, Curon alludes in some way to cab drivers' involvement as go-betweens in the commercial sex trade.

52. Frederick H. Whitin, General Secretary, Committee of Fourteen, to Rosenstern, New York, October 14, 1913, box 1, C14P, quoted in Gilfoyle, *City of Eros*, 304; and Rosen, *The Lost Sisterhood*, 1–13.

53. Nesbitt, unpublished manuscript, 56, folder 1, box 1, CTNP.

54. Herbert Asbury, *The Gangs of New York: An Informal History of the Underworld* (Garden City, NY: Garden City Publishing Co., Inc., 1928), 177; William T. Stead, *Satan's Invisible World Displayed; or, Despairing Democracy* (New York: R. F. Fenno & Co., 1897), 99; and H. L. Mencken, *The American Language: A Preliminary Inquiry into the Development of English in the United States*, 3rd ed. (New York: Alfred A. Knopf, 1929), 163n64. See also the introductory

material of *Mazet*, which paraphrases this statement somewhat differently: "It [the Tenderloin District] derives its name from the remark of Police Captain Williams when he was sent thither from an uptown precinct, that he was leaving the rump to feed on the tenderloin, his reference being to the richness of the precinct in pecuniary opportunities for police captains" (45).

55. On the white slavery panic, see especially Mark Thomas Connelly, *The Response to Prostitution in the Progressive Era* (Chapel Hill: University of North Carolina Press, 1980), 114–35; Edward J. Bristow, *Prostitution and Prejudice: The Jewish Fight Against White Slavery, 1870–1939* (New York: Oxford University Press, 1982),146–80; Rosen, *The Lost Sisterhood*, 112–35; Barbara Meil Hobson, *Uneasy Virtue: The Politics of Prostitution and the American Reform Tradition* (1987; repr., with new preface, Chicago: University of Chicago Press, 1990), 139–64; Gilfoyle, *City of Eros*, 270–97; and Keire, "The Vice Trust."

56. Jane Addams, *The Spirit of Youth and the City Streets* (New York: Macmillan Company, 1909), 13, 7.

57. On Progressive-era reformers' attacks on the urban political machine, see especially Wiebe, *The Search for Order*, 164–95; and Daniel T. Rodgers, "In Search of Progressivism," *Reviews in American History* 10.4 (December 1982): 113–32.

58. On the reform campaign of the Reverend Charles Parkhurst, see Robert F. Walsh, *Dr. Parkhurst's Crusade; or, New York after Dark* (New York: Commonwealth Publishing Co., 1892); Gardner, *The Doctor and the Devil*; Charles H. Parkhurst, *Our Fight with Tammany* (New York: Charles Scribner's Sons, 1895); idem, *My Forty Years in New York* (New York: Macmillan Company, 1923); Timothy J. Gilfoyle, "The Moral Origins of Political Surveillance: The Preventive Society in New York City, 1867–1918," *American Quarterly* 38.4 (Autumn 1986): 637–52; idem, *City of Eros*, 298–302; and Warren Sloat, *A Battle for the Soul of New York: Tammany Hall, Police Corruption, Vice, and Reverend Charles Parkhurst's Crusade against Them, 1892–1895* (New York: Cooper Square Press, 2002). Gardner was the detective hired by Parkhurst to lead his many slumming excursions.

On the Chicago reform campaign fueled by William T. Stead, see his *If Christ Came to Chicago!*; and Joseph O. Baylen, "A Victorian's Crusade in Chicago, 1893–94," *Journal of American History* 51.3 (December 1964): 418–34. Both Parkhurst and Stead are addressed in Boyer, *Urban Masses and Moral Order*, 162–87.

59. Samuel P. Orth, *The Boss and the Machine: A Chronicle of the Politicians and Party Organization* (New Haven, CT: Yale University Press, 1919), 63–92; and Gilfoyle, *City of Eros*, 301.

60. Curon, *Chicago, Satan's Sanctum*, 200–10 (quotes from 202); and Vice Commission of Chicago, *The Social Evil in Chicago*. Aside from brief mentions of these committees and their final reports in the published records of the

Illinois state legislature, I have been able to turn up next to nothing about the hearings and investigations they conducted. According to archivists at the Illinois State Archives, neither committee ever published its findings, and no original committee papers have been preserved (Kim Efird, Illinois State Archives, e-mail message to author, November 16, 2004).

Although pressured by local prosecutors to release the key to its code, the Chicago Vice Commission never did and it was apparently destroyed. Still, the report was so full of salacious details that Chicago postal officials initially forbade its distribution through the mail. See "Wayman Pushes Fight on Resort Property Owners," *CT*, October 7, 1912, 1; and "Vice Reports Barred," *CRH*, September 15, 1911, 3. On the public reception of *The Social Evil in Chicago*, see also Walter Lippman, *A Preface to Politics* (New York: M. Kennerly, 1913), 123–31; and Connelly, *The Response to Prostitution in the Progressive Era*, 91–113.

Not until 1913 did a government-funded investigation of Chicago moral conditions and police graft, headed by Lieutenant Governor Barratt O'Hara (a Chicago Democrat), provide the public with anything approaching the same level of shocking detail that the Lexow and Mazet committee reports had presented to New Yorkers more than a decade earlier. Employing the unorthodox tactic of questioning the patrons and proprietors of popular Levee resorts immediately after their apprehension in those venues, the Illinois Senate Vice Committee's late-night sessions generated so many sensationalistic headlines that it was accused of attempting to boost newspaper sales, if not the popularity of the Levee itself. Noting that O'Hara was in the pocket of publisher William Randolph Hearst, Chicago reformer Graham Taylor remarked that he "had no trouble . . . in telling them straight out that their methods were hysterical and the publicity into which they are dragging women is scandalous" (Graham Taylor to William Kent, Chicago, May 26, 1913, "Letters 1913" folder, box 1, GTP). Given the detailed newspaper coverage of the committee's proceedings, it seems likely that readers had little trouble using these sources to search out a little scandal of their own. (The O'Hara committee's final report was published as *Report of the Senate Vice Committee, Created under the Authority of the Senate of the Forty-ninth General Assembly, As a Continuation of the Committee Created under the Authority of the Senate of the Forty-eighth General Assembly, State of Illinois* [Chicago: 1916].)

61. My understanding of the modus operandi of private anti-vice organizations in turn-of-the-century Chicago and New York, as well as their impact on the practice of slumming in these two cities, is based on my own examination of the records of several such organizations (including, but not limited to, those discussed at length in succeeding paragraphs), as well as the following: Thomas James Riley, "A Study of the Higher Life of Chicago" (PhD diss., University of Chicago, 1905), 49–50, 54; Walter C. Reckless,

Vice in Chicago (Chicago: University of Chicago Press, 1933), 254–68; Boyer, *Urban Masses and Moral Order*, 191–219; Duis, *The Saloon*, 230–73; D'Emilio and Freedman, *Intimate Matters*, 202–21; Gilfoyle, "The Moral Origins of Political Surveillance"; idem, *City of Eros*, 185–96; Chauncey, *Gay New York*, 131–49; and Mara L. Keire, "The Committee of Fourteen and Saloon Reform in New York City, 1905–1920," *Business and Economic History* 26.2 (Winter 1997): 573–83.

62. Edwin R. A. Seligman, ed., *The Social Evil: With Special Reference to Conditions Existing in the City of New York*, 2nd ed. (New York: G. P. Putnam's Sons, 1912), ix.

63. Gilfoyle, *City of Eros*, 186–88.

64. Clifford W. Barnes, "The Story of the Committee of Fifteen," *Journal of Social Hygiene* 4.1 (April 1918): 145–47; *Annual Report of the Committee of Fifteen for the year ending April 30, 1913*, 1–3; *Annual Report of the Committee of Fifteen for the year ending April 30, 1914*, 1; and Reckless, *Vice in Chicago* 255–58.

The Committee of Fifteen used this publicity tactic for approximately two years, from June 1913 until July 1915. By the end of the program, when the state's new Injunction and Abatement Law codified the practice of holding real estate owners responsible for the goings-on that occurred on their property, the committee boasted that its informal tactics had "dislodged the undesirable tenants in more than 800 resorts" ("The Committee of Fifteen; What It Has Done and Its Method of Operation," unpublished manuscript, n.d., 1, third "Material Concerning the Committee of Fifteen" folder, box 26, GTP).

65. Reckless, *Vice in Chicago*, 262; and Louise de Koven Bowen, *The Public Dance Halls of Chicago*, rev. ed. (Chicago: The Juvenile Protective Association, 1917).

66. "Gypsy Leads 10 Thousand through Red Light District," *CRH*, October 19, 1909, 1.

67. "Police in Carriages Descend on Chinatown," *NYT*, April 24, 1905, 1. For examples of similar crowds gathering to watch raids in the Tenderloin, see "Raid in the Tenderloin," *NPG*, May 11, 1895, 7; and "Raid on the Newmarket," *NYT*, March 6, 1897, 2.

68. On the successful closure of vice districts in numerous U.S. cities, including New York and Chicago, between 1912 and 1917, see Joseph Mayer, "Passing of the Red Light District," *Social Hygiene* 4.2 (April 1918), 199; Rosen, *The Lost Sisterhood*, esp. 14–37; and Boyer, *Urban Masses and Moral Order*, 191–219. On the anti-vice war against Chicago's Levee, see also Herbert Asbury, *Gem of the Prairie*, esp. 281–319.

69. Erenberg, *Steppin' Out*, esp. 111–75. On the emergence of cabarets in Chicago, see Reckless, *Vice in Chicago*, 101; and "At Last the Cabaret Has Arrived to Gladden Chicago 'Bohemians,'" *CT*, June 30, 1912, A6.

CHAPTER 2

1. "At Last the Cabaret Has Arrived to Gladden Chicago 'Bohemians,'" *CT*, June 30, 1912, A6; "Legal Light Sees Cabaret," *CT*, August 1, 1913, 3; and Erenberg, *Steppin' Out*, esp. 75–175.
2. On the Castles, see especially Erenberg, *Steppin' Out*, 146–75; Mr. and Mrs. Vernon Castle, *Modern Dancing* (New York: The World Syndicate Co., by arrangement with Harper & Brothers, 1914); and Irene Castle, as told to Bob and Wanda Duncan, *Castles in the Air* (Garden City, NY: Doubleday, 1958).
3. On Chicago's attempts to regulate cabarets in the summer of 1913, see "Whispers Shelve Cabaret Measure," *CT*, July 22, 1913, 2; "Cermak Sponsor for Cabaret Law?" *CT*, July 25, 1913, 4; "Legal Light Sees Cabaret," *CT*, August 1, 1913, 3; "Good-by, Cabaret!" *CT*, August 21, 1913, 3. On the apparent failure of this attempt to regulate Chicago cabarets and a renewed effort in the spring of 1918, see "The Law and the Cabarets," *CT*, April 23, 1918, 10. On New York's losing battle to police cabarets, see Erenberg, *Steppin' Out*, esp. 77–87.
4. [Richard Fletcher], "The Value of 'Slumming,'" "The Commentaries" column, *The Chronicle*, March 1917, 3; and *Chicago for the Tourist*, issued by The Passenger Department, Illinois Central, 1925, 14, CHM. For other examples of the marketing of these neighborhoods to tourists, see especially Anna Alice Chapin, *Greenwich Village* (New York: Dodd, Mead & Company, 1917) and John Drury, *Seven Days in Chicago* (New York: R. M. McBride & Company, 1928). Jan Seidler Ramirez discusses the proliferation of guidebooks to Greenwich Village that followed Chapin's publication in "The Tourist Trade Takes Hold," in Rick Beard and Leslie Cohen Berlowitz, eds., *Greenwich Village: Culture and Counterculture* (New Brunswick, N J: Museum of the City of New York in association with Rutgers University Press, 1993), 377–78.
5. My understanding of the physical, demographic, and cultural characteristics of Greenwich Village, in this and subsequent paragraphs, relies heavily upon the following sources: Parry, *Garrets and Pretenders*; Caroline Ware, *Greenwich Village, 1920–1930: A Comment on American Civilization in the Post-War Years* (Boston: Houghton Mifflin, 1935); Allen Churchill, *The Improper Bohemians* (New York: Dutton, 1959); Humphrey, *Children of Fantasy*; Fishbein, *Rebels in Bohemia*; Beard and Berlowitz, eds., *Greenwich Village*; Chauncey, *Gay New York*, 227–44; and Stansell, *American Moderns*.
6. My understanding of Chicago's Towertown is drawn largely from Zorbaugh, *The Gold Coast and the Slum*; Reckless, *Vice in Chicago*; Bernard Duffey, *The Chicago Renaissance in American Letters: A Critical History* (East Lansing: Michigan State College Press, 1954); Kenneth Rexroth, *An Autobiographical Novel*, rev. and expanded, ed. Linda Hamalian (1964; New York: New Directions Publishing Corporation, 1991); Dale Kramer, *Chicago Renaissance: The Literary Life in the Midwest, 1900–1930* (New York: Appleton-Century,

1966); James Albert Gazell, "The High Noon of Chicago's Bohemia," *Journal of the Illinois State Historical Society* 65.1 (Spring 1972): 54–68; Meyerowitz, *Women Adrift*; and Johnson, "The Kids of Fairytown" in Beemyn, ed., *Creating a Place for Ourselves*, 97–118.

7. Erenberg, *Steppin' Out*, 253.

8. On the Golden Swan Saloon, commonly known to Villagers as the "Hell Hole," see Parry, *Garrets and Pretenders*, 269; Humphrey, *Children of Fantasy*, 24; Malcolm Cowley, *Exile's Return: A Literary Odyssey of the 1920's* (1934; repr. New York: Viking Press, 1951), 69; and John Sloan, "Hell Hole," 1917 (etching, reproduced in John Sloan, *New York Etchings [1905–1949]*, Helen Farr Sloan, ed. [New York: Dover Publications, Inc., 1978], plate 36). On Madame Galli's, see John Drury, *Dining in Chicago* (New York: John Day Company, 1931), 44–48; "Famous Mme. Galli's Restaurant to Leave Old Home This Week," *CT*, March 31, 1935; and "That Was Bohemia," *Chicago Sun*, February 12, 1947.

9. Zorbaugh, *The Gold Coast and the Slum*, 41–44, 102–4; Walter S. Ross, "The Magic District," *North Central Magazine*, November 1929, 28; Ware, *Greenwich Village*, 16–22, 249–52; Alfreda Gordon, "Bohemia with a Haircut," *Chicago Sunday Times*, March 24, 1940, 5–M; and Samuel Putnam, *Paris Was Our Mistress: Memoirs of a Lost and Found Generation* (New York: Viking Press, 1947), 19–20.

10. Lynn Dumenil, *Modern Temper: American Culture and Society in the 1920s* (New York: Hill and Wang, 1995), 233.

11. Chauncey, *Gay New York*, 233, 304–9; Ware, *Greenwich Village*, 15–17, 56–58; Zorbaugh, *The Gold Coast and the Slum*, 98–102, 159–81; George Chauncey, "Long-Haired Men and Short-Haired Women: Building a Gay World in the Heart of Bohemia," in Beard and Berlowitz, eds., *Greenwich Village*, 151–63; and Lewis Erenberg, "Greenwich Village Nightlife, 1910–1950," in Beard and Berlowitz, eds., *Greenwich Village*, 357–70.

12. Memorandum from Major Thomas B. Crockett to the Director of Military Intelligence, Chicago, April 7, 1919; D. H. Campbell, Report on the Dill Pickle Club, 18 Tooker Place, a Suspicious Organization, April 5, 1919; and Informants #309–I449 and I420 of the Patriotic American League, Report In Re: Meeting—Dill Pickle Club, 18 Tooker Place, December 9, 1919; all of which are included in Record #10110–551, Box 2775, Declassified General Correspondence, 1917–1941, Military Intelligence Division, Records of the War Department General and Special Staffs, Record Group 165, National Archives at College Park, College Park, MD.

13. Edna Fine Dexter, quoted in Parry, *Garrets and Pretenders*, 202; and P. J. M. [Peter J. Mallon], Report on the Black Parrot, 131 Washington Place, April 11, 1919, sixth 1919 investigative reports folder, box 34, C14P.

14. Poster for the dance "A Night in Bohemia, The Dill Pickle Masked Ball," October 31, 1916; Placard advertising "St. Patrick's Costume Ball," March 1925; and Placard advertising the "Adam and Eve Costume" contest at the

Dill Pickle Club's Halloween Party, October 31 [1923 or 1928]—all included in folder 29, box 1, DPCP; Advertisement for Dill Pickle Club, *The Daily Maroon*, October 26, 1928, 5; J. A. S. [James A. Seaman], Report of Investigator, The Saraband of Apes and Ivory, Renee La Coste Webster Hall Dance, March 23, 1917, "Special Inspections" folder, box 31, C14P; "Greenwich Village Affairs," Resume of reports on cabarets, 1917, 16, "Inv. Reports on Cabarets" folder, box 31, C14P; J. A. S. [James A. Seaman], Report of Investigator, The Liberal Club Ball, Webster Hall, 8th [*sic*] St., February 11, 1917, "Special Inspections" folder, box 31, C14P; and "The Greenwich Village Dances at Webster Hall," Resume of Cabaret Situation, 1917, 12, "Inv. Reports of Cabarets" folder, box 31, C14P.

15. Report on Derby Cabaret, Huron and Clark Sts., December 7, 1923, folder 92, JPAP; Report on Erie Cabaret, Erie and North Clark, December 7, 1923, folder 92, JPAP; J. A. S. [James A. Seaman], Report of Investigator, Greenwich Village—shops, March 31, 1917, "Special Inspections" folder, box 31, C14P; H. K. [Harry Kahan], Report on Greenwich Village Hearth, 129 McDougal [*sic*] Str. betw. W. 3rd & W. 4th Str., May 31, 1921, fourth 1920 [*sic*] investigative reports folder, box 34, C14P; "Village Raid Nets 4 Women And 9 Men," *NYT*, February 5, 1923, 17; and F. Aery, "Villagers Go Down," *Brevities*, August 8, 1932, 16.

16. Chauncey, *Gay New York*, 235–37; J. A. S. [James A. Seaman], Report of Investigator, The Greenwich Village Carnival By Glenn Coleman, Webster Hall, April 6, 1917, "Special Inspections" folder, box 31, C14P; "Greenwich Village Affairs"; H. K. [Harry Kahan], Report on The Jungle, 11 Cornelia St., July 4, 1922, 1922 investigative reports folder, box 34, C14P; [Benjamin] Blinstrub, Report on Derby Cabaret, 680 N. Clark St., December 12, 1922, folder 93, JPAP; and Rexroth, *An Autobiographical Novel*, 162, 166–67. For more on The Jungle cabaret in Greenwich Village, see Chauncey, *Gay New York*, 238; Carl Van Vechten, Diary, October 22, 1922, box 111, CVVP; and "Rum Chasers Get 4th Boat in Week," *NYT*, September 18, 1922, 26. Van Vechten, who attended The Jungle with the playwright Avery Hopwood and his lover John Floyd, makes no mention of any fairy entertainment, noting only that it was "a tough gangster resort" where Hopwood's coat was stolen. The *New York Times* article relates a raid on the resort in which The Jungle's "singing waiter," Ronald S. Macdiarmid, was arrested by Federal Prohibition agents for serving liquor. The Jungle's July 4th entertainer, Rosebud, is most likely the same Rosebud, Arthur C. Budd, who was arrested in a raid on the Black Parrot Tea Shoppe Hobo-Hemia in February 1923 (see chapter 4, note 56) and who, during the pansy craze of the late 1920s and early 1930s, performed with Jackie Maye and Jean Malin in various Times Square cabarets (see the final section of this chapter).

17. Frederick H. Whitin, General Secretary, Committee of Fourteen, to Dr. William Adams Brown, Union Theological Seminary, New York City, November 14,

1917, second 1917 correspondence folder, box 4, C14P; Samuel P. Thrasher, Report to the Executive Committee of the Committee of Fifteen, 1921, 2, enclosed with Samuel P. Thrasher to Frederick H. Whitin, Chicago, December 8, 1921, Committee of Fifteen (Chicago) correspondence folder, box 10, C14P; and carbon copy of Mary K. Simhkovitch to John F. Hylan, New York, June 9, 1921, first 1921 correspondence folder, box 5, C14P.

18. Report on 606 Cabaret, 606 North Clark St., December 7, 1923, folder 92, JPAP; H. K. [Harry Kahan], Report on Greenwich Village Hearth, 129 McDougal [sic] Str. betw. W. 3rd & W. 4th Str., May 31, 1921, fourth 1920 [sic] investigative reports folder, box 34, C14P; Frederick H. Whitin to Harry Salvin, New York, August 31, 1918, second 1918 correspondence folder, box 4, C14P. For more extensive and artful analyses of the distinction between prostitution and "charity," see Peiss, *Cheap Amusements*, 108–14; and Elizabeth Clement, *Love for Sale: Courting Couples, Charity Girls, and Sex Workers and the Making of Modern Heterosexuality in New York City, 1900–1945* (Chapel Hill: University of North Carolina Press, 2006), 45–75.

19. Frederick H. Whitin to Harry Salvin, New York, August 31, 1918, second 1918 correspondence folder, box 4, C14P; Frederick H. Whitin to Mrs. V. G. [Mary] Simkhovitch, New York, June 13, 1921, first 1921 correspondence folder, box 5, C14P; Leslie L. Lewis, "Superintendent's Report 1925," in *Seventeenth Annual Report of the Committee of Fifteen for the year ended December 31, 1925* (Chicago: Committee of Fifteen, 1926), 7; and Reckless, *Vice in Chicago*, 113.

20. "Nab 11 Young Girls in West Dance Raid," *NYT*, January 22, 1923, 17; "7 Arrested in Raid Paroled," *NYT*, January 24, 1923, 8; and "Dance Hall Owner Is Found Guilty," *NYT*, April 21, 1923, 12.

21. "When the Village Robs the Cradle," *NYT Magazine*, February 18, 1923, 6.

22. Report on [Wind Blew] Inn, [116] E. Ohio St., March 9, 1922, 11:30 p.m., in *Conditions in Chicago* (Chicago: Juvenile Protective Association, 1922), 7, folder 145, JPAP. For examples of advertisements for Towertown nightspots in campus newspapers, see Announcement of the Dill Pickle Club's Halloween dance, *The Art Student* (School of the Art Institute), Fall 1916, 270; Advertisement for Bert Kelly's Stables, *The Daily Maroon* (University of Chicago), October 17, 1924, 3; ibid., January 9, 1925, 2; Advertisements for the Dill Pickle Club, *The Daily Maroon*, October 26, 1928, 5; and ibid., October 8, 1929, 4.

    The JPA's concerns about the bohemian influence on local youth extended beyond the boundaries of Towertown. In its 1924 annual report, the organization noted that, after several Near North Side resorts had been closed down, the bohemian influence seemed to spread throughout the city. In the Uptown neighborhood, they discovered "a bizarre place in an alley at Broadway and Clifton" called the Side Show, which was quite popular with North Side high school students who no longer had to travel to the Near North Side for a taste of bohemian revelry (*Annual Report of the*

Juvenile Protective Association for 1924 [Chicago: Juvenile Protective Association, 1925], 11–12, folder 126, JPAP).

23. See newspaper clippings in scrapbook vol. 22, WEDP. Of the thirty-two revocations of cabaret licenses in Chicago between 1923 and July 1930, sociologist Walter Reckless found that Mayor Dever was responsible for all but four; and all but two of his twenty-eight revocations came during the first two years of his term, 1923 and 1924. Dever's cabaret closures equaled the total number of cabarets padlocked by federal authorities between September 1925 and March 1930 (Reckless, *Vice in Chicago*, 114–15). However, both of these statistics pertain not just to Towertown but to the entire city of Chicago and, in Dever's case at least, are heavily weighted toward the black-and-tan cabarets of Bronzeville. So the total number of license revocations and padlocks in Towertown during the 1920s was fairly limited.

24. "Air Village Doings," *NYT*, June 2, 1921, 13; and "Unite for New War on Village Evils," *NYT*, January 25, 1923, 20. For additional coverage of raids in 1921 and 1922, see "Says 'Village' Life Caused 11 Suicides," *NYT*, June 3, 1921, 32; "That Vicious Village," editorial, *NYT*, June 4, 1921, 12; "Village Defended in New Manifesto," *NYT*, June 8, 1921, 20; "All's Quiet in the Village," *NYT*, June 10, 1921, 3; and "Conservatives Have a Grievance," editorial, *NYT*, May 13, 1922, 12.

25. Petition against the Gold Coast House of Correction, April 22, [1925], and a memorandum from the Acting Captain Commanding 28th Distr. to the Superintendent [of Police], May 4, 1925, both attached to a letter from Morgan A. Collins, Superintendent of Police, to William E. Dever, Mayor, Chicago, May 11, 1925, folder 28, box 4, WEDP.

26. Report on Cabaret Palace Gardens, Ontario & N. Clark, April 30, 1923, folder 92, JPAP.

27. Hal, "Plantation, Chicago," "Cabaret Reviews" column, *Variety*, April 21, 1926, 45; Johnson, *Black Manhattan*, 160; and Langston Hughes, *The Big Sea: An Autobiography* (New York: Alfred A. Knopf, 1940), 223.

28. On the effects of the Great Migration in Chicago and New York, see Drake and Cayton, *Black Metropolis*; Osofsky, *Harlem*; Spear, *Black Chicago*; Grossman, *Land of Hope*; and Gregory, *The Southern Diaspora*. In Chicago, where the population of "foreign-born Negroes" grew from 664 in 1910 to 1,138 in 1930, the impact of West Indian immigration on the development of the city's black community was relatively negligible. But in New York, where the population of "foreign-born Negroes" swelled from 11,757 to 54,754 during this same twenty-year period, West Indians came to constitute as much as twenty percent of the city's black population (in 1920; by 1930, they made up slightly less than seventeen percent) and played a significant role in shaping Harlem's black nightlife and culture (*Fifteenth Census of the United States: 1930; Population, Volume II: General Report; Statistics by Subjects* [Washington, DC: United States Government Printing Office, 1933] 67, 70; see also Philip Kasinitz, *Caribbean New York: Black Immigrants and the Poli-*

tics of Race [Ithaca, NY: Cornell University Press, 1992]; and Irma Watkins-Owens, "Early-Twentieth-Century Caribbean Women: Migration and Social Networks in New York City," in Nancy Foner, ed., *Islands in the City: West Indian Migration to New York* [Berkeley: University of California Press, 2001], 25–51).

29. Osofsky, *Harlem*, 71–91; and Johnson, *Black Manhattan*, 146, 158.
30. Osofsky, *Harlem*, 92–123; and Johnson, *Black Manhattan*, 145–69.
31. Chicago Commission on Race Relations, *The Negro in Chicago*, 107–8; Grossman, *Land of Hope*, 123–26; Drake and Cayton, *Black Metropolis*, 63 (map), 8; Spear, *Black Chicago*, 11–27, 142–46; and Eddie Condon, with Thomas Sugrue, *We Called It Music: A Generation of Jazz*, rev. ed. (1947; repr., New York: Da Capo Press, 1992), 133. According to Drake and Cayton, while "most of the ordinary people in the Black Belt refer[red] to their community as 'the South Side,'" they were all "familiar with another name for the area—Bronzeville," apparently coined by an editor of the *Chicago Bee* in 1930 when the newspaper "sponsored a contest to elect a 'Mayor of Bronzeville'" (383).
32. Karl K. Kitchen, "Karl K. Kitchen Presents: Gracie Fields Is Finding Out About New York—Tales of the Town," unknown newspaper clipping, n.d. [late 1930?], in scrapbook 24, CVVP.
33. Eric Garber, "A Spectacle in Color," in Duberman, Vicinus, and Chauncey, eds., *Hidden from History*, 322. See also Bricktop with Haskins, *Bricktop*, which describes Chicago's buffet flats as "after-hours spots that were usually in someone's apartment—the type of place where gin was poured out of milk pitchers" (57).

   The proliferation of buffet flats attracted the attention of both black and white reformers. As early as 1913, in a letter to New York's Committee of Fourteen, a black detective bureau in Harlem reported the presence of no fewer than 371 buffet flats in Harlem where "women and young girls are kept for various entertaining purposes," and during that same year, the *Chicago Defender* attacked local buffet flats for enticing "young women . . . to come and meet a 'live' one" and turning the young men into "p.l.'s (prostitute lovers)" who "throw their manhood to the dogs" (Shepard N. Edmonds, General Manager, Edmonds' National Detective Bureau, to Walter G. Hooke, Secretary, Committee of Fourteen, New York, May 22, 1913, General Correspondence—May 1913 folder, box 2, C14P; and Little Bo Peep, "The Buffet Flats," *CD*, November 8, 1913, 4).
34. Ronald L. Morris, *Wait Until Dark: Jazz and the Underworld, 1880–1940* (Bowling Green, OH: Bowling Green University Popular Press, 1980), esp. 25–36, 58–62, 117, 120, 138–47; Jim Haskins, *The Cotton Club* (1977; repr., New York: Hippocrene Books, 1994), 30–33, 74–75; and Kenney, *Chicago Jazz*, 150–51.
35. Bingham Dai, *Opium Addiction in Chicago* (Shanghai: The Commercial Press, Limited, 1937), 90–94; John Landesco, *Organized Crime in Chicago* (1929;

repr., Chicago: University of Chicago Press, 1968); Joseph Spillane, "The Making of an Underground Market: Drug Selling in Chicago, 1900–1940," *Journal of Social History* 32.1 (Autumn 1998): 27–48; "Black Belt's Nite Life," *Variety*, October 16, 1929, 1, 12, quoted in "Is This Really Harlem?" *NYAN*, October 23, 1929, repr. in Allon Schoener, ed., *Harlem on My Mind: Cultural Capital of Black America, 1900–1968* (New York: Random House, 1968), 80; Mezz Mezzrow, *Really the Blues* (1946; repr., London: Flamingo, 1993), 71–77, 208–16; and Edgar M. Grey, "White Cabaret Keepers Conduct Dives," *New York News*, December 10, 1927, newspaper clipping, "Harlem Report on Conditions" folder, box 82, C14P.

Among the famous whites that participated in the drug culture of Harlem and Bronzeville were the actress Tallulah Bankhead, playwright Avery Hopwood, and jazz clarinetist Mezz Mezzrow. During the late 1920s and early 1930s, Bankhead sought out cocaine in Harlem's brightest nightspots, while Hopwood was known to indulge in opium smoking during the mid-1920s at Harlem cabarets such as Small's Paradise. Mezz Mezzrow's drug of choice was "tea" (marijuana), which he first started smoking in Bronzeville before becoming a dealer to some of Harlem's most prominent entertainers in the 1930s (Lee Israel, *Miss Tallulah Bankhead* [New York: G. P. Putnam's Sons, 1972], 132; Van Vechten, Diary, March 19, 1925, box 111, CVVP; and Mezzrow, *Really the Blues*, 71–77, 208–16).

36. Report on [Royal] Gardens, [459] E. [31st] St., Chicago, February 25–26, 1922, in "Conditions in Chicago," published by Juvenile Protective Association, June 30, 1922, 9–10, folder 145, JPAP (emphasis added); and Bulletin #1513: Innocent Girls, [April 1922], in bulletin book 14, April 1922 to December 1, 1922, box 88, C14P.
37. "Night Raid Nets 83 in Harlem," *CW*, December 16, 1922, 2.
38. Ibid.; and Treasurer, Committee of Fourteen, to William F. Fuerst, Secretary, The New York Foundation, New York, October 28, 1927, second 1927 correspondence folder, box 6, C14P.
39. Chicago Commission on Race Relations, *The Negro in Chicago*, 323; "Black and Tans and Race Riots," black Chicago newspaper editorial, [1920], reprinted in ibid., 324–25. In a similar editorial, the *Chicago Whip* remarked: "The continual tirade is made because these agencies object to SOCIAL EQUALITY even though it be in a cabaret. The attack is not made on CABARETS, but on BLACK AND TAN CABARETS. More ridiculous than all is the effort to name them among the causes of race hatred when one recalls how well the 'blacks and tans' get along together after midnight" ("Black and Tan," editorial, *CW*, April 24, 1920, 8).
40. "Time for Action," unnamed Chicago newspaper editorial clipping, [January 1923], folder 109, JPAP.
41. "Mayor Closes Entertainers' and 5 Cafes," *CA*, May 8, 1923, scrapbook vol. 20, WEDP; "6 Black and Tan Cafes Divested Of Licenses," *CT*, May 9,

1923, scrapbook vol. 20, WEDP; and "Mayor Orders Drive on All Vice Cafes," *CA*, May 9, 1923, scrapbook vol. 20, WEDP. For further examples of the use of such rhetoric in prompting a January 1923 special grand jury investigation of police corruption and illicit activities in Chicago only two months before the mayoral election, see "Vice Laid to Mayor," *CT*, January 18, 1923, 1, folder 109, JPAP; and Jessie F. Binford, "Director's Annual Report for Fiscal Year 1922–1923," 2, supplement I, folder 13, JPAP.

42. "'Whitewash' Cabaret to Balk City Closing," *CDN*, May 10, 1923, scrapbook vol. 20, WEDP; and "Cafe Adopts New Rules to Stave Off Closing Order," *Chicago Post*, May 10, 1923, scrapbook vol. 20, WEDP. When Bronzeville cabarets actually followed through on such pledges to bar black patrons, they could even obtain the seal of approval from local reform organizations. During the spring of 1926, JPA officer and investigator Elizabeth Crandall reported that both she and her female companions were quite pleased with the conduct and entertainment they observed at Bronzeville's Plantation Café. "The show given at this place was clean and full of life and fire," she noted, in terms suggestive of the "primitive" qualities many slummers associated with Bronzeville nightspots. Yet the acceptability of this cabaret clearly hinged upon the fact that blackness and whiteness were kept carefully separated. On the first night Crandall visited, "no colored patrons were present" to partake of the lively entertainment offered by the club's black singers, dancers, and musicians. On the second, there was only one black party—"men and women in evening clothes" who, according to Crandall, "appeared to be of intelligence and importance among their group" (Elizabeth L. Crandall, Juvenile Protective Officer, Juvenile Protective Association of Chicago, to William E. Dever, Mayor of the City of Chicago, Chicago, May 12, 1926, folder 29, box 4, WEDP). On the ability of black and tans to operate without licenses or to continue their operations by obtaining injunctions against the police, see Kenney, *Chicago Jazz*, 150.

43. William E. Dever, "Black Belt," unpublished campaign speech, 1927, 7, folder 61, box 8, WEDP. For coverage of the arrests of Williams and Glaser and related raids on Chicago black and tans, see "Black and Tan Cafes in Chicago Raided," *BAA*, January 8, 1927, 9; Gentle Jimmy, "Williams Denies Seducing Girl," "News and Views of Shows" column, *TLAHJ*, January 15, 1927, 21; and "Black and Tan Raids on Chi's Mixed Places," *Variety*, January 19, 1927, 47.

44. Jessie F. Binford, *Annual Report of the Juvenile Protective Association of Chicago from January 1, 1927, to January 1, 1928* (Chicago: Juvenile Protective Association, 1928), 11–12, folder 126, JPAP; Kenney, *Chicago Jazz*, 151–52; Samuel B. Charters and Leonard Kunstadt, *Jazz: A History of the New York Scene* (1962; repr., New York: Da Capo Press, 1981), 232; "Squeeze Me," *TLAHJ*, September 3, 1927, 5; and "The Rambler," *TLAHJ*, August 6, 1927, 24–25. Noting the continued absence of such major black and tans as the

Plantation, Sunset, and Entertainers' cafés during the spring of 1928, "The Rambler" proclaimed, "How naked it now looks, and forlorn! The blinking lights from scattered shops are sparks from dying embers which reveal yesterday's dead pleasures as shadowy spectres" (ibid., March 24, 1928, 8). One notable exception in the trend toward smaller black-and-tan dives was the December 1928 opening of the Grand Terrace by Ed Fox (an original owner of the Sunset Café) at 3955 South Parkway. The Grand Terrace drew sizable white audiences throughout the late 1920s and 1930s (see Kenney, *Chicago Jazz*, 154).

45. Committee of Fourteen, *Annual Report for 1926* (New York: Committee of Fourteen, 1927), 31; George E. Worthington, General Secretary, Committee of Fourteen, to Raymond B. Fosdick, Bureau of Social Hygiene, New York, December 5, 1927, second 1927 correspondence folder, box 6, C14P; Application for position as investigator for the Committee of Fourteen, completed by Raymond Alexander Claymes, 1928 correspondence folder, box 7, C14P; [Raymond A. Claymes], "A Brief Summary of Conclusions of Vice Conditions in Harlem, Based on Personal Observations by Investigator," [1928], 4, 6, "Harlem Report on Conditions" folder, box 82, C14P; Committee of Fourteen, *Annual Report for 1928* (New York: Committee of Fourteen, 1929), 33–34, "Committee Minutes, October 1925–December 1929" notebook, box 86, C14P; and Minutes, Annual Meeting, January 24, 1929, 2, "Committee Minutes, October 1925–December 1929" notebook, box 86, C14P.

Raymond Claymes's employment application indicates that at the time he was hired in early 1928, this Howard- and Yale-educated investigator was on leave from his job as a teacher of languages in the New York City school system (a position he had held for five years) to pursue a career as a classical baritone. A thirty-five year-old native Texan, Claymes was unmarried and lived in Harlem, where he helped support his sister and an aged uncle (see Application for position as investigator for the Committee of Fourteen, completed by Raymond Alexander Claymes; and program for Second Song Recital by Raymond Claymes, Baritone, Grace Congregational Church of Harlem, March 11, 1928, 1928 correspondence folder, box 7, C14P).

46. [Claymes], "A Brief Summary of Conclusions of Vice Conditions in Harlem," 4; Minutes, Directors' Meeting, May 24, 1929, 2, "Committee Minutes, October 1925–December 1929" notebook, box 86, C14P; Committee of Fourteen, *Annual Report for 1928*, 6, 34; and Report on the Swanee Club (N.C. [night club]), 253 West 125th Street, in "Night Clubs and Speakeasies Located on Numbered Streets," 1929, 66, "Speakeasies & Nightclubs" folder, box 37, C14P (further examples of January 1929 raids on white-owned Lenox Avenue black and tans, including the Olympic, the Blue Point Grill, the Victoria Café, and the Three Friends Inn, can also be found in this folder). Despite the January 1929 raid on the Swanee Club,

it apparently managed to reopen; *Variety* counted it among the "11 class white trade night clubs" still operating in Harlem in October 1929 ("Black Belt's Nite Life," repr. in Schoener, ed., *Harlem on My Mind*, 80).

On the previous reluctance of federal authorities to prosecute white-owned black and tans, see [Claymes], "A Brief Summary of Conclusions of Vice Conditions in Harlem," 5–6. In a section of this manuscript which was not published in the Committee of Fourteen's *Annual Report for 1928*, Claymes noted that "The few negro owned and operated 'speakeasies' are continually watched and hounded by the police while the 95% owned and operated by whites are unmolested" (5–6). Claymes further reported, again in a section marked for intentional exclusion from the published report by the committee's general secretary, that a "very prominent lawyer" informed him that "an active public negro, friend of his . . . had gone to the office of one of the Federal attorneys where a negro counselor was employed to protest against the public speakeasy situation in Harlem. He said that negro Federal agent caused to be raided and closed about three places and then was himself 'shaken down' by his superior officers, being ordered to occupy his time with other activities" (6).

47. "Black Belt's Nite Life," repr. in Schoener, ed., *Harlem on My Mind*, 80; Lewis, *When Harlem Was in Vogue*, 242; Lewis A. Erenberg, *Swingin' the Dream: Big Band Jazz and the Rebirth of American Culture* (Chicago: University of Chicago Press, 1998), 13–14; "The Dying Nite Clubs," *Variety*, December 31, 1930, 32; and Max Ewing to his parents, New York, November 8, 1931, letter 718, box 4, MEP.

48. On the pansy and lesbian craze, see Chauncey, *Gay New York*, esp. 301–29; Garber, "A Spectacle in Color," 318–33; Faderman, *Odd Girls and Twilight Lovers*, 67–79; Mumford, "Homosex Changes," 395–414; idem, *Interzones*, 73–92; Johnson, "The Kids of Fairytown," in Beemyn, ed., *Creating a Place for Ourselves*, 97–118; and Drexel, "Before Paris Burned," in Beemyn, ed., *Creating a Place for Ourselves*, 119–44.

Following George Chauncey, most scholars refer to this final slumming vogue simply as the "pansy craze," but given the significant role that lesbians played in the popular spectacle of homosexuality that permeated the era's cabarets, theatrical productions, pulp fiction, and tabloid headlines, I have rechristened it the "pansy and lesbian craze." Chauncey has suggested that the term "pansy craze" was used by participants and observers in the late 1920s and early 1930s, but I have found no evidence of this particular term either in the primary sources quoted by Chauncey in *Gay New York* or in my own research. Admittedly, pansies comprised a larger proportion of the spectacle that attracted urban thrill seekers than lesbians did, and published accounts of this trend described an audience that was becoming increasingly "pansy conscious" (see "Reversed 'Pansy' Co. By Impersonators," *Variety*, October 15, 1930, 38; "Female Impersonators En Masse Play as Show For School Children," *Variety*, June 2, 1931,

1; and Alma Mater, "Hollywood Lowdown," *Brevities*, April 18, 1932, 10).

49. "As told to Harry by Herman," unpublished field notes, n.d., folder 3, box 98, EWBP.

50. Chauncey, *Gay New York*, 227–44; Faderman, *Odd Girls and Twilight Lovers*, 67–79; and Stephen Graham, *New York Nights* (New York: George H. Doran Company, 1927), 114. Chauncey mistakenly attributes this "Village song" to the "late 1910s" (*Gay New York*, 227), but British travel writer Stephen Graham clearly situates this line in the context of his mid-1920s visit to New York, setting it up with a remark that suggests the line comes from poetry rather than song. Even more interestingly, Graham's reference to "fairies" here seems to apply, perhaps mistakenly, to lesbians rather than feminine men. The relevant passage from Graham's *New York Nights* reads:

> Women dance together at the dining-dancings on Broadway but at the more fashionable resorts twi-feminine partnership is not tolerated. In the Village they dance together unashamed to a murmurous chorus of 'fairies, fairies,' and the Greenwich Village poet 'plains—"Fairyland's not far from Washington Square."

> This is something not imitated in London, where it may still be a charming compliment to call a girl a fairy. (114)

51. Zorbaugh, *The Gold Coast and the Slum*, 100; and Earle W. Bruce, "Comparison of Traits of the Homosexual from Tests and from Life-History Materials" (MA thesis, University of Chicago, 1942), 11. See also Johnson, "The Kids of Fairytown," 97–118; Faderman, *Odd Girls and Twilight Lovers*, 67–79; and Chad Heap, "The City as a Sexual Laboratory: The Queer Heritage of the Chicago School," *Qualitative Sociology* 26.4 (December 2003): 457–87.

52. George Chauncey, "The Policed: Gay Men's Strategies of Everyday Resistance," in William R. Taylor, ed., *Inventing Times Square: Commerce and Culture at the Crossroads of the World* (1991; repr., Baltimore: Johns Hopkins University Press, 1996), 317–19; idem, *Gay New York*, 301–4; Daniel O'L., quoted in George W. Henry, MD, *Sex Variants: A Study of Homosexual Patterns* (1941; repr., New York: Paul B. Hoeber, Inc., 1948), 431–32; and Paul Sweinhart, "Along Broadway," *ZTN*, April 12, 1930, 17. In Chicago, the equivalent cheap lodging-house and residential hotel district frequented by homosexual theatrical performers and service-industry workers was roughly coincident with bohemian Towertown on the Near North Side. At least as early as 1923, the Lawson YMCA hotel on Chicago Avenue had already acquired a reputation for housing "a bunch of prick lickers" ([unknown author], "Conversation with Edwin A. Teeter, [on the commuter rail from] Chicago to LaPorte," September 7, 1923, 4, folder 11, box 98, EWBP). On the furnished rooms and lodging houses of Chicago's Near North Side, see Zorbaugh, *The Gold Coast and the Slum*, 69–86; and Meyerowitz, *Women*

Adrift, 108–15; and idem, "Sexual Geography and Gender Economy: The Furnished Room Districts of Chicago, 1890–1930," *Gender and History* 2.3 (1990): 274–96.

53. On the living arrangements of black lesbians and gay men in 1920s and 1930s Harlem and Bronzeville, see Garber, "A Spectacle in Color," 318–33; Faderman, *Odd Girls and Twilight Lovers*, 67–79; Chauncey, *Gay New York*, 244–67; Mumford, "Homosex Changes," 395–414; idem, *Interzones*, 73–92; and Drexel, "Before Paris Burned," 119–44. On the greater level of acceptance and toleration historically granted to lesbians and gay men within the black community, see bell hooks, "Homophobia in Black Communities," in her *Talking Back: Thinking Feminist, Thinking Black* (Boston: South End Press, 1989), 120–26; and Drexel, "Before Paris Burned," 119–44. Chauncey explicates the class-based differences in the level of toleration granted to lesbians and gay men in black Harlem in *Gay New York*, 253–57, 263–67.

54. "'Nosey' Sees All Knows All," *CW*, January 29, 1921, 2; and *IST*, May 24, 1929, 10, quoted in Chauncey, *Gay New York*, 256 (emphasis added).

55. Edward Franklin Frazier, "The Negro Family in Chicago" (PhD diss., University of Chicago, 1931), 233. Although the content of the original field notes that Frazier quotes here has apparently been lost to history, his use of an ellipsis followed by an inserted parenthetical phrase—" . . . (female homo-sexuals)"—in published excerpts from this document suggests that he was "translating" one of the slang terms ("bulldaggers" or "bulldykes") commonly used by blacks during this era to refer to lesbians.

56. "Village 'Joints' Out or Tame," *Variety*, May 6, 1925, 19; Ware, *Greenwich Village*, 238; placard advertising John Loughman's Dill Pickle Club lecture entitled "Buzzing a Broad in Bohemia," folder 27, box 1, DPCP; placard advertising a Dill Pickle Club lecture entitled "Capturing a Millionaire by One who lost one," October 12 [1932], folder 37, box 2, DPCP; Ben L. Reitman, *Sister of the Road: An Autobiography of Box-Car Bertha as Told to Dr. Ben L. Reitman* (New York: The Macaulay Company, 1937), 210; placard advertising Elizabeth Davis's Dill Pickle Club lecture entitled, "Will Amazonic Women Usurp Man's Sphere?" January 14 [1931], folder 33, box 2, DPCP; and placard advertising a Dill Pickle Club debate between William H. Seed and Jack Ryan entitled, "Shall Society accept Intermediates?" February 23 [1930], folder 34, box 2, DPCP. The Newberry Library's extensive collection of Dill Pickle Club handbills and placards provides numerous other examples of such sexually charged lectures and debates during the 1920s and early 1930s (see folders 22–30, box 1, and folders 31–40, box 2, DPCP).

57. Jack "Ziggy" Mason, "Malin Was Not Queer!" *BT*, September 1933, 16, 11; and Chauncey, *Gay New York*, 314–18.

58. See Chauncey, *Gay New York*, 318–21; "'Pansy' Places on Broadway," *Variety*, September 10, 1930, 1; "Cabaret Bills," *Variety*, November 26, 1930, 71; "'Pansy Club' Now With Racket Getting Bolder," *Variety*, December 17,

1930, 57; "'Pansy' Stuff Slipping," *Variety*, December 31, 1930, 31; "The
Dying Night Clubs," *Variety*, December 31, 1930, 32; "Broadway" section,
"Chatter" column, *Variety*, January 21, 1931, 50; Investigator B, Report on
night club, Coffee Cliff, 45th St., just east of B'way., December 2, 1930,
1:15–2:55 a.m., "1930" folder, box 35, C14P; "'Rival' Punches Nose of Slain
'Jackie' Moss' Girl Friend," *CA*, January 21, 1931, 19; and "Boy" Solomon,
"On and Off Broadway," *ZTN*, January 31, 1931, 16.

59. See Chauncey, *Gay New York*, 318–21; "'Pansy' Places on Broadway,"
Variety, September 10, 1930, 1; "'Francis' on Floor," *Variety*, November 26,
1930, 67; "Cabaret Bills," *Variety*, November 26, 1930, 71; "'Pansy Club'
Now With Racket Getting Bolder," *Variety*, December 17, 1930, 57; "'Pansy'
Stuff Slipping," *Variety*, December 31, 1930, 31; "Broadway" section,
"Chatter" column, *Variety*, January 21, 1931, 50; Advertisement for "Karyl
Norman and his 'Pansy' Club," *ZTN*, January 10, 1931, 85; and "Boy" Solo-
mon, "On and Off Broadway," *ZTN*, January 31, 1931, 16.

60. Reitman, *Sister of the Road*, 65; "Shut 2 Night Clubs, with Girls Garbed as
Men, and Theater," unidentified newspaper clipping, the lesbian scrap-
book, Kinsey Institute for Research in Sex, Gender and Reproduction,
Indiana University, Bloomington; Faderman, *Odd Girls and Twilight Lovers*,
107; untitled field document beginning "Told to me by a Mr. X. who has
visited some of the queer night clubs," n.d., folder 11, box 98, EWBP; and
"Pansy Parlors, Tough Chicago Has Epidemic of Male Butterflies," *Variety*,
December 10, 1930, 1.

61. Schwanda Schweik, "Chicago World's Fairies," *Brevities*, December 7,
1931,1, 13; Charlie Dawn, "He Thrills 'Em as Brunette or Blonde," *CA*,
April 1, 1932, 32; idem, "Bright Spots," *CA*, February 13, 1932, 8; Advertisement for Karyl Norman's Supper Club at the New Parody, 1023 N. State St.,
CA, February 6, 1932, 8; [Earle Bruce], Field report on the Ballyhoo [Café],
1942 N. Halsted, Wednesday Nov. 22nd, 1933, 11:30 p.m., Cover charge
$.25, folder 3, box 98, EWBP; idem, Field report on the Ballyhoo Café,
1942 N. Halsted, 9/24/33, 11:30 p.m., folder 2, box 98, EWBP; [Unknown
author], Field report on "Visitors, At the Subway Bar, Grand at Wabash
Avenues, Told to me by Don," n.d., folder 11, box 98, EWBP; Bill to Jimmie, [Saginaw, Mich.], [summer 1934], typescript, folder 11, box 98, EWBP;
[Unknown author], "Some Characteristics of the Lower North Community," unpublished student paper, n.d., 18, folder 4, box 156, EWBP; and
Charlie Dawn, "Stan Myers Becomes Master of Ceremonies in Morrison
Revue," *CA*, December 5, 1934, 15. Although the K-9 Club (located at 105
East Walton Place) opened some three years before the beginning of the
1933–34 Century of Progress World's Fair, its peak popularity coincided
with the arrival of this exposition.

62. George E. Worthington, General Secretary and Counsel, Committee of
Fourteen, to Mrs. J. Nelson Borland, New York, February 4, 1931, third
1931 correspondence folder, box 7, C14P; and Chauncey, *Gay New York*,

160–61, 346–47. In a last-ditch effort in 1932 to secure continued funding for its regulatory activities, the Committee of Fourteen distributed a bulletin to its board members and patrons entitled, "Why the Committee of Fourteen is needed." Reprinting a letter from an anonymous "American Citizen and Tax payer," this bulletin detailed the threat that pansies and lesbians supposedly posed to "decent people . . . from uptown and society" by taking them to queer joints where "gangsters . . . rob[bed] them at the point of guns, taking the jewelry, money and other valuables of the unsuspecting guests" (Bulletin #2043, "Why the Committee of Fourteen is needed," March 4, 1932, bulletin book 23, box 89, C14P).

63. Chauncey, *Gay New York*, 334–42; "Club Richman Penalized," *NYT*, July 25, 1936, 16; "Club Richman Asks Stopper on N.Y. Cops," *Variety*, May 6, 1936, 54; and "Club Richman Loses License," *ZTN*, August 1, 1936, 8.

64. Roger Biles, *Big City Boss in Depression and War: Mayor Edward J. Kelly of Chicago* (DeKalb, IL: Northern Illinois University Press, 1984), 90; and the Juvenile Protective Association of Chicago, "The Return of the Saloon," published report, February 1, 1935, 5, folder 134, JPAP. Although both the JPA and Chicago's Committee of Fifteen survived the Depression (the former until the present day; the latter until at least early 1942, based on correspondence in the Ernest W. Burgess papers at the Special Collections Research Center, University of Chicago Library), like New York's Committee of Fourteen, their attempts to regulate the pansy and lesbian craze were limited by the economic constraints of the era. In the summer of 1934, an outside group of advisors encouraged the Committee of Fifteen to focus its energies and dwindling finances primarily on the continuing problem of female prostitution, paying less attention than before to the city's "taverns" and to the "homosexual practices" that were "promoted through contacts made at [such] identified locations" (Memorandum to Officers, Directors and Members Protective Services Committee, from Charles E. Miner, General Director, Committee of Fifteen, June 14, 1934, folder 8, box 6, EWBP).

65. As early as late August 1934, the Chicago correspondent for *Zit's Theatrical Newspaper* noted that a clean-up of Chicago nightlife was beginning: "Censoring seems to be in vogue . . . . Authorities have . . . made inquiries on things hereabouts . . . [including] the Fan dancers and nudists upon whom the budding nighteries depend for business . . . . Uptown vaudeville theatres are cautious to keep the fur brushed the right way and the delete signs are up backstage . . . and there is no particular desire for Mae West imitations" (A.R.F., "Chicago News and Views," *ZTN*, August 25, 1934, 7).

66. "Chi Lily-White in Sudden Morals Drive, While Philly Is Livening Up," *Variety*, January 8, 1935, 51; "Four More Niteries in Chi Get Sluffoed," *Variety*, January 8, 1935, 9; and "Shut 2 Night Clubs, with Girls Garbed as Men, and Theater," unidentified and undated newspaper clipping, the lesbian

scrapbook, Kinsey Institute for Research in Sex, Gender and Reproduction, Indiana University, Bloomington.

67. On the early drag balls in Harlem and Bronzeville, see Abram Hill, "The Hamilton Lodge Ball," August 30, 1939, "New York City and Its People" section, reel 4, NNY; "Hamilton Lodge Ball an Unusual Spectacle," *NYA*, March 6, 1926, 3; Chauncey, *Gay New York*, 257–63; and Drexel, "Before Paris Burned," 119–44.

68. Richard Bruce Nugent, "On 'Gloria Swanson,' Real name Mr. Winston," 1–2, biographies section, reel 1, NNY; "Chatter in Chi," *Variety*, March 27, 1929, 47; "'Gloria Swanson' Buried in Harlem," *CD*, May 4, 1940, 21; and "'Gloria Swanson', Impersonator, Dies," *NYAN*, April 27, 1940, 1, 20. For more on the Sepia Gloria Swanson, see Garber, "A Spectacle in Color," 320; and Chauncey, *Gay New York*, 251–52.

69. Wilbur Young, "Gladys Bentley," biographies section, reel 1, NNY; Van Vechten Diaries, November 7 & December 5, 1929, and January 25, February 2 & May 24, 1930, box 111, CVVP; and "Broadway" section, "Chatter" column, *Variety*, May 30, 1933, 60. It is unclear exactly when Bentley left the Clam House, but by July 1931, she was performing at Gladys' Exclusive Club, in which she may have held part-interest. By February 1933, she had left the Exclusive Club to perform downtown at the King's Terrace. (See Ted Yates, "Around the Town," *IST*, July 16, 1931; Edward G. Perry, "Impressions," *NYAN*, October 28, 1931, 10; "Seek to Ban Songs of Gladys Bentley," *NYAN*, February 22, 1933, 1; "Broadway" section, "Chatter" column, *Variety*, May 30, 1933, 60; "King's Terrace" review, "Night Club Reviews," *Variety*, June 13, 1933, 48; Sid Weiss, "Night Clubs," *ZTN*, October 14, 1933, 6; and Gladys Bentley, "I Am a Woman Again," *Ebony*, August 1952, 92–98.")

    For more on Gladys Bentley, see especially Eric Garber, "Gladys Bentley: The Bulldagger Who Sang the Blues," *Out/look* (Spring 1988): 52–61; Chauncey, *Gay New York*, 251–53; and David Serlin, *Replaceable You: Engineering the Body in Postwar America* (Chicago: University of Chicago Press, 2004), 111–58. Serlin analyzes Bentley's claim in her 1952 essay for *Ebony* that post–World War II hormone treatments helped her to renounce her lesbianism and become "a woman again," marrying a heterosexual man.

70. Nugent, "On 'Gloria Swanson,'" 2; Roi Ottley, "This Hectic Harlem," *NYAN*, August 9, 1933, 9; and Augustus Austin, "Fletcher Henderson's Band Pleases At Opera House," *NYA*, September 1, 1934, 4. The Sepia Gloria Swanson continued to perform at the Theatrical Grill and on the stages of Harlem's vaudeville theaters until 1935. After a series of gigs in Philadelphia and Baltimore, he returned to the Harlem cabaret scene in late 1936 as a headline act at the Brittwood Grill and later at the 101 Ranch and Clark Monroe's, performing as his health permitted until at least early 1938 (see Marcus Wright, "The Talk of the Town," *NYA*, December 1, 1934, 5; Roi Ottley, "Hectic Harlem," *NYAN*, March 7, 1936, 13; Archie Seale, "Around

Harlem," *NYAN*, November 14, 1936, 11; Florence Ingram, "Around Harlem," *NYAN*, January 23, 1937, 9; "'Gloria' Swanson Tops At Brittwood," *CD*, September 25, 1937, 11; "Gloria Goes To 101 Ranch," *CD*, January 29, 1938; "Night Life On Wane," *NYAN*, December 31, 1938, 16; "'Gloria Swanson' Buried in Harlem," *CD*, May 4, 1940, 21; and "'Gloria Swanson', Impersonator, Dies," *NYAN*, April 27, 1940, 1, 20).

71. Young, "Gladys Bentley," 1; and Roi Ottley, "This Hectic Harlem," *NYAN*, April 21, 1934, 9. See also The Wagon, "Wagon Review Diamond-Studded Ubangi Club Show," *CD*, June 20, 1936, 11.

72. See advertisement for Lafayette Theatre, noting the appearance of "Gloria Swanson, Greatest Colored Female Impersonator," *NYAN*, January 10, 1934, 7; V. E. J. [Vere E. Johns], "Lafayette Theatre," *NYA*, April 14, 1934, 5; Romeo L. Dougherty, "My Observations," NYAN, April 14, 1934, 6; Vere E. Johns, "In the Name of Art," *NYA*, March 3, 1934, 6; Advertisement for the Harlem Opera House, noting the appearance of "Clara Bow, Greatest of All Female Impersonators" and Jackie Mabley, *NYAN*, March 15, 1934, 7; Roi Ottley, "This Hectic Harlem," *NYAN*, July 28, 1934, 9; and Marcus Wright, "The Talk of the Town," *NYA*, April 7, 1934, 4 & September 1, 1934, 4.

73. The Harlem race riot of 1935 started after a Puerto Rican youth named Lino Rivera was manhandled by white clerks who caught him shoplifting in their West 135th Street store on March 19, and rumors quickly spread that he had been beaten to death. Already frustrated with their treatment by local white business owners and landlords, nearly ten thousand Harlem residents took to the streets to protest the alleged murder, ransacking white-owned stores and destroying property to the tune of $2 million. Their actions met with a swift police response, and by morning, three black Harlem residents had been killed, thirty hospitalized and more than one hundred arrested. In the aftermath of this violence, white attendance at Harlem cabarets fell off dramatically, despite the attempts of columnists such as Ed Sullivan to allay the fears of white patrons. But the riots did not bring a complete end to affluent whites' uptown slumming excursions (see Greenberg, *"Or Does It Explode?"*; Roi Ottley, "This Hectic Harlem," *NYAN*, April 13, 1935, 9; and Erenberg, *Swingin' the Dream*, 26–27.)

74. "Goings on about Town" column, *The New Yorker*, throughout 1936; and Myrtle Evangeline Pollard, "Harlem As Is: Volume II: The Negro Business and Economic Community" (BA thesis, The College of the City of New York, 1937), 376–77 (emphasis added).

75. Lou Layne, "Moon Over Harlem," *NYA*, February 16, 1935, 5; "The Ubangi Club Loses License to Sell Liquor," *New York Herald Tribune*, April 16, 1937; and "Club Loses Liquor License," *NYT*, 16 April 1937. Although the raids on Harlem's pansy and lesbian nightspots were sporadic, local authorities spearheaded a particularly active and virulent crackdown during the summer of 1934 (see "One-Man-Raid Battles Does a Carrie Nation," *NYAN*, May 12, 1934, 1; Roi Ottley, "This Hectic Harlem," *NYAN*, May 26,

1934, 9, and September 15, 1934, 9; and Marcus Wright, "The Talk of the Town," *NYA*, May 12, 1934, 5; May 19, 1934, 5; June 9, 1934, 4; July 7, 1934, 4; July 14, 1934, 4; July 21, 1934, 4; and September 15, 1934, 4).

76. Clarenz's suicide in March 1936 occurred after a late night's work at the 101 Ranch. Returning to his fourth-floor Harlem apartment, he scrawled a quick note before jumping from his kitchen window, apparently distraught over the problems that his romantic attention to men was creating with his new wife of five weeks (see "Night Club Entertainer Dies in Fall from Window," *NYA*, March 21, 1936, 1, 12; and "Clarenz Scrawls Poem to Admirer," *NYAN*, March 21, 1936, 1, 5). On the hospitalizations that interrupted the Sepia Gloria Swanson's career and his eventual death in 1940, see Archie Seale, "Around Harlem," *NYAN*, January 2, 1937, 9; "Night Life On Wane," *NYAN*, December 31, 1938, 16; "'Gloria Swanson' Buried in Harlem," *CD*, May 4, 1940, 21; and "'Gloria Swanson', Impersonator, Dies," *NYAN*, April 27, 1940, 1, 20.)

77. "Night Life On Wane," *NYAN*, December 31, 1938, 16; Advertisement for the Hamilton Lodge Ball, Rockland Palace, *NYAN*, February 18, 1939; Hill, "The Hamilton Lodge Ball"; and Chauncey, *Gay New York*, 332–33.

78. Advertisement for the 7–11 Club, Northwest Corner 31st St. and Indiana Ave. (upstairs), featuring the Sepia Mae West, in Franz Hoffmann, comp., *Jazz Advertised in the Negropress*, vol. 4, *The Chicago Defender 1910–1934* (Berlin: F. Hoffmann, 1980), 309; advertisement for 7–11 Club, featuring "The Sepia Peggy Joyce, World's Greatest Female Impersonator," in ibid., 311; advertisement for the Annex Buffet, 2840 S. State St., featuring the "Sepia Mae West (Come up and See Her)," in ibid., 318; "Annex Buffet Is A Cool 'Hot' Spot Patrons Learn," *CD*, September 1, 1934, 9; "'Mae West' Stars at Annex Buffet," *CD*, September 15, 1934, 9; advertisement for the Annex Buffet, announcing, "New Café at 2300 So. State Street, Presenting The One and Only 'Sepia' Mae West (Doin' 'Em Wrong) in Her Own Musical Revue, 'The Gay Nineties,' Staged and Directed by Mae West," in Hoffmann, *Jazz Advertised in the Negropress*, 4:321; advertisement for the Cozy Cabin Club, 3119 Cottage Grove Ave., "The South Side's ?? Oddest Nite Club ??" featuring "'Luzetta Hall,' Sensational Blues Singer," "'Joan Crawford,' Soubrette," and "'Gilda Grey,' Fan Dancer," in ibid., 321; "A Unique Show at Cozy Cabin," *CD*, September 1, 1934, 8; and Hilda See, "'Around the Town' Brings Treat In Dance and Song," *CD*, November 3, 1934, 9.

79. Advertisement for Annex Café, featuring the Sepia Mae West and her Easter Parade, in Franz Hoffmann, *Jazz Advertised in the Negropress*, vol. 5, *The Chicago Defender 1935–1949* (Berlin: F. Hoffmann, 1981), 333; advertisement for the Cabin Inn, 3353 S. State Street, featuring Dick Barrow, "Marlene Dietrich," Luzetta Hall, Jean Archer, Dixie Gene, Stella Johnson and "Bullfrog Shorty" Burch (ibid., 340); Advertisement for the Club DeLisa, 5512-14-16 S. State St., featuring "Valda" (ibid., 336); advertisement for the

Club DeLisa, featuring Peggy Joyce (ibid., 342); "Chicago Puts Lid On and Then Takes It Off," *NYAN*, November 2, 1935, 12; "Chicago Clamps Down Lid on Girly-Girlies," *NYAN*, December 14, 1935, 10; and John Loughery, *The Other Side of Silence: Men's Lives and Gay Identities: A Twentieth-Century History* (New York: Henry Holt, 1998), 79.

80. "'Mae West' To Invade The Coast," *CD*, October 19, 1935, 9; "Mae West Is Back From Coast Trip," CD, September 12, 1936; Advertisement for Cabin Inn, featuring Valda Gray and Petete Swanson, in Hoffmann, *Jazz Advertised in the Negropress*, 5:352; "Kicking At Cabin," *CD* November 7, 1936, 25; "Cabin Inn Celebrate 4th Anniversary With Red Hot Show and Plenty 'Imps,'" *CD*, July 10, 1937, 10; "'Imps' At Cabin Inn," *CD*, May 28, 1938, 19; "Valda Gray Revue Tops At Cabin Inn," *CD*, November 19, 1938, 18; and Billy Jones, "Big New Revue Tops Cabin Inn," *CD*, January 7, 1939, 18.

81. Conrad Bentzen, "Notes on the Homosexual in Chicago," unpublished student paper, March 14, 1938, 5–6, folder 10, box 145, EWBP; Full-page advertisement for *Chicago Defender* and 8th Annual Goodfellows' Club Midnight Benefit Show, at the Regal Theatre, 47th & South Parkway (featuring the Sepia Mae West), in Hoffmann, *Jazz Advertised in the Negropress*, 5:357; Full-page advertisement for the *Defender* Christmas Benefit Show, 8th Regiment Armory (featuring entertainers from the Cabin Inn), in ibid., 388; and Ben L. Reitman, VDC #99, Chicago Syphilis Control Program VD reports, August 5, 1937, 525, supplement II, folder 23, BLRP. For more on the Chicago Health Department's late 1930s campaign against syphilis, see Suzanne Poirier, *Chicago's War on Syphilis, 1937–1940: The Times, the Trib, and the Clap Doctor* (Urbana: University of Illinois Press, 1995).

82. "Swingland's New Sensation," *CD*, April 9, 1938, 18; "Noone's Ork and New Show At Swingland," *CD*, April 23, 1938, 18; Advertisement for Doc Jennings' 33rd St. Café, featuring "Luzette Hall, Female Impersonator," in Hoffmann, *Jazz Advertised in the Negropress*, 5:372; Advertisement for the Creole Inn, 60 E. 30th Street, featuring "MC and Producer Dickie Mae West) Barrows [sic]" and Dixie Jean Westmore, in ibid., 379; "Dick Barrow Has Snappy Xmas Revue," *CD*, December 31, 1938, 7; and Advertisement for the Tuxedo Inn, 342 E. 31st St., featuring "Jean Collins, Female Impersonator," in Hoffmann, *Jazz Advertised in the Negropress*, 5: 385.

83. "Producer, Dickie Barrow," *CD*, April 8, 1939, 21; "At Joe's," *CD*, December 9, 1939, 20; "Joe Hughes Set For Big Time This Friday Night," *CD*, September 12, 1942, 21; Advertisement for Joe's DeLuxe Club, 6323 So. Parkway, featuring Valda Gray, in Hoffmann, *Jazz Advertised in the Negropress*, 5:427, 461, 486, 512; and Advertisement for Joe's DeLuxe Club, featuring Valda Gray, Petite Swanson and Dixie Lee (ibid., 560). The Cabin Inn made one final move to 3520 S. State Street sometime in mid-1939 but had closed by early 1940 (*Chicago Classified Telephone Directory* [Chicago: Reuben H. Donnelley Corp., September 1939 & February 1940]).

CHAPTER 3

1. "Unfashionable 'Slumming,'" *NYT*, April 30, 1893, 12; Ernest A. Bell, "The Story of the Midnight Mission," in Bell, ed., *Fighting the Traffic in Young Girl*, 412–31; photograph with caption "Old Glory and Older Glory—'These Dives Must Go': The author, Rev. Ernest A. Bell, holding a meeting in the vice district—at the open door of a notorious resort," ibid., page facing 226 (in some editions of this book; other editions carry a photograph of "Bishop of London Preaching in Wall Street, New York"); "Women Go Slumming," *The [Chicago] Daily Inter-Ocean*, October 23, 1893, 1; and "Purity Band in the Levee," *CT*, October 12, 1906, 1.
2. "Divinity Students 'Slumming,'" *NYT*, May 5, 1899, 8; and "Prof. Bailey's Class Here Again to See Us," *NYT*, May 4, 1906, 5. For a bibliography of apparently earnest, early sociological studies of U.S. slums and tenement districts, see Wm. Howe Tolman and Wm. I. Hull, *Handbook of Sociological Information with Especial Reference to New York City, Prepared for the City Vigilance League, New York City* (New York, 1894), 93–97.
3. "Prof. Bailey's Class Here Again to See Us," *NYT*, May 4, 1906, 5; and Alexander Woollcott, *The Story of Irving Berlin* (New York: G. P. Putnam's Sons, 1925), 40.
4. Gardner, *The Doctor and the Devil*, 58–60, 66–67; "Dr. Parkhurst Goes Slumming," editorial, *WP*, April 8, 1892, 4; and Duff, *Side Lights on Darkest Chicago*, 17.
5. "Slumming Curate Gets into a Cell," *NYT*, March 14, 1907, 3; and "Seize Reformers When Police Raid Resort in Levee," *CT*, October 8, 1912, 1. For similar accusations, both implied and more direct, see also "Women Go Slumming," *The [Chicago] Daily Inter-Ocean*, October 23, 1893, 1; and "Gaynor Holds His Critics Up to Scorn," *NYT*, November 13, 1912, 6.
6. Ford, *Forty-Odd Years in the Literary Shop*, 202–3. The frequently conflicting explanations offered by these authors for their slumming excursions through the Bowery, the Tenderloin, and the Levee can be found in Stephen Crane, "Adventures of a Novelist," repr. in *The New York City Sketches of Stephen Crane*, ed. R.W. Stallman and E.R. Hagemann (New York: New York University Press, 1966), 226–31; Theodore Dreiser, *Dawn* (New York: H. Liveright, 1931); Hutchins Hapgood, *A Victorian in the Modern World* (New York: Harcourt, Brace and Co., 1939); and Josiah Flynt, *My Life* (New York: The Outing Publishing Company, 1908). For examples of the works produced by these authors based on their slumming excursions through the red-light and tenement districts of New York and Chicago, see Stephen Crane, *Maggie: A Girl of the Streets* (New York: D. Appleton, 1896); Theodore Dreiser, *Sister Carrie* (New York: Doubleday, Page & Co., 1900); Hutchins Hapgood, *The Spirit of the Ghetto*; idem, *The Autobiography of a Thief* (New York: Fox, Duffield & Company, 1903); idem, *The Spirit of Labor* (New York: Duffield & Company, 1907); idem, *An Anarchist Woman* (New York:

Duffield & Company, 1909); idem, *Types from the City Streets* (New York: Funk & Wagnalls, 1910); George Ade, *Artie: A Story of the Streets and Town* (Chicago: H. S. Stone & Co., 1896); idem, *Pink Marsh: A Story of the Streets and Town* (Chicago: H. S. Stone, 1897); idem, *Fables in Slang* (Chicago: H. S. Stone and Company, 1900); idem, *In Babel: Stories of Chicago* (New York: McClure, Phillips & Co., 1903); Josiah Flynt, *Tramping with Tramps: Studies and Sketches of Vagabond Life* (New York: The Century Co., 1899); idem, *Notes of an Itinerant Policeman* (Boston: L. C. Page, 1900); and idem, *The World of Graft* (New York: McClure, Phillips & Co., 1901). For recent insightful analyses of this literature of the slum and the red-light district and its relation to historical conditions, see especially Christopher P. Wilson, "Stephen Crane and the Police," *American Quarterly* 48.2 (1996): 273–315; Keith Gandal, *The Virtues of the Vicious;* and Carrie Tirado Bramen, "The Urban Picturesque and the Spectacle of Americanization," *American Quarterly* 52.3 (2000): 444–77.

7. Rufus S. Simmons, President of The Midnight Mission, to Victor F. Lawson, Chicago, September 30, 1909, folder 9: "The Midnight Mission: Minutes, 1906–1909," box 4, Ernest Albert Bell papers, CHM; William T. Stead, *If Christ Came to Chicago!,* 259–60; and Bell, "Chicago's White Slave Market" in Bell, ed., *Fighting the Traffic in Young Girls,* 257.

8. Wooldridge, *Hands Up!,* 43–49, 148, 195–202, 237–42, 297–99; Ingersoll, *A Week in New York,* 202; *Rand, McNally & Co.'s Handy Guide to Chicago,* 104–5; Rev. Orrin R. Jenks, statement, included in "Dance Hall Evils Deplored by Chicago Pastors," *CRH,* January 30, 1905, 3; and Rufus S. Simmons to Victor F. Lawson, September 30, 1909.

By October 1906, a short story in the literary magazine of the Sunday edition of the *Chicago Tribune* mocked the notion that *anything* dangerous still existed in Chicago's Levee or in New York's once-infamous Bowery or Tenderloin, for that matter. Describing a series of ultimately unnecessary precautions undertaken by "Frederick Rockhold, banker and broker, a New Yorker of New York," before venturing into the Windy City's most notorious resorts, the story's protagonist ultimately resolved: "Well, of all the false alarms as a wicked town, Chicago is the limit. I'm going back to New York, join Rockefeller's Sunday school class, and get tough—or go slumming up to Dr. Parkhurst's church" ("New Yorker Who Tried to Find Something Really Wicked in Chicago," *CT,* October 21, 1906, F2).

For a rare example of male slummers' attempts to hide their visits to the cities' most popular slumming resorts, see "Sees Vice Peril in Freiberg's," *CT,* December 22, 1914, 8. This article notes that a chauffeur for one Chicago livery company reported that "the tickets of the 'fares'" that he "carried from the loop to Freiberg's" popular Levee dance hall "were marked 'by the hour' because the customers did not like to have the record of their charge account show they had been 'slumming.'"

9. Dreiser, *Dawn,* 443.

10. Ruth Ashmore, "What You Want to Know," *Ladies' Home Journal*, December 1891, 16.

11. "Life in New York City," *BDE*, February 15, 1891, 13. On the popularity of such organized tours through the immigrant districts of New York and Chicago and the increasing use of automated touring cars in those and other cities, see Cocks, *Doing the Town*, esp. 156–73 and 186–203.

12. "Trade Opens With Cuba," *CT*, September 2, 1898, 5; J. Douglas Wetmore to Frederick H. Whitin, Executive Secretary, Committee of Fourteen, New York, September 21, 1908, July–December 1908 correspondence folder, box 1, C14P; and George B. Van Cleve, President, The George B. Van Cleve Company, Advertising, to Frederick H. Whitin, Secretary, Committee of Fourteen, New York, September 22, 1908, July–December 1908 correspondence folder, box 1, C14P.

13. James Clarence Harvey, *In Bohemia* (New York: H. M. Caldwell Co., 1905), 118; and "Slumming Parties," editorial, *CT*, June 4, 1907, 8. On the advent of dating among the urban middle class in turn-of-the-century America, see Beth L. Bailey, *From Front Porch to Back Seat: Courtship in Twentieth-Century America* (Baltimore: The Johns Hopkins University Press, 1988), esp. 13–24.

14. *Chicago's Dark Places*, 57; "Chicago as Seen by Herself," *McClure's Magazine*, May 1907, 69; and *Annual Report of the Committee of Fifteen for the Year Ending April 30, 1916* (Chicago, 1916), 9. Similar reform tactics can be found in Rev. R. A. White, statement, included in "Dance Hall Evils Deplored by Chicago Pastors," *CRH*, January 30, 1905, 3; "Arrest Men Found Slumming with Two Girls, Both Young," *CT*, June 1, 1908, 3; and Emma Norine Law, *The Shame of a Great Nation: The Story of the "White Slave Trade"* (Harrisburg, PA: United Evangelical Publishing House, 1909), 192. For a discerning scholarly interpretation of the use of similar sensationalist rhetoric in turn-of-the-century reform exposés and popular romance novels, see Meyerowitz, *Women Adrift*, 60–64.

15. "Slumming Parties," editorial, *CT*, June 4, 1907, 8. On the rise of nativism in turn-of-the-century America, see especially Higham, *Strangers in the Land*, 68–263; and Jacobson, *Whiteness of a Different Color*, 68–90.

16. John C. Van Dyke, *The New New York: A Commentary on the Place and the People* (New York: The Macmillan Company, 1909), 242. On the behavior of working-class women and men in urban amusements, see especially Addams, *The Spirit of Youth and the City Streets*, 12–13, 67–103; Peiss, *Cheap Amusements*, 88–162; McBee, *Dance Hall Days*, 51–156; and Clement, *Love for Sale*, 13–75.

17. L. Perry Curtis Jr., *Apes and Angels: The Irishman in Victorian Caricature*, rev. ed. (Washington, DC: Smithsonian Institution Press, 1997), 58–67; "The 'Dangerous Classes' of New York, and What Is Being Done for Them," *Appletons' Journal of Literature, Science and Art*, March 5, 1870, 270; "Fox's

Illustrated Week's Doings," *NPG*, August 23, 1884, 7; and H. H. M., "In Our Neighborhood," *Christian Union*, February 1, 1883, 89. On the intermediate racial positioning of the Irish and their struggle to "become white," see especially David R. Roediger, *The Wages of Whiteness: Race and the Making of the American Working Class* (London: Verso, 1991); Lott, *Love and Theft;* Noel Ignatiev, *How the Irish Became White* (New York: Routledge, 1995); Catherine Mary Eagan, "'I Did Imagine . . . We Had Ceased to Be Whitewashed Negroes': The Racial Formation of Irish Identity in Nineteenth-Century Ireland and America" (PhD diss., Boston College, 2000); and Kevin Kenny, "Race, Violence, and Anti-Irish Sentiment in the Nineteenth Century," in J. J. Lee and Marion R. Casey, eds., *Making the Irish American: History and Heritage of the Irish in the United States* (New York: New York University Press, 2006), 364–78. On German Americans' assimilation to whiteness and "hundred-percent" status, see Russell A. Kazal, *Becoming Old Stock: The Paradox of German-American Identity* (Princeton, NJ: Princeton University Press, 2004).

18. "Life in New York City," *BDE*, February 24, 1884, 3; and "Life in New York City," *BDE*, February 15, 1891, 13.

19. James Huneker, *New Cosmopolis: A Book of Images* (New York: Charles Scribner's Sons, 1915), 7.

20. On the racialized notions of "civilization" and "primitivism" that permeated turn-of-the-century American culture, see especially Marianna Torgovnick, *Gone Primitive: Savage Intellects, Modern Lives* (Chicago: University of Chicago Press, 1990), 21–22, 45–48; and Gail Bederman, *Manliness and Civilization: A Cultural History of Gender and Race in the United States, 1880–1917* (Chicago: University of Chicago Press, 1995), 20–22, 31–37.

21. Ingersoll, *A Week in New York*, 202–13; and *Rand, McNally & Co.'s Handy Guide to Chicago and the World's Columbian Exposition*, 105–9.

22. Stuart C. Wade, *A Bird's-eye View of Greater New York and Its Most Magnificent Store; Being a Concise and Comprehensive Visitors' Guide to Greater New York, its Myriad Sights and Scenes, and its Grandest Emporium of Commerce, The Big Store of Siegel-Cooper Co.; Illustrated with Maps, Plans, and Diagrams; A description of the Big Store, and a Complete Directory and Finding List of its Various Departments, and the Merchandise on Sale there* (New York: Siegel-Cooper Co., 1898), 77; Allan Forman, "Celestial Gotham," *The Arena*, April 1893, 620; and *Chicago's Dark Places*, 1.

23. *Hull-House Maps and Papers; A Presentation of Nationalities and Wages in a Congested District of Chicago, Together with Comments and Essays on Problems Growing Out of the Social Conditions, by Residents of Hull-House, a Social Settlement at 335 South Halsted Street, Chicago, Ill.* (New York: T. Y. Crowell & Co., 1895); and Philpott, *The Slum and the Ghetto*, 136–37. In his close examination of the Hull House maps, Philpott found, "The average number of 'nations' to a block is eight. Incredibly, four out of five *lots* are mixed"

(137). Similar observations about the diversity of Chicago's Italian districts and the Chinatowns of New York and Chicago can be found in Vecoli, "The Formation of Chicago's 'Little Italies,'" 5–20; Guglielmo, *White on Arrival*, 16–21; Lui, *The Chinatown Trunk Mystery*, 33–51, 143–74; and McKeown, *Chinese Migrant Networks and Cultural Change*, 193–98.

24. On the supposed containment of racial difference in reified immigrant communities, see especially Kay J. Anderson, *Vancouver's Chinatown: Racial Discourse in Canada, 1875–1980* (Montreal: McGill-Queen's University Press, 1991); Shah, *Contagious Divides*, 17–44; Henry Yu, *Thinking Orientals: Migration, Contact, and Exoticism in Modern America* (New York: Oxford University Press, 2001), 47–71; Donna R. Gabaccia, "A Global Geography of 'Little Italy': Italian Neighbourhoods in Comparative Perspective," *Modern Italy* 11.1 (February 2006): 9–24; and idem, "Inventing 'Little Italy,'" *Journal of the Gilded Age and Progressive Era* 6.1 (January 2007): 7–41.

25. Bederman, *Manliness and Civilization*, 35–36; and Gary Gerstle, *American Crucible: Race and Nation in the Twentieth Century* (Princeton, NJ: Princeton University Press, 2001), 104–8.

26. Bederman, *Manliness and Civilization*, 29–31, 48–50.

27. Forman, "New York Niggertown"; Rupert Hughes, *The Real New York* (New York: The Smart Set Publishing Company, 1904), 246–48; Campbell, Knox, and Byrnes, *Darkness and Daylight*, 472; and Duff, *Side Lights on Darkest Chicago*, 47.

28. Forman, "New York Niggertown."

29. I. B. Stockdale, Report on "Bernie's Place," N/E cor. 47 st. & 7 ave., 11:55 [p.m.], August 21, 1911, 3, 1910–12 investigative reports folder, box 28, C14P; and Forman, "New York Niggertown."

30. Ibid.; and Hughes, *The Real New York*, 246–48.

31. "Seitz in Chinatown," *Frank Leslie's Popular Monthly*, May 1893, 614; Meloney, "Slumming in New York's Chinatown," 233; and Beck, *New York's Chinatown*, 25.

32. Paul Bourget, *Outre-Mer: Impressions of America* (London: T. Fisher, 1895), 190.

33. Riis, *How the Other Half Lives*, 94; and Hughes, *The Real New York*, 148.

34. On the distinctions between race and color, see Jacobson, *Whiteness of a Different Color*, 5–7; and Guglielmo, *White on Arrival*, 7–9. For a rejoinder to this debate, see Roediger, *Working Toward Whiteness*, 12–13, 27–32.

35. Frank M. Bristol, "The Rev. Dr. Bristol in the Slums," *Chicago Times*, February 14, 1892, 9; and "Low Life; Scenes and Incidents in Little Italy," *NPG*, July 23, 1887, 7.

36. Ibid.; and Chas. S. Briggs, Report on 13 Bayard St., S. Goldberg, prop., Eve., January 29, 1914, 3, 1913–14 investigative reports folder, box 28, C14P. The Committee of Fourteen's investigative reports from the early 1910s contain numerous references to Italians that identify them in

.

contradistinction to whites and blacks. Investigator Charles S. Briggs routinely drew such distinctions, noting at one point that they prevented him from adequately doing his job. "There is something going on in these premises," he reported in reference to a saloon located at the corner of Fourth Avenue and Twenty-sixth Street, "but a white man cannot make it as the patrons of the place are almost exclusively Italians" (Chas. S. Briggs, Investigative report on A. Parachini & Co., 4th ave. & 26th St. N.W. cor., Eve., February 27, 1914, 4, 1913–14 investigative reports folder, box 28, C14P). Another of the committee's investigators, I. B. Stockdale, used more overtly racist terms to invoke the same distinctions, recounting an occasion when "a white woman well 'stewed' talk[ed] to two Italians" at a Tenderloin resort "packed with . . . white men with nigger women & white women with nigger men" (I. B. Stockdale, Investigative report on #342–7 Ave, 11.07 [p.m.], September 2, 1911, 3–4, 1910–12 investigative reports folder, box 28, C14P). Further references to Italians as swarthy, dark-skinned, olive-skinned, and "yellow—almost greenish—from the heat of their natal sun" (Bourget, *Outre-Mer*, 189) can be found in Joseph Kirkland, "Among the Poor of Chicago," *Scribner's Magazine*, July 1892, 6; Elisabeth Irwin, "Where the Players are Marionettes and the Age of Chivalry is Born Again in a Little Italian Theater in Mulberry Street," *The Craftsman*, September 1907, 667; Riis, *How the Other Half Lives*, 53; Campbell, Knox, and Byrnes, *Darkness and Daylight*, 194, 398, 409; and Bourget, *Outre-Mer*, 189. On racial in-betweenness and related conceptions of "differentiated whiteness," see Orsi, "The Religious Boundaries of an Inbetween People," 313–47; Barrett and Roediger, "In Between Peoples," 3–44; Jacobson, *Whiteness of a Different Color*, 168–70; and Roediger, *Working Toward Whiteness*, 127–30.

37. "A Cosmopolitan Market—New York Sunday Star," *Current Literature*, October 1889, 348; John Mathews, "The New York Puller-In," orig. pub. *Leslie's Weekly*, repr. in *Current Literature*, June 1903, 711; and Bourget, *Outre-Mer*, 192.

38. Campbell, Knox, and Byrnes, *Darkness and Daylight*, 471–72.

39. [C. H. Cooper], Investigative report on 125 McDougal [*sic*] St., March 8, 1907, 1906–7 investigative reports folder, box 28, C14P; I. B. Stockdale, Investigative report on #342–7 Ave., 11.07 [p.m.], September 2, 1911, 3, 1910–12 investigative reports folder, box 28, C14P; H.W.N., Committee of Fourteen, to Arthur Wood, Police Commissioner, New York, October 27, 1914, 2, second 1914 investigative reports folder, box 28, C14P; Chas. S. Briggs, Report, Eve., January 29, 1914, 6, 1913–14 investigative reports folder, box 28, C14P. See also "A Detective Roughly Handled," *NYT*, April 4, 1889, 5; I. B. Stockdale, Investigative report on #2 Carmine St., 10.25 p.m., August 26, 1911, 3, 1910–12 investigative reports folder, box 28, C14P; and "They Want the 'Levee' Purified," *CT*, August 10, 1890, 3

(emphasis added). Jacob Riis expressed similar sentiments in *How the Other Half Lives*, noting that the portion of lower Manhattan where "the old 'Africa' . . . is now fast becoming a modern Italy" (150) was the primary locus of "the aptly-named black-and-tan saloon" (156).

40. General Secretary, Committee of Fourteen, to Lewis W. Hine, New York, [July 1914], "General Correspondence, 1914, July" folder, box 3, C14P (emphasis added).

41. "Vice Ring Flourishes," *CRH*, October 28, 1907, 1, 4.

42. Vynne, *Chicago by Day and Night*, 202–3; Wooldridge, *Hands Up!*, 43, 60, 288; and Blair, "Vicious Commerce," 4.

43. *Mazet*, 1622, 2351–65, 2509–17. New York Police Commissioner William McAdoo (1904–6) similarly noted, "There is also, in the Tenderloin especially, a very dangerous band of colored women who prey on white men. There was at one time quite a number of 'creep joints' there. A white victim was robbed and the robber escaped through the cellar or the back yard. A great number of these women were arrested, convicted, and sent to prison, but, unless carefully watched, new ones will take up the work" (William McAdoo, *Guarding a Great City* [New York: Harper & Brothers, 1906], 98–99).

44. *Chicago's Dark Places*, 102. See also Henry B. Gibbud, "72," *The Story of Nellie Conroy: Leaves from the Journal of an All-Night Missionary* (New York: Florence Night Mission, 1887), 4–6; and "Alleged White Slavers Bound Over," *[Chicago] Day Book*, November 15, 1911, 24. Historian Mara L. Keire makes a similar point in "The Vice Trust," 8. Reports of black women subjecting their white sisters to sexual enslavement, though also rare, were nearly as prevalent as those detailing the involvement of black men in white slavery. See, for example, *Chicago's Dark Places*, 140; and "Alleged White Slavers Bound Over," *[Chicago] Day Book*, November 15, 1911, 24.

45. Walling, *Recollections of a New York Chief of Police*, 428. On the murder of Elsie Siegel, see Lui, *The Chinatown Trunk Mystery*, 1–16. On the Sing double-murder by a Chinese rival for Alice Davis Sing's affections, see "Murder Brings Chinese Tong War to Close," *[Chicago] Day Book*, September 3, 1913, 32; "The Sing Murder Case," *[Chicago] Day Book*, September 4, 1913, 5; "The Sing Murder Case," *[Chicago] Day Book*, September 5, 1913, 28; and "New Feature in the Sing Murder Case," *[Chicago] Day Book*, September 6, 1913, 4.

46. Turner, "The City of Chicago: A Study of the Great Immoralities," 580; "Five 'White Slave' Trade Investigations: The Revelations Made and Results Obtained by the Study of This Serious Question by Federal, State, and City Authorities," *McClure's Magazine*, July 1910, 347; Bell, "Chicago's White Slave Market," in Bell, ed., *Fighting the Traffic in Young Girls*, 262; B. C., "The White Slave Trade in New York City," in Bell, ed., *Fighting the Traffic in Young Girls*, 186–87; and "White Slavers in Fear of the Penitentiary,"

CRH, June 20, 1908, 11. See also Charles Byron Chrysler, *White Slavery* (no publisher, 1909), 23; George Kibbe Turner, "Daughters of the Poor: A Plain Story of the Development of New York City as a Leading Center of the White Slave Trade of the World, under Tammany Hall," *McClure's Magazine*, November 1909, 45–47; *White Slave Traffic*, 61st Cong., 2d Sess., 1909, H. Rept. 47, 12–13, 30; and Theodore A. Bingham, *The Girl That Disappears: The Real Facts about the White Slave Traffic* (Boston: Richard G. Badger and the Gorham Press, 1911), 32–40. Syndicates of "French importers, procurers, and pimps" were also accused of ruining young white American women, although the role of such *macquereaux* in the white slave trade of Chicago and New York was largely restricted to the importation and exploitation of women from France ("Five 'White Slave' Trade Investigations," 347). For scholarly analyses of the association of these racialized immigrant groups with the threat of white slavery, see Egal Feldman, "Prostitution, the Alien Woman, and the Progressive Imagination, 1910–1915," *American Quarterly* 19.2 (Summer 1967): 192–206; Bristow, *Prostitution and Prejudice*; Rosen, *The Lost Sisterhood,* 44, 119; Mary de Young, "Help, I'm Being Held Captive! The White Slave Fairy Tale of the Progressive Era," *Journal of American Culture* 6.1 (Spring 1983): 96–99; Frederick K. Grittner, *White Slavery: Myth, Ideology, and American Law* (New York: Garland Publishing, 1990), 20–23, 30, 64; and Keire, "The Vice Trust," 7–8.

47. Clifford G. Roe, *The Great War on White Slavery, or Fighting for the Protection of Our Girls* (Clifford G. Roe and E. S. Steadwell, 1911), 63.
48. "Lament about Reform," *New York Herald*, repr. in *WP*, March 13, 1892, 10; and Vice Commission of Chicago, *The Social Evil in Chicago,* 32.
49. Harvey, *In Bohemia*, 137–38.
50. Bowen, *The Public Dance Halls of Chicago*, 5; Peiss, *Cheap Amusements*, 102; and "Beside Saturday Evening 'Club Dance' First Ward Ball Was Almost Chaste," *CT*, October 9, 1910, 11. For a nuanced analysis of tough dancing, see Peiss, *Cheap Amusements*, 88–114.
51. *Bowery Waltz*, prod. William Heise (Edison Manufacturing Co., 1897); and *A Tough Dance* (American Mutoscope and Biograph Company, 1902).
52. "Find 'Dago Frank' Levee Insurgent," *CT*, May 1, 1911, 3.
53. Report of an investigation of a ball in a resort on D Avenue, February 16, 1912, quoted in Kneeland, *Commercialized Prostitution in New York City*, 70; and Peiss, *Cheap Amusements*, 106. On the simultaneous emergence of more respectable, middle-class-oriented public amusements and dances, in the form of cabarets and modified, desensualized dance steps such as the long Boston and the fox trot, see Erenberg, *Steppin' Out*, 111–75; Elsie Janis, "How to Dance the New Steps," *WP*, November 2, 1913, magazine section, 4; Mr. and Mrs. Vernon Castle, *Modern Dancing*; and "New Dances that Have a Smoothness as a Keynote," *NYT Sunday Magazine*, November 1, 1914, 2.

54. On "treating," see especially Peiss, *Cheap Amusements*, 108–14; Meyero-witz, *Women Adrift*, 101–7; Clement, *Love for Sale*, 45–75; and idem, "Trick or Treat: Prostitution and Working-Class Women's Sexuality in New York City, 1900–1932" (PhD diss., University of Pennsylvania, 1998), 67–130. "Preceding the middle-class flapper by at least twenty years," Clement notes, "treating girls were pivotal in the changes in sexual and gender ideology that were firmly in place by the Roaring Twenties" (ibid., 4).
55. Beck, *New York's Chinatown*, 156.
56. Wooldridge, *Hands Up!*, 169; and Beck, *New York's Chinatown*, 34, 38. In an 1895 article, the *Chicago Daily News* described a similarly diverse opium den, where "a select coterie, black, white and yellow, clubbed together and rented an old coal cellar on Clark Street" in Chicago's Chinese quarter (Dick Griffin, "Opium Addiction in Chicago: 'The Noblest and the Best Brought Low,'" *Chicago History* 6.2 [1977]: 113). On the romantic relations and marriages of white (especially Irish) women to Chinese men, see "Why 200 Chicago Women Are Married to Chinamen," *CT*, September 30, 1906, F2; and Lui, *The Chinatown Trunk Mystery*, 143–74. For representations of purportedly inappropriate intimacy between white women and Chinese men in the opium joints and streets of the Chinatowns of New York and Chicago, see Gardner, *The Doctor and the Devil*, 36–40; Beck, *New York's Chinatown*, 116–20; and Wooldridge, *Hands Up!*, 171–72.
57. Nesbitt, unpublished manuscript, 116–17, folder 1, box 1, CTNP.
58. Meloney, "Slumming in New York's Chinatown," 231; and Bessie Casebeer, quoted in E. C. Bishop, *Twenty-first Biennial Report of the State Superintendent of Public Instruction to the Governor of the State of Nebraska; For the Biennium Beginning January 7, 1909 and Ending January 5, 1911* (Lincoln: State of Nebraska, Department of Public Instruction, 1911), 387.
59. Ben Hecht, *A Child of the Century* (1954; repr., New York: Signet Books, 1960), 171; Junius Wood, *The Negro in Chicago: How He and His Race Kindred Came to Dwell in Great Numbers in a Northern City; How He Lives and Works; His Successes and Failures; His Political Outlook: A First-Hand Study* (Chicago: Chicago Daily News, 1916), 25; and George Francis O'Neill to Walter Hooke, Executive Secretary, Committee of Fourteen, In Re. James Marshall, New York, September 28, 1912, "Invest. Rep. 1912" folder, box 28, C14P. Three years before assisting the Committee of Fourteen with its investiga-tion, George Francis O'Neill had risen to fame as the attorney who chal-lenged New York City's forced quarantine of Irish immigrant Mary Mallon, also known as "Typhoid Mary" (Judith Walzer Leavitt, *Typhoid Mary: Captive to the Public's Health* [1996; repr., Boston: Beacon Press, 1997], 70–95).
60. Curon, *Chicago, Satan's Sanctum*, 58; and "Bullet Ends 'Slumming Tour,'" *CT*, May 27, 1903, 3. In her recent popular history of the Everleigh Club, Karen Abbott recounts both the more famous 1905 shooting of department store heir Marshall Field Jr. and the incident described here, the latter of

which she attributes to Robinson's having insulted the woman in the second slumming party (*Sin in the Second City*, 80–82, 89–102). The 1939 memoirs of writer Hutchins Hapgood appear to confirm the Everleigh sisters' willingness to welcome non-sexual customers to their establishment. While teaching at the University of Chicago in 1897, Hapgood recalled, it was not unusual for him and some of the young instructors who "were fond of the Bohemian life, including the traditional sex and drink" to stop by the Everleigh Club "to seek free conversation and convivial drinks with the Everly [*sic*] sisters and some of the young girls. . . . We young men felt that we, by paying for drinks, did not need to patronize the house further, and the Everly [*sic*] sisters, who seemed to appreciate our society, apparently felt the same way. Of course, once in a while, some one of us, overcome by wine and desire, would disappear with one of the young women, but not often" (Hapgood, *A Victorian in the Modern World*, 135–36).

61. Curon, *Chicago, Satan's Sanctum*, 60–61; May Churchill Sharpe, *Chicago May: Her Story* (New York: Macaulay Company, 1928), 37; Civil Service Commission, City of Chicago, *Final Report, Police Investigation, 1911–1912* [Chicago, 1912], 17, "Chicago, Police, Pamphlets concerning, 1904–1913" folder, box 19, GTP; and Report of a Disorderly Tenement House in the City of New York, 106 West 40th Street, August 20, 1901, "106 West 40th St.–Prost." folder, box 20, CFP. Linking the upsurge of "circuses," or, live sexual performances, in Chicago to the influx of laborers and tourists associated with the World's Columbian Exposition, former prostitute and thief May Churchill Sharpe recalled, "The World's Fair was a gold mine for me and my friends, during the years 1892 and 1893. The first of those years we nicked the builders, the second the visitors. And what dreadful things were done by some of the girls! It always makes me sick even to think of them. The mere mention of the details of some of the 'circuses' is unprintable. I think Rome at its worst had nothing on Chicago during those lurid days" (*Chicago May*, 37).

Further examples of French immigrants' actual participation in the performance of the "French perversion," may be found in Report of J. W. Earl, 130 W. 31st St., July 31, 1901, "128 West 31st St.-Prost." folder, box 19, CFP; Report of E. C. Becherer, 130 W. 31st St., July 31, 1901, "128 West 31st St.–Prost." folder, box 19, CFP; and A Resident to the Vice Crusade Committee [Committee of Fifteen], New York, February 5, 1901, "152 West 38th St.–Prost., 101 West 40th St.–Prost." folder, box 20, CFP; and Bell, "Chicago's White Slave Market," in Bell, ed., *Fighting the Traffic in Young Girls*, 261–62. On the increasing association of fellatio with "French" prostitutes and brothels, whether because of their nationality or because the term was simply applied to those who specialized in the practice, see especially Elizabeth Alice Clement, "Trick or Treat" (PhD diss., University of Pennsylvania, 1998), 49, 345–50; idem, *Love for Sale*, 80, 116; and Heather Lee Miller, "The Teeming Brothel: Sex Acts, Desires, and Sexual Identities in the United States, 1870–1940" (PhD diss., Ohio State University, 2002), 202–7.

62. J. Richardson Parke, ScB, PhG, MD, *Human Sexuality: A Medico-Literary Treatise on the Laws, Anomalies, and Relations of Sex with Especial Reference to Contrary Sexual Desire* (Philadelphia: Professional Publishing Company, 1906), 313; Unidentified investigative report, "Investigative Reports— untitled—1905–1910" folder, box 38, C14P, quoted in Clement, "Trick or Treat," 49; Bell, "Chicago's White Slave Market," in Bell, ed., *Fighting the Traffic in Young Girls*, 261–62; Vice Commission of Chicago, *The Social Evil in Chicago*, 73; and G. Frank Lydston, MD, *The Diseases of Society: The Vice and Crime Problem* (Philadelphia and London: J. B. Lippincott Company, 1904), 309.

63. *Mazet*, 1394; Vice Commission of Chicago, *The Social Evil in Chicago*, 139; I. B. Stockdale, Investigative report on #8 Mott St., 11:45 p.m., June 29, 1912, 1912 investigative reports folder, box 28, C14P; and Curon, *Chicago, Satan's Sanctum*, 147.

64. On the turn-of-the-century gendered framework of sexual norms predominant among immigrant and working-class men, see George Chauncey, *Gay New York*, esp. 47–97.

65. *Mazet*, 1394.

66. Mary Casal, *The Stone Wall: An Autobiography* (Chicago: Eyncourt Press, 1930), 184–85.

67. Ibid., 165.

68. Howells, *Impressions and Experiences*, 135–36.

69. "Tired of the 'Slummers,'" *CT*, June 17, 1906, 1. See also "Robbed the Railways" (*WP*, March 4, 1898, 16), in which a New York workingman vowed to "throw a bucket of water on the next batch of persons who invaded his rooms against his wishes."

70. "The Famous Banquet at a Swell New York Hotel Given by Bill M'Glory," *NPG*, January 11, 1902, 3. See also "Revelry Wild and Shameless," *NYT*, March 16, 1883, 5.

71. "Will Go Slumming," *CT*, April 25, 1892; and "Slumming among the Rich," *NYT*, April 25, 1892, 8.

72. "An Indecent Spectacle," *L'Italia*, July 23, 1892, Chicago Foreign Language Press Survey, compiled by the Chicago Public Library Omnibus Project, Works Progress Administration, Special Collections Research Center, University of Chicago Library, Chicago.

73. "Jews Launch Bolt at White Slavers," *CT*, October 3, 1909, 1; and "Reformation of the Great East Side," *NYT*, November 19, 1900, 5.

74. Adolf Kraus, *Reminiscences and Comments: The Immigrant, the Citizen, a Public Officer, the Jew* (Chicago: Toby Rubovits Inc., 1925), 177; "Frank Brothers Spurned by Jews," *CT*, September 25, 1909, 2. See also "Purify the West Side," *Daily Jewish Courier*, July 14, 1914, Chicago Foreign Language Press Survey, compiled by the Chicago Public Library Omnibus Project, Works

Progress Administration, Special Collections Research Center, University of Chicago Library, Chicago; "Join Hands in War on White Slavery," *CT*, October 6, 1909, 3; "Anti-Vice Mass Meeting," *NYT*, April 23, 1900, 5; and "To Uplift White Slaves," *NYT*, May 15, 1910, 9.

75. A. Clayton Powell Sr., *Against the Tide: An Autobiography* (New York: Richard R. Smith, 1938), 50; The Citizens' Protective League, *Story of the Riot* (1900; New York: Arno Press & The New York Times, 1969), 1; "Negroes Wound a Policeman," *NYT*, August 13, 1900, 10; and "Harris Alleges Self-Defense," *NYT*, October 27, 1900, 14, and Sacks, *Before Harlem*, 39–42. In November 1900, Arthur Harris was convicted of the second-degree murder of police-man R. J. Thorpe and sentenced to life imprisonment in Sing Sing ("Life Imprisonment for Murderer Harris," *NYT*, November 3, 1900, 14).

   Chicago largely escaped such dramatic racial violence until 1919. Yet when the 1908 race riot in the Illinois capital of Springfield was blamed on the proliferation of commercialized sex in that city's black district, a group of prominent "colored people" resolved to prevent a similar outrage in the Windy City. Establishing the Lincoln Law and Order League, they undertook "the 'cleaning up' of the south side levee district between Twelfth street and Thirty-ninth street as far as negro resorts are concerned." According to the Reverend H. E. Stewart of the Institutional Church, the downstate violence taught "the colored man a lesson" that "there is much for him to do in the fight against lawlessness" ("Negroes Form Society for War against Vice," *CRH*, August 24, 1908, 4; see also "Colored Men to Join League," *CRH*, August 29, 1908, 5).

76. Wilson, Report on McNally's (or, Callahan's) saloon, 12 Chatham Square, March 19, 1901, "12 Chatham Square—'Dive'" folder, box 4, CFP; Sum-mary report of Chinatown conditions provided by Quan Yick Nam, February 19, 1901, "7 Mott St.—'Prostitution'" folder, box 4, CFP; Bulletin #54, August 14, 1911, "Committee Minutes, March 1905–1913" notebook, box 86, C14P; *Annual Report of the Committee of Fourteen for 1911* (New York: 1912), n.p.; The Committee of Fourteen in New York City, *Annual Report for 1915–1916* (New York: 1917), 85–86; and copy of probation agreement for Barron Wilkins, September 23, 1909, enclosed in Frederick H. Whitin, Committee of Fourteen to Mrs. William H. Baldwin, New York, August 10, 1910, Mrs. Wm. H. Baldwin correspondence folder, box 10, C14P. For more on the activities and motivations of the Chinese men who assisted New York's Committee of Fifteen, see Jennifer Fronc, "'I Led Him On': Under-cover Investigation and the Politics of Social Reform in New York City, 1900–1919" (PhD diss., Columbia University, 2005), 91–104.

   The establishment of the Committee of Fourteen's "Auxiliary Negro Committee" provided Fred R. Moore with an institutional base from which to formalize the efforts that he had initiated in the *New York Age* to crack down on illicit activities in the black Tenderloin and Harlem. But the primary impetus for the auxiliary's founding, as the committee's annual report for 1911 noted, was to inoculate the committee against allegations of racism. After asking Booker T. Washington to convince New York's black saloonkeepers that its actions against them were not racially motivated, a proposition that he refused, the Committee of Fourteen announced that "an advisory Committee of representative men of their race in this city has been formed" to address the claims of "the proprietors of negro resorts" who "felt or claimed that they were victims of race prejudice" (Booker T. Washington to Ruth S. Baldwin, Huntington, NY, August 14, 1910, Mrs. Wm. H. Baldwin correspondence folder, box 10, C14P; and *Annual Report of the Committee of Fourteen for 1911*). For more on the Committee of Fourteen's "Auxiliary Negro Committee," also known as the "Committee of Five" and, later, as the "Committee of Seven," see Jennifer Fronc, "The Horns of the Dilemma: Race Mixing and the Enforcement of Jim Crow in New York City," *Journal of Urban History* 33.1 (November 2006): 9–14, 19–20.

77. D. E. Tobias, Editor, *The Searcher: A Journal of Thought and Opinion*, to Walter G. Hooke, Superintendent, Committee of Fourteen, New York, September 10, 1913, David Elliot Tobias correspondence folder, box 15, C14P. See also the many other letters and pamphlets produced by Tobias between 1910 and 1918 in the David Elliot Tobias correspondence folder, box 15, C14P. Evidence of Tobias's first interaction with the Committee of Fourteen in 1908, defending Barron Wilkins's Little Savoy against the committee's racially biased regulatory practices, can be found in the copy of a letter from Frederick H. Whitin, Secretary, Committee of Fourteen, to D. E. Tobias, New York, July 8, 1908, enclosed with Frederick H. Whitin, Secretary, Committee of Fourteen, to Wm. Jay Schieffelin, Treasurer, Committee of Fourteen, New York, July 8, 1908, in the Wm. Jay Schieffelin correspondence folder, box 14, C14P.

In addition to Tobias, both W. E. B. Du Bois and Gilchrist Stewart, chairman of the New York Vigilance Committee of the New York Branch of the NAACP, attacked the Committee of Fourteen for pressuring black saloonkeepers to eliminate race mixing from their establishments as a precondition for doing business, while allowing white-owned black and tans to operate with relative impunity despite their promotion of similar conditions. See Clement, *Love for Sale*, 81–86; Fronc, "The Horns of the Dilemma," 14–21; and Sacks, *Before Harlem*, 64–66.

78. Burgess, "A Study of the Characteristics of the Cantonese Merchants in Chinatown, New York, as Shown by Their Use of Leisure Time," 28; L., Investigative report "In re. Saloons, etc., Manhattan," August 8, 1913, 1, 1913 Aug.–Sept. investigative reports folder, box 28, C14P; and Nascher, *The Wretches of Povertyville*, 58.

79. "Answers to Correpndnc [*sic*]," *The Tenderloin*, January 28, 1899, 5; advertisements for "expert guides" for "parties wishing to see the inter-

esting parts of New York," *The Tenderloin*, January 28, 1899, 10; April 1, 1899, 14; April 8, 1899, 2, 15; April 15, 1899, 15; April 22, 1899, 3, 12, 13; *Mazet*, 185–86; and "Levee Cleaning Crusade Begins," *CT*, May 28, 1905, 6. On slumming guides, see also Nascher, *The Wretches of Povertyville*, 33.

80. Durante and Kofoed, *Night Clubs*, 95–96. On Connors, see also Sante, *Low Life*, 125–32. On "lobbygows," see Light, "From Vice District to Tourist Attraction," 389–90; and Fronc, "'I Led Him On,'" 94–98.

81. John Corbin, "How the Other Half Laughs," *Harper's New Monthly Magazine*, December 1898, 30–48; F. H. McLean, "Bowery Amusements," in *Yearbook of the University Settlement Society of New York* (1899), 17–18; Jacob Gordin, "The Yiddish Stage," in *Fifteenth Annual Report of the University Settlement Society of New York* (1901), 26–30; "In Little Italy," in *The Week in New York*, July 16–22, 1905, 12; James, Flynn, Paulding, Patton, and Andrews, *The Immigrant Jew in America*, 226–30, 249–52; Nina Warnke, "Immigrant Popular Culture as Contested Sphere: Yiddish Music Halls, the Yiddish Press, and the Processes of Americanization, 1900–1910," *Theatre Journal* 48.3 (1996): 321–35; Sabine Haenni, "The Immigrant Scene: The Commercialization of Ethnicity and the Production of Publics in Fiction, Theater, and the Cinema, 1890–1915" (PhD diss., University of Chicago, 1998), 181–255; Bettina Warnke, "Reforming the New York Yiddish Theater: The Cultural Politics of Immigrant Intellectuals and the Yiddish Press, 1887–1910" (PhD diss., Columbia University, 2001); Riv-Ellen Prell, "The Ghetto Girl and the Erasure of Memory," in Hasia R. Diner, Jeffrey Shandler, and Beth S. Wenger, eds., *Remembering the Lower East Side: American Jewish Reflections* (Bloomington: Indiana University Press, 2000), 86–112; and Owen Kildare, *My Mamie Rose: The Story of My Regeneration* (New York: The Baker & Taylor Company, 1903), 138.

82. Durante and Kofoed, *Night Clubs*, 95–97; and Meloney, "Slumming in New York's Chinatown," 233. A similar performance featuring a "young woman, probably a southerner, who makes a good living by showing visitors how to 'hit the pipe'" can be found in Nascher, *The Wretches of Povertyville*, 181.

In the mid-1930s, one popular account of Chinatown suggested that local residents were outraged by the presence of such performances. "It is rumored in several cities that bus companies maintain opium dens as a show for their rubberneck patrons," Leong Gor Yun wrote. "If the Chinese could substantiate this rumor, they would tear the performers limb from limb. . . . Smokers and non-smokers alike are outraged by this false local color daubed on Chinatown by bus companies, but they are powerless, beyond a sneer or a smirk, against the lies they hear being fobbed off on groups of gullible tourists" (Leong Gor Yun, *Chinatown Inside Out* [New York: Barrows Mussey, 1936], 217). Given the vehemence of emotions expressed in this quote, it seems likely that many Chinatown residents harbored similar sentiments at the turn of the century, but doubtless many of them also participated in this money-making venture.

83. "The Theatrical Week," *NYT*, December 16, 1894, 10; "Mr. Harrigan's New Play," *NYT*, December 11, 1894, 5; and "Bookings at Columbia," *BDE*, September 10, 1899, 23. At least one other burlesque company appears to have employed Chinese actors to lend a sense realism to its opium den scenes. In a 1901 review of Ed F. Rush's Victoria Burlesquers, the *Brooklyn Daily Eagle* noted, "It is a popular company . . . and usually worth seeing. Its burlesque this year is called 'Slumming in Chinatown;' shows the interior of an opium den and is said to be provided with real Chinamen and real victims" ("The Theaters Open," *BDE*, September 1, 1901, 20; see also "The Drama," *CT*, November 3, 1901, 46).

84. Robert Neilson Stephens, *On the Bowery: A Comedy Drama in Five Acts* ([New York], 1893); "Fourteenth Street Theatre," *NYT*, September 11, 1894, 5; "'Chuck' Connors Departs," *NYT*, August 21, 1897, 7; *Cincinnati Tribune*, January 20, 1895, quoted in Gilfoyle, *A Pickpocket's Tale*, 268; "Theatrical Gossip," *NYT*, October 16, 1894, 8; Gilfoyle, *A Pickpocket's Tale*, 260–70; and idem, "Staging the Criminal: *In the Tenderloin*, Freak Drama, and the Criminal Celebrity," *Prospects: An Annual of American Culture Studies* 30 (2005): 285–307. Gilfoyle notes that "no published or copyrighted version of *In the Tenderloin* exists" (*A Pickpocket's Tale*, 419n3).

85. "Plays and Players," *BDE*, April 1, 1900, 24; "In the Vaudevilles," *NYT*, December 29, 1901, 9; "Summer Amusements," *BDE*, August 10, 1902, sec. 2, 17; and "News of the Theater and its People," *BDE*, February 16, 1902, sec. 4, 8. See also "At the Play," *CT*, April 30, 1899, 41; "'The Cuckoo' in Brooklyn," *BDE*, September 12, 1899, 5; "Theatres and Music Halls," *NYT*, November 7, 1899, 5; "Notes of the Week," *NYT*, November 12, 1899, 18; "Dramatic and Musical," *NYT*, March 20, 1900, 7; advertisement for The Dewey, E. 14th Street, *NYT*, December 30, 1901, 8; "News of the Theater and its People," *BDE*, March 16, 1902, sec. 2, 14; and advertisement for Sid J. Euson's Theater, N. Clark & Kinzie, *CT*, February 11, 1906, 12.

86. *The Deceived Slumming Party*, directed by D. W. Griffith and Wallace McCutcheon (American Mutoscope and Biograph Co., 1908); Sabine Haenni, "Filming 'Chinatown': Fake Visions, Bodily Transformations," in Peter X. Feng, ed., *Screening Asian Americans* (New Brunswick, NJ: Rutgers University Press, 2002), 25–26, 37–41; and Rabinovitz, *For the Love of Pleasure*, 18–19. As Haenni notes, the cross-racial perils of the scenes set in Chinatown were mitigated in *The Deceived Slumming Party* by the racist practice of employing white actors in yellowface to represent Chinese men ("Filming 'Chinatown,'" in Feng, ed., *Screening Asian Americans*, 44).

Another example of an early film that mocked slummers' excursions on the Lower East Side is *Lifting the Lid* (American Mutoscope and Biograph Co., 1905). While the film's promotional materials warned that its "subject is somewhat spicy," American Mutoscope and Biograph Co.

assured potential screeners that their production was "unobjectionable in everyway and has made a decided hit wherever shown." This film tracked "the experiences of a country couple who come to New York to see the sights," including "a Bowery dance hall, a Chinese restaurant, a Chinese opium den and an Oriental dance hall" (Biograph summary of *Lifting the Lid*, in AFI Catalog of Silent Films, http://www.afi.com/members/catalog/ AbbrView.aspx?s=1&Movie=29785&bhcp=1 [accessed October 28, 2007]). For more on *Lifting the Lid*, see Rabinovitz, *For the Love of Pleasure*, 18–19; and Haenni, "Filming 'Chinatown,'" in Feng, ed., *Screening Asian Americans*, 21–52.

87. Asbury, *Gem of the Prairie*, 273–74.

88. O'Connor, *Hell's Kitchen*, 93 (on short-changing at the Tivoli dance hall in the Tenderloin); "Teach Has Trio Arrested; Prof. J. W. Shields of Springfield Goes 'Slumming' and Is Robbed of $180—Chauffeur Among Prisoners," *CT*, September 4, 1911, 3; and "'Slumming Tour' Brings Fine," *CT*, February 9, 1907, 9.

89. "Loses Gem By Slumming," *CT*, January 3, 1906, 4; and "'Auntie' Loses Gems at 'Party,'" *CT*, September 30, 1915, 13. In a front-page story in the summer of 1911, the *Chicago Tribune* reported a case in which a woman slummer and her male companion both claimed to have been drugged and robbed by another woman in their party, whom they later learned already had an arrest record for theft (see "Drugged, Robbed in Mrs. Romadka Slumming Party," *CT*, July 24, 1911, 1).

90. S. W. L., Investigative report on Baron [*sic*] Wilkins' Cafe, (331 West 37th Street) 253 W. 35th Street, March 16, 1910, 9 to 2:30 p.m., 1910–12 investigative reports folder, box 28, C14P.

91. Hapgood, *A Victorian in the Modern World*, 153–54.

92. Ogden, NI, and C. Stack, Investigative report on 342 Seventh Ave., N.W. Cor 29th St., May 9, 1917, 9.45 p.m., "Broadway–East Houston; E. 3rd–E. 8th; Second–Seventh" investigative reports folder, box 32, C14P.

93. [David Oppenheim], Investigative report on George Lee, 234 W. 61st bet Amsterdam & West End Ave., June 10–11, 1916, 11:40 p.m. to 2:15 a.m., second 1916 investigative reports folder, box 31, C14P; Nascher, *The Wretches of Povertyville*, 46; and Kneeland, *Commercialized Prostitution in New York City*, 69.

As at McGurk's, patrons of the Tenderloin's most popular dance hall, The Haymarket, were also protected from ill-behaved women. According to local politico Dick Butler, the Haymarket's regular female habitués were required to pass "a sort of civil service examination" instituted by the proprietor of the establishment, Ed Corey, and had to agree to two major house rules. "Rule No. 1 was that no man who fell for them was to be robbed on the premises. Rule No. 2 was that if they stole from a patron after taking him elsewhere, and the man put a rap in against them with the police, then they had to pay the money back to calm the patron and save the police undue embarrassment" (Richard J. Butler and Joseph Driscoll, *Dock Walloper* [New York, 1933], quoted in O'Connor, *Hell's Kitchen*, 90).

CHAPTER 4

1. Hapgood, *The Spirit of the Ghetto*, 5.
2. Hecht, *A Child of the Century*, 171. See also Hapgood, *Types from City Streets*; idem, *A Victorian in the Modern World*, esp. 153–56, 162–71; John Sloan, *John Sloan's New York Scene: From the Diaries, Notes, and Correspondence, 1906–1913*, ed. Bruce St. John (New York: Harper and Row, 1965); *Sherwood Anderson's Memoirs: A Critical Edition,* ed. Ray Lewis White (Chapel Hill: University of North Carolina Press, 1969); Crane, *Maggie*; and Ben Hecht, *A Thousand and One Afternoons in Chicago* (Chicago: Covici-McGee, 1922).
3. For examples of the slogans of the Mad Hatter and the Dill Pickle Club, see Corinne Lowe, "The Village in a City," *Ladies' Home Journal*, March 1920, 29; and photograph of the door of the Dill Pickle Club, emblazoned with its slogan, folder 32, box 2, DPCP.
4. On the imaginary worlds created in Village and Towertown cabarets, see Lewis Erenberg, "Greenwich Village Nightlife, 1910–1950," in Beard and Berlowitz, eds., *Greenwich Village,* 357–70; Jan Seidler Ramirez, "The Tourist Trade Takes Hold," in Beard and Berlowitz, eds., *Greenwich Village,* 371–91; J. A. S. [James A. Seaman], Report of Investigator, Greenwich Village— shops, March 31, 1917, "Special Inspections" folder, box 31, C14P; Ben Reitman, "Life and Death of the Dill Pickle Club," *Chicago Sunday Times,* August 22, 1937, 20–21; and Zorbaugh, *The Gold Coast and the Slum,* 101.
5. M. B. [Maxwell Bodenheim], "Soulful Flirtation Between 'Beauty And the Beast,'" *Chicago Literary Times*, May 15, 1923, 5; and idem, "Peeping Tom In Verbal Dressing Rooms of Bohemia," *Chicago Literary Times*, May 15, 1923, 2.
6. According to historian Jerrold Seigel, the terms "Bohemia," "*la Bohème*," and "Bohemian" were first used to refer to artistic communities in France in the 1830s and 1840s. Seigel notes that this "new vocabulary played on the common French word for gypsy—*bohémien*—which erroneously identi- fied the province of Bohemia . . . as the gypsies' place of origin" (Jerrold Seigel, *Bohemian Paris: Culture, Politics, and the Boundaries of Bourgeois Life, 1830–1930* [New York: Viking, 1986], 5; see also Parry, *Garrets and Pretend- ers*, xxi).
7. For more on the development of dating as a twentieth-century, white middle-class cultural practice, see Paula Fass, *The Damned and the Beauti- ful: American Youth in the 1920s* (New York: Oxford University Press, 1977); Bailey, *From Front Porch to Back Seat;* and John Modell, *Into One's Own: From Youth to Adulthood in the United States, 1920–1975* (Berkeley, CA: University of California Press, 1989).

8. Harry Kemp, *More Miles: An Autobiographical Novel* (New York: Boni and Liveright, 1926), 110; and Margaret C. Anderson, "Mrs. Ellis's Failure," *The Little Review*, March 1915, 18. On bohemians' extensive interest in Freudian psychoanalysis and their responsibility for popularizing his (vulgarized) ideas, see especially Leslie Fishbein, "The Culture of Contradiction: The Greenwich Village Rebellion," in Beard and Berlowitz, eds., *Greenwich Village*, 212–28. On the important role that Margaret Anderson and Jane Heap played in shaping bohemian ideas about sexuality, both through their *Little Review* and through their open lesbianism, see Holly A. Baggett, "'Someone to Talk Our Language': Jane Heap, Margaret Anderson, and the *Little Review* in Chicago," in Allida M. Black, ed., *Modern American Queer History* (Philadelphia: Temple University Press, 2001), 24–35; and Katz, *Gay/Lesbian Almanac*, 363–64.

9. Margaret C. Anderson, "Mrs. Ellis's Failure," 17–18 (emphasis in the original); Sada Cowan, letter to the editor, *The Little Review*, April 1915, 53; and "What Is the Greatest Need Now in the Sex Life of the Nation? A Symposium," *The Quill*, December 1926, 8. See also William Thurston Brown, letter to the editor, *The Little Review*, April 1915, 52; E. C. A. Smith, letter to the editor, *The Little Review*, April 1915, 54; Baggett, "'Someone to Talk Our Language,'" 31–33; and Katz, *Gay/Lesbian Almanac*, 363–64.

10. Ellen Kay Trimberger, "Feminism, Men, and Modern Love: Greenwich Village, 1900–1925," in Snitow, Stansell, and Thompson, eds., *Powers of Desire,* 131–52; and Document XXVI, a first-person narrative "written verbatim from several conferences" with a "woman [who] desired to tell her life's story rather than write it," quoted in Reckless, "The Natural History of Vice Areas in Chicago," 243–46.

11. Hutchins Hapgood to Neith Boyce, "Late, Saturday night," 1914 [?], Hapgood Family Papers, Beinecke Rare Book Library, Yale University, quoted in Stansell, *American Moderns,* 292; and Neith Boyce to Hutchins Hapgood, 1916, Hapgood Family Papers, Beinecke Rare Book Library, Yale University, quoted in Trimberger, "Feminism, Men, and Modern Love," 142 (emphasis in original).

12. Fishbein, *Rebels in Bohemia*, 94–99; idem, "The Culture of Contradiction," 223–25; Trimberger, "Feminism, Men, and Modern Love," 136–48; Floyd Dell, *Women as World Builders: Studies in Modern Feminism* (Chicago: Forbes and Company, 1913), 20; idem, *Homecoming: An Autobiography* (New York: Farrar and Rinehart, 1933), 290; Max Eastman, *Enjoyment of Living* (New York: Harper and Row, 1948), 315; and Henrietta Rodman to Harry Kemp, quoted in Humphrey, *Children of Fantasy,* 241.

13. Mina Loy, "Colossus," unpublished manuscript, Mina Loy papers, Collection of American Literature, Beinecke Rare Book and Manuscript Library, Yale University, quoted in Carolyn Burke, *Becoming Modern: The Life of Mina Loy* (New York: Farrar, Straus and Giroux, 1996), 241; Zorbaugh, *The Gold*

Coast and the Slum, 91–92; and Ware, *Greenwich Village, 1920–1930,* 245. Zorbaugh further noted, "Towertown, like Greenwich Village, is predominantly a woman's bohemia. In Paris the 'Quarter' is a bohemia of young men students. In London bohemia belongs to the man about town, to the older artists—cultivated, clever—who like the adventure of the night life of the city. But of late years, in New York and Chicago, with changing mores and the emancipation of the younger generation of American women, Greenwich Village and Towertown have become women's bohemias" (*The Gold Coast and the Slum*, 91).

14. Cowley, *Exile's Return,* 70; and "3 Pints of Gin Put Artist in Pickle (Dill), But He 'Takes Rap' Rather than Betray Source of Supply," *CDN,* March 18, 1931, 4.

15. Ben L. Reitman, "Homosexuality (To Be Added on Part IV)," 11, from "Living with Social Outcasts," unpublished manuscript, [March 1933], supplement IV, folder 34, BLRP. George Chauncey makes similar arguments in *Gay New York*, 230–32; and in "Long-Haired Men and Short-Haired Women: Building a Gay World in the Heart of Bohemia," in Beard and Berlowitz, eds., *Greenwich Village*, 152–55. For additional analysis of the "fellowship" shared by fairies, lesbians, and bohemians in Chicago's Towertown, see Johnson, "The Kids of Fairytown," in Beemyn, ed., *Creating a Place for Ourselves*, 97–118; Zorbaugh, *The Gold Coast and the Slum,* esp. 87–104; and "Two Pictures of the Rise and Fall of Bohemianism," unpublished student paper, folder 1, box 161, EWBP. The last, which paraphrases page 100 of Zorbaugh's work, notes that "distorted forms of sex behavior are found in the shelter of the unconventionality of the village [here referring to Towertown], principally among the homo-sexuals who frequent the village tea-rooms and studios" (ibid., 7).

16. Floyd Dell, *The Briary-Bush: A Novel* (New York: Alfred A. Knopf, 1921), 34, 31–32.

17. Otto Weininger, quoted in Margaret C. Anderson, "Mrs. Ellis's Failure," 18; Sigmund Freud, *Three Essays on Sexuality*, trans. and ed. James Strachey (New York: Basic Books, 1962), 10n1 (the footnote in question was added to the 3rd edition in 1915; translated into English in 1918); Dell, *Homecoming*, 295; and White, ed., *Sherwood Anderson's Memoirs*, 339–40. See also Baggett, "'Someone to Talk Our Language,'" 31–33; and Katz, *Gay/Lesbian Almanac*, 363–64.

18. See Bruce Kellner, *Carl Van Vechten and the Irreverent Decades* (Norman, OK: University of Oklahoma Press, 1968); Carl Van Vechten and Fania Marioff's correspondence with each other, 1912–1959, boxes 26–41, CVVP; and Document 22, quoted in Zorbaugh, *The Gold Coast and the Slum,* 100.

In her 1995 "bisexualist" revision of the history of sexuality, *Vice Versa: Bisexuality and the Eroticism of Everyday Life* (New York: Simon & Schuster, 1995), Marjorie Garber takes lesbian and gay historians to task for interpreting women and men like those discussed in this paragraph as *homosexuals* whose historical situation prevented them from fully escaping society's "compulsory heterosexuality" (to use Adrienne Rich's term from "Compulsory Heterosexuality and Lesbian Existence," in Snitow, Stansell, and Thompson, eds., *Powers of Desire,* 177–205), arguing that the complicated sexual histories of these individuals are more properly categorized as bisexual. While I am sympathetic to Garber's assertion that the discounting of individuals' varied sexual desires in favor of the creation of "an imagined utopia of same-sex (or opposite-sex) consistency" results in the "writ[ing] out [of] human richness, diversity, pleasure, and loss, replacing them with mere ideology" (118), I refrain from adopting the designation *bisexual* for two reasons. First, during the period under consideration, the term *bisexual* was more often used to refer to the presence of both male and female characteristics in one person, than to the presence of sexual desires for both women and men (Chauncey, *Gay New York,* 49). Second, I believe that the transhistorical application of the term *bisexual,* as it is currently understood, constitutes a type of essentialism that fails to tease out the historical specificity of the ever-changing social and cultural contexts of individuals who might be so classified. For these reasons, I refer only to women and men whose sexual histories defy simple sexual categorization as either heterosexual or homosexual—a position more in line with the Möbius strip-model of sexuality that Garber proposes in her introduction but largely loses sight of in her analysis (130).

19. "Document #52: Dill Pickle Club," unpublished document, n.d., 6, in "Documents: History of Lower North Side Community, Chicago," CNS; Cowley, *Exile's Return,* 52; and White, ed., *Sherwood Anderson's Memoirs,* 521–22. (I thank David Johnson for pointing out the differences between the original, expurgated publication of *Sherwood Anderson's Memoirs* [New York: Harcourt, Brace and Company, 1942] and the later, more complete edition cited above.) Italian poet Emanuel Carnevali, who spent several years in Towertown and the Village, similarly defended his youthful homoerotic relationship with a fellow schoolboy from insinuations of homosexuality in his posthumously published memoir (Emanuel Carnevali, *The Autobiography of Emanuel Carnevali,* comp. and with a preface by Kay Boyle [New York: Horizon Press, 1967]). On Greenwich Village bohemians' negative reactions toward homosexuality, see also Chauncey, *Gay New York,* 229–31.

20. Tennessee Mitchell Anderson, unpublished and undated autobiographical manuscript, 77, folder 17, box 3, Sherwood Anderson papers, Newberry Library, Chicago. Tennessee Mitchell married Sherwood Anderson in 1914, following Anderson's divorce from his first wife.

21. Robert Edwards, letter to the editor, quoted in Peter Pater, "Local Color," *The Quill,* May 1927, 25.

22. "The Greenwich Village Dances at Webster Hall," Resume of Cabaret Situation, 1917, 12, "Inv. Reports of Cabarets" folder, box 31, C14P; M. B. [Maxwell Bodenheim], "Peeping Tom In Verbal Dressing Rooms of Bohemia,"

2; and John Corbin, "Village Morality," *NYT*, February 23, 1919, sec. IV, 2. Examples of popular magazine articles about the bohemian districts of New York and Chicago include "Hunt for Bohemia," *Bookman*, May 1915, 245–47; Robert C. Benchley, "The Art of Being a Bohemian," *Vanity Fair*, March 1916, 43; Floyd Dell, "The Passing Glories of Greenwich Village," *Vanity Fair*, March 1916, 49, 126; Anne O'Hagan, "Where Is Greenwich Village?", *Vanity Fair*, July 1916, 65; "Disillusioned by Bohemia?" *Literary Digest*, September 16, 1916, 688–89; "Inevitable Adventure," *Bookman*, July 1917, 540–43; "Lure of Greenwich Village," *Literary Digest*, May 8, 1920, 46–47; and Frank Ward O'Malley, "Greenwich Village Virus," *Saturday Evening Post*, October 15, 1921, 14–15.

23. Lowe, "The Village in a City," 28–29, 107–8; and Helen "Jimmie" Criswell, et al., Diary for the Mad Hatter, March 4 and 11, 1920, January 10, 1921, and June 10, 1920, box 64, Hendrik Willem van Loon Papers, #3292, Division of Rare Books and Manuscript Collections, Cornell University Library, Ithaca, NY.

24. Ramirez, "The Tourist Trade Takes Hold," in Beard and Berlowitz, eds., *Greenwich Village*, 386–87; *The Trufflers*, directed by Fred E. Wright (Essanay Film Mfg. Co., 1917); *The Broken Melody*, directed by William P. S. Earle (Selznick Pictures Corp., 1919); *A Girl in Bohemia*, directed by Howard M. Mitchell (Fox Film Corp., 1919); *Toby's Bow*, directed by Harry Beaumont (Goldwyn Pictures Corp., 1919); *Woman, Woman!*, directed by Kenean Buel (Fox Film Corp.; A Standard Picture, 1919); *Harriet and the Piper*, directed by Bertram Bracken (Louis B. Mayer Productions and Anita Stewart Productions, Inc., 1920); *Within the Cup*, directed by Raymond B. West (W. W. Hodkinson Corp. and General Film Co., 1918); *The Dangerous Moment*, directed by Marcel De Sano (Universal Film Manufacturing Co., 1921); and *Smiling All the Way*, directed by Fred J. Butler (D. N. Schwab Productions, Inc., 1920).

25. Ogden, Investigator Report, Webster Hall, 119 E. 11th St., near Third Ave., March 6, 1917, 11 p.m., "Broadway–East Houston; E. 3rd–E. 84th; Second–Seventh" folder, box 32, C14P; and P. J. M. [Peter J. Mallon], report on Webster Hall, 119 East 11th Street, March 14, 1919, 11:30, p.m., eighth 1919 investigative reports folder, box 34, C14P.

26. Paul Cressey, notes, folder 6, box 129, EWBP, quoted in Randy D. McBee, "'Struggling, Petting, Muzzling, Mushing, Loving, Fondling, Feeling, or Whatever You Wish to Call It': A Social History of Working-Class Heterosexuality in the United States, 1890s–1930s" (PhD diss., University of Missouri, Columbia, 1996), 212; and J. A. S. [James A. Seaman], Report of Investigator, Greenwich Village—shops, March 31, 1917, "Special Inspections" folder, box 31, C14P.

27. Chapin, *Greenwich Village*, 221.

28. Allen M. Brandt, *No Magic Bullet: A Social History of Venereal Disease in the United States Since 1880*, expanded ed. (New York: Oxford University Press, 1987), 52–121; and "The Greenwich Village Dances at Webster Hall,"

Resume of Cabaret Situation, 1917, 12, "Inv. Reports of Cabarets" folder, box 31, C14P. See also "Greenwich Village Affairs," Resume of reports on cabarets, 1917, 16, "Inv. Reports of Cabarets" folder, box 31, C14P; and Humphrey, *Children of Fantasy*, 254n25. The latter recounts a May 1976 conversation with the early Village bohemian Kenneth R. Chamberlain, who claimed that "Greenwich Village was probably the best informed community in America on birth-control measures—condoms and diaphragms were the most popular devices."

29. Rexroth, *An Autobiographical Novel*, 137; Roger A. Bruns, *The Damndest Radical: The Life and World of Ben Reitman, Chicago's Celebrated Social Reformer, Hobo King, and Whorehouse Physician* (Urbana: University of Illinois Press, 1987), 230–45; Report on 606 Cabaret, 606 North Clark Street, December 7, 1923, folder 92, JPAP; Report on saloon, 606 N. Clark Street, December 5, 1922, folder 93, JPAP; Benjamin Blinstrub, Follow-up Work on Mr. Kinsie's Investigation, December 24, 1923, 3, folder 96, JPAP; H. K. [Harry Kahan], Report on Greenwich Village tearooms, September 23, 1919, sixth 1919 investigative reports folder, box 34, C14P; and P. J. M. [Peter J. Mallon], Report on Golden Eagle, 135 McDougal [*sic*] St., April 11, 1919, 8:10 p.m., seventh 1919 investigative reports folder, box 34, C14P. In another report, this investigator likewise notes that after a waiter at Gonfarone's told him that he "may be able to pick up a woman at the Black Cat," another warned that "the Greenwich Village girls did not go there, telling me that they all had their own sweethearts" (idem, report on Gonfarone's, 179 MacDougal St., April 11, 1919, 6:30 to 8 p.m., seventh 1919 investigative reports folder, box 34, C14P). Similarly, James A. Seaman remarked that a "number of Broadway prostitutes in civilian clothes" could usually be found at the Webster Hall masquerade balls. "They have been noticeable at the last few dances in increasing numbers. These dances are comi[n]g so often and the girls are appearing so often at them that it looks as if they were finding it a lucrative place to get men" (J. A. S. [James A. Seaman], Report on Greenwich Village Ball, "Silver Ball" by Bobby Brown and his well known woman, December 21, 1917, second 1918 [*sic*] investigative reports folder, box 33, C14P).

30. Frederick H. Whitin, General Secretary, Committee of Fourteen, to Dr. James A. Seaman, New York, February 17, 1919, second 1919 correspondence folder, box 4, C14P; Document 22, quoted in Zorbaugh, *The Gold Coast and the Slum*, 99; M. B. [Maxwell Bodenheim], "Peeping Tom in Verbal Dressing Rooms of Bohemia," 2; and J. A. S. [James A. Seaman], Report of Investigator, The Liberal Club Ball, Webster Hall, 8th [*sic*] St., February 11, 1917, "Special Inspections" folder, box 31, C14P.

31. Document 26, quoted in Zorbaugh, *The Gold Coast and the Slum*, 117; and Graham, *New York Nights*, 277. The prevalence of well-to-do women frequenting the Village and Towertown led bohemian writer Maxwell Bodenheim to incorporate this topic in his 1925 novel, *Replenishing Jessica* (New York: Boni

and Liveright, 1925). Longing for the sexual satisfaction which her philandering husband was no longer providing her, the title character "drove down to a tea room in the 'bohemian' section" of New York while her husband was in Chicago, "and coolly selected the most handsome and sprightly tongued, unattended man in the place, and spent the night at his studio, and felt hilariously relieved afterwards. He had been a slender, Italian youth, with a loosely dissipated, long-nosed face, and graceful manner . . . ." (233–34).

32. Dorothy Day, *The Eleventh Virgin* (New York: A. Boni & Company, 1924), 167, quoted in Humphrey, *Children of Fantasy*, 243; J. A. S. [James A. Seaman], Report of Investigator, The Liberal Club Ball, Webster Hall, 8th [*sic*] St., February 11, 1917, "Special Inspections" folder, box 31, C14P.

33. Yvonne ("Eve") Blue, Diary, November 8, 1926, December 6, 1931, and December 23, 1931, YBSP; and Rexroth, *An Autobiographical Novel*, 302–3. Among the six men Blue kissed and petted on that fateful night in December 1931 was John Drury, the "author of that tremendously popular book *Dining in Chicago*," as Blue gleefully noted (Diary, December 23, 1931, YBSP). For another example of Blue's earlier, less explicitly sexual fascination with bohemia, see her diary entry for March 26, 1927, in which she records her excitement at learning about the existence of "queer Bohemian restaurants in the immediate vicinity" of a family friend's Near North Side home. "Sometime," she confided enthusiastically, "we are going to some of them." (Blue, Diary, March 27, 1927, YBSP.)

34. Fass, *The Damned and the Beautiful*, 294; and "Greenwich Village Affairs," Resume of reports on cabarets, 1917, 16, "Inv. Reports on Cabarets" folder, box 31, C14P. For more on young women's adoption of the symbols and trappings of bohemian fashion and social practices during the 1920s, see Fass, *The Damned and the Beautiful*, esp. 291–326; and Modell, *Into One's Own*, esp. 67–120.

35. "Wind Blew Inn Burns," *CDN*, April 22, 1922, 1; "Wind Blew Inn Burns," *Chicago Examiner*, April 22, 1922, in the "Restaurant and Taverns" clipping file, CHM; and Report of Miss Florence L. Rose, New York City, June 19, 1919, box 34, C14P. A report on the Liberal Club Ball noted similar behavior at Village masquerades: "Later in the morning there were many hugging and kissing parties going on up in the balcony" (J. A. S. [James A. Seaman], Report of Investigator, The Liberal Club Ball, Webster Hall, 8th [*sic*] St., February 11, 1917, "Special Inspections" folder, box 31, C14P).

36. "Village Defended in New Manifesto," *NYT*, June 8, 1921, 20.

37. "Collins Faces Test of Power to Curb Cafes," clipping from unnamed newspaper, July 24, 1923, scrapbook vol. 22, WEDP; and "Collins Sorry for 'Innocent' in 'Tent' Raid," clipping from unnamed and undated newspaper [July 1923], scrapbook vol. 22, WEDP.

38. Dr. I. L. Nascher to Frederick H. Whitin, General Secretary, Committee of Fourteen, New York, March 16, 1919, first 1919 correspondence folder, box 4, C14P; Dr. I. L. Nascher, to Frederick H. Whitin, General Secretary, Com-

mittee of Fourteen, New York, March 10, 1918, first 1918 correspondence folder, box 4, C14P; I. L. Nascher, "Esthesiomania: A Study of Some of the Queer Folks in New York's Latin Quarter," *Medical Times* 47 (February 1919): 34–40; Helen Bullitt Lowry, "Medical Diagnosis of the True Greenwich Villager," *NYT Magazine*, December 21, 1919, 8; and Charles J. Rosebault, "The Rumpus in Greenwich Village," *NYT Book Review and Magazine*, June 12, 1921, 6.

39. Bailey, *From Front Porch to Back Seat*, 3. My understanding of the development of dating relies heavily on Bailey's history of American courtship.

40. Phyllis Blanchard and Carlyn Manasses, *New Girls for Old* (1930; repr., New York: The Macaulay Company, 1937), 69–71. Other studies reaching similar conclusions include: Ira S. Wile, "Introduction," in Ira S. Wile, ed., *The Sex Life of the Unmarried Adult: An Inquiry into and an Interpretation of Current Sex Practices* (1934; repr., Garden City, NY: Garden City Publishing Company, 1946); Winifred Richmond, *The Adolescent Boy* (New York: Farrar and Rinehart, 1933); and R. H. Edward, J. M. Artman, and Galen M. Fisher, *Undergraduates* (Garden City, NY: Doubleday, Doran, 1928). See also Fass, *The Damned and the Beautiful*, 260–90; Bailey, *From Front Porch to Back Seat*, 77–96; and Modell, *Into One's Own*, 97–105.

41. Blue, Diary, March 21, 1932, YBSP.

42. "The Greenwich Village Dances at Webster Hall," Resume of Cabaret Situation, 1917, 12, "Inv. Reports of Cabarets" folder, box 31, C14P; J. A. S. [James A. Seaman], Report of Investigator, The Saraband of Apes and Ivory, Renee La Coste Webster Hall Dance, March 23, 1917, "Special Inspections" folder, box 31, C14P; and "Greenwich Village Affairs," Resume of reports on cabarets, 1917, 16, "Inv. Reports on Cabarets" folder, box 31, C14P. The continuing importance of gender in structuring sexual normativity can also be found in the comments of those who were well aware of the medical and psychological distinctions that experts were beginning to make between heterosexuality and homosexuality. When the author of many of the above reports, James A. Seaman, a medical student moonlighting as an investigator for the Committee of Fourteen, ran into some college friends at a Webster Hall ball, he invoked the hetero/homo sexual dichotomy by noting that one of his acquaintances "spent much time with a couple of the above mentioned 'Homos.'" But in trying to determine whether his friend was likewise homosexual, Seaman resorted—like most people of his day—to an examination of the man's gender performance, remarking that he was "a rather effeminate type but whether he is one of their kind I do not know for sure; however he seemed to be. He seemed more effeminate than when he was in college" (J. A. S. [James A. Seaman], Report of Investigator, The Liberal Club Ball, Webster Hall, 8th [sic] St., February 11, 1917, "Special Inspections" folder, box 31, C14P).

43. J. A. S. [James A. Seaman], Report of Investigator, The Saraband of Apes and Ivory, Renee La Coste Webster Hall Dance, March 23, 1917, "Special

Inspections" folder, box 31, C14P; "The Greenwich Village Dances at Webster Hall," Resume of Cabaret Situation, 1917, 12, "Inv. Reports of Cabarets" folder, box 31, C14P; and Report on the Black Cat Ball at Webster Hall, March 15, [1918], quoted in Frederick H. Whitin, General Secretary, Committee of Fourteen, to John F. Gilchrist, Commissioner, Department of Licenses, New York City, n.d., first 1918 correspondence folder, box 4, C14P. On the probable effect that World War I campaigns against venereal disease had in steering men who were searching for illicit sex away from female prostitutes and toward fairies, see Chauncey, *Gay New York*, 143–44; Frederick H. Whitin, "Sexual Perversion Cases in New York City Courts, 1916–1921," bulletin #1480, November 12, 1921, bulletin book 13, box 88, C14P; Frederick H. Whitin, General Secretary, Committee of Fourteen, to Miss Eddingsfield, The Commonwealth Fund, New York, January 18, 1922, first 1922 correspondence folder, box 5, C14P; and idem, to Whitcomb H. Allen, February 8, 1926, "A, 1916–26" correspondence folder, box 9, C14P.

44. Nels Anderson, "Document 120: Young Man, Twenty-two, Well Dressed, Homosexual Prostitute, Loafs in Grant Park (W. B. P.)," unpublished field notes, n.d., folder 2, box 127, EWBP (when Anderson refers to "the art gallery," he probably means the Art Institute of Chicago); and copy of the transcript of The People of the State of New York, on the complaint of Edgar X. Frost, Police Officer, *v.* Leon Mirabeau, Charge: Vis. Code of Crim. Proc. Sec. 887 Subd. 4–3, City Magistrates Court, Second District of Manhattan, City of New York, Before: Hon. Jean H. Norris, City Magistrate, June 27, 1924, box 62, C14P. The male prostitute involved in this case "plead guilty to an act of degeneracy," and the tearoom's manager Leon Mirabeau, who had earlier been convicted (in 1916) for vagrancy and indecency, was sentenced to six months in the workhouse. On appeal before the Court of Special Sessions of the City of New York, however, Mirabeau's conviction was overturned, because the presiding judge in the original case committed a "reversible error" in mentioning "a plea of guilty of a defendant in another case involving certain facts and circumstances connected with the alleged illegal use of a part of the premises in the case at bar," namely that of the male prostitute arrested in Mirabeau's tearoom, without allowing the latter man to cross-examine the former (see copy of the transcript of #60–N.Y.1924, Court of Special Sessions of the City of New York, Appellate Part—First Judicial Department, Memorandum of Decision in The People of the State of New York, Respondent, against Leon Mirabeau, Defendant-Appellant, October 17, 1924, box 62, C14P).

45. White, ed., *Sherwood Anderson's Memoirs*, 357; "Where to Go," *The New Majority*, November 18, 1919, 16; placard advertising a Dill Pickle Club lecture by Betty, Lizzie, Znubia and Nancy entitled, "Men Who Have Approached Us," folder 35, box II, DPCP; placard advertising the Dill Pickle Club's "Sensational Discussion, 'How Should Women Treat Men?' By a Medley

of Bohemia's Noted Man-Killers," folder 36, box II, DPCP; Slim Brundage, "Step High, Stoop Low; And Leave Your Dignity Outside," *Panorama*, the weekly magazine of the *Chicago Daily News*, February 29, 1964, 5; Frederick H. Whitin, General Secretary, Committee of Fourteen, to Mrs. Henry Moskowitz, New York City, February 17, 1919, first 1919 correspondence folder, box 4, C14P; "Greenwich Village Affairs," Resume of reports on cabarets, 1917, 16, "Inv. Reports on Cabarets" folder, box 31, C14P; and J[ames] A. Seaman to Frederick H. Whitin, General Secretary, Committee of Fourteen, New York City, February 14, 1919, second 1919 correspondence folder, box 4, C14P. A 1918 letter to *The Quill* confirms that balls organized by Village bohemians became increasingly frequent events, a development which not all area residents found desirable: "Once upon a time there were two or three dances at Webster Hall during the season," a man calling himself Horace Longhair wrote to *The Quill*'s Bobby Edwards. "I dropped in there not long ago and in the manager's office A. Moss [editor of *The Quill*] and six other dance magnates were haggling over dates while their chauffeurs waited for them" (Horace Longhair, undated letter to the editor, published in "Bobby Edwards' Column," *The Quill*, March 1918, 21). See also Sherwood Anderson, "Jack Jones—'The Pickler,'" *CDN*, June 18, 1919, 12; and Slim Brundage, quoted in Lee Sustar, "When Speech Was Free (And Usually Worth It)," *The Reader* (Chicago), October 21, 1983, sec. 1, 20; and Bruns, *The Damndest Radical*, 230–45.

46. Zorbaugh, *The Gold Coast and the Slum*, 101; Ramirez, "The Tourist Trade Takes Hold," 378; "Two Pictures of the Rise and Fall of Bohemianism," unpublished student paper, 7–8, folder 1, box 161, EWBP; and "Village Raid Nets 4 Women and 9 Men," *NYT*, February 5, 1923, 17. The last article notes that Smith and Rogers were pseudonyms used by Vera Black and Nan Paddock, respectively. "Ruby" was revealed to be "Harry Bernhammer, 21 years old, living at 36 Hackensack Avenue, West Hoboken, N. J." Also among the individuals arrested was Arthur C. Budd, a twenty-one-year-old New York City resident, who was employed as a female impersonator in the Broadway show, *The Lady in Ermine*. Budd, who was not attired in women's clothing on this particular evening, also performed in Village cabarets under the stage name "Rosebud" (ibid). The following day, the *New York Times* noted that a local magistrate dismissed charges against all but the proprietors of the Black Parrot and revealed that the tearoom's coproprietor Patricia Rogers hailed from Chicago ("Board Ship to Get Big Liquor Agent," *NYT*, February 6, 1923, 23). *Variety* also covered this raid in its "Cabaret" column, but it noted the arrests of only the nine men, including one who "was found to be togged up in complete female attire at the station house." Contradicting the *Times* account, *Variety* reported that the man in drag "answered to the name of 'Rosebud'" and "claimed to be in the chorus of 'The Lady in Ermine' at the Century, which was verified

by the police, and it cost the chorister his job" ("Cabaret" column, *Variety*, February 15, 1923, 30).

47. J[ames] A. Seaman to Frederick H. Whitin, General Secretary, Committee of Fourteen, New York City, February 14, 1919, second 1919 correspondence folder, box 4, C14P; and "Bobby Edward's Column," *The Quill*, September 1, 1917, 13.

48. William Targ, *Indecent Pleasures: The Life and Colorful Times of William Targ* (New York: Macmillan Publishing Co., Inc., 1975), 37–38; Kemp, *More Miles*, 363; and Blue, Diary, December 6, 1931, YBSP.

49. Ben L. Reitman, "The Joys and Hazards of Sex," unpublished manuscript, n.d., 28–29, supplement IV, folder 33, BLRP; Dell, *Homecoming*, 288; Harold Stearns, *The Street I Know* (New York: Lee Furman, Inc., 1935), 127; and Humphrey, *Children of Fantasy*, 247–48. Reitman's description of "Peter Pan" closely resembles the similarly named Timothy "Tiny Tim" Felter, a Village personality who traveled from one bohemian tearoom to another, selling "soul candies" and entertaining patrons. For more on "Tiny Tim," see Ramirez, "The Tourist Trade Takes Hold," 383; and the photo essay by Rick Beard and Jan Seidler Ramirez, "'Greenwich Thrillage': Village Commerce," in Beard and Berlowitz, eds., *Greenwich Village*, 338.

50. Ogden, Investigator Report, Webster Hall, 119 E. 11th St., near Third Ave., March 6, 1917, 11 p.m., "Broadway–East Houston; E. 3rd–E. 84th; Second–Seventh" folder, box 32, C14P; and H. K. [Harry Kahan], Report on Zinas Restaurant, 144 Macdugall [*sic*] Street, September 28, 1919, seventh 1919 investigative reports folder, box 34, C14P.

51. Charles Hanson Towne, *This New York of Mine* (New York: Cosmopolitan Book Corporation, 1931), 267; and Putnam, *Paris Was Our Mistress,* 19–20. Although this particular quote from *Paris Was Our Mistress* refers specifically to changes in Greenwich Village, Putnam recounted the demise of Chicago's literary bohemia in a similar fashion (41). Similar disdain for the commercialization of bohemia can be found in Floyd Dell, *Love in Greenwich Village* (New York: George H. Doran Company, 1926), 296; and Max Ewing to Edgar H. Ailes, Somewhere East of Syracuse, New York, December 9, 1924, letter #23, "Letters to Edgar H. Ailes, 1–25" folder, box 5, MEP.

52. A. H. M. [Arthur H. Moss], editorial, *The Quill*, April 1918, 4; and May Swenson, Report on her December 1938 interview with Harry Kemp, Tramp Poet, New York City, January 11, 1939, 38, New York Folklore project, Federal Writers' Project, Library of Congress, transcript accessed online through the Library of Congress's American Life Histories: Manuscripts from the Federal Writers' Project, 1936–1940 Web site, http://memory.loc.gov/ammem/wpainto/wpahome.html; accessed April 26, 1999. The owners of Towertown's Green Mask also had an aversion to slummers. "No rubberneck buses unloaded at the door," Kenneth Rexroth noted in *An Autobiographical Novel*. "June [Wiener] simply refused to seat tourists, and if they got past her she had such a devastating way with her that they quickly left" (168).

53. "Artists Ban 'Glanders,'" clipping from unnamed newspaper, folder 20, box 1, DPCP. It is not clear how many men of the era actually participated in the "monkey gland" craze—which involved the transplantation or surgical grafting of slices of monkey or ape testicles onto those of impotent men— but it was certainly a hot topic of discussion at the Dill Pickle Club and in the popular press. The operation was pioneered in 1920 by Serge Voronoff, a French surgeon of Russian heritage, at the Collège de France in Paris (see Serge Voronoff, *Life: A Study of the Means of Restoring Vital Energy and Prolonging Life*, trans. Evelyn Bostwick Voronoff [New York: Dutton, 1920]; idem, *Rejuvenation by Grafting*, ed. and trans. Fred F. Imianitoff [New York: Adelphi, 1925]; placard advertising Henry J. Shireson, MD's Dill Pickle Club lecture and presentation of "the Famous Sex Gland Film 'Rejuvenation Increasing Human Efficiency,'" folder 34, box 2, DPCP; placard advertising Dr. Thomas F. Gallagher's Dill Pickle Club lecture entitled, "The Male Sex Hormone," folder 34, box 2, DPCP; "Monkey Gland Pioneer Heard Here in April," *New York American*, January 30, 1931, 18; Dr. Max Thorek, "Monkey Glands," *Variety*, December 31, 1920, 15; "Famous Dr. Voronoff Latest Broadcasting; Monkey Gland Pioneer Heard Here in April," *New York American*, January 30, 1931, 18; Wainwright Evans, "Rejuvenation: The monkey gland legend gives way to the Steinach method of reactivating the aging human," *Esquire*, December 1935, 44+; and Kate Summerscale, *The Queen of Whale Cay: The Eccentric Story of "Joe" Carstairs, Fastest Woman on Water* [1997; repr., New York: Viking, 1998], 35–44).

54. H. K. [Harry Kahan], Report on 28 Sixth Avenue, September 27, 1920, fourth 1920 investigative reports folder, box 34, C14P; Howard G. Grey to Morgan A. Collins, Superintendent of Police, Chicago, October 2, 1923, folder 24, WEDP; and Morgan A. Collins, Superintendent of Police, to William E. Dever, Mayor, Chicago, October 4, 1923, folder 24, WEDP. See also John F. Stacey to William E. Dever, Chicago, October 1, 1923, folder 24, WEDP.

55. On nativism, see Higham, *Strangers in the Land*. On bohemians' interactions with southern and eastern European immigrants in Greenwich Village and Towertown, see Parry, *Garrets and Pretenders,* esp. 200–8, 269–80; Fishbein, *Rebels in Bohemia*, 168–73, 223–26; Rexroth, *An Autobiographical Novel*, esp. 129–34, 161–71, 260–61; and Putnam, *Paris Was Our Mistress*, 43–45.

56. Steven Watson, *The Harlem Renaissance: Hub of African-American Culture, 1920–1930* (New York: Pantheon Books, 1995), 35–38, 90–91; Max Eastman, *Love and Revolution: My Journey Through an Epoch* (New York: Farrar, Straus & Cudahy, 1964), 222; Claude McKay, *A Long Way from Home* (New York: L. Furman, Inc., 1937), esp. 96–105, 116–33; and Tyrone Tillery, *Claude McKay: A Black Poet's Struggle for Identity* (Amherst: University of Massachusetts Press, 1992), 48–49, 82–83. A fictionalized Richard Bruce Nugent (as Paul Arbian) can also be found flitting from Harlem to the Village in Wallace Thurman's *Infants of the Spring* (New York: The Macaulay Company, 1932).

57. Rexroth, *An Autobiographical Novel*, 165–67; "Bishop Fallows Rakes K.K.K. Before Dill Pickle Club," *CT*, September 5, 1921, 13; and Harry Haywood, *Black Bolshevik: Autobiography of an Afro-American Communist* (Chicago: Liberator Press, 1978), 115, 129. See also Nels Anderson, "Document 120," in which Anderson, while doing fieldwork for his landmark study on hobos, observes a white male prostitute trying to pick up "a fine-looking Negro" at Towertown's Grey Cottage.

58. Edna Dexter Fine, quoted in Parry, *Garrets and Pretenders*, 204–5; and Rexroth, *An Autobiographical Novel*, 269–71, 210–12.

59. On the Arabic influence on North Clark Street, see Rexroth, *An Autobiographical Novel*, 176. On the Sioux T. Room, see H. K. [Harry Kahan], Report on Greenwich Village tearooms, September 16, 1919, 1, sixth 1919 investigative reports folder, box 34, C14P. The Russian character of the Band Box is covered in H. K. [Harry Kahan], Report on Greenwich Village tearooms, September 23, 1919, 1, sixth 1919 investigative reports folder, box 34, C14P. Sonia the Cigarette Girl's masquerade is addressed in H. K. [Harry Kahan], Report on Zinas Restaurant, 144 Macdugall [*sic*] Street, September 28, 1919, seventh 1919 investigative reports folder, box 34, C14P; and Ramirez, "The Tourist Trade Takes Hold," 389. In the former source, the Russian owner of Zina's Restaurant unmasks her counterfeit competitor, Sonia, to the Committee of Fourteen's Russian-speaking undercover investigator, Harry Kahan. On the increasingly exaggerated performance of "Romany Marie," see Parry, *Garrets and Pretenders*, 306 (quoted in text); Maxwell Bodenheim, *My Life and Loves in Greenwich Village* (New York: Bridgehead Books, 1954), 12–13; Ramirez, "The Tourist Trade Takes Hold," 384; and Robert Schulman, *Romany Marie: The Queen of Greenwich Village* (Louisville, KY: Butler Books, 2006), 17, 63–65.

60. "Justice Assails Greenwich Village," *NYT*, September 14, 1919, sec. II, 1. The *New York Times* engaged in a similar—albeit, more positive—racialization of bohemia even before the war had ended. Coming to the defense of a population they referred to as "another maltreated nationality" in the spring of 1918, the newspaper's editors compared a series of police raids on Village nightspots to the "general obliteration of small nations which German armies are carrying out" ("Another Maltreated Nationality," editorial, *NYT*, March 5, 1918, 10). In late 1923, Ben Hecht, editor of the *Chicago Literary Times*, turned the tables on such representations of bohemians by publishing a humorous attack on hundred-percenters in his Towertown newspaper ("The 100%er," *Chicago Literary Times*, vol. 1, no. 20 [December 1923], 1, 6).

61. M. B. [Maxwell Bodenheim], "Poet Faces New Crises in Diary," *Chicago Literary Times*, January 1, 1924, 2; Rexroth, *An Autobiographical Novel*, 161–64, 260, 277; Gail Borden, "Ahead of the Times," *Chicago Daily Times*, November 28, 1934, 12; "Mr. Quill's Guide," *The Quill*, March 1925, 28; "'Eve's Tea Room' Boss Ran into Policewoman," *Variety*, June 23, 1926, 35;

Chauncey, *Gay New York*, 240–41; and Ruth Shoule, Case study of Natalie Feinberg, born 1901, U.S.A., father and mother born in Russia, Orthodox Jews, as adapted by and quoted in Reckless, "The Natural History of Vice Areas in Chicago," 374–75. For Eva Kotchever/Eve Addams, the name change served a double purpose. It not only helped to obscure her immigrant status but, through its gender wordplay, also served to dramatize the mannish proprietor's lesbianism. Addams is unveiled as Eve Czlotcheber, a "woman . . . born in Poland," in the *New York Times* coverage of her 1926 arrest ("Sentenced for Giving Book," *NYT*, July 3, 1926, 13). However, she is most often referred to as Eva Kotchever in present-day sources, owing to George Chauncey's reinstatement of her name in lesbian and gay history. Chauncey appears to have found the name Eva Kotchever in the record books of the Society for the Suppression of Vice (Chauncey, *Gay New York*, 432n40).

62. "When the Village Robs the Cradle," *NYT Magazine*, February 18, 1923, 6; H. K. [Harry Kahan], Report on Greenwich Village tearooms, September 23, 1919, sixth 1919 investigative reports folder, box 34, C14P; and Graham, *New York Nights*, 271–78.

63. "When the Village Robs the Cradle," *NYT Magazine*, February 18, 1923, 6; and advertisement for the Dil-Pickle [*sic*] Club, noting the presence of "Big Babe's Congo Beauts," *The Daily Maroon*, October 8, 1929, 4.

CHAPTER 5

1. Eddie Barefield, quoted in Jeff Kisseloff, *You Must Remember This: An Oral History of Manhattan From the 1890s to World War II* (New York: Harcourt Brace Jovanovich, 1989), 325; and Wallace Thurman, *Negro Life in New York's Harlem: A Lively Picture of a Popular and Interesting Section*, Little Blue Book No. 494 (Girard, KS: Haldeman-Julius Publications, n.d.), 24.

2. On the black-and-tan slumming craze in Philadelphia, see H. K. [Harry Kahan], Report on Investigation Made in Philadelphia, PA on July 26, 27 and 28, 1923, enclosed with Frederick H. Whitin, General Secretary, Committee of Fourteen, to Karl de Schweinitz, Secretary, Philadelphia Society for Organizing Charity, New York, August 1, 1923, third "P" correspondence folder, box 12, C14P; and "Briefs," in "Amusements" column, *TLAHJ*, February 26, 1927, 21. For examples of the same vogue in Pittsburgh, see "'Little Paris' Must Not Mix Clientele," *NYAN*, March 10, 1926, 1. On Detroit, see "Police Close Detroit Cabarets," *BAA*, May 29, 1926, 7. Examples of black-and-tan venues in Cleveland can be found in Katrina Hazzard-Gordon, *Jookin': The Rise of Social Dance Formations in African-American Culture* (Philadelphia: Temple University Press, 1990). The popularity of black-and-tan nightlife in Atlantic City is noted in "Atlantic City Orgies Rival Babylon," *CW*, September 16, 1922, 3; "Hold Rich Man in Murder of Cabaret Queen," *CW*,

December 16, 1922; and "Black and Tans," *BAA*, August 22, 1925, 5. For similar examples in Baltimore, see Ralph Matthews, "Reporter Finds Gay Spots In Baltimore Night Life," *BAA*, December 26, 1925, 16. On Los Angeles, see "Black And Tan Road House Raided In Los Angeles," *BAA*, October 9, 1926, 19; "Mixed Cabaret Now for Whites," *TLAHJ*, January 15, 1927, 25; "Stop 'Humming Bird' Hum," in "Amusements" column, *TLAHJ*, June 4, 1927, 20; and "Ebony Club, L.A." review, *Variety*, July 18, 1933, 64, 74.

3. "The Rambler," *TLAHJ*, April 14, 1928, 8.

4. Ibid.

5. Howard "Stretch" Johnson, quoted in Kisseloff, *You Must Remember This*, 309.

6. In its *Annual Report for 1926*, New York's Committee of Fourteen noted, "White people are beginning to discover this section [Harlem], moved by the witnessing of plays such as 'Miss Lulu Belle,' and the influence of novels such as 'Nigger Heaven'" (Committee of Fourteen, *Annual Report for 1926*, in "Committee Minutes, October 1925–December 1929" notebook, box 86, C14P; see also Treasurer, Committee of Fourteen, to William F. Fuerst, Secretary, The New York Foundation, New York, October 28, 1927, second 1927 correspondence folder, box 6, C14P). Although the white invasion of Harlem and Bronzeville was well underway before the publication of Van Vechten's *Nigger Heaven*, the novel's extraordinary popularity among white readers, as demonstrated by several sold-out printings of the book, clearly spurred an increased interest in black nightlife. On novels and film featuring black-and-tan nightspots, see Carl Van Vechten, *Nigger Heaven* (New York: Alfred A. Knopf, 1926); Claude McKay, *Home to Harlem* (New York: Harper, 1928); Rudolph Fisher, *The Walls of Jericho* (New York: Alfred A. Knopf, 1928); Nella Larsen, *Passing* (New York: Alfred A. Knopf, 1929); Thurman, *Infants of the Spring*; Thomas Beer, *The Road to Heaven: A Romance of Morals* (New York: Alfred A. Knopf, 1928); Katherine Brush, *Young Man of Manhattan* (New York: Farrar & Rinehart, 1930); and Lee Israel, *Miss Tallulah Bankhead* (New York: G. P. Putnam's Sons, 1972).

7. Clarence Williams, quoted in Marshall Stearns, *The Story of Jazz* (1956; repr., New York: Oxford University Press, 1979), 168; Van Vechten, Diary, August 18, 1925, April 20, April 29, May 12, June 9, September 23, November 27 & December 6, 1926, and May 4, 1929, box 111, CVVP; Rexroth, *An Autobiographical Novel*, 302; and Mezz Mezzrow, *Really the Blues* (1946; repr., London: Flamingo, 1993), 118–20.

8. Bruce A. Linton, "A History of Chicago Radio Station Programming, 1921–1931, with Emphasis on Stations WMAQ and WGN" (PhD diss., Northwestern University, 1953), 29, 99; and Haskins, *The Cotton Club*, 55–57.

9. Document XXIX, "'Cabareting—First Glimpses,' written by a girl, college student, middle class family from small town," quoted in Reckless, "The

Natural History of Vice Areas in Chicago," 275; and Blue, Diary, May 24, 1932, YBSP.

10. Drury, *Dining in Chicago,* 251; and Graham, *New York Nights,* 242–43. Similar arguments that have informed my thinking on this topic have been advanced by Huggins, *Harlem Renaissance;* Lewis, *When Harlem Was in Vogue;* Douglas, *Terrible Honesty;* and Mumford, *Interzones.* For more on the crisis instigated by transformations in middle-class work, see T. J. Jackson Lears, *No Place of Grace: Antimodernism and the Transformation of American Culture, 1880–1920* (Chicago: University of Chicago Press, 1981); idem, "Some Versions of Fantasy: Toward a Cultural History of Advertising, 1880–1930," *Prospects* 9 (1984): 349–405; and idem, "Sherwood Anderson: Looking for the White Spot," in Richard Wightman Fox and T. J. Jackson Lears, eds., *The Power of Culture: Critical Essays in American History* (Chicago: University of Chicago Press, 1993), 13–37.

11. Dame Rogue [pseud. Louise Norton], "Philisophic Fashions," *The Rogue,* May 15, 1915, 18. On the rage for primitivism and the important role it played in early-twentieth-century art and thought, see especially Torgovnick, *Gone Primitive*; and idem, *Primitive Passions: Men, Women, and the Quest for Ecstasy* (New York: Alfred A. Knopf, 1997).

12. Document XXIX, quoted in Reckless, "The Natural History of Vice Areas in Chicago," 277.

13. Durante and Kofoed, *Night Clubs,* 113.

14. The People of the State of Illinois *v.* Julia Rector, Before the Hon. Arnold Heap, Judge, in the Municipal Court of Chicago, Morals Branch, Opinion of the Court Delivered on January 28, 1922, recorded in a pamphlet printed by the Committee of Fifteen, Chicago, in "Legal Decisions & Memoranda, 1920–24, Part 2, Subjects 9–12" folder, box 61, C14P.

15. H. K. [Harry Kahan], Report on investigation "Cooperating with Officers Kaufman and Rullman," February 24, 1922, 1922 investigative reports folder, box 34, C14P (omission in the original). An investigator for the JPA noted similar behavior at a Chicago black and tan: "Five or six of the couples went through all the suggestive motions of a regular sex act. Two or three couples were really gymnastic, going through rapid motions for a while, they would then stand perfectly still for a while, close their eyes, and show evidence of extreme satisfaction" (Daniel Russell, report on Pioneer Cabaret, #45204.27, 3532 South State Street, 11:30 p.m., December 16, 1923, folder 96, JPAP).

16. H. K. [Harry Kahan], Report on Baron Wilkins, S.E. cor. 134th Str & VII Ave., July 30, 1920, about 1.00 a.m., second 1920 investigative reports folder, box 34, C14P; and Dr. Magnus Hirschfeld, in dialogue with George Sylvester Viereck, "'Einstein of Sex' Finds Beauty Rules in Harlem," *Chicago Herald and Examiner,* February 3, 1931, 4. In 1923, a black investigator hired jointly by the New York Urban League and the Committee of Fourteen

also noted that white slummers tended to behave more wildly than black patrons at Happy Rhone's Cabaret, 143rd Street and Lenox Avenue: "The whites at Happy Rhone's are somewhat careless in their manner of dancing and some of them use vulgar language on the floor. The floor-man handles all alike however and manages to keep fairly good order" ([Mr. Fladger], Report of Investigation of Vice Conditions in Harlem, [1923], 2, Urban League correspondence folder, box 15, C14P).

17. E. J. S., Report on Diana Dance Hall, 150 E. 14th Street, May 12, 1927, "Dance Halls 1927–30" folder, box 37, C14P. In a similar incident, Investigator F for the Committee of Fourteen reported that when he asked a Bronx dance hall hostess "if she would step out for a wild time," she first said she could not talk about it right then, but "added that she would like to be taken to a negro cabaret in Harlem as she had never been to one" (Investigator F, report on Aster Dance Palace, Boston Road, West Farms, Bronx, N.Y., May 19, 1928, "Dance Halls 1927–30" folder, box 37, C14P).

18. Jacquelyn Dowd Hall expertly analyzes the ways that white Southern men used lynching and the myth of the black male sexual predator as means of controlling white Southern women. See Hall, "'The Mind That Burns in Each Body,'" 328–49. Other important studies on the complex racial, sexual and gendered dynamics of lynching include: Gail Bederman, "'Civilization,' the Decline of Middle-Class Manliness, and Ida B. Wells's Antilynching Campaign (1892–94)," *Radical History Review* 52 (Winter 1992): 5–30; MacLean, "The Leo Frank Case Reconsidered"; and Williamson, *A Rage for Order.*

19. Document XXIX, quoted in Reckless, "The Natural History of Vice Areas in Chicago," 276–78.

20. Graham, *New York Nights*, 242, 246–47, 244; report on Edmund's Theatrical Club, (called Douglas Club also), 28th St. near 7th Ave., [1916], first 1916 investigative reports folder, box 31, C14P; report on ——Gardens, ——E. —— St., February 25–26, 1922, in *Conditions in Chicago* (Chicago: Juvenile Protection Association, 1922), 10, folder 145, JPAP; and Daniel Russell, Report on Pioneer Cabaret, December 16, 1923, folder 96, JPAP.

21. The People of the State of Illinois *v.* Julia Rector, box 61, C14P, 7.

22. Investigator 7, Report on Lenox Avenue Club, 652 Lenox Avenue, September 26 (27), 1929, 4:15–5:10 a.m., "G-R" folder, box 36, C14P. "Tall, Tan and Terrific" was the logo used by the Cotton Club to advertise its chorus line of light-skinned beauties—a logo that was immortalized in Cab Calloway's 1937 recording "She's Tall, She's Tan, She's Terrific" (Watson, *The Harlem Renaissance,* 127; Haskins, *The Cotton Club,* 73; and Cab Calloway and His Orchestra, "She's Tall, She's Tan, She's Terrific," Variety 643/Vocalion 32787, 78 rpm). On white chorus lines in urban cabarets and stage revues, see especially Linda Mizejewski, *Ziegfeld Girl: Image and Icon in Culture and Cinema* (Durham, NC: Duke University Press, 1999).

23. Paul M. Kinsie, American Social Hygiene Association, New York, "Investigation Made for the Juvenile Protective Association: Vice Conditions in Chicago, December 3rd to December 11th, 1923," December 10, 1923, 4, folder 110, JPAP; and [Paul M. Kinsie], Report on Paradise Cabaret, Prairie and 35th, Chicago, Illinois, December 3, 1922, folder 93, JPAP.

24. Geo. E. Taylor, "Adams and Eves Arrested, Blame It On The Weather," *BAA*, June 13, 1925, 3; Report on Pioneer Cabaret, 3532 S. State, December 16, 1923, folder 96, JPAP; and Report on Elks Cafe (S.E. [speakeasy]), 2454 Seventh Avenue, May and July 1928, included in the compilation report of Night Clubs and Speakeasies Located on Avenues and Named Streets, 1929, 112, "Speakeasies and Nightclubs" folder, box 37, C14P. See also R. A. C. [Raymond A. Claymes], Report on Elks Cafe, 2454 7th Av., May 18, 1928, 1:45 to 2:30 a.m., "Sa-Su" folder, box 36, C14P.

25. Report on —— Gardens, —— E. —— St., February 25–26, 1922, in *Conditions in Chicago*, 9–10, folder 145, JPAP; J. A. Rogers, *Sex and Race: A History of White, Negro, and Indian Miscegenation in the Two Americas, Volume II: The New World* (New York: Helga M. Rogers, 1942), 291; Investigator 25, Report H-10, 1241 N. Clark St. 2d floor (1 up), front south, May 8 (May 9), 1933, 1, folder 97, JPAP; and Investigator 25, Report H-9, 650 E. 33d Street, May 8, 1933, 2, folder 97, JPAP.

26. James Craig Gordon, "A White Man's View of America's Negro Problem," *New York Graphic*, repr. in *TLAHJ*, January 15, 1927, 11; Report on Schiller Cafe, December 3, 1922, folder 93, JPAP; and Report on —— Gardens, —— E. —— St., Chicago, February 25–26, 1922, in *Conditions in Chicago*, 9–10, folder 135, JPAP. See also Wm. J. Mabin, "God's Stepchildren," *People* (London), March 15, 1931, newspaper clipping, scrapbook 24, CVVP; and Rogers, *Sex and Race*, 290.

27. Walter Winchell, quoted in Bennie Butler, "Walter Winchell Gets 'On Harlem,'" *IST*, August 3, 1929, 9. Responding to Winchell, Butler pointed out the racial bias of his comments: "Well, whose business is it, anyway, Mr. Winchell if these 'gorgeous looking white girls unashamedly neck with dapper sepias'? Why should they be ashamed? And to the majority of Sepia Sheiks, 'the coarse and tough types' do not appeal. I hold and I believe that the Constitution supports my claim, that every citizen has the inalienable rights to life and to the pursuits of happiness. . . . And how about the Ofay Papas who seek the company of Ebony Mamas, Mr. Winchell? Why not write of this as well as the Sepia Papas and the Gorgeous White Girls? But that's never worried many white men's conscience. Black women have always been legitimate sex prey. Up to thirty years ago, they were victims of impending violence if they did not give of their bodies. Today, many of them have to give in order to earn a decent living" (ibid.).

28. Bricktop, with Haskins, *Bricktop*, 59.

29. Rogers, *Sex and Race*, 293, 294; "Personal Experiences of a Well-Known Negro," reproduced in ibid., 305 (omission in the original); Rogers, *Sex and*

Race, 295; Report on the Green Leaf Melody Club, a Night Club—White and Colored, 108 West 129th Street, Upstoop, included in the compilation report of Night Clubs and Speakeasies Located on Numbered Avenues and Streets, 1929, 68, "Speakeasies and Nightclubs" folder, box 37, C14P; and R. A. C. [Raymond A. Claymes], Report on Green Leaf Melody Club, Inc., 108 W. 129th St., June 14 & 15, 1928, 2 to 4 a.m. and 11:30 to 1 a.m., "117–134 St." folder, box 36, C14P.

30. Frederick H. Whitin, Secretary, Committee of Fourteen, to Ernest Boas, Esq., Mt. Sinai Hospital, New York, August 30, 1915, "1915 Jan–Dec" correspondence folder, box 3, C14P; and Roi Ottley, "This Hectic Harlem," NYAN, November 8, 1933, 9. On a similar Los Angeles "Gigolo House" run by "an enterprising colored woman," who provided her women clients with "representatives of various races and 'types,' all of whom had 'IT,'" see "Wealthy Women Rent Lovers to Ease Loneliness," TLAHJ, December 24, 1927, 19.

31. On the sexual misuse of black female slaves, see Angela Davis, "Reflections on the Black Woman's Role in the Community of Slaves," The Black Scholar 3 (December 1971): 2–15.

32. Bertram Pollens, The Sex Criminal (New York: Macaulay Company, 1938), 60–61; and [Paul M. Kinsie], Report on Officer 1474, April 28, 1923, folder 92, JPAP. Although Pollens's book was published in the late 1930s, it was based upon studies gathered by the author, a psychologist at New York's City College, for several years preceding its publication.

33. Clement, Love for Sale, 80–86, 202–4, 208–10; Mumford, Interzones, 108–13; and Reckless, Vice in Chicago, 55.

34. "Exploiting of Vice," editorial, NYA, September 9, 1922, 4; and "Under the Lash of the Whip," editorial, CW, August 5, 1922, 8.

35. "Exploiting of Vice," editorial, NYA, September 9, 1922, 4; "Under the Lash of the Whip," editorial, CW, August 5, 1922, 8; and Thurman, Negro Life in New York's Harlem, 25–26. A similar sentiment can be found in a 1926 New York Age editorial which asserted that "most of these resorts are alien establishments foisted upon Harlem for commercial purposes only and maintained through the patronage of white pleasure seekers, weary of the white lights of Broadway" ("The Slumming Hostess," editorial, NYA, November 6, 1926, 4).

36. On the white ownership of buffet flats catering to white men, see Edgar M. Grey, "White Cabaret Keepers Conduct Dives," New York News, December 10, 1927, newspaper clipping, "Harlem Report on Conditions" folder, box 82, C14P; The Committee of Fourteen in New York City, Annual Report for 1916, 86; "Under the Lash of the Whip," editorial, CW, July 8, 1922, 8; and "Find 'Buffet Flats' Near Best Homes," CW, August 26, 1922, 1.

37. "Underworld Color Line Laid Bare,'" CW, December 2, 1922, 1. From the late 1910s through the late 1920s, Williams owned or managed

such nightspots as the Royal Gardens, located at 459 East 31st Street, De Luxe Gardens at 3508 South State, and the Dreamland Café at 3520 South State.

38. "Under the Lash of the Whip," editorial, *CW*, December 24, 1921, 8.

39. "Vice May Cause More Riots," *CW*, December 23, 1922, 1; and "Giving Harlem a Bad Name," editorial, *NYA*, July 23, 1927, 4. See also "Under the Lash of The Whip," editorial, *CW*, July 8, 1922, 8; and Bill Chase, "House Rent Parties Were an Institution," *NYA*, October 29, 1949, 30. Even some white observers asserted that white slummers were responsible for the perversion of Harlem's black nightlife. British writer Stephen Graham noted that "the Whites who go there rather than the Blacks who live there are to blame for [the sex perversion]" (*New York Nights,* 242), while Robert Sylvester's popular history of New York's 1920s nightlife insisted that "Harlem was in the business to cater to the weird whites" (*No Cover Charge: A Backward Look at the Night Clubs* [New York: Dial Press, 1956], 46).

40. Edgar M. Grey, "White Cabaret Keepers Conduct Dives," *New York News*, December 10, 1927, newspaper clipping, "Harlem Report on Conditions" folder, box 82, C14P. For indictments of black politicians, see "Underworld Color Line Laid Bare," *CW*, December 2, 1922, 1.

41. "The 'Fixers,'" editorial, *CD*, October 27, 1917; and "The Slumming Hostess," editorial, *NYA*, November 6, 1926, 4. (See also Kenney, *Chicago Jazz,* 19, 189n38; and Osofsky, *Harlem*, 185.) The *New York Age* reprinted the text of an invitation bearing "the full length picture of a [black] lady in a close fitting black gown" which was mailed to whites throughout New York, announcing: "I am in a position to carry you through Harlem as you would go slumming through Chinatown. My guides are honest and have been instructed to give the best of service, and I can give the best of references of being both capable and honest so as to give you a night or day of pleasure. Your season is not completed with thrills until you have visited Harlem through Miss ——'s representatives" ("The Slumming Hostess," editorial, *NYA*, November 6, 1926, 4). Probably responding to the same invitation, the *Pittsburgh Courier* printed a report on "Miss Anita Handy[,] editor of a new magazine in New York called 'A Guide to Harlem and Its Amusements' . . . whose plan to have hostesses under her direction conduct tours for visitors to see Harlem sights has been criticized" ("Her Idea Criticised," *Pittsburgh Courier*, November 20, 1926, clipping, scrapbook 20, CVVP).

42. "Under the Lash of the Whip," editorial, *CW*, August 5, 1922, 8. In a 1932 column, black journalist Bennie Butler similarly indicted white male slummers for soiling the virtue of both black and white women. "For a score of years and even longer," Butler claimed, "white men have been very frequent visitors of Negro cabarets in this city as in all other big centres. . . . Consequently, Negro womanhood was atrociously treated—for there is no

more vicious despoiler than the white man, even with his own women. His aberration is too well known for me to attempt to elaborate on it" ("This Harlem Urge," *IST*, March 10, 1932, 12).

43. "Theatre Goers Protest Alleged Vulgar Dancing," *NYA*, November 6, 1926, 1. See also "Find 'Buffet Flats' Near Best Homes," *CW*, August 26, 1922, 1.

44. R. A. C. [Raymond A. Claymes], Report on Sheep Club, 2166 7th Av., Basement, rear, April 10, 1928, 3 to 4:10 a.m., "Sa-Su" folder, box 36, C14P. This nightclub is also referred to as the Sheik Club in another Committee of Fourteen report (Report on Sheik Club, 2166 Seventh Avenue, April 9 and November 18, 1928, included in the compilation report of Night Clubs and Speakeasies Located on Avenues and Named Streets, 1929, 108, "Speakeasies and Nightclubs" folder, box 37, C14P).

45. Report on Schiller Cabaret, 318 East 31st Street, November 25, 1922, about 11:30 p.m., folder 93, JPAP. The director of the JPA agreed with the black woman's assessment, drawing particular attention to this incident by citing it in the JPA's petition to the Criminal Court of Cook County to convene a special grand jury in January 1923 to investigate the police protection of vice organizations throughout Chicago (see Jessie F. Binford, petition to the Criminal Court of Cook County, January term, 1923, folder 92, JPAP).

46. Roi Ottley, "This Hectic Harlem," *NYAN*, May 5, 1934, 9; and "Broken Hearted Wife" to the Committee of Fourteen, New York, March 17, 1916, fifth 1916 correspondence folder, box 3, C14P. According to the letter, the dives in question were "Doyle's saloon at 126 st & Lenox Av and also . . . the dive at the s.e. cor. 134 st & 7 Ave" (ibid.).

47. Butler, "This Harlem Urge," 12; and Roi Ottley, "This Hectic Harlem," *NYAN*, May 19, 1934, 9. An investigator for New York's Committee of Fourteen observed a similarly violent response to a black man's solicitations of a white woman in October 1915, reporting that "a white man punched a black man sitting at the next table to him" in Barron Wilkins's Astoria Café in Harlem, when the black man supposedly "insulted the white woman that was sitting with the white man" ([David Oppenheim], Report on Astoria Café [Baron (*sic*) Wilkins], 2275 7th Ave., [October 1915], 17, third 1916 [*sic*] investigative reports folder, box 31, C14P).

48. Floyd Snelson, "Cruising Reporter Remembers," *NYA*, October 29, 1949, 12. Recounting this cross-racial dance over twenty years after the fact, Snelson recalled, "She said she had never danced with a colored man before, and expressed her enjoyment—and needless to say, I was pleased and somewhat flattered—which all makes for a wholesome democratic life" (ibid.). And Snelson was not alone in suggesting that such acts of slumming could ease racial prejudice and injustice. *Inter-State Tattler* columnist Bennie Butler held out similar hopes for white female slummers. "Unlike the white man," he wrote, "the white woman invading Harlem was sympathetic and

sought to alleviate. She did not try to subdue and cruelly wound or ruth-
lessly trample underfoot those whom she came in contact with. Gradually
there came a broader understanding of the Negro. She now saw the better
side of the Aframerican, which the white man in his ignorance and arro-
gance, was totally blind to. Her sympathy and understanding was followed
by appreciation and admiration" ("This Harlem Urge," 12).

49. Condon, with Sugrue, *We Called It Music*, 100, 110–12, 122–23; Dave Peyton, "The Musical Bunch," *CD*, January 23, 1926, 6; Kenney, *Chicago Jazz*,
58, 87–116; and Bud Freeman, as told to Robert Wolf, *Crazeology: The Autobiography of a Chicago Jazzman* (Urbana: University of Illinois Press, 1989),
6, 8, 10. Kenney notes that white Chicago jazzmen George Wettling and
Francis "Muggsy" Spanier began attending South Side clubs even earlier
while still in their early teens—Wettling stopping off in the area on his way
home to Woodlawn from the Loop, and Spanier sitting outside the Pekin
Inn at the age of only eleven or twelve to hear King Oliver play his cornet
(Kenney, 102). On the friendships that developed between black and white
musicians, see especially Kenney, *Chicago Jazz*; Peretti, *The Creation of Jazz*;
and Neil Leonard, *Jazz and the White Americans* (Chicago: University of
Chicago Press, 1962).

50. Mezzrow, *Really the Blues*, 103, 48.

51. Peretti, *The Creation of Jazz*, 88. On Mezzrow's complicated relationship
with black culture and jazz musicians, see also Gayle Wald, *Crossing the
Line: Racial Passing in Twentieth-Century U.S. Literature and Culture* (Durham,
NC: Duke University Press, 2000), 53–81.

52. Art Hodes and Chadwick Hansen, eds., *Selections from the Gutter: Portraits
from the "Jazz Record"* (Berkeley: University of California Press, 1977), 18;
Mezzrow, *Really the Blues*, 115, 143–44, 159–60, 208–16; Francis "Doll"
Thomas and Howard "Stretch" Johnson, quoted separately in Kisseloff, *You
Must Remember This*, 319; Pops Foster and Tom Stoddard, *Pops Foster: The
Autobiography of a New Orleans Jazzman as Told to Tom Stoddard* (Berkeley:
University of California Press, 1971), 124; and Louis Metcalf, quoted in
Douglas, *Terrible Honesty*, 417.

53. Tom Piazza, interview with Milt Hinton, Washington, DC, January 1977,
transcript, housed at the Institute of Jazz Studies, Rutgers University–
Newark, quoted in Kenney, *Chicago Jazz*, 108. Kenney notes that several
other black musicians, including Red Saunders and Ralph E. Brown, recalled
drinking with white musicians in Bronzeville cabarets after their night's
work was finished, but they stressed that these relationships were very
casual (Kenney, *Chicago Jazz*, 111).

54. Lil Hardin Armstrong, quoted in Wayne Jones and Don DeMichael, in-
terview with Bud Freeman, November 3, 1980, untranscribed audio tape,
Chicago Jazz Archive, Music Division, Regenstein Library, University of
Chicago, quoted in Kenney, *Chicago Jazz*, 111.

55. Dempsey J. Travis, *An Autobiography of Black Jazz* (Chicago: Urban Research Institute, 1983), 66; Peretti, *The Creation of Jazz*, 188–90; Kenney, *Chicago Jazz*, 110–14; and Mezzrow, *Really the Blues*, 146, 159.

56. Travis, *An Autobiography of Black Jazz*, 68, 70; Peretti, *The Creation of Jazz*, 87, 198; and Kenney, *Chicago Jazz*, 103. Peretti quotes an interview with black clarinetist Ralph Brown which describes white musicians' theft of black jazz arrangements: "As Ralph Brown remembered, 'they didn't let us [blacks] play certain places, and [white] guys would steal, some guy would steal what someone was playing, there was some friction, but there wasn't much you could do about it.' Nevertheless, despite segregation in downtown nightclubs, Brown and other blacks resolved to 'steal some of theirs, too'" (Peretti, 198). The concept of "love and theft" is derived from Eric Lott's analysis of the similar mechanics of nineteenth-century blackface minstrelsy (see Lott, *Love and Theft*, esp. 3–12).

57. George S. Schuyler, "Phylon Profile, XXII: Carl Van Vechten," *Phylon* 11.4 (1950): 363–64. In his autobiography *The Big Sea*, Langston Hughes recalled attending numerous downtown parties, including those held in the homes of Carl Van Vechten and Fania Marinoff, Rita Romilly, Muriel Draper, Eddie Wassermann, Mr. and Mrs. Arthur Spingarn, Charlie Studin, Florine Stettheimer, V. F. Calverton, Bob Chanler, and Colin McPhee and Jane Belo (249–55). For records of scores of racially mixed parties hosted by Van Vechten and a wide variety of his friends during the 1920s and early 1930s, see also Van Vechten, Diary, box 111, CVVP; and Kellner, *Carl Van Vechten and the Irreverent Decades*, 200–2.

58. Hughes, *The Big Sea*, 251.

59. Geraldyn Dismond, "All-Americans Go To Town For Ritzy Rent Rag," *IST*, June 9, 1932, newspaper clipping, scrapbook 25, CVVP; Hughes, *The Big Sea*, 244, 249; and Max Ewing to Mr. and Mrs. J. C. Ewing, New York, April 29, 1929, letter 546, box 3, MEP.

60. See Lewis, *When Harlem Was in Vogue*, 98–103, 179, 182–88, 195; Carl Van Vechten, "The Folksongs of the American Negro," *Vanity Fair*, July 1925, 52, 92; idem, "The Black Blues," *Vanity Fair*, August 1925, 57, 86, 92; idem, "Langston Hughes: A Biographical Note," *Vanity Fair*, September 1925, 62; and idem, " 'Moanin' Wid a Sword in Ma Han,' " *Vanity Fair*, February 1926, 61, 100, 102. On some of the loans that Van Vechten engineered or made to Paul and Eslanda Robeson, Langston Hughes, and other black artists, see Carl Van Vechten to Fania Marinoff, New York, June 18, June 19 & June 29, 1925, folder 11, box 36, CVVP; and Van Vechten, Diary, May 13, 1926, December 29, 1927, and May 26, 1930, box 111, CVVP. On the involvement of New York's white society in the Scottsboro case, see Prentiss Taylor to Langston Hughes, New York, December 18, 1932, folder 12, box 9, PTP; Langston Hughes to Prentiss Taylor, Moscow, March 5, 1933, folder 13, box 9, PTP; and Watson, *The Harlem Renaissance*, 157–58.

61. *London Sunday Herald*, May 22, 1927, quoted in Watson, *The Harlem Renaissance*, 100; Max Ewing to Mr. and Mrs. J. C. Ewing, New York, May 12, 1929, letter 549, box 3, MEP; and idem, May 8, [1928], letter 479, box 3, MEP.

62. G. O. H., Report on 2728 So. Wabash, [Apt.] 213, 2nd [floor], January 5, 1921, 4:20 to 4:30 p.m., 68, volume 20, C15P; Report on Connie's Inn, 2221 Seventh Avenue (Night Club) (White & Colored), January & March 1928, included in the compilation report of Night Clubs and Speakeasies Located on Avenues and Named Streets, 1929, 110, "Speakeasies and Nightclubs" folder, box 37, C14P; and Report on 2262–Fifth, [December 13–14, 1918, 9 p.m.–2 a.m.], enclosed with a letter from an unidentified man to Mr. Whiting [*sic*], General Secretary, Committee of Fourteen, Philadelphia, December 15, 1918, seventh investigative reports folder box 32, C14P.

63. "O'fay Girls 'Turn Colored' in Order to Land Harlem Jobs," *CW*, October 10, 1931, 10. For an example of a white woman discovered by local authorities to be making false claims to blackness in an effort to disguise her relationship with a black man, see the partial transcript of a trial, involving "Defendant—Harry Johnson" and "Complainant—Eva Chilton," January 13, 1923, folder 108, JPAP.

64. [David Oppenheim], Report on The Snug Cafe, 2120 Madison Ave, SW Cor 133rd St., [October 16, 1915], 11:45 p.m., 11, third 1916 investigative reports folder, box 31, C14P. Noting that the black landlady of the boarding house where she took men for sex did not "want to let out her rooms to any white men," a black woman employed a similar tactic, telling the landlady that the white undercover investigator who accompanied her was Cuban ([David Oppenheim], report on John & Joes Cafe, 535 Lenox Ave, SW Cor 137th St., [October 30, 1915], about 11:45 [p.m.], 21–22, third 1916 investigative reports folder, box 31, C14P).

65. On blacks passing both temporarily and permanently for white, Spanish, Italian, or Jewish, see Drake and Cayton, *Black Metropolis*, 159–71; "To the You Know 'Em Editor," *CW*, March 12, 1921, 2; "'Nosey' Sees All Knows All," *CW*, December 30, 1922, 5; and idem, June 10, 1922, 5. In the last of these sources, the *Chicago Whip*'s gossip columnist, Nosey, reported the arrest of four black couples that claimed to be "Hebrew" at a "real lively place on the West Side." While the police accepted the self-identifications of all four women and three of the men, they doubted the explanation of the darkest man in the group, "saying that he was the queerest looking Hebrew that they had ever seen." "When asked further about his nationality," the columnist remarked, this man "explained that he was a Hawaiian Jew. The Hawaiian part explained features about his face and hair that had mystified the investigators. He stuck to his story and spluttered much using a dialect and got away with it" ("'Nosey' Sees All Knows All," *CW*, June 10, 1922, 5).

66. Erenberg, *Steppin' Out,* 257. My argument here is particularly indebted to Eric Lott's analysis of the dynamics of nineteenth-century minstrelsy (Lott, *Love and Theft,* esp. 67).

67. Report on Baron [*sic*] Wilkins Astoria Cafe, S.E. cor. 7 Ave. & 134, 12:30–4:15 a.m., July 31, 1914, first 1914 investigative reports folder, box 28, C14P; and "'Nosey' Sees All Knows All," *CW,* August 14, 1920, 2.

68. Agent S. B., U.S. Interdepartmental Social Hygiene Board, Corroborative Testimony by Agent, January 29–February 25, 1922, 10, folder 108, JPAP; and Report on Paradise Cabaret, December 3, 1922, 1:00 a.m., folder 93, JPAP (emphasis added).

69. G. E. Taylor, "Bartenders' Union after More Jobs," *BAA,* February 6, 1926, 3; Morris, *Wait Until Dark,* 25–36, 58–62; Kenney, *Chicago Jazz,* 150–51; and Travis, *An Autobiography of Black Jazz,* 39–49. In his 1928 report on Harlem vice conditions, the black investigator hired by the Committee of Fourteen, Raymond A. Claymes, reported that he had been informed by a "very prominent lawyer" that "approximately 80% of the open speakeasies [in Harlem] are owned by a syndicate of Italians" ([Raymond A. Claymes], "A Brief Summary of Conclusions of Vice Conditions in Harlem, Based on Personal Observations by Investigator," [unpublished, 1928], 5, "Harlem Report on Conditions" folder, box 82, C14P). On in-betweenness, see Orsi, "The Religious Boundaries of an Inbetween People"; and Barrett and Roediger, "In Between Peoples."

70. "H-A-S-H," *IST,* January 13, 1928, 8; "'Squeeze Me,'" editorial, *TLAHJ,* September 3, 1927, 5; Kenney, *Chicago Jazz,* 149; Tony Langston, "Joe Gorman Dead," *CD,* October 11, 1924, 8; Claude McKay, *Harlem: Negro Metropolis* (New York: E. P. Dutton and Company, 1940), 118; and "George Immerman Aids Many Harlem Families," *IST,* November 2, 1924, 9.

71. Lady Nicotine [Geraldyn Dismond], "Between Puffs," *IST,* January 13, 1928, 9; and Roi Ottley, "This Hectic Harlem," *NYAN,* October 4, 1933, 9.

72. Hasia R. Diner, *In the Almost Promised Land: American Jews and Blacks, 1915–1935* (Westport, CT: Greenwood Press, 1977), 65. On the passage of immigration quotas during the 1920s and their effect on Jews and Italians in the United States, see esp. Higham, *Strangers in the Land*; John Bodnar, *The Transplanted: A History of Immigrants in Urban America* (Bloomington: Indiana University Press, 1985); and Ngai, *Impossible Subjects.*

73. [Harry Kahan], Report on The Star Dancing Academy, 116 East 59th Street, January 6, 1925, 1924 [*sic*] investigative reports folder, box 35, C14P; Paul Goalby Cressey, "The Closed Dance Hall in Chicago" (MA thesis, University of Chicago, 1929), 128–29; and Paul G. Cressey, *The Taxi-Dance Hall: A Sociological Study in Commercialized Recreation and City Life* (Chicago: University of Chicago Press, 1932), 35–36. On relationships between Asian men and white women in the taxi-dance halls of Prohibition-era Chicago and New York and their public acceptance (or lack thereof), see especially

NOTES TO PAGES 224–225

Bulletin #1796 "Notes from Women's Court Bulletin," May 1923, June 6, 1923, bulletin book 15, November 1923 to January–June 1923 [*sic*], box 88, C14P; "N.Y. Daily News Wants Color Line Drawn in City," *CD*, July 7, 1923, 8; "Court Frees Girls Arrested in Raid; Dismisses Charges against Sixteen Dancers Caught in Oriental Hall," *NYT*, August 13, 1923, 15; [Daniel] Russell, Report on the Athenian, December 15, 1923, folder 103, JPAP; H. K. [Harry Kahan], Report on Happyland Dancing Academy, 88/90 Columbus Avenue, June 16, 1924, 1924 investigative reports folder, box 35, C14P; Elizabeth K. Taft, Executive Secretary, Inwood House, to the Committee of Fourteen, New York, December 16, 1924, 1924 investigative reports folder, box 35, C14P; Paul G. Cressey, Report #49531.10, Oakley Dancing Academy, May 3, July 1 & July 2, 1927, folder 103, JPAP; "30 Dance Hall Girls Freed," *NYT*, August 26, 1927, 15; "Policewomen Find Dance Halls Quiet," *NYT*, January 28, 1930, 19; "Vice Report Scores Dance Hall Evils," *NYT*, May 21, 1930, 23; Mumford, *Interzones*, 53–72; Derek Vaillant, *Sounds of Reform: Progressivism and Music in Chicago, 1873–1935* (Chapel Hill: University of North Carolina Press, 2003), 184–233; Clement, *Love for Sale*, 177–211; and Linda España-Maram, *Creating Masculinity in Los Angeles's Little Manila: Working-Class Filipinos and Popular Culture, 1920s–1950s* (New York: Columbia University Press, 2006), 105–33.

74. Cressey, "The Closed Dance Hall in Chicago," 128–29, 334–36, 355; and Cressey, *The Taxi-Dance Hall*, 35–36. Not all blacks welcomed Filipinos in their neighborhoods or looked upon Filipinos' relationships with white women as unproblematic. The *Chicago Defender* published a letter from one reader suggesting that at least some blacks thought that Filipino immigrants' initial inclination to ally themselves with downtrodden blacks in the United States evaporated when they "developed what is commonly known among Negroes as 'white fever' and began to carry on many clandestine affairs with white women." In short order, the reader noted, "the white man decided that the little islander had gone past the limit and needed a severe chastisement," but until this occurred, the Filipino found himself "enjoying social privileges that are rigidly denied the American Negro, [and] developed a superiority complex over his friend of an earlier day" (Eugene Henry Huffman to Arthur Brisbane, Los Angeles, n.d., reprinted as "Sidelights: What Some See and Others Pass Over," *CD*, April 12, 1930, 14).

75. Cressey, *The Taxi-Dance Hall*, 218–19; and *Chicago Journal*, September 8, 1928, quoted in Cressey, "The Closed Dance Hall in Chicago," 355.

76. Consolidated Detective Bureau, Report, Case-1034, March 19, 1923, 5, first 1923 correspondence folder, box 5, C14P. The white investigators of New York's Committee of Fourteen were so oblivious to the differences between native-born and West Indian blacks in Harlem that I have found only two references to West Indians among the hundreds of reports on black cabarets and buffet flats which the committee generated during the

1910s and 1920s (see Report on Panama Cafe, 2461 Seventh Ave., N.E. corner of 143rd Street, January 8, 1919, seventh 1919 investigative reports folder, box 34, C14P; and Committee of Fourteen, *Annual Report for 1928* (New York: 1929), 32, "Committee Minutes, October 1925–December 1929" folder, box 86, C14P).

77. "Things That Should Be Considered," *CD*, October 20, 1917, 12; Grossman, *Land of Hope*, 123–60; Osofsky, *Harlem*, 43–44; Drake and Cayton, *Black Metropolis*, 379–97; and Ogren, *The Jazz Revolution*, 114–15.

78. Grossman, *Land of Hope*, 146, 150–55; Ogren, *The Jazz Revolution*, 113–14; Mrs. B. S. Gaten, "Standards of Looseness in Public Places," *CD*, July 13, 1918, 8 (emphasis in original); "Monogram a Den of Filth and Vulgarity," *CW*, July 31, 1920, 1; Hazel Carby, "Policing the Black Woman's Body in an Urban Context," *Critical Inquiry* 18.4 (Summer 1992): 738–55; and idem, "'On the Threshold of Woman's Era': Lynching, Empire, and Sexuality in Black Feminist Theory," in Henry Louis Gates Jr., ed., *"Race," Writing, and Difference* (Chicago: University of Chicago Press, 1986), 301–16. On black reform efforts to police migrant women's sexuality, see also Christina Simmons, "African Americans and Sexual Victorianism in the Social Hygiene Movement, 1910–40," *Journal of the History of Sexuality* 4.1 (July 1993): 51–75; and Victoria W. Wolcott, *Remaking Respectability: African American Women in Interwar Detroit* (Chapel Hill: University of North Carolina Press, 2001).

79. On black nativist attitudes toward—and animosities directed against— Harlem's West Indian immigrants, see Osofsky, *Harlem*, 131–35; and Jervis Anderson, *This Was Harlem: A Cultural Portrait, 1900–1950* (New York: Farrar Straus Giroux, 1982), 299–304. On the names that native-born blacks called West Indians, see also Watson, *The Harlem Renaissance*, 32; and Van Vechten, *Nigger Heaven*, 285–86.

80. "'Nosey' Sees All Knows All," *CW*, April 2, 1921, 2. Howard and Olive, a black middle-class couple in Carl Van Vechten's *Nigger Heaven*, use this same approach to explain their attendance at a lowdown Harlem cabaret that other characters had associated with "too many pink-chasers an' bulldikers" (that is, with too many blacks seeking the company of whites [pink-chasers] and lesbians [bulldikers]). "Where did you go [last night]?" the couple's friend Mary asked them. "Atlantic City Joe's," Howard replied. "We felt like slumming" (Van Vechten, *Nigger Heaven*, 137).

81. Alberta Hunter, Smithsonian Jazz Oral History Project interview transcript, housed at the Institute of Jazz Studies, Rutgers University–Newark, 6:6–7, quoted in Peretti, *The Creation of Jazz*, 67–68.

82. "Under the Lash of the Whip," *CW*, January 10, 1920, 3. The locus for this New Year's Eve gathering was Bronzeville's notorious Entertainers' Café, perhaps the most popular Chicago black and tan of the early 1920s.

83. "'Nosey' Sees All Knows All," *CW*, December 23, 1922, 5. "Nosey" expressed a similar skepticism for black middle-class slumming in Bronzeville

cabarets on several other occasions in the early 1920s. See "'Nosey' Sees All Knows All," *CW*, October 9, 1920, 2; January 1, 1921, 2; March 4, 1922, 5; and July 29, 1922, 5.

84. Although Peretti focuses specifically on jazz musicians to show how music helped to overcome class, color, and regional differences among blacks, his argument can easily be extended to the larger black community (Peretti, *The Creation of Jazz*, 58–75).

85. J.D.B.P., "Club Ebony Opens with a Flash," *TLAHJ*, October 15, 1927, 32; and Mamie L. Briggs, "Mamie L. Briggs' Society Pages; Club Ebony Opens," *IST*, September 30 and October 14, 1927. On the artistic appreciation and appropriation of jazz performance and techniques by Harlem Renaissance figures, see Ogren, *The Jazz Revolution*, 111–38.

86. "Square's Harlem Club," *Variety*, November 20, 1929, 67; "Invades Chicago Loop District with Cabaret," *NYAN*, October 26, 1932, 8; "Village Atmospheric Black Belt Brodies," *Variety*, February 19, 1930, 49; "3 of 5 Places Survive in Village's Harlem Attempt," *Variety*, October 29, 1930, 55; "Connie's Bows Out," *Variety*, September 19, 1933; "Connie's a Beer Spot," *Variety*, September 26, 1933, 43; "Connie's Inn (New York)," in "Night Club Reviews" column, *Variety*, May 1, 1935, 40; "C. C. Folds after Decade in Harlem," *Variety*, February 19, 1936, 61; "Cotton Club Follows Connie's to Broadway," *Variety*, July 1, 1936, 38; and Abel Green, "Niteries on Road Back," *Variety*, January 6, 1937, 195.

CHAPTER 6

1. Paul Yawitz, "Fakes, Foneys, Flops, Femmes Expose Village as Gin Pan Alley," *New York Evening Graphic*, August 24, 1931, 25.

2. "Reversed 'Pansy' Co. By Impersonators," *Variety*, October 15, 1930, 38; "Female Impersonators En Masse Play as Show For School Children," *Variety*, June 2, 1931, 1; Alma Mater, "Hollywood Lowdown," *Brevities*, April 18, 1932, 10; and La Forest Potter, MD, *Strange Loves: A Study in Sexual Abnormalities* (New York: Robert Dodsley Co., 1933), 8.

3. Evelyn Nesbit, article in *BT*, quoted in Potter, *Strange Loves*, 5, 6n1.

4. Potter, *Strange Loves*, 4–5.

5. Kaier Curtin, *"We Can Always Call Them Bulgarians": The Emergence of Lesbians and Gay Men on the American Stage* (Boston: Alyson Publications, 1987), 63, 105–14; "New York Exchange," review, *Variety*, January 5, 1927, 44; "Chicago" section, "News from the Dailies," *Variety*, March 23, 1927, 36; "'The Drag' as Play with 40 of 'Our Sex,'" *Variety*, November 24, 1926, 1; "Sensational New Plays In Sight—1 Refused," *Variety*, January 19, 1927, 1, 55; "Rialto Gossip," *NYT*, January 16, 1927, sec. 7, 1; Rush, "The Drag," review, "Plays out of Town" column, *Variety*, February 2, 1927, 49; and Hamilton, *When I'm Bad, I'm Better*, 55–69. On the early 1927 crackdown on Broadway's "dirt shows," see Curtin, *"We Can Always Call Them*

Bulgarians," 91–104; Chauncey, *Gay New York*, 311–13; Hamilton, *When I'm Bad, I'm Better*, 70–103; Leslie A. Taylor, "Veritable Hotbeds: Lesbian Scandals in the United States, 1926–1936" (PhD diss., University of Iowa, 1998), 104–211; and Andrea Friedman, *Prurient Interests: Gender, Democracy, and Obscenity in New York City, 1909–1945* (New York: Columbia University Press, 2000), 95–115.

6. "The Captive," review, *Variety*, October 6, 1926, 80; Rush, "The Drag"; Tom Fulbright, "Mae West Has the Last Laugh," *Hollywood Studio Magazine*, November 1978, 21; *Variety*, January 12, 1927, 37, quoted in Hamilton, *When I'm Bad, I'm Better*, 61; "The Pansy Bugle," *BT*, February 1933, 12; Connie Lingle, "Sapphic Sisters Scram!" *Brevities*, November 16, 1931, 1, 10; Jack "Ziggy" Mason, "Malin Was Not Queer!" *BT*, September 1933, 16, 11; and Chauncey, *Gay New York*, 314–15.

7. "Unique Nut Club for Laughs on Spot And Air, Turns 'Em Away in Village," *Variety*, December 19, 1928, 1, 3; and Rian James, *All About New York* (New York: The John Day Company, 1931), 215. For more on La Belle Rose's 1928–33 reign at the Village Nut Club, see "On the Square," *Variety*, January 16, 1929, 46; "La Belle Rose's Act," *Variety*, February 6, 1929, 43; "Nut Club Enlarging," *Variety*, July 31, 1929, 56; "Nut Club Growing," *Variety*, August 21, 1929, 58; "New Village Nut Club (New York)," review, *Variety*, September 3, 1930, 75; "Broadway Chatter" column, *Variety*, October 29, 1930, 79; Charles Weller, "Night Club Buzz," *ZTN*, April 18, 1931, 11; "New York" section, "Cabaret Bills" column, *Variety*, February 16, 1932, 78; June 28, 1932, 35; and July 26, 1932, 52; "Broadway" section, "Chatter" column, *Variety*, September 12, 1933, 59; and "Nut Club, N.Y.," review, *Variety*, September 19, 1933, 39.

8. Sustar, "When Speech Was Free (And Usually Worth It)," 25; John Drury, *A Century of Progress Authorized Guide to Chicago* (Chicago: Consolidated Book Publishers, 1933), 184; Schwanda Schweik, "Chicago World's Fairies," *Brevities*, December 7, 1931, 1; Leo Adams to Merle Macbain, New York, November 29, 1931, first Merle Macbain correspondence folder, box 1, Leo Adams papers, NYPL; Burton J. Barnett, "Towertown—The Last Hope of Bohemia," *The Daily Northwestern*, January 8, 1931, 3; and Constance Weinberger and S[aul] D. Alinsky, Report on "Diamond Lil's," part of their larger study, "The Public Dance Hall," Autumn 1928, folder 10, box 126, EWBP. See also Jon-Henri Damski, "Chicago Queers Circa 1931," *Windy City Times*, September 15, 1994, 15.

9. Mark Hellinger, "People I've Met" column, *New York Daily Mirror*, undated clipping, quoted in Chauncey, *Gay New York*, 315; unidentified newspaper clipping, [August 1933], the lesbian scrapbook, Kinsey Institute for Research in Sex, Gender, and Reproduction, Indiana University, Bloomington; "Goings on about Town," *The New Yorker*, August 23, 1930, 2; and Drury, *Dining in Chicago*, 187–88. Drury's reference to the K-9 Club as an "odd sort of place" was easily recognizable to readers as part of the code

employed by the cabaret's owners who regularly advertised their nightly revue of female impersonators as the "oddest show in town" (e.g., Advertisement for the K-9 Club, *CA*, December 1, 1934, 10).

10. "Some Characteristics of the Lower North Community," unpublished student paper, n.d., 18, folder 4, box 156, EWBP; and Julian Jerome, "Floor-Show," *Vanity Fair*, February 1931, 68. In an unpublished manuscript, Dr. Ben L. Reitman recalled the nonchalance with which sophisticated slummers attempted to greet even the most outrageous introduction to Towertown's white lesbians and pansies. "I have said to a casual visitor to the Dill Pickle, 'I want you to meet these boys, they are a couple of the best known Michigan Avenue "bitches" in town,'" Reitman recounted, "and everybody [simply] smiled" ("Homosexuality [To Be Added on Part IV]," 12, in "Living with Social Outcasts," unpublished manuscript, [March 1933], supplement IV, folder 34, BLRP).

11. "Taverns," October 19, 1934, 2, folder 89, JPAP; and Investigator B, Report on night club, Coffee Cliff, 45th St., just east of B'way, December 2, 1930, 1:15–2:55 a.m., 1930 investigative reports folder, box 35, C14P.

12. Untitled field report beginning, "Case is a rather well built young girl of nineteen. . . . ," folder 6, box 98, EWBP (the author of this document is most likely Cynthia Cohen, a graduate of the University of Chicago who conducted a study of Chicago public health clinics during the early 1930s). On "pseudo-lesbians," see Ware, *Greenwich Village*, 253; Bobby Edwards, "Loves Lesbians," letter to the editor, *Brevities*, December 21, 1931, 15; and Lingle, "Sapphic Sisters Scram!", 1, 10. Lillian Faderman uses the term "lesbian chic" to denote women's increased sexual experimentation with other women during the 1920s and 1930s (*Odd Girls and Twilight Lovers*, 62–92.)

13. Barry Bishop, "Swinging Wide," *Brevities*, August 1, 1932, 6 (recurring ellipses have been removed from this quote); and "As told to Harry by Herman," folder 3, box 98, EWBP. On the supposed lesbian threat to young women who participated in the pansy and lesbian craze, see also Mrs. Yvonne Garneau to Mr. G[eorge] E. Worthington, Montreal, Canada, July 18, 1931, "1930–31 Police" correspondence folder, box 13, C14P; Edwards, "Loves Lesbians," 15; and Lingle, "Sapphic Sisters Scram!", 10.

14. Jerome, "Floor-Show," 68, 86.

15. White, *The First Sexual Revolution,* esp. 16–35. In her study of the cosmetics industry, historian Kathy Peiss demonstrates that advertisers faced an uphill battle to convince American men to purchase fragrances and skin creams, because they continued to associate such products with femininity and homosexuality. But some beauty products were quite successfully marketed to men. By the mid-1930s, Peiss notes, a survey of "two hundred white-collar New Yorkers" found that "one in two used an aftershave talc or lotion" (*Hope in a Jar: The Making of America's Beauty Culture* [New York: Metropolitan Books, 1998], 158–66).

16. "Jackie Maye Gets Cops' O.K.," *ZTN*, February 11, 1933, 1.

17. [Earle W. Bruce], Field report on the Ballyhoo [Café], Wednesday Nov. 22nd, 1933, 11:30 p.m., Cover charge $.25, folder 3, box 98, EWBP; and idem, Field report on the Ballyhoo Café, 1942 N. Halsted, 9/24/33, 11:30 p.m., folder 2, box 98, EWBP.

18. Lew Weiss, "Night Club News," *ZTN*, March 19, 1932, 14; Paul Swein-hart, "Along Broadway," *ZTN*, April 9, 1932, 8; Souvenir noisemaker from Café Folies Bergére, 157 W. 56th St., N.Y.C., in possession of the author; Frank O. Beck, *Hobohemia* (Rindge, NH: Richard R. Smith Publisher, 1956), 86–87; and "World's Fair Ladies Peel!! (Letter to the Editor from a Friendly Lass in Chicago)," *BT*, September 1933, 3. For further examples of female impersonators and pansy entertainers appearing on the same bill as fan and bubble dancers, see Joe Kolling, "Cincy's Rhineland Night Life Does a Comeback," *Variety*, November 27, 1934, 59; and Dan Goldberg, "Chi's Nocturnal Side Roars Again After Slumbering for 10 Years," *Variety*, December 11, 1934, 47, 57. In a study of the men's magazine *Esquire*, Kenon Breazeale documents a similar strategy on the part of the magazine's editors during the 1930s to offset any potentially feminizing effects of their efforts to promote middle-class male consumerism by publishing erotic pinups of buxom blondes to reinforce their male readers' heterosexual identity ("In Spite of Women: *Esquire* Magazine and the Construction of the Male Consumer," *Signs* 20.1 [Autumn 1994]: 1–22).

19. Unpublished field document beginning, "Told to me by a Mr. X. . . . ," n.d., folder 11, box 98, EWBP.

20. A New York lesbian similarly reported that men often dropped by lesbian nightspots in the Village and in Midtown "mostly for queer women" and the titillation they provided (Molly N., quoted in Henry, *Sex Variants,* 647).

21. Clement, "Trick or Treat," 359–62; and Ben L. Reitman, VDC #104, Chicago Syphilis Control Program VD reports, [1937], 536 3/4, supplement II, folder 23, BLRP.

22. Helen Lawrenson, *Whistling Girl* (New York: Doubleday and Company, 1978), 26–27. Alfred C. Kinsey's landmark studies on sexual behavior remain the best source for tracking the increasing inclusion of oral sex among "normal" sexual practices. Although numerous scholars have questioned the accuracy of Kinsey's methodology, if one assumes that his sampling methods were relatively similar across the various age cohorts studied in his surveys, a comparison of the figures attributed to older and younger groups still reveals important generational shifts in sexual practices. In *Sexual Behavior in the Human Female*, Kinsey and his associates found that women's experience with "oral stimulation of male genitalia" was increasing with each generation during the early twentieth century. Among those women born before 1900, the study found that 38 percent had performed oral sex on men more than twenty-five times during their lives. Among those women born between 1900 and 1909, the figure rose to 42 percent

and again to 43 percent among those born in 1910 and after. But these latter figures represented only a portion of the women in those cohorts who
had engaged in fellatio; Kinsey also found that 5 percent of women born
between 1900 and 1909 and 16 percent of those born in 1910 and after
had experienced "oral stimulation of male genitalia" less than twenty-five
times. It is the dramatic shift in these percentages that suggests that those
women who came of age during the late 1920s and 1930s were more likely
to engage in oral sexual practices than the women who preceded them
were. And the more highly educated the women were (in all cohorts),
the more likely they were to have tried these practices (Alfred C. Kinsey,
Wardell B. Pomeroy, Clyde E. Martin, and Paul H. Gebhard, *Sexual Behavior
in the Human Female* [Philadelphia: W. B. Saunders Company, 1953], 281).

23. "'Rival' Punches Nose of Slain 'Jackie' Moss' Girl Friend," *CA*, January 21,
    1931, 19.
24. Molly N., quoted in Henry, *Sex Variants*, 647. On the importance of public
    spaces in the building of the lesbian and gay communities of New York and
    Chicago, see Chauncey, *Gay New York*, 151–329; and Johnson, "The Kids of
    Fairytown," in Beemyn, ed., *Creating a Place for Ourselves*, 101–4.
25. In announcing Gladys Bentley's engagement at the King's Terrace, the
    Broadway Tattler encouraged readers to "Take the G.F. [girlfriend] along
    and give these Niteries the O.O. [once-over]!" while calling attention to the
    novelty of having a black queer entertainer headlining at a Times Square
    cabaret. The "Brownskinned Gladys Bentley, smart-smut-songstress, one of
    the svelte decorations," the column noted in a telegraphed description of
    the club. "She's a mantee" ("Snoopin' Around with The Tattler," *BT*, Au-
    gust 1933, 3). For more on Bentley's engagement at the King's Terrace, see
    "Broadway" section, "Chatter" column, *Variety*, May 30, 1933, 60; "King's
    Terrace" review, "Night Club Reviews" column, *Variety*, June 13, 1933,
    48; Sid Weiss, "Night Clubs," *ZTN*, October 14, 1933, 6; "With the Sun
    Dodgers: A Guide to Night-Life of the Metropolis," *BT*, December 1933, 2;
    and Zit, "Headlines That Tell a Story," *ZTN*, February 24, 1934, 8. On the
    appearance of the Sepia Gloria Swanson at Towertown's Monte Carlo and
    other Jim Crow cabarets on Chicago's Near North Side, see the announce-
    ment in *ZTN*, winter 1931–32; and "'Gloria Swanson' Buried in Harlem,"
    CD, May 4, 1940, 21.
26. "Colored Love," *Brevities*, July 25, 1932, 7.
27. Document 20, quoted in Zorbaugh, *The Gold Coast and the Slum*, 96.
28. On the role of benevolent organizations, mutual aid societies, religious
    institutions, and newspapers in building a sense of ethnic community in
    early-twentieth-century U.S. cities, see especially Lizabeth Cohen, *Making a
    New Deal: Industrial Workers in Chicago, 1919–1939* (New York: Cambridge
    University Press, 1991). There are at least three references to the existence
    of homosexual newspapers or similar community-oriented publications
    in Chicago during the 1920s and 1930s, but no extant copies of these

publications have yet been located. In 1925, the Society for Human Rights, founded by Chicagoan and early homosexual rights activist Henry Gerber, published the short-lived *Friendship and Freedom,* the existence of which has been verified by historian Jonathan Ned Katz through a photograph of homosexual publications published by Magnus Hirschfeld in 1927 (*Gay American History: Lesbians and Gay Men in the U. S. A.,* rev. ed. [New York: Meridian, 1992], 385–93). A second reference to a community newspaper, possibly also referring to *Friendship and Freedom,* can be found in the annual report of the JPA for 1925. Investigating "the homo-sexual group of men and boys who have their headquarters in Grant Park" during the summer of 1925, sociologist Nels Anderson reported that these men were "publishing a paper of their own, using a vocabulary which no one outside the group could easily understand" (Jessie F. Binford, "The Year's Work—1925," in *Annual Report of the Juvenile Protective Association* [Chicago, 1925], 12). The final reference to a homosexual newspaper dates to the early 1930s. In an unpublished manuscript on "social outcasts," Dr. Ben L. Reitman remarked that "the Homos publish a paper in Chicago, and some idea of their activities can be gleaned from excerpts from one of the editions." Seemingly indicating the name of the newspaper to which he referred, Reitman reproduced those excerpts under the heading, "THE CARPET SWEEPER (It picks up all the Dirt!)" (unpublished manuscript section entitled "Homosexuality [To Be Added on Part IV]," 19[a]).

29. [Earle W. Bruce], Field report on the Ballyhoo Café, 1942 N. Halsted, 9/24/33, 11:30 p.m., in folder 2, box 98, EWBP; and Unpublished field document beginning, "Told to me by a Mr. X. . . ," n.d., folder 11, box 98, EWBP.

30. Marian to Ben Reitman, June 2, 1931, in possession of Ruth Surgal, Chicago, quoted in Poirier, *Chicago's War on Syphilis, 1937–1940,* 154; and Bruce Scott, interviewed by Gregory Sprague, Chicago, August 26, 1985, cassette tape, box II (cassettes), GASP.

31. [Unknown author], "Told to me by Clarence," n.d., unpublished field document, folder 3, box 98, EWBP.

32. [Earle W. Bruce], Field report on the Ballyhoo Café, 1942 N. Halsted, 9/24/33, 11:30 p.m., folder 2, box 98, EWBP; and Paul Yawitz, "Greenwich Village Sin Dives Lay Traps For Innocent Girls and Ambitious Youths," *Evening Graphic,* August 25, 1931, 4 (this clipping is included in the lesbian scrapbook, Kinsey Institute for Research in Sex, Gender and Reproduction, Indiana University, Bloomington; the order of the two sentences in the quote from Yawitz has been reversed). On the effects of the repeal of Prohibition on lesbian and gay nightlife, see Chauncey, *Gay New York,* 335–54.

33. [Ernest W. Burgess], Notes on the 1932 New Year's Eve drag ball at Johnny Ryan's, January 26, 1933, folder 11, box 98, EWBP; [Harry Kahan], Investigation of Jewel Restaurant, 43 West 48th Street, October 5, 1926, 1926 investigative reports folder, box 35, C14P; Lingle, "Sapphic Sisters Scram!"

1, 10; Leon (Nazie) Mirabeau, "The Pansy Bugle," *BT*, March 1933, 12, 14; "Sunday School Teacher Arrested with Others in 'Queer' 6th Ave. Joint," *Variety*, July 2, 1930, 59; Paul Sweinhart, "Along Broadway," *ZTN*, January 30, 1932, 8; Advertisement for the Club Piccardy, 4308 Cottage Grove, featuring "Miss Billie Le Roy And Her Gang of Female Impersonators," *CA*, December 1, 1934, 11; Charles Borin, interviewed by Gregory A. Sprague, Chicago, September 3, 1980, cassette tape, box I (cassettes), GASP; and Jim Holden, "After 3 a.m.," *Brevities*, April 3, 1933, 6.

34. See Chauncey, *Gay New York*, 316–17; "Ohmygod! Jean Malin Has a Fight," *ZTN*, August 20, 1932, 1; and "Streetwalker and Elite Meet in Bughouse Square," *Chicago HUSH,* September 18, 1932, 15.

35. Gene S., quoted in Henry, *Sex Variants*, 255–56 (the sentences in this quote have been rearranged); unidentified "Californian who moved to New York," quoted in Loughery, *The Other Side of Silence,* 40. Similar expressions of disgust for the "bells or bitches who paint and powder up and go this way on the street" can be found in the 1930s life histories of homosexual men housed in the Ernest W. Burgess papers at the Special Collections Research Center, University of Chicago Library ("Regarding the love affair of Jim and Rodey. Told me by Rodey," n.d., folder 3, box 98, EWBP; see also untitled life history, April 18, 1933, folder 3, box 98, EWBP; and untitled life history, May 5, [1933], folder 3, box 98, EWBP).

36. Chauncey, *Gay New York*, 100–2. In his essay on Chicago's 1930s homosexual male subculture, David K. Johnson charts a similar dynamic in the working-class "City of Big Shoulders" ("The Kids of Fairytown," in Beemyn, ed., *Creating a Place for Ourselves,* 104–8).

37. Fred [Ritter] to Max Ewing, New York, December 25, 1933, "Misc. Letters to Max Ewing—unidentified correspondents" folder, box 7, MEP.

38. Lingle, "Sapphic Sisters Scram!" 1, 10. On the emergence of a more conservative sense of "lesbian discretion" and public comportment among Depression-era white middle-class women, see Kennedy, "'But we would never talk about it,'" in Lewin, ed., *Inventing Lesbian Cultures in America,* 15–40.

39. On the practice adopted by white middle-class gay men and lesbians beginning in the mid-1930s of appearing in public primarily in mixed couplings, see Elizabeth Lapovsky Kennedy and Madeline D. Davis, *Boots of Leather, Slippers of Gold: The History of a Lesbian Community* (New York: Routledge, 1993), 48–50, 61–62; Chauncey, *Gay New York*, 280; Kennedy, "'But we would never talk about it,'" in Lewin, ed., *Inventing Lesbian Cultures in America,* 37–38; and Gean Harwood, *The Oldest Gay Couple in America: A Seventy-Year Journey through Same-Sex America* (Secaucus, NJ: Carol Publishing Group, 1997), 57–58.

40. Robert Brennan, as interviewed by Gregory A. Sprague, Chicago, January 28, 1984, cassette tape, box I (cassettes), GASP; Handbill advertising a drag ball sponsored by Gene Robbins, Wesley O. Mann, George Burns, and Maxie Lengel at the Rockland Palace, 155th St. and Eighth Ave., Saturday

night, June 14th, [1930], 10 p.m., in the lesbian scrapbook, Kinsey Institute for Research in Sex, Gender, and Reproduction, Indiana University, Bloomington; "Strictly Confidential," *Brevities*, March 28, 1932, 2. Despite the decreased regulation of black urban districts, doing business in Harlem could still prove dangerous for white queers. As early as 1928, the black press reported the arrest of several white drag entertainers at two different Harlem black and tans, the Lulu Belle Club, located at 341 Lenox Avenue, and the Pullman Café at 351 Lenox Avenue (see "Citizens Claim That Lulu Belle Club on Lenox Avenue Is Notorious Dive," *NYAN*, February 15, 1928, 1; and "Forty-one Arrested in Raid on Club," *NYAN*, July 11, 1928, 1). The neighborhood proved even more dangerous for Village impresario George Burns, who was shot in the left foot while "kicking up a little fun in one of those uptown whoopee joints known as 'The Nook,' at 169 West 133rd street" ("Guns and Razors Flash in Debate at 'The Nook,'" *New York Telegraph*, March 29, 1928, clipping, in scrapbook 22, CVVP).

41. Alan Lomax, *Mister Jelly Roll* (1950; repr., London: Virgin Books, 1991), 45. George Chauncey advances a similar argument to explain the development of the black homosexual community in Harlem (*Gay New York*, 245). On the freedom and economic opportunities that Southern black migrants associated with the urban North, see especially Drake and Cayton, *Black Metropolis*, 31–57; Grossman, *Land of Hope*, 66–119; and Gregory, *The Southern Diaspora*, 115–52.

42. Dr. James G. Kiernan, "Sexology. . . . Theory of Inversion. . . . Classification of Homosexuality," *Urologic and Cutaneous Review* 20.6 (1916): 345–46, 348–50, quoted in Katz, *Gay/Lesbian Almanac*, 367; Minutes from the Board of Directors Meeting, Friday, November 12, 1926, 182, supplement I, folder 27, JPAP; Louis Sobol, "Your Broadway and Mine," *New York Evening Graphic*, April 6, 1931, 21; Irving Marcus, quoted in Ted Yates, "Around the Town," *IST*, July 23, 1931, 9; and Ted Yates, "Around the Town," *IST*, July 30, 1931, 8. A front-page headline in a November 1920 issue of the black-owned *Chicago Whip* alluded to the city's new and sizable black homosexual population by asking, "Have We A New Sex Problem Here?" Although specifically referring to the story of a black Chicago man who had successfully sued his wife for divorce "on the grounds that she had forsaken him to run away with another woman," this headline implied an expected recurrence of such predicaments as migrants adjusted to modern urban life and sexual practices ("Have We A New Sex Problem Here?" *CW*, November 27, 1920, 1).

43. Blair Niles, *Strange Brother* (New York: Horace Liveright, 1931), 34, 38–62; and John Dos Passos, *The Big Money* (New York: Harcourt, Brace and Company, 1936), 514, 516.

44. Nugent, "On 'Gloria Swanson,' Real name Mr. Winston," 1; Danny Barker, quoted in Howard Reich, "Hotter Near the Lake," *CT Magazine*, September

5, 1993, 16; "One-Man-Raid Battles Does a Carrie Nation," *NYAN*, May 12, 1934, 1; and Roi Ottley, "This Hectic Harlem," *NYAN*, December 20, 1933, 9; and January 17, 1934, 9.

45. Roi Ottley, "This Hectic Harlem," *NYAN*, April 21, 1934, 9; Nugent, "On 'Gloria Swanson,' Real Name Mr. Winston," 2–3; "'Mae West' Stars At Annex Buffet," *CD*, September 15, 1934, 9; and "Cabin Inn Celebrates 4th Anniversary With Red Hot Show And Plenty 'Imps,'" *CD*, July 10, 1937, 10. On the opening of the Ubangi Club featuring Gladys Bentley, see also V. E. J. [Vere E. Johns], "Lafayette Theatre," *NYA*, April 14, 1934, 5.

46. Dick Barrow with Dott Scott's Rhythm Band, "Down at the Cabin Inn," music and lyrics by Scott, Decca 7226 (78A), 78 rpm, recorded September 29, 1936; Lou Layne, "Moon Over Harlem," *NYA*, June 22, 1935, 4; and Archie Seale, "Man About Harlem," NYA, February 15, 1936, 4. Similar promotional recordings included Louis Armstrong and his Hot Five, with vocal chorus by May Alix, "Sunset Café Stomp (From 'Sunset Café Revue')," music and lyrics by Percy Venable and Louis Armstrong, Okeh 8423–B, 78 rpm, recorded November 16, 1926; and Jimmie Noone's Apex Club Orchestra, accompanied by Earl Hines on piano, "Apex Blues," music and lyrics by Jimmie Noone, Vocalion 2779/Brunswick 4966/Brunswick 7096, 78 rpm, recorded July 11, 1929.

47. Helen Lawrenson, *Stranger at the Party: A Memoir* (New York: Random House, 1975), 170; Richard Bruce Nugent, interviewed by Eric Garber, undated partial transcript, EGP; Edouard Roditi to Eric Garber, Paris, August 26, 1983, EGP; Garber, "A Spectacle in Color," in Duberman, Vicinus, and Chauncey, eds., *Hidden from History*, 323; Hank Fuller, "In One Ear," *Brevities*, March 21, 1932, 5; Geraldyn Dismond and Jean Louise Simon, "Social Snapshots," *IST*, October 31, 1930, 5; and January 16, 1931, 5; and "Under Hypnosis" section of "My First Meeting of The Homo—Sept. 1927," unpublished manuscript, September 24, 1932, 4, folder 4, box 98, EWBP. In his short story, "Just Boys," James T. Farrell portrays a party in the Chicago home of a woman much like Madame Block: "In a three-story building, a few doors north of the Prairie Theatre at Fifty-eighth and Prairie," Princess Amy hosted a candle-lit salon of black and white homosexual men, to which the white pansy protagonist, Baby Face, took his newly acquired black lover, Sammy Lincoln, one Saturday evening ("Just Boys," 1931–34, in *The Short Stories of James T. Farrell* [Garden City, NY: Halcyon House, 1941], 48–58).

Similar Harlem gatherings could be found in the antique-laden home of a couple of "old maid" gentlemen known as Jap and Saul, as well as in the apartments of several other queer Harlem luminaries, including Caska Bonds, Eddie Manchester, and the pianist David Fontaine (see Garber, "A Spectacle in Color," in Duberman, Vicinus, and Chauncey, eds., *Hidden from History*, 323; Edouard Roditi to Eric Garber, Paris, August 26, 1983,

EGP; and Edouard Roditi, interviewed by Ray Gerard Koskovich, Paris, May 23, 1983, transcript included in box 28, GASP). Roditi claimed that Manchester's apartment was in midtown Manhattan, but Garber locates it in Harlem. One Harlem columnist referred to a Caska Bonds party as "one of them 'love feast' things" (Ted Yates, "Around the Town," *IST*, November 19, 1931, 13).

48. Jack Moore, "Harlem Browns Busy!" *Brevities*, September 19, 1932, 16, 14; Garber, "A Spectacle of Color," in Duberman, Vicinus, and Chauncey, eds., *Hidden from History*, 323; Report on Lenox Avenue Club, 652 Lenox Avenue, 1928, in "Night Clubs and Speakeasies Located on Avenues and Named Streets," 1929, 100, "Speakeasies & Nightclubs" folder, box 37, C14P; and Ben L. Reitman, VDC #99. Eric Garber suggests that the "Daisy Chain" on 140th Street was also known as the "101 Ranch" and that the enormous transvestite featured in Valentine's sex circus was named "Clarenz." But either Garber or his informant has confused two distinct Harlem institutions. The 101 Ranch was a popular Harlem cabaret during the mid-1930s; run by Leroy McDonald and located at 101 West 139th Street, it featured a popular, "svelte," transvestite master of ceremonies known as Clarenz (née Clarence Henderson). During the mid-1930s, 140th Street in Harlem was apparently famous for its circuses; in his serialized short story, "Flowers of Sin," African American writer George S. Schuyler mentioned them prominently in a list of famous Harlem nightspots of the era (Garber, "A Spectacle of Color," in Duberman, Vicinus, and Chauncey, eds., *Hidden from History*, 323; advertisement for the 101 Ranch, featuring "Clarenz, 'Toast of Night Flight,'" *NYAN*, September 15, 1937; and George S. Schuyler, "Flowers of Sin," chapter IV, *NYAN*, July 13, 1935, magazine section, 2–A).

   Further references to the sex circuses and freak shows of 1930s Harlem and Bronzeville can be found in Stretch Johnson, quoted in Kisseloff, *You Must Remember This*, 322; Investigator 25, Report H-16 (Colored), 67 East 49th St., 1st floor, front, east, May 11, 1933, folder 97, JPAP; and Drake and Cayton, *Black Metropolis*, 610.

49. Bentzen, "Notes on the Homosexual in Chicago," 5, 8.

50. Commenting on black society's willingness to tolerate homosexuals, as long as they exhibited good breeding and public discretion, Harlem Renaissance writer and artist Richard Bruce Nugent, himself a member of a prominent African American family from the nation's capital, later remarked, "This 'class' acceptance quite negated for me that I was doing anything more reprehensible than being naughty. . . . Homosexual activities were perhaps socially taboo but actually 'winked' at," as long as one were not too indiscreet (Richard Bruce Nugent to Eric Garber, September 18, 1981, EGP). On the class dynamics of homosexuality in Harlem and Bronzeville, see also Chauncey, *Gay New York*, 248–67; Drexel, "Before Paris Burned," in Beemyn, ed., *Creating a Place for Ourselves*, 124–25; Charles Michael Smith, "Bruce Nugent: Bohemian of the Harlem Renaissance," in Joseph Beam,

ed., *In the Life: A Black Gay Anthology* (Boston: Alyson, 1986), 209–20; and Bruce Nugent, *Gay Rebel of the Harlem Renaissance: Selections from the Work of Richard Bruce Nugent*, ed. Thomas H. Wirth (Durham, NC: Duke University Press, 2002), 20–30.

51. "Hamilton Lodge Ball Draws 7,000," *NYAN*, March 2, 1932, 2.

52. Lorenzo Banyard [a.k.a. Nancy Kelly], interviewed by Allen Drexel, Chicago, February 27, 1994, quoted in Drexel, "Before Paris Burned," in Beemyn, ed., *Creating a Place for Ourselves*, 124. Joanne, the Cabin Inn performer to whom Banyard/Kelly referred, is almost certainly "Joan Crawford," also billed on occasion as "Joanne Crawford," and known by family and the law as George Manus. For an account of Manus's late-night arrest at the corner of 35th and State streets, see "Cocktails Get Female Impersonator In 'Dutch,'" *CD*, July 15, 1939, 24.

53. The Three Moral Monkeys, "The World, The Flesh & The Devil," *IST*, November 27, 1925, 8; and Thomas A. Dorsey, "Sissy Blues," as transcribed from the Gertrude "Ma" Rainey recording, in Angela Y. Davis, *Blues Legacies and Black Feminism: Gertrude "Ma" Rainey, Bessie Smith, and Billie Holiday* (New York: Pantheon, 1998), 242–43. Thomas A. "Georgia Tom" Dorsey had a successful career as a blues composer and performer in Chicago in the 1920s, before renouncing such secular music and achieving even greater success as "the father of black gospel music." See Michael W. Harris, *The Rise of Gospel Blues: The Music of Thomas Andrew Dorsey in the Urban Church* (New York: Oxford University Press, 1992); and Wallace D. Best, *Passionately Human, No Less Divine: Religion and Culture in Black Chicago, 1915–1952* (Princeton, NJ: Princeton University Press, 2005), 104–8.

54. W[ilbur] Young, "Dances Originating in Harlem," n.d., 2, "The dance" section, reel 2, NNY.

55. George Hannah and Meade Lux Lewis, "The Boy in the Boat," October 1931, on *"Sissy Man Blues": 25 Authentic Straight & Gay Blues & Jazz Vocals*, Jass compact disc 13, Jass Records, 1989, quoted in Faderman, *Odd Girls and Twilight Lovers*, 77; and Marcus Wright, "The Talk Of The Town," *New York Age*, May 26, 1934, 5.

56. My argument here follows that of George Chauncey, who contends that "the transition from one sexual regime to the next was an uneven process," occurring as much as two generations earlier in middle-class culture than in "much of Euro-American and African-American working-class culture." Not until at least the middle of the twentieth century, Chauncey argues, did the shift in sexual regimes become complete (*Gay New York*, 13–14).

57. Agent S. B., U.S. Interdepartmental Social Hygiene Board, "Corroborative Testimony by Agent," Chicago, Illinois, January 29–February 25, 1922, 8, folder 108, JPAP (emphasis in original).

58. Marian J., quoted in Henry, *Sex Variants*, 724; and Myrtle K., quoted in Henry, *Sex Variants*, 783. Given undeniable similarities in their family histories and childhoods, Henry's pseudonymous "Myrtle K." is almost

certainly the black vaudeville comedian Jackie "Moms" Mabley. For the most complete biography of Mabley, albeit a version that limits allusions to her lesbianism or bisexuality to one brief reference, see Elsie A. Williams, *The Humor of Jackie Moms Mabley: An African American Comedic Tradition* (New York: Garland Publishing, 1995).

59. Marian J., quoted in Henry, *Sex Variants*, 725–26; and Myrtle K., quoted in Henry, *Sex Variants*, 783. On the tendency of social reformers to represent "African American women prisoners as masculine or aggressive and their white lovers as 'normal' feminine women who would return to heterosexual relations upon release from prison," see Estelle B. Freedman, "The Prison Lesbian: Race, Class, and the Construction of the Aggressive Female Homosexual, 1915–1965," *Feminist Studies* 22.2 (Summer 1996): 399.

60. "Masquerade Ball Draws 5,000 People," *NYAN*, February 20, 1929, 2; and Sydney H., quoted in Henry, *Sex Variants*, 56.

61. Myles Vollmer, "The New Year's Eve Drag," unpublished student paper, n.d., 1, folder 2, box 139, EWBP; Hughes, *The Big Sea*, 273; Chauncey, *Gay New York*, 261; and W. Dorr Legg, "Exploring Frontiers: An American Tradition," *New York Folklore* 19.1–2 (1993): 223. Noting the police protection at the Coliseum balls, Samuel Steward recalled, "The police would make as many jokes about the costumes as the onlookers would outside" (Samuel M. Steward, interviewed by Gregory A. Sprague, Berkeley, CA, May 20, 1982, cassette tape, box II [cassettes], GASP).

62. "Hamilton Lodge Ball Draws 7,000," *NYAN*, March 2, 1932, 2; Chauncey, *Gay New York*, 260; Edgar T. Rouzeau, "Snow and Ice Cover Streets," *NYAN*, February 28, 1934, 3; and Marion Moore Day, quoted in Kisseloff, *You Must Remember This*, 323. Ironically, the expanded newspaper coverage of the Hamilton Lodge ball during the 1930s and its close attention to the fashions on display threw male reporters' masculinity and heterosexuality into question. At least one reporter noted this anxiety with a parenthetical statement after a particularly detailed fashion report: "Don't get me wrong, boys," he wrote, "I got this description from a woman" (St. Clair Bourne, "Pansies Cavort in Most Delovely Manner," *NYAN*, March 6, 1937, 5).

63. "Annex Buffet Is A Cool 'Hot' Spot Patrons Learn," *CD*, September 1, 1934, 9; The Unknown Lady, "Gang Chatter," *NYA*, February 24, 1934, 9; Roi Ottley, "This Hectic Harlem," *NYAN*, July 12, 1933, 9.

64. Roi Ottley, "This Hectic Harlem," *NYAN*, December 15, 1934, 9; and "Clarenz Scrawls Poem to Admirer," *NYAN*, March 21, 1936, 5.

65. "Abnormal Perverts and What They Mean In The Light of Scriptures Preached On By Bish. Lawson Sunday," *NYA*, March 1, 1930, 1, 7.

66. Moore, "Harlem Browns Busy!" 14; and Roi Ottley, "This Hectic Harlem," *NYAN*, May 19, 1934, 9.

67. Terence E. Williams, "Writer Scores Best Girls Who Entertain 'Nordics,'" *Pittsburgh Courier*, October 1, 1927; Harry B. Webber, "'Skirted' Men Featured N.Y.'s Biggest Party," *BAA*, April 16, 1927, 1; and Editorial, *CW*,

December 18, 1926, clipping, scrapbook 19, CVVP. A. W. B. expressed a similar viewpoint in the *Inter-State Tattler*, noting that "the sordid practices of the racketeers, rich degenerates and sophisticated females seeking a thrill from contact with the heterogeneous aggregation constituting a fringe of shameless sin" needed to be exposed in Harlem (A.W.B., "The outlinE [*sic*]," *IST*, August 6, 1931, 6). For further black commentary on the Fort Valley Industrial School benefit ball, see "The Fort Valley Spectacle," *New York News*, April 23, 1927; clipping, scrapbook 21, CVVP; and "Renaissance," *CW*, April 23, 1927, clipping, scrapbook 21, CVVP. See also Chauncey's analysis of this ball and the black coverage of it in *Gay New York*, 260–61. Despite objections to the ball, Jimmy Harris and his "Tomboys of Greenwich Village" repeated the Fort Valley Benefit Masque at the Renaissance Casino in November 1927, on the very same night that the Urban League's Annual Masque Ball was held (see Charmaine, "Harlem Town," *TLAHJ*, November 19, 1927, 41).

68. George S. Schuyler, "Society—A Sort of Duke's Mixture—A Conglomerate of 'Hot Stuff' Vendors, Bootleggers, Professional Men, Etc.," *NYAN*, December 18, 1929, sec. 3, 3. Richard Bruce Nugent seems to confirm Schuyler's assertion, noting, "We did not find it either amusing or interesting to *not* go to house-rent parties, 'low' dives and bars, speakeasies, etc. who [*sic*] spoke against the very thing that we should have attended and abetted. You know the scene. In this as in everything else we copied [*sic*] the white society with tragic fidelity" (Richard Bruce Nugent to Eric Garber, September 18, 1981, 2, EGP).

69. Roi Ottley, "This Hectic Harlem," *NYAN*, August 25, 1934, 9.

70. Frank Marshall Davis, *Livin' the Blues: Memoirs of a Black Journalist and Poet*, ed. with an introduction by John Edgar Tidwell (Madison: University of Wisconsin Press, 1992), 219–20.

71. Potter, *Strange Loves*, 187–88. On the segregated whites-only drag balls of New York and Chicago, see Chauncey, *Gay New York*, 291–99; Paul Sweinhart, "Along Broadway," *ZTN*, May 10, 1930, 17 (on Jack Mason's Continental Costume Ball, scheduled for Madison Square Garden on May 17); "Madison Sq. Garden's 'Drag' Financial Bust," *Variety*, May 21, 1930, 41; George E. Worthington, General Secretary and Counsel, Committee of Fourteen, to Mrs. J. Nelson Borland, New York, February 4, 1931, third 1931 correspondence folder, box 7, C14P; idem to Edward P. Mulrooney, Police Commissioner, New York, November 25, 1930, and attached report on the Mummers-Carbeck Costume Ball, to be held at the Star Casino, 107th St. & Park Ave., on Thanksgiving Eve, Wednesday, November 26, 1930, third 1931 correspondence folder, box 7, C14P; and Harvey K. and George P., interviewed by Gregory A. Sprague, ONE Institute, Los Angeles, June 3, 1983, GASP (who discuss a drag ball held at the "Merry Garden Ballroom" on Chicago's North Side, by which they probably meant the Marigold Ballroom in Chicago's Lakeview neighborhood).

For more on the popularity of the interracial drag balls held in Harlem and Bronzeville, as well as at the Coliseum Annex on Chicago's Near South Sides, see Miss Gerry [Geraldyn Dismond], *BAA*, February 1930, quoted in "Abnormal Perverts and What They Mean In The Light of Scriptures Preached On By Bish. Lawson Sunday," *NYA*, March 1, 1930, 7; "Hamilton Lodge Ball Is Scene of Splendor," *NYA*, February 22, 1930, 6; "Hamilton Lodge Ball Draws 7,000," *NYAN*, March 2, 1932, 2; [Ernest W. Burgess], Report on The Goblins, Coliseum Annex, October 30, 1932, folder 11, box 98, EWBP; "Leo, Age 18, Colored, One sister about 19 and one older brother 21 yrs of age," unpublished life history, n.d., 7, folder 11, box 98, EWBP; Myles Vollmer, "The New Year's Eve Drag," unpublished student paper, n.d., 2, folder 2, box 139, EWBP; Garber, "A Spectacle in Color," in Duberman, Vicinus, and Chauncey, eds., *Hidden from History*, 318–33; Chauncey, *Gay New York*, 257–63, 291–99; and Drexel, "Before Paris Burned," in Beemyn, ed., *Creating a Place for Ourselves*, 119–44.

72. Gene S., quoted in Henry, *Sex Variants*, 255; Chauncey, *Gay New York*, 298; and Harvey K. and George P., interviewed by Gregory A. Sprague, GASP. Henry's informant Theodore S. provided yet another example of a white gay man who professed to both enjoying and disliking Harlem's famous interracial masquerades. "I've been to a couple of drags in Harlem," he told Henry, "but I enjoyed it only once." Suggesting that his appreciation (or lack thereof) of the Harlem balls was linked to his experiences with cross-racial sex, Theodore quickly added that he had "seen attractive colored people but had only one experience" (Theodore S., quoted in Henry, *Sex Variants*, 239). Paralleling the account of the restroom antics at Chicago's Halloween grag, another of Henry's informants recounted a similarly active restroom at one of Harlem's popular interracial balls, insisting that sexual activity was so widespread that it might have spilled into the dance hall's more public spaces if the police had not "tried to keep the sex in the toilet" (Sydney H., quoted in Henry, *Sex Variants*, 56).

73. "Mere Male Blossoms Out in Garb of Milady at Big Hamilton Lodge Ball," *NYAN*, February 19, 1930, 3 (lists "Gene Mallin [*sic*], George Denny and Francis Dunn . . . [as] the three leading prize winners"); Lady Nicotine [Geraldyn Dismond], "Between Puffs," *IST*, February 25, 1932, 12; Maurice Dancer, "Nite Life Shadows," *IST*, March 31, 1932, 12; Garber, "A Spectacle in Color," in Duberman, Vicinus, and Chauncey, eds., *Hidden from History*, 329; and Legg, "Exploring Frontiers," 225. In making this argument, Garber draws on a statement uttered by a character in Blair Niles's semi-autobiographical 1931 novel, *Strange Brother*. "In Harlem I found courage and joy and tolerance," the character Mark Thornton remarked. "I can be myself there. . . . They know all about me, and I don't have to lie" (Niles, *Strange Brother*, 152).

74. Robert Brennan, as interviewed by Gregory A. Sprague, GASP; Parker Tyler to Charles Henri Ford, New York, ca. December 1929, quoted in Watson,

The Harlem Renaissance, 134; Lou Layne, "Moon Over Harlem," *NYA*, March 2, 1935, 5; Carl Van Vechten, *The Splendid Drunken Twenties: Selections from the Daybooks, 1922–1930*, ed. Bruce Kellner (Urbana: University of Illinois Press, 203); and James Smalls, *The Homoerotic Photography of Carl Van Vechten: Public Face, Private Thoughts* (Philadelphia: Temple University Press, 2006), 4, 7. The adjective "'phay" is a contraction of "ofay," a term commonly used by blacks to refer to whites during the 1920s and 1930s, although in this particular instance it aptly suggests the adjective "fey," as well.

75. Van Vechten, Diary, March 23, 1929, box 111, CVVP; and R. A. C. [Raymond Alexander Claymes], Report on speakeasy at 109 W. 136th St., basement, May 27, 1928, 1 to 1:30 a.m., "135–207 St." investigative reports folder, box 36, C14P.

76. Earle W. Bruce, "Observations of a Homosexual Party," unpublished student paper written for Sociology 309, Methods of Social Research, n.d., 1–2, folder 8, box 127, EWBP; Maurice Chideckel, *Female Sex Perversion: The Sexually Aberrated Woman as She Is* (New York: Eugenics Publishing Company, 1935), 122–23; and Mumford, *Interzones*, 84–85. The recording that Chideckel refers to is almost certainly Ruth Green's 1924 recording of "Mama's Got Something, I Know You Want It" (see Ron Sweetman, "Recording Activity in New Orleans in the 'Twenties," August 12, 2001, available at http://www.bluesworld.com/NODiscog.html; accessed August 27, 2006). On the queer-themed blues recordings of Gertrude "Ma" Rainey, George Hannah, and others and their importance in urban homosexual culture in the late 1920s and 1930s, see Sandra Lieb, *Mother of the Blues: A Study of Ma Rainey* (Amherst: University of Massachusetts Press, 1981); Hazel Carby, "It Just Be's Dat Way Sometime: The Sexual Politics of Women's Blues," *Radical America* 20.4 (June–July 1986): 9–22; Faderman, *Odd Girls and Twilight Lovers*, 74–79; Chauncey, *Gay New York*, 250–51; and Davis, *Blues Legacies and Black Feminism*, 39–41.

77. Bentzen, "Notes on the Homosexual in Chicago, 5, 6, 8."

EPILOGUE

1. See Kenneth T. Jackson, *Crabgrass Frontier: The Suburbanization of the United States* (New York: Oxford University Press, 1985), 190–218, 231–45; Thomas J. Sugrue, *The Origins of the Urban Crisis: Race and Inequality in Postwar Detroit* (Princeton, NJ: Princeton University Press, 1996), 125–53; Rosalyn Baxandall and Elizabeth Ewen, *Picture Windows: How the Suburbs Happened* (New York: Basic Books, 2001), 117–38; and Arnold R. Hirsch, "Less Than *Plessy*: The Inner City, Suburbs, and State-Sanctioned Residential Segregation in the Age of *Brown*," in Kevin M. Kruse and Thomas J. Sugrue, eds., *The New Suburban History* (Chicago: University of Chicago Press, 2006), 33–56.

2. See especially Jackson, *Crabgrass Frontier*, 190–218; Salvatore J. LaGumina, *From Steerage to Suburbs: Long Island Italians* (New York: Center for Migration Studies, 1988); Sugrue, *The Origins of the Urban Crisis*, 33–56; Theresa J. Mah, "Buying into the Middle Class: Residential Segregation and Racial Formation in the United States, 1920–1964" (PhD diss., University of Chicago, 1999); Karen Brodkin, "How Did Jews Become White Folks?" in Michelle Fine, Lois Weis, Linda Powell Pruitt, and April Burns, eds., *Off White: Readings on Power, Privilege, and Resistance* (New York: Routledge, 2004), 26–29; Andrew Wiese, *Places of Their Own: African American Suburbanization in the Twentieth Century* (Chicago: University of Chicago Press, 2005), 94–109; and Hasia R. Diner, *The Jews of the United States, 1654–2000* (Berkeley: University of California Press, 2006), 283–304.

3. Campbell Gibson and Kay Jung, "Historical Census Statistics on Population Totals by Race, 1790 to 1990, and by Hispanic Origin, 1970 to 1990, for Large Cities and Other Urban Places in the United States," Population Division, Working Paper No. 76 (Washington, DC: U.S. Census Bureau, 2005), http://www.census.gov/population/www/documentation/twps0076.html (accessed October 31, 2007); and Janet L. Abu-Lughod, *New York, Chicago, Los Angeles: America's Global Cities* (Minneapolis: University of Minnesota Press, 1999), 197–207, 218–28. On the Second Great Migration of Southern blacks, see also Arnold R. Hirsch, *Making the Second Ghetto: Race and Housing in Chicago, 1940–1960* (New York: Cambridge University Press, 1983); Roger Biles, "Race and Housing on Chicago," *Journal of the Illinois State Historical Society* 94.1 (Spring 2001): 31–38; Wendy Plotkin, "'Hemmed In': The Struggle against Racial Restrictive Covenants and Deed Restrictions in Post-WWII Chicago," *Journal of the Illinois State Historical Society* 94.1 (Spring 2001): 39–69; and Amanda I. Seligman, *Block by Block: Neighborhoods and Public Policy on Chicago's West Side* (Chicago: University of Chicago Press, 2005).

4. Virginia E. Sánchez Korrol, *From Colonia to Community: The History of Puerto Ricans in New York City* (Berkeley: University of California Press, 1994), 213; Clarence Senior, "Too Many People? Migration and Puerto Rico's Population Problem," *Annal of the American Academy of Political and Social Science* 285 (January 1953): 130; Maura I. Toro-Morn, "Boricuas en Chicago: Gender and Class in the Migration and Settlement of Puerto Ricans," in Carmen Teresa Whalen and Victor Vázquez-Hernández, eds., *The Puerto Rican Diaspora: Historical Perspectives* (Philadelphia: Temple University Press, 2005), 134; and Nicholas De Genova and Ana Y. Ramos-Zayas, *Latino Crossings: Mexicans, Puerto Ricans, and the Politics of Race and Citizenship* (New York: Routledge, 2003), 35–36.

5. On the 1935 uprising in Harlem and its effects on local nightlife, see Roi Ottley, "This Hectic Harlem," *NYA*, April 13, 1935, 9; Archie Seale, "Man About Harlem," *NYA*, October 26, 1935, 6; Cheryl Greenberg, *"Or Does It Explode?"* 3–6, 131–33; and Erenberg, *Swingin' the Dream*, 26–27. On neigh-

borhood tensions in Bronzeville during the Depression and the Second World War, see Drake and Cayton, *Black Metropolis*, 83–97, 182–95; and Hirsch, *Making the Second Ghetto*, 1–67.

6. "Navy Sets Up 'Jim Crow' Area in Chicago," *CD*, July 25, 1942, 1–2; Hirsch, *Making the Second Ghetto*, 49–50; Erenberg, *Swingin' the Dream*, 206–08; Malcolm X with Alex Haley, *The Autobiography of Malcolm X* (New York, 1963), as quoted in ibid., 207; Dominic J. Capeci, Jr., *The Harlem Riot of 1943* (Philadelphia: Temple University Press, 1977); and Sugrue, *The Origins of the Urban Crisis*, esp. 28–31.

7. Ruth Padnos, "The Case of Sex-Morons (so-called): Crime Waves and Publicity," term paper for Sociology 270: Social Pathology, Winter 1937, folder 7, box 145, EWBP; Estelle Freedman, "'Uncontrolled Desires': The Response to the Sexual Psychopath, 1920–1960," in Kathy Peiss and Christina Simmons, eds., *Passion and Power: Sexuality in History* (Philadelphia: Temple University Press, 1989), 199–225; George Chauncey, "The Post-War Sex Crime Panic," in William Graebner, ed., *True Stories from the American Past* (New York: Praeger, 1993), 160–78; Jennifer Terry, *An American Obsession: Science, Medicine, and Homosexuality in Modern Science* (Chicago: University of Chicago Press, 1999), 268–96; Chad Heap, *Homosexuality in the City: A Century of Research at the University of Chicago*, an exhibition catalog (Chicago: University of Chicago Library, 2000), 28–31; Stephen Robertson, *Crimes against Children: Sexual Violence and Legal Culture in New York City, 1880–1960* (Chapel Hill: University of North Carolina Press, 2005), 205–32; and idem, "'Boys, of Course, Cannot be Raped': Age, Homosexuality and the Redefinition of Sexual Violence, 1880–1955," *Gender & History* 18.2 (August 2006): 357–79.

8. "Ban on Femme Imps, Says Det. M.D., 1 Way To Stop Sex Murders," *Variety*, April 7, 1937, 53. The Illinois state legislature adopted a sexual psychopath law in 1938. The New York City Mayor's Committee on Sex Offenses first recommended passage of similar legislation in 1939, but the state legislature did not pass a sexual psychopath bill until 1947. Governor Thomas Dewey vetoed this first bill but signed a significantly amended version into law in April 1950. See Edwin H. Sutherland, "The Diffusion of Sexual Psychopath Laws," *American Journal of Sociology* 56.2 (September 1950): 142–48; and Robertson, *Crimes against Children*, 218–22.

9. On post-World War II ideologies of containment and domesticity, see especially Elaine Tyler May, *Homeward Bound: American Families in the Cold War Era*, rev. ed. (1988; repr., New York: Basic Books, 1999).

10. Nasaw, *Going Out*, 248–56; Lynn Spigel, *Make Room for TV: Television and the Family Ideal in Postwar America* (Chicago: University of Chicago Press, 1992), 36–72, 99–135; and Gary Edgerton, *The Columbia History of American Television* (New York: Columbia University Press, 2007), 103, 178.

11. William Severini Kowinski, *The Malling of America: An Inside Look at the Great Consumer Paradise* (New York: W. Morrow, 1985); Anne Friedberg,

"Cinema and the Postmodern Condition," in Linda Williams, ed., *Viewing Positions: Ways of Seeing Film* (New Brunswick, NJ: Rutgers University Press, 1995), 59–83; Paul Monaco, *The Sixties, 1960–1969* (New York: Charles Scribner's Sons, 2001); Lizabeth Cohen, *A Consumers' Republic: The Politics of Mass Consumption in Postwar America* (New York: Knopf, 2003), 257–89; John Koval, et al., eds., *The New Chicago: A Social and Cultural Analysis* (Philadelphia: Temple University Press, 2006); and Jerliou Hammett and Kingsley Hammett, eds., *The Suburbanization of New York: Is the World's Greatest City Becoming Just Another Town?* (New York: Princeton Architectural Press, 2007)

12. Edward Lewine, "Is Downtown Dead?" *NYT*, May 25, 1997, CY1; José Germosen, "Survival of the Fiercest," *Village Voice*, September 4, 2001, 59; David Kirby, "S & M Cafe Sign Too Saucy for Some Neighbors' Palates," *NYT*, August 24, 1997, CY7; Mike Thomas, "Life's Not a Drag at the Kit Kat," *Chicago Sun Times*, December 16, 2007, D1; Judith Halberstam, *Female Masculinity* (Durham, NC: Duke University Press, 1998), 256; Del LaGrace Volcano and Judith Halberstam, *The Drag King Book* (New York: Serpent's Tail, 1999), 67; Andrew Jacobs, "At a Lounge, the Tables Are Turned on Drag Queens," *NYT*, April 5, 1998, CY6; Bill Roundy, "King of the Hill: Drag Kings Come to New York for Murray Hill's Drag Fest," *New York Blade*, October 5, 2001, http://www.billroundy.com/kings.html (accessed January 14, 2008); and Kate Zambreno, "It's Ladies' Night: The Chicago Kings Usher in a New Lesbian Scene," *Newcity Chicago*, June 25, 2003, http://www.newcitychicago.com/chicago/2621.html (accessed January 14, 2008).

13. On the fashion for holding bachelorette parties at drag clubs in New York and Chicago, see Lucky Cheng's Web site, "Lucky Cheng's is the Bachelorette Party Capital of the Universe!!!" http://www.planetluckychengs.com/bachlorettes.html (accessed January 14, 2008); Lips' Web site, "Bachelorettes," http://www.lipsnyc.com/bachelorettes.html (accessed January 14, 2008); Yelp Chicago Web site, "Kit Kat Lounge," customer reviews, http://www.yelp.com/biz/kit-kat-lounge-chicago (accessed January 14, 2008); and Rachel Devitt, "Glamour Queens," *Time Out Chicago*, November 22–28, 2007, http://www.timeout.com/chicago/articles/museums-culture/24433/glamour-queens (accessed January 14, 2008).

14. Pamela Newkirk, "A 'Must See' for Foreigners: Harlem," *NYT*, August 18, 1996, 53, 56. Dinitia Smith, "Cashing In on Gotham's Culture-Hungry Guests," *NYT*, April 15, 1996, C11; Frank Bruni, "At Harlem Churches, Flocks of Tourists," *NYT*, November 24, 1996, 37; and Don Babwin (Associated Press), "'Ghetto Tour' Showcases Chicago Projects," *Yahoo! News*, July 23, 2007, http://news.yahoo.com/ (accessed July 23, 2007).

15. Amelia Gentleman, "Slum Tours: A Day Trip Too Far?" *The Observer*, May 7, 2006, http://www.guardian.co.uk/travel/2006/may/07/delhi.india.ethicalliving (accessed January 8, 2008); John Otis, "Rio Tours Give Meaning to Phrase 'Slumming It': Gangsters Allow Visitors to View Shantytowns,"

San Francisco Chronicle, August 27, 2006, G-8, http://sfgate.com/ (accessed January 8, 2008); "From Safaris to 'Slum Tours,'" *Sydney Morning Herald*, February 19, 2007, http://www.smh.com.au/news/travel/from-safaris-to-slum-tours/2007/02/19/1171733643239.html (accessed January 8, 2008); Anya Yurchyshynm, "A Dose of Reality," *Budget Travel*, February 2008, http://www.budgettravel.com/bt-dyn/content/article/2008/01/07/AR2008010701680.html (accessed March 9, 2008); Eric Weiner, "Slum Visits: Tourism or Voyeurism?" *NYT*, March 9, 2008, http://www.nytimes.com/2008/03/09/travel/09heads.html (accessed March 9, 2008); and Victoria Safaris Web site, 'Pro Poor Tourism in Africa," http://www.victoriasafaris.com/kenyatours/propoor.htm (accessed January 8, 2008).

16. Reality Tours & Travel Web site, "Dharavi Slum Tours," http://realitytoursandtravel.com/slumtours.html (accessed January 8, 2008); Wiley Cooper, *Lusty Traveler: The Complete Sex Tourism Guide of Erotic Vacations for Men, Rio de Janeiro* (United States: Sex Tourism Publishing, 2008), 56, 85; Klaus de Albuquerque, "Sex, Beach Boys and Female Tourists in the Caribbean," *Sexuality & Culture* 2 (1998): 87–111; Chris Ryan and Colin Michael Hall, *Sex Tourism: Marginal People and Liminalities* (New York: Routledge, 2001); Edward Herold, Rafael Garcia, and Tony DeMoya, "Female Tourists and Beach Boys: Romance or Sex Tourism?" *Annals of Tourism Research* 28.4 (October 2001): 978–97; and Jasbir Kaur Puar, "Circuits of Queer Mobility: Tourism, Travel, and Globalization," *GLQ* 8.1–2 (2002): 101–37.

Abbreviations in Notes

BAA	*[Baltimore] Afro-American*
BT	*Broadway Tattler*
BDE	*Brooklyn Daily Eagle*
CA	*Chicago American*
CD	*Chicago Defender*
CDN	*Chicago Daily News*
CRH	*Chicago Record-Herald*
CT	*Chicago Tribune*
CW	*Chicago Whip*
IST	*Inter-State Tattler*
NPG	*National Police Gazette*
NYA	*New York Age*
NYAN	*New York Amsterdam News*
NYT	*New York Times*
TLAHJ	*The Light and "Heebie Jeebies":* *America's News Magazine*
WP	*Washington Post*
ZTN	*Zit's Theatrical Newspaper*

LEGISLATIVE REPORTS

Lexow	*Report and Proceedings of the Senate Committee* *Appointed to Investigate the Police Department of the* *City of New York.* Albany: James B. Lyon, State Printer, 1895. 5 vols.
Mazet	*Report of the Special Committee of the Assembly* *Appointed to Investigate the Public Offices and* *Departments of the City of New York and of the Counties*

Therein Included, Transmitted to the Legislature January 15, 1900.
Albany: James B. Lyon, State Printer, 1900. 5 vols.

ARCHIVES AND ARCHIVAL COLLECTIONS

BLRP   Dr. Ben L. Reitman Papers, Special Collections, University of
Illinois, Chicago

C14P   Committee of Fourteen Papers, Rare Books and Manuscripts
Division, The New York Public Library, Astor, Lenox, and Tilden
Foundations, New York

C15P   Committee of Fifteen Papers (Chicago), Special Collections
Research Center, University of Chicago Library, Chicago

CFP   Committee of Fifteen Papers (New York), Rare Books and
Manuscripts Division, The New York Public Library, Astor, Lenox,
and Tilden Foundations, New York

CHM   Chicago History Museum, Chicago

CNS   Chicago Neighborhood Studies (prepared for the Chicago Historical
Society and the Local Community Research Committee, University
of Chicago, under the direction of Vivien M. Palmer), Chicago
History Museum, Chicago

CTNP   Charles Torrence Nesbitt Papers, Rare Book, Manuscript, and
Special Collections Library, Duke University, Durham, North
Carolina

CVVP   Carl Van Vechten Papers, Rare Books and Manuscripts Division,
The New York Public Library, Astor, Lenox, and Tilden
Foundations, New York

DPCP   Dill Pickle Club Papers, Newberry Library, Chicago

EGP   Eric Garber Papers, Gay and Lesbian Historical Society of Northern
California, San Francisco

EWBP   Ernest W. Burgess Papers, Special Collections Research Center,
University of Chicago Library, Chicago

GASP   Gregory A. Sprague Papers, Chicago History Museum, Chicago

GTP   Graham Taylor Papers, Newberry Library, Chicago

JPAP   Juvenile Protective Association Papers, Special Collections,
University of Illinois, Chicago

MEP   Max Ewing Papers, Collection of American Literature, Beinecke
Rare Books and Manuscripts Library, Yale University, New Haven,
Connecticut

NNY   Negroes in New York, Federal Writers Project New York, Special
Collections, Schomburg Center for Research in Black Culture, New
York Public Library, New York

NYPL   Rare Books and Manuscripts Division, The New York Public
Library, Astor, Lenox, and Tilden Foundations, New York

PTP	Prentiss Taylor Papers, Archives of American Art, Smithsonian Institution, Washington, DC
WEDP	William E. Dever Papers, Chicago History Museum, Chicago
YBSP	Yvonne ("Eve") Blue Skinner Papers, Schlesinger Library, Radcliffe College, Cambridge, Massachusetts

Index

Bronzeville (Chicago) (*cont.*)
resistance to slumming in, 206–11,
267–69; buffet flats, 76, 94, 200–1, 205,
207–8, 218, 258–60, 379–80n47; circuses, 201, 259; cross-racial friendships
in, 211–14; cross-racial intimacy and,
77–82, 195, 200–5, 208–11, 270; drugs
accessible in, 76–77, 315–16n35; as
economic and cultural center, 75; Great
Migration and, 73, 75–76, 189–91, 205,
218, 254; homosexuals in, 85–86, 95,
254–55, 260–67, 270–72, 378n42; Italians in, 219–23; Jews in, 76, 79–80, 195,
207, 219–23; map, *74*; musical slumming in, 12, 211–14; origin of name
Bronzeville, 315n31; pansy and lesbian
craze in, 91–92, 94–96, 233, 253–60;
socio-cultural heterogeneity in, 225–29;
spatial and demographic transformation
of, 73, *74*; white business proprietors in,
76, 79–80, 124–25, 206–8, 221. *See also*
Negro vogue
Brooklyn, 147, 187, 231, 279
brothels, 25, 33, 36–37, 40, 204–6. *See also*
prostitution; red-light districts
Broun, Heywood, 216
Brown, Lilian, 93
Brown, Ralph E., 365n53
Bruce, Earle W., 83, 273
Brundage, Slim, 177
Brush, Katherine, 193
Bryant, Louise, 184
Budd, Arthur "Rose," 87, 310n16, 353–54n46
buffet flats: cross-racial sex and, 81, 135,
200–1, 204–5, 259, 273; defined, 76;
Jewish proprietors of, 207; pansy and
lesbian craze and, 258–59, 270–71, 273,
379–80n47; primitivism and, 208, 273;
prostitution and, 76, 81, 135, 204–5,
207; raids on, 200; as slumming attrac-
tion, 76, 82, 191, 200–1; as target of
reformers, 81, 315n33; white proprietors of, 207–8
bulldaggers, 12, 84, 260–64, 269, 382n59
Bungalow, The, 249
Bunner, Henry Cuyler, 31
bunny hug, 56
Bureau of Social Hygiene, 81
burlesque, 29
Burns, George, 253, 378n40
Busse, Fred A., 49

Butler, Bennie, 361n27, 363–64n42,
364–65n48
Butler, Nicholas Murray, 106
Buxbaum's Resort, 52

cabarets: as Harlem/Bronzeville attraction,
70, 73, 75–81, 191, 207–10, 317n42,
359–60nn16–17; mainstream cabarets
and pansy and lesbian craze, 83–84, 231,
236–41, 245–46, 249–51, 253; mainstream cabarets and the Negro vogue,
229; racial discrimination in, 213,
317n42; raids on, 56, 353n46; relocation
of prostitution to, 67, 77; slumming
as legitimization of, 56–57; as target of
reformers, 52, 56, 314n23; as upscale
public amusement, 53–55. *See also* black
and tans; pansy and lesbian craze
Cabin Inn, 94–96, 258, 259, 261, *275*,
327n83
Café Folies Bergére, 241
call houses, 67, 77. *See also* brothels; pros-
titution
Calloway, Cab, *192*
Camp, The, 250
Canadians, 296–97n13
Capone, Al, 221
Captive, The (Bourdet), 234–35
Carby, Hazel, 226
Carnegie, Andrew, 50
Carnevali, Emanuel, 347n19
Carpenter, Edward, 158
Carr, Johnny, 259
Carter, June (June Wiener), 186
Cartier, Mademoiselle, 258
Casal, Mary, 139
Casebeer, Bessie, 134
Castle, Irene and Vernon, 55–56
casual sex, 28, 41, 50, 101, 109, 125, 132,
152, 187, 197, 209, 238. *See also* charity;
charity girls; free love; prostitution;
treating
Catholics, 8
Central Park (New York), 57
Century of Progress World's Fair, 68, 88, 90,
94, 201, 243
Cermak, Anton J., 90
Chanler, Robert Winthrop, 214
Chapin, Anna Alice, 166, *167*
charity (sexual practice), 67, 179. *See also*
treating

class (*cont.*)
113–14, 227–28; transitions in sexual regimes and, 381n56; undercover anti-vice investigators and, 50–51; whiteness and, 114–16. *See also* middle class; upper class; working class
Classic Café, *60*, 182–83
Claymes, Raymond A., 81, 318–19nn45–46
Clement, Elizabeth, 34, 243
Club Abbey, 87, 236–38
Club Anna, 204
Club Calais, 87
Club Casanova, 282
Club Delisa, 95
Club D'Orsay, 87, 244, 249–50
Club Ebony, 228
Club Le Masque, 241–42
Club New Yorker, *237*
Club Piccardy, 250
Club Richman, 89, 241
Coal Scuttle, 155
Coffee Cliff, 87, 238
Cohen, Lester, 184, 234
Coke village (Harlem), 77
Cole, Louis, 273
Coliseum Annex, 265, 271
Colisimo's Café, 154
College Inn, 213
Colley, Lillian, *172*
Columbia Hall, 43–44
commercial leisure, 7, 45–46, 101, 282. *See also* heterosocialization
Committee of Fifteen (Chicago), 51, 66–68, 199, 218, 323n64
Committee of Fifteen (New York), 50, 143–44
Committee of Five (New York), 144. *See also* Committee of Fourteen
Committee of Fourteen (New York): on black and tans, 124, 210; black auxiliary of, 144; black views of, 339–40nn76–77; bohemians and, 66–68, 165, 173, 177, 180–82, 187; on buffet flats, 315n33; on circuses, 259; on cross-racial intimacy, 78–79, 81, 135, 203–4; on dance halls, 360n17; disbanding of, 89, 322–23n62; on free love, 166, 169, 171; on homosexuality, 89, 175; on literary/theatrical depictions of slumming, 358n6; on oral sex, 137; origin of, 50; property owners as target, 309n64; on prostitution, 46,

168, 177; on public intimacy, 196, 273; racial identity as problem for, 219–20, 225, 333n36; resistance to, 144; undercover investigations, 13, 151; on white male sexual aggressiveness, 209–10
communists, 184, 216
concert halls (concert-saloons): Bowery concert halls, 31–32, 302n30; displacement by sexual entertainment, 28; slumming party excursions to, 17
condoms, 167
Condon, Eddie, 212
Connie's Inn: exploitation of black women at, 209; Jewish proprietors of, 222–23; presentation of blackness in, 1, 218; promotional material, 93; relocation to midtown Manhattan, 229; slumming at, 1, 189; Ubangi Club at site of, 257
Connors, Chuck, 145–47
Cook, Will Marion, 209
Cotton Club: association with sexual availability, 197; presentation of blackness in, 1, 191, 255; promotional material, 93, *192*; radio broadcasts of, 194; relocation to midtown, 229; slumming at, 1, 189, 257; Ubangi Club connections with, 257
Covarrubias, Miguel, 215
Cozy Cabin Club, 94
Crandall, Elizabeth, 315n42
Crane, Stephen, 107, 154
Crawford, Joan (George Manus), 94
Crenshaw, Bob, 184
Criswell, Helen, 164
cross-dressing. *See* drag balls; female impersonators; masquerades
cross-racial intimacy: black and tans and, 1, 34, 78–80, 125, 135, 200–4; bohemian support for, 184–85; buffet flats and, 76, 81, 135, 200–1, 205; in the Chicago Black Belt, 42–43; grenades, 203; interracial marriage, 158; miscegenation laws, 121–22; primitivism and, 102–3, 118, 190–91, 197–98; racial differentiation and, 125–26; sexual norms and, 102–3; Tenderloin resorts and, 37;
—Asian men/white women: in Chinatown opium dens, 34; female respectability and, 132–33; Harlem/Bronzeville slumming and, 224–25; white female slumming and, 127–28

Dos Passos, John, 255–56
double standard, 29, 34, 108–9, 158, 174, 179
Douglas, Aaron, 228–29
Douglas Club, 37
Drag, The (West), 234–35
drag balls, 91, 94, 261, 264–66, 271. *See also* female impersonators; masquerades
drag kings, 282–83. *See also* male impersonators
drag queens, 233, 241, 261, *275*, 282–83. *See also* female impersonators
Draper, Muriel, 214, 216
Dreamland Café, 80, 191, 212, 214, 221
Dreiser, Theodore, 107, 109, 215
drugs, 76–77, 315–16n35. *See also particular drugs*
Drury, John, 236–37, 350n33, 372–73n9
Du Bois, W. E. B., 228–29, 340n77
Duff, P. J., 106
Duggan, Lisa, 10
dumb-bell tenements, 20–21, 122
Dunn, Francis (Helen Morgan), 87, 185
Durante, Jimmy, 145, 196

East Harlem (New York), 25, 279
Eastman, Crystal, 184
Eastman, Max, 159–60, 184
Edison Manufacturing Company, 130
Edmund's Theatrical Club, 37
Edwards, Bobby, *58*, 163, 178–79, 239, 353n45
Eilers, Sally, *237*
Elks Café, 200–1
Ellington, Duke, 194
Elliott, John Lovejoy, 294n21
Ellis, Edith, 158
Ellis, Havelock, 64, 157
English, 118
Entertainers' Café, 79, 196, 199, 220, 221, 317n42
Erenberg, Lewis A., 219
Erin, The, *40*, 40
escorts/guides: bohemian tour guides, 177–79, *178*, 353–54n46; commercial tour companies, 110, 145, 363n41; employed by wholesale houses, 108; Harlem/Bronzeville guides, 208; hired by reformers, 106; police as slumming escorts, *6*, 17–18, 109; rubberneck wagons, 145, 341–42n82. *See also* tourism

Everglades, 87
Everleigh Club, 40, 135–36, 336–37n60
Eve's Hangout, 186
Ewing, Max, 82, 216–17

faggots, 260–64, 266–67, 269
fairies: in bohemian districts, 65, 84, 160–61, 175–76, 234; bohemian men compared to, 161–62; bohemian men's views of, 162–63; bohemian women's views of, 161, 163; circuses, 44, 138–39; faggots, 260–64, 266–67, 269; fairy cultural type, 10–11; fairy entertainers, 43–44, 65, 137–38, 243; fairy resorts, 28, 43–44, 137–39; *fairy* term, 12, 232, 320n50; fairy truck (dance style), 262; female slummers and, 139; femininity of (gender nonconformity), 44–45, 65, 137–39, 175, 232, 251, 260–63, 270; in Harlem/Bronzeville, 254–55, 260; homosexual class distinctions and, 139, 251, 260; literary depictions of, 161; male slummers and, 44–45, 138, 175–76; at masquerades, 44–45, 65, 175–76, 234; oral sex and, 176; pansies compared to, 232, 241; prostitution and, 28, 176; sexual practices of, 28, 65, 138, 176; as target of reformers, 43–44, 137–38; as *third sex*, 161; as victim of violence, 175–76. *See also* female impersonators; homosexuality; pansy and lesbian craze
Fallows, Samuel, 184
fan dancers, 90, 94, 241–42
Farrell, James T., 379–80n47
Farway, Jean (Natalie Feinberg), 186
Fass, Paula, 170
Favela Tour, 284
Feinberg, Natalie (Jean Farway), 186
Felter, Timothy "Tiny Tim," 168, 354n49
female impersonators: in black and tans, 84, 91–94, 259, 261, 266, 270, 274; in bohemian districts, 87, 177, 234–35; as Bowery entertainment, 138; drag queen restaurants, 283; drag queens, 233, 241, 261, *275*, 281, 283; fairy resorts and, 28, 43–44; as Levee entertainment, 43; men's cosmetics associated with, 373n10; pansy and lesbian craze and, 84, 87–94, 230, 232, 234, 236, 238, 240–41, 249, 250, 259, 261; sex crime

lady lovers, 65, 85, 163, 234. *See also* lesbians
Lambert, Helen, 252
LaMonte, Lestra, 87
Langner, Lawrence, 215
Larsen, Nella, 193, 215–16
Lascars, 123
LaVerde, Leon, 88
Law, Jackie, 235
Lawrence, Richard Hoe, *124*
Lawrenson, Helen, 243, 258
Lawson, R. C., 267–68
Layne, Lou, 93
Lederer, George Washington, 147–48
Legg, W. Dorr, 272
Lenox Club, 1, 199, 259
LeRoy, Billie, 250
lesbians: association with circuses, 136, 201, 243, 259; black homosexual community and, 254–55; in bohemian districts, 84, 163–64, 234–35; in the Bowery, 44; bull-daggers, 12, 84, 260–64, 269, 382n59; as cabaret proprietors, 250; Chicago settlements of, 84–86; claims to middle-class respectability and privilege, 253–54; class distinctions among, 139, 252–53, 260; cross-racial relationships and, 263–64; as display/entertainment, 136–37; drag kings, 283–84; female slummers and, 83, 238–39, 242, 264; femininity/gender conformity of, 139, 251–53; formation of slums and, 9; Greenwich Village as lesbian paradise, 239; lady lovers, 65, 85, 163, 234; literary depictions of, 83; male heterosexual privilege and, 242; male impersonators, 87, 90–91, 93, 96, 232, 240, 244, *257*, 264; mannish women, 10–11, 84, 90, 230, 250–52, 255–56, 260–63; *mantees* term, 249; masculinity of (gender nonconformity), 45, 260–64; at masquerades, 45, 233–34, 261, 265, 270–71; New York settlements of, 84–85, 163–64; nightlife catering to, 83, 87–88, 90–91, 238–39, 242, 247–48; normative femininity and, 252–53; pseudolesbianism, 162, 239; sexual practices of, 264; as sexual threat to women, 239; as target of reformers, 90–91, 267–68; temperamental resorts, 86; theatrical depictions of, 234–35; as *third sex*, 161; as threat to men, 244,

262; white homosexual community and, 245, 247–53. *See also* pansy and lesbian craze
Levee (Chicago): overview, 37–48, *38*, *112*; black and tans, 70, 125, 135; blacks in, 42–43, 120, 126, 146; bohemian slummers in, 154; circuses, 42–43, 136; closure of, 53, 76–77, 155; dance halls, *112*, 149; dance steps popular in, 56, 130–31; dangers in, 126, 135–36, 150–51, 329n8; drawing of street scene, *40*; escorted tours to, 108–10, 145–46; fairies in, 43–45, 137–38; French in, 41, 138; immigrants in, 41, 122, 125, 131, 305n42; increased public intimacy in, 135; location of, 37–39, 40; masquerades in, 45; muckraking journalism in, 39, 107; oral sex in, 136–37; origin of *Levee* term, 39; photo of dance halls, *40*; prostitution in, 39–42, 48, 51, 135–37; Protestant evangelical slumming in, 104, *105*, 106, 122; racialization of, 117–20, 125; resistance to slumming in, 140, 143; slumming excursions to, 52, 107–8, 111; spatial overlap with Black Belt, 42, 71, 117; spatial overlap with Chinatown, 41–42, 117; as target of reformers, 47–49, 51–52, 111, *112*, 155; white female slumming and, 39–41, 113, 128
Levee Districts (Chicago): financial revenue from slumming, 129, 144–45; map, *38*. *See also* Levee; North Side Levee; West Side Levee
Lewis, "Dago" Frank, 51, 131
Lewis, Dolly, 181–82
Lexow, Clarence, 48
Lexow Committee, 48, 148, 307–8n60
Liberal Club, 65, 169, 183
Lido Cabaret, 240–41
Lincoln Gardens, 214
Lincoln Law and Order League, 338n75
Lips, 283
Little Africa (New York), 24, 28–29, *30*, 117–20, *124*
Little Buck's, 44
Little Italy (Chicago), 37, *38*, 117–18, 122
Little Italy (New York), 17, 26–27, *30*, 33–34, 116–18, 122–23
Little Sicily (Chicago), 25, *60*
Liveright, Horace, 216

and, 89, 92, 233, 249, 253, 274; popular association with slumming, 1–2; post-Prohibition social climate, 89–96, 253, 274, 279–81. *See also* alcohol
prophylactic sexual measures, 137, 167–68
prostitution: black prostitution rates, 81, 205–6, 209; black social critics on, 206–9, 269; charity compared with, 67; concentration in black districts, 26–27, 77, 253; covert forms in cabarets and call houses, 67, 77; cross-racial intimacy confused with, 78; financial revenue from, 129; free love compared with, 67–68, 166–69, 177, 181–82; post-Prohibition regulations against, 89; sex tourism and, 285; as target of reformers, 4, 46–53, 66–68, 111, 205, 323n64; treating compared with, 131–32
—female prostitution: "bachelor society" and, 27–28; black prostitutes and cross-racial sex, 39, 42, 81, 204, 205; black prostitutes as foil for white female virtue, 205–6; black prostitutes as sexual threat, 125–27; in bohemian nightspots, 163–64, 168–69; in buffet flats, 76, 81, 135, 204–5, 207; Chinese female prostitution, 28, 34; circuses and, 42–43, 106, 136–37, 259; dance halls as path to, 46–47, 111, 131; as deterrent vs. cause of sexual crime, 46, 51, 205; female slummers' casual intimacy compared to, 135–36; Great Migration and black prostitution, 205, 209; immigrant trafficking in, 128–29, 142–43; at masquerades, 347n29; oral sex and, 136–37; venereal disease and, 95, 137, 167–68; white prostitutes and cross-racial sex, 81, 210; white prostitutes in black districts, 207, 210, 253; white slavery panic, 46–47, 53, 127–29, 205
—male prostitution: "bachelor society" and, 28; black male prostitutes (white female clients), 204; fairies, 28, 176; oral sex and, 176, 351n42. *See also* brothels; *particular red-light districts*; red-light districts
psychoanalysis, 157–58, 161, 195
public intimacy: bohemian attitudes toward, 156, 171; class differentiation and, 113–14; cross-racial intimacy and, 77–79, 200–2; at masquerades,

271, 384n72; sensual dancing, 195–97, 273–74, 359–60nn15–16; sexual respectability and, 131, 134–35, 173, 195–96, 206
"public woman" term, 4
Puerto Ricans, 279, 325n73
Pullman Café, 378n40
Purple Pup, 61, 166, *167*
Putnam, Samuel, 62, 180, 354n51

queers: bohemian sexuality and, 161–62, 268–69; claims to middle-class respectability/privilege, 253–54; disdain for fairies/pansies, 250–51; historical use of term, 12, 251; homosexual class distinctions and, 251; masculinity/gender conformity of, 251–53; queer resorts, 251–52. *See also* homosexuality
Quill, The, 58, 158, 163, 177, 178, 353n45

race: black and tans, racial differentiation and, 75, 123–25, 190–91; blackness, 117–21, 191, 198, 208, 217–20, 225–29, 263–64, 273, 367n65; bohemian views on, 183–88; defined in sexual terms, 80, 118, 120–23, 191–98; defined in terms of civilization and primitivism, 118–19; hierarchy of, 118; identifiable characteristics of, 118–24; in-betweenness, 10, 114–15, 123, 218–25, 333n36, 367nn64–65, 369n74; legal definitions of, 114, 121–22; marking of, 8, 292n16; racial display in black cabarets, 1, 191; racialization of urban space, 23–25, 54, 71–75, 96, 116–23, 156, 183, 211, 217–18; racialized sexual threats, 125–29; skin color and, 114, 118–20, 121–23, 218–19, 291n17, 367nn64–65; slumming as contestation of racial difference, 190, 195, 211; slumming as racial differentiation, 2–3, 75, 97, 101–3, 115–19, 190–91, 204–6, 211, 217–21, 223–29, 296–97n13. *See also* blacks; cross-racial sex; race riots; white/black racial axis; whiteness
race records, 193, 273–74
race riots, 8, 79, 93, 143, 279–80, 316n39, 325n73, 338n75. *See also* violence
racial in-betweenness, 10, 114–15, 123, 218–25, 367nn64–65, 369n74
racism, 7–8, 8, 185

radio broadcasts, 194, 258

ragtime music, 29, 36–37, 42, 146

raids: on black and tans, 78–79, 81–82, 317n42, 318–19n46; on bohemian tearooms, 68–69, 171–72, 182–83, 312n16, 353–54n46, 356n60; on buffet flats, 200; on cabarets, 56, 353n46; in Chinatown, 53; on circuses, 177; film depictions of, 149; on pansy and lesbian nightspots, 93, 95, 268, 272, 325–26n75; in red-light districts, 47, 52–53, 107, 143; as slumming spectacle, 52–53

Raines Law of 1896, 50

Rainey, Gertrude "Ma," 193, 261, 273

Ramirez, Jan Seidler, 165

rape, 46, 205

rap music, 284

Reality Tours and Travel, 285

Reckless, Walter, 194–95, 206

Rector's cabaret, 56

Red Lantern, 61

red-light districts: city officials' toleration of, 46; closure of, 53–55, 77, 166, 253, 269; conflation with slums, 18, 25–27; financial revenue from slumming, 129; legally sanctioned in New Orleans, 25; origin of *red-light* term, 25, 297n18; police raids in, 47, 52–53; raids in, 47, 52–53, 107, 143; slumming excursions to, 18; spatial segregation of, 19, 51, 299–300n19. *See also* brothels; *particular red-light districts*; prostitution

Red Mask, 235

Red Scare, 7–8, 185

Reed, John, 183

Regal, The, 194

Reitman, Ben L., 158, 161, 179, 243, 247–48, 354n49, 373n10, 376n28

religion: evangelical Protestant moral reform, 4–6, 47, 52, 96, 103–8, *105*; evangelical Protestant slumming, 103–4, *105*; Harlem gospel tours, 284–85; immigrants as religious deviants, 128; nativism and, 7–8; Negro vogue and, 208; opposition to drag balls and, 267–68; resistance to slumming and, 142–43; suburban homogeneity and, 278

Renaissance Casino, 253

Renault, Francis, 87

Replenishing Jessica (Bodenheim), 349–50n31

resistance: black critics on female slumming, 210–11, 364–65n48; black resistance to slumming, 144, 191, 206–11, 267–69, 362n35, 363–64n42; bohemian resistance to tourism, 180–81, 354n52; Harlem opposition to pansy and lesbian craze, 267–69, 383n68; homosexual community and, 247, 250; immigrant residents' views of slummers, 140–44; reverse-slumming, 141–42, 269–70; slumming as anti-nativist act, 103

restaurants: on the Bowery, 29, 31–32; cabarets' relation to, 53–56; in Chinatown (Chicago), 41–42, 224; in Chinatown (New York), 17, 34–35, 105, 133, *134*, 149, 224, 342–43n86; drag-oriented restaurants, 283; in Greenwich Village, 63, 66; in Harlem, 255; Italian restaurants, 37, 61, 63; queer-oriented restaurants, 245; in Towertown, 57, 61

reverse-slumming, 141–42, 269–70

Rexroth, Kenneth, 170, 184, 354n52

Rich, Adrienne, 346–47n18

Richman, Harry, 258

Riis, Jacob A., 21, 24, *124*

Rio de Janeiro, 285

Rivers, Lena, 241–42

Road to Heaven, The (Beer), 193

Robeson, Paul, 215–16

Rocco's Grill, 266–67

Rockefeller, John D., Jr., 50

Rockland Palace, 253, 265

Rodman, Henrietta, 160

Roe, Clifford G., 128

Roediger, David R., 9

Rogers, J. A., 201, 203–4

Rogers, Patricia, 177, 353n46

Romanians, 185

Romilly, Rita, 214

Roosevelt, Theodore, 240

Rose, Florence, 171

Rosebault, Charles J., 173

Rosebud (Arthur "Rose" Budd), 87, 312n16, 353–54n46

Rosebud (cabaret), 93

Roselle Inn, 87–88, 90, 242, 244

Rosenwald, Julius, 216

Roxy, The, 283

rubberneck wagons, 145, 341–42n82

Rubinstein, Helena, 215

Rush Street entertainment district, 83–84

women (*cont.*)
144, 159–60, 163, 197–98, 204–6, 242,
244; as moral reformers, 4–6, 19, 21,
50, 52, 66, 104; protective/restrictive
measures for female slummers, 151–52;
robbery/deception of female slummers,
150; sexual independence of, 153, 159,
169–70, 180, 197–98, 204, 206, 238–39,
349–50n31; slum shopping as gendered
activity, 32; as targets of reform, 104,
108–13; as tearoom proprietors, 160,
177, 345–46n13; white slavery panic
and, 46–47, 53, 127, 132–33; white
women as sexual predators, 128. *See also*
feminism; gender; lesbians; prostitution
Women's Christian Temperance Union,
104
women's suffrage movement, 8
Woolcott, Alexander, 106
Wooldridge, Clifton R., 126
working class: association with primitivism,
102; association with white slavery,
46–47, 127; "bachelor society" and,
27–28; blacks and, 225–26, 227–28,
260–64, 266–67, 269; in bohemian
districts, 57–62; buffet flats and, 201;
dancing and, 130–31; development of
industrial suburbs, 19–20; emergence
of heterosocial commercial leisure and,
28–29, 45, 47; financial revenue from
slumming, 144–50; gendered sexual
regime and, 10, 137–39, 241, 260–64;
homosexuals, 85–86, 251–53, 260–64;
interracial sociability and, 34; male
homosocial public leisure and, 5, 28;
neighborhoods and resorts as slumming
attractions, 2–6, *6*, 9, 17, 22, 24, 29–45,

30, *36*, *38*, 40, 101–2, 109–10; neighborhoods coincident with red-light districts, 25–27; recipients of benevolence,
4–6; resistance to slumming in, 140–43;
sexual norms of "charity" and "treating," 67, 131–33, 334n54; as target of
reformers, 46–53, 62–63, 66; tenement
life and, 22–23; urban spatial segregation and, 3–4, 18–20; women's sexual
availability, 35, 131–32
World's Columbian Exposition, 39, 47,
305n42, 337n61
world's fairs. *See* Century of Progress
World's Fair; World's Columbian
Exposition
Wright, Marcus, 262
Wylie, Elinor, 215

Yale Club, 62
Yawitz, Paul, 249
Yee, Georgie, 146
Yellow Fish, 61
yellow peril, 127
Young Man of Manhattan (Brush), 193
young people: at bohemian tearooms,
68–69, 171, 313n22; corrupted youths
as reformers' concern, 52, 68–69, 90,
146, 171, 208; corrupted youths as tour
attractions, 146; Great Migration and,
76; as Harlem/Bronzeville slummers,
78, 80; petting parties and, 171, *172*,
173–74, 350n33

Ziegfeld Follies, 87, 199
Zina's Restaurant, 180
Zorbaugh, Harvey Warren, 160, 162,
168–69, 246, 345–46n13, 346n15